P9-CFV-426

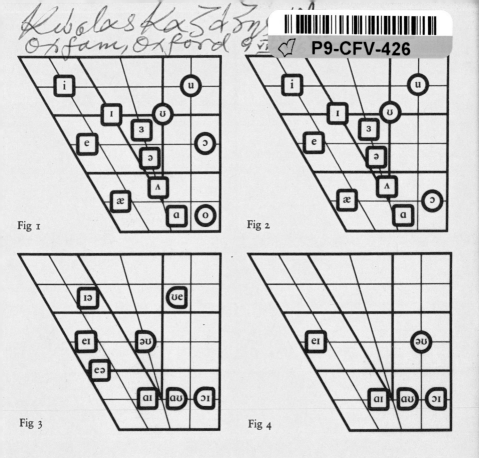

Fig 1

Fig 2

Fig 3

Fig 4

Fig 1 The General British simple vowels

Fig 2 The General American simple vowels

Fig 3 The General British diphthongs (starting-areas)

Fig 4 The General American diphthongs (starting-areas)

The form of these diagrams is meant to suggest the area through which the highest point of the tongue passes in producing the total possible range of the vowel sounds of human speech. Each square represents the very approximate position and some of the possible range of variation for the highest point of the tongue in making an English unrounded vowel. Similarly each circle represents a vowel made with some degree of rounding of the lips.

A diphthong symbol in an enclosure which is square to the left begins with unrounded lips; a diphthong in an enclosure which is circular to the left begins with rounded lips and so on. The diagrams give the relative values in the two varieties of English of all the 20 vowel symbols of the list of the keywords.

Vowel symbol 6 **ɒ** of the joint list of British and American sounds does not appear on Fig 2 because it has exactly the same value in General American pronunciation as symbol 5 **ɑ**. It would also have been possible to omit symbol 10 **ʌ** from Fig 2 because for most General American speakers it scarcely differs from **ə** in quality.

Diphthong symbols 18 to 20 do not appear on Fig 4 because the sound sequences of the General American pronunciations of *near*, *hair* and *pure* do not contain diphthongs as the term is usually defined.

A full explanation of the significance of these diagrams may be consulted in the author's *Guide to English Pronunciation*, Chapter II.

A Concise Pronouncing Dictionary of British and American English

A Concise Pronouncing Dictionary
of British and American English

J WINDSOR LEWIS

London
Oxford University Press
1972

Oxford University Press, Ely House, London W.1
GLASGOW NEW YORK TORONTO MELBOURNE WELLINGTON
CAPE TOWN IBADAN NAIROBI DAR ES SALAAM LUSAKA
ADDIS ABABA DELHI BOMBAY CALCUTTA MADRAS KARACHI
LAHORE DACCA KUALA LUMPUR SINGAPORE HONG KONG TOKYO

ISBN 019 431123 6

© *Oxford University Press* 1972
*All rights reserved. No part of this publication may be reproduced,
stored in a retrieval system, or transmitted, in any form or by any
means, electronic, mechanical, photocopying, recording or otherwise,
without the prior permission of Oxford University Press*

Set in Sabon at The Lancashire Typesetting Co Ltd
and printed at the University Press, Oxford
by Vivian Ridler, Printer to the University

Foreword

English now holds an undisputed place as the first international language. If it is to remain an efficient instrument of world communication, those who speak it, especially as a second language, must conform to certain accepted rules of pronunciation. There can be little doubt that on the grounds of general influence it is the British or American styles of pronunciation which provide the most appropriate models to follow. It is for this reason that Mr Windsor Lewis's *Concise Pronouncing Dictionary*, showing both types of pronunciation in a carefully selected word list, is particularly valuable.

He has not sought to show the whole complexity of pronunciation even within the traditional British and American standards, but has wisely chosen to recommend only one form for the foreign speaker to adopt. Too often, English dictionaries persist in showing pronunciations which are seriously archaic. The forms given by Mr Windsor Lewis consistently reflect current usage; and the phonetic transcription which he employs is both simple and economical. His decision to emphasize the differences of quality rather than of quantity between vowels is especially welcome, since the former have a greater practical relevance for the foreign learner.

This is a reference book which is sure to be widely used abroad; it is also certain that many who have English as their native language will consult its pages with profit.

A C GIMSON
Professor of Phonetics
University College, London

Preface

Two broad types of English have been recorded, a British and an American. Each represents the fluent, spontaneous, everyday usage of those educated speakers on either side of the Atlantic whose speech is of the most generally accepted kind and least restricted in terms of geographical region or social grouping.

The question will no doubt be asked why a new dictionary has been prepared when we already have such excellent reference works as the Daniel Jones *English Pronouncing Dictionary* (the EPD) and the Kenyon and Knott *Pronouncing Dictionary Of American English* (the PDAE). An immediate answer is that neither of these was planned solely for the benefit of users of English as a foreign or second language. Each is offered as 'a record of facts' and these can be of such complexity that an interpretation and to some extent simplification of these facts in the form of a limited set of recommendations can be of value to the learner.

Many teachers of English as a foreign language and others with an academic interest in this book may wish to know something of how it was planned: they are referred to the account below of The design of the dictionary, p xiv.

Acknowledgments

There is no doubt that this dictionary would not exist at all if it were not for Professor A C Gimson whose kind encouragement and invaluable advice have to my good fortune been readily forthcoming ever since its preparation was begun in 1964. I offer him my sincerest thanks.

I am also grateful to Mrs Muriel Higgins who undertook the laborious job of typing the whole of the first draft of the manuscript and to Mr David Gibbons for advice on American pronunciations.

J WINDSOR LEWIS
University of Leeds

Contents

Advice to the learner

Very often it is only the pronunciation of a word that you need to refer to. Using a general dictionary with its very long word list and searching within involved paragraphs or following up cross-references can waste time. This is why you should use a pronouncing dictionary. This one has been designed so that it is quick and easy to refer to. To get the most out of it you should always try to keep it within reach, look up any words you are in doubt about with the least possible delay and, if circumstances permit you to, *read the transcription aloud*. Even muttering to yourself under your breath is much better than just imagining what it sounds like. Best of all, repeat it two or three times clearly so that you store it in all three memory 'banks' involved – the visual, the auditory and the muscular. Remember that the more common the word is the more important it is to get it right, the more unusual the word is the less you need worry about it.

This book has been planned not only as a reference book to be consulted but as a companion to your English pronunciation textbook. You should find some time to read it every day if possible, say a page a day. This should not be too time consuming because you can pay less attention to words that are unfamiliar to you in print and concentrate your attention on those you know well by sight. You will no doubt get a number of 'shocks'. Most teachers are only too familiar with the painful experience of hearing learners mispronounce words they are supposed to have learnt in the first few months of their English studies. By reading the text you will come across many things it would never have occurred to you to look up. Did you know, for instance, that the regularly spelt plural form of *house* is irregular phonetically? Do you know what might be unexpected about the pronunciations of *bedroom* and *rectangle*? Are you absolutely certain that you know the right vowels for *pretty, said, broad, bury, tongue, worse, break, height, pear* or *were*? Should you omit the h in *human*? Does *use* have s or z? (This answer is not straightforward.)

A word of warning: if in conversation various people around you repeatedly use a word with a pronunciation not given here, either raise the matter for discussion or join them in their usage. Only an insensitive person prides himself on being 'the only soldier in step'.

The arrangement of the entries

A prime objective has been to make this dictionary self-explanatory. In general it should only be necessary to consult the key to symbols and notes immediately inside the covers at either end to check the values of the phonetic symbols until the user is familiar with them. The extended explanations which follow are given to ensure that there is no possibility of misunderstanding. The terms British English pronunciation and American English pronunciation in these notes stand for what may be termed more exactly as the 'General British' and 'General American' pronunciations of English, as explained below in B The accents represented p xiv.

1 Pronunciations common to British and American English

At the majority of entries a single pronunciation is shown in **bold type**. For example:

abolish əˈbolɪʃ   advice ədˈvaɪs

2 Alternative pronunciations

In many cases one or more alternative pronunciations are shown in medium weight type. Any of these, while not being the preferred recommendation, need not be avoided if the user has already adopted it or would prefer to do so. For example:

again əˈgen əˈgeɪn   applicable ˈæplɪkəbl əˈplɪkəbl

3 British-American differences

Contrasts between British and American English are frequent. In such cases the recommended British pronunciation appears in bold type immediately after the headword, and the recommended American pronunciation follows preceded by the symbol $. This symbol indicates that the pronunciation is, or pronunciations are, chiefly or solely American. For example:

asthma ˈæsmə $ ˈæzmə   ate *past of 'eat'* et $ eɪt
docile ˈdəʊsaɪl $ ˈdosl   half hɑf $ hæf

4 Recommended American forms also current in British usage

Where the recommended American pronunciation of a word can also be given as an alternative British form, the symbol $ for the American pronunciation is immediately followed by £. For example:

room rʊm $ £ rum   version ˈvɜʃn $ £ ˈvɜʒn

5 British-only alternatives

All forms of words which are not preferred recommendations are shown in medium weight type. If such a form is recommended for British English only, it is identified by a preceding £. For example:

default dɪˈfɔlt £ dɪˈfolt   tissue ˈtɪʃu £ ˈtɪsju

6 American-only alternatives

An alternative pronunciation for American English only is identified by a preceding $ in its medium weight form. For example:

adamant ˈædəmənt $ ˈædəmænt   drama ˈdrɑmə $ ˈdræmə

If these alternatives follow an American preferred recommendation, the American currency symbol is not repeated. For example:

armada ɑˈmɑdə $ ɑr- ɑrˈmeɪdə   café ˈkæfeɪ $ kæˈfeɪ kə-

7 American alternatives which are recommended British forms

If a word given a separate American preferred pronunciation has an alternative form which corresponds to what has already been shown as the preferred British form, the previous transcription is not repeated but the abbreviation *etc* appears. For example:

suggest səˈdʒest $ səgˈdʒest *etc*   wheel wil $ hwil *etc*

8 Gradation words

There are fifty or so very important words listed such as *can, from*, etc which have two or more pronunciations that are shown in bold type because there is no single form suitable for all situations. The vital selection in turn, according to the word's prominence, of either the more usual weak-form or the less usual but still frequent strong-form, can only be summarized here. For a full treatment see my *Guide to English Pronunciation*, Chapter IV.

9 Hyphens showing part repetition

When alternative British forms, or recommended and alternative American forms, differ in part only from the preferred British transcription already given, often only that part of the transcription which differs is repeated. This is indicated by preceding and/or following hyphens. For example:

ceremony ˈserəmənɪ $ -məʊnɪ   realization ˈrɪəlaɪˈzeɪʃn $ -lɪˈz-
appreciation əˈpriʃɪˈeɪʃn -ɪsɪ-   explosive ɪkˈspləʊsɪv -zɪv

10 Hyphens showing syllable separation

Hyphens also appear occasionally within full phonetic transcriptions. Here their function is the completely usual one of indicating that there is a greater degree of separation between the syllables on either side of the hyphen than might be taken to be the case if it were not present and no space was left between the parts of the word. For example:

biped ˈbaɪ-ped   cartridge ˈka-trɪdʒ

If the hyphen had been omitted at *biped*, the stressed vowel aɪ could be expected to have the value it has in *type* when in fact it is considerably longer, more or less as in *eye*. In *cartridge* the hyphen is used to suggest that the following tr has the value it has beginning syllables, as in *trip*, rather than the value with a longer, more separate t, as in *heart-rending*.

11 Syllabic consonants

When it would not otherwise be clear that an m, n, l, or r constitutes by itself a full syllable, a short vertical stroke appears beneath the letter. Such marks would be superfluous in the cases of e.g. *button* ˈbʌtn̩, *bottle* ˈbɒtl̩, *novelty* ˈnɒvltɪ, *novelette* 'nɒvl̩ˈet, etc. They are essential, however, in such cases as government ˈgʌvṃənt, (contrast *pavement* ˈpeɪvmənt which can only be two syllables), *modernize* ˈmɒdṇaɪz, *novelist* ˈnɒvl̩ɪst, *passionate* ˈpæʃṇət, *temporary* ˈtempṛɪ, etc.

It is noteworthy that all words with syllabic consonants which have been marked as such are also very often pronounced with unsyllabic forms of those consonants, especially in situations where they are passed over lightly owing to rhythmic pressures and/or lack of prominence of the word in which they occur. Almost always the last fully stressed word of a sentence, however, retains any syllabic consonant with which it has been transcribed.

12 R-sounds

In the transcriptions of words like *car, or, over, sailor, fire, cure,* etc which, in British English, only have r in their pronunciation when a word following immediately afterwards begins with a vowel sound, the frequent absence of the r is indicated by enclosing it in brackets. American English always has this r and these brackets should therefore be ignored by those adopting that accent. For example:

car kɑ(r)   over ˈəʊvə(r)
cure kjʊə(r)   stir stɜ(r)

An r follows the symbol ɜ in a few words because, for users of British English only, it represents an extra sound which should never be omitted. American English users may ignore it. For them ɜ on its own always means a sound with r-quality. For example:

furry ˈfɜrɪ

13 The principal stress

Each word of more than one syllable is shown with an angled stress mark placed immediately before the beginning of that one and only principal stressed syllable which any such word must contain whenever it is uttered in isolation. For example:

about əˈbaʊt   twenty ˈtwentɪ
capacity kəˈpæsətɪ   syllable ˈsɪləbl

14 Subordinate stresses

In addition to their principal stresses, words of two or more syllables may contain at least one further stressed syllable previous to the principal stress. Immediately in front of such subordinate stressed syllables upright stress marks are placed. For example:

pre-war ˈpriˈwɔ(r)   uphill ˈʌpˈhɪl
pronunciation prəˈnʌnsɪˈeɪʃn   university ˈjunɪˈvɜsətɪ
individuality ˈɪndɪˈvɪdʒʊˈælətɪ   misapprehension ˈmɪsˈæprɪˈhenʃn

In connected speech any syllable bearing a stress mark in this dictionary may have its stress reduced from principal to subordinate, or even entirely suppressed. For example, 'prɪnˈses may become in the sequence *Princess Anne* 'prɪnˈses ˌæn or 'prɪnses ˈæn or prɪnses ˈæn. Even in isolation the second of two subordinate stresses may be dropped at a very slightly faster than average pace.

15 Suspension points

Very occasionally a word or compound is rarely used in complete isolation and so the stress pattern is shown without a principal stress mark. For example:

whacking great 'wækɪŋ 'greɪt . . .

16 Variant spellings

If a word in this dictionary has more than one common spelling, as occurs most often with British and American differences, it is given separate entries at the appropriate alphabetical places. To avoid the waste of time that would be involved in following up a cross-reference, full information on pronunciation is given at each entry. An exception to this is that many verbs which have an alternative form of the suffix *-ize* (*-ise*) in British usage are listed only with *-ize*. At the entries of some compound words, the alternative forms given at the entries for their component parts may not be included, at least in full, in order to save space. Where two variant spellings would otherwise require separate entries immediately following or very close to one another, they have been incorporated in a single line with the alternative, usually American, form in parentheses. For example:

centre($ -er) ˈsentə(r)   colour($ -or) ˈkʌlə(r)

17 Proper nouns

Most proper nouns, British and American, have their own entries in the dictionary. However, when a word has, besides its common form, a 'proper' form spelt with an initial capital letter, this proper noun does not have a separate entry but is indicated immediately after the common form. For example:

dickens, D– ˈdɪkɪnz   victor, V– ˈvɪktə(r)

18 Compound words

Whether compound words are written as separate words, hyphenated or as a single unit is notoriously unpredictable in English. Broadly speaking the halfway house of hyphenation is more characteristic of British than American usage. I have shown British usage following, as a rule, the *Concise Oxford Dictionary* for want of better information in cases of doubt and ordinarily giving one style only.

In view of the innumerable compounds in use in English, the items offered are of necessity only a generous selection of examples of types which exist. They include notably such 'invisible' compounds as *at all*, *child's play*, *May Day*, *stock exchange* and other such traps for the unwary.

19 Derivatives

Straightforward derivatives such as *needless*, *kindness*, *hopeful*, *quickly*, etc where the transcription of the original word is not altered by the addition of a suffix, are generally omitted from this dictionary. So also are all phonetically regular inflections: plurals, genitives and past tense forms. However, when any of these are phonetically irregular they receive separate strictly alphabetical entries, as at *mice*, *crises*, *wives*, *termini*, *stigmata*, *says*, *sang*, *sought*, *driven*, etc. This is so even if they are orthographically regular as for *circumstances*, *consequences*, etc but not if they are orthographically irregular but phonetically quite straightforward as for *echoes*, *skies*, etc.

20 Suffixes

To provide assistance with derivatives which are not included in this dictionary, any common suffix is entered at its alphabetical position so long as it is possible to make a useful generalisation about its phonetic value. This is so for *-able*, *-ably*, *-ible*, *-ically*, *-ist*, *-ment*, *-ship*, *-shire*, etc but not for *-ade*, *-age*, *-ess*, *-ine*, *-land*, etc which do not have regular predictable pronunciations. A few prefixes are also included.

21 Abbreviations

The dictionary includes a selection of common British and American abbreviations that the learner is likely to meet in general literature and conversation such as *a.m.*, *BBC*, *USSR*, *FBI*, *Dr*, *Inc.*, *Ltd*, *Dept*, etc.

22 Alphabetical ordering

All items in the dictionary are incorporated into a single alphabet in the strictest alphabetical order, regardless of the presence of any hyphens, spaces, capital letters, etc.

The design of the dictionary

A The contents

In order to keep the size of this volume to reasonable proportions, it was necessary to eliminate all specialised and technical expressions and to include only such words and such names of places and persons as were considered to be familiar over the whole of the educated English-speaking world. The total number of entries is approximately 24 000.

B The accents represented

Both the EPD and the PDAE display a much wider range of pronunciations than the present book. The PDAE records 'several different types of speech used by large bodies of educated and cultivated Americans' and the EPD the speech of 'Southern English people who have been educated at the public (i.e. residential) schools'.

By contrast the present dictionary excludes all American pronunciations with any specific association with either the Eastern or the Southern regions of the USA giving only those which are most general in the USA and Canada. This kind of American pronunciation is often referred to, with a looseness convenient to our purposes, as 'General American' pronunciation (GA).

Again by contrast this dictionary excludes any British pronunciations which are associated specifically and only with a public boarding-school or any socially conspicuous background. In general it also excludes pronunciations which clearly represent the usage solely of a relatively small minority (say less than 20%) of British speakers. For example, the pronunciations of *fire-engine, forearm, hair-oil, overawe, rear-admiral,* etc omitting the linking r. Also excluded are usages of even very slightly old-fashioned types and usages of any type associated solely with any particular, even very broad, regional subdivision of Great Britain. This most general type of educated British pronunciation, referred to popularly as 'BBC English', is described fully in Professor A C Gimson's *Introduction to the Pronunciation of English* (revised edition 1970) and more briefly in my *Guide to English Pronunciation* (1969). This variety of British pronunciation is fully specified in Gimson's terminology as the general Received Pronunciation of British English. It is a convenient parallelism with the term General American and a welcome avoidance of the 'less than happy' archaic-sounding term 'Received' to abbreviate this to simply General British pronunciation (GB).

C The basis for the recommendations

Like all other compilers of such works I have relied primarily on general observations of as many different speakers as possible. Present-day television and radio broadcasting have facilitated this as never before. But

I have in particular sought to render my observations of General British as free from misjudgement as possible by a systematic collection of data on the pronunciation of a limited number of individual speakers. There was little difficulty in deciding who these individuals should be. A certain small group of speakers existed, selected with great care specifically for the widest national or international acceptability of their speech: the BBC and ITV national newsreaders and the newsreaders of the BBC World Service. Since the autumn of 1963, when the BBC discontinued its policy of anonymity for announcers in everything but continuity work, I have attempted to collect the most complete data possible on announcers' usages. These collections have proved useful correctives to the general impressions of myself and colleagues I have consulted. Such speech features as have to be displayed in a pronouncing dictionary which aims to represent the usages of fluent spontaneous everyday conversation differ very little on the whole from those involved in newsreading. I have been able to collect data on well over a hundred such speakers altogether. Many of them have been kind enough to complete questionnaires on their linguistic backgrounds which provided valuable checks on my impressions of current British pronunciation tendencies as revealed in their speech and I am glad of the opportunity to thank them now.

For the American pronunciations I have in almost all cases deferred to the judgments of the American authorities. In particular, I am pleased to record my great indebtedness to the meticulous observations of Mr Edward Artin, the pronunciation editor of the *Webster's Third New International Dictionary*. On the differences between GA and GB see my article 'The American and British Accents of English' in the June 1971 issue of *English Language Teaching* (OUP) pp 239–248, my note on 'The So-Called Broad A' in the same journal for October 1968, p 65 and my *Guide to English Pronunciation*.

D Trends of change in pronunciation (a) extraneous words

With the highly developed mass-media communications and geographical and social mobility we have today, linguistic changes can be very rapid. The pronunciation of *Majorca* recommended, which was relatively unusual, perhaps even likely to sound affected twenty years ago, will quite possibly be the only one heard except from a minority of elderly speakers within the next twenty years. Similar cases are *Lyons, Marseilles,* etc. From around the period of the First World War there has been a steadily increasing tendency to adopt presumed Continental sound values in words of obviously non-English origin. An earlier example was the word *armada* which is shown in the current edition of the *Concise Oxford Dictionary* in only one pronunciation rhyming with *Ada*. This form of the word seems to have almost entirely disappeared in Britain quite soon after the First World War. Such archaisms are to be found in very large numbers in general dictionaries designed essentially for the English speaking public.

Now rarely heard, except from the elderly, is the substitution of non-nasal vowel followed by ŋ for a nasal vowel in words borrowed from the French:

ˈpɑŋsiɒŋ for ˈpõsiõ (pension) is now likely to sound amusingly old-fashioned possibly even incomprehensible to many educated speakers below retirement age. One or two popular words such as *meringue* and *charabanc* have settled into such pronunciations firmly but in most words with French nasal vowel origins a nasalized English vowel is heard. Our transcriptions containing nasalization signs are not to be interpreted in terms of a French sound system (as it seems they are in EPD). The number of educated English speakers who can pronounce such words exactly after the French fashion is minute and few of them would be disposed to do so in ordinary English conversation.

E Trends of change in pronunciation (b) the main word stock

Any change must have a point of equilibrium between old and new: this is the approximate state of thousands of English words at any one point of time. The rate of exchange of an older type of pronunciation for a newer one is not the same for all words and where two pronunciations in my judgment have seemed likely to maintain their relative state of equilibrium, as very often happens, for a very long time then I have been on the whole inclined to recommend the more conservative form. Such is the case for example with the words *absorb*, *explosive* and *forehead*.

Equilibrium or near equilibrium forms only are offered as alternatives. I have unhesitatingly omitted the British single-syllable unit ɔə formerly widely heard in e.g. *four*, *more*, *board*, etc which, except under regional influence, is now used regularly only by a small minority of the elderly and also the 'saw' vowel in such words as *soft*, *loss*, *frost*, *cloth*, etc now extremely unusual (except in *off*) in speakers under retirement age in Great Britain (though still the predominant type in America).

Among other such items are the important structural words *were* and *weren't* which have now become too unusual with ɛə to recommend. The -*shire* suffix for English counties is now very little heard in GB as ʃiə. (In GA ʃiər seems to predominate except in the name *New Hampshire*.) Many more such examples, especially ones involving the spread of ə in unstressed syllables, may be found by comparing the entries in this dictionary with the forms given within square brackets in the EPD.

F The phonetic symbols

The phonetic transcription employed is fully in accordance with the principles of the International Phonetic Association and makes use of only their authorised symbols. There was no question of using the indefensibly outdated EPD transcription which Daniel Jones inherited so long ago from Henry Sweet. Jones never used it himself in any new book for the last fifty years of his life and was fully aware of its unsuitability for EFL use. He said of the EPD: 'If the book had been designed solely for the use of the foreign learner needing a representation of one particular kind of pronunciation which he can take as a model, a simpler notation might have been used.' There is no doubt that his simplifications would have included the symbols o and eə as used in this dictionary.

The most unfortunate feature of the EPD transcription as regards its
suitability for the EFL user is its highly misleading emphasis on the
relatively trivial contrasts of length between the vowels of such pairs of
words as *bit/beat, not/nought, soot/suit* when other pairings equally
deserving of such representation (e.g. *come/calm*) and far more vital length
contrasts (particularly those of shortness in syllables closed by p, t, k, tʃ,
f, θ, s or ʃ versus greater length in syllables not so checked) are not
exhibited. This problem has been dealt with by adopting Professor A C
Gimson's transcription of *An Introduction to English Pronunciation* with
simplifications which, though they would have been unsuitable there, are
highly appropriate to a non-comparative work like the present. One of
these simplifications, ə, Professor Gimson has used himself (in his
contribution to Professor Randolph Quirk's *Use of English*). Others, such
as non-differentiation of the initial elements of aɪ and aʊ, we may expect
to see when the EPD is next re-set. Professor Gimson informs me that he
wishes then to employ a transcription which, like the one in this dictionary,
is a slight simplification of that used in his *Introduction to English
Pronunciation*. As this type of transcription has distinctive symbols for the
vowels distinguished only by colons in the EPD, any colons used with it
are dispensable: they are dispensed with in this dictionary.

G The transcriptions

On the principle that the simplest and therefore most readily comprehensible transcriptions will be those running least counter to what
the ordinary orthography suggests, I have shown very few pronunciations
displaying contextual adjustments of the adjacent sounds of compound
words etc to each other even though such phenomena are very common
in colloquial English. Assimilations, elisions and compressions are very
common but are relatively rarely the only acceptable forms within the
range of our 'unhurried' style. Examples of unavoidable cases may be seen
at *newspaper, horse-shoe, rest-cure, breast-stroke, postscript, postman,
first-class* and *tortoise-shell*. I have not shown most similar words with
elided forms because the proper value of a plosive consonant in such
situations produces a perfectly acceptable alternative. Such very common
variants as ˈtripmənt, əˈdʒʌsmənt, ʌmˈpleznt, əbˈmɪt for *treatment,
adjustment, unpleasant, admit* I have usually ignored altogether. So also
with the trivially modified compressions of e.g. *radio* to reɪdjəʊ, *soloist* to
ˈsəʊlʊɪst, *usually* to ˈjuʒwəlɪ, etc.

Similarly no attempt has been made to offer the common alternative
pronunciations ˈemtɪ, ˈfʌŋʃn, ˈrestrɔ̃nt, mɪnts, tʃeɪnʒ, benʃ for *empty,
function, restaurant, mince, change, bench*, etc where presence or absence
of a sound from a cluster makes a negligible auditory effect.

Some types of reduced pronunciation such as əʊpm for *open* or spəʊz for
suppose have been avoided not merely from desire to simplify the
presentation but from fear that in serious speech they might seem
undignified or clumsy, though in markedly informal styles they are very
frequent indeed.

Although my general practice has been to present a realistic representation of actual phonetic values rather than a more phonologically 'true' picture where the two aims clashed, I have in certain cases represented sounds which are not ordinarily heard in the 'unhurried colloquial' isolated or 'lexical' pronunciation because (i) they are present in the orthography and a transcription representing them will be likely to give rise to least puzzlement, (ii) they represent the underlying phonological values which could at least theroetically come to the surface in less 'normal' rhythmic contexts than the lexical, (iii) they seem certain to be unconsciously eliminated by the EFL learner as they are by the native English speaker. This applies to expressions like *Brussels sprout, primus stove, pumice stone,* etc which are lexically ˈbrʌsl ˈsprɑʊts, etc and only potentially as displayed in the dictionary.

In the case of such words as *always, Monday,* etc it seems possible that of the total number of occurrences of each word the majority may well nowadays take eɪ as the vowel of the second syllable. However, the version with that vowel as ɪ rather than eɪ is recommended since (i) it is completely unobtrusive in all situations, (ii) most of those who use eɪ seem to operate such words with gradation, e.g. preferring ɪ when no suggestion of pause follows in mentioning a succession of days as when BBC announcers who use eɪ use it only the second time in expressions of the common type *the outlook for Thursday and Friday.*

H The stress notation

The 'statements' involved in the marking of principal stresses and subordinate stresses are of quite different orders. The one type is absolute the other relative. In every 'lexical' pronunciation of a word of two or more syllables one and one only will normally bear a falling tone: this is the principle stressed syllable. The presence or absence of the level tones which may occur before the tonic is much less firmly predictable: as a rule the maximum number of stresses considered to be appropriate to an unstudied articulation has been given, but any English vowel (even ə) may carry stress, especially the 'long' vowels and diphthongs, so that the occurrence of /ˈ/ must be interpreted as a suggestion of likelihood rather than certainty. A minute increase of tempo eliminates the second of two subordinate stresses: ˈmɪsæprɪˈhenʃn is scarcely less frequent if at all than ˈmɪsˈæprɪˈhenʃn.

Those familiar with the stress notations of the EPD and PDAE will notice that, whereas they distinguish what might be called four degrees of stress (tonic, pre-tonic primary and secondary, post-tonic) this dictionary distinguishes only two, tonic and pretonic stresses. The marks for these two stress types were adopted from the set of 'tonetic' stress marks developed by Mr Roger Kingdon. They have the advantage of visually distinguishing the more important tonic stress sign from the sign for subordinate stresses. Its being angled, and thus occupying slightly more space horizontally, usefully helps to emphasise its great importance. Professor Gimson informs me that he wishes to adopt a simpler notation for stress when the EPD is next re-set.

I Word rhythmic patterns

It is only practicable for a pronouncing dictionary to represent in general one form of a word even though longer words with unstressed syllables tend to behave in a highly 'elastic' manner in English. The learner will ordinarily pick up most of these patterns of variation more or less unconsciously but if he has doubts about his handling of rhythm he must consult a teacher and/or a textbook on English pronunciation.

The rhythmic pattern of our transcriptions represents the typical way an English speaker would say the word in question in isolation without any special contrasts with what has been said before and in a manner which suggests that the topic is of definite interest and/or importance, but does not suggest extraordinary vivacity or emphasis, not studied care. Where two or more possible ways of utterance fall within this *unhurried colloquial style* I have given preference to the slower of them.

Perhaps I should warn those familiar with older representations of English pronunciation that they may receive the opposite impression. The fact is that spoken English style in Britain has perceptibly speeded up in the last generation or so. For example a pronunciation such as four-syllabled ˈtempərərɪ, which Daniel Jones in 1917, no doubt with some exaggeration, classified as 'approximately equally frequent' with three-syllabled ˈtemprərɪ, nowadays usually has an effect of sounding quite studied. One now hears usually three syllables for the word in situations of full prominence as ˈtempr̩ɪ and elsewhere more often two syllables as ˈtemprɪ. Recordings of BBC news bulletins made even as recently as the forties now tend to sound almost ceremonial compared with the current styles of most announcers.

Less familiar expressions, however, are generally uttered more carefully and so more slowly. Today if one hears ˈtempərəlɪ or ˈlɪtərəl they are more likely to be *temporally* or *littoral* than *temporarily* or *literal* (ˈtempr̩lɪ and ˈlɪtrl). This should be borne in mind by the reader when he notices that sometimes many words with similar spellings may have slightly different transcriptions.

J Syllable boundaries

Besides identifying which syllables receive stress, the stress marks also offer information on the relationships of syllables to each other. In particular, it should be noted that, although it has been suggested that a word like *astray* should be divided into its two syllables by a stress mark placed as in əsˈtreɪ, because a *minimum of prominence continues through the whole of the 'stop' of the t*, I have preferred to place the mark as in əˈstreɪ. This is because, although in terms of its own phonetic value, the s in such a cluster may be considered as belonging to the previous syllable, it more often has the more important auditory effect of reducing or eliminating aspiration of a voiceless plosive it precedes. The policy of assigning such an s visually to the following syllable enables us to represent clearly the contrast between e.g. mɪˈsteɪk and ˈmɪsˈtaɪm (*mistake* and *mistime*): the t of *mistake* has the value it has in *stake* rather than in *take*, whereas the t of *mistime* has the value it has in *time* rather than in *sty*. The sound value of the t of dɪs'teɪst is usually more different from that of dɪ'stɪŋkt than is the second d of dis'deɪn, the latter two sounds being ordinarily indistinguishable. Compare *disperse* with *disburse* which has to be pronounced rather artificially if it is made audibly different from the commoner word.

A

A a eɪ
AA 'eɪ ˋeɪ
A1 'eɪ ˋwʌn
a *the article; usual form:* ə
    strong-form: eɪ
Aaron ˋeərən
aback əˋbæk
abacus ˋæbəkəs
abandon əˋbændən
abase əˋbeɪs
abash əˋbæʃ
abate əˋbeɪt
abattoir ˋæbətwɑ(r) $ 'æbəˋtwɑr -ˋtwɔr
abbess ˋæbes -ɪs
abbey ˋæbɪ
abbot ˋæbət
abbreviate əˋbrivɪeɪt
abbreviation əˋbrivɪˋeɪʃn
ABC 'eɪ bi ˋsi
abdicate ˋæbdɪkeɪt
abdication 'æbdɪˋkeɪʃn
abdomen ˋæbdəmən -en -ɪn
    æbˋdəʊmən -en -ɪn
abdominal æbˋdɒmɪnl
abduct æbˋdʌkt əb-
abduction æbˋdʌkʃn əb-
Abel ˋeɪbl
Aberdeen 'æbəˋdin $ 'æbərˋdin
aberration 'æbəˋreɪʃn
Aberystwyth 'æbəˋrɪstwɪθ
abet əˋbet
abeyance əˋbeɪəns
abhor əbˋhɔ(r) əˋbɔ(r)
abide əˋbaɪd
ability *n, suffix* əˋbɪlətɪ
abject ˋæbdʒekt
abjure əbˋdʒʊə(r)
ablative ˋæblətɪv
ablaze əˋbleɪz
able ˋeɪbl
-able *suffix* əbl
-ably *suffix* əblɪ
abnormal 'æbˋnɔml $ -ˋnɔrml
abnormality 'æbnɔˋmælətɪ $ 'æbnɔr-
aboard əˋbɔd $ əˋbɔrd
abode əˋbəʊd
abolish əˋbɒlɪʃ
abolition 'æbəˋlɪʃn
A-bomb ˋeɪ bɒm
abominable əˋbɒmɪnəbl

abomination əˋbɒmɪˋneɪʃn
aboriginal 'æbəˋrɪdʒnl -dʒɪnl
aborigines 'æbəˋrɪdʒɪniz
abortion əˋbɔʃn $ əˋbɔrʃn
abortive əˋbɔtɪv $ əˋbɔrtɪv
abound əˋbaʊnd
about əˋbaʊt
about-face əˋbaʊt ˋfeɪs
above əˋbʌv
above-board əˋbʌv ˋbɔd $ ˋbɔrd
above-mentioned əˋbʌv ˋmenʃnd
abracadabra 'æbrəkəˋdæbrə
Abraham ˋeɪbrəhæm -həm
abrasion əˋbreɪʒn
abrasive əˋbreɪsɪv -eɪzɪv
abreast əˋbrest
abridge əˋbrɪdʒ
abroad əˋbrɔd
abrupt əˋbrʌpt
abscess ˋæbses -ɪs -əs ˋæps-
abscond əbˋskɒnd æb-
absence ˋæbsns ˋæps-
absent *adj* ˋæbsnt ˋæp-
absent *v* əbˋsent æb-
absentee 'æbsnˋti 'æp-
absinth ˋæbsɪnθ
absolute ˋæbsəlut 'æbsəˋlut 'æp-
absolutely *as an emphatic*
    equivalent of 'yes': 'æbsəˋlutlɪ
absolution 'æbsəˋluʃn 'æp-
absolve əbˋzɒlv æb- -ˋsɒlv
absorb əbˋsɔb əbˋz- əpˋs-
abstain əbˋsteɪn
abstemious əbˋstimɪəs
abstention əbˋstenʃn
abstinence ˋæbstɪnəns
abstract *adj* ˋæbstrækt
abstract *v* əbˋstrækt æb-
abstruse əbˋstrus
absurd əbˋsɜd əbˋz- əpˋs-
abundance əˋbʌndəns
abuse *n* əˋbjus
abuse *v* əˋbjuz
abusive əˋbjusɪv
abut əˋbʌt
abysmal əˋbɪzml
abyss əˋbɪs
Abyssinia 'æbɪˋsɪnɪə -bəˋs-
acacia əˋkeɪʃə
academic 'ækəˋdemɪk

2 academy

academy ə'kædəmɪ
accede ək'sid
accelerate ək'seləreɪt æk-
acceleration ək'selə'reɪʃn æk-
accelerator ək'seləreɪtə(r) æk-
accent n 'æksnt $ £ 'æksent
accent v æk'sent ək-
accentuate ək'sentʃueɪt
accept ək'sept ɪk-
acceptance ək'septəns
access 'ækses
accessary ək'sesərɪ
accession ək'seʃn
accessory ək'sesərɪ
accident 'æksɪdnt -səd- -dənt
accidental 'æksɪ'dentl -sə'd-
accidentally 'æksɪ'dentlɪ -|ɪ
acclaim ə'kleɪm
acclamation 'æklə'meɪʃn
acclimatise ə'klaɪmətaɪz
accolade 'ækəleɪd -lad $ 'ækə'leɪd -'lad
accommodate ə'komədeɪt
accommodation ə'komə'deɪʃn
accompaniment ə'kʌmpnɪmənt
accompanist ə'kʌmpənɪst -pn-
accompany ə'kʌmpnɪ -pən-
accomplice ə'kʌmplɪs $ £ -kom-
accomplish ə'kʌmplɪʃ $ £ -kom-
accord ə'kɔd $ ə'kɔrd
accordance ə'kɔdns -dəns $ ə'kɔr-
accordion ə'kɔdɪən $ ə'kɔr-
accost ə'kost $ ə'kɔst
account ə'kaʊnt
accountant ə'kaʊntənt
Accra ə'krɑ
accredit ə'kredɪt
accretion ə'kriʃn
accrue ə'kru
accumulate ə'kjumjʊleɪt -jəl-
accumulation ə'kjumjʊ'leɪʃn -jə'l-
accuracy 'ækjərəsɪ -jʊr-
accurate 'ækjərət -jʊr- -ɪt
accursed ə'kɜsɪd ə'kɜst
accusation 'ækjʊ'zeɪʃn
accusative ə'kjuzətɪv
accuse ə'kjuz
accustom ə'kʌstəm
ace eɪs
acetic ə'sitɪk -set- æs-
acetylene ə'setəlin $ -tlin -ɪn
ache eɪk
achieve ə'tʃiv
Achilles ə'kɪliz

achromatic 'ækrə'mætɪk -krəʊ-
acid 'æsɪd
acidify ə'sɪdɪfaɪ
-acious suffix 'eɪʃəs
acknowledge ək'nolɪdʒ
acme 'ækmɪ
acne 'æknɪ
acorn 'eɪkɔn $ 'eɪkərn
acoustic ə'kustɪk $ -'kaʊ- -'kju-
acquaint ə'kweɪnt
acquaintance ə'kweɪntəns
acquiesce 'ækwɪ'es
acquire ə'kwaɪə(r)
acquisition 'ækwɪ'zɪʃn
acquisitive ə'kwɪzətɪv -zɪt-
acquit ə'kwɪt
acquittal ə'kwɪtl
acre 'eɪkə(r)
acreage 'eɪkərɪdʒ
acrid 'ækrɪd
acrimonious 'ækrɪ'məʊnɪəs
acrimony 'ækrɪmənɪ $ -məʊnɪ
acrobat 'ækrəbæt
acropolis ə'kropəlɪs
across ə'kros $ ə'krɔs etc
acrostic ə'krostɪk $ ə'krɔstɪk etc
act ækt
action 'ækʃn
action stations 'ækʃn steɪʃnz
activate 'æktɪveɪt
active 'æktɪv
activity æk'tɪvətɪ -vɪtɪ
actor 'æktə(r)
actress 'æktrəs -ɪs
actual 'æktʃʊəl 'æktʃl
actuality 'æktʃʊ'ælətɪ
actually 'æktʃəlɪ -tʃʊlɪ
actuate 'æktʃueɪt
acuity ə'kjuətɪ
acumen ə'kjumən -en 'ækjʊmən -en
acute ə'kjut
ad æd
AD 'eɪ 'di
Ada 'eɪdə
adage 'ædɪdʒ
adagio ə'dadʒəʊ -aʒ- -ʒɪəʊ -dʒɪəʊ
Adam 'ædəm
adamant 'ædəmənt $ 'ædəmænt
adapt ə'dæpt
adaptation 'ædæp'teɪʃn
add æd
addenda ə'dendə
addendum ə'dendəm

adder ˈædə(r)
addict ˈædɪkt
addicted əˈdɪktɪd
addiction əˈdɪkʃn
adding-machine ˈædɪŋ məʃin
Addis Ababa ˈædɪs ˈæbəbə
addition əˈdɪʃn
addle ˈædl
address n əˈdres $ ˈædres etc
address v əˈdres
addressee ˈædreˈsi
adduce əˈdjus $ əˈdus
Adelaide ˈædɪleɪd -dəl-
Aden ˈeɪdn
adenoid ˈædɪnɔɪd $ £ -dn̩-
adept ˈædept əˈdept æˈd-
adequate ˈædɪkwət
adhere ədˈhɪə(r)
adherent ədˈhɪərnt
adhesion ədˈhiʒn
adhesive ədˈhisɪv -zɪv əˈdi-
ad hoc ˈæd ˈhok
adieu əˈdju æˈdjɜ $ əˈdu
ad infinitum ˈæd ɪnfɪˈnaɪtəm
adipose ˈædɪpəʊs
adjacent əˈdʒeɪsnt
adjectival ˈædʒɪkˈtaɪvl -dʒək-
adjective ˈædʒɪktɪv -dʒək-
adjoin əˈdʒɔɪn
adjourn əˈdʒɜn
adjudicate əˈdʒudɪkeɪt
adjudication əˈdʒudɪˈkeɪʃn
adjunct ˈædʒʌŋkt
adjust əˈdʒʌst
adjutant ˈædʒətənt -dʒʊt-
ad lib ˈæd ˈlɪb
administer ədˈmɪnɪstə(r)
administration ədˈmɪnɪˈstreɪʃn
administrative ədˈmɪnɪstrətɪv
$ -reɪtɪv
administrator ədˈmɪnɪstreɪtə(r)
admirable ˈædmrəbl -mər-
admiral ˈædmr̩l -mərl
admiralty ˈædmr̩ltɪ -mərl-
admiration ˈædməˈreɪʃn -mɪˈr-
admire ədˈmaɪə(r)
admissible ədˈmɪsəbl
admission ədˈmɪʃn
admit ədˈmɪt
admittance ədˈmɪtns -təns
admonish ədˈmonɪʃ
ad nauseam ˈæd ˈnɔsɪæm -ɔzɪ- -ɪəm
$ -ɔʃɪ- -ɔʒɪ-

ado əˈdu
adobe əˈdəʊbɪ
adolescence ˈædəˈlesns
adolescent ˈædəˈlesnt
Adonais ˈædəˈneɪɪs -dəʊˈn-
Adonis əˈdəʊnɪs $ əˈdonɪs etc
adopt əˈdopt
adoption əˈdopʃn
adoration ˈædəˈreɪʃn
adore əˈdɔ(r)
adorn əˈdɔn $ əˈdɔrn
adrenalin(e) əˈdrenəlɪn
Adrian ˈeɪdrɪən
Adriatic ˈeɪdrɪˈætɪk
adrift əˈdrɪft
adroit əˈdrɔɪt
adulation ˈædjʊˈleɪʃn $ ˈædʒʊˈleɪʃn
adult ˈædʌlt əˈdʌlt
adulterate əˈdʌltəreɪt
adultery əˈdʌltərɪ -trɪ
advance ədˈvans $ -ˈvæns
advantage ədˈvantɪdʒ $ -ˈvæn-
advantageous
ˈædvənˈteɪdʒəs -væn- £ -van-
advent ˈædvent -vənt
adventitious ˈædvenˈtɪʃəs
adventure ədˈventʃə(r)
adverb ˈædvɜb
adverbial ədˈvɜbɪəl
adversary ˈædvəsərɪ -srɪ $ -ərserɪ
adverse ˈædvɜs
adversity ədˈvɜsətɪ
advert colloq n ˈædvɜt
advert v ədˈvɜt
advertise ˈædvətaɪz $ ˈædvərtaɪz
advertisement ədˈvɜtɪsmənt -ɪzm-
$ ˈædvərˈtaɪzmənt etc
advice ədˈvaɪs
advisability ədˈvaɪzəˈbɪlətɪ
advisable ədˈvaɪzəbl
advise ədˈvaɪz
advisory ədˈvaɪzərɪ -zrɪ
advocacy ˈædvəkəsɪ
advocate n ˈædvəkət -kɪt -keɪt
advocate v ˈædvəkeɪt
Aegean iˈdʒiən ɪˈdʒ-
aegis ˈidʒɪs
Aeneas iˈniəs ɪˈn- -æs ˈiniæs
Aeneid ˈiniɪd ɪˈn-
aeon ˈiən ˈion
aerate ˈeəreɪt ˈeɪər-
aerial ˈeərɪəl
aerodrome ˈeərədrəʊm

4 aerodynamic

aerodynamic 'eərəʊdaɪ'næmɪk
aeronautic 'eərəʊ'nɔtɪk
aeroplane 'eərəpleɪn
aerosol 'eərəsol $ -sɔl -səʊl
Aeschylus 'iskɪləs $ 'es-
Aesop 'isop $ 'isəp
aesthete 'isθit $ 'es-
aesthetic is'θetɪk ɪs- $ es-
afar ə'fa(r)
affable 'æfəbl
affair(e) ə'feə(r)
affect ə'fekt
affectation 'æfek'teɪʃn
affection ə'fekʃn
affiliate ə'fɪlɪeɪt
affiliation ə'fɪlɪ'eɪʃn
affinity ə'fɪnətɪ
affirm ə'fɜm
affix n 'æfɪks
affix v ə'fɪks
afflict ə'flɪkt
affliction ə'flɪkʃn
affluence 'æfluəns
affluent 'æfluənt
afford ə'fɔd $ ə'fɔrd
affray ə'freɪ
affront ə'frʌnt
Afghan 'æfgæn -gan
Afghanistan æf'gænɪ'stan $ -'stæn etc
afield ə'fild
afire ə'faɪə(r)
aflame ə'fleɪm
afloat ə'fləʊt
afoot ə'fʊt
afore-mentioned ə'fɔ 'menʃnd $ ə'fɔr
afore-said ə'fɔ sed $ ə'fɔr
afraid ə'freɪd
afresh ə'freʃ
Africa 'æfrɪkə
Afrikaans 'æfrɪ'kans $ -'kanz etc
Afrikaner 'æfrɪ'kanə(r) $ -'kænər
Afro- prefix 'æfrəʊ
aft aft $ æft
after 'aftə(r) $ 'æftər
after-care 'aftə keə(r) $ 'æftər keər
after-effect 'aftər ɪfekt $ 'æftər
afternoon 'aftə'nun $ 'æftər'nun
afterthought 'aftəθɔt $ 'æftər-
afterward(s) 'aftəwəd(z) -wʊd(z)
  $ 'æftərwərd(z)
again ə'gen ə'geɪn
against ə'genst ə'geɪnst
agape ə'geɪp

agate 'ægət
Agatha 'ægəθə
age eɪdʒ
aged adj 'a man aged 30': 'eɪdʒd
aged attrib adj 'an aged man': 'eɪdʒɪd
agency 'eɪdʒənsɪ
agenda ə'dʒendə
agent 'eɪdʒənt
agent provocateur 'æʒõ prə'vokə'tɜ
aggrandize ə'grændaɪz 'ægrən-
aggravate 'ægrəveɪt
aggregate 'ægrɪgət -grəgɪt -geɪt
aggression ə'greʃn
aggressive ə'gresɪv
aggrieve ə'griv
aghast ə'gast $ ə'gæst
agile 'ædʒaɪl $ 'ædʒl
agitate 'ædʒɪteɪt
agitation 'ædʒɪ'teɪʃn
aglow ə'gləʊ
Agnes 'ægnɪs -nəs
agnostic æg'nostɪk
agnosticism æg'nostɪsɪzm
ago ə'gəʊ
agog ə'gog
agonise 'ægənaɪz
agony 'ægənɪ
agoraphobia 'ægərə'fəʊbɪə -grə-
agrarian ə'greərɪən
agree ə'gri
agricultural 'ægrɪ'kʌltʃərl
agriculture 'ægrɪkʌltʃə(r)
aground ə'graʊnd
ague 'eɪgju
ah a
aha 'a'ha
ahead ə'hed
ahem conventionally as in reading
  aloud: ə'hem but in spontaneous
  manner ə'hm mhm or a realistic
  throat-clearing noise
ahoy ə'hɔɪ
aid eɪd
aide-de-camp 'eɪd də 'kõ $ 'kæmp etc
aide-memoire 'eɪd mem'wa(r)
ail eɪl
aim eɪm
air eə(r)
aircraft 'eəkraft $ 'eərkræft
Airedale 'eədeɪl $ 'eər-
air hostess 'eə həʊstes -ɪs -əs $ 'eər
airline 'eəlaɪn $ 'eər-
airmail 'eəmeɪl $ 'eər-

airplane 'eəpleın $ 'eər-
airport 'eəpɔt $ 'eərpɔrt
air-raid 'eə reıd $ 'eər
airtight 'eətaıt $ 'eər-
airy 'eərı
aisle aıl
aitch eıtʃ
ajar ə'dʒɑ(r)
akimbo ə'kımbəʊ
akin ə'kın
Alabama 'ælə'bæmə £ -'bɑmə
alabaster 'æləbastə(r) $ £ -bæstə(r)
à la carte 'ɑ lɑ 'kat $ 'kɑrt
Aladdin ə'lædın $ -dn
à la mode 'ɑ lɑ 'məʊd
Alan 'ælən
alarm ə'lɑm $ ə'lɑrm
alas ə'læs £ ə'lɑs
Alaska ə'læskə
Alastair 'æləstə(r) -steə(r)
Albania æl'beınıə
albatross 'ælbətros
albeit ɔl'biıt
Alberta æl'bɜtə
albino 'æl'binəʊ $ 'æl'baınəʊ
album 'ælbəm
albumen 'ælbjʊmen -mən -mın
alchemist 'ælkımıst -kəm-
alcohol 'ælkəhol $ -hɔl etc
alcove 'ælkəʊv
alderman 'ɔldəmən $ -dərmən
Alderney 'ɔldənı £ 'ol- $ -dərn-
Aldershot 'ɔldəʃot £ 'ol- $ -dər-
Aldous 'ɔldəs £ 'ol-
ale eıl
Alec 'ælık
alert ə'lɜt
Alex 'ælıks
Alexander 'ælıg'zandə(r) $ -'zændər
Alfred 'ælfrıd
alfresco æl'freskəʊ
algae 'ældʒi -dʒaı
algebra 'ældʒıbrə
algebraic 'ældʒı'breıık
Algeria æl'dʒıərıə
Algernon 'ældʒənən $ -ərnon -nən
Algiers æl'dʒıəz $ -'dʒıərz
alias 'eılıəs 'eılıæs
Ali Baba 'ælı 'babə
alibi 'ælıbaı -ləb-
Alice 'ælıs
alien 'eılıən
alight ə'laıt

align ə'laın
alike ə'laık
alimentary 'ælı'mentrı $ £ -tərı
alimony 'ælımənı $ -məʊnı
Alison 'ælısn
Alistair 'æləstə(r) -steə(r)
alive ə'laıv
alkali 'ælkəlaı
all ɔl
Allah 'ælə
allay ə'leı
allegation 'ælı'geıʃn
allege ə'ledʒ
allegiance ə'lidʒəns
allegory 'ælıgərı -grı $ -gɔrı
allegro ə'leıgrəʊ -'leg-
alleluia 'ælı'lujə
allergy 'ælədʒı $ 'ælər-
alleviate ə'livıeıt
alley 'ælı
alliance ə'laıəns
allied attrib 'ælaıd ə'laıd
alligator 'ælıgeıtə(r)
alliteration ə'lıtə'reıʃn
allocate 'æləkeıt
allot ə'lot
allow ə'laʊ
alloy n 'ælɔı
alloy v ə'lɔı
all right 'ɔl 'raıt
All Saints Day 'ɔl 'seınts deı
allspice 'ɔlspaıs
allude ə'lud £ -ljud
allure ə'ljʊə(r) $ £ ə'lʊə(r)
allusion ə'luʒn £ -lju-
alluvial ə'luvıəl
ally n 'ælaı ə'laı
ally v ə'laı $ 'ælaı
Alma Mater 'ælmə 'matə(r) 'meıtə(r)
almanac 'ɔlmənæk
almighty 'ɔl'maıtı
almond 'amənd $ 'ælm- 'æm-
almoner 'ɔlmənə(r) 'amənə(r)
 $ £ 'ælmənə(r)
almost 'ɔlməʊst £ 'ol-
alms amz
aloft ə'loft $ ə'lɔft
alone ə'ləʊn
along ə'loŋ $ ə'lɔŋ etc
alongside ə'loŋ'saıd $ ə'lɔŋ- etc
aloof ə'luf
aloud ə'laʊd
alpaca æl'pækə

alpha ˈælfə
alphabet ˈælfəbet -bət -bɪt
alpine ˈælpaɪn
Alps ælps
already ɔlˈredɪ
alright ˈɔlˈraɪt
Alsatian ælˈseɪʃn
also ˈɔlsəʊ £ ˈolsəʊ
altar ˈɔltə(r) £ ˈol-
alter ˈɔltə(r) £ ˈol-
alteration ˈɔltəˈreɪʃn £ ˈol-
altercation ˈɔltəˈkeɪʃn £ ˈol- $ -tər-
alternate adj ɔlˈtɜnət £ ol-
alternate v ˈɔltəneɪt £ ˈol- $ -tɜrn-
alternative ɔlˈtɜnətɪv £ ol-
although ɔlˈðəʊ £ ol-
altimeter ˈæltɪmɪtə(r) ˈɔl-
    $ ælˈtɪmɪtər etc
altitude ˈæltɪtjud -tʃud $ -tud
alto ˈæltəʊ
altogether ˈɔltəˈgeðə(r)
altruism ˈæltruɪzm
alum ˈæləm
aluminium ˈæləˈmɪnɪəm £ -ljʊ-
aluminum əˈlumɪnəm
always ˈɔlwɪz -weɪz -wəz
am usual form after 'I': m
    otherwise: əm strong-form: æm
a.m. ˈeɪ ˈem
amalgam əˈmælgəm
amalgamation əˈmælgəˈmeɪʃn
Amanda əˈmændə
amanuenses əˈmænjuˈensiz
amanuensis əˈmænjuˈensɪs
amass əˈmæs
amateur ˈæmətə(r) -tɜ(r)
    $ £ -ətʃə(r) -ətʃʊə(r) etc
amaze əˈmeɪz
Amazon ˈæməzn $ -zon etc
ambassador æmˈbæsədə(r)
ambassadorial æmˈbæsəˈdɔrɪəl
amber ˈæmbə(r)
ambidextrous ˈæmbɪˈdekstrəs
ambiguity ˈæmbɪˈgjuətɪ
ambiguous æmˈbɪgjʊəs
ambition æmˈbɪʃn
ambitious æmˈbɪʃəs
ambivalent æmˈbɪvələnt
amble ˈæmbl
Ambrose ˈæmbrəʊz
ambrosia æmˈbrəʊzɪə $ -əʊʒə
ambulance ˈæmbjələns -bjʊ-
ambush ˈæmbʊʃ

Amelia əˈmilɪə
ameliorate əˈmilɪəreɪt
amen ˈɑˈmen ˈeɪˈmen
amenable əˈminəbl
amend əˈmend
amenity əˈmenətɪ £ əˈminətɪ
America əˈmerɪkə
American əˈmerɪkən
amethyst ˈæmɪθɪst -məθ-
amiable ˈeɪmɪəbl
amicable ˈæmɪkəbl
amidships əˈmɪdʃɪps
amidst əˈmɪdst
amiss əˈmɪs
amity ˈæmɪtɪ ˈæmətɪ
ammonia əˈməʊnɪə
ammunition ˈæmjʊˈnɪʃn
amnesia æmˈnizɪə $ £ -iʒə
amnesty ˈæmnəstɪ -nɪs-
amoeba əˈmibə
amok əˈmok
among əˈmʌŋ
amoral ˈeɪˈmorl ˈæˈm- $ ˈeɪˈmɔrl etc
amorous ˈæmərəs
amorphous əˈmɔfəs $ -ˈmɔr-
amount əˈmaʊnt
amour əˈmʊə(r)
Amos ˈeɪmos $ ˈeɪməs
ampere ˈæmpeə(r) $ -pɪər
amphibian æmˈfɪbɪən
amphitheatre($ -ter) ˈæmfɪθɪətə(r)
ample ˈæmpl
amplify ˈæmplɪfaɪ
amplitude ˈæmplɪtʃud -tjud $ -tud
ampoule ˈæmpul
ampul(e) ˈæmpjul
amputate ˈæmpjʊteɪt
amuck əˈmʌk
amulet ˈæmjʊlɪt -lət
amuse əˈmjuz
Amy ˈeɪmɪ
an usual form: ən strong-form: æn
-ana suffix ˈɑnə $ ˈænə
anachronism əˈnækrənɪzm
anaconda ˈænəˈkondə
anaemia əˈnimɪə
anaemic əˈnimɪk
anaesthesia ˈænɪsˈθizɪə $ £ -iʒə
anaesthetic ˈænɪsˈθetɪk
anaesthetist əˈnisθətɪst $ əˈnes-
anaesthetize əˈnisθətaɪz $ əˈnes-
anagram ˈænəgræm
analogue ˈænəlog $ -lɔg

analogous ə'næləgəs
analogy ə'nælədʒɪ
analyse($ -lyze) 'ænəlaɪz
analyses ə'næləsiz
analysis ə'næləsɪs
analyst 'ænəlɪst
analytic 'ænə'lɪtɪk
analytical 'ænə'lɪtɪkl
analyze 'ænəlaɪz
anarchy 'ænəkɪ $ 'ænərkɪ
anathema ə'næθəmə
anatomical 'ænə'tomɪkl
anatomy ə'nætəmɪ
-ance suffix əns
ancestor 'ænsɪstə(r) $ £ -sestə(r)
anchor 'æŋkə(r)
anchovy 'æntʃəʊvɪ -tʃəvɪ æn'tʃəʊvɪ
ancient 'eɪnʃnt
ancillary æn'sɪlərɪ $ 'ænsɪlerɪ etc
and usual form: ən also often after t,
    d, f, v, θ, ð, s, z, ʃ, ʒ (the alveolar
    plosives and all fricatives): n
    strong-form: ænd
andante æn'dæntei -tɪ
Andes 'ændiz
Andrew 'ændru
anecdote 'ænɪkdəʊt
anemia ə'nimɪə
anemic ə'nimɪk
anemone ə'nemənɪ
anesthesia 'ænəs'θiziə -nɪs- $ -iʒə
anesthetic 'ænəs'θetɪk
anesthetist ə'nisθətɪst $ ə'nes-
anesthetize ə'nisθətaɪz $ ə'nes-
anew ə'nju $ ə'nu
angel 'eɪndʒl
Angela 'ændʒələ
anger 'æŋgə(r)
angina æn'dʒaɪnə
angle 'æŋgl
Anglican 'æŋglɪkən
Anglicise 'æŋglɪsaɪz
Anglo- prefix 'æŋgləʊ
Anglo-Saxon 'æŋgləʊ 'sæksn
Angola æŋ'gəʊlə
angora æŋ'gɔrə
angostura 'æŋgə'stjʊərə
    $ -'stʊə- etc
angry 'æŋgrɪ
anguish 'æŋgwɪʃ
angular 'æŋgjʊlə(r)
Angus 'æŋgəs
animal 'ænəml 'ænɪml

animate adj 'ænɪmət -nəm -mɪt
animate v 'ænɪmeɪt
animosity 'ænɪ'mosətɪ -nə'm-
anise 'ænɪs
Anita ə'nitə
Ankara 'æŋkərə
ankle 'æŋkl
Ann(e) æn
Anna 'ænə
Annabel 'ænəbel
Annabella 'ænə'belə
annals 'ænlz
annex(e) n 'æneks
annex v ə'neks
annihilate ə'naɪəleɪt -'naɪl-
anniversary 'ænɪ'vɜsrɪ -nə'v- $ £ -sərɪ
Anno Domini 'ænəʊ 'domɪnaɪ -ɪnɪ
annotate 'ænəteɪt
announce ə'naʊns
annoy ə'nɔɪ
annual 'ænjʊəl
annuity ə'njuətɪ $ -'nu-
annul ə'nʌl
annunciation ə'nʌnsɪ'eɪʃn
anoint ə'nɔɪnt
anomalous ə'nomələs
anon. ə'nonɪməs mainly jocular: ə'non
anonymous ə'nonɪməs
anopheles ə'nofəliz
anorak 'ænəræk
another ə'nʌðə(r)
answer 'ɑnsə(r) $ 'ænsər
ant ænt
antagonism æn'tægənɪzm
antagonize æn'tægənaɪz
antarctic æn'taktɪk $ æn'tarktɪk
ante- prefix 'æntɪ
antecedent 'æntɪ'sidnt
antedate 'æntɪ'deɪt
antediluvian 'æntɪdɪ'luvɪən £ -'lju-
antelope 'æntɪləʊp
antenatal 'æntɪ'neɪtl
antenna æn'tenə
antennae æn'teni -naɪ
anterior æn'tɪərɪə(r)
ante-room 'æntɪ rʊm $ £ rum etc
anthem 'ænθəm
anthology æn'θolədʒɪ
Anthony 'æntənɪ $ -nθə- etc
anthracite 'ænθrəsaɪt
anthropoid 'ænθrəpɔɪd
anthropological 'ænθrəpə'lodʒɪkl
anthropology 'ænθrə'polədʒɪ

anti- *prefix* ˈæntɪ $ ˈæntaɪ
anti-aircraft ˈæntɪˈeəkrɑft $ ˈeərkræft
antibiotic ˈæntɪbaɪˈotɪk $ -taɪ-
antibody ˈæntɪbodɪ
antic ˈæntɪk
anticipate ænˈtɪsəpeɪt -sɪp-
anticipation ænˈtɪsəˈpeɪʃn -sɪˈp-
anticlimax ˈæntɪˈklaɪmæks $ -taɪ-
anti-clockwise ˈæntɪˈklokwaɪz $ -taɪ
anticyclone ˈæntɪˈsaɪkləun $ -taɪ-
antidote ˈæntɪdəut
antifreeze ˈæntɪfriz $ -taɪ-
Antilles ænˈtɪliz
antimony ˈæntɪmənɪ $ -məunɪ
antipathetic ˈæntɪpəˈθetɪk
antipathy ænˈtɪpəθɪ
Antipodes ænˈtɪpədiz
antiquarian ˈæntɪˈkweərɪən
antiquary ˈæntɪkwərɪ $ -kwerɪ
antiquated ˈæntɪkweɪtɪd
antique ænˈtik
antiquity ænˈtɪkwətɪ
antirrhinum ˈæntɪˈraɪnəm
anti-Semitism ˈæntɪ ˈsemɪtɪzm $ ˈæntaɪ
antiseptic ˈæntɪˈseptɪk
anti-social ˈæntɪ ˈsəuʃl $ æntaɪ
antithesis ænˈtɪθəsɪs
antler ˈæntlə(r)
Antoinette ˈæntwəˈnet £ ˈöt-
Antony ˈæntənɪ
antonym ˈæntənɪm
Antwerp ˈæntwəp
anus ˈeɪnəs
anvil ˈænvɪl
anxiety æŋˈzaɪətɪ æŋgˈz-
anxious ˈæŋkʃəs
any ˈenɪ
anybody ˈenɪbodɪ -bədɪ
any case, in ɪn ˈenɪ keɪs
anyhow ˈenɪhau
anyone ˈenɪwʌn *weak-form:* ˈenɪwən
any place($ anyplace) ˈenɪ pleɪs
any rate, at əˈtenɪ reɪt $ £ ət ˈenɪ *etc*
anything ˈenɪθɪŋ
anytime ˈenɪtaɪm
anyway ˈenɪweɪ
anywhere ˈenɪweə(r) $ -hweər *etc*
aorta eɪˈɔtə $ eɪˈɔrtə
apart əˈpat $ əˈpart
apartheid əˈpatheɪt -teɪt -haɪt -taɪt
  $ əˈpar-
apartment əˈpatmənt $ əˈpart-
apathetic ˈæpəˈθetɪk

apathy ˈæpəθɪ
ape eɪp
aperitive əˈperətɪv
aperture ˈæpətʃə(r) -tʃuə(r) $ ˈæpər- *etc*
apex ˈeɪpeks
aphorism ˈæfərɪzm
apiary ˈeɪpɪərɪ $ ˈeɪpɪerɪ
apiece əˈpis
aplomb əˈplom əˈplö
apocalypse əˈpokəlɪps
apocryphal əˈpokrɪfl
Apollo əˈpoləu
apologetic əˈpoləˈdʒetɪk
apologise əˈpolədʒaɪz
apology əˈpolədʒɪ
apoplectic ˈæpəˈplektɪk
apoplexy ˈæpəpleksɪ
apostate ˈæpəsteɪt $ əˈposteɪt
a posteriori ˈeɪ ˈpostɪərɪˈɔraɪ
apostle əˈposl
apostrophe əˈpostrəfɪ
appal($ -all) əˈpɔl
apparatus ˈæpəˈreɪtəs $ -ˈræt-
apparent əˈpærnt əˈpeərnt
apparition ˈæpəˈrɪʃn
appeal əˈpil
appear əˈpɪə(r)
appearance əˈpɪərns
appease əˈpiz
append əˈpend
appendices əˈpendɪsiz
appendicitis əˈpendɪˈsaɪtɪs -təs
appendix əˈpendɪks
appertain ˈæpəˈteɪn $ -pər-
appetite ˈæpətaɪt -pɪt-
applaud əˈplɔd
applause əˈplɔz
apple ˈæpl
apple sauce ˈæpl ˈsɔs $ ˈæpl sɔs
appliance əˈplaɪəns
applicable ˈæplɪkəbl əˈplɪkəbl
applicant ˈæplɪkənt
application ˈæplɪˈkeɪʃn
application form ˈæplɪˈkeɪʃn fɔm
  $ fɔrm
apply əˈplaɪ
appoint əˈpɔɪnt
apportion əˈpɔʃn $ əˈpɔrʃn
apposite ˈæpəzɪt
appraisal əˈpreɪzl
appreciable əˈpriʃəbl
appreciate əˈpriʃɪeɪt
appreciation əˈpriʃɪˈeɪʃn -ɪsɪ-

apprehend 'æprɪ'hend
apprehension 'æprɪ'henʃn
apprehensive 'æprɪ'hensɪv
apprentice ə'prentɪs
apprise ə'praɪz
approach ə'prəʊtʃ
approbation 'æprə'beɪʃn
appropriate adj ə'prəʊprɪət
appropriate v ə'prəʊprɪeɪt
approval ə'pruvl
approve ə'pruv
approximate adj ə'prɒksɪmət
approximate v ə'prɒksɪmeɪt
apricot 'eɪprɪkɒt $ 'æp-
April 'eɪprl
a priori 'eɪ praɪ'ɔraɪ
apron 'eɪprən
apron-strings 'eɪprən strɪŋz
apropos 'æprə'pəʊ
apse æps
apt æpt
aptitude 'æptɪtjud -tʃud $ -tud
aqualung 'ækwəlʌŋ
aquamarine 'ækwəmə'rin
aquarium ə'kweərɪəm
aquatic ə'kwætɪk $ ə'kwɒtɪk
aqueduct 'ækwɪdʌkt
aqueous 'eɪkwɪəs 'æk-
aquiline 'ækwɪlaɪn
Arab 'ærəb
arabesque 'ærə'besk
Arabia ə'reɪbɪə
Arabian ə'reɪbɪən
Arabic 'ærəbɪk
arable 'ærəbl
arbiter 'ɑbɪtə(r) $ 'ɑr-
arbitrary 'ɑbɪtrərɪ -tr̩ɪ $ 'ɑrbɪtrerɪ
arbitrate 'ɑbɪtreɪt $ 'ɑr-
arboreal ɑ'bɔrɪəl $ ɑr-
arbour($ -bor) 'ɑbə(r) $ 'ɑrbər
arc ɑk $ ɑrk
arcade ɑ'keɪd $ ɑr-
arch ɑtʃ $ ɑrtʃ
arch- prefix ɑtʃ $ ɑrtʃ
archaeological 'ɑkɪə'lɒdʒɪkl $ 'ɑrkɪə-
archaeologist 'ɑkɪ'ɒlədʒɪst $ 'ɑrkɪ-
archaeology 'ɑkɪ'ɒlədʒɪ $ 'ɑrkɪ-
archaic ɑ'keɪɪk $ ɑr-
archangel ɑk'eɪndʒl $ ɑrk-
archbishop ɑtʃ'bɪʃəp $ ɑrtʃ-
archbishopric ɑtʃ'bɪʃəprɪk $ ɑrtʃ-
archdeacon ɑtʃ'dikən $ ɑrtʃ-
archduke ɑtʃ'djuk $ ɑrtʃ'duk etc

archer 'ɑtʃə(r) $ 'ɑrtʃər
archetype 'ɑkɪtaɪp $ 'ɑrkɪ-
Archibald 'ɑtʃɪbɔld $ 'ɑrtʃɪ-
Archie 'ɑtʃɪ $ 'ɑrtʃɪ
archipelago 'ɑkɪ'peləgəʊ $ 'ɑr- 'ɑrtʃɪ-
architect 'ɑkɪtekt $ 'ɑrk-
architectural 'ɑkɪ'tektʃərl $ 'ɑrkɪ-
architecture 'ɑkɪtektʃə(r) $ 'ɑrkɪ-
archives 'ɑkaɪvz $ 'ɑrk-
archway 'ɑtʃweɪ $ 'ɑrtʃ-
arc lamp 'ɑk læmp $ 'ɑrk
arc light 'ɑk laɪt $ 'ɑrk
arctic 'ɑktɪk $ 'ɑrk-
Arden 'ɑdn $ 'ɑrdn
ardent 'ɑdnt $ 'ɑrdnt
ardour 'ɑdə(r) $ 'ɑrdər
arduous 'ɑdjʊəs $ 'ɑrdʒʊəs
are usual form: ə(r) strong-form: ɑ(r)
    see also: they're, we're, you're, aren't
area 'eərɪə
arena ə'rinə
aren't ɑnt $ ɑrnt
Argentina 'ɑdʒən'tinə $ 'ɑrdʒ-
argue 'ɑgju $ 'ɑrgju
argument 'ɑgjʊmənt $ 'ɑrg-
argumentative 'ɑgjʊ'mentətɪv $ 'ɑrg-
aria 'ɑrɪə $ 'ærɪə
-arian suffix 'eərɪən
arid 'ærɪd
aright ə'raɪt
arise ə'raɪz
aristocracy 'ærɪ'stɒkrəsɪ
aristocrat 'ærɪstəkræt $ ə'rɪst- etc
aristocratic 'ærɪstə'krætɪk $ ə'rɪst- etc
Aristophanes 'ærɪs'tɒfəniz
Aristotle 'ærɪstɒtl
Arizona 'ærɪ'zəʊnə
arithmetic ə'rɪθmətɪk
arithmetical 'ærɪθ'metɪkl
ark ɑk $ ɑrk
Arkansas 'ɑkənsɔ $ 'ɑrk-
arm ɑm $ ɑrm
armada ɑ'mɑdə $ ɑr- ɑr'meɪdə
armadillo 'ɑmə'dɪləʊ $ 'ɑrm-
armament 'ɑməmənt $ 'ɑrm-
armchair 'ɑmtʃeə(r) ɑm'tʃeə(r) $ 'ɑrm-
arm-in-arm 'ɑm ɪn 'ɑm $ 'ɑrm ɪn 'ɑrm
armistice 'ɑmɪstɪs $ 'ɑrm-
armour($ -mor) 'ɑmə(r) $ 'ɑrmər
armpit 'ɑmpɪt $ 'ɑrm-
army 'ɑmɪ $ 'ɑrmɪ
Arnold 'ɑnld $ 'ɑrnld
aroma ə'rəʊmə

arose ə'rəʊz
around ə'raʊnd
arouse ə'raʊz
arpeggio ɑ'pedʒəʊ -ʒɪəʊ $ ar-
arrange ə'reɪndʒ
arrangement ə'reɪndʒmənt
array ə'reɪ
arrears ə'rɪəz $ ə'rɪərz
arrest ə'rest
arrival ə'raɪvl
arrive ə'raɪv
arrogance 'ærəgəns
arrogant 'ærəgənt
arrow 'ærəʊ
arrowroot 'ærəʊrut
arsenal 'ɑsnl $ 'ɑrs-
arsenic 'ɑsnɪk $ 'ɑrs-
arson 'ɑsn $ 'ɑrsn
art ɑt $ ɑrt
arterial ɑ'tɪərɪəl $ ɑr't-
artery 'ɑtərɪ -trɪ $ 'ɑrt-
artesian ɑ'tizɪən $ ɑr'tiʒn
artful 'ɑtfl -fʊl $ 'ɑrt-
arthritic ɑ'θrɪtɪk $ ar-
arthritis ɑ'θraɪtɪs -təs $ ar-
Arthur 'ɑθə(r) $ 'ɑrθər
artichoke 'ɑtɪtʃəʊk $ 'ɑrt-
article 'ɑtɪkl 'ɑtəkl $ 'ɑrt-
articulate adj ɑ'tɪkjʊlət -jəl- $ ar-
articulate v ɑ'tɪkjʊleɪt -jəl- $ ar-
artifact 'ɑtɪfækt $ 'ɑrt-
artifice 'ɑtɪfɪs -təf- $ 'ɑrt-
artificial 'ɑtɪ'fɪʃl -təf- $ 'ɑrt-
artillery ɑ'tɪlərɪ $ ar-
artisan 'ɑtɪ'zæn 'ɑtɪzæn $ 'ɑrtɪzn
artist 'ɑtɪst $ 'ɑrtɪst
artiste ɑ'tist $ ɑr'tist
artistic ɑ'tɪstɪk $ ar-
artistry 'ɑtɪstrɪ $ 'ɑrt-
Aryan 'eərɪən
as usual form: əz strong-form: æz
asbestos æs'bestəs æz- £ -tos
ascend ə'send
ascension ə'senʃn
Ascension Day ə'senʃn deɪ
ascent ə'sent
ascertain 'æsə'teɪn $ 'æsər-
ascetic ə'setɪk
Ascot 'æskət -kot
ascribe ə'skraɪb
aseptic æ'septɪk $ £ eɪ'septɪk
ash æʃ
ashamed ə'ʃeɪmd

ashen 'æʃn
ashore ə'ʃɔ(r)
ash-tray 'æʃ treɪ
Ash Wednesday 'æʃ 'wenzdɪ -deɪ
Asia 'eɪʃə $ £ 'eɪʒə etc
Asian 'eɪʃn $ £ 'eɪʒn etc
Asiatic 'eɪʃɪ'ætɪk $ £ 'eɪʒɪ-
aside ə'saɪd
asinine 'æsɪnaɪn
ask ɑsk $ æsk
askance ə'skæns £ ə'skɑns
asked 'ɑst 'ɑskt $ 'æs-
askew ə'skju
asleep ə'slip
asp æsp
aspect 'æspekt
aspersion ə'spɜʃn $ £ -ʒn
asphalt 'æsfælt $ £ -fɔlt
asphyxia əs'fɪksɪə -kʃə $ æs-
asphyxiate əs'fɪksɪeɪt $ æs-
asphyxiation əs'fɪksɪ'eɪʃn $ æs-
aspic 'æspɪk
aspidistra 'æspə'dɪstrə
aspirant 'æspɪrənt $ £ ə'spaɪərnt etc
aspirate n 'æspərət
aspirate v 'æspəreɪt
aspiration 'æspə'reɪʃn
aspire ə'spaɪə(r)
aspirin 'æsprɪn $ -pər- etc
ass animal æs
ass term of abuse ɑs $ £ æs
assail ə'seɪl
assailant ə'seɪlənt
Assam æ'sæm
assassin ə'sæsɪn $ ə'sæsn
assassinate ə'sæsɪneɪt $ £ -sn̩eɪt
assault ə'sɔlt £ ə'sɒlt
assemble ə'sembl
assembly ə'semblɪ
assembly-hall ə'semblɪ hɔl
assembly-line ə'semblɪ laɪn
assent ə'sent
assert ə'sɜt
assertion ə'sɜʃn
assertive ə'sɜtɪv
assess ə'ses
assessor ə'sesə(r)
asset 'æset 'æsɪt
assiduity 'æsɪ'djuətɪ $ -'du-
assiduous ə'sɪdjʊəs $ -dʒʊ-
assign ə'saɪn
assignment ə'saɪnmənt
assimilate ə'sɪmɪleɪt

assimilation ə'sɪmə'leɪʃn
assist ə'sɪst
assistant ə'sɪstənt
assize ə'saɪz
associate n ə'səuʃɪət -ʃɪeɪt
associate v ə'səuʃɪeɪt
association ə'səuʃɪ'eɪʃn ə'səusɪ-
assonance 'æsənəns
assorted ə'sɔtɪd $ -'sɔrt-
assortment ə'sɔtmənt $ -'sɔrt-
assuage ə'sweɪdʒ
assume ə'sjum $ £ ə'sum
assumption ə'sʌmpʃn -mʃn
assurance ə'ʃuərns £ -'ʃɔr-
assure ə'ʃuə(r) £ ə'ʃɔ(r)
assuredly ə'ʃuərɪdlɪ £ ə'ʃɔr-
Assyria ə'sɪrɪə
aster 'æstə(r)
asterisk 'æstərɪsk
astern ə'stɜn
asthma 'æsmə $ 'æzmə
asthmatic æs'mætɪk $ æz-
astigmatic 'æstɪg'mætɪk
astigmatism ə'stɪgmətɪzm
astonish ə'stonɪʃ
astonishment ə'stonɪʃmənt
astound ə'staund
astrakhan 'æstrə'kæn -'kɑn
   $ 'æstrəkən etc
astray ə'streɪ
astride ə'straɪd
astringent ə'strɪndʒənt æ's-
astrological 'æstrə'lodʒɪkl
astrology ə'strolədʒɪ
astronaut 'æstrənɔt
astronomical 'æstrə'nomɪkl
astronomy ə'stronəmɪ
astute ə'stjut $ ə'stut
asunder ə'sʌndə(r)
asylum ə'saɪləm
at usual form: ət strong-form: æt
at all adv phrase ə'tɔl $ ət 'ɔl
at all events ə'tɔl ɪvents $ ət 'ɔl
-ate n adj suffix ət ɪt eɪt
-ate v suffix eɪt
ate past of 'eat' et $ eɪt
atheism 'eɪθɪɪzm
atheist 'eɪθɪɪst
atheistic 'eɪθɪ'ɪstɪk
Athenian ə'θinɪən
Athens 'æθnz -ɪnz
athlete 'æθlit
athletic æθ'letɪk

-ation suffix 'eɪʃn
atishoo ə'tɪʃu or a more realistic
   sound of a 'sneeze'
Atlanta ət'læntə
Atlantic ət'læntɪk
atlas, A– 'ætləs
atmosphere 'ætməsfɪə(r)
atmospheric 'ætməs'ferɪk
atoll 'ætol $ 'ætɔl -təul etc
atom 'ætəm
atomic ə'tomɪk
atonal æ'təunl ə't- $ 'eɪ'təunl etc
atone ə'təun
atrocious ə'trəuʃəs
atrocity ə'trosətɪ
atrophy 'ætrəfɪ
attach ə'tætʃ
attaché ə'tæʃeɪ $ 'ætə'ʃeɪ
attaché case ə'tæʃɪ keɪs
attack ə'tæk
attain ə'teɪn
attempt ə'tempt
attend ə'tend
attendance ə'tendəns
attendant ə'tendənt
attention ə'tenʃn
attentive ə'tentɪv
attest ə'test
attic, A– 'ætɪk
attire ə'taɪə(r)
attitude 'ætɪtjud -tʃud $ -tud
attorney ə'tɜnɪ
attract ə'trækt
attributable ə'trɪbjutəbl
attribute n 'ætrɪbjut
attribute v ə'trɪbjut
attribution 'ætrɪ'bjuʃn
attrition ə'trɪʃn
auburn 'ɔbən $ 'ɔbərn
auction 'ɔkʃn £ 'okʃn
auctioneer 'ɔkʃə'nɪə(r) £ 'ok-
audacious ɔ'deɪʃəs
audacity ɔ'dæsətɪ
Auden 'ɔdn
audible 'ɔdəbl
audience 'ɔdɪəns
audit 'ɔdɪt
audition ɔ'dɪʃn
auditor 'ɔdɪtə(r)
auditorium 'ɔdɪ'tɔrɪəm
aught ɔt
augment ɔg'ment
August 'ɔgəst

august ɔˈgʌst
Augustus əˈgʌstəs ɔˈg-
Auld Lang Syne 'ɔld 'læŋ ˈzaɪn ˈsaɪn
aunt ɑnt $ ænt
auntie, aunty ˈɑntɪ $ ˈæntɪ
au pair 'əʊ ˈpeə(r)
aura ˈɔrə
aurora ɔˈrɔrə əˈr-
auspices ˈɔspɪsɪz £ ˈos-
auspicious ɔˈspɪʃəs £ oˈs-
Austen ˈostɪn $ £ ˈɔstɪn
austere ɔˈstɪə(r) £ oˈs-
austerity ɔˈsterətɪ £ oˈs-
Austin ˈostɪn $ £ ˈɔstɪn
Australasia 'ostrəˈleɪʃə $ £ ˈɔs-
Australia oˈstreɪlɪə $ £ ɔˈs-
Australian oˈstreɪlɪən $ £ ɔˈs-
Austria ˈostrɪə $ £ ˈɔs-
authentic ɔˈθentɪk
authenticity 'ɔθenˈtɪsətɪ
author ˈɔθə(r)
authorise ˈɔθəraɪz
authoritarian ɔˈθorɪˈteərɪən $ ɔˈθɔr-
authoritative ɔˈθorətətɪv
  $ ɔˈθɔrəteɪtɪv etc
authority ɔˈθorətɪ $ ɔˈθɔr-
authorship ˈɔθəʃɪp $ ˈɔθərʃɪp
autobiographical 'ɔtəˈbaɪəˈgræfɪkl
autobiography 'ɔtəbaɪˈogrəfɪ
autocracy ɔˈtokrəsɪ
autocrat ˈɔtəkræt
autocratic 'ɔtəˈkrætɪk
autograph ˈɔtəgrɑf $ -græf
automatic 'ɔtəˈmætɪk
automation 'ɔtəˈmeɪʃn
automaton ɔˈtomətən $ -ton etc
automobile ˈɔtəməbil 'ɔtəˈməʊbil
  $ 'ɔtəməˈbil etc
autonomous ɔˈtonəməs
autopsy ˈɔtopsɪ -təp-
autumn ˈɔtəm
autumnal ɔˈtʌmnl
auxiliary ɔgˈzɪlɪərɪ -lərɪ £ og- $ -lɪerɪ
avail əˈveɪl
availability əˈveɪləˈbɪlətɪ

avalanche ˈævəlɑnʃ -lɔnʃ $ -læntʃ etc
avarice ˈævərɪs
avaricious 'ævəˈrɪʃəs
Av(e) abbr ˈævənju $ -nu etc
avenge əˈvendʒ
avenue ˈævənju $ -nu etc
average ˈævrɪdʒ -vər-
averse əˈvɜs
aversion əˈvɜʃn $ £ -ʒn
avert əˈvɜt
aviary ˈeɪvɪərɪ $ -vɪerɪ
aviation 'eɪvɪˈeɪʃn
avid ˈævɪd
avoid əˈvɔɪd
avoirdupois 'ævədəˈpɔɪz $ 'ævər-
Avon ˈeɪvən
avouch əˈvaʊtʃ
avow əˈvaʊ
avowedly əˈvaʊɪdlɪ
await əˈweɪt
awake əˈweɪk
awaken əˈweɪkən
award əˈwɔd $ əˈwɔrd
aware əˈweə(r)
awash əˈwoʃ $ əˈwɔʃ etc
away əˈweɪ
awe ɔ
awful ˈɔfl
awhile əˈwaɪl $ əˈhwaɪl etc
awkward ˈɔkwəd £ -wʊd $ -ərd
awning ˈɔnɪŋ
awoke əˈwəʊk
awry əˈraɪ
ax(e) æks
axes pl of 'axe' ˈæksɪz
axes pl of 'axis' ˈæksiz
axiom ˈæksɪəm
axiomatic 'æksɪəˈmætɪk
axis ˈæksɪs
axle ˈæksl
ay ever eɪ
aye yes aɪ
azalea əˈzeɪlɪə
Azores əˈzɔz $ əˈzɔrz
azure ˈæʒə(r)

B

B b bi
B.A. 'bi ˈeɪ

baa bɑ or a more realistic suggestion
  of a 'bleat'

babble ˈbæbl
babe beɪb
babel, B– ˈbeɪbl $ ˈbæbl
baboon bəˈbun $ bæˈbun
baby ˈbeɪbɪ
babyhood ˈbeɪbɪhʊd
Babylon ˈbæbəlon -ɪl- -lən
baby-sitter ˈbeɪbɪ sɪtə(r)
Bacchus ˈbækəs
Bach bɑk
   instead of this k *many use* x,
   the corresponding fricative
bachelor ˈbætʃələ(r)
bacilli bəˈsɪlɑɪ
bacillus bəˈsɪləs
back bæk
backache ˈbækeɪk
backbite ˈbækbaɪt
backbone ˈbækbəʊn
back-cloth ˈbæk klɒθ $ klɔθ
back-door bæk ˈdɔ(r)
back-fire bæk ˈfaɪə(r)
background ˈbækɡraʊnd
backhand ˈbækhænd
backhanded ˈbækˈhændɪd
backlash ˈbæklæʃ
backlog ˈbæklog $ -lɔg *etc*
backslide ˈbækˈslaɪd
backside ˈbæksaɪd bækˈsaɪd
backstroke ˈbækstrəʊk
backward(s) ˈbækwəd(z) £ -wʊd(z)
   $ -wərd(z)
backwater ˈbækwɔtə(r)
bacon, B– ˈbeɪkən
bacteria bækˈtɪərɪə
bad bæd
bade bæd beɪd
badge bædʒ
badger ˈbædʒə(r)
badminton, B– ˈbædmɪntən
bad-tempered ˈbæd ˈtempəd $ -pərd
baffle ˈbæfl
bag bæg
bagatelle ˈbægəˈtel
baggy ˈbægɪ
Baghdad bægˈdæd $ ˈbægdæd
baggage ˈbægɪdʒ
bagpipes ˈbægpaɪps
bah bɑ *or a similar gruff vocal eruption*
Bahamas bəˈhɑməz $ bəˈheɪməz *etc*
bail beɪl
bailiff ˈbeɪlɪf
bait beɪt

baize beɪz
bake beɪk
bakelite ˈbeɪkəlaɪt
bakery ˈbeɪkərɪ
baking powder ˈbeɪkɪŋ paʊdə(r)
balaclava, B– ˈbæləˈklɑvə $ -ˈklævə
balalaika ˈbæləˈlaɪkə
balance ˈbæləns
balance-sheet ˈbæləns ʃit
balcony ˈbælkənɪ
bald bɔld
balderdash ˈbɔldədæʃ $ -dərd-
bale beɪl
baleful ˈbeɪlfl -fʊl
balk bɔk
Balkan(s) ˈbɔlkən(z)
ball bɔl
ballad ˈbæləd
ballast ˈbæləst
ball bearing ˈbɔl ˈbeərɪŋ
ballerina ˈbæləˈrinə
ballet ˈbæleɪ $ bæˈleɪ *etc*
ballet dancer ˈbæleɪ dɑnsə(r)
   $ bæˈleɪ dænsər *etc*
Balliol ˈbeɪlɪəl
balloon bəˈlun
ballot ˈbælət
ballpoint ˈbɔlpɔɪnt
ballpoint-pen ˈbɔlpɔɪnt ˈpen
ballyhoo ˈbælɪˈhu $ ˈbælɪhu *etc*
balm bɑm
Balmoral bælˈmorl $ -ˈmɔrl *etc*
balsam ˈbɔlsəm £ ˈbolsəm
Baltic ˈbɔltɪc £ ˈbol-
baluster ˈbæləstə(r)
balustrade ˈbæləˈstreɪd
bamboo bæmˈbu
bamboozle bæmˈbuzl
ban bæn
banal bəˈnɑl $ ˈbeɪnl ˈbænl *etc*
banana bəˈnɑnə $ bəˈnænə
band bænd
bandage ˈbændɪdʒ
bandit ˈbændɪt
bandstand ˈbændstænd
bandy ˈbændɪ
bane beɪn
bang bæŋ
banger ˈbæŋə(r)
Bangkok ˈbæŋˈkok $ ˈbæŋkok *etc*
Bangladesh ˈbæŋɡləˈdeʃ
bangle ˈbæŋgl
Bangor ˈbæŋɡə(r) $ -gɔr

banish ˋbænıʃ
banishment ˋbænıʃmənt
banister ˋbænıstə(r)
banjo ˈbænˋdʒəʊ ˋbændʒəʊ
bank bæŋk
bank-holiday ˈbæŋk ˋholədı $ £ -deı
banknote ˋbæŋknəʊt
bankrupt ˋbæŋkrʌpt
bankruptcy ˋbæŋkrʌptsı -rəp-
banner ˋbænə(r)
banns bænz
banquet ˋbæŋkwıt
Banquo ˋbæŋkwəʊ
bantam ˋbæntəm
banter ˋbæntə(r)
Bantu ˈbænˋtu
baptism ˋbæptızm
baptismal bæpˋtızml
Baptist ˋbæptıst
baptize bæpˋtaız
bar bɑ(r)
Barabbas bəˋræbəs
barb bɑb $ barb
Barbados bɑˋbeıdəs -dos $ £ -dəʊz
 $ bar-
Barbara ˋbɑbrə $ ˋbarbr̥ə
barbarian bɑˋbeərıən $ bar-
barbaric bɑˋbærık $ bar-
barbarism ˋbɑbərızm $ ˋbar-
barbarity bɑˋbærətı $ bar-
barbarous ˋbɑbərəs $ ˋbar-
barbecue(-eque) ˋbɑbıkju $ ˋbar-
barber ˋbɑbə(r) $ ˋbarbər
Barbirolli ˈbɑbəˋrolı $ ˋbar-
Barcelona ˈbɑsəˋləʊnə $ ˋbar-
Barclay ˋbɑklı -kleı $ ˋbar-
bard bɑd $ bard
bare beə(r)
bareback ˋbeəbæk $ ˋbeər-
barefaced ˋbeəfeıst $ ˋbeər-
barefoot ˋbeəfʊt $ ˋbeər-
barefooted ˈbeəˋfʊtıd $ ˈbeər-
bareheaded ˈbeəˋhedıd $ ˈbeər-
bargain ˋbɑgın $ ˋbar-
barge ˋbɑdʒ $ ˋbardʒ
baritone ˋbærıtəʊn
bark bɑk $ bark
barley ˋbɑlı $ ˋbarlı
barley-sugar ˋbɑlı ʃʊgə(r) $ ˋbarlı
barley-water ˋbɑlı wɔtə(r) $ ˋbarlı
barmaid ˋbɑmeıd $ ˋbar-
barman ˋbɑmən $ ˋbar-
barn bɑn $ barn

barnacle ˋbɑnəkl $ ˋbarn-
barn-yard ˋbɑn jɑd $ ˋbarn jard
barometer bəˋromıtə(r)
baron ˋbærən
baroness ˋbærənəs -nes -nıs
baronet ˋbærənıt -nət -net
baronial bəˋrəʊnıəl
barony ˋbærənı
baroque bəˋrok bəˋrəʊk
barrack ˋbærək
barrage ˋbærɑʒ $ bəˋrɑʒ
barrel ˋbærl
barrel-organ ˋbærl ɔgən $ ɔrgən
barren ˋbærən
Barrett ˋbærət
barricade n ˋbærəkeıd -rık-
barricade v ˈbærəˋkeıd -rıˋk-
Barrie ˋbærı
barrier ˋbærıə(r)
barrister ˋbærıstə(r)
barrow ˋbærəʊ
bartender ˋbɑtendə(r) $ ˋbar-
barter ˋbɑtə(r) $ ˋbartər
Bartholemew bɑˋθoləmju $ bar-
basalt ˋbæsɔlt
base beıs
baseball ˋbeısbɔl
basement ˋbeısmənt
bases pl of 'basis' ˋbeısız
bases pl of 'base' ˋbeısız
bash bæʃ
basic ˋbeısık
basically ˋbeısıklı
basil, B– ˋbæzl
basin ˋbeısn
basis ˋbeısıs
bask bɑsk $ bæsk
basket ˋbɑskıt $ ˋbæskıt
basket-ball ˋbɑskıt bɔl $ ˋbæskıt
bas-relief ˈbɑ rıˋlif
bass in music beıs
bass fish bæs
bassoon bəˋsun $ bæˋsun etc
bastard ˋbɑstəd £ ˋbæs- $ ˋbæstərd
baste beıst
Bastille bæˋstil
bastion ˋbæstıən $ -tʃən etc
Basutoland bəˋsutəʊlænd
bat bæt
Batavia bəˋteıvıə
batch bætʃ
bated ˋbeıtıd
bath, B– bɑθ $ bæθ

bathe beɪð
bathed *past of 'bathe'* ˋbeɪðd
bathed *past of 'bath'* ˋbaθt $ ˋbæθt
bathing-costume ˋbeɪðɪŋ kostʃum -tjum
  $ -tum
bathing-suit ˋbeɪðɪŋ sut £ sjut
bathos ˋbeɪθos
bathrobe ˋbaθrəʊb $ ˋbæθ-
bathroom ˋbaθrʊm $ £ ˋbæθrum *etc*
baths baðz $ bæðz bæθs
bathtub ˋbaθtʌb $ ˋbæθ-
batman ˋbætmən
baton ˋbætõ -tən -tn $ bæˋton -õ bə-
batsman ˋbætsmən
battalion bəˋtælɪən
batten ˋbætn
batter ˋbætə(r)
battering ram ˋbætrɪŋ ræm
battery ˋbætrɪ
battle ˋbætl
battle-axe ˋbætl æks
battle-cry ˋbætl kraɪ
battle-field ˋbætl fild
battle-ground ˋbætl graʊnd
battlement ˋbætlmənt
battle-ship ˋbætl ʃɪp
bauble ˋbɔbl
baulk bɔk
bauxite ˋbɔksaɪt $ ˋbəʊzaɪt
Bavaria bəˋveərɪə
bawdy ˋbɔdɪ
bawl bɔl
bay beɪ
bayonet ˋbeɪənɪt -ət
Bayreuth baɪˋrɔɪt $ ˋbaɪrɔɪt
bazaar bəˋza(r)
BBC 'bi bi ˋsi
BC 'bi ˋsi
BEA 'bi i ˋeɪ
beach bitʃ
beach-comber ˋbitʃ kəʊmə(r)
beacon ˋbikən
bead bid
beadle ˋbidl
beagle ˋbigl
beak bik
beaker ˋbikə(r)
beam bim
bean bin
bear beə(r)
beard bɪəd $ bɪərd
bearings ˋbeərɪŋz
beast bist

beat bit
beaten ˋbitn
beatific bɪəˋtɪfɪk
beatify bɪˋætɪfaɪ
beatitude bɪˋætɪtjud $ -tud
beatnik ˋbitnɪk
Beatrice ˋbɪətrɪs
beau bəʊ
beautiful ˋbjutəfl -tɪfl
beautify ˋbjutəfaɪ -tɪf-
beauty ˋbjutɪ
beauty-parlour ˋbjutɪ palə(r) $ parlər
beaver ˋbivə(r)
becalmed bɪˋkamd
became bɪˋkeɪm bə-
because bəˋkoz bɪ- $ bəˋkɔz *etc*
Bechuanaland 'betʃuˋanəlænd
beck bek
Becket(t) ˋbekɪt
beckon ˋbekən
become bɪˋkʌm bə-
bed bed
bedclothes ˋbedkləʊðz $ £ -kləʊz
bedeck bɪˋdek
Bedford ˋbedfəd $ ˋbedfərd
bedlam ˋbedləm
Bedouin ˋbeduɪn
bedraggled bɪˋdrægld
bedridden ˋbedrɪdn
bedrock ˋbedˋrok
bedroom ˋbedrʊm $ £ -rum *etc*
  with dr *as in 'dry'*
bedside ˋbedsaɪd
bedsitter 'bedˋsɪtə(r)
bed-sitting-room 'bed ˋsɪtɪŋ rʊm
  $ £ rum *etc*
bedspread ˋbedspred
bedstead ˋbedsted
bedtime ˋbedtaɪm
bee bi
beech bitʃ
beef bif
beefeater ˋbifitə(r)
beefsteak ˋbifsteɪk £ 'bifˋsteɪk
beehive ˋbihaɪv
beeline ˋbilaɪn
been bin $ bɪn *etc*
beer bɪə(r)
beeswax ˋbizwæks
beet bit
Beethoven ˋbeɪthəʊvən -təʊ-
beetle ˋbitl
beetroot ˋbit-rut

befall bɪ'fɔl
befit bɪ'fɪt
before bɪ'fɔ(r) bə-
beforehand bɪ'fɔhænd bə- $ -'fɔr-
befriend bɪ'frend
befuddle bɪ'fʌdl
beg **beg**
began bɪ'gæn bə-
beget bɪ'get
beggar 'begə(r)
beggary 'bəgərɪ
begin bɪ'gɪn bə-
begrime bɪ'graɪm
begrudge bɪ'grʌdʒ
beguile bɪ'gaɪl
begun bɪ'gʌn bə-
behalf bɪ'haf bə- $ -'hæf
behave bɪ'heɪv bə-
behaviour($ -or) bɪ'heɪvɪə(r) bə-
behead bɪ'hed
behind bɪ'haɪnd bə-
behindhand bɪ'haɪndhænd bə-
beige beɪʒ
being 'biɪŋ
Beirut beɪ'rut $ 'beɪrut
belabour bɪ'leɪbə(r)
belated bɪ'leɪtɪd
belch beltʃ
beleaguer bɪ'ligə(r)
Belfast 'belfast bel'fast $ -fæst
belfry 'belfrɪ
Belgian 'beldʒən
Belgium 'beldʒəm
Belgrade 'bel'greɪd
belie bɪ'laɪ
belief bɪ'lif bə-
believe bɪ'liv bə-
Belinda bə'lɪndə
belittle bɪ'lɪtl
bell **bel**
belle **bel**
belles lettres 'bel 'letr *with unsyllabic* r
bell-hop 'bel hop
bellicose 'belɪkəʊs
belligerent bə'lɪdʒərənt
bellow 'beləʊ
bellows 'beləʊz
bell-ringer 'bel rɪŋə(r)
bell-tent 'bel tent
belly 'belɪ
belly-ache 'belɪ eɪk
belong bɪ'lɒŋ bə- $ -'lɔŋ *etc*
belongings bɪ'lɒŋɪŋz bə- $ -'lɔŋ *etc*

beloved bɪ'lʌvɪd bə- -vd
below bɪ'ləʊ bə-
belt **belt**
bemoan bɪ'məʊn
bemuse bɪ'mjuz
bench bentʃ
bend **bend**
bended 'bendɪd
beneath bɪ'niθ bə-
Benedict 'benədɪkt
Benedictine *liqueur* 'benɪ'dɪktin -nə-
Benedictine *monk* 'benɪ'dɪktɪn -taɪn -nə-
benediction 'benɪ'dɪkʃn -nə-
benefaction 'benɪ'fækʃn -nə-
benefactor 'benɪfæktə(r) -nə-
benefice 'benɪfɪs -nə-
beneficent bə'nefɪsnt bɪ-
beneficial 'benɪ'fɪʃl -nə-
beneficiary 'benɪ'fɪʃərɪ -nə- $ -ʃɪerɪ
benefit 'benɪfɪt -nə-
benevolence bə'nevələns bɪ-
benevolent bə'nevələnt bɪ-
Bengal beŋ'gɔl
benign bɪ'naɪn
benignant bɪ'nɪgnənt
Benjamin 'bendʒəmɪn
Bennett 'benɪt
bent **bent**
benumb bɪ'nʌm
benzedrine 'benzədrɪn -drin
benzene 'benzin ben'zin
benzine 'benzin ben'zin
bequeath bɪ'kwið
bequest bɪ'kwest
berate bɪ'reɪt
bereave bɪ'riv bə-
bereavement bɪ'rivmənt bə-
Berber 'bɜbə(r)
bereft bɪ'reft bə-
beret 'bereɪ -rɪ -rɪt $ bə'reɪ
Bergen 'bɜgən 'beəgən
Berkeley 'bɑklɪ
   $ *and* £ *for US place* 'bɜklɪ
Berkshire 'bɑkʃə(r) $ 'bɜkʃɪər -ʃər
beriberi 'berɪ'berɪ
Berlin bɜ'lɪn
Berlioz 'beəlɪəʊz $ 'beərl-
Bermuda bə'mjudə $ bər-
Bernard 'bɜnəd $ -ərd bə'nɑrd
Berne bɜn beən $ beərn
berry 'berɪ
berserk bɜ'sɜk $ 'bɜsɜk *etc*
berth bɜθ

Bertha ˋbɜθə
Berwick ˋberɪk $ ˋbɜwɪk
Beryl ˋberl
beseech bɪˋsitʃ
beset bɪˋset
beside(s) bɪˋsaɪd(z) bə-
besiege bɪˋsidʒ bə-
besotted bɪˋsotɪd
besought bɪˋsɔt
bespoke bɪˋspəʊk
best best
bestial ˋbestɪəl $ ˋbestʃl etc
bestir bɪˋstɜ(r)
bestow bɪˋstəʊ
bestrew bɪˋstru
bestride bɪˋstraɪd
best-seller 'best ˋselə(r)
bet bet
beta ˋbitə $ ˋbeɪtə etc
betake bɪˋteɪk
Bethlehem ˋbeθlɪhem $ -lɪəm etc
betide bɪˋtaɪd
betoken bɪˋtəʊkən
betook bɪˋtʊk
betray bɪˋtreɪ
betroth bɪˋtrəʊð $ bɪˋtrɔθ etc
betrothal bɪˋtrəʊðl $ bɪˋtrɔθl etc
better ˋbetə(r)
Betty ˋbetɪ
between bɪˋtwin bə-
bevel ˋbevl
beverage ˋbevrɪdʒ
bevy ˋbevɪ
bewail bɪˋweɪl
beware bɪˋweə(r)
bewilder bɪˋwɪldə(r)
bewilderment bɪˋwɪldəmənt $ -dərm-
bewitch bɪˋwɪtʃ
beyond bɪˋjond
bi- prefix baɪ-
bias ˋbaɪəs
bias(s)ed ˋbaɪəst
bib bɪb
Bible ˋbaɪbl
biblical ˋbɪblɪkl
bibliography 'bɪblɪˋogrəfɪ
bicarbonate 'baɪˋkabənət -bn̩- -ɪt
    $ -ˋkarb-
bicentenary 'baɪsenˋtinərɪ -nr̩ɪ
    $ 'baɪˋsentn̩erɪ 'baɪsenˋtenərɪ
biceps ˋbaɪseps
Bicester ˋbɪstə(r)
bicker ˋbɪkə(r)

bicycle ˋbaɪsəkl
bid bɪd
bide baɪd
biennial baɪˋenɪəl
bier bɪə(r)
bifocal ˋbaɪˋfəʊkl
big bɪg
bigamist ˋbɪgəmɪst
bigamous ˋbɪgəməs
bigamy ˋbɪgəmɪ
bight baɪt
bigot ˋbɪgət
bigotry ˋbɪgətrɪ
bike baɪk
bikini bɪˋkinɪ
bilateral baɪˋlætrl -tərl
bile baɪl
bilge bɪldʒ
bilharzia bɪlˋhazɪə $ -ˋharzɪə
bilingual baɪˋlɪŋgwl
bilious ˋbɪlɪəs
bill, B- bɪl
bill-board ˋbɪl bɔd $ bɔrd
billet ˋbɪlɪt
billet-doux 'bɪleɪ ˋdu -lɪ ˋbeɪ
billiards ˋbɪlɪədz $ -ɪərdz
billion ˋbɪlɪən
bill-of-fare 'bɪl əv ˋfeə(r)
billow ˋbɪləʊ
billy goat ˋbɪlɪ gəʊt
bin bɪn
bind baɪnd
bindweed ˋbaɪndwid
binge bɪndʒ
bingo ˋbɪŋgəʊ
binoculars bɪˋnokjʊləz $ -lərz
biochemistry 'baɪəʊˋkemɪstrɪ
biographer baɪˋogrəfə(r)
biographical 'baɪəˋgræfɪkl
biography baɪˋogrəfɪ
biological 'baɪəˋlodʒɪkl
biologist baɪˋolədʒɪst
biology baɪˋolədʒɪ
biped ˋbaɪ-ped
birch bɜtʃ
bird bɜd
Birmingham ˋbɜmɪŋəm $ -ɪŋhæm
birth bɜθ
birth-control ˋbɜθ kəntrəʊl
birthday ˋbɜθdeɪ
birthplace ˋbɜθpleɪs
birth-rate ˋbɜθ reɪt
Biscay ˋbɪskɪ -keɪ

biscuit ˈbɪskɪt
bisect baɪˈsekt
bisection baɪˈsekʃn
bishop ˈbɪʃəp
bison ˈbaɪsn
Bismarck ˈbɪzmak $ -mark
bit bɪt
bitch bɪtʃ
bite baɪt
bitten ˈbɪtn
bitter ˈbɪtə(r)
bitumen ˈbɪtʃʊmən -men -mɪn -tjum-
bivouac ˈbɪvuæk ˈbɪvwæk
bizarre bɪˈza(r)
blab blæb
black blæk
black-beetle ˈblæk bitl
blackberry ˈblækbrɪ $ -berɪ etc
blackbird ˈblækbəd
black box 'blæk ˈboks
blackboard ˈblækbɔd $ -bɔrd
black-currant blæk ˈkʌrnt $ ˈkərnt
blacken ˈblækən
Blackfriars ˈblækfraɪəz $ -fraɪərz
blackguard ˈblægad $ -gard
blackguardly ˈblægədlɪ $ -gərd-
blackhead ˈblækhed
blackleg ˈblækleg
blacklist ˈblæklɪst
blackmail ˈblækmeɪl
black market 'blæk ˈmakɪt $ ˈmarkɪt
blackout ˈblækaʊt
Blackpool ˈblækpul
blacksmith ˈblæksmɪθ
bladder ˈblædə(r)
blade bleɪd
Blake bleɪk
blame bleɪm
blameworthy ˈbleɪmwɜðɪ
blanch blantʃ $ blæntʃ
blancmange bləˈmonʒ
bland ˈblænd
blandishments ˈblændɪʃmənts
blank blæŋk
blanket ˈblæŋkɪt
blare bleə(r)
blarney ˈblanɪ $ ˈblarnɪ
blasé ˈblazeɪ $ 'blaˈzeɪ
blaspheme blæsˈfim £ blas-
blasphemous ˈblæsfəməs £ ˈblas-
blasphemy ˈblæsfəmɪ £ ˈblas-
blast blast $ blæst
blatant ˈbleɪtnt

blaze bleɪz
blazer ˈbleɪzə(r)
blazon ˈbleɪzn
bleach blitʃ
bleak blik
bleary ˈblɪərɪ
bleary-eyed 'blɪərɪ ˈaɪd
bleat blit
bled bled
bleed blid
bleep blip
blemish ˈblemɪʃ
blench blentʃ
blend blend
bless bles
blessed adj ˈblesɪd
blessed pp blest
blew blu
blight blaɪt
blind blaɪnd
blindfold ˈblaɪndfəʊld
blind man's buff 'blaɪnd mænz ˈbʌf
blink blɪŋk
bliss blɪs
blister ˈblɪstə(r)
blithe blaɪð
blithering ˈblɪðərɪŋ
blizzard ˈblɪzəd $ ˈblɪzərd
bloat bləʊt
blob blob
bloc blok
block blok
blockade bloˈkeɪd blə-
blockhead ˈblokhed
bloke bləʊk
blond(e) blond
blood blʌd
blood-donor ˈblʌd dəʊnə(r)
bloodhound ˈblʌdhaʊnd
blood poisoning ˈblʌd pɔɪznɪŋ
bloodshed ˈblʌdʃed
bloodshot ˈblʌdʃot
blood-sucker ˈblʌd sʌkə(r)
bloodthirsty ˈblʌdθɜstɪ
blood-vessel ˈblʌd vesl
bloody ˈblʌdɪ
bloom blum
bloomers ˈbluməz $ ˈblumərz
Bloomsbury ˈblumzbrɪ $ -berɪ
blossom ˈblosəm
blot blot
blotch blotʃ
blotting-paper ˈblotɪŋ peɪpə(r)

blouse blaʊz $ blaʊs *etc*
blow bləʊ
blow-fly ˋbləʊ flaɪ
blown bləʊn
blow-out ˋbləʊ aʊt
blowzy ˋblaʊzɪ
blubber ˋblʌbə(r)
bludgeon ˋblʌdʒən
blue blu
bluebell ˋblubel
bluebottle ˋblubotl
blue-collar ˈblu ˋkolə(r)
blueprint ˋblu-prɪnt
blue-stocking ˋblu stokɪŋ
bluff blʌf
bluish ˋbluɪʃ
blunder ˋblʌndə(r)
blunderbuss ˋblʌndəbʌs $ -dərb-
blunt blʌnt
blur blɜ(r)
blurb blɜb
blurt blɜt
blush blʌʃ
bluster ˋblʌstə(r)
B.O. ˈbi ˋəʊ
boa ˋbəʊə bɔ
BOAC ˈbi əʊ eɪ ˋsi
boa-constrictor ˋbəʊə kənstrɪktə(r) ˋbɔ
boar bɔ(r)
board bɔd $ bɔrd
boarding-house ˋbɔdɪŋ haʊs $ ˋbɔrd-
boarding school ˋbɔdɪŋ skul $ ˋbɔrd-
boast bəʊst
boat bəʊt
boatman ˋbəʊtmən
boatswain ˋbəʊsn
bob bob
bobbin bobɪn
bob-sled ˋbob sled
bob-sleigh ˋbob sleɪ
bobtail ˋbobteɪl
Boccaccio bəˋkætʃɪəʊ
bode bəʊd
bodice ˋbodɪs
bodily ˋbodəlɪ -dļɪ
body ˋbodɪ
body-guard ˋbodɪ gad $ gard
Boeing ˋbəʊɪŋ
Boer bɔ(r) ˋbəʊə(r)
bog bog $ bɔg
boggle ˋbogl
bogus ˋbəʊgəs
bog(e)y ˋbəʊgɪ

Bohème, la ˈla bəʊˋeəm -ˋeɪm
Bohemia bəʊˋhimɪə
Bohemian bəʊˋhimɪən
boil bɔɪl
boiling-point ˋbɔɪlɪŋ pɔɪnt
boisterous ˋbɔɪstrəs
Boleyn bəˋlɪn $ £ ˋbʊlɪn
bold bəʊld
bolero *dance* bəˋleərəʊ
bolero *garment* ˋbolərəʊ
bollard ˋboləd $ -lərd
boll-weevil ˈbəʊl ˋwivl
Bolivia bəˋlɪvɪə
boloney bəˋləʊnɪ
Bolshevik ˋbolʃəvɪk -ʃɪv-
bolster ˋbəʊlstə(r)
bolt bəʊlt
Bolton ˋbəʊltən -tn
bomb bom
bombard bomˋbad bəm- $ -ˋbard
bombardment bomˋbadmənt bəm-
   $ -ˋbard-
bombastic bomˋbæstɪk
Bombay bomˋbeɪ
bomber ˋbomə(r)
bombshell ˋbomʃel
bona fide ˋbəʊnə ˋfaɪdɪ
bonanza bəˋnænzə
Bonaparte ˋbəʊnəpat $ -part
bond bond
bondage ˋbondɪdʒ
bone bəʊn
bone-dry ˈbəʊn ˋdraɪ
bonfire ˋbonfaɪə(r)
bongo-drum ˋboŋgəʊ drʌm
bonhomie ˋbonəmɪ $ ˈbonəˋmi *etc*
bon mot ˈbõ ˋməʊ ˈbon
bonnet ˋbonɪt
bonny ˋbonɪ
bonus ˋbəʊnəs
bony ˋbəʊnɪ
boo(h) bu
booby-trap ˋbubɪ træp
book bʊk
bookcase ˋbʊkkeɪs
book ends ˋbʊk endz
booking-clerk ˋbʊkɪŋ klak $ klɜk
booking-office ˋbʊkɪŋ ofɪs $ ɔfɪs
book-keeper ˋbʊk kipə(r)
book-keeping ˋbʊk kipɪŋ
booklet ˋbʊklət -ɪt
book-maker ˋbʊkmeɪkə(r)
bookmark ˋbʊkmak $ -mark

bookseller ˈbʊksələ(r)
bookshelf ˈbʊkʃelf
bookstall ˈbʊkstɔl
bookstore ˈbʊkstɔ(r)
book token ˈbʊk təʊkən
bookworm ˈbʊkwɜm
boom bum
boomerang ˈbuməræŋ
boon bun
boor bʊə(r) £ bɔ(r)
boost bust
boot but
bootblack ˈbutblæk
booth buð $ £ buθ
bootlegger ˈbutlegə(r)
booty ˈbutɪ
booze buz
boracic bəˈræsɪk
borax ˈbɔræks
Bordeaux bɔˈdəʊ $ bɔr-
border ˈbɔdə(r) $ ˈbɔr-
borderland ˈbɔdəlænd $ ˈbɔrdər-
borderline ˈbɔdəlaɪn $ ˈbɔrdər-
bore bɔ
boredom ˈbɔdəm $ ˈbɔr-
boric acid ˈbɔrɪk £ ˈborɪk
born bɔn $ bɔrn
borne bɔn $ bɔrn
Borneo ˈbɔnɪəʊ $ ˈbɔrn-
borough ˈbʌrə $ ˈbɜəʊ ˈbɜə etc
borrow ˈborəʊ
Borstal ˈbɔstl $ ˈbɔrstl
bosh boʃ
Bosnia ˈboznɪə
bosom ˈbʊzəm
boss bos $ bɔs
Boston ˈbostən $ ˈbɔstən
Boswell ˈbozwel -wəl
botanical bəˈtænɪkl
botanist ˈbotənɪst $ £ -tn̩ɪst
botany ˈbotənɪ $ £ -tn̩ɪ
botch botʃ
both bəʊθ
bother ˈboðə(r)
botheration ˌboðəˈreɪʃn
bothersome ˈboðəsəm $ ˈboðərsəm
Botticelli ˌbotɪˈtʃelɪ
bottle ˈbotl
bottom ˈbotəm
boudoir ˈbudwa(r)
bough baʊ
bought bɔt
boulder ˈbəʊldə(r)

boulevard ˈbuləvad -va(r) $ -vard etc
Boulogne bəˈlɔɪn bʊ-
bounce baʊns
bound baʊnd
boundary baʊndrɪ $ £ -dərɪ
bounteous ˈbaʊntɪəs
bountiful ˈbaʊntɪfl
bounty ˈbaʊntɪ
bouquet bʊˈkeɪ ˈbʊkeɪ bəʊˈkeɪ
bourbon *whisky* ˈbɜbən
bourgeois ˈbʊəʒwa £ ˈbɔ- $ ˈbɜʒwa
Bournemouth ˈbɔnməθ $ ˈbɔrn-
bout baʊt
boutique buˈtik
bovine ˈbəʊvaɪn -vin
bow *weapon, knot* bəʊ
bow *stoop, ship's* baʊ
bowdlerize ˈbaʊdləraɪz
bowel baʊl
bowl bəʊl
bowler hat ˌbəʊlə ˈhæt $ -lər
bowling-green ˈbəʊlɪŋ grin
bowsprit ˈbəʊsprɪt
bow-tie ˈbəʊ ˈtaɪ
bow-wow ˈbaʊ ˈwaʊ *or a more
   realistic imitation of 'barking'*
box boks
boxer ˈboksə(r)
box-office ˈboks ofɪs $ ɔfɪs
Boxing Day ˈboksɪŋ deɪ
boxing-gloves ˈboksɪŋ glʌvz
boxing-match ˈboksɪŋ mætʃ
boy bɔɪ
boycott ˈbɔɪkot -kət
boyfriend ˈbɔɪ-frend
boyhood ˈbɔɪhʊd
bra bra
bracelet ˈbreɪslət -lɪt
bracken ˈbrækən
bracket ˈbrækɪt
brackish ˈbrækɪʃ
brag bræg
braggart ˈbrægət -gat $ -gərt
Brahmin ˈbramɪn
braid breɪd
Braille breɪl
brain breɪn
brainstorm ˈbreɪn-stəm $ -stɔrm
brain-washing ˈbreɪn wɔʃɪŋ
brainwave ˈbreɪnweɪv
braise breɪz
brake breɪk
bramble ˈbræmbl

bran bræn
branch brɑntʃ $ bræntʃ
brand brænd
brandish `brændɪʃ
brand new 'brænd `nju $ `nu
brandy `brændɪ
brandy-snap `brændɪ snæp
brash bræʃ
brass brɑs $ bræs
brass band 'brɑs `bænd $ 'bræs
brassière `bræzɪə(r) -sɪə(r)
   $ brə`zɪər etc
brat bræt
bravado brə`vɑdəʊ
brave breɪv
bravery `breɪvərɪ
bravo 'brɑ`vəʊ $ `brɑvəʊ etc
brawl brɔl
brawn brɔn
bray breɪ
brazen `breɪzn
brazier `breɪzɪə(r) $ £ `breɪʒə(r)
Brazil brə`zɪl
Brazil-nut brə`zɪl nʌt
breach britʃ
bread bred
bread-crumb `bred krʌm
breadth bretθ bredθ
bread winner `bred wɪnə(r)
break breɪk
breakaway `breɪkəweɪ
breakdown `breɪkdaʊn
breakfast `brekfəst
breakneck ... 'breɪk`nek
breakthrough `breɪkθru
breakwater `breɪkwɔtə(r)
bream brim
breast brest
breastplate `brestpleɪt
breast-stroke `bres strəʊk
breath breθ
breathalyser `breθəlaɪzə(r)
breathe brið
breathing space `briðɪŋ speɪs
bred bred
breech britʃ
breeches `brɪtʃɪz $ £ `britʃɪz
breed brid
breeze briz
Bren gun `bren gʌn
brethren `breðrɪn -rən
Breton `bretən
breve briv

breviary `brivɪərɪ $ -vɪerɪ
brevity `brevətɪ
brew bru
Brian `braɪən
briar `braɪə(r)
bribe braɪb
bribery `braɪbərɪ
bric-a-brac `brɪk ə bræk
brick brɪk
bricklayer `brɪkleɪə(r)
brickwork `brɪkwɜk
bridal `braɪdl
bride braɪd
bridegroom `braɪdgrum -grʊm
bridesmaid `braɪdzmeɪd
bridge brɪdʒ
Bridget `brɪdʒɪt
bridle `braɪdl
bridle path `braɪdl pɑθ $ pæθ
brief brif
brigade brɪ`geɪd
brigadier 'brɪgə`dɪə(r)
brigand `brɪgənd
bright braɪt
brighten `braɪtn
Brighton `braɪtn
brilliance `brɪlɪəns
brilliant `brɪlɪənt
brim brɪm
brimstone `brɪmstən $ £ -stəʊn
brindled `brɪndld
brine braɪn
bring brɪŋ
brink brɪŋk
briquette brɪ`ket
Brisbane `brɪzbən -beɪn
brisk brɪsk
brisket `brɪskɪt
bristle `brɪsl
Bristol `brɪstl
Britain `brɪtn -tən
Britannia brɪ`tænɪə
British `brɪtɪʃ
Briton `brɪtən -tn
Brittany `brɪtənɪ $ £ -tnɪ
brittle `brɪtl
broach brəʊtʃ
broad brɔd
broadcast `brɔdkɑst $ -kæst
broaden `brɔdn
broadsheet `brɔdʃit
broadside `brɔdsaɪd
Broadway `brɔdweɪ

brocade brə`keɪd $ £ brəʊ-
broccoli `brokəlɪ
brochure `brəʊʃʊə(r) -ʃə(r) brə`ʃʊə(r)
broderie anglaise 'brəʊdərɪ `ɒŋgleɪz
   $ ɒŋ`gleɪz
broil brɔɪl
broke brəʊk
broken `brəʊkən
bromide `brəʊmaɪd
bronchial `brɒŋkɪəl
bronchitis brɒŋ`kaɪtɪs -təs
Brontë `brɒntɪ `brɒnteɪ
bronze brɒnz
Bronze Age `brɒnz eɪdʒ
brooch brəʊtʃ
brood brud
brook brʊk
broom brum brum
Bros `brʌðəz $ -ðərz jocular: bros
broth brɒθ $ brɔθ etc
brothel `brɒθl
brother `brʌðə(r)
brotherhood `brʌðəhʊd $ `brʌðər-
brother-in-law `brʌðr ɪn lɔ
brought brɔt
brow braʊ
browbeat `braʊbit
brown, Brown(e) braʊn
brownie, B– `braʊnɪ
browse braʊz
Bruce brus
bruin `bruɪn
bruise bruz
brunette bru`net
brunt brʌnt
brush brʌʃ
brushwood `brʌʃwʊd
brusque brusk brʊsk $ £ brʌsk etc
Brussels `brʌslz
Brussels sprouts 'brʌslz `spraʊts
brutal `brutl
brutality bru`tælətɪ
brute brut
Brute, et tu 'et `tu bruteɪ
Brutus `brutəs
B.Sc. 'bi es `si
bubble `bʌbl
bubonic bju`bɒnɪk
buccaneer 'bʌkə`nɪə(r)
Buchanan bju`kænən bə`k-
Bucharest 'bjukə`rest $ `bukərest etc
buck bʌk
bucket `bʌkɪt

Buckingham `bʌkɪŋəm $ -ɪŋhæm
buckle `bʌkl
buckram `bʌkrəm
buck-skin `bʌkskɪn
buckwheat `bʌkwit
bucolic bju`kolɪk
bud bʌd
Budapest 'bjudə`pest $ `budəpest etc
Buddha `bʊdə $ `budə etc
Buddhism `bʊd-ɪzm $ `bud- etc
Buddist `bʊdɪst $ `budɪst etc
budge bʌdʒ
budgerigar `bʌdʒərɪga(r)
budget 'bʌdʒɪt -ət
Buenos Aires 'bweɪnəs `eəriz 'bwenəs
   'bəʊn- `aɪər- -rɪz £ `eəz $ `eərz
buff bʌf
buffaloe `bʌfələʊ
buffer `bʌfə(r)
buffet food `bʊfeɪ 'bu- $ bə`feɪ bu- etc
buffet strike `bʌfɪt
buffoon bə`fun $ bʌ`fun
buffoonery bə`funerɪ $ bʌ-
bug bʌg
bugbear `bʌgbeə(r)
buggy `bʌgɪ
bugle `bjugl
build bɪld
building society `bɪldɪŋ səsaɪətɪ
built bɪlt
Bulawayo 'bʊlə`weɪəʊ -`waɪ-
bulb bʌlb
bulbous `bʌlbəs
Bulgaria bʌl`geərɪə bʊl-
bulge bʌldʒ
bulk bʌlk
bulkhead `bʌlkhed
bull bʊl
bullfight `bʊl-faɪt
bulldog `bʊldɒg $ -dɔg etc
bulldozer `bʊldəʊzə(r)
bullet `bʊlɪt -ət
bulletin `bʊlətɪn $ -tn
bullet-proof `bʊlɪt pruf
bull frog `bʊl frog $ frɔg etc
bullion `bʊlɪən
bullock `bʊlək
bullring `bʊlrɪŋ
bull's-eye `bʊlz aɪ
bull-terrier `bʊl `terɪə(r)
bully `bʊlɪ
bulrush `bʊlrʌʃ
bulwark `bʊlwək $ -wərk

bum bʌm
bumble-bee ˋbʌmbl bi
bump bʌmp
bumper ˋbʌmpə(r)
bumpkin ˋbʌmpkɪn
bumptious ˋbʌmpʃəs
bun bʌn
bunch bʌntʃ
bundle ˋbʌndl
bung bʌŋ
bungalow ˋbʌŋgələʊ
bungle ˋbʌŋgl
bunion ˋbʌnɪən
bunk bʌŋk
bunkum ˋbʌŋkəm
bunny ˋbʌnɪ
Bunsen-burner ˋbʌnsn bɜnə(r)
Bunyan ˋbʌnjən
buoy bɔɪ $ ˋbuɪ
buoyancy ˋbɔɪənsɪ $ ˋbujənsɪ
buoyant ˋbɔɪənt $ ˋbujəṅt
burberry ˋbɜbrɪ -bərɪ $ -berɪ etc
burble ˋbɜbl
burden ˋbɜdn
burdensome ˋbɜdnsəm
bureau ˋbjʊərəʊ £ bjʊəˋrəʊ
bureaucracy bjʊəˋrokrəsɪ
bureaucrat ˋbjʊərəkræt -rəʊk-
bureaucratic ˌbjʊərəˋkrætɪk
burgher ˋbɜgə(r)
burglar ˋbɜglə(r)
burglary ˋbɜglərɪ
burgundy, B– ˋbɜgəndɪ
burial ˋberɪəl
burial-ground ˋberɪəl graʊnd
burial-service ˋberɪəl sɜvɪs
burlesque bɜˋlesk
burly ˋbɜlɪ
Burma ˋbɜmə
Burmese bɜˋmiz
burn bɜn
burnish ˋbɜnɪʃ
Burns bɜnz
burnt bɜnt
burp bɜp
bur(r) bɜ(r)
burrow ˋbʌrəʊ $ ˋbɜəʊ
bursar ˋbɜsə(r)

burst bɜst very colloquially: bʌst
bury, B– ˋberɪ
bus bʌs
bush bʊʃ
bushel ˋbʊʃl
business ˋbɪznəs -nɪs -z -ṇ-
bust bʌst
bustle ˋbʌsl
bus stop ˋbʌs stop
busy ˋbɪzɪ
busybody ˋbɪzɪ bodɪ
but usual form: bət strong-form: bʌt
butane ˋbjuteɪn
butcher ˋbʊtʃə(r)
butler ˋbʌtlə(r)
butt bʌt
butter ˋbʌtə(r)
buttercup ˋbʌtəkʌp $ ˋbʌtər-
butter-fingers ˋbʌtə fɪŋgəz
   $ ˋbʌtər fɪŋgərz
butterfly ˋbʌtəflaɪ $ ˋbʌtər-
buttermilk ˋbʌtəmɪlk $ ˋbʌtər-
buttocks ˋbʌtəks
button ˋbʌtn
buttonhole ˋbʌtnhəʊl
buttress ˋbʌtrəs -ɪs
buxom ˋbʌksəm
buy baɪ
buzz bʌz
buzzard ˋbʌzəd $ ˋbʌzərd
by baɪ
by(e)- prefix baɪ
bye bye ˌbaɪ ˋbaɪ
bye byes ˋbaɪ baɪz
by-election ˋbaɪ ɪlekʃn əl-
bygone ˋbaɪgon $ -gɒn etc
by-law ˋbaɪ lɔ
by-pass ˋbaɪ pas $ pæs
by-path ˋbaɪ paθ $ pæθ
by-product ˋbaɪ prodʌkt
by-road ˋbaɪ rəʊd
Byron ˋbaɪərən
by-stander ˋbaɪ stændə(r)
by-way ˋbaɪ weɪ
by-word ˋbaɪ wɜd
Byzantine bɪˋzæntaɪn baɪ- -tɪn -tin
   ˋbɪzntaɪn

C

C c si
ca. *abbr* ˈsɑkə əˈbɑʊt
cab kæb
cabal kəˈbæl
cabaret ˈkæbəreɪ $ ˈkæbəˈreɪ
cabbage ˈkæbɪdʒ
caber ˈkeɪbə(r)
cabin ˈkæbɪn
cabin-cruiser ˈkæbɪn ˈkruzə(r)
cabinet ˈkæbɪnət -bənɪt -bn̩-
cabinet minister ˈkæbɪnət mɪnɪstə(r)
cable ˈkeɪbl
cable-car ˈkeɪbl kɑ(r)
cablegram ˈkeɪblɡræm
cacao kəˈkɑʊ $ £ kəˈkeɪɑʊ
cachet ˈkæʃeɪ $ kæˈʃeɪ
cachou ˈkæʃu $ kəˈʃu ˈkæ-
cackle ˈkækl
cacophonous kəˈkofənəs
cacophony kəˈkofənɪ
cacti ˈkæktaɪ -ti
cactus ˈkæktəs
cad kæd
cadaverous kəˈdævərəs
caddy ˈkædɪ
cadence ˈkeɪdns
cadenza kəˈdenzə
cadet kəˈdet
cadge kædʒ
Cadillac ˈkædⱼæk
Cadiz kəˈdɪz ˈkeɪdɪz
cadre ˈkɑdə ˈkædrɪ
  with unsyllabic r: ˈkɑdr
Caesar ˈsizə(r)
Caesarean sɪˈzeərɪən
café ˈkæfeɪ $ kæˈfeɪ kə-
café-au-lait ˈkæfeɪ ɑʊ ˈleɪ
cafeteria ˈkæfəˈtɪərɪə -fɪ-
caffeine ˈkæfin $ kæˈfin *etc*
caftan ˈkæftæn
cage keɪdʒ
cagey ˈkeɪdʒɪ
Cain keɪn
cairn keən $ keərn
Cairo ˈkaɪərɑʊ ˈkaɪrɑʊ
cajole kəˈdʒɑʊl
cake keɪk
calabash ˈkæləbæʃ
Calais ˈkæleɪ $ kæˈleɪ
calamity kəˈlæmətɪ

calcify ˈkælsɪfaɪ
calcium ˈkælsɪəm
calculable ˈkælkjələbl -jʊl-
calculate ˈkælkjəleɪt -jʊl-
calculation ˈkælkjəˈleɪʃn -jʊl-
calculus ˈkælkjələs -jʊ-
Calcutta kælˈkʌtə
Caledonian ˈkælɪˈdɑʊnɪən
calendar ˈkælɪndə(r)
calender ˈkælɪndə(r)
calf kɑf $ kæf
calibrate ˈkælɪbreɪt
calibre($ -ber) ˈkælɪbə(r)
calico ˈkælɪkɑʊ
California ˈkæləˈfɔnɪə -lɪf-
calipers ˈkælɪpəz $ -pərz
caliph ˈkælɪf ˈkeɪlɪf
caliphate ˈkælɪfeɪt ˈkeɪ-
call kɔl
calligraphy kəˈlɪɡrəfɪ
callipers ˈkælɪpəz $ -pərz
callisthenics ˈkælɪsˈθenɪks
callous ˈkæləs
callus ˈkæləs
callow ˈkælɑʊ
calm kɑm $ kɑlm
Calor gas ˈkælə ɡæs $ ˈkælər
calorie ˈkælərɪ
calumny ˈkæləmnɪ
calve kɑv $ kæv
Calvinism ˈkælvɪnɪzm
Calvinist ˈkælvɪnɪst
calypso kəˈlɪpsɑʊ
calyx ˈkeɪlɪks ˈkælɪks
cam kæm
camaraderie ˈkæməˈrɑdərɪ
Cambridge ˈkeɪmbrɪdʒ
camber ˈkæmbə(r)
cambric ˈkeɪmbrɪk
came keɪm
camel ˈkæml
camellia kəˈmɪlɪə -ˈmel-
Camembert ˈkæməmbeə(r) -mõm-
cameo ˈkæmɪɑʊ
camera ˈkæmrə -mərə
Cameron ˈkæmərən
Cameroon ˈkæməˈrun
camouflage ˈkæməflɑʒ
camp kæmp
campaign kæmˈpeɪn

campanile 'kæmpə`nilı -leı

camp-bed 'kæmp `bed

Campbell `kæmbl

camp-fire `kæmp faɪə(r)

camphor `kæmfə(r)

campus `kæmpəs

can kæn

can *auxiliary v usual form:* kən
  strong-form: kæn

Canada `kænədə

Canadian kə`neɪdɪən

canal kə`næl

canapé `kænəpeɪ -pɪ

canary kə`neərɪ

canasta kə`næstə

Canberra `kænbərə

cancan `kænkæn

cancel `kænsl

cancer, C– `kænsə(r)

cancerous `kænsərəs

candelabra 'kændə`labrə -`læb- £ -`leɪb-

candid `kændɪd

candidate `kændədɪt `kændɪdət
  $ £ -deɪt *etc*

candidature `kændɪdeɪtʃə(r)

candied `kændɪd

candle `kændl

candle-light `kændl laɪt

candlestick `kændlstɪk

candour($ -or) `kændə(r)

candy `kændɪ

candyfloss `kændɪflos $ -flɔs

candy store `kændɪ stɔ(r)

candy-stripe `kændɪ straɪp

cane keɪn

canine `keɪnaɪn `kæn-

canister `kænɪstə(r)

canker `kæŋkə(r)

cannabis `kænəbɪs

cannibal `kænəbl

cannibalistic 'kænəbə`lɪstɪk

cannon `kænən

cannot `kænot kant `kænət

canny `kænɪ

canoe kə`nu

canon `kænən

canonical kə`nonɪkl

canonize `kænənaɪz

canopy `kænəpɪ

cant kænt

can't kant $ kænt

cantaloup($ -lope) `kæntəlup
  $ -ləup *etc*

cantankerous kæn`tæŋkərəs

cantata kæn`tatə

canteen kæn`tin

canter `kæntə(r)

Canterbury `kæntəbrɪ $ `kæntərberɪ

canticle `kæntɪkl

cantilever `kæntɪlivə(r)

canto `kæntəʊ

canvas(s) `kænvəs

canyon `kænjən

cap kæp

capability 'keɪpə`bɪlətɪ

capable `keɪpəbl

capacious kə`peɪʃəs

capacitor kə`pæsɪtə(r)

capacity kə`pæsətɪ

cape keɪp

caper `keɪpə(r)

Cape Town `keɪp taʊn

capillary kə`pɪlərɪ $ `kæpʃerɪ

capital `kæpɪtl

capitalism `kæpɪtlɪzm

capitalize `kæpɪtlaɪz

capitation 'kæpɪ`teɪʃn

Capitol `kæpɪtl

capitulate kə`pɪtʃuleɪt

capitulation kə`pɪtʃʊ`leɪʃn

capon `keɪpən $ `keɪpon *etc*

caprice kə`pris

capricious kə`prɪʃəs

Capricorn `kæprɪkɔn $ -kɔrn

capsicum `kæpsɪkəm

capsize kæp`saɪz

capstan `kæpstən

capsule `kæpsjul $ `kæpsl *etc*

captain, Capt. `kæptɪn *nautical*
  colloquial before names: `kæpm
  $ `kæptən *etc*

caption `kæpʃn

captious `kæpʃəs

captivate `kæptɪveɪt

captive `kæptɪv

captivity kæp`tɪvətɪ

captor `kæptə(r) `kæptɔ(r)

capture `kæptʃə(r)

car ka(r)

Caracas kə`rækəs $ kə`rakəs

carafe kə`ræf kə`raf

caramel `kærəml -mel

carat `kærət

caravan `kærəvæn £ 'kærə`væn

caraway-seed `kærəweɪ sid

carbide `kabaɪd $ `kar-

carbine ˈkabaın $ ˈkɑrbin
carbolic kaˈbolık kə- $ kɑr-
carbon ˈkabən $ ˈkɑr-
carbonic kaˈbonık kə- $ kɑr-
carboniferous ˌkabəˈnıfərəs $ ˈkɑr-
carborundum ˌkabəˈrʌndəm $ ˈkɑr-
carbuncle ˈkabʌŋkl $ ˈkɑrb-
carburettor (-tter) ˈkabjuˈretə(r) -bəˈr-
   $ ˈkɑrbəreıtər -bjə-
carcase ˈkakəs $ ˈkɑr-
carcass ˈkakəs $ ˈkɑr-
card kad $ kɑrd
cardamom ˈkadəməm $ ˈkɑrd- -mom
cardboard ˈkadbɔd $ ˈkɑrdbɔrd
cardiac ˈkadıæk $ ˈkɑrd-
Cardiff ˈkadıf $ ˈkɑrdıf
cardigan, C– ˈkadıgən $ ˈkɑrd-
cardinal ˈkadnl -dınl $ ˈkɑrd-
card-sharper ˈkad ʃapə(r)
   $ ˈkɑrd ʃɑrpər
care keə(r)
career kəˈrıə(r)
carefree ˈkeəfri $ ˈkeər-
careful ˈkeəfl $ ˈkeərfl
caress kəˈres
caret ˈkæret
caretaker ˈkeəteıkə(r) $ ˈkeər-
cargo ˈkagəu $ ˈkɑrgəu
Caribbean ˌkærıˈbıən -rə- kəˈrıbıən
caricature ˈkærıkəˈtʃuə(r) -rə-
   ˈkærıkətʃə(r)
caricaturist ˈkærıkəˈtʃuərıst
caries ˈkeəriz -rız -riiz
carillon ˈkærıljən ˈkærıõ
   $ ˈkærɭon etc
Carlisle kaˈlaıl $ kɑr-
Carlyle kaˈlaıl $ kɑr-
Carmen ˈkamen $ ˈkɑrmən
carmine ˈkamaın $ ˈkɑr- -mın
carnage ˈkanıdʒ $ ˈkɑr-
carnal ˈkanl $ ˈkɑrnl
carnation kaˈneıʃn $ kɑr-
carnival ˈkanəvl -nıvl $ ˈkɑr-
carnivore ˈkanıvɔ(r) $ ˈkɑr-
carnivorous kaˈnıvərəs $ kɑr-
carol, C– ˈkærl
Caroline ˈkærəlaın
carouse kəˈrauz
carousel ˈkærəˈsel
carp kap $ kɑrp
carpenter ˈkapıntə(r) $ ˈkɑrp-
carpentry ˈkapıntrı $ ˈkɑrp-
carpet ˈkapıt $ ˈkɑrpıt

carpet-sweeper ˈkapıt swipə(r)
   $ ˈkɑrp-
carriage ˈkærıdʒ
carriage-way ˈkærıdʒ weı
carrier ˈkærıə(r)
carrier-pigeon ˈkærıə pıdʒən
   $ ˈkærıər
carrion ˈkærıən
carrion-crow ˈkærıən krəu
carrot ˈkærət
carry ˈkærı
cart kat $ kɑrt
carte blanche ˈkat ˈblanʃ ˈblãʃ ˈblonʃ
   ˈblõʃ ˈblɔ̃ʃ ˈblonʃ $ ˈkɑrt
cartel kaˈtel $ kɑr-
cart-horse ˈkat hɔs $ ˈkɑrt hɔrs
cartilage ˈkatɭıdʒ -təl- -tıl- $ ˈkɑrt-
cartilaginous ˈkatıˈlædʒınəs -dʒŋ̩-
   $ ˈkɑrt-
cartography kaˈtogrəfı $ kɑr-
carton ˈkatn $ ˈkɑrtn
cartoon kaˈtun $ kɑr-
cartridge ˈka-trıdʒ $ ˈkɑr-
cartridge-belt ˈka-trıdʒ belt $ ˈkɑr-
cartridge-paper ˈka-trıdʒ peıpə(r)
   $ ˈkɑr-
carve kav $ kɑrv
carving-knife ˈkavıŋ naıf $ ˈkɑrv-
caryatid ˈkærıˈætıd
cascade kæˈskeıd
case keıs
case-hardened ˈkeıs hadnd $ hɑrdnd
case-history ˈkeıs hıstrı
casement ˈkeısmənt
cash kæʃ
cash-box ˈkæʃ boks
cashew ˈkæʃu $ kəˈʃu
cashier kəˈʃıə(r) $ £ kæˈʃıə(r)
cashmere kæʃˈmıə(r) $ ˈkæʒmıər etc
cash-register ˈkæʃ ˈredʒıstə(r) ˈk- r-
casing ˈkeısıŋ
casino kəˈsinəu
cask kask $ kæsk
casket ˈkaskıt $ ˈkæskıt
cassava kəˈsavə
casserole ˈkæsərəul
Cassius ˈkæsıəs $ ˈkæʃəs -ʃıəs
cassock ˈkæsək
cassowary ˈkæsəwərı $ £ -werı
cast kast $ kæst
castanets ˈkæstəˈnets
castaway ˈkastəweı $ ˈkæst-
caste kast $ kæst

castellated ˈkæstəleɪtɪd
caster ˈkɑstə(r) $ ˈkæstər
castigate ˈkæstɪgeɪt
castigation ˌkæstɪˈgeɪʃn
cast-iron ˈkɑst ˈaɪən $ ˈkæst ˈaɪərn
castle ˈkɑsl $ ˈkæsl
castor ˈkɑstə(r) $ ˈkæstər
castor oil ˈkɑstər ˈɔɪl $ ˈkæstər ɔɪl
castrate kæˈstreɪt $ £ ˈkæstreɪt
castration kæˈstreɪʃn
casual ˈkæʒʊəl
casualty ˈkæʒʊəltɪ -ʒl-
casuist ˈkæzjʊɪst $ £ ˈkæʒʊɪst
cat kæt
catacomb ˈkætəkəʊm £ -kum
cataclysm ˈkætəklɪzm
catafalque ˈkætəfælk
catalog(ue) ˈkætəlɒg $ -lɔg etc
catalysis kəˈtæləsɪs
catalyst ˈkætəlɪst $ £ -tl̩-
catamaran ˈkætəməˈræn
catapult ˈkætəpʌlt
cataract ˈkætərækt
catarrh kəˈtɑ(r)
catastrophe kəˈtæstrəfɪ
catastrophic ˈkætəˈstrɒfɪk
cat-burglar ˈkæt bəglə(r)
catcall ˈkætkɔl
catch kætʃ
catchment ˈkætʃmənt
catchup ˈkætʃəp
catechism ˈkætəkɪzm
catechize ˈkætəkaɪz
categorical ˈkætəˈgɒrɪkl $ -ˈgɔr- etc
category ˈkætəgrɪ -tɪg- -gərɪ $ -gɔrɪ
cater ˈkeɪtə(r)
caterpillar ˈkætəpɪlə(r) $ -tər- -təp-
caterwaul ˈkætəwɔl $ -tər-
catfish ˈkætfɪʃ
catgut ˈkætgʌt
catharsis kəˈθɑsɪs $ -ˈθɑrsɪs
cathedral kəˈθidrl
Catherine ˈkæθrɪn -r̩-
cathode ˈkæθəʊd
cathode-ray-tube ˈkæθəʊd ˈreɪ tjub
  $ tub
catholic, C– ˈkæθl̩ɪk
catholicism, C– kəˈθɒləsɪzm
catholicity ˈkæθəˈlɪsətɪ
catkin ˈkætkɪn
catnap ˈkætnæp
cat-o'-nine-tails ˈkæt ə ˈnaɪn teɪlz
cat's-eye ˈkæts aɪ

cat's-paw ˈkæts pɔ
cattle ˈkætl
catwalk ˈkætwɔk
Caucasian kɔˈkeɪzɪən $ £ -ˈkeɪʒn
Caucasus ˈkɔkəsəs
caucus ˈkɔkəs
caught kɔt
cauldron ˈkɔldrən £ ˈkol-
cauliflower ˈkɒlɪflaʊə(r) $ ˈkɔl-
causal ˈkɔzl
cause kɔz
causeway ˈkɔzweɪ
caustic ˈkɔstɪk £ ˈkos-
cauterize ˈkɔtəraɪz
caution ˈkɔʃn
cautious ˈkɔʃəs
cavalcade ˈkævlˈkeɪd
cavalier ˈkævəˈlɪə(r)
cavalry ˈkævlrɪ
cave keɪv
Cave! ˈkeɪvɪ keɪˈvi
cave-dweller ˈkeɪv dwelə(r)
cavern ˈkævən $ ˈkævərn
caviare ˈkævɪə(r) $ £ ˈkævɪˈa(r) etc
cavil ˈkævl -vɪl
cavity ˈkævətɪ
cavort kəˈvɔt $ -ˈvɔrt
caw kɔ
cayenne ˈkeɪˈen $ kaɪˈen -ˈæn etc
CBE ˈsi bi ˈi
C of E ˈsi əv ˈi
cease sis
cease-fire ˈsis ˈfaɪə(r)
Cecil ˈsesl $ ˈsɪsl etc £ ˈsɪsl
Cecily ˈsesəlɪ ˈsɪsəlɪ -sl̩-
cedar ˈsidə(r)
cede sid
cedilla səˈdɪlə sɪ-
Cedric ˈsedrɪk ˈsid-
ceiling ˈsilɪŋ
celanese ˈseləˈniz
celebrate ˈseləbreɪt -lɪb-
celebration ˈseləˈbreɪʃn -lɪˈb-
celebrity səˈlebrətɪ
celerity səˈlerətɪ sɪ-
celery ˈselərɪ
celestial səˈlestɪəl $ -stʃl
Celia ˈsilɪə
celibacy ˈselɪbəsɪ
celibate ˈselɪbət
cell sel
cellar ˈselə(r)

cellist ˈtʃelɪst
cell-mate ˈsel meɪt
cello ˈtʃeləu
cellophane ˈseləfeɪn
cellular ˈseljələ(r) -ljulə(r)
celluloid ˈseljəlɔɪd -ljul-
cellulose ˈseljələus -ljul-
Celt kelt $ £ selt
Celtic ˈkeltɪk $ £ ˈseltɪk
    football team: ˈseltɪk
cement səˈment sɪˈment
cemetery ˈsemətrɪ $ -terɪ etc
cenotaph ˈsenətaf $ £ -tæf
censer ˈsensə(r)
censor ˈsensə(r)
censorship ˈsensəʃɪp $ -sərʃ-
censure ˈsenʃə(r)
census ˈsensəs
cent sent
centaur ˈsentɔ(r)
centenarian ˌsentəˈneərɪən
centenary senˈtinərɪ -ˈten-
    $ ˈsentṇerɪ etc
centennial senˈtenɪəl
centigrade ˈsentɪgreɪd
centigram(me) ˈsentɪgræm
centime ˈsontim ˈsötɪm
centimetre($ -ter) ˈsentɪmitə(r)
centipede ˈsentɪpid
central ˈsentrl
centralize ˈsentrəlaɪz
centre($ -er) ˈsentə(r)
centre-piece ˈsentə pis $ ˈsentər
centrifugal senˈtrɪfjugl £ ˈsentrɪˈfjugl
centripetal senˈtrɪpɪtl £ ˈsentrɪˈpitl
centurion senˈtjuərɪən $ -ˈtu-
century ˈsentʃərɪ
ceramic səˈræmɪk sɪ- se-
cereal ˈsɪərɪəl
cerebral ˈserəbrl $ səˈribrl etc
cerement ˈsɪəmənt $ ˈserəmənt
ceremonial ˌserəˈməunɪəl
ceremonious ˌserəˈməunɪəs
ceremony ˈserəmənɪ $ -məunɪ
cerise səˈriz $ £ səˈris
certain ˈsɜtn
certainty ˈsɜtntɪ
certifiable ˈsɜtɪˈfaɪəbl ˈsɜtɪfaɪəbl
certificate n səˈtɪfɪkət -fəkɪt -fɪkɪt
certificate v səˈtɪfɪkeɪt
certify ˈsɜtɪfaɪ
certitude ˈsɜtɪtjud $ -tud
cerulean səˈrulɪən

cessation seˈseɪʃn
cession ˈseʃn
cesspit ˈsespɪt
cesspool ˈsespul
cetacean sɪˈteɪʃn
Ceylonese ˈseləˈniz
cf. kəmˈpeə(r) ˈsi ˈef
c/f ˈkærɪd ˈfɔwəd $ ˈfɔrwərd
chafe tʃeɪf
chaff tʃaf $ £ tʃæf
chaffinch ˈtʃæfɪntʃ
chagrin ˈʃægrɪn $ ʃəˈgrɪn
chain tʃeɪn
chain-gang ˈtʃeɪn gæŋ
chain-mail ˈtʃeɪn ˈmeɪl
chain reaction ˈtʃeɪn rɪˈækʃn
chain-smoker ˈtʃeɪn sməukə(r)
chain-stitch ˈtʃeɪn stɪtʃ
chain-store ˈtʃeɪn stɔ(r)
chair tʃeə(r)
chair-lift ˈtʃeə lɪft $ ˈtʃeər
chairman ˈtʃeəmən $ ˈtʃeər-
chaise ʃeɪz
chaise longue ˈʃeɪz ˈloŋ $ ˈlɔŋ etc
chalet ˈʃæleɪ -lɪ $ ʃæˈleɪ etc
chalice ˈtʃælɪs
chalk tʃɔk
challenge ˈtʃæləndʒ -ɪndʒ
chamber ˈtʃeɪmbə(r)
chamberlain ˈtʃeɪmbəlɪn -leɪn $ -bərl-
chamber-maid ˈtʃeɪmbə meɪd $ -bər
chamber music ˈtʃeɪmbə mjuzɪk $ -bər
chamber-pot ˈtʃeɪmbə pot $ -bər
chameleon kəˈmilɪən
chamois ˈʃæmwa $ ˈʃæmɪ
chamois-leather ˈʃæmɪ leðə(r)
champ tʃæmp
champagne ʃæmˈpeɪn
champion ˈtʃæmpɪən
championship ˈtʃæmpɪənʃɪp
chance tʃans $ tʃæns
chancellery ˈtʃanslrɪ $ ˈtʃæn-
chancellor ˈtʃanslə(r) $ tʃæn-
chancery ˈtʃansərɪ $ ˈtʃæn-
chandelier ˈʃændəˈlɪə(r) -dɪˈl-
chandler ˈtʃandlə(r) $ ˈtʃændlər
change tʃeɪndʒ
changeling ˈtʃeɪndʒlɪŋ
channel ˈtʃænl
chant tʃant $ tʃænt
chanticleer ˈtʃæntɪklɪə(r) ˈtʃæntɪˈklɪə(r)
    £ ˈtʃan-
chantry ˈtʃantrɪ $ ˈtʃæntrɪ

chaos ˈkeɪɒs
chap tʃæp
chapel ˈtʃæpl
chaperon ˈʃæpərəʊn
chaplain ˈtʃæplɪn
chaplet ˈtʃæplət -lɪt
chapter ˈtʃæptə(r)
char tʃɑ(r)
charabanc ˈʃærəbæŋ
character ˈkærɪktə(r)
characteristic ˈkærɪktəˈrɪstɪk
characterization ˈkærɪktəraɪˈzeɪʃn $ -ɪˈz-
characterize ˈkærɪktəraɪz
charade ʃəˈrɑd $ ʃəˈreɪd
charcoal ˈtʃɑkəʊl $ ˈtʃɑr-
charge tʃɑdʒ $ tʃɑrdʒ
charge-account ˈtʃɑdʒ əkaʊnt $ ˈtʃɑrdʒ
chargé d'affaires ˈʃɑʒeɪ dəˈfeə(r) dæˈf-
  $ ˈʃɑr-
charger ˈtʃɑdʒə(r) $ ˈtʃɑr-
charge-sheet ˈtʃɑdʒ ʃiːt $ ˈtʃɑrdʒ
Charing Cross ˈtʃærɪŋ ˈkrɒs $ ˈkrɔs
chariot ˈtʃærɪət
charisma kəˈrɪzmə
charismatic ˈkærɪzˈmætɪk
charitable ˈtʃærɪtəbl -rt-
charity ˈtʃærətɪ
charlady ˈtʃɑleɪdɪ $ ˈtʃɑr-
charlatan ˈʃɑlətən $ ˈʃɑr-
Charles ˈtʃɑlz $ ˈtʃɑrlz
Charleston ˈtʃɑlstən $ ˈtʃɑrl-
charlotte, C– ˈʃɑlət -lot $ ˈʃɑrlət
charm tʃɑm $ tʃɑrm
charnel ˈtʃɑnl $ ˈtʃɑrnl
chart tʃɑt $ tʃɑrt
charter ˈtʃɑtə(r) $ ˈtʃɑr-
charter flight ˈtʃɑtə(r) flaɪt $ ˈtʃɑrt-
chartreuse ʃɑˈtrɜz $ ʃɑrˈtruz
charwoman ˈtʃɑwʊmən $ ˈtʃɑr-
chary ˈtʃeərɪ
Charybdis kəˈrɪbdɪs
chase tʃeɪs
chasm ˈkæzm
chassis ˈʃæsɪ $ ˈtʃæsɪ
chaste tʃeɪst
chasten ˈtʃeɪsn
chastise tʃæˈstaɪz
chastisement tʃæˈstaɪzmənt
chastity ˈtʃæstətɪ
chasuble ˈtʃæzjʊbl $ -zəbl -sə- -ʒə-
chat tʃæt
château ˈʃætəʊ $ ʃæˈtəʊ
chattel ˈtʃætl

chatter ˈtʃætə(r)
chatterbox ˈtʃætəboks $ ˈtʃætər-
Chaucer ˈtʃɔsə(r)
chauffeur ˈʃəʊfə(r) $ £ ʃəʊˈfɜ(r)
chauvinism ˈʃəʊvɪnɪzm
chauvinistic ˈʃəʊvɪˈnɪstɪk
cheap tʃip
cheapen ˈtʃipən
cheat tʃit
check tʃek
check-list ˈtʃek lɪst
checkmate ˈtʃekmeɪt
check-up ˈtʃek ʌp
Cheddar ˈtʃedə(r)
cheek tʃik
cheep tʃip
cheer tʃɪə(r)
cheerio ˈtʃɪərɪˈəʊ
cheese tʃiz
cheese-cake ˈtʃiz keɪk
cheese-paring ˈtʃiz peərɪŋ
cheetah ˈtʃitə
chef ʃef
chef d'oeuvre ˈʃeɪ ˈdɜvr
  with unsyllabic r
Chekhov ˈtʃekof -ov $ -kɔf etc
Chelsea ˈtʃelsɪ
chemical ˈkemɪkl
chemise ʃəˈmiz
chemist ˈkemɪst
chemistry ˈkemɪstrɪ
chenille ʃəˈnil
cheque tʃek
chequered ˈtʃekəd $ ˈtʃəkərd
chequers, C– ˈtʃekəz $ -kərz
cherish ˈtʃerɪʃ
cheroot ʃəˈrut
cherry ˈtʃerɪ
cherub ˈtʃerəb
cherubim ˈtʃerəbɪm
chervil ˈtʃɜvɪl
Cheshire ˈtʃeʃə(r) $ -ʃɪər
chess tʃes
chessman ˈtʃesmæn
chest tʃest
Chester ˈtʃestə(r)
Chesterfield ˈtʃestəfild $ -tər-
Chesterton ˈtʃestətən $ -tər-
chestnut ˈtʃesnʌt
chest-of-drawers ˈtʃest əv ˈdrɔz
  $ ˈdrɔrz
cheval-glass ʃəˈvæl glɑs $ glæs
chevalier ˈʃevəˈlɪə(r) ʃəˈvælɪeɪ

Chevrolet ˈʃevrəleɪ $ ˌʃevrəˈleɪ
chevron ˈʃevrən
chevy ˈtʃevɪ
chew tʃu
chewing-gum ˈtʃuɪŋ gʌm
Chianti kɪˈæntɪ
chiarascuro kɪˈarəˈskjʊərəʊ -ˈskʊər-
chic ʃik
Chicago ʃɪˈkagəʊ $ ʃɪˈkɔgəʊ etc
chicanery ʃɪˈkeɪnərɪ
chichi ˈʃiʃi
chick tʃɪk
chicken ˈtʃɪkɪn
chicken-feed ˈtʃɪkɪn fid
chicken-hearted ˈtʃɪkɪn ˈhɑtɪd $ ˈhɑrtɪd
chickenpox ˈtʃɪkɪnpoks
Chichester ˈtʃɪtʃɪstə(r)
chicory ˈtʃɪkərɪ
chide tʃaɪd
chief tʃif
chieftain ˈtʃiftən
chiffon ˈʃɪfon $ ʃɪˈfon ˈʃɪfən
chiffonier ˈʃɪfəˈnɪə(r)
chilblain ˈtʃɪlbleɪn
child ˈtʃaɪld
child-bearing ˈtʃaɪld beərɪŋ
childbirth ˈtʃaɪldbɜθ
childhood ˈtʃaɪldhʊd
childish ˈtʃaɪldɪʃ
childlike ˈtʃaɪldlaɪk
children ˈtʃɪldrən ˈtʃʊl- ˈtʃl- -rn
child's play ˈtʃaɪldz pleɪ
Chile ˈtʃɪlɪ
chill tʃɪl
chilli ˈtʃɪlɪ
chime ˈtʃaɪm
chim(a)era ˈkaɪˈmɪərə ˈkɪ-
chimney ˈtʃɪmnɪ
chimney-pot ˈtʃɪmnɪ pot
chimney-stack ˈtʃɪmnɪ stæk
chimney-sweep ˈtʃɪmnɪ swip
chimpanzee ˈtʃɪmpænˈzi
chin tʃɪn
china, C– ˈtʃaɪnə
chinchilla tʃɪnˈtʃɪlə
chin-chin ˈtʃɪn ˈtʃɪn
chine tʃaɪn
Chinese ˈtʃaɪˈniz
chink tʃɪŋk
chintz ˈtʃɪnts
chip tʃɪp
chipolata ˈtʃɪpəˈlatə
chipmunk ˈtʃɪpmʌnk

Chippendale ˈtʃɪpəndeɪl
chiropodist kɪˈropədɪst ʃɪˈr- $ kaɪˈr-
chiropody kɪˈropədɪ ʃɪˈr- $ kaɪˈr-
chirp tʃɜp
chirrup ˈtʃɪrəp
chisel ˈtʃɪzl
chit tʃɪt
chit-chat ˈtʃɪt tʃæt
chivalrous ˈʃɪvlrəs
chivalry ˈʃɪvlrɪ
chive tʃaɪv
chivy ˈtʃɪvɪ
Chloe ˈkləʊɪ
chloride ˈklɔraɪd
chlorinate ˈklorɪneɪt $ £ ˈklɔr-
chlorine ˈklɔrin
chloroform ˈklorəfɔm $ ˈklɔrəfɔrm
chlorophyll ˈklorəfɪl $ ˈklɔr-
chock tʃok
chock-a-block ˈtʃok ə ˈblok
chock-full ˈtʃok ˈfʊl
choc-ice ˈtʃok aɪs
chocolate ˈtʃoklət -ɪt
choice tʃɔɪs
choir ˈkwaɪə(r)
choke tʃəʊk
choler ˈkolə(r)
cholera ˈkolərə
choose tʃuz
choosey ˈtʃuzɪ
chop tʃop
Chopin ˈʃəʊpæ̃ ˈʃo- $ ˈʃəʊpæn
chopper ˈtʃopə(r)
chopsticks ˈtʃopstɪks
chop-suey ˈtʃop ˈsuɪ
choral ˈkɔrl
chorale kəˈral $ kəˈræl kəʊ- etc
chord kɔd $ kɔrd
chore tʃɔ(r)
choreography ˈkorɪˈogrəfɪ $ ˈkɔr-
chorister ˈkorɪstə(r) $ ˈkɔ-
chortle ˈtʃɔtl $ ˈtʃɔrtl
chorus ˈkɔrəs
chose ˈtʃəʊz
chosen ˈtʃəʊzn
chow tʃaʊ
chowder ˈtʃaʊdə(r)
Christ kraɪst
christen ˈkrɪsn
Christendom ˈkrɪsndəm
christening ˈkrɪsnɪŋ -sŋɪŋ
Christian ˈkrɪstʃən £ -stɪən
Christianity ˈkrɪstɪˈænətɪ

Christian name ˈkrɪstʃən neɪm -stɪən
Christina krɪˈstinə
Christine ˈkrɪstin krɪˈstin
Christmas ˈkrɪsməs
Christmas-box ˈkrɪsməs bɒks
Christmas Day ˈkrɪsməs ˈdeɪ
Christmas-tree ˈkrɪsməs tri
Christopher ˈkrɪstəfə(r)
chromatic krəˈmætɪk $ krəʊˈmætɪk etc
chrome krəʊm
chromium ˈkrəʊmɪəm
chronic ˈkrɒnɪk
chronicle ˈkrɒnɪkl -nəkl
chronological ˈkrɒnəˈlɒdʒɪkl
chronology krəˈnɒlədʒɪ
chronometer krəˈnɒmɪtə(r)
chrysalis ˈkrɪsəlɪs
chrysanthemum krɪˈsænθəməm -ˈzæn-
Chrysler ˈkraɪzlə(r)
chubby ˈtʃʌbɪ
chuck tʃʌk
chuckle ˈtʃʌkl
chug tʃʌg
chukker ˈtʃʌkə(r)
chum tʃʌm
chump tʃʌmp
chunk tʃʌŋk
church tʃɜtʃ
church-goer ˈtʃɜtʃ gəʊə(r)
Churchill ˈtʃɜtʃɪl
churchman ˈtʃɜtʃmən
church-warden tʃɜtʃ ˈwɔdn $ ˈwɔrdn
churchyard ˈtʃɜtʃjad $ -jard
churl tʃɜl
churlish ˈtʃɜlɪʃ
churn tʃɜn
chute ʃut
chutney ˈtʃʌtnɪ
CIA ˈsi aɪ ˈeɪ
cicada sɪˈkadə $ sɪˈkeɪdə etc
cicatrice ˈsɪkətrɪs
Cicero ˈsɪsərəʊ
CID ˈsi aɪ ˈdi
cider ˈsaɪdə(r)
cigar sɪˈga(r)
cigarette ˈsɪgəˈret $ ˈsɪgəret etc
cigarette-case ˈsɪgəˈret keɪs $ ˈsɪgəret etc
cigarette-holder ˈsɪgəˈret həʊldə(r)
    $ ˈsɪgəret etc
cinch sɪntʃ
Cincinnati ˈsɪnsɪˈnætɪ
cinder ˈsɪndə(r)
Cinderella ˈsɪndəˈrelə

cine ˈsɪnɪ ˈsɪneɪ
cine-camera ˈsɪnɪ kæmrə
cine-film ˈsɪnɪ fɪlm
cinema ˈsɪnəmə
cine-projector ˈsɪnɪ prədʒektə(r)
cinnamon ˈsɪnəmən
cipher ˈsaɪfə(r)
circa ˈsɜkə
circle ˈsɜkl
circuit ˈsɜkɪt
circuitous sɜˈkjuɪtəs
circular ˈsɜkjələ(r) -jʊlə(r)
circularize ˈsɜkjələraɪz -jʊl-
circulate ˈsɜkjəleɪt -jʊl-
circulation ˈsɜkjəˈleɪʃn -jʊˈl-
circumcise ˈsɜkəmsaɪz
circumcision ˈsɜkəmˈsɪʒn
circumference sɜˈkʌmfrəns -rns
circumflex ˈsɜkəmfleks
circumlocution ˈsɜkəmləˈkjuʃn -ləʊˈk-
circumnavigate ˈsɜkəmˈnævɪgeɪt
circumscribe ˈsɜkəmskraɪb
circumscription ˈsɜkəmˈskrɪpʃn
circumspect ˈsɜkəmspekt
circumspection ˈsɜkəmˈspekʃn
circumstance ˈsɜkəmstəns £ -stɑns
    $ £ -stæns
circumstances ˈsɜkəmstænsɪz £ -stən-
    -stɑn-
circumstantial ˈsɜkəmˈstænʃl
circumvent ˈsɜkəmˈvent
circumvention ˈsɜkəmˈvenʃn
circus ˈsɜkəs
cirrhosis sɪˈrəʊsɪs
cirrus ˈsɪrəs
cistern ˈsɪstən $ ˈsɪstərn
citadel ˈsɪtədl -del
citation saɪˈteɪʃn
cite saɪt
citizen ˈsɪtɪzn $ £ -təzn $ -təsn
citizenship ˈsɪtɪznʃɪp
citric ˈsɪtrɪk
Citroën ˈsɪtrʊən
citron ˈsɪtrən
citrus ˈsɪtrəs
city ˈsɪtɪ
civet ˈsɪvɪt
civic ˈsɪvɪk
civil ˈsɪvl
Civil Defence Corps ˈsɪvl dɪˈfens kɔ(r)
civilian səˈvɪlɪən
civility səˈvɪlətɪ
civilization ˈsɪvļaɪˈzeɪʃn $ ˈsɪvļɪˈzeɪʃn

civilize ˈsɪvḷaɪz
Civil Servant ˈsɪvl ˈsɜvnt
Civil Service ˈsɪvl ˈsɜvɪs
civil war ˈsɪvl ˈwɔ(r)
clack klæk
clad klæd
claim kleɪm
claimant ˈkleɪmənt
clairvoyant kleəˈvɔɪənt $ kleər-
clam klæm
clamber ˈklæmbə(r)
clammy ˈklæmɪ
clamorous ˈklæmərəs
clamour($ -or) ˈklæmə(r)
clamp klæmp
clan klæn
clandestine klænˈdestɪn
clang klæŋ
clangour($ -or) ˈklæŋə(r)
clank klæŋk
clannish ˈklænɪʃ
clansman ˈklænzmən
clap klæp
clapboard ˈklæpbɔd
   $ ˈklæbɔrd -bərd etc
claptrap ˈklæptræp
Clara ˈkleərə ˈklɑrə
Clare kleə(r)
Clarence ˈklærəns
claret ˈklærət
Clark(e) klɑk $ klɑrk
clarification ˈklærəfɪˈkeɪʃn -rɪf-
clarify ˈklærəfaɪ -rɪf-
clarinet ˈklærɪˈnet $ ˈklærɪnet
clarion ˈklærɪən
clarity ˈklærətɪ
clash klæʃ
clasp klɑsp $ klæsp
class klɑs $ klæs
class-conscious ˈklɑs konʃəs $ ˈklæs
classic ˈklæsɪk
classical ˈklæsɪkl
classicist ˈklæsɪsɪst
classification ˈklæsɪfɪˈkeɪʃn
classified ˈklæsɪfaɪd
classify ˈklæsɪfaɪ -səf-
classmate ˈklɑsmeɪt $ ˈklæs-
classroom ˈklɑsrʊm -rum
   $ ˈklæsrum -rʊm
class-warfare ˈklɑs ˈwɔfeə(r)
   $ ˈklæs ˈwɔrfeər
clatter ˈklætə(r)
Claud(e) klɔd

Claudia ˈklɔdɪə
Claudius ˈklɔdɪəs
clause klɔz
claustrophobia ˈklɔstrəˈfəʊbɪə £ ˈklos-
clavichord ˈklævɪkɔd $ -kɔrd
clavicle ˈklævɪkl
claw klɔ
clay kleɪ
claymore ˈkleɪmɔ(r)
clean klin
cleanliness ˈklenlɪnəs
cleanly adj ˈklenlɪ
cleanly adv ˈklinlɪ
cleanse klenz
clean-shaven ˈklin ˈʃeɪvn
clear klɪə(r)
clearance ˈklɪərns
clear-headed ˈklɪə ˈhedɪd $ ˈklɪər
clearing ˈklɪərɪŋ
clearing-house ˈklɪərɪŋ haʊs
clear-sighted ˈklɪə ˈsaɪtɪd $ ˈklɪər
cleavage ˈklivɪdʒ
cleave kliv
clef klef
cleft kleft
cleft palate ˈkleft ˈpælət -lɪt
clematis ˈklemətɪs kləˈmeɪtɪs $ -ˈmæt-
clemency ˈklemənsɪ
clement ˈklemənt
clench klentʃ
Cleopatra klɪəˈpætrə -ˈpɑtrə
clerestory ˈklɪəstɔrɪ $ ˈklɪərstɔrɪ
clergy ˈklɜdʒɪ
clergyman ˈklɜdʒɪmən
cleric ˈklerɪk
clerical ˈklerɪkl
clerk klɑk $ klɜk
Cleveland ˈklivlənd
clever ˈklevə(r)
cliché ˈkliʃeɪ $ kliˈʃeɪ
click klɪk
client ˈklaɪənt
clientele ˈkliənˈtel ˈkliõ- $ ˈklaɪən-
cliff klɪf
cliff-hanger ˈklɪf hæŋə(r)
Clifford ˈklɪfəd $ ˈklɪfərd
climate ˈklaɪmɪt -mət
climatology ˈklaɪməˈtolədʒɪ
climax ˈklaɪmæks
climb klaɪm
clime klaɪm
clinch klɪntʃ
cling klɪŋ

clinic ˈklɪnɪk
clinical ˈklɪnɪkl
clink klɪŋk
clip klɪp
clique klik $ klɪk
Clive klaɪv
cloak kləʊk
cloak-room ˈkləʊk rʊm $ £ rum etc
cloche kləʊʃ kloʃ
clock klok
clockwise ˈklokwaɪz
clockwork ˈklokwɜk
clod klod
clodhopper ˈklodhopə(r)
clog klog $ klɔg
cloisonné klwaˈzoneɪ $ ˈklɔɪzəˈneɪ
cloister ˈklɔɪstə(r)
close adj, n kləʊs
close v kləʊz
close-fitting ˈkləʊs ˈfɪtɪŋ
close-set ˈkləʊs ˈset
close-shaven ˈkləʊs ˈʃeɪvn
closet ˈklozɪt -zət
close-up ˈkləʊs ʌp
closure ˈkləʊʒə(r)
clot klot
cloth kloθ $ klɔθ etc
clothe kləʊð
clothes kləʊðz $ £ kləʊz etc
clothes-basket ˈkləʊðz baskɪt
　　$ £ ˈkləʊz etc $ bæskɪt
clothes brush ˈkləʊðz brʌʃ $ £ ˈkləʊz
clothes-horse ˈkləʊðz hɔs
　　$ £ ˈkləʊz etc $ hɔrs
clothes-line ˈkləʊðz laɪn $ £ ˈkləʊz etc
clothes-peg ˈkləʊðz peg $ £ ˈkləʊz etc
clothier ˈkləʊðɪə(r)
clothing ˈkləʊðɪŋ
cloths kloθs $ klɔðz
cloud klaʊd
cloud-burst ˈklaʊd bɜst
clout klaʊt
clove kləʊv
clove hitch ˈkləʊv hɪtʃ
cloven ˈkləʊvn
clover ˈkləʊvə(r)
clown klaʊn
cloy klɔɪ
club klʌb
club-foot ˈklʌb ˈfʊt
clubland ˈklʌblænd
cluck klʌk
clue klu

clump klʌmp
clumsy ˈklʌmzɪ
clung klʌŋ
cluster ˈklʌstə(r)
clutch klʌtʃ
clutter ˈklʌtə(r)
Clyde klaɪd
co- prefix kəʊ
coach kəʊtʃ
coachman ˈkəʊtʃmən
coagulate kəʊˈægjʊleɪt
coagulation kəʊˈægjʊˈleɪʃn
coal kəʊl
coalesce ˈkəʊəˈles
coal-field ˈkəʊl fild
coal-gas ˈkəʊl gæs
coalition ˈkəʊəˈlɪʃn
coal-mine ˈkəʊl maɪn
coal-scuttle ˈkəʊl skʌtl
coarse kɔs $ kɔrs
coast kəʊst
coast-guard ˈkəʊst gad $ gard
coast-line ˈkəʊst laɪn
coat kəʊt
coatee kəʊˈti ˈkəʊti
coat-hanger ˈkəʊt hæŋə(r)
coat of arms ˈkəʊt əv ˈamz $ ˈarmz
coax kəʊks
coaxial kəʊˈæksɪəl -kʃl
cob kob
cobalt ˈkəʊbɔlt kəʊˈb- £ -bolt
cobble ˈkobl
cobbler ˈkoblə(r)
cobra ˈkəʊbrə £ ˈkobrə
cobweb ˈkobweb
coca-cola ˈkəʊkə ˈkəʊlə
cocaine kəʊˈkeɪn
cochineal ˈkotʃɪˈnil ˈkotʃinil
cock kok
cockade koˈkeɪd
cock-a-doodle-doo ˈkok ə ˈdudl ˈdu
cook-a-hoop ˈkok ə ˈhup
cockatoo ˈkokəˈtu
cockchafer ˈkoktʃeɪfə(r)
cock-crow ˈkok krəʊ
cockerel ˈkokrl
cocker spaniel ˈkokə ˈspænɪəl
　　$ ˈkokər
cock-eyed ˈkok aɪd kok ˈaɪd
cock-fighting ˈkok faɪtɪŋ
cockle ˈkokl
Cockney ˈkoknɪ
cockpit ˈkokpɪt

cockroach ˈkokrəʊtʃ
cockscomb ˈkokskəm
cocksure ˈkokˈʃʊə(r) £ -ˈʃɔ(r)
cocktail ˈkokteɪl
coco ˈkəʊkəʊ
cocoa ˈkəʊkəʊ
coconut ˈkəʊkənʌt
cocoon kəˈkun
cod kod
coda ˈkəʊdə
coddle ˈkodl
code kəʊd
codex ˈkəʊdeks
codices ˈkəʊdɪsiz
codicil ˈkəʊdəsɪl -dɪs- $ ˈkodəsl
codify ˈkəʊdɪfaɪ $ ˈkodəfaɪ etc
codling ˈkodlɪŋ
cod-liver-oil ˈkod lɪvər ˈɔɪl
co-ed ˈkəʊ ˈed $ ˈkəʊ ed
co-education ˈkəʊ ˈedʒʊˈkeɪʃn £ -ˈedjʊ-
co-efficient ˈkəʊ ɪˈfɪʃnt
coerce kəʊˈɜs
coercion kəʊˈɜʃn $ kəʊˈɜʒn
coeval kəʊˈivl
coexist ˈkəʊɪgˈzɪst
coexistence ˈkəʊɪgˈzɪstəns
coffee ˈkofɪ $ ˈkɔfɪ
coffee-bean ˈkofɪ bin $ ˈkɔfɪ
coffee-mill ˈkofɪ mɪl $ ˈkɔfɪ
coffer ˈkofə(r) $ ˈkɔfər etc
coffin ˈkofɪn $ ˈkɔfɪn
cog kog $ kɔg
cogent ˈkəʊdʒənt
cogitate ˈkodʒɪteɪt
cogitation ˈkodʒɪˈteɪʃn
cognac ˈkonjæk ˈkəʊn-
cognate ˈkogneɪt
cognition kogˈnɪʃn
cognizance ˈkognɪzns ˈkon-
cog-wheel ˈkog wil $ hwil etc
cohabit kəʊˈhæbɪt
cohabitation ˈkəʊhæbɪˈteɪʃn
Cohen ˈkəʊɪn
cohere kəʊˈhɪə(r)
coherence kəʊˈhɪərns
coherent kəʊˈhɪərnt
cohesion kəʊˈhiʒn
cohesive kəʊˈhisɪv -ˈhizɪv
cohort ˈkəʊhɔt $ -hɔrt
coiffure kwaˈfjʊə(r) kwæ-
coign kɔɪn
coil kɔɪl
coin kɔɪn

coinage ˈkɔɪnɪdʒ
coincide ˈkəʊɪnˈsaɪd
coincidence kəʊˈɪnsɪdəns -səd-
coincidental kəʊˈɪnsɪˈdentl -səˈd-
coke kəʊk
cokernut ˈkəʊkənʌt $ -kərn-
col kol
colander ˈkʌləndə(r) ˈkol-
Colchester ˈkəʊltʃɪstə(r) kol- -tʃəs-
cold kəʊld
cold-blooded ˈkəʊld ˈblʌdɪd
cold-hearted ˈkəʊld ˈhatɪd $ ˈhartɪd
cold shoulder ˈkəʊld ˈʃəʊldə(r)
colic ˈkolɪk
Colin ˈkolɪn
Coliseum ˈkolɪˈsɪəm
collaborate kəˈlæbəreɪt
collaboration kəˈlæbəˈreɪʃn
collapse kəˈlæps
collapsible kəˈlæpsəbl
collar ˈkolə(r)
collar-bone ˈkolə bəʊn $ ˈkolər
collar-stud ˈkolə stʌd $ ˈkolər
collate kəˈleɪt koˈl-
collateral kəˈlætərl
collation kəˈleɪʃn koˈl-
colleague ˈkolig
collect n ˈkolekt
collect v kəˈlekt
collection kəˈlekʃn
collective kəˈlektɪv
collector kəˈlektə(r)
colleen ˈkolin
college ˈkolɪdʒ
collegiate kəˈlidʒɪət -dʒət
collide kəˈlaɪd
collie ˈkolɪ
collier ˈkolɪə(r)
colliery ˈkoljərɪ
collision kəˈlɪʒn
collocation ˈkoləˈkeɪʃn
colloquial kəˈləʊkwɪəl
colloquialism kəˈləʊkwɪəlɪzm
colloquy ˈkoləkwɪ
collusion kəˈluʒn
collusive kəˈlusɪv
cologne, C- kəˈləʊn
colon ˈkəʊlən
colonel ˈkɜnl
colonial kəˈləʊnɪəl
colonialism kəˈləʊnɪəlɪzm
colonist ˈkolənɪst
colonization ˈkolənaɪˈzeɪʃn $ -ɪˈz-

colonize ˈkolənɑɪz
colonnade ˈkoləˈneɪd $ ˈkoləneɪd
colony ˈkolənɪ
Colorado ˈkoləˈrɑdəʊ $ -ˈræd- etc
colossal kəˈlosl
Colosseum ˈkoləˈsɪəm
colossus kəˈlosəs
colour($ -or) ˈkʌlə(r)
colour-bar($ -or) ˈkʌlə bɑ(r) $ ˈkʌlər
colour-blind($ -or) ˈkʌlə blɑɪnd $ ˈkʌlər
colt kəʊlt
Columbia kəˈlʌmbɪə
columbine ˈkoləmbɑɪn
Columbus kəˈlʌmbəs
column ˈkoləm
columnist ˈkoləmɪst -mnɪst
coma ˈkəʊmə
comatose ˈkəʊmətəʊs $ ˈkom-
comb kəʊm
combat ˈkombæt -bət ˈkʌm-
    $ kəmˈbæt
combatant ˈkombətənt $ kəmˈbætənt
combative ˈkombətɪv $ kəmˈbætɪv
combination ˈkombɪˈneɪʃn
combine n ˈkombɑɪn
combine v kəmˈbɑɪn
combine harvester ˈkombɑɪn ˈhɑvɪstə(r)
    $ ˈhɑrv-
combustible kəmˈbʌstəbl
combustion kəmˈbʌstʃən
come kʌm
comeback ˈkʌmbæk
comedian kəˈmidɪən
comedienne kəˈmidɪˈen -ˈmeɪd-
    $ kəˈmidɪən etc
comedown ˈkʌmdɑʊn
comedy ˈkomədɪ
comely ˈkʌmlɪ
comestible kəˈmestəbl
comet ˈkomɪt
comfit ˈkʌmfɪt ˈkom-
comfort ˈkʌmfət $ ˈkʌmfərt
comfortable ˈkʌmftəbl $ -fərt-
comfy ˈkʌmfɪ
comic ˈkomɪk
comical ˈkomɪkl
comity ˈkomɪtɪ $ £ -ətɪ
comma ˈkomə
command kəˈmɑnd $ kəˈmænd
commandant ˈkomənˈdænt £ -ˈdɑnt
    $ £ ˈkoməndænt etc
commandeer ˈkomənˈdɪə(r)
commander kəˈmɑndə(r) $ -ˈmæn-

commemorate kəˈmeməreɪt
commemoration kəˈmeməˈreɪʃn
commemorative kəˈmemrətɪv
    $ -məreɪtɪv
commence kəˈmens
commend kəˈmend
commendable kəˈmendəbl
commendation ˈkomenˈdeɪʃn
commensurate kəˈmenʃərət £ -sjərət
comment n ˈkoment
comment v ˈkoment $ kəˈment
commentary ˈkoməntrɪ $ -terɪ
commentator ˈkomənteɪtə(r)
commerce ˈkomɜs
commercial kəˈmɜʃl
commercialize kəˈmɜʃlɑɪz
commiserate kəˈmɪzəreɪt
commiseration kəˈmɪzəˈreɪʃn
commissar ˈkomɪsɑ(r)
commissariat ˈkomɪˈseərɪət -ɪæt
commissary ˈkomɪsrɪ -məs- -sərɪ $ -serɪ
commission kəˈmɪʃn
commissionaire kəˈmɪʃnˈeə(r)
commissioner kəˈmɪʃnə(r)
commit kəˈmɪt
committee kəˈmɪtɪ
commode kəˈməʊd
commodious kəˈməʊdɪəs
commodity kəˈmodətɪ
commodore ˈkomədɔ(r)
common ˈkomən
commoner ˈkomənə(r)
Common Market ˈkomən ˈmɑkɪt
    $ ˈmɑrkɪt
common-room ˈkomən rʊm
    $ £ rum etc
commonplace ˈkomənpleɪs
Commons, the ðə ˈkomənz
Commonwealth ˈkomənwelθ
commotion kəˈməʊʃn
communal ˈkomjʊnl kəˈmjunl
commune n ˈkomjun
commune v kəˈmjun
communicant kəˈmjunɪkənt
communicate kəˈmjunɪkeɪt
communication kəˈmjuniˈkeɪʃn
communicative kəˈmjunɪkətɪv
    $ -keɪtɪv
communion, C– kəˈmjunɪən
communique kəˈmjunɪkeɪ
communism ˈkomjʊnɪzm
communist ˈkomjʊnɪst
community kəˈmjunətɪ

community centre($ -ter)
 kə'mjunətɪ sentə(r)
commutation 'komjʊ'teɪʃn
commute kə'mjut
compact *adj* kəm'pækt
compact *n* 'kompækt
companion kəm'pæniən
companionship kəm'pæniənʃɪp
companion-way kəm'pæniən weɪ
company 'kʌmpənɪ -pnɪ
comparable 'komprəbl
comparative kəm'pærətɪv
compare kəm'peə(r)
comparison kəm'pærɪsn
compartment kəm'patmənt $ -'part-
compass 'kʌmpəs
compassion kəm'pæʃn
compassionate kəm'pæʃɲət
compatibility kem'pætə'bɪlətɪ
compatible kəm'pætəbl
compatriot kəm'pætrɪət $ -'peɪt-
compel kəm'pel
compendious kəm'pendɪəs
compendium kəm'pendɪəm
compensate 'kompənseɪt $ -pen-
compensation 'kompən'seɪʃn $ -pen-
compensatory 'kompən'seɪtərɪ -pen-
 kəm'pensətərɪ $ kəm'pensətɔrɪ
compere 'kompeə(r)
compete kəm'pit
competence 'kompətəns -pɪt-
competent 'kompətənt -pɪt-
competition 'kompə'tɪʃn -pɪt-
competitive kəm'petətɪv
competitor kəm'petɪtə(r)
compilation 'kompɪ'leɪʃn
compile kəm'paɪl
complacence kəm'pleɪsns
complacency kəm'pleɪsnsɪ
complacent kəm'pleɪsnt
complain kəm'pleɪn
complaint kəm'pleɪnt
complaisance kəm'pleɪzns -eɪsns
complement 'komplɪmənt -ləm-
complementary 'komplɪ'mentrɪ -ləm-
complete kəm'plit
completion kəm'pliʃn
complex 'kompleks $ kəm'pleks *etc*
complexion kəm'plekʃn
complexity kəm'pleksətɪ
compliance kəm'plaɪəns
compliant kəm'plaɪənt
complicate 'komplɪkeɪt

complication 'komplɪ'keɪʃn
complicity kəm'plɪsətɪ
compliment *n* 'komplɪmənt -ləm-
compliment *v* 'komplɪment -ləm-
complimentary 'komplɪ'mentrɪ -lə'm-
 $ -tərɪ
comply kəm'plaɪ
component kəm'pəʊnənt
comport kəm'pɔt $ -'pɔrt
compose kəm'pəʊz
composite 'kompəzɪt -sɪt -aɪt
 $ kəm'pozɪt kom-
composition 'kompə'zɪʃn
compositor kəm'pozɪtə(r)
compos mentis 'kompəs 'mentɪs
compost 'kompost $ 'kompəʊst
composure kəm'pəʊʒə(r)
compote 'kompəʊt
compound *adj* 'kompaʊnd
 $ kom'paʊnd
compound *n* 'kompaʊnd
compound *v* kəm'paʊnd
comprehend 'komprɪ'hend
comprehensible 'komprɪ'hensəbl
comprehension 'komprɪ'henʃn
comprehensive 'komprɪ'hensɪv
compress *n* 'kompres
compress *v* kəm'pres
compression kəm'preʃn
comprise kəm'praɪz
compromise 'komprəmaɪz
comptometer komp'tomɪtə(r)
compulsion kəm'pʌlʃn
compulsive kəm'pʌlsɪv
compulsorily kəm'pʌlsɽlɪ -srɪlɪ
compulsory kəm'pʌlsrɪ -sərɪ
compunction kəm'pʌŋkʃn
computation 'kompjʊ'teɪʃn
compute kəm'pjut
computer kəm'pjutə(r)
comrade 'komreɪd -rɪd £ 'kʌm-
 $ 'komræd *etc*
comradeship 'komreɪdʃɪp -rɪd-
 $ 'komrædʃɪp
con kon
concave 'kon'keɪv 'konkeɪv
conceal kən'sil
concede kən'sid
conceit kən'sit
conceited kən'sitɪd
conceive kən'siv
concentrate 'konsntreɪt
concentration 'konsn'treɪʃn

concentric kən'sentrık kon-
concept 'konsept
conception kən'sepʃn
concern kən'sɜn
concert 'konsət $ 'konsɜrt
concerted kən'sɜtıd
concertina 'konsə'tinə $ -sər't-
concerto kən'tʃɜtəʊ -'tʃeə- $ -'tʃeər-
concession kən'seʃn
concessionaire kən'seʃn'eə(r)
conch koŋk kontʃ
concierge 'kõsı'eəʒ 'kon- $ -'eərʒ
conciliate kən'sılıeıt
conciliation kən'sılı'eıʃn
conciliatory kən'sılıətrı $ kən'sılıətɔrı
concise kən'saıs
conclave 'konkleıv
conclude kən'klud
conclusion kən'kluʒn
conclusive kən'klusıv
concoct kən'kokt $ £ kon'kokt etc
concoction kən'kokʃn
concomitant kən'komıtənt
concord 'koŋkɔd $ -kɔrd
concordance kən'kɔdns $ -'kɔrdns
concordat kon'kɔdæt $ -'kɔrd-
concourse 'koŋkɔs $ -kɔrs
concrete 'koŋkrit
concubine 'koŋkjʊbaın
concupiscence kən'kjupısns
concur kən'kɜ(r)
concurrence kən'kʌrns $ -'kɜəns
concurrent kən'kʌrnt $ -'kɜənt
concuss kən'kʌs
concussion kən'kʌʃn
condemn kən'dem
condemnation 'kondem'neıʃn -dəm-
condensation 'konden'seıʃn -dən-
condense kən'dens
condescend 'kondı'send
condescension 'kondı'senʃn
condign kən'daın kon'daın
condiment 'kondımənt
condition kən'dıʃn
conditional kən'dıʃnl
condole kən'dəʊl
condolence kən'dəʊləns
condominium 'kondə'mınıəm
condone kən'dəʊn
conduce kən'djus $ kən'dus
conduct n 'kondʌkt
conduct v kən'dʌkt
conduction kən'dʌkʃn

conductor kən'dʌktə(r)
conductress kən'dʌktrəs -ıs
conduit 'kondıt 'kʌn- -djʊıt
    $ -duıt -dıt
cone kəʊn
coney 'kəʊnı
confection kən'fekʃn
confectionery kən'fekʃnrı $ -ņerı
confederacy kən'fedrəsı
confederate n kən'fedŗət
confederate v kən'fedəreıt
confederation kən'fedə'reıʃn
confer kən'fɜ(r)
conference 'konfrns
confess kən'fes
confession kən'feʃn
confessional kən'feʃnl
confessor kən'fesə(r)
confetti kən'fetı
confidant(e) 'konfı'dænt 'konfıdænt
confide kən'faıd
confidence 'konfıdəns
confidence man 'konfıdəns mæn
confidence trick 'konfıdəns trık
confidential 'konfı'denʃl
configuration kən'fıgjə'reıʃn -gjʊr-
confine n 'konfaın
confine v kən'faın
confinement kən'faınmənt
confirm kən'fɜm
confirmation 'konfə'meıʃn $ -fər-
confiscate 'konfıskeıt
confiscation 'konfı'skeıʃn
conflagration 'konflə'greıʃn
conflict n 'konflıkt
conflict v kən'flıkt
confluence 'konfluəns
conform kən'fɔm $ -'fɔrm
conformist kən'fɔmıst $ -'fɔrm-
conformity kən'fɔmətı $ -'fɔrm-
confound kən'faʊnd
confront kən'frʌnt
Confucian kən'fjuʃn
Confucius kən'fjuʃəs
confuse kən'fjuz
confusion kən'fjuʒn
confute kən'fjut
congeal kən'dʒil
congenial kən'dʒinıəl
congenital kən'dʒenıtl
conger-eel 'koŋgər 'il
congested kən'dʒestıd
congestion kən'dʒestʃən

conglomerate kən'gloməreɪt
conglomeration kən'glomə'reɪʃn
Congo 'koŋgəʊ
Congolese 'koŋgə'liz
congratulate kən'grætʃʊleɪt
congratulation kən'grætʃʊ'leɪʃn
congratulatory kən'grætʃʊ'leɪtərɪ
  $ kən'grætʃʊlətɔrɪ
congregate 'koŋgrɪgeɪt
congregation 'koŋgrɪ'geɪʃn
congress, C– 'koŋgres $ -grɪs
congressional kən'greʃnl
congressman 'koŋgrɪsmən
Congreve 'koŋgriv
congruent 'koŋgrʊənt
congruous 'koŋgrʊəs
conical 'konɪkl
conifer 'konɪfə(r) $ £ 'kəʊnɪfə(r)
coniferous kə'nɪfərəs -fr-
conjectural kən'dʒektʃərl
conjecture kən'dʒektʃə(r)
conjoin kən'dʒɔɪn kon-
conjoint kon'dʒɔɪnt kən-
conjugal 'kondʒʊgl
conjugate 'kondʒʊgeɪt
conjugation 'kondʒʊ'geɪʃn
conjunction kən'dʒʌŋkʃn
conjure *do tricks* 'kʌndʒə(r)
conjure *appeal* kən'dʒʊə(r)
conjurer(-or) 'kʌndʒərə(r)
conk koŋk $ kɔŋk
conker 'koŋkə(r) $ 'kɔŋkər
connect kə'nekt
Connecticut kə'netɪkət
connection(-xion) kə'nekʃn
connivance kə'naɪvns
connive kə'naɪv
connoisseur 'konə'sɜ(r) -nɪ's- -'sjʊə(r)
connotation 'konə'teɪʃn
connubial kə'njubɪəl $ -'nu- *etc*
conquer 'koŋkə(r)
conqueror 'koŋkərə(r)
conquest 'koŋkwest
Conrad 'konræd
consanguinity 'konsæŋ'gwɪnətɪ
conscience 'konʃns
conscientious 'konʃɪ'enʃəs
conscious 'konʃəs
conscript *n* 'konskrɪpt
conscript *v* kən'skrɪpt
conscription kən'skrɪpʃn
consecrate 'konsɪkreɪt
consecration 'konsɪ'kreɪʃn

consecutive kən'sekjʊtɪv
consensus kən'sensəs
consent kən'sent
consequence 'konsɪkwəns $ -kwens
consequences 'konsɪkwensɪz £ -ənsɪz
consequential 'konsɪ'kwenʃl
conservancy kən'sɜvənsɪ
conservation 'konsə'veɪʃn $ -sər-
conservatism kən'sɜvətɪzm
conservative, C– kən'sɜvətɪv
Conservatoire kən'sɜvətwɑ(r)
conservatory kən'sɜvətrɪ $ -tɔrɪ
conserve kən'sɜv
consider kən'sɪdə(r)
considerable kən'sɪdrəbl
considerate kən'sɪdɽət
consideration kən'sɪdə'reɪʃn
considering kən'sɪdɽɪŋ
consign kən'saɪn
consignment kən'saɪnmənt
consist kən'sɪst
consistency kən'sɪstənsɪ
consistent kən'sɪstənt
consistory kən'sɪstərɪ
consolation 'konsə'leɪʃn
consolation prize 'konsə'leɪʃn praɪz
consolatory kən'səʊlətrɪ -'sol- $ -tɔrɪ
console *n* 'konsəʊl
console *v* kən'səʊl
consolidate kən'solɪdeɪt
consolidation kən'solɪ'deɪʃn
consols 'konsolz kən'solz
consommé kən'someɪ $ 'konsə'meɪ
consonant 'konsənənt -sn-
consort *n* 'konsɔt $ -sɔrt
consort *v* kən'sɔt $ -'sɔrt
consortium kən'sɔtɪəm $ -'sɔrʃɪəm -ʃm
conspectus kən'spektəs
conspicuous kən'spɪkjʊəs
conspiracy kən'spɪrəsɪ
conspirator kən'spɪrətə(r)
conspire kən'spaɪə(r)
constable 'kʌnstəbl $ £ 'kon- *etc*
constabulary kən'stæbjʊlərɪ -lɽɪ $ -lerɪ
Constance 'konstəns
constancy 'konstənsɪ
constellation 'konstə'leɪʃn
consternation 'konstə'neɪʃn $ -stər-
constipate 'konstɪpeɪt
constipation 'konstɪ'peɪʃn
constituency kən'stɪtʃʊənsɪ
constituent kən'stɪtʃʊənt
constitute 'konstɪtjut -tʃ- $ -tut

constitution 'kɒnstɪ'tʃuʃn -'tju- $ -'tu-
constitutive kən'stɪtʃʊtɪv
$ 'kɒnstɪtutɪv etc
constrain kən'streɪn
constraint kən'streɪnt
constrict kən'strɪkt
constriction kən'strɪkʃn
construct kən'strʌkt
construction kən'strʌkʃn
constructive kən'strʌktɪv
construe kən'stru
consul 'kɒnsl
consular 'kɒnsjʊlə(r) -jələ(r)
consulate 'kɒnsjʊlət -jəl- $ 'kɒnsələt
consult kən'sʌlt
consultant kən'sʌltənt
consultation 'kɒnsl'teɪʃn
consultative kən'sʌltətɪv $ 'kɒnslteɪtɪv
consume kən'sjum $ £ -'sum
consumer kən'sjumə(r) $ £ -'su-
consummate adj kən'sʌmət -ɪt
consummate v 'kɒnsəmeɪt £ -sjʊm-
consummation 'kɒnsə'meɪʃn £ -sjʊ-
consumption kən'sʌmpʃn
consumptive kən'sʌmptɪv
contact n 'kɒntækt
contact v 'kɒntækt kən'tækt kon-
contagion kən'teɪdʒən
contagious kən'teɪdʒəs
contain kən'teɪn
container kən'teɪnə(r)
contaminate kən'tæmɪneɪt -mən-
contamination kən'tæmɪ'neɪʃn
contemn kən'tem
contemplate 'kɒntəmpleɪt
contemplation 'kɒntəm'pleɪʃn
contemplative kən'templətɪv
$ 'kɒntəmpleɪtɪv etc
contemporaneous kən'tempə'reɪnɪəs
contemporary kən'temprɪ -rərɪ
$ kən'tempərerɪ
contempt kən'tempt
contemptible kən'temptəbl
contemptuous kən'temptʃʊəs
contend kən'tend
content adj kən'tent
content n 'kɒntent kən'tent
contention kən'tenʃn
contentious kən'tenʃəs
contentment kən'tentmənt
contest n 'kɒntest
contest v kən'test
contestant kən'testənt

context 'kɒntekst
contextual kən'tekstʃʊəl
contiguous kən'tɪgjʊəs
contiguity 'kɒntɪ'gjuətɪ
continent, C– 'kɒntɪnənt $ -tn̩ənt etc
continental 'kɒntɪ'nentl -tn'entl
contingency kən'tɪndʒənsɪ
contingent kən'tɪndʒənt
continual kən'tɪnjʊəl
continuance kən'tɪnjʊəns
continuation kən'tɪnjʊ'eɪʃn
continue kən'tɪnju
continuity 'kɒntɪ'njuətɪ $ -'nu-
continuous kən'tɪnjʊəs
contort kən'tɔt $ -'tɔrt
contortion kən'tɔʃn $ -'tɔrʃn
contour 'kɒntʊə(r)
contour line 'kɒntʊə laɪn $ 'kɒntʊər
contour map 'kɒntʊə mæp $ 'kɒntʊər
contra 'kɒntrə
contraband 'kɒntrəbænd
contraception 'kɒntrə'sepʃn
contraceptive 'kɒntrə'septɪv
contract n 'kɒntrækt
contract v kən'trækt
$ agree 'kɒntrækt
contract out 'kɒntrækt 'aʊt
contractile kən'træktaɪl $ -tl
contraction kən'trækʃn
contradict 'kɒntrə'dɪkt
contradiction 'kɒntrə'dɪkʃn
contradictory 'kɒntrə'dɪktərɪ
contralto kən'træltəʊ
contraption kən'træpʃn
contrapuntal 'kɒntrə'pʌntl
contrariety 'kɒntrə'raɪətɪ
contrariness kən'treərɪnəs
contrariwise kən'treərɪwaɪz
contrary obstinate kən'treərɪ
contrary opposite 'kɒntrɪ -rərɪ $ -rerɪ
contrast n 'kɒntrɑst $ -træst
contrast v kən'trɑst $ -'træst
contravene 'kɒntrə'vin
contravention 'kɒntrə'venʃn
contretemps 'kɒntrətõ -'kõt-
contribute kən'trɪbjut
contribution 'kɒntrɪ'bjuʃn -trə'b-
contributor kən'trɪbjʊtə(r) -jətə(r)
contributory kən'trɪbjʊtərɪ $ -tɔrɪ
contrite 'kɒntraɪt
contrition kən'trɪʃn
contrivance kən'traɪvns
contrive kən'traɪv

control kən'trəʊl
controller kən'trəʊlə(r)
controversial 'kontrə'vɜʃl
controversy 'kontrəvɜsɪ £ kən'trovəsɪ
controvert 'kontrə'vɜt
contumacious 'kontjʊ'meɪʃəs
 $ -tə'm- -tʃə'm-
contumacy 'kontjʊməsɪ $ -təm- -tʃəm-
 $ kən'tuməsɪ etc
contumelious 'kontjʊ'milɪəs
 $ -tə'm- -tʃə'm-
contumely 'kontjumlɪ $ £ -məl-
contuse kən'tjuz $ -'tuz
conundrum kə'nʌndrəm
conurbation 'konɜ'beɪʃn
convalesce 'konvə'les
convalescence 'konvə'lesns
convalescent 'konvə'lesnt
convection kən'vekʃn
convector kən'vektə(r)
convene kən'vin
convenience kən'vinɪəns
convenient kən'vinɪənt
convent 'konvənt $ £ -vent etc
convention kən'venʃn
conventional kən'venʃnl
conventionality kən'venʃn'ælətɪ
converge kən'vɜdʒ
convergent kən'vɜdʒənt
conversant kən'vɜsnt 'konvəsnt $ -vər-
conversation 'konvə'seɪʃn $ -vər-
conversational 'konvə'seɪʃnl $ -vər-
conversazione 'konvə'sætsɪ'əʊneɪ -nɪ
 $ -vər-
converse adj, n 'konvɜs
converse v kən'vɜs
conversion kən'vɜʃn $ £ kən'vɜʒn
convert n 'konvɜt
convert v kən'vɜt
convertibility kən'vɜtə'bɪlətɪ
convertible kən'vɜtəbl
convex 'konveks
convexity kən'veksətɪ
convey kən'veɪ
conveyance kən'veɪəns
conveyor-belt kən'veɪə belt $ -'veɪər
convict n 'konvɪkt
convict v kən'vɪkt
conviction kən'vɪkʃn
convince kən'vɪns
convivial kən'vɪvɪəl
conviviality kən'vɪvɪ'ælətɪ
convocation 'konvə'keɪʃn

convolution 'konvə'luʃn
convolvulus kən'volvjʊləs
convoy 'konvɔɪ
convulse kən'vʌls
convulsion kən'vʌlʃn
convulsive kən'vʌlsɪv
cony 'kəʊnɪ
coo ku
cook kʊk
cooker 'kʊkə(r)
cookery 'kʊkərɪ
cook-house 'kʊk haʊs
cookie 'kʊkɪ
cool kul
cooler 'kulə(r)
coolie 'kulɪ
coon kun
coop kup
co-op 'kəʊ op kəʊ 'op
cooper 'kupə(r)
co-operate kəʊ 'opəreɪt £ 'ɔp-
co-operation kəʊ 'opə'reɪʃn £ 'ɔp-
co-operative kəʊ 'oprətɪv £ 'ɔp-
 $ -pəreɪtɪv
co-opt kəʊ 'opt
co-ordinate n kəʊ 'ɔdɪnət $ 'ɔr- -dn̩-
co-ordinate v kəʊ 'ɔdɪneɪt $ 'ɔr- -dn̩-
co-ordination kəʊ 'ɔdɪ'neɪʃn $ 'ɔr-
coot kut
cop kop
cope kəʊp
copeck 'kəʊpek 'kopek
Copernican kə'pɜnɪkən
Copernicus kə'pɜnɪkəs
copious 'kəʊpɪəs
copper 'kopə(r)
Copperfield 'kopəfild $ -pərf-
copper-plate 'kopə pleɪt $ 'kopər
coppice 'kopɪs
copra 'koprə $ 'kəʊprə etc
copse kops
Copt kopt
Coptic 'koptɪk
copula 'kopjʊlə
copulate 'kopjʊleɪt
copy 'kopɪ
copy-book 'kopɪ bʊk
copyhold 'kopɪhəʊld
copyright 'kopɪraɪt
coquetry 'kokɪtrɪ $ £ 'kəʊk-
coquette ko'ket £ kəʊ-
coquettish kə'ketɪʃ
coracle 'korəkl $ 'kɔr- etc

coral ˈkɔrl $ ˈkɔrl etc
coral-reef ˈkɔrl rif $ ˈkɔrl etc
cor anglais ˈkɔr ˈɒŋgleɪ $ ɒŋˈgleɪ
corbel ˈkɔbl $ ˈkɔrbl
cord kɔd $ ˈkɔrd
Cordelia kɔˈdiliə $ kɔr-
cordial ˈkɔdɪəl $ ˈkɔrdʒl
cordite ˈkɔdaɪt $ ˈkɔr-
cordon ˈkɔdn $ ˈkɔrdn
corduroy ˈkɔdərɔɪ £ -djʊr- $ ˈkɔr-
core kɔ(r)
co-respondent ˈkəʊ rɪˈspɒndənt
corgi ˈkɔgɪ $ ˈkɔrgɪ
coriander ˈkɒrɪˈændə(r) $ ˈkɒrɪˈændər
Corinth ˈkɒrɪnθ $ ˈkɔr-
Corinthian kəˈrɪnθɪən
Coriolanus ˈkɒrɪəˈleɪnəs -ˈlɑnəs $ ˈkɔr-
cork kɔk $ kɔrk
corkage ˈkɔkɪdʒ $ ˈkɔrk-
cormorant ˈkɔmərənt $ ˈkɔr-
corn kɔn $ kɔrn
corn-cob ˈkɔn kɒb $ ˈkɔrn
corn-crake ˈkɔn kreɪk $ ˈkɔrn
cornea ˈkɔnɪə $ ˈkɔrnɪə
corned-beef ˈkɔnd ˈbif $ ˈkɔrnd
cornelia kɔˈniliə $ kɔr-
Cornelius kɔˈnilɪəs $ kɔr-
corner ˈkɔnə(r) $ ˈkɔr-
corner-stone ˈkɔnə stəʊn $ ˈkɔrnər
cornet ˈkɔnɪt $ kɔrˈnet etc
corn-exchange ˈkɔn ɪkstʃeɪndʒ $ ˈkɔrn
cornflour ˈkɔnflaʊə(r) $ ˈkɔrn-
corn-laws ˈkɔn lɔz $ ˈkɔrn
cornice ˈkɔnɪs $ ˈkɔrnɪs
Cornish ˈkɔnɪʃ $ ˈkɔrnɪʃ
corn-starch ˈkɔn stɑtʃ $ ˈkɔrn stɑrtʃ
cornucopia ˈkɔnjuˈkəʊpɪə $ ˈkɔrnəˈk-
Cornwall ˈkɔnwl $ ˈkɔrnwl -wɔl
corollary kəˈrɒlərɪ $ ˈkɒrəlerɪ ˈkɔr-
corona kəˈrəʊnə
coronation ˈkɒrəˈneɪʃn $ ˈkɔrə- etc
coroner ˈkɒrənə(r) $ ˈkɔrənər
coronet ˈkɒrənet -nɪt ˈkɔrəˈnet
$ ˈkɔrənet etc
corporal ˈkɔprl $ ˈkɔrprl
corporate ˈkɔpərət $ ˈkɔrp-
corporation ˈkɔpəˈreɪʃn $ ˈkɔrp-
corporeal kɔˈpɔrɪəl $ kɔr-
corps kɔ(r)
corpse kɔps $ kɔrps
corpulence ˈkɔpjʊləns $ ˈkɔr-
corpulent ˈkɔpjʊlənt $ ˈkɔr-
corpus ˈkɔpəs $ ˈkɔrpəs

corpuscle ˈkɔpʌsl $ ˈkɔr-
corral kəˈral kɔˈr- $ kəˈræl
correct kəˈrekt
correction kəˈrekʃn
correctitude kəˈrektɪtjud $ -tud
corrective kəˈrektɪv
correlate ˈkɒrəleɪt -rɪl- $ ˈkɔr- etc
correlation ˈkɒrəˈleɪʃn -rɪˈl- $ ˈkɔr- etc
correlative kəˈrelətɪv
correspond ˈkɒrɪˈspɒnd $ ˈkɔr- etc
correspondence ˈkɒrɪˈspɒndəns $ ˈkɔr-
correspondent ˈkɒrɪˈspɒndənt $ ˈkɔr-
corridor ˈkɒrɪdə(r) -də(r) $ ˈkɔr- etc
corrigenda ˈkɒrɪˈdʒendə $ ˈkɔr- etc
corrigendum ˈkɒrɪˈdʒendəm $ ˈkɔr- etc
corrigible ˈkɒrɪdʒəbl -rdʒ- $ ˈkɔr- etc
corroborate kəˈrɒbəreɪt
corroboration kəˈrɒbəˈreɪʃn
corrode kəˈrəʊd
corrosion kəˈrəʊʒn
corrosive kəˈrəʊsɪv -zɪv
corrugated ˈkɒrəgeɪtɪd $ ˈkɔr- etc
corrugation ˈkɒrəˈgeɪʃn $ ˈkɔr- etc
corrupt kəˈrʌpt
corruptible kəˈrʌptəbl
corruption kəˈrʌpʃn
corsage kɔˈsaʒ ˈkɔsaʒ $ kɔr-
corsair, C– ˈkɔseə(r) $ ˈkɔr-
corset ˈkɔsɪt -ət $ ˈkɔr-
Corsica ˈkɔsɪkə $ ˈkɔr-
Corsican ˈkɔsɪkən $ ˈkɔr-
cortège kɔˈteɪʒ $ kɔr-
cortex ˈkɔteks $ ˈkɔr-
cortical ˈkɔtɪkl $ ˈkɔr-
corvette kɔˈvet kɔr-
cosh kɒʃ
co-signatory ˈkəʊ ˈsɪgnətrɪ -tərɪ $ -tɔrɪ
cosine ˈkəʊsaɪn
cosmetic kɒzˈmetɪk
cosmic ˈkɒzmɪk
cosmogony kɒzˈmɒgənɪ
cosmography kɒzˈmɒgrəfɪ
cosmonaut ˈkɒzmənɔt
cosmopolitan ˈkɒzməˈpɒlɪtən -tn
cosmos ˈkɒzmɒs $ ˈkɒzməs etc
cosset ˈkɒsɪt
cost kɒst $ kɔst etc
costermonger ˈkɒstəmʌŋgə(r)
costly ˈkɒstlɪ $ ˈkɔstlɪ
costume ˈkɒstʃum $ ˈkɒstum
costumier kɒˈstjumɪə(r) -ɪər $ -ˈstu-
cosy ˈkəʊzɪ
cot kɒt

cote kəʊt
coterie ˈkəʊtərɪ $ ˈkəʊtəˈri
coterminous ˈkəʊˈtɜmɪnəs
cottage ˈkotɪdʒ
cotton ˈkotn
cotton-wool ˈkotn ˈwʊl
cotyledon ˈkotɪˈlidn
couch kaʊtʃ
couchette kuˈʃet
couch-grass ˈkaʊtʃ gras ˈkutʃ $ græs
cougar ˈkugə(r)
cough kof $ kɔf etc
cough-drop ˈkof drop $ ˈkɔf etc
cough-mixture ˈkof mɪkstʃə(r) $ ˈkɔf etc
could usual form: kəd
  strong-form: kʊd
couldn't ˈkʊdnt
coulter ˈkəʊltə(r)
council ˈkaʊnsl
council-house ˈkaʊnsl haʊs
council(l)or ˈkaʊnslə(r) -sələ(r) -sɪlə(r)
counsel ˈkaʊnsl
counsellor ˈkaʊnslə(r)
count kaʊnt
count-down ˈkaʊnt daʊn
countenance ˈkaʊntɪnəns $ -tɲəns
counter ˈkaʊntə(r)
counteract ˈkaʊntərˈækt
counteraction ˈkaʊntərˈækʃn
counter-attack ˈkaʊntər ətæk
counter-attraction ˈkaʊntər ətrækʃn
counterbalance v ˈkaʊntəˈbæləns $ -tər-
counter-claim n ˈkaʊntə kleɪm $ -tər
counter-espionage ˈkaʊntər ˈespɪənaʒ
  $ ˈespɪənɪdʒ
counterfeit ˈkaʊntəfɪt £ -fit $ -tərf-
counterfoil ˈkaʊntəfɔɪl $ -tərf-
counter-irritant ˈkaʊntər ˈɪrɪtənt
countermand ˈkaʊntəˈmand
  $ ˈkaʊntərmænd ˈkaʊntərˈmænd
counterpane ˈkaʊntəpeɪn $ -tərp-
counterpart ˈkaʊntəpat $ -tərpart
counterplot ˈkaʊntəplot $ -tərp-
counterpoint ˈkaʊntəpɔɪnt $ -tərp-
counterpoise ˈkaʊntəpɔɪz $ -tərp-
counter-revolution ˈkaʊntər revəluʃn
countersign ˈkaʊntəsaɪn $ -tərs-
counter-tenor ˈkaʊntə tenə(r) $ -tər
countervail ˈkaʊntəˈveɪl $ -tərˈv-
countess ˈkaʊntes $ £ -ɪs -əs
counting-house ˈkaʊntɪŋ haʊs
countless ˈkaʊntləs
countrified ˈkʌntrɪfaɪd

country ˈkʌntrɪ
countryman ˈkʌntrɪmən
countryside ˈkʌntrɪsaɪd
county ˈkaʊntɪ
coup ku
coup de grâce ˈku də ˈgras
coup d'état ˈku deɪˈta
coupé ˈkupeɪ $ kuˈpeɪ kup etc
couple ˈkʌpl
couplet ˈkʌplət -ɪt
coupling ˈkʌplɪŋ
coupon ˈkupon $ ˈkju-
courage ˈkʌrɪdʒ $ ˈkɜɪdʒ
courageous kəˈreɪdʒəs
courgette kʊəˈʒet $ kʊər-
courier ˈkʊrɪə(r) $ ˈkɜɪər
course kɔs $ kɔrs
court kɔt $ kɔrt
court-card ˈkɔt kad $ ˈkɔrt kard
courteous ˈkɜtɪəs ˈkɔt-
courtesan ˈkɔtɪˈzæn $ ˈkɔrtɪzn -zæn etc
courtesy ˈkɜtəsɪ £ ˈkɔt-
courtier ˈkɔtɪə(r) $ ˈkɔr-
court-martial ˈkɔt ˈmaʃl $ ˈkɔrt ˈmarʃl
courtship ˈkɔt-ʃɪp $ ˈkɔrt-
court-yard ˈkɔt jad $ ˈkɔrt jard
cousin ˈkʌzn
couth kuθ
cove kəʊv
covenant ˈkʌvənənt -vɲ-
Covent Garden ˈkovnt ˈgadn £ ˈkʌv-
  $ ˈgardn
Coventry ˈkovntrɪ £ ˈkʌv-
cover ˈkʌvə(r)
coverage ˈkʌvərɪdʒ -vr-
coverlet ˈkʌvələt -ɪt -et
covert ˈkʌvət $ ˈkʌvərt ˈkəʊv- -vɜt
covet ˈkʌvɪt -ət
covetous ˈkʌvɪtəs -vət-
covey ˈkʌvɪ
cow kaʊ
coward ˈkaʊəd $ ˈkaʊərd
cowardice ˈkaʊədɪs $ ˈkaʊərdɪs
cowboy ˈkaʊbɔɪ
cower ˈkaʊə(r)
cowl kaʊl
co-worker kəʊ ˈwɜkə(r)
Cowper poet ˈkupə(r) ˈkaʊpə(r)
cowrie ˈkaʊrɪ
cowslip ˈkaʊslɪp
cox koks
coxcomb ˈkokskəʊm
coxswain ˈkoksn ˈkoksweɪn

coy kɔɪ
coyote ˋkɔɪəʊt kɔɪˋəʊt kɔɪˋəʊtɪ
$ kaɪˋəʊt -tɪ ˋkaɪəʊt
cozen ˋkʌzn
crab kræb
crab-apple ˋkræb æpl
crabbed *adj* ˋkræbɪd -bd
crack kræk
crack-brained 'kræk ˋbreɪnd
crackle ˋkrækl
crackling ˋkræklɪŋ
cradle ˋkreɪdl
craft krɑft $ kræft
crafty ˋkrɑftɪ $ ˋkræftɪ
crag kræg
craggy ˋkrægɪ
cram kræm
cramp kræmp
crampon ˋkræmpon $ -pən
cranberry ˋkrænbrɪ $ -berɪ
crane kreɪn
cranefly ˋkreɪn flɑɪ
cranial ˋkreɪnɪəl
cranium ˋkreɪnɪəm
crank kræŋk
cranny ˋkrænɪ
crape kreɪp
crash kræʃ
crash-dive ˋkræʃ daɪv
crash-helmet ˋkræʃ helmɪt -ət
crass kræs
crate kreɪt
crater ˋkreɪtə(r)
cravat krəˋvæt
craven ˋkreɪvən
craving ˋkreɪvɪŋ
crawfish ˋkrɔfɪʃ
crawl krɔl
crayfish ˋkreɪ-fɪʃ
crayon ˋkreɪon -ən
craze kreɪz
crazy ˋkreɪzɪ
creak krik
cream krim
creamery ˋkrimərɪ
crease kris
create krɪˋeɪt
creation krɪˋeɪʃn
creative krɪˋeɪtɪv
creator krɪˋeɪtə(r)
creature ˋkritʃə(r)
crèche kreɪʃ kreʃ
credence ˋkridns

credentials krɪˋdenʃlz
credibility 'kredəˋbɪlətɪ
credible ˋkredəbl
credit ˋkredɪt
creditable ˋkredɪtəbl
creditor ˋkredɪtə(r)
credit squeeze ˋkredɪt skwiz
credo ˋkreɪdəʊ ˋkridəʊ
credulity krəˋdjulətɪ $ -ˋdul-
credulous ˋkredjʊləs $ ˋkredʒʊləs
creed krid
creek krik $ krɪk
creel kril
creep krip
creeper ˋkripə(r)
cremate krɪˋmeɪt
cremation krɪˋmeɪʃn
crematorium 'kreməˋtɔrɪəm
crème de menthe 'kreɪm də ˋmonθ
    krem mõθ menθ mõt
crenellated($ -ela-) ˋkrenəleɪtɪd
creole, C– ˋkriəʊl
creosote ˋkrɪəsəʊt
crêpe kreɪp
crept krept
crepuscular krəˋpʌskjʊlə(r)
crescendo krəˋʃendəʊ
crescent ˋkresnt ˋkreznt
cress kres
crest krest
crested ˋkrestɪd
crest-fallen ˋkrest fɔlən
cretacious krɪˋteɪʃəs
Cretan ˋkritən -tn
Crete krit
cretin ˋkretɪn
cretonne kreˋton ˋkreton $ krɪˋton
    ˋkriton
crevasse krəˋvæs
crevice ˋkrevɪs
crew kru
crib krɪb
cribbage ˋkrɪbɪdʒ
crick krɪk
cricket ˋkrɪkɪt
cricket-ball ˋkrɪkɪt bɔl
cricket-match ˋkrɪkɪt mætʃ
cried kraɪd
crier ˋkraɪə(r)
crime kraɪm
Crimea kraɪˋmɪə
crime fiction ˋkraɪm fɪkʃn
criminal ˋkrɪmənl -mnl -mɪnl

criminology ˈkrɪməˈnolədʒɪ
crimp krɪmp
crimson ˈkrɪmzn
cringe krɪndʒ
crinkle ˈkrɪŋkl
crinoline ˈkrɪnəlɪn -lin ˈkrɪnəˈlin
cripple ˈkrɪpl
crises ˈkraɪsiz
crisis ˈkraɪsɪs
crisp krɪsp
criss-cross ˈkrɪs kros $ krɔs
criteria kraɪˈtɪərɪə
criterion kraɪˈtɪərɪən
critic ˈkrɪtɪk
critical ˈkrɪtɪkl
criticism ˈkrɪtɪsɪzm
criticize ˈkrɪtɪsaɪz
critique krɪˈtik
croak krəʊk
crochet ˈkrəʊʃeɪ -ʃɪ $ krəʊˈʃeɪ
crochet-hook ˈkrəʊʃɪ hʊk £ -ʃeɪ
    $ krəʊˈʃeɪ
crock krok
crockery ˈkrokərɪ
crocodile ˈkrokədaɪl
crocodile tears ˈkrokədaɪl tɪəz
    $ tɪərz
crocus ˈkrəʊkəs
croft kroft $ krɔft etc
Cromwell ˈkromwel -wl
crony ˈkrəʊnɪ
crook krʊk
crooked adj ˈkrʊkɪd
croon krun
crop krop
cropper ˈkropə(r)
croquet ˈkrəʊkeɪ -kɪ $ krəʊˈkeɪ
croquette krəʊˈket
cross kros $ krɔs
cross-bar ˈkros bɑ(r) $ ˈkrɔs bɑr
cross-beam ˈkros bim $ ˈkrɔs
crossbench ˈkrosbentʃ $ ˈkrɔs-
cross(-)bow ˈkros bəʊ $ ˈkrɔs
crossbred ˈkrosbred $ ˈkrɔs-
crossbreed ˈkrosbrid $ ˈkrɔs-
cross bun, hot ˈhot kros ˈbʌn $ krɔs
cross-check ˈkros ˈtʃek $ ˈkrɔs
cross-country ˈkros ˈkʌntrɪ $ ˈkrɔs
cross-examination ˈkros ɪgˈzæmɪˈneɪʃn
    $ ˈkrɔs
cross-examine ˈkros ɪgˈzæmɪn $ ˈkrɔs
cross-eyed ˈkros ˈaɪd ˈkros aɪd $ ˈkrɔs
cross-fertilize ˈkros ˈfɜtɪlaɪz $ ˈkrɔs -tl̩-

cross-fire ˈkros faɪə(r) $ ˈkrɔs
cross-grained ˈkros ˈgreɪnd $ ˈkrɔs
crossing ˈkrosɪŋ $ ˈkrɔsɪŋ
cross-legged ˈkros ˈlegd ˈlegɪd $ ˈkrɔs
cross-question kros ˈkwestʃən $ krɔs
crosspatch ˈkrospætʃ $ ˈkrɔs-
cross-purposes kros ˈpɜpəsɪz $ krɔs
cross-reference ˈkros ˈrefrns $ ˈkrɔs
cross-road ˈkros rəʊd $ ˈkrɔs
cross-section ˈkros ˈsekʃn $ ˈkrɔs
crossword ˈkroswɜd $ ˈkrɔs-
crossword puzzle ˈkroswɜd pʌzl $ ˈkrɔs-
crotch krotʃ
crotchet ˈkrotʃɪt -ət
crouch krautʃ
croup krup
croupier ˈkrupɪə(r) £ ˈkrupɪeɪ
crow krəʊ
crowbar ˈkrəʊbɑ(r)
crowd kraʊd
crown kraʊn
crown-land ˈkraʊn ˈlænd
crow's-feet ˈkrəʊz fit
crow's-nest ˈkrəʊz nest
crozier ˈkrəʊzɪə(r) $ ˈkrəʊʒər
crucial ˈkruʃl
crucible ˈkrusəbl
crucifix ˈkrusɪfɪks
crucifixion, C- ˈkrusɪˈfɪkʃn
cruciform ˈkrusɪfɔm $ -fɔrm
crucify ˈkrusɪfaɪ
crude krud
crudity ˈkrudətɪ
cruel krʊəl ˈkruḷ
cruelty ˈkrʊəltɪ ˈkruḷtɪ
cruet ˈkruɪt
cruise kruz
crumb krʌm
crumble ˈkrʌmbl
crummy ˈkrʌmɪ
crumpet ˈkrʌmpɪt
crunch krʌntʃ
crupper ˈkrʌpə(r)
crusade kruˈseɪd
crush krʌʃ
crust krʌst
crustacean krʌˈsteɪʃn
crutch krʌtʃ
crux krʌks
cry kraɪ
cry-baby ˈkraɪ beɪbɪ
crypt krɪpt
cryptic ˈkrɪptɪk

crypto- *prefix* ˈkrɪptəʊ ˈkrɪptə
cryptogram ˈkrɪptəgræm
crystal ˈkrɪstl
crystal-gazer ˈkrɪstl geɪzə(r)
crystalline ˈkrɪstəlaɪn
crystallization ˌkrɪstəlaɪˈzeɪʃn
$ -ɪˈzeɪʃn
crystallize ˈkrɪstəlaɪz
cub kʌb
Cuba ˈkjubə
Cuban ˈkjubən
cubby-hole ˈkʌbɪ həʊl
cube kjub
cubic ˈkjubɪk
cubicle ˈkjubɪkl
cubism ˈkjub-ɪzm
cubist ˈkjubɪst
cubit ˈkjubɪt
cuckold ˈkʌkəʊld $ £ ˈkʌkld
cuckoo ˈkʊku $ ˈkuku
cuckoo-clock ˈkʊku klok $ ˈkuku
cucumber ˈkjukʌmbə(r)
cud kʌd
cuddle ˈkʌdl
cuddly ˈkʌdlɪ
cudgel ˈkʌdʒl
cue kju
cuff kʌf
cuff(-)link ˈkʌf lɪŋk
cuisine kwɪˈzin
cul de sac ˈkʊl də ˈsæk ˈkʌl
culinary ˈkʌlɪnərɪ $ ˈkjulənerɪ ˈkʌlɪnerɪ
cull kʌl
cullender ˈkʌlɪndə(r)
culminate ˈkʌlmɪneɪt
culmination ˌkʌlmɪˈneɪʃn
culpable ˈkʌlpəbl
culprit ˈkʌlprɪt
cult kʌlt
cultivate ˈkʌltɪveɪt
cultivation ˌkʌltɪˈveɪʃn
cultural ˈkʌltʃərl
culture ˈkʌltʃə(r)
culture pearl ˈkʌltʃə pɜl $ -tʃər
culvert ˈkʌlvət $ ˈkʌlvərt
cumber ˈkʌmbə(r)
Cumberland ˈkʌmbələnd $ -bərl-
cumbersome ˈkʌmbəsm $ -bərsm
cumbrous ˈkʌmbrəs
cummerbund ˈkʌməbʌnd $ -mərb-
cumulative ˈkjumjʊlətɪv -jəl- $ -leɪtɪv
cumulus ˈkjumjʊləs -jəl-
cuneiform ˈkjuniɪfɔm kjuˈniɪfɔm $ -fɔrm

cunning ˈkʌnɪŋ
cup kʌp
cupboard ˈkʌbəd $ ˈkʌbərd
cupboard love ˈkʌbəd lʌv $ ˈkʌbərd
cup final ˈkʌp ˈfaɪnl
cupful ˈkʌpfʊl
Cupid ˈkjupɪd
cupidity kjuˈpɪdətɪ
cupola ˈkjupələ
cupric ˈkjuprɪk
cup-tie ˈkʌp taɪ
cur kɜ(r)
curable ˈkjʊərəbl
curaçao ˈkjʊərəsəʊ $ ˈkjʊrəˈsaʊ
curacy ˈkjʊərəsɪ
curate ˈkjʊərət
curative ˈkjʊərətɪv
curator kjʊəˈreɪtə(r) $ ˈkjʊəreɪtər
curb kɜb
curd kɜd
curdle ˈkɜdl
cure kjʊə(r)
curé ˈkjʊəreɪ $ kjʊˈreɪ
curfew ˈkɜfju
curio ˈkjʊərɪəʊ
curiosity ˌkjʊərɪˈosətɪ
curious ˈkjʊərɪəs
curl kɜl
curlew ˈkɜlju $ ˈkɜlu *etc*
curly ˈkɜlɪ
curmudgeon kɜˈmʌdʒən
currant ˈkʌrənt $ ˈkɜənt
currency ˈkʌrənsɪ $ ˈkɜənsɪ
current ˈkʌrənt $ ˈkɜənt
curriculum kəˈrɪkjʊləm
curriculum vitae kəˈrɪkjʊləm ˈvaɪti
ˈvitaɪ ˈwitaɪ
curry ˈkʌrɪ $ ˈkɜɪ
curry-powder ˈkʌrɪ paʊdə(r) $ ˈkɜɪ
curse kɜs
cursed *adj* kɜst ˈkɜsɪd
cursive ˈkɜsɪv
cursory ˈkɜsərɪ ˈkɜsrɪ
curt kɜt
curtail kɜˈteɪl
curtailment kɜˈteɪlmənt
curtain ˈkɜtn
curtain-call ˈkɜtn kɔl
curtain-raiser ˈkɜtn reɪzə(r)
curtsy ˈkɜtsɪ
curvature ˈkɜvətʃə(r) $ £ ˈkɜvətʃʊə(r)
curve kɜv
curvet kɜˈvet

cushion ˈkʊʃn -ʃɪn
cushy ˈkʊʃɪ
cusp kʌsp
cuss kʌs
cussed adj ˈkʌsɪd
custard ˈkʌstəd $ -tərd
custard-pie ˈkʌstəd ˈpaɪ $ -tərd
custard-powder ˈkʌstəd paʊdə(r)
  $ -tərd
custodian kəˈstəʊdɪən
custody ˈkʌstədɪ
custom ˈkʌstəm
customary ˈkʌstəmərɪ -mrɪ $ -merɪ
customer ˈkʌstəmə(r)
custom-house ˈkʌstəm haʊs
cut kʌt
cute kjut
cuticle ˈkjutɪkl
cutlass ˈkʌtləs
cutler ˈkʌtlə(r)
cutlet ˈkʌtlət -lɪt
cut-throat ˈkʌt θrəʊt
cuttle-fish ˈkʌtl fɪʃ
cyclamen ˈsɪkləmən $ ˈsaɪk- etc
cycle ˈsaɪkl
cyclist ˈsaɪklɪst
cyclone ˈsaɪkləʊn

cyclopaedia ˈsaɪkləʊˈpidɪə ˈsaɪkləˈp-
cyclostyle ˈsaɪkləʊstaɪl ˈsaɪkləs-
cyclotron ˈsaɪkləʊtron ˈsaɪklət-
cygnet ˈsɪgnɪt -nət
cylinder ˈsɪlɪndə(r)
cylindrical sɪˈlɪndrɪkl -rəkl
cymbal ˈsɪmbl
Cymbeline ˈsɪmbəlin
cynic ˈsɪnɪk
cynical ˈsɪnɪkl
cynicism ˈsɪnɪsɪzm
cynosure ˈsɪnəzjʊə(r) -ʒʊə(r) -ʃʊə(r)
  $ £ ˈsaɪnəʃʊər -ʒʊər
Cynthia ˈsɪnθɪə
cypress ˈsaɪprəs
Cyprian ˈsɪprɪən
Cypriot ˈsɪprɪət
Cyprus ˈsaɪprəs
Cyril ˈsɪrl
Cyrillic sɪˈrɪlɪk
cyst sɪst
czar zɑ(r)
Czech tʃek
Czechoslovak ˈtʃekəʊˈsləʊvæk
Czechoslovakia ˈtʃekəʊsləˈvækɪə
  -sləˈvakɪə

D

D d di
dab dæb
dabble ˈdæbl
dace deɪs
dachshund ˈdækshʊnd -sʊnd -snd
  $ ˈdaks- etc
dactyl ˈdæktɪl
dad dæd
daddy ˈdædɪ
daddy-long-legs ˈdædɪ ˈloŋ legz
daffodil ˈdæfədɪl
daft dɑft $ dæft
dagger ˈdægə(r)
dahlia ˈdeɪlɪə $ ˈdælɪə ˈdalɪə etc
Dail Eireann ˈdɔɪl ˈeərən
daily ˈdeɪlɪ
Daimler ˈdeɪmlə(r)
dainty ˈdeɪntɪ
dairy ˈdeərɪ
dairy-cattle ˈdeərɪ kætl

dairy farm ˈdeərɪ fam $ farm
dairy farming ˈdeərɪ famɪŋ $ far-
dairymaid ˈdeərɪmeɪd
dairyman ˈdeərɪmən
dais ˈdeɪɪs deɪs
daisy, D– ˈdeɪzɪ
Dakota dəˈkəʊtə
dale deɪl
dalliance ˈdælɪəns
dally ˈdælɪ
dam dæm
damage ˈdæmɪdʒ
Damascus dəˈmæskəs
damask ˈdæməsk
dame deɪm
damn dæm
damnable ˈdæmnəbl
damnation dæmˈneɪʃn
damned dæmd
damp dæmp

dampen ˈdæmpən
damsel ˈdæmzl
damson ˈdæmzn
dance dɑns $ dæns
dance-band ˈdɑns bænd $ ˈdæns
dance-hall ˈdɑns hɔl $ ˈdæns
dance-orchestra ˈdɑns ɔkɪstrə $ ˈdæ- ɔr-
dancing-master ˈdɑnsɪŋ mɑstə(r)
$ ˈdænsɪŋ mæstər
dancing-partner ˈdɑnsɪŋ pɑtnə(r)
$ ˈdænsɪŋ partnər
dancing-shoes ˈdɑnsɪŋ ʃuz $ ˈdænsɪŋ
dandelion ˈdændɪlɑɪən
dandle ˈdændl
dandruff ˈdændrʌf -əf
dandy ˈdændɪ
Dane deɪn
danger ˈdeɪndʒə(r)
danger-money ˈdeɪndʒə mʌnɪ $ -dʒər
dangerous ˈdeɪndʒərəs
dangle ˈdæŋgl
Daniel ˈdænɪəl
Danish ˈdeɪnɪʃ
dank dæŋk
Dante ˈdæntɪ -teɪ $ ˈdɑntɪ
Danube ˈdænjub
daphne, D– ˈdæfnɪ
dapper ˈdæpə(r)
dapple ˈdæpl
Darby and Joan ˈdɑbɪ ən ˈdʒəʊn $ ˈdɑr-
dare ˈdeə(r)
dare-devil ˈdeə devl $ ˈdeər
daren't deənt $ deərnt
daring ˈdeərɪŋ
dark dɑk $ dɑrk
dark-haired ˈdɑk ˈheəd $ ˈdɑrk ˈheərd
dark horse ˈdɑk ˈhɔs $ ˈdɑrk ˈhɔrs
dark-room ˈdɑk rʊm
$ ˈdɑrk $ £ rum etc
darken ˈdɑkən $ ˈdɑrkən
darling ˈdɑlɪŋ $ ˈdɑrlɪŋ
darn dɑn $ dɑrn
darning-needle ˈdɑnɪŋ nidl $ ˈdɑrn-
dart dɑt $ dɑrt
dart-board ˈdɑt bɔd $ ˈdɑrt bɔrd
Dartmoor ˈdɑtmʊə(r) -mɔ(r) $ ˈdɑrt-
Darwin ˈdɑwɪn $ ˈdɑrwɪn
Darwinian dɑˈwɪnɪən $ dɑr-
dash dæʃ
dash-board ˈdæʃ bɔd $ bɔrd
dastardly ˈdæstədlɪ $ -tərdlɪ
data ˈdeɪtə ˈdɑtə $ ˈdætə
date deɪt

date-line ˈdeɪt lɑɪn
dative ˈdeɪtɪv
datum ˈdeɪtəm ˈdɑtəm $ ˈdætəm
daub dɔb
daughter ˈdɔtə(r)
daughter-in-law ˈdɔtr ɪn lɔ
daunt dɔnt
dauphin ˈdɔfɪn ˈdəʊfæ
davenport ˈdævnpɔt $ -pɔrt
David ˈdeɪvɪd
Da Vinci də ˈvɪntʃɪ
davit ˈdævɪt
daw dɔ
dawdle ˈdɔdl
dawn dɔn
day deɪ
daybreak ˈdeɪbreɪk
daydream ˈdeɪdrim
day-labourer ˈdeɪ leɪbrə(r) -bərə(r)
daylight ˈdeɪlɑɪt
day-return ˈdeɪ rɪˈtɜn
day-ticket ˈdeɪ tɪkɪt
day-time ˈdeɪ tɑɪm
daze deɪz
dazzle ˈdæzl
D-Day ˈdi deɪ
DDT ˈdi di ˈti
deacon ˈdikən
dead ded
deaden ˈdedn
dead heat ˈded ˈhit
dead-line ˈded lɑɪn
deadlock ˈdedlok
deadly ˈdedlɪ
dead-pan ˈded ˈpæn
dead set ˈded ˈset
dead-weight ˈded ˈweɪt
deadwood ˈdedwʊd
deaf def
deaf-aid ˈdef eɪd
deafen ˈdefn
deal dil
dealt delt
dean din
deanery ˈdinərɪ
dear dɪə(r)
dearie ˈdɪərɪ
dearth dɜθ
death deθ
death-bed ˈdeθ bed
death-duties ˈdeθ djutɪz $ dutɪz
deathly ˈdeθlɪ
death-mask ˈdeθ mɑsk $ mæsk

death-rate ˈdeθ reɪt
death-roll ˈdeθ rəʊl
death's-head ˈdeθs hed
death-trap ˈdeθ træp
death-warrant ˈdeθ wornt $ wɔrnt
débâcle deɪˈbɑkl *this* l *may be unsyllabic*
debar dɪˈbɑ(r)
debase dɪˈbeɪs
debatable dɪˈbeɪtəbl
debate dɪˈbeɪt
debauch dɪˈbɔtʃ
debentures dɪˈbentʃəz $ -tʃərz
debilitate dɪˈbɪlɪteɪt
debility dɪˈbɪlətɪ
debit ˈdebɪt
debonair ˈdebəˈneə(r)
Deborah ˈdebərə ˈdebrə
de-briefing diˈbrifɪŋ
debris ˈdebri ˈdeɪbri $ dəˈbri
debt det
debtor ˈdetə(r)
debunk ˈdiˈbʌŋk
début ˈdeɪbu ˈdebu -bju $ dɪˈbju *etc*
débutante ˈdebjʊtɑnt -tɔnt -tõt
$ ˈdebjʊˈtɑnt ˈdebjʊtænt
decade ˈdekeɪd deˈkeɪd
decadence ˈdekədəns
decadent ˈdekədənt
decamp dɪˈkæmp
decant dɪˈkænt
decapitate dɪˈkæpɪteɪt ˈdi-
decapitation dɪˈkæpɪˈteɪʃn ˈdi-
decarbonize ˈdiˈkabənaɪz $ -ˈkarb-
decasyllable ˈdekəsɪləbl
decasyllabic ˈdekəsɪˈlæbɪk
decay dɪˈkeɪ
decease dɪˈsis
deceit dɪˈsit
deceitful dɪˈsitfl
deceive dɪˈsiv
decelerate ˈdiˈseləreɪt
deceleration ˈdiˈseləˈreɪʃn
December dɪˈsembə(r)
decency ˈdisnsɪ
decent ˈdisnt
decentralization ˈdiˈsentrəlaɪˈzeɪʃn
$ -lɪˈzeɪʃn
decentralize ˈdiˈsentrəlaɪz
deception dɪˈsepʃn
deceptive dɪˈseptɪv
decibel ˈdesɪbel -bl
decide dɪˈsaɪd
deciduous dɪˈsɪdjʊəs $ dɪˈsɪdʒʊəs

decimal ˈdesɪml
decimate ˈdesɪmeɪt
decipher dɪˈsaɪfə(r)
decision dɪˈsɪʒn
decisive dɪˈsaɪsɪv
deck dek
deck-chair ˈdek tʃeə(r)
declaim dɪˈkleɪm
declamation ˈdekləˈmeɪʃn
declamatory dɪˈklæmətrɪ $ -tɔrɪ
declaration ˈdekləˈreɪʃn
declare dɪˈkleə(r)
declassify ˈdiˈklæsɪfaɪ
declension dɪˈklenʃn
decline dɪˈklaɪn
declivity dɪˈklɪvətɪ
declutch ˈdiˈklʌtʃ
decode ˈdiˈkəʊd
décolleté deɪˈkolteɪ $ ˈdeɪkolˈteɪ
decompose ˈdikəmˈpəʊz
decomposition ˈdiˈkompəˈzɪʃn
decontaminate ˈdikənˈtæmɪneɪt
decontamination ˈdɪkənˈtæmɪˈneɪʃn
decontrol ˈdikənˈtrəʊl
décor ˈdeɪkɔ(r) $ deɪˈkɔr dəˈkɔr
decorate ˈdekəreɪt
decoration ˈdekəˈreɪʃn
decorative ˈdekrətɪv $ ˈdekəreɪtɪv
decorous ˈdekərəs $ dɪˈkɔrəs
decorum dɪˈkɔrəm
decoy *n* ˈdikɔɪ dɪˈkɔɪ
decoy *v* dɪˈkɔɪ
decrease *n* ˈdikris
decrease *v* dɪˈkris
decree dɪˈkri
decree nisi dɪˈkri ˈnaɪsaɪ $ ˈnisi
decrepit dɪˈkrepɪt
decrepitude dɪˈkrepɪtjud $ -tud
decry dɪˈkraɪ
dedicate ˈdedɪkeɪt
dedication ˈdedɪˈkeɪʃn
deduce dɪˈdjus $ dɪˈdus
deduct dɪˈdʌkt
deduction dɪˈdʌkʃn
deductive dɪˈdʌktɪv
deed did
deem dim
deep dip
deepen ˈdipən
deep-freeze ˈdip ˈfriz
deep-rooted ˈdip ˈrutɪd
deep-seated ˈdip ˈsitɪd
deer dɪə(r)

deerstalker ˈdɪəstɔkə(r) $ ˈdɪərstɔkər
deface dɪˈfeɪs
de facto ˈdeɪ ˈfæktəʊ ˈdi
defamation ˈdefəˈmeɪʃn
defamatory dɪˈfæmətrɪ $ -tɔrɪ
defame dɪˈfeɪm
default dɪˈfɔlt £ dɪˈfolt
defeat dɪˈfit
defeatism dɪˈfitɪzm
defeatist dɪˈfitɪst
defect ˈdifekt dɪˈfekt
defection dɪˈfekʃn
defective dɪˈfektɪv
defence($ -ense) dɪˈfens
defend dɪˈfend
defendant dɪˈfendənt
defensible dɪˈfensəbl
defensive dɪˈfensɪv
defer dɪˈfɜ(r)
deference ˈdefrəns
deferential ˈdefəˈrenʃl
defiance dɪˈfaɪəns
defiant dɪˈfaɪənt
deficiency dɪˈfiʃnsɪ
deficit ˈdefəsɪt -fɪs-
defile n ˈdifaɪl
defile v dɪˈfaɪl
define dɪˈfaɪn
definite ˈdefənɪt -nət -fn̩-
definition ˈdefəˈnɪʃn
definitive dɪˈfɪnətɪv
deflate dɪˈfleɪt di-
deflect dɪˈflekt
deflection dɪˈflekʃn
deflower dɪˈflaʊə(r)
deforest diˈforɪst $ -ˈfɔr-
deform dɪˈfɔm $ dɪˈfɔrm
deformity dɪˈfɔmətɪ $ -ˈfɔrm-
defraud dɪˈfrɔd
defray dɪˈfreɪ
defrock ˈdiˈfrok
defrost ˈdiˈfrost $ ˈdiˈfrɔst
deft deft
defunct dɪˈfʌŋkt
defy dɪˈfaɪ
degenerate adj dɪˈdʒenərət
degenerate v dɪˈdʒenəreɪt
degeneration dɪˈdʒenəˈreɪʃn
degradation ˈdegrəˈdeɪʃn
degrade dɪˈgreɪd
degree dɪˈgri
dehumanize ˈdiˈhjumənaɪz
dehydrate ˈdiˈhaɪdreɪt

de-ice ˈdiˈaɪs
deification ˈdeɪfɪˈkeɪʃn $ £ ˈdiːfɪ-
deify ˈdeɪfaɪ $ £ ˈdiːfaɪ
deign deɪn
deism ˈdi-ɪzm ˈdeɪ-ɪzm
deist ˈdiɪst ˈdeɪɪst
deity ˈdeɪətɪ $ £ ˈdiətɪ
deject dɪˈdʒekt
dejection dɪˈdʒekʃn
delay dɪˈleɪ
delectable dɪˈlektəbl
delectation ˈdilekˈteɪʃn
delegacy ˈdelɪgəsɪ
delegate n ˈdelɪgət -ləg- -ɪt
  $ £ ˈdeləgeɪt etc
delegate v ˈdeləgeɪt
delegation ˈdeləˈgeɪʃn -lɪˈg-
delete dɪˈlit di-
deleterious ˈdeləˈtɪərɪəs
delft delft
Delhi ˈdelɪ
deliberate adj dɪˈlɪbrət
deliberate v dɪˈlɪbəreɪt
deliberation dɪˈlɪbəˈreɪʃn
deliberative dɪˈlɪbrətɪv $ -bəreɪtɪv
delicacy ˈdelɪkəsɪ
delicate ˈdelɪkət -lək- -kɪt
delicatessen ˈdelɪkəˈtesn -lək-
delicious dɪˈlɪʃəs də-
delight dɪˈlaɪt də-
delightful dɪˈlaɪtfl də-
delimit ˈdiˈlɪmɪt
delimitation ˈdiˈlɪmɪˈteɪʃn
delineate dɪˈlɪnɪeɪt
delineation dɪˈlɪnɪˈeɪʃn
delinquency dɪˈlɪŋkwənsɪ
delinquent dɪˈlɪŋkwənt
deliquescent ˈdelɪˈkwesnt
delirious dɪˈlɪrɪəs də-
delirium dɪˈlɪrɪəm də-
deliver dɪˈlɪvə(r) də-
deliverance dɪˈlɪvrns də-
delivery dɪˈlɪvrɪ də-
dell del
delouse ˈdiˈlaʊs -z
Delphi ˈdelfaɪ
Delphic ˈdelfɪk
delphinium delˈfɪnɪəm
delta ˈdeltə
delude dɪˈlud £ -ˈljud
deluge ˈdeljudʒ
delusion dɪˈluʒn £ -ˈljuʒn
delusive dɪˈlusɪv £ -ˈljusɪv

de luxe dı 'lʌks -lʊks -luks də-
delve delv
demagnetize 'di'mægnıtaız
demagogue 'deməgog $ -gɔg etc
demand dı'mɑnd $ dı'mænd
demarcate 'dimakeıt $ 'di'mar- 'dimar-
demarcation 'dima'keıʃn $ 'dimar-
demean dı'min
demeanour dı'minə(r)
demented dı'mentıd
demerara 'demə'reərə -'rarə
demerit di'merıt
demesne dı'meın
demi- prefix demı
demigod 'demıgod
demilitarized 'di'mılıtəraızd
demimonde 'demı'mõd
demise dı'maız dı'miz
demist 'di'mıst
demob dı'mob
demobilization dı'məubļaı'zeıʃn
    $ dı'məubļı'zeıʃn
demobilize dı'məubļaız
democracy dı'mokrəsı
democrat, D– 'deməkræt
democratic 'demə'krætık
démodé deı'məudeı $ 'deıməu'deı
demographic 'demə'græfık
demography dı'mogrəfı
demolish dı'molıʃ
demolition 'demə'lıʃn
demon 'dimən
demoniacal 'demə'naıəkl
demonstrable dı'monstrəbl
    'demənstrəbl
demonstrate 'demənstreıt
demonstration 'demən'streıʃn
demonstrative dı'monstrətıv
demonstrator 'demənstreıtə(r)
demoralization dı'morļaı'zeıʃn
    $ dı'morļı'zeıʃn
demoralize dı'morļaız $ -'mor-
demote 'di'məut
demotic dı'motık
demur dı'mɜ(r)
demure dı'mjʊə(r)
den den
denationalization 'di'næʃnəlaı'zeıʃn
    $ 'di'næʃnəlı'zeıʃn
denationalize 'di'næʃnəlaız
denatured 'di'neıtʃəd $ -tʃərd
deniable dı'naıəbl
denial dı'naıļ

denigrate 'denıgreıt
denim 'denım
Denis 'denıs
Denise də'niz
denizen 'denızn
Denmark 'denmak $ -mark
denominate dı'nomıneıt
denomination dı'nomı'neıʃn
denominator dı'nomıneıtə(r)
denotation 'dinəu'teıʃn
denote dı'nəut
dénouement deı'numõ $ 'deınu'mõ etc
denounce dı'naʊns
dense dens
density 'densətı
dent dent
dental 'dentl
dentifrice 'dentıfrıs
dentist 'dentıst
dentistry 'dentıstrı
denture 'dentʃə(r)
denude dı'njud $ dı'nud
denunciation dı'nʌnsı'eıʃn
deny dı'naı
deodorant 'di'əudərənt
depart dı'pat $ dı'part
department dı'patmənt $ -'part-
departmental 'dipat'mentl $ -part-
departure dı'patʃə(r) $ -'partʃər
depend dı'pend
dependant dı'pendənt
dependence dı'pendəns
dependency dı'pendənsı
dependent dı'pendənt
depict dı'pıkt
depiction dı'pıkʃn
depilatory dı'pılətrı $ -tɔrı
deplete dı'plit
depletion dı'pliʃn
deplorable dı'plɔrəbl
deplore dı'plɔ(r)
deploy dı'plɔı
deponent dı'pəunənt
depopulate 'di'popjʊleıt
depopulation 'di'popjʊ'leıʃn
deport dı'pɔt $ dı'pɔrt
deportation 'dipɔ'teıʃn $ -pɔr-
deportment dı'pɔtmənt $ -'pɔrt-
depose dı'pəuz
deposit dı'pozıt
deposit account dı'pozıt əkaunt
deposition 'depə'zıʃn 'di-
depositor dı'pozıtə(r)

depository dɪˈpozɪtrɪ $ -tɔrɪ
depot ˈdepəʊ $ ˈdipəʊ
deprave dɪˈpreɪv
depravity dɪˈprævətɪ
deprecate ˈdeprəkeɪt -rɪk-
deprecation ˈdeprəˈkeɪʃn -rɪˈk-
depreciate dɪˈpriʃɪeɪt
depreciation dɪˈpriʃɪˈeɪʃn -isi-
depreciatory dɪˈpriʃətərɪ $ -tɔrɪ
depredation ˈdeprəˈdeɪʃn
depress dɪˈpres
depressed area dɪˈprest ˈeərɪə
depression dɪˈpreʃn
deprivation ˈdeprɪˈveɪʃn
deprive dɪˈpraɪv
Dept. dɪˈpatmənt $ -ˈpart-
depth depθ
depth-charge ˈdepθ tʃadʒ $ tʃardʒ
deputation ˈdepjʊˈteɪʃn
depute dɪˈpjut
deputize ˈdepjʊtaɪz
deputy ˈdepjʊtɪ
derail dɪˈreɪl di-
derailment dɪˈreɪlmənt di-
derange dɪˈreɪndʒ
derangement dɪˈreɪndʒmənt
derby, D– ˈdabɪ $ ˈdɜbɪ
Derek ˈderɪk
derelict ˈderəlɪkt
derestrict ˈdirɪˈstrɪkt
deride dɪˈraɪd
de rigueur də rɪˈgɜ(r) ˈdə
derision dɪˈrɪʒn
derisive dɪˈraɪsɪv -aɪzɪv
derisory dɪˈraɪsərɪ -aɪzə-
derivation ˈderɪˈveɪʃn
derivative dɪˈrɪvətɪv
derive dɪˈraɪv
dermatologist ˈdɜməˈtolədʒɪst
dermatology ˈdɜməˈtolədʒɪ
derogatory dɪˈrogətrɪ $ -tɔrɪ
derrick ˈderɪk
dervish ˈdɜvɪʃ
descant ˈdeskænt
descend dɪˈsend
descendant dɪˈsendənt
descent dɪˈsent
describe dɪˈskraɪb
description dɪˈskrɪpʃn
descriptive dɪˈskrɪptɪv
descry dɪˈskraɪ
Desdemona ˈdezdɪˈməʊnə
desecrate ˈdesɪkreɪt

desecration ˈdesɪˈkreɪʃn
desert n ˈdezət $ ˈdezərt
desert v dɪˈzɜt
desertion dɪˈzɜʃn
deserve dɪˈzɜv
deservedly dɪˈzɜvɪdlɪ
desiccate ˈdesɪkeɪt
desiderata dɪˈzɪdəˈreɪtə -ˈratə
design dɪˈzaɪn
designate adj ˈdezɪgneɪt -nət -nɪt
designate v ˈdezɪgneɪt
designation ˈdezɪgˈneɪʃn
designedly dɪˈzaɪnɪdlɪ
desirable dɪˈzaɪərəbl
desirability dɪˈzaɪərəˈbɪlətɪ
desire dɪˈzaɪə(r)
desirous dɪˈzaɪərəs
desist dɪˈzɪst
desk desk
Desmond ˈdezmənd
desolate adj ˈdesələt
desolate v ˈdesəleɪt
desolation ˈdesəˈleɪʃn
despair dɪˈspeə(r)
despatch dɪˈspætʃ
desperado ˈdespəˈradəʊ $ -ˈreɪd-
desperate ˈdesprət
desperation ˈdespəˈreɪʃn
despicable dɪˈspɪkəbl ˈdespɪkəbl
despise dɪˈspaɪz
despite dɪˈspaɪt
despoil dɪˈspɔɪl
despondence dɪˈspondəns
despondency dɪˈspondənsɪ
despondent dɪˈspondənt
despot ˈdespot $ ˈdespət etc
despotism ˈdespətɪzm
dessert dɪˈzɜt
dessert-spoon dɪˈzɜt spun
destination ˈdestɪˈneɪʃn
destine ˈdestɪn
destiny ˈdestɪnɪ
destitute ˈdestɪtjut $ -tut
destitution ˈdestɪˈtjuʃn $ -ˈtuʃn
destroy dɪˈstrɔɪ
destructibility dɪˈstrʌktəˈbɪlətɪ
destructible dɪˈstrʌktəbl
destruction dɪˈstrʌkʃn
destructive dɪˈstrʌktɪv
desultory ˈdesltrɪ $ -tɔrɪ
detach dɪˈtætʃ
detachment dɪˈtætʃmənt
detail n ˈditeɪl $ dɪˈteɪl etc

detail v `diteɪl dɪ`teɪl
detain dɪ`teɪn
detainee 'diteɪ`nɪ dɪ't-
detect dɪ`tekt
detection dɪ`tekʃn
detective dɪ`tektɪv
detective story dɪ`tektɪv stɔrɪ
detention dɪ`tenʃn
deter dɪ`tɜ(r)
detergent dɪ`tɜdʒənt
deteriorate dɪ`tɪərɪəreɪt
deterioration dɪ'tɪərɪə`reɪʃn
determination dɪ'tɜmɪ`neɪʃn
determine dɪ`tɜmɪn
determinedly dɪ`tɜmɪndlɪ
deterrent dɪ`terənt $ -`tɜr- etc
detest dɪ`test
detestation 'dite`steɪʃn
dethrone 'di`θrəʊn
detonate `detəneɪt
detonation 'detə`neɪʃn
detonator `detəneɪtə(r)
detour `dituə(r) £ -tɔ(r) `deɪ- $ dɪ`tuər
detract dɪ`trækt
detraction dɪ`trækʃn
detractor dɪ`træktə(r)
detribalize 'di`traɪblaɪz
detriment `detrɪmənt
detrimental 'detrɪ`mentl
de trop də `trəʊ
deuce djus $ dus
deuced adj djust `djusɪd $ dust `dusɪd
Deuteronomy 'djutə`ronəmɪ $ 'dut- etc
devaluation 'di'vælju`eɪʃn
devalue 'di`vælju
devastate `devəsteɪt
devastation 'devə`steɪʃn
develop dɪ`veləp
development dɪ`veləpmənt
deviate `divɪeɪt
deviation 'divɪ`eɪʃn
deviationist 'divɪ`eɪʃnɪst
devil `devl
devilish `devlɪʃ
devil-may-care 'devl meɪ `keə(r)
devilry `devlrɪ
devious `divɪəs
devise dɪ`vaɪs
devitalization 'di'vaɪtlaɪ`zeɪʃn
  $ -lɪ`zeɪʃn
devitalize 'di`vaɪtlaɪz
devoid dɪ`vɔɪd
devolution 'divə`luʃn £ -`lju- $ 'dev-

devolve dɪ`volv
Devon `devn
devote dɪ`vəʊt
devotee 'devə`ti
devotion dɪ`vəʊʃn
devour dɪ`vaʊə(r)
devout dɪ`vaʊt
dew dju $ du
dew-drop `dju drop $ `du
dewy `djuɪ $ `duɪ
dexterity 'dek`sterətɪ
dext(e)rous `dekstrəs
dhoti `dəʊtɪ
dhow daʊ
diabetes 'daɪə`bitiz
diabetic 'daɪə`betɪk
diabolic 'daɪə`bolɪk
diacritic 'daɪə`krɪtɪk
diadem `daɪədem
diagnose 'daɪəg`nəʊz $ `daɪəgnəʊs etc
diagnoses 'daɪəg`nəʊsiz
diagnosis 'daɪəg`nəʊsɪs
diagnostic 'daɪəg`nostɪk
diagonal daɪ`ægənl
diagram `daɪəgræm
diagrammatic 'daɪəgrə`mætɪk
dial `daɪəl
dialect `daɪəlekt
dialectal 'daɪə`lektl
dialectic 'daɪə`lektɪk
dialectician 'daɪəlek`tɪʃn
dialogue($ -og) `daɪəlog $ -lɔg etc
diameter daɪ`æmɪtə(r)
diametrical 'daɪə`metrɪkl
diamond `daɪəmənd
Diana daɪ`ænə
Diane daɪ`æn dɪ`æn di`an
diaper `daɪəpə(r)
diaphanous daɪ`æfənəs
diaphragm `daɪəfræm
diarist `daɪərɪst
diarrh(o)ea 'daɪə`rɪə
diary `daɪərɪ
Diaspora daɪ`æspərə
diatribe `daɪətraɪb
dibble `dɪbl
dice daɪs
dicey `daɪsɪ
dickens, D– `dɪkɪnz
dicky `dɪkɪ
dicky-bird `dɪkɪ bɜd
dictaphone `dɪktəfəʊn
dictate n `dɪkteɪt

dictate v dɪk'teɪt $ 'dɪkteɪt etc
dictation dɪk'teɪʃn
dictator dɪk'teɪtə(r)
dictatorial 'dɪktə'tɔːrɪəl
diction 'dɪkʃn
dictionary 'dɪkʃnrɪ $ -ɳerɪ
dictum 'dɪktəm
did dɪd
didactic dɪ'dæktɪk
diddle 'dɪdl
didn't 'dɪdnt
die daɪ
die-hard 'daɪ hɑːd $ hɑːrd
Diesel 'dizl $ 'diːsl
diesel-engine 'dizl endʒɪn $ 'diːsl
diesel oil 'dizl ɔɪl $ 'diːsl
diet 'daɪət
dietary 'daɪətrɪ $ -terɪ
dietetics 'daɪə'tetɪks
dietician 'daɪə'tɪʃn
differ 'dɪfə(r)
difference 'dɪfrns
different 'dɪfrnt
differential 'dɪfə'renʃl
differentiate 'dɪfə'renʃɪeɪt
differentiation 'dɪfə'renʃɪ'eɪʃn -ensɪ-
difficult 'dɪfɪklt -fək- $ -kʌlt
difficulty 'dɪfɪkltɪ -fk- -fək- $ 'dɪfəkʌltɪ
diffidence 'dɪfɪdəns -fəd-
diffident 'dɪfɪdənt -fəd-
diffract dɪ'frækt
diffraction dɪ'frækʃn
diffuse adj dɪ'fjuːs
diffuse v dɪ'fjuːz
diffusion dɪ'fjuːʒn
dig dɪg
digest n 'daɪdʒest
digest v daɪ'dʒest dɪ-
digestion daɪ'dʒestʃən dɪ-
digestive daɪ'dʒestɪv dɪ-
digit 'dɪdʒɪt
dignify 'dɪgnɪfaɪ
dignitary 'dɪgnɪtrɪ $ -terɪ
dignity 'dɪgnətɪ
digraph 'daɪgrɑːf $ £ -græf
digress daɪ'gres
digression daɪ'greʃn
dike daɪk
dilapidated dɪ'læpɪdeɪtɪd
dilapidation dɪ'læpɪ'deɪʃn
dilate daɪ'leɪt
dilation daɪ'leɪʃn
dilatory 'dɪlətrɪ $ -tɔrɪ

dilemma dɪ'lemə daɪ-
dilettante 'dɪlɪ'tæntɪ -teɪ $ -'tɑːn-
diligence 'dɪlɪdʒəns
diligent 'dɪlɪdʒənt
dill dɪl
dilly-dally 'dɪlɪ 'dælɪ
dilute daɪ'ljuːt $ £ -'luːt
dilution daɪ'ljuːʃn $ £ -'luːʃn
dim dɪm
dime daɪm
dimension dɪ'menʃn daɪ-
diminish dɪ'mɪnɪʃ
diminution 'dɪmɪ'njuːʃn $ -'nuːʃn
diminutive dɪ'mɪnjətɪv -jʊt- $ -nət-
dimity 'dɪmətɪ
dimple 'dɪmpl
din dɪn
Dinah 'daɪnə
dine daɪn
diner 'daɪnə(r)
ding-dong 'dɪŋ 'dɒŋ $ 'dɔːŋ etc
dinghy 'dɪŋgɪ 'dɪŋɪ
dingle 'dɪŋgl
dingy 'dɪndʒɪ
dining-room 'daɪnɪŋ rʊm $ £ rum etc
dinky 'dɪŋkɪ
dinner 'dɪnə(r)
dinner-bell 'dɪnə bel $ 'dɪnər
dinner-jacket 'dɪnə dʒækɪt $ 'dɪnər
dinner-party 'dɪnə pɑːtɪ $ 'dɪnər pɑːrtɪ
dinner-service 'dɪnə sɜːvɪs $ 'dɪnər
dinner-set 'dɪnə set $ 'dɪnər
dinner-time 'dɪnə taɪm $ 'dɪnər
dinosaur 'daɪnəsɔː(r)
dint dɪnt
diocesan daɪ'ɒsɪsn -ɪzn
diocese 'daɪəsɪs
Diogenes daɪ'ɒdʒɪniːz
dioxide daɪ'ɒksaɪd
dip dɪp
diphtheria dɪf'θɪərɪə dɪp'θ-
diphthong 'dɪfθɒŋ 'dɪpθ- $ -θɔːŋ etc
diploma dɪ'pləʊmə
diplomacy dɪ'pləʊməsɪ
diplomat 'dɪpləmæt
diplomatic 'dɪplə'mætɪk
diplomatist dɪ'pləʊmətɪst
dipsomania 'dɪpsə'meɪnɪə
dipsomaniac 'dɪpsə'meɪnɪæk
dire 'daɪə(r)
direct adj, v dɪ'rekt daɪ- də-
direction dɪ'rekʃn daɪ- də-
direction finder dɪ'rekʃn faɪndə(r)

directive dɪˈrektɪv dɑɪ- də-
directly dɪˈrektlɪ -klɪ
director dɪˈrektə(r) dɑɪ- də-
directorate dɪˈrektərət dɑɪ- də-
directory dɪˈrektrɪ dɑɪ- də-
dirge dɜdʒ
dirigible ˈdɪrɪdʒəbl dɪˈrɪdʒəbl
dirk dɜk
dirt dɜt
dirt-cheap ˈdɜt ˈtʃip
dirt-track ˈdɜt træk
dirty ˈdɜtɪ
dis- prefix dɪs
disability ˈdɪsəˈbɪlətɪ
disable dɪsˈeɪbl
disabuse ˈdɪsəˈbjuz
disadvantage ˈdɪsədˈvɑntɪdʒ $ -ˈvæn-
disadvantageous ˈdɪsˈædvənˈteɪdʒəs
 -væn- £ -van-
disaffected ˈdɪsəˈfektɪd
disaffection ˈdɪsəˈfekʃn
disafforest ˈdɪsəˈfɒrɪst $ -ˈfɔr-
disafforestation ˈdɪsəˈfɒrɪˈsteɪʃn $ -ˈfɔr- etc
disagree ˈdɪsəˈgri
disagreement ˈdɪsəˈgrimənt
disallow ˈdɪsəˈlaʊ
disappear ˈdɪsəˈpɪə(r)
disappearance ˈdɪsəˈpɪərns
disappoint ˈdɪsəˈpɔɪnt
disappointment ˈdɪsəˈpɔɪntmənt
disapproval ˈdɪsəˈpruvl
disapprove ˈdɪsəˈpruv
disarm dɪsˈɑm $ dɪsˈɑrm
disarmament dɪsˈɑməmənt $ -ˈɑrm-
disarrange ˈdɪsəˈreɪndʒ
disarray ˈdɪsəˈreɪ
disaster dɪˈzɑstə(r) $ -ˈzæs-
disastrous dɪˈzɑstrəs $ -ˈzæs-
disavow ˈdɪsəˈvaʊ
disband dɪsˈbænd
disbelief ˈdɪsbɪˈlif -bə-
disbelieve ˈdɪsbɪˈliv -bə-
disburse dɪsˈbɜs
disc dɪsk
discard dɪˈskɑd $ dɪˈskɑrd
discern dɪˈsɜn
discernible dɪˈsɜnəbl
discharge n ˈdɪsʃtɑdʒ dɪsˈtʃɑdʒ $ -ɑrdʒ
discharge v dɪsˈtʃɑdʒ $ -ɑrdʒ ˈdɪstʃɑrdʒ
disciple dɪˈsaɪpl
disciplinarian ˈdɪsəplɪˈneərɪən
disciplinary ˈdɪsəplɪnrɪ ˈdɪsəˈplɪnərɪ
 $ ˈdɪsəplɪnerɪ

discipline ˈdɪsəplɪn
disc jockey ˈdɪsk dʒɒkɪ
disclaim dɪˈskleɪm
disclose dɪˈskləʊz
disclosure dɪˈskləʊʒə(r)
discoloration ˈdɪskʌləˈreɪʃn
discolour($ -or) dɪˈskʌlə(r)
discomfit dɪˈskʌmfɪt
discomfiture dɪˈskʌmfɪtʃə(r)
discomfort dɪˈskʌmfət $ -fərt
discommode ˈdɪskəˈməʊd
discompose ˈdɪskəmˈpəʊz
discomposure ˈdɪskəmˈpəʊʒə(r)
disconcert ˈdɪskənˈsɜt
disconnect ˈdɪskəˈnekt
disconnection ˈdɪskəˈnekʃn
disconsolate dɪsˈkɒnsələt -lɪt
discontent ˈdɪskənˈtent
discontinuance ˈdɪskənˈtɪnjuəns
discontinue ˈdɪskənˈtɪnju
discontinuous ˈdɪskənˈtɪnjuəs
discord ˈdɪskɔd $ ˈdɪskɔrd
discothèque ˈdɪskəˈtek ˈdɪskətek
discount n ˈdɪskaʊnt
discount v dɪˈskaʊnt
discountenance dɪˈskaʊntɪnəns
discourage dɪˈskʌrɪdʒ $ -ˈskɜr-
discourse n ˈdɪskɔs $ ˈdɪskɔrs
discourse v dɪˈskɔs $ dɪˈskɔrs
discourteous dɪˈskɜtɪəs
discover dɪˈskʌvə(r)
discovery dɪˈskʌvrɪ
discredit dɪˈskredɪt
discreet dɪˈskrit
discrepancy dɪˈskrepənsɪ
discrete dɪˈskrit
discretion dɪˈskreʃn
discriminate dɪˈskrɪmɪneɪt
discrimination dɪˈskrɪmɪˈneɪʃn
discursion dɪˈskɜʃn $ dɪˈskɜʒn
discursive dɪˈskɜsɪv
discursory dɪˈskɜsərɪ
discus ˈdɪskəs
discuss dɪˈskʌs
discussion dɪˈskʌʃn
disdain dɪsˈdeɪn
disease dɪˈziz
disembark ˈdɪsɪmˈbɑk $ -ˈbɑrk
disembarkation ˈdɪsˈembɑˈkeɪʃn
 $ -bɑr-
disembarrass ˈdɪsɪmˈbærəs
disembody ˈdɪsɪmˈbɒdɪ
disembowel ˈdɪsɪmˈbaʊl

disenchant 'dɪsɪn'tʃɑnt $ -ænt
disenfranchise 'dɪsɪn'fræntʃaɪz
disengage 'dɪsɪn'geɪdʒ
disentangle 'dɪsɪn'tæŋgl
disestablish 'dɪsɪ'stæblɪʃ
disfavour($ -or) dɪs'feɪvə(r)
disfigure dɪs'fɪgə(r) $ -gjər
disfranchise dɪs'fræntʃaɪz
disgorge dɪs'gɔdʒ $ -'gɔrdʒ
disgrace dɪs'greɪs
disgruntled dɪs'grʌntld
disguise dɪs'gaɪz
disgust dɪs'gʌst
dish dɪʃ
disharmony 'dɪs'hamənɪ $ -'harm-
dishabille 'dɪsə'bil
dish-cloth `dɪʃ klɒθ $ klɔθ
dishearten dɪs'hɑtn $ -'hartn
dishevelled dɪ'ʃevld
dishonest dɪs'ɒnɪst
dishonour($ -or) dɪs'ɒnə(r)
dish-water `dɪʃ wɔtə(r)
disillusion 'dɪsɪ'luʒn
disincentive 'dɪsɪn'sentɪv
disinclination 'dɪsɪnklɪ'neɪʃn
disincline 'dɪsɪn'klaɪn
disinfect 'dɪsɪn'fekt
disinfectant 'dɪsɪn'fektənt
disinflation 'dɪsɪn'fleɪʃn
disingenuous 'dɪsɪn'dʒenjuəs
disinherit 'dɪsɪn'herɪt
disintegrate dɪs'ɪntɪgreɪt
disintegration dɪs'ɪntɪ'greɪʃn
disinter 'dɪsɪn'tɜ(r)
disinterest(ed) dɪs'ɪntrəst(ɪd) -ɪst(ɪd)
disjoint dɪs'dʒɔɪnt
disjunctive dɪs'dʒʌŋktɪv
disk dɪsk
dislike dɪs'laɪk
dislocate `dɪsləkeɪt
    $ -ləʊk- dɪs'ləʊkeɪt etc
dislocation 'dɪslə'keɪʃn $ -ləʊ'k etc
dislodge dɪs'lɒdʒ
disloyal dɪs'lɔɪl
dismal `dɪzml
dismantle dɪs'mæntl
dismast dɪs'mɑst $ -'mæst
dismay dɪs'meɪ
dismember dɪs'membə(r)
dismiss dɪs'mɪs £ dɪz-
dismissal dɪs'mɪsl £ dɪz-
dismount dɪs'maʊnt
Disney `dɪznɪ

disobedience 'dɪsə'bidɪəns
disobedient 'dɪsə'bidɪənt
disobey 'dɪsə'beɪ
disoblige 'dɪsə'blaɪdʒ
disorder dɪs'ɔdə(r) $ -'ɔrd-
disorganization 'dɪs'ɔgənaɪ'zeɪʃn
    $ -'ɔrgənɪ'zeɪʃn
disorganize dɪs'ɔgənaɪz $ -'ɔrg-
disorientate dɪs'ɔrɪənteɪt
disown dɪs'əʊn
disparage dɪ'spærɪdʒ
disparate `dɪspərət -eɪt -ɪt
disparity dɪ'spærətɪ
dispassionate dɪ'spæʃnət -ɪt
dispatch dɪ'spætʃ
dispatch-box dɪ'spætʃ bɒks
dispatch-rider dɪ'spætʃ raɪdə(r)
dispel dɪ'spel
dispensable dɪ'spensəbl
dispensary dɪ'spensərɪ
dispensation 'dɪspen'seɪʃn
dispense dɪ'spens
dispersal dɪ'spɜsl
disperse dɪ'spɜs
dispersion dɪ'spɜʃn $ dɪ'spɜʒn etc
dispirit dɪ'spɪrɪt
displace dɪ'spleɪs
display dɪ'spleɪ
displease dɪ'spliz
displeasure dɪ'spleʒə(r)
disport dɪ'spɔt $ -'spɔrt
disposable dɪ'spəʊzəbl
disposal dɪ'spəʊzl
dispose dɪ'spəʊz
disposition 'dɪspə'zɪʃn
dispossess 'dɪspə'zes
dispossession 'dɪspə'zeʃn
disproof dɪ'spruf
disproportion 'dɪsprə'pɔʃn $ -'pɔrʃn
disproportionate 'dɪsprə'pɔʃnət
    $ -'pɔrʃ-
disprove dɪ'spruv
disputable dɪ'spjutəbl `dɪspjutəbl
disputant dɪ'spjutənt `dɪspjutənt
disputation 'dɪspju'teɪʃn
dispute dɪ'spjut $ n `dɪspjut
disqualification 'dɪskwolɪfɪ'keɪʃn
disqualify dɪ'skwolɪfaɪ
disquiet dɪ'skwaɪət
disquietude dɪ'skwaɪətjud $ -tud
disquisition 'dɪskwɪ'zɪʃn
disregard 'dɪsrɪ'gɑd $ -'gɑrd
disrepair 'dɪsrɪ'peə(r)

disreputable dɪsˋrepjʊtəbl
disrepute ˈdɪsrɪˋpjut
disrespect ˈdɪsrɪˋspekt
disrespectful ˈdɪsrɪˋspektfl
disrobe dɪsˋrəʊb
disrupt dɪsˋrʌpt
disruption dɪsˋrʌpʃn
disruptive dɪsˋrʌptɪv
dissatisfaction ˈdɪˋsætɪsˋfækʃn
dissatisfy dɪˋsætɪsfaɪ
dissect dɪˋsekt
dissection dɪˋsekʃn
dissemble dɪˋsembl
disseminate dɪˋsemɪneɪt
dissemination dɪˋsemɪˋneɪʃn
dissension dɪˋsenʃn
dissent dɪˋsent
dissertation ˈdɪsəˋteɪʃn $ ˈdɪsər-
disservice dɪˋsɜvɪs
dissever dɪˋsevə(r)
dissidence ˋdɪsɪdəns
dissident ˋdɪsɪdənt
dissimilar dɪˋsɪmlə(r)
dissimilitude ˈdɪsɪˋmɪlɪtjud $ -tud
dissimulate dɪˋsɪmjʊleɪt
dissipate ˋdɪsɪpeɪt
dissipation ˈdɪsɪˋpeɪʃn
dissociate dɪˋsəʊʃɪeɪt
dissociation dɪˋsəʊʃɪˋeɪʃn -ˈsəʊsɪ-
dissoluble dɪˋsoljʊbl
dissolute ˋdɪsəlut -ljut
dissolution ˈdɪsəˋluʃn
dissolve dɪˋzolv
dissolvent dɪˋzolvnt -ˋsol-
dissonance ˋdɪsənəns
dissuade dɪˋsweɪd
dissuasive dɪˋsweɪsɪv -zɪv
dissuasion dɪˋsweɪʒn
dissyllable dɪˋsɪləbl daɪ-
distaff ˋdɪstaf $ -æf
distance ˋdɪstəns
distant ˋdɪstənt
distaste dɪsˋteɪst
distasteful dɪsˋteɪstfl
distemper dɪˋstempə(r)
distend dɪˋstend
distension dɪˋstenʃn
distil dɪˋstɪl
distillation ˈdɪstɪˋleɪʃn
distiller dɪˋstɪlə(r)
distillery dɪˋstɪlərɪ
distinct dɪˋstɪŋkt
distinction dɪˋstɪŋkʃn

distinctive dɪˋstɪŋktɪv
distinguish dɪˋstɪŋgwɪʃ
distort dɪˋstɔt $ -ˋstɔrt
distortion dɪˋstɔʃn $ -ˋstɔrʃn
distract dɪˋstrækt
distraction dɪˋstrækʃn
distrain dɪˋstreɪn
distrait dɪˋstreɪ ˋdɪstreɪ
distraught dɪˋstrɔt
distress dɪˋstres
distribute dɪˋstrɪbjut
distribution ˈdɪstrɪˋbjuʃn
distributive dɪˋstrɪbjʊtɪv
distributor dɪˋstrɪbjʊtə(r)
district ˋdɪstrɪkt
District Attorney ˈdɪstrɪkt əˋtɜnɪ
distrust dɪˋstrʌst
disturb dɪˋstɜb
disturbance dɪˋstɜbəns
disunion dɪsˋjunɪən
disunite ˈdɪsjʊˋnaɪt
disuse *n* dɪsˋjus
disuse *v* dɪsˋjuz
disyllabic ˈdaɪsɪˋlæbɪk ˈdɪ-
disyllable daɪˋsɪləbl dɪ-
ditch dɪtʃ
dither ˋdɪðə(r)
ditto ˋdɪtəʊ
ditty ˋdɪtɪ
diurnal daɪˋɜnl
divagate ˋdaɪvəgeɪt
divagation ˈdaɪvəˋgeɪʃn
divan dɪˋvæn daɪ- $ £ ˋdaɪvæn
divan-bed dɪˋvæn ˋbed daɪ-
dive daɪv
dive-bomber ˋdaɪv bomə(r)
diverge daɪˋvɜdʒ dɪ-
divergence daɪˋvɜdʒənt dɪ-
divergent daɪˋvɜdʒəns dɪ-
divers ˋdaɪvəz $ -vərz
diverse daɪˋvɜs dɪ-
diversification daɪˋvɜsɪfɪˋkeɪʃn dɪ-
diversify daɪˋvɜsɪfaɪ dɪ-
diversion daɪˋvɜʃn dɪ- $ -ˋvɜʒn
diversity daɪˋvɜsətɪ dɪ-
divert daɪˋvɜt dɪ-
divest daɪˋvest dɪ-
divide dɪˋvaɪd
dividend ˋdɪvɪdend
divination ˈdɪvɪˋneɪʃn
divine dɪˋvaɪn
diving-board ˋdaɪvɪŋ bɔd $ bɔrd
divinity dɪˋvɪnətɪ

divisible dɪˈvɪzəbl
division dɪˈvɪʒn
divisor dɪˈvaɪzə(r)
divorce dɪˈvɔs $ -ˈvɔrs
divorcee dɪˈvɔˈsi -ˈseɪ ˈdɪvɔ- $ -ˈvɔr-
divot ˈdɪvət
divulge daɪˈvʌldʒ dɪ-
dixie, D– ˈdɪksɪ
dizzy ˈdɪzɪ
do *auxiliary v, usual forms:*
  before consonants: de
  before vowels: du *strong-form:* du
do *n, v* du
do *musical note* dəʊ
dobbin ˈdobɪn
docile ˈdəʊsaɪl $ ˈdosl
docility dəʊˈsɪlətɪ
dock dok
dockyard ˈdokjad $ -jard
doctor ˈdoktə(r)
doctorate ˈdoktərət
doctrinaire ˈdoktrɪˈneə(r)
doctrinal ˈdoktrɪnl dokˈtraɪnl
doctrine ˈdoktrɪn
document ˈdokjʊmənt
documentation ˈdokjʊmenˈteɪʃn
documentary ˈdokjʊˈmentrɪ
dodder ˈdodə(r)
dodge dodʒ
dodgems ˈdodʒəmz
dodgy ˈdodʒɪ
dodo ˈdəʊdəʊ
doe dəʊ
doer ˈduə(r)
does *usual form:* dəz *strong-form:* dʌz
doeskin ˈdəʊ-skɪn
doesn't ˈdʌznt *weak-form:* dəznt
doff dof $ dɔf
dog dog $ dɔg *etc*
dog-days ˈdog deɪz $ ˈdɔg *etc*
doge dəʊdʒ
dog-eared ˈdog ɪəd $ ˈdɔg ɪərd
dogfight ˈdogfaɪt $ ˈdɔg- *etc*
dog-fish ˈdog fɪʃ $ ˈdɔg *etc*
dogged *adj* ˈdogɪd $ ˈdɔgɪd *etc*
doggerel ˈdogərl $ ˈdɔg- *etc*
dogma ˈdogmə $ ˈdɔgmə *etc*
dogmatic dogˈmætɪk $ dɔg- *etc*
dogmatism ˈdogmətɪzm $ ˈdɔg- *etc*
dogmatize ˈdogmətaɪz $ ˈdɔg- *etc*
dog's-body ˈdogz bodɪ $ ˈdɔgz *etc*
dog-tired ˈdog ˈtaɪəd $ ˈdɔg ˈtaɪərd
dog-tooth ˈdog tuθ $ ˈdɔg *etc*

doh dəʊ
doily ˈdɔɪlɪ
doings ˈduɪŋz
do-it-yourself ˈdu ɪt jəˈself $ jər-
dolce vita ˈdoltʃeɪ ˈvitə
doldrums ˈdoldrəmz
dole dəʊl
doleful ˈdəʊlfl
doll dol $ dɔl
dollar ˈdolə(r)
dollop ˈdoləp
doll's house ˈdolz haʊs
dolly ˈdolɪ $ ˈdɔlɪ
dolorous ˈdolərəs $ ˈdəʊlərəs
dolour($ -or) ˈdəʊlə(r)
dolphin ˈdolfɪn $ ˈdɔlfɪn
dolt dəʊlt
-dom *suffix* dəm
domain dəʊˈmeɪn dəˈmeɪn
dome dəʊm
Domesday Book ˈdumzdeɪ bʊk ˈdəʊmz-
domestic dəˈmestɪk
domesticate dəˈmestɪkeɪt
domesticity ˈdəʊmeˈstɪsətɪ
domicile ˈdomɪsaɪl $ -sl
domiciliary ˈdomɪˈsɪlɪərɪ $ -lɪerɪ
dominance ˈdomɪnəns
dominant ˈdomɪnənt
dominate ˈdomɪneɪt
domination ˈdomɪˈneɪʃn
domineer ˈdomɪˈnɪə(r)
dominion dəˈmɪnɪən
domino ˈdomɪnəʊ
don don
Donald ˈdonld
donate dəʊˈneɪt $ ˈdəʊneɪt
donation dəʊˈneɪʃn
done dʌn
Don Giovanni ˈdon dʒɔˈvanɪ -ˈvænɪ
Don Juan ˈdon ˈdʒuən $ ˈhwan ˈwan
donkey ˈdoŋkɪ
donkey-engine ˈdoŋkɪ endʒɪn
donor ˈdəʊnə(r)
Don Quixote ˈdon ˈkwɪksət -əʊt
  $ £ kɪˈhəʊtɪ
don't dəʊnt
doodle ˈdudl
doom dum
Doomsday ˈdumzdeɪ
door dɔ(r)
door-bell ˈdɔ bel $ ˈdɔr
door-keeper ˈdɔ kipə(r) $ ˈdɔr
door-mat ˈdɔ mæt $ ˈdɔr

door-nail `dɔ neɪl $ `dɔr
door-post `dɔ pəʊst $ `dɔr
doorstep `dɔ step $ `dɔr
doorway `dɔweɪ $ `dɔrweɪ
dope dəʊp
Dora `dɔrə
Doreen dɔ`rin `dɔrin
Doric `dorɪk $ £ `dɔrɪk
Doris `dorɪs $ `dɔrɪs
dormant `dɔmənt $ `dɔr-
dormer `dɔmə(r) $ `dɔr-
dormice `dɔmaɪs $ `dɔr-
dormitory `dɔmɪtrɪ $ `dɔrmɪtɔrɪ
dormouse `dɔmaʊs $ `dɔr-
Dorothy `dorəθɪ $ `dɔrəθɪ
dorsal `dɔsl $ `dɔrsl
Dorset `dɔsɪt -sət $ `dɔr-
dosage `dəʊsɪdʒ
dose dəʊs
doss dos
doss-house `dos haʊs
dossier `dosɪeɪ -sɪə(r) $ `dɔs- dɔs`jeɪ
dost dʌst only as a weak-form: dəst
dot dot
dotage `dəʊtɪdʒ
dote dəʊt
doth dʌθ
dotty `dotɪ
douane du`an
double `dʌbl
double-barrelled `dʌbl `bærld
double-bass `dʌbl `beɪs
double-breasted `dʌbl `brestɪd
double-cross `dʌbl `kros $ `krɔs
double-dealing `dʌbl `dilɪŋ
double-decker `dʌbl `dekə(r)
double Dutch `dʌbl `dʌtʃ
double-faced `dʌbl `feɪst
double-jointed `dʌbl `dʒɔɪntɪd
double-quick `dʌbl `kwɪk
doublet `dʌblɪt -lət
double-talk `dʌbl tɔk
doubloon də`blun
doubly `dʌblɪ `dʌbl̩ɪ
doubt daʊt
doubtful `daʊtfl
douche duʃ
dough dəʊ
doughnut `dəʊnʌt $ `dəʊnət etc
doughty `daʊtɪ
Douglas `dʌgləs
dour dʊə(r)
douse daʊs $ daʊz

dove dʌv
dove past of 'dive' dəʊv
dove-cot `dʌv kot
dove-cote `dʌv kəʊt
Dover `dəʊvə(r)
dovetail `dʌvteɪl
dowager `daʊɪdʒə(r)
dowdy `daʊdɪ
dowel `daʊl̩
down daʊn
downcast `daʊnkast $ -kæst
downfall `daʊnfɔl
downgrade n `daʊngreɪd
downgrade v `daʊn`greɪd
downhearted `daʊn`hatɪd $ -`hart-
downhill `daʊn`hɪl
Downing Street `daʊnɪŋ strit
downpour `daʊnpɔ(r)
downright `daʊnraɪt
downstairs `daʊn`steəz $ -`steərz
downstream `daʊn`strim
downtown `daʊn`taʊn `daʊntaʊn
downtrodden `daʊn`trodn
downward(s) `daʊnwəd(z) £ -wʊd(z)
    $ -wərd(z)
downy `daʊnɪ
dowry `daʊərɪ
dowse put out daʊs $ daʊz
dowse divine daʊz
doxology doks`olədʒɪ
doyen `dɔɪən `dɔɪen `dwaɪæ̃
    $ dɔɪ`en dwaɪ`en dwaɪ`æ̃ etc
doyley `dɔɪlɪ
doze dəʊz
dozen `dʌzn
Dr person `doktə(r)
drab dræb
drachm dræm
drachma `drækmə
draft draft $ dræft
draftsman `draftsmən $ `dræf-
drag dræg
dragnet `drægnet
dragon `drægən
dragonfly `drægənflaɪ
dragoon drə`gun
drain dreɪn
drainage `dreɪnɪdʒ
draining-board `dreɪnɪŋ bɔd $ bɔrd
drain-pipe `dreɪn paɪp
drake dreɪk
dram dræm
drama `dramə $ `dræmə

dramatic drə`mætɪk

dramatis personae 'dræmətɪs pɜ`səʊnɪ
    dram- -naɪ

dramatist `dræmətɪst `dram-

dramatization 'dræmətaɪ`zeɪʃn 'dram-
    $ -tɪ`zeɪʃn etc

dramatize `dræmətaɪz `dram-

drank dræŋk

drape dreɪp

drapery `dreɪpərɪ

drastic `dræstɪk £ `dra-

drat dræt

draught draft $ dræft

draught-board `draft bɔd $ `dræft bɔrd

draughtsman `draftsmən $ `dræfts-

draw drɔ

drawback `drɔbæk

drawbridge `drɔbrɪdʒ

drawer person `drɔɔ(r)

drawer thing drɔ(r)

drawing `drɔ-ɪŋ

drawing-board `drɔ-ɪŋ bɔd $ bɔrd

drawing-pin `drɔ-ɪŋ pɪn

drawing-room `drɔ-ɪŋ rʊm $ £ rum etc

drawl drɔl

drawn drɔn

dray dreɪ

dread dred

dreadful `dredfl

dreadnought `drednɔt

dream drim

dreamland `drimlænd

dreamlike `drimlaɪk

dreamt dremt

dreamworld `drimwɜld

dreary `drɪərɪ

dredge dredʒ

dregs dregz

drench drentʃ

dress dres

dressage `dresaʒ $ dre`saʒ drə-

dress circle 'dres `sɜkl `d- s-

dressing-gown `dresɪŋ gaʊn

dressing-table `dresɪŋ teɪbl

dressmaker `dresmeɪkə(r)

dress rehearsal 'dres rɪ`hɜsl `d- r-

drew dru

dribble `drɪbl

driblet `drɪblɪt -ət

dried draɪd

drier `draɪə(r)

drift drɪft

drift-net `drɪft net

drift-wood `drɪft wʊd

drill drɪl

drily `draɪlɪ

drink drɪŋk

drinking-fountain `drɪŋkɪŋ faʊntɪn
    $ faʊntn

drinking-song `drɪŋkɪŋ sɔŋ $ sɔŋ

drip drɪp

drip-dry 'drɪp `draɪ

dripping wet 'drɪpɪŋ `wet

drive draɪv

drivel `drɪvl

driven `drɪvn

driving-wheel `draɪvɪŋ wil $ hwil etc

drizzle `drɪzl

droll drəʊl

drollery `drəʊlərɪ

dromedary `dromədərɪ `drʌm- $ -derɪ

drone drəʊn

drool drul

droop drup

drop drop

drop-kick `drop kɪk

drop-out `drop aʊt

dropsical `dropsɪkl

dropsy `dropsɪ

dross dros $ drɔs

drought draʊt

drove drəʊv

drover `drəʊvə(r)

drown draʊn

drowse draʊz

drowsy `draʊzɪ

drub drʌb

drudge drʌdʒ

drudgery `drʌdʒərɪ

drug drʌg

drug(-)store `drʌg stɔ(r)

druggist `drʌgɪst

Druid `druɪd

drum drʌm

drum major drʌm `meɪdʒə(r)

drum majorette 'drʌm meɪdʒə`ret

drumstick `drʌm-stɪk

drunk drʌŋk

drunkard `drʌŋkəd $ -kərd

drunken `drʌŋkən

dry draɪ

dry-clean 'draɪ `klin

dryad `draɪəd `draɪæd

dryer `draɪə(r)

dry-rot 'draɪ `rot

dry-walling 'draɪ `wɔlɪŋ

dual `djuļ $ `dul
dual carriageway 'djuļ `kærɪdʒweɪ
  $ 'duļ
dub dʌb
dubbin `dʌbɪn
dubiety dju`baɪətɪ $ du- etc
dubious `djubɪəs $ `du- etc
ducal `djukl $ `du- etc
ducat `dʌkət
duchess `dʌtʃɪs `dʌtʃəs
duchy `dʌtʃɪ
duck dʌk
duck-bill `dʌk bɪl
duck-boards `dʌk bɔdz $ bɔrdz
duckling `dʌklɪŋ
duckweed `dʌkwid
duct dʌkt
ductile `dʌktaɪl $ `dʌktl
ductility dʌk`tɪlətɪ
dud dʌd
dude djud $ dud etc
dudgeon `dʌdʒən
due dju $ du etc
duel `djuļ $ `duļ etc
duel(l)ist `djuəlɪst $ `duəlɪst etc
duenna dju`enə $ du`enə etc
duet dju`et $ du`et etc
duffelcoat `dʌflkəʊt
duffer `dʌfə(r)
dug dʌg
dug-out `dʌg aʊt
duke djuk $ duk etc
dukedom `djukdəm $ `duk- etc
dulcet `dʌlsɪt
dulcimer `dʌlsɪmə(r)
dull dʌl
dullard `dʌləd $ `dʌlərd
duly `djulɪ $ `dulɪ etc
dumb dʌm
dumbbell `dʌmbel
dumbfound dʌm`faʊnd
dumb-waiter 'dʌm `weɪtə(r)
dummy `dʌmɪ
dump dʌmp
dumpling `dʌmplɪŋ
dumpy `dʌmpɪ
dun dʌn
Duncan `dʌŋkən
dunce dʌns
dune djun $ dun
dung dʌŋ
dungarees 'dʌŋgə`riz
dungeon `dʌndʒən

dunghill `dʌŋhɪl
dunk dʌŋk
Dunlop `dʌnlop
duodecimal 'djuə`desɪml
  $ 'duə- etc
duodenal 'djuə`dinl $ 'duə- etc
duodenum 'djuə`dinəm $ 'duə- etc
duologue `djuəlog $ `duəlɔg etc
dupe djup $ dup etc
duplex `djupleks $ `du- etc
duplicate n `djuplɪkət $ `du-
duplicate v `djuplɪkeɪt $ `du- etc
duplication 'djuplɪ`keɪʃn $ 'du- etc
duplicator `djuplɪkeɪtə(r) $ `du-
duplicity dju`plɪsətɪ $ du- etc
durability 'djuərə`bɪlətɪ $ 'duərə- etc
durable `djuərəbl $ `duərəbl etc
durance `djuərəns $ `duərəns etc
duration dju`reɪʃn $ du- etc
Durban `dɜbən
durbar `dɜba(r)
duress djuə`res $ du`res
Durham `dʌrəm $ `dɜrəm etc
during `djuərɪŋ $ `duərɪŋ etc
durst dɜst
dusk dʌsk
dust dʌst
dustbin `dʌstbɪn
dust-bowl `dʌst bəʊl
dust-coat `dʌst kəʊt
duster `dʌstə(r)
dust-jacket `dʌst dʒækɪt
dustman `dʌstmən
dustpan `dʌstpæn
Dutch dʌtʃ
Dutch courage 'dʌtʃ `kʌrɪdʒ $ `kɜɪdʒ
Dutchman `dʌtʃmən
dutiable `djutɪəbl $ `du- etc
dutiful `djutɪfl $ `du- etc
duty `djutɪ $ `dutɪ etc
dwarf dwɔf $ dwɔrf
dwell dwel
dwelling `dwelɪŋ
dwelling house `dwelɪŋ haʊs
dwindle `dwɪndl
dye daɪ
dying `daɪɪŋ
dyke daɪk
dynamic daɪ`næmɪk
dynamism `daɪnəmɪzm
dynamite `daɪnəmaɪt
dynamo `daɪnəməʊ
dynastic dɪ`næstɪk $ £ daɪ`næstɪk

dynasty ˈdɪnəstɪ $ ˈdaɪnəstɪ -næs-
dysentery ˈdɪsntrɪ $ -terɪ

dyspepsia dɪsˈpepsɪə $ dɪsˈpepʃə *etc*
dyspeptic dɪsˈpeptɪk

E

E e i
each itʃ
each other itʃ ˈʌðə(r)
eager ˈigə(r)
eagle ˈigl
eagle-eyed ˈigl ˈaɪd
eaglet ˈiglɪt -ət
Eamon ˈeɪmən
ear ɪə(r)
ear-ache ˈɪər eɪk
ear-drum ˈɪə drʌm $ ˈɪər
earl ɜl
earldom ˈɜldəm
early ˈɜlɪ
earmark ˈɪəmɑk $ ˈɪərmɑrk
earn ɜn
earnest ˈɜnɪst
ear-phone ˈɪə fəʊn $ ˈɪər
ear-ring ˈɪə rɪŋ $ ˈɪər
earshot ˈɪə ʃot $ ˈɪər
earth ɜθ
earthen ˈɜθn $ ˈɜðn
earthenware ˈɜθnweə(r) $ ˈɜðn-
earthquake ˈɜθkweɪk
earthworm ˈɜθwɜm
earthy ˈɜθɪ
earwig ˈɪəwɪg $ ˈɪər-
ease iz
easel ˈizl
easily ˈizḷɪ
east ist
Easter ˈistə(r)
Easter Monday ˈistə ˈmʌndi $ ˈistər
Easter Sunday ˈistə ˈsʌndɪ $ ˈistər
Easter week ˈistə wik $ ˈistər
Easter egg ˈistər eg
eastern ˈistən $ ˈistərn
easy ˈizɪ
easy chair ˈizɪ tʃeə(r)
easy-going ˈizɪ ˈgəʊɪŋ
eat it
eaten ˈitn
eau-de-cologne ˈəʊ də kəˈləʊn
eaves ivz
eavesdropper ˈivzdropə(r)

ebb eb
ebb-tide ˈeb ˈtaɪd ˈeb taɪd
ebony ˈebənɪ
ebullience ɪˈbʌlɪəns ɪˈbʊl-
ebullient ɪˈbʌlɪənt ɪˈbʊl-
eccentric ɪkˈsentrɪk ek-
eccentricity ˈeksenˈtrɪsətɪ
Ecclesiastes ɪˈklizɪˈæstiz
ecclesiastical ɪˈklizɪˈæstɪkl
echelon ˈeʃəlon ˈeɪʃ-
echo ˈekəʊ
echo-sounding ˈekəʊ saʊndɪŋ
éclair eɪˈkleə(r) ˈeɪkleə(r) ɪˈk-
eclectic ɪˈklektɪk
eclipse ɪˈklɪps
ecology iˈkolədʒɪ
economic(s) ˈikəˈnomɪk(s) ˈek-
economical ˈikəˈnomɪkl ˈek-
economist iˈkonəmɪst ɪˈk-
economize iˈkonəmaɪz ɪˈk-
economy iˈkonəmɪ
ecstasy ˈekstəsɪ
ecstatic ɪkˈstætɪk
ectoplasm ˈektəplæzm
Ecuador ˈekwədɔ(r) ˈekwəˈdɔ(r)
ecumenical ˈɪkjuˈmenɪkl $ ˈek-
eczema ˈeksɪmə $ ˈegzəmə ɪgˈzimə
eddy ˈedɪ
Eden ˈidn
edge edʒ
edgeways ˈedʒweɪz
edgewise ˈedʒwaɪz
edgy ˈedʒɪ
edibility ˈedəˈbɪlətɪ
edible ˈedəbl
edict ˈidɪkt
edification ˈedɪfɪˈkeɪʃn
edifice ˈedɪfɪs
edify ˈedɪfaɪ
Edinburgh ˈednbrə -dɪn- -bərə
    $ ˈednbɜrəʊ -bər- -rə
edit ˈedɪt
Edith ˈidɪθ
edition ɪˈdɪʃn əˈd-
editor ˈedɪtə(r)

editorial ˈedɪˈtɔːrɪəl
educate ˈedʒʊkeɪt £ ˈedjʊk-
education ˈedʒʊˈkeɪʃn £ ˈedjʊ-
educationist ˈedʒʊˈkeɪʃn̩ɪst £ ˈedjʊ-
educe ɪˈdjuːs i- $ ɪˈduːs i- *etc*
Edward ˈedwəd £ -wʊd $ ˈedwərd
Edwardian edˈwɔːdɪən $ -ˈwɔːrd-
EEC ˈi i ˈsi
eel il
e'en in
e'er eə(r)
eerie ˈɪərɪ
efface ɪˈfeɪs
effect ɪˈfekt əˈf-
effective ɪˈfektɪv əˈf-
effectual ɪˈfektʃʊəl əˈf-
effectuate ɪˈfektʃʊeɪt əˈf-
effeminate ɪˈfemɪnət əˈf-
effervesce ˈefəˈves
effervescence ˈefəˈvesns
effervescent ˈefəˈvesnt
effete ɪˈfiːt eˈfiːt
efficacious ˈefɪˈkeɪʃəs
efficacy ˈefɪkəsɪ
efficiency ɪˈfɪʃnsɪ əˈf-
efficient ɪˈfɪʃnt əˈf-
effigy ˈefɪdʒɪ
efflorescence ˈefləˈresns £ ˈeflɔˈr-
effluent ˈeflʊənt
effort ˈefət $ ˈefərt
effrontery ɪˈfrʌntərɪ əˈf-
effusion ɪˈfjuːʒn
effusive ɪˈfjuːsɪv
e.g. ˈi ˈdʒi
egalitarianism ɪˈɡælɪˈteərɪənɪzm
egg eg
egg-cup ˈeg kʌp
egg-head ˈeg hed
egg-plant ˈeg plɑːnt $ plænt
egg-shell ˈeg ʃel
egg-whisk ˈeg wɪsk $ hwɪsk *etc*
eglantine ˈeɡləntaɪn $ -tɪn
ego ˈeɡəʊ $ £ ˈiɡəʊ
egocentric ˈeɡəʊˈsentrɪk $ £ ˈiɡəʊ-
egoism ˈeɡəʊɪzm $ £ ˈiɡ-
egoistic ˈeɡəʊˈɪstɪk $ £ ˈiɡəʊ-
egotism ˈeɡətɪzm $ £ ˈiɡ-
egotistic ˈeɡəʊˈtɪstɪk $ £ ˈiɡəʊ-
egregious ɪˈɡriːdʒɪəs
egress ˈiɡres
egret ˈiɡret -ɪt -ət
Egypt ˈiːdʒɪpt
Egyptian ɪˈdʒɪpʃn

eh eɪ
eiderdown ˈaɪdədaʊn $ -dərd-
eight eɪt
eighteen eɪˈtin
eighth eɪtθ
eightieth ˈeɪtɪəθ
eightpence ˈeɪtpəns $ -pens *etc*
eightpenny ˈeɪtpənɪ $ -penɪ *etc*
eightsome ˈeɪtsm
Einstein ˈaɪnstaɪn
eighty ˈeɪtɪ
eighty-one ˈeɪtɪ ˈwʌn
Eire ˈeərə
Eisenhower ˈaɪznhaʊə(r)
eisteddfod aɪˈsteðvod $ eɪˈst- eˈst-
either ˈaɪðə(r) $ ˈiðər
ejaculate ɪˈdʒækjʊleɪt
eject ɪˈdʒekt
ejection ɪˈdʒekʃn
ejector ɪˈdʒektə(r)
ejector-seat ɪˈdʒektə sit $ -tər
eke ik
elaborate *adj* ɪˈlæbrət -ɪt
elaborate *v* ɪˈlæbəreɪt
elapse ɪˈlæps əl-
elastic ɪˈlæstɪk əl- £ -ˈlɑːs-
elasticity ˈelæˈstɪsətɪ ˈil- $ £ ɪˈlæˈst-
elate ɪˈleɪt
elation ɪˈleɪʃn
elbow ˈelbəʊ
elbow-room ˈelbəʊ rʊm $ £ rum *etc*
elder ˈeldə(r)
elderberry ˈeldəberɪ $ ˈeldər-
elderly ˈeldəlɪ $ ˈeldərlɪ
eldest ˈeldɪst -əst
El Dorado ˈel dəˈrɑːdəʊ
Eleanor ˈelɪnə(r) ˈelənə(r)
elect ɪˈlekt əˈlekt
election ɪˈlekʃn əˈl-
electioneering ɪˈlekʃnˈɪərɪŋ əˈl-
elective ɪˈlektɪv əˈl-
elector ɪˈlektə(r) əˈl-
electoral ɪˈlektərl
electorate ɪˈlektərət əˈl-
electric ɪˈlektrɪk əˈl-
electrical ɪˈlektrɪkl əˈl-
electrician ɪˈlekˈtrɪʃn ˈelɪk- ˈelək- əˈl-
electricity ɪˈlekˈtrɪsətɪ ˈelɪk- ˈelək- əˈl-
electrification ɪˈlektrɪfɪˈkeɪʃn əˈl-
electrify ɪˈlektrɪfaɪ əˈl-
electrocute ɪˈlektrəkjut əˈl-
electrocution ɪˈlektrəˈkjuʃn əˈl-
electrode ɪˈlektrəʊd əˈl-

electrolysis ɪˈlekˈtrɒləsɪs ˈelɪk- ˈeləkˈ
electro-magnet ɪˈlektrəʊ ˈmægnɪt əˈlˈ
electron ɪˈlektrɒn əˈl-
electronic ɪˈlekˈtrɒnɪk ˈelɪk- ˈeləkˈ
electroplate ɪˈlektrəʊpleɪt ɪˈlektrəʊˈpleɪt
elegance ˈelɪgəns ˈeləˈ
elegant ˈelɪgənt ˈeləˈ
elegiac ˈelɪˈdʒaɪək -aɪæk $ ɪˈlidʒɪæk
elegy ˈelədʒɪ
element ˈeləmənt ˈelɪmˈ
elementary ˈeləˈmentrɪ ˈelɪˈ
elephant ˈeləfnt ˈelɪˈ
elephantine ˈeləˈfæntaɪn ˈelɪ- $ -tin etc
elevate ˈeləveɪt ˈelɪˈ
elevation ˈeləˈveɪʃn ˈelɪˈ
elevator ˈeləveɪtə(r) ˈelɪˈ
eleven ɪˈlevn əˈlevn
elevenses ɪˈlevnzɪz əˈl-
eleventh ɪˈlevnθ əˈl-
elf elf
elfin ˈelfɪn
Elgar ˈelgɑ(r)
elicit ɪˈlɪsɪt əˈl-
elide ɪˈlaɪd
eligible ˈelɪdʒəbl
eligibility ˈelɪdʒəˈbɪlətɪ
Elijah ɪˈlaɪdʒə
eliminate ɪˈlɪmɪneɪt
elimination ɪˈlɪmɪˈneɪʃn
elision ɪˈlɪʒn
élite eɪˈlit $ ɪˈlit etc
elixir ɪˈlɪksə(r) eˈl-
Elizabeth ɪˈlɪzəbəθ əˈl-
Elizabethan ɪˈlɪzəˈbiθn əˈl-
elk elk
Ellen ˈelən
ellipse ɪˈlɪps əˈl-
ellipses ɪˈlɪpsiz əˈl-
ellipsis ɪˈlɪpsɪs əˈl-
elliptical ɪˈlɪptɪkl əˈl-
elm elm
elocution ˈeləˈkjuʃn
elocutionist ˈeləˈkjuʃn̩ɪst
elongate ˈilɒŋgeɪt $ ɪˈlɒŋgeɪt
elope ɪˈləʊp əˈl-
eloquence ˈeləkwəns
eloquent ˈeləkwənt
else els
elsewhere elsˈweə(r) ˈelsweə(r)
$ elsˈhweər etc
elucidate ɪˈlusɪdeɪt
elucidation ɪˈlusɪdeɪʃn
elude ɪˈlud £ ɪˈljud

elusive ɪˈlusɪv
elusory ɪˈlusərɪ
elves elvz
Elysium ɪˈlɪzɪəm
emaciate ɪˈmeɪʃɪeɪt ɪˈmeɪsɪeɪt
emaciation ɪmeɪʃɪˈeɪʃn ɪˈmeɪsɪ-
emanate ˈeməneɪt
emancipate ɪˈmænsɪpeɪt
emancipation ɪˈmænsɪˈpeɪʃn
Emanuel ɪˈmænjʊəl
emasculate ɪˈmæskjʊleɪt
emasculation ɪˈmæskjʊˈleɪʃn
embalm ɪmˈbam
embankment ɪmˈbæŋkmənt
embargo ɪmˈbagəʊ $ -arg-
embark ɪmˈbak $ -ˈbark
embarkation ˈembaˈkeɪʃn $ -bar-
embarrass ɪmˈbærəs
embarrassment ɪmˈbærəsmənt
embassy ˈembəsɪ
embed ɪmˈbed
embellish ɪmˈbelɪʃ
embellishment ɪmˈbelɪʃmənt
ember ˈembə(r)
embezzle ɪmˈbezl
embezzlement ɪmˈbezlmənt
embitter ɪmˈbɪtə(r)
emblazon ɪmˈbleɪzn
emblem ˈembləm
embodiment ɪmˈbodɪmənt
embody ɪmˈbodɪ
embolden ɪmˈbəʊldn
emboss ɪmˈbos $ ɪmˈbɔs
embrace ɪmˈbreɪs
embrocation ˈembrəˈkeɪʃn -brəʊˈk-
embroider ɪmˈbrɔɪdə(r)
embroidery ɪmˈbrɔɪdərɪ -drɪ
embroil ɪmˈbrɔɪl
embryo ˈembrɪəʊ
embryonic ˈembrɪˈonɪk
emend ɪˈmend əˈm-
emerald ˈemərld
emerge ɪˈmɜdʒ
emergence ɪˈmɜdʒəns
emergency ɪˈmɜdʒənsɪ
emergent ɪˈmɜdʒənt
emeritus ɪˈmerɪtəs
emery ˈemərɪ
emetic ɪˈmetɪk
emigrant ˈemɪgrənt
emigrate ˈemɪgreɪt
emigration ˈemɪˈgreɪʃn
emigré ˈemɪgreɪ $ ˈeməˈgreɪ ˈeɪm- etc

Emily ˈeməlɪ
eminence ˈemɪnəns
eminent ˈemɪnənt
emir eˈmɪə(r) ɪˈm- ˈemɪə(r)
emissary ˈemɪsrɪ -sərɪ $ -serɪ
emission ɪˈmɪʃn
emit ɪˈmɪt
Emma ˈemə
emolument ɪˈmoljʊmənt
emotion ɪˈməʊʃn
emotional ɪˈməʊʃnl
emotive ɪˈməʊtɪv
emperor ˈemprə(r)
emphasis ˈemfəsɪs
emphasize ˈemfəsaɪz
emphatic ɪmˈfætɪk
empire ˈempaɪə(r)
empiric emˈpɪrɪk ɪm-
empirical emˈpɪrɪkl ɪm-
empiricism emˈpɪrɪsɪzm ɪm-
employ ɪmˈplɔɪ
employee ɪmˈplɔɪˈi ɪmˈplɔɪi
employment ɪmˈplɔɪmənt
employment agency
  ɪmˈplɔɪmənt eɪdʒənsɪ
employment exchange
  ɪmˈplɔɪmənt ɪksteɪndʒ
emporium emˈpɔrɪəm
empower ɪmˈpaʊə(r)
empress ˈemprəs -rɪs
emptiness ˈemptɪnəs
empty ˈemptɪ
empty-handed ˈemptɪ ˈhændɪd
empty-headed ˈemptɪ ˈhedɪd
emu ˈimju
emulate ˈemjʊleɪt
emulation ˈemjʊˈleɪʃn
emulsify ɪˈmʌlsɪfaɪ
emulsion ɪˈmʌlʃn
enable ɪˈneɪbl
enact ɪˈnækt
enamel ɪˈnæml
enamour($ -or) ɪˈnæmə(r)
encamp ɪnˈkæmp
encampment ɪnˈkæmpmənt
encase ɪnˈkeɪs
encaustic ɪnˈkɔstɪk
-ence suffix əns
encephalitis ˈensefəˈlaɪtɪs ˈenkef-
enchain ɪnˈtʃeɪn
enchant ɪnˈtʃɑnt $ ɪnˈtʃænt
enchantress ɪnˈtʃɑntrəs -rɪs
  $ -ˈtʃæn-

encircle ɪnˈsɜkl
enclave ˈenkleɪv ˈon- ˈŏk- -lɑv
enclitic enˈklɪtɪk
enclose ɪnˈkləʊz
enclosure ɪnˈkləʊʒə(r)
encompass ɪnˈkʌmpəs
encore ˈoŋkɔ(r) £ onˈkɔ(r)
encounter ɪnˈkaʊntə(r)
encourage ɪnˈkʌrɪdʒ $ ɪnˈkɜ-
encouragement ɪnˈkʌrɪdʒmənt $ ɪnˈkɜ-
encroach ɪnˈkrəʊtʃ
encrust ɪnˈkrʌst
encumber ɪnˈkʌmbə(r)
encumbrance ɪnˈkʌmbrəns
-ency suffix ənsɪ
encyclical ɪnˈsɪklɪkl -ˈsaɪk-
encyclop(a)edia ɪnˈsaɪkləˈpidɪə
encyclop(a)edic ɪnˈsaɪkləˈpidɪk
end end
endanger ɪnˈdeɪndʒə(r)
endear ɪnˈdɪə(r)
endeavour ɪnˈdevə(r)
endemic enˈdemɪk
endive ˈendɪv $ ˈendaɪv
endorse ɪnˈdɔs $ ɪnˈdɔrs
endorsement ɪnˈdɔsmənt $ -ˈdɔrs-
endow ɪnˈdaʊ
endowment ɪnˈdaʊmənt
endurance ɪnˈdjʊərəns $ ɪnˈdʊər- etc
endure ɪnˈdjʊə(r) $ ɪnˈdʊər etc
enema ˈenəmə
enemy ˈenəmɪ
energetic ˈenəˈdʒetɪk $ ˈenər-
energy ˈenədʒɪ $ ˈenərdʒɪ
enervate ˈenəveɪt $ ˈenərv-
enfeeble ɪnˈfibl en-
enfold ɪnˈfəʊld
enforce ɪnˈfɔs $ -ˈfɔrs
enforcement ɪnˈfɔsmənt $ -ˈfɔrs-
enfranchise ɪnˈfræntʃaɪz
enfranchisement ɪnˈfræntʃɪzmənt
engage ɪnˈgeɪdʒ
engagement ɪnˈgeɪdʒmənt
engagement ring ɪnˈgeɪdʒmənt rɪŋ
engender ɪnˈdʒendə(r)
engine ˈendʒɪn
engine-driver ˈendʒɪn draɪvə(r)
engineer ˈendʒɪˈnɪə(r)
England ˈɪŋglənd
English ˈɪŋglɪʃ
Englishman ˈɪŋglɪʃmən
engraft ɪnˈgrɑft $ ɪnˈgræft
engrave ɪnˈgreɪv

engross ɪnˈɡrəʊs
engulf ɪnˈɡʌlf
enhance ɪnˈhɑns $ £ ɪnˈhæns
enigma ɪˈnɪɡmə
enigmatic ˈenɪɡˈmætɪk
enjoin ɪnˈdʒɔɪn
enjoy ɪnˈdʒɔɪ
enjoyment ɪnˈdʒɔɪmənt
enlarge ɪnˈlɑdʒ $ ɪnˈlɑrdʒ
enlargement ɪnˈlɑdʒmənt $ -ˈlɑrdʒ-
enlighten ɪnˈlaɪtn
enlightenment ɪnˈlaɪtnmənt
enlist ɪnˈlɪst
enliven ɪnˈlaɪvn
en masse ˈɒ̃ ˈmæs $ £ ˈɒn ˈmæs ˈen etc
enmesh ɪnˈmeʃ
enmity ˈenmətɪ
ennoble ɪˈnəʊbl
ennui ˈonwi $ onˈwi etc
enormity ɪˈnɔmətɪ $ -ˈnɔrm-
enormous ɪˈnɔməs $ ɪˈnɔrməs
enough ɪˈnʌf əˈnʌf
en passant ˈɒ̃ ˈpæsɒ̃ $ pæˈsɒ̃
enquire ɪnˈkwaɪə(r)
enquiry ɪnˈkwaɪərɪ
    $ ˈɪnkwaɪərɪ -kwərɪ etc
enrage ɪnˈreɪdʒ
enrapture ɪnˈræptʃə(r)
enrich ɪnˈrɪtʃ
enrichment ɪnˈrɪtʃmənt
enroll ɪnˈrəʊl
enrolment ɪnˈrəʊlmənt
en route ˈɒ̃ ˈrut ˈon $ ˈon en ɪn etc
ensconce ɪnˈskons
ensemble usually with unsyllabic l:
    ˈɒ̃ ˈsɒ̃bl $ £ ˈon ˈsombl etc
enshrine ɪnˈʃraɪn
enshroud ɪnˈʃraʊd
ensign badge, flag ˈensaɪn
ensign naval flag, US officer ˈensn etc
enslave ɪnˈsleɪv
ensnare ɪnˈsneə(r)
ensue ɪnˈsju $ £ ɪnˈsu
ensure ɪnˈʃʊə(r) £ -ˈʃɔ(r)
-ent suffix ənt
entail ɪnˈteɪl
entangle ɪnˈtæŋɡl
entente ɒ̃ˈtɒ̃t ɒ̃ˈtɔ̃t $ £ onˈtont
entente cordiale ˈɒ̃tɒ̃t ˈkɔdɪˈal $ ˈkɔr-
enter ˈentə(r)
enteric enˈterɪk
enteritis ˈentəˈraɪtɪs -təs
enterprise ˈentəpraɪz $ ˈentər-

entertain ˈentəˈteɪn $ ˈentər-
entertainment ˈentəˈteɪnmənt $ ˈentər-
enthral(l) ɪnˈθrɔl
enthrone ɪnˈθrəʊn
enthronement ɪnˈθrəʊnmənt
enthuse ɪnˈθjuz $ -ˈθu-
enthusiasm ɪnˈθjuzɪæzm $ £ -ˈθu-
enthusiast ɪnˈθjuzɪæst $ £ -ˈθu-
enthusiastic ɪnˈθjuzɪˈæstɪk $ £ -ˈθu-
entice ɪnˈtaɪs
enticement ɪnˈtaɪsmənt
entire ɪnˈtaɪə(r)
entirety ɪnˈtaɪərətɪ ɪnˈtaɪətɪ
entitle ɪnˈtaɪtl
entity ˈentətɪ
entomb ɪnˈtum
entomology ˈentəˈmolədʒɪ
entr'acte ˈɒ̃trækt ˈont- $ onˈtrækt
entrails ˈentreɪlz
entrain ɪnˈtreɪn
entrance n ˈentrns
entrance v ɪnˈtrans $ -æns
entrance fee ˈentrns fi
entrant ˈentrənt
entrap ɪnˈtræp
entreat ɪnˈtrit
entreaty ɪnˈtritɪ
entrée ˈɒ̃treɪ $ £ ˈontreɪ $ onˈtreɪ
entrench ɪnˈtrentʃ
entrepreneur ˈɒ̃trəprəˈnɜ(r) $ £ ˈontrə-
entrust ɪnˈtrʌst
entry ˈentrɪ
entwine ɪnˈtwaɪn
enumerate ɪˈnjuməreɪt $ ɪˈnum- etc
enumeration ɪˈnjuməˈreɪʃn $ ɪˈnum- etc
enunciate ɪˈnʌnsɪeɪt
envelop ɪnˈveləp
envelope ˈenvələʊp ˈon-
envenom ɪnˈvenəm
enviable ˈenvɪəbl
envious ˈenvɪəs
environ(s) ɪnˈvaɪərən(z) ˈenvɪrən(z)
environment ɪnˈvaɪərənmənt
envisage ɪnˈvɪzɪdʒ $ enˈvɪzɪdʒ
envoy ˈenvɔɪ
envy ˈenvɪ
enwrap ɪnˈræp
enzyme ˈenzaɪm
eon ˈiən ˈion
epaulet(te) ˈepɔˈlet -pəʊˈl- -pəˈl-
    $ ˈepəlet -lɪt ˈepəˈlet
ephemeral ɪˈfemərl £ ɪˈfim-
epic ˈepɪk

epicure ˈepɪkjʊə(r)
epicurean ˈepɪkjuˈrɪən
epidemic ˈepɪˈdemɪk
epidermis ˈepɪˈdɜmɪs
epidiascope ˈepɪˈdaɪəskəʊp
epiglottis ˈepɪˈglotɪs ˈepɪglotɪs
epigram ˈepɪgræm
epilepsy ˈepɪlepsɪ
epileptic ˈepɪˈleptɪk
epilogue($ -og) ˈepɪlog $ -lɔg
Epiphany ɪˈpɪfənɪ
episcopal ɪˈpɪskəpl
episcopalian ɪˈpɪskəˈpeɪlɪən
episode ˈepɪsəʊd
episodic ˈepɪˈsodɪk
epistle ɪˈpɪsl
epitaph ˈepɪtæf £ -af
epithet ˈepɪθet
epitome ɪˈpɪtəmɪ
epoch ˈipok $ ˈepək
epoch-making ˈipok meɪkɪŋ $ ˈepək
epsilon epˈsaɪlən $ £ ˈepsɪlən $ -lon
equable ˈekwəbl
equal ˈikwl
equality ɪˈkwolətɪ
equalize ˈikwəlaɪz
equanimity ˈekwəˈnɪmətɪ ˈik-
equate ɪˈkweɪt
equation ɪˈkweɪʒn -eɪʃn
equator ɪˈkweɪtə(r)
equatorial ˈekwəˈtɔrɪəl ˈik-
equerry ɪˈkwerɪ ˈekwərɪ
equestrian ɪˈkwestrɪən
equidistant ˈikwɪˈdɪstənt
equilateral ˈikwɪˈlætərl
equilibrium ˈikwɪˈlɪbrɪəm
equine ˈikwaɪn ˈek-
equinoctial ˈikwɪˈnokʃl ˈek-
equinox ˈikwɪnoks ˈek-
equip ɪˈkwɪp
equipment ɪˈkwɪpmənt
equipoise ˈekwɪpɔɪz ˈik-
equitable ˈekwɪtəbl
equity ˈekwətɪ
equivalent ɪˈkwɪvḷənt
equivocal ɪˈkwɪvəkl
equivocation ɪˈkwɪvəˈkeɪʃn
-er suffix ə(r)
era ˈɪərə $ ˈerə
eradicate ɪˈrædɪkeɪt
eradication ɪˈrædɪˈkeɪʃn
erase ɪˈreɪz $ ɪˈreɪs
eraser ɪˈreɪzə(r) $ ɪˈreɪsər

Erasmus ɪˈræzməs
erasure ɪˈreɪʒə(r) $ ɪˈreɪʃər
ere eə(r)
erect ɪˈrekt
erection ɪˈrekʃn
ergo ˈɜgəʊ
Eric ˈerɪk
Erin ˈerɪn
ermine ˈɜmɪn
Ernest ˈɜnɪst
erode ɪˈrəʊd
erosion ɪˈrəʊʒn
erotic ɪˈrotɪk $ eˈr-
err ɜ(r) $ eər
errand ˈerənd
errand-boy ˈerənd bɔɪ
errant ˈerənt
errata eˈrɑtə $ £ ɪˈreɪtə $ -ˈrætə
erratic ɪˈrætɪk
erratum eˈrɑtəm $ £ ɪˈreɪtəm eˈr-
   $ -ˈrætəm
erroneous ɪˈrəʊnɪəs
error ˈerə(r)
Erse ɜs
erudite ˈerʊdaɪt ˈerjʊ-
erudition ˈerʊˈdɪʃn ˈerjʊ-
erupt ɪˈrʌpt
eruption ɪˈrʌpʃn
escalate ˈeskəleɪt
escalator ˈeskəleɪtə(r)
escapade ˈeskəˈpeɪd
escape ɪˈskeɪp əˈs-
escapist ɪˈskeɪpɪst əˈs-
escarpment ɪˈskɑpmənt $ ɪˈskɑrp-
-escence suffix ˈesns
eschew ɪsˈtʃu esˈtʃu
escort n ˈeskɔt $ ˈeskɔrt
escort v ɪˈskɔt $ ɪˈskɔrt
escutcheon ɪˈskʌtʃən
-ese suffix ˈiz $ ˈis
Eskimo ˈeskɪməʊ
Esmé ˈezmɪ ezˈmeɪ
esophagus iˈsofəgəs ɪˈs-
esoteric ˈesəʊˈterɪk ˈis-
especial ɪˈspeʃl əˈs-
Esperanto ˈespəˈræntəʊ $ -ˈran-
espionage ˈespɪənaʒ -nadʒ
   $ -nɪdʒ ˈespɪəˈnaʒ
esplanade ˈespləneɪd -nad
espouse ɪˈspaʊz
espresso eˈspresəʊ £ ekˈs-
esprit de corps ˈespri də ˈkɔ(r)
   $ eˈspri əˈs- etc

espy ɪˈspaɪ
Esq. ɪˈskwaɪə(r)
-esque suffix ˈesk
esquire ɪˈskwaɪə(r) $ ˈeskwaɪər etc
essay n ˈeseɪ
essay v ɪˈseɪ
essence ˈesns
essential ɪˈsenʃl əˈs-
Essex ˈesɪks
establish ɪˈstæblɪʃ
establishment ɪˈstæblɪʃmənt
estate ɪˈsteɪt
estate agent ɪˈsteɪt eɪdʒənt
estate car ɪˈsteɪt kɑ(r)
esteem ɪˈstim
esthete ˈisθit $ ˈesθit
esthetic ɪsˈθetɪk $ es-
estimable ˈestɪməbl
estimate n ˈestɪmət -meɪt -əmɪt
estimate v ˈestɪmeɪt
estimation ˈestɪˈmeɪʃn
Estonia eˈstəʊnɪə
estrange ɪˈstreɪndʒ
estuary ˈestʃʊərɪ $ -ʊerɪ
etc(etera), &c ɪtˈsetrə ekˈs- ɪkˈs-
$ £ etˈsetrə etc
etch etʃ
etching ˈetʃɪŋ
eternal ɪˈtɜnl
eternity ɪˈtɜnətɪ
ether ˈiθə(r)
ethereal ɪˈθɪərɪəl
ethic ˈeθɪk
ethical ˈeθɪkl
Ethiopia ˈiθɪˈəʊpɪə
ethnic ˈeθnɪk
ethnography eθˈnogrəfɪ
ethnological ˈeθnəˈlodʒɪkl
ethnology eθˈnolədʒɪ
ethos ˈiθos
etiquette ˈetɪket $ -kɪt ˈetɪˈket
Eton ˈitn
-ette suffix ˈet
etymological ˈetɪməˈlodʒɪkl
etymology ˈetɪˈmolədʒɪ
eucalyptus ˈjukəˈlɪptəs
Eucharist ˈjukərɪst
Eugene juˈʒeɪn $ £ juˈdʒin
eugenics juˈdʒenɪks
eulogistic ˈjuləˈdʒɪstɪk
eulogize ˈjulədʒaɪz
eulogy ˈjulədʒɪ
Eunice ˈjunɪs

eunuch ˈjunək $ -nɪk
euphemism ˈjufəmɪzm
euphemistic ˈjufəˈmɪstɪk
euphony ˈjufənɪ
euphoria juˈfɔrɪə
Eurasia juˈreɪʒə
eureka juˈrikə
eurhythmics juˈrɪðmɪks
Europe ˈjʊərəp
European ˈjʊərəˈpɪən
euthanasia ˈjuθəˈneɪzɪə $ -neɪʒə
evacuate ɪˈvækjʊeɪt
evacuation ɪˈvækjʊˈeɪʃn
evacuee ɪˈvækjuˈi
evade ɪˈveɪd
evaluate ɪˈvæljʊeɪt
evaluation ɪˈvæljʊˈeɪʃn
evanescent ˈivəˈnesnt
evangelical ˈivænˈdʒelɪkl
evangelist ɪˈvændʒəlɪst
evaporate ɪˈvæpəreɪt
evaporation ɪˈvæpəˈreɪʃn
evasion ɪˈveɪʒn
evasive ɪˈveɪsɪv -zɪv
eve, E– iv
Evelyn ˈivlɪn $ ˈevlɪn
even ˈivn
evening ˈivnɪŋ
evening dress ˈivnɪŋ ˈdres ˈe- d-
evensong ˈivnsoŋ $ -soŋ
event ɪˈvent əˈv-
eventual ɪˈventʃʊəl əˈv-
eventuality ɪˈventʃʊˈælətɪ əˈv-
ever ˈevə(r)
Everest ˈevərɪst
evergreen ˈevəgrin
everlasting ˈevəˈlastɪŋ $ ˈevərˈlæstɪŋ
evermore ˈevəˈmɔ(r) $ ˈevər-
every ˈevrɪ
everybody ˈevrɪbodɪ
everyday ˈevrɪˈdeɪ
everyone ˈevrɪwʌn
everything ˈevrɪθɪŋ
everywhere ˈevrɪweə(r) $ -hweər etc
evict ɪˈvɪkt
eviction ɪˈvɪkʃn
evidence ˈevɪdəns
evident ˈevɪdənt
evidently ˈevɪdəntlɪ $ -den- ˈevɪˈdentlɪ
evil ˈivl
evil-minded ˈivl ˈmaɪndɪd
evince ɪˈvɪns
evocation ˈivəʊˈkeɪʃn ˈev- -vəˈk-

68 **evocative**

evocative ɪˈvokətɪv
evoke ɪˈvəʊk
evolution ˈiːvəˈluːʃn $ ˈevˈə-
evolutionary ˈiːvəˈluːʃṇərɪ $ ˈevə- -ṇerɪ
evolve ɪˈvɒlv
ewe juː
ewer juːə(r)
exacerbate ɪgˈzæsəbeɪt $ -sərb-
exacerbation ɪgˈzæsəˈbeɪʃn $ -sərˈb-
exact ɪgˈzækt
exactitude ɪgˈzæktɪtjuːd $ -tuːd etc
exaggerate ɪgˈzædʒəreɪt
exaggeration ɪgˈzædʒəˈreɪʃn
exalt ɪgˈzɔːlt £ -ɒlt
exaltation ˈegzɔlˈteɪʃn £ -ɒl-
exam ɪgˈzæm
examination ɪgˈzæmɪˈneɪʃn
examine ɪgˈzæmɪn
example ɪgˈzɑːmpl $ ɪgˈzæmpl
exasperate ɪgˈzæspəreɪt £ -ˈzɑs-
excavate ˈekskəveɪt
excavation ˈekskəˈveɪʃn
excavator ˈekskəveɪtə(r)
exceed ɪkˈsiːd
excel ɪkˈsel
excellence ˈeksələns -sl̩-
excellency, E– ˈeksələnsɪ -sl̩-
excellent ˈeksələnt -sl̩-
excelsior ekˈselsɪɔ(r) $ £ ɪkˈselsɪə(r)
except ɪkˈsept
exception ɪkˈsepʃn
exceptional ɪkˈsepʃnl
excerpt ˈeksəpt
excess ɪkˈses
excessive ɪkˈsesɪv
exchange ɪksˈtʃeɪndʒ
exchequer ɪksˈtʃekə(r) eks-
excise n ˈeksaɪz
excise v ɪkˈsaɪz
excision ɪkˈsɪʒn ek-
excitable ɪkˈsaɪtəbl
excitability ɪkˈsaɪtəˈbɪlətɪ
excite ɪkˈsaɪt
excitement ɪkˈsaɪtmənt
exclaim ɪkˈskleɪm
exclamation ˈekskləˈmeɪʃn
exclamatory ɪksˈklæmətrɪ $ -tɔrɪ
exclude ɪksˈkluːd
exclusion ɪkˈskluːʒn
exclusive ɪkˈskluːsɪv $ -zɪv
excommunicate ˈekskəˈmjuːnɪkeɪt
excommunication ˈekskəˈmjuːnɪˈkeɪʃn
excrement ˈekskrəmənt

excrescence ɪkˈskresns
excreta ɪkˈskriːtə
excrete ɪkˈskriːt
excretion ɪkˈskriːʃn
excruciating ɪkˈskruːʃɪeɪtɪŋ
exculpate ˈekskʌlpeɪt
excursion ɪkˈskɜːʃn $ £ ɪkˈskɜːʒn
excuse n ɪkˈskjuːs
excuse v ɪkˈskjuːz
execrable ˈeksɪkrəbl
execrate ˈeksɪkreɪt
execration ˈeksɪˈkreɪʃn
executant ɪgˈzekjʊtənt
execute ˈeksɪkjuːt
execution ˈeksɪˈkjuːʃn
executive ɪgˈzekjʊtɪv
executor ɪgˈzekjʊtə(r)
exegesis ˈeksɪˈdʒiːsɪs
exemplary ɪgˈzemplərɪ
exemplification ɪgˈzemplɪfɪˈkeɪʃn
exemplify ɪgˈzemplɪfaɪ
exempt ɪgˈzempt
exemption ɪgˈzempʃn
exercise ˈeksəsaɪz
exert ɪgˈzɜːt
exertion ɪgˈzɜːʃn
exhalation ˈekshəˈleɪʃn -səˈl- -sheɪˈl-
exhale eksˈheɪl
exhaust ɪgˈzɔːst
exhaustion ɪgˈzɔːstʃən
exhaustive ɪgˈzɔːstɪv
exhibit ɪgˈzɪbɪt
exhibition ˈeksɪˈbɪʃn
exhilarate ɪgˈzɪləreɪt
exhilaration ɪgˈzɪləˈreɪʃn
exhort ɪgˈzɔːt $ -ˈzɔrt
exhortation ˈeksɔːˈteɪʃn ˈegzɔ-
$ ˈegzər- ˈeksər- -ɔr-
exhumation ˈeksjuːˈmeɪʃn ˈegz-
exhume ɪgˈzjuːm ɪkˈsjuːm eksˈhjuːm
$ ɪgˈzuːm etc
exigency ˈeksɪdʒənsɪ ɪgˈzɪdʒənsɪ ˈegz-
exigent ˈeksɪdʒənt ˈegz-
exile ˈeksaɪl ˈegzaɪl
exist ɪgˈzɪst
existence ɪgˈzɪstəns
existent ɪgˈzɪstənt
existentialism ˈegzɪˈstenʃl̩ɪzm
exit ˈeksɪt
exodus ˈeksədəs
ex officio ˈeks əˈfɪʃɪəʊ
exonerate ɪgˈzonəreɪt
exoneration ɪgˈzonəˈreɪʃn

exorbitant ɪg'zɔbɪtənt $ -'zɔrb-
exorcize 'eksɔsaɪz 'eksəs- $ -sɔrs -sərs-
exotic ɪg'zotɪk
expand ɪk'spænd
expanse ɪk'spæns
expansion ɪk'spænʃn
expansive ɪk'spænsɪv
expatiate ɪk'speɪʃɪeɪt
expatriate eks'pætrɪeɪt
expect ɪk'spekt
expectancy ɪk'spektənsɪ
expectant ɪk'spektənt
expectation 'ekspek'teɪʃn
expectorate ɪk'spektəreɪt
expediency ɪk'spidɪənsɪ
expedient ɪk'spidɪənt
expedite 'ekspɪdaɪt
expedition 'ekspɪ'dɪʃn
expeditionary 'ekspɪ'dɪʃnrɪ $ -n̩erɪ
expeditious 'ekspɪ'dɪʃəs
expel ɪk'spel
expend ɪk'spend
expenditure ɪk'spendɪtʃə(r)
expense ɪk'spens
expense account ɪk'spens əkaʊnt
expensive ɪk'spensɪv
experience ɪk'spɪərɪəns
experiment n ɪk'sperɪmənt
experiment v ɪk'sperɪment
experimental ɪk'sperɪ'mentl
expert 'ekspɜt
expertise 'ekspɜ'tiz
expiate 'ekspɪeɪt
expiation 'ekspɪ'eɪʃn
expiration 'ekspɪ'reɪʃn
expire ɪk'spaɪə(r)
expiry ɪk'spaɪərɪ
 $ 'ek- 'ekspaɪərɪ 'ekspərɪ
explain ɪk'spleɪn
explanation 'eksplə'neɪʃn
explanatory ɪk'splænətrɪ $ -tɔrɪ
expletive ɪk'splitɪv $ 'eksplɪtɪv
explicable 'eksplɪkəbl ek'splɪkəbl
explicit ɪk'splɪsɪt
explode ɪk'spləʊd
exploit n 'eksplɔɪt
exploit v ɪk'splɔɪt
explore ɪk'splɔ(r)
exploration 'eksplə'reɪʃn -plɔr-
exploratory ɪk'splɔrətrɪ -plor- $ -tɔrɪ
explosion ɪk'spləʊʒn
explosive ɪk'spləʊsɪv -zɪv
exponent ɪk'spəʊnənt

export n 'ekspɔt $ 'ekspɔrt
export v ɪk'spɔt $ ɪk'spɔrt
exportation 'ekspɔ'teɪʃn $ -spɔr-
expose ɪk'spəʊz
exposé ek'spəʊzeɪ $ 'ekspəʊ'zeɪ
exposition 'ekspə'zɪʃn
expostulate ɪk'spostʃʊleɪt
exposure ɪk'spəʊʒə(r)
expound ɪk'spaʊnd
express ɪk'spres
expression ɪk'spreʃn
expressionism ɪk'spreʃn̩ɪzm
expressive ɪk'spresɪv
expropriate eks'prəʊprɪeɪt
expropriation 'eks'prəʊprɪ'eɪʃn
expulsion ɪk'spʌlʃn
expunge ɪk'spʌndʒ
expurgate 'ekspəgeɪt $ -spər-
exquisite ɪk'skwɪzɪt ek- 'ekswɪzɪt
ex-service eks 'sɜvɪs
extant ek'stænt $ £ 'ekstənt -stænt etc
extemporaneous 'eks'tempə'reɪnɪəs
extemporary ɪk'stempərərɪ -prɪ $ -pərerɪ
extempore ɪk'stempərɪ
extend ɪk'stend
extension ɪk'stenʃn
extensive ɪk'stensɪv
extent ɪk'stent
extenuate ɪk'stenjʊeɪt
exterior ɪk'stɪərɪə(r)
exterminate ɪk'stɜmɪneɪt
extermination ɪk'stɜmɪ'neɪʃn
external ek'stɜnl
extinct ɪk'stɪŋkt
extinction ɪk'stɪŋkʃn
extinguish ɪk'stɪŋgwɪʃ
extirpate 'ekstəpeɪt $ -stərp-
extol ɪk'stəʊl
extort ɪk'stɔt $ ɪk'stɔrt
extortion ɪk'stɔʃn $ ɪk'stɔrʃn
extortionate ɪk'stɔʃnət $ -'stɔr-
extra 'ekstrə
extra- prefix 'ekstrə
extract n 'ekstrækt
extract v ɪk'strækt
extraction ɪk'strækʃn
extradite 'ekstrədaɪt
extradition 'ekstrə'dɪʃn
extramarital 'ekstrə'mærɪtl
extramural 'ekstrə'mjʊərl
extraneous ɪk'streɪnɪəs
extraordinarily ɪk'strɔdnrəlɪ
 $ ɪk'strɔrdn̩'erəlɪ

extraordinary ık'strɔdnrı $ -'ɔrdn̩erı
extra-ordinary 'ekstrə 'ɔdnrı
$ 'ɔrdn̩erı
extrasensory 'ekstrə'sensərı
extravagance ık'strævəgəns -vıg-
extravagant ık'strævəgənt -vıg-
extreme ık'strim
extremist ık'strimıst
extremity ık'stremətı
extricate 'ekstrıkeıt
extrinsic ek'strınsık -zık
extrovert 'ekstrəvɜt -trəʊv-
extrude ık'strud
extrusion ık'struʒn
exuberance ıg'zjubərəns $ -'zu-
exuberant ıg'zjubərənt $ -'zu-
exude ıg'zjud $ -'zud
exult ıg'zʌlt

exultant ıg'zʌltənt
exultation 'egzʌl'teıʃn
eye aı
eyeball 'aıbɔl
eye-bath 'aı baθ $ 'aı bæθ
eyebrow 'aıbraʊ
eyeful 'aı-fʊl
eyelash 'aılæʃ
eyelet 'aılət -lıt
eyelid 'aılıd
eye-opener 'aı əʊpnə(r)
eyepiece 'aı-pis
eyesight 'aı-saıt
eyesore 'aı-sɔ(r)
eye-strain 'aı streın
eye-wash 'aı wɒʃ
eye-witness 'aı wıtnəs aı 'wıtnəs -nıs
eyrie 'aıərı 'eərı

F

F f ef
fa fɑ
Fabian 'feıbıən
fable 'feıbl
fabric 'fæbrık
fabricate 'fæbrıkeıt
fabrication 'fæbrı'keıʃn
fabulous 'fæbjʊləs -jəl-
façade fæ'sad fə'sad
face feıs
face-lift 'feıs lıft
facet 'fæsıt -et -ət
facetious fə'siʃəs
facial 'feıʃl
facile 'fæsaıl $ -sl
facilitate fə'sılıteıt
facility fə'sılətı
facsimile fæk'sıməlı -mılı
fact fækt
faction 'fækʃn
factious 'fækʃəs
factitious fæk'tıʃəs
factor 'fæktə(r)
factory 'fæktrı -tr̩ı
factotum fæk'təʊtəm
factual 'fæktʃʊəl
faculty 'fækltı
fad fæd
fade feıd

faeces 'fisiz
fag fæg
fag-end fæg 'end 'fæg end
faggot 'fægət
Fahrenheit 'færənhaıt 'far-
fail feıl
failure 'feıljə(r)
faint feınt
fair feə(r)
fair-haired 'feə 'heəd $ 'feər 'heərd
fair-minded 'feə 'maındıd $ 'feər
fairy 'feərı
fairy-tale 'feərı teıl
fait accompli 'feıt ə'komplı $ əkom'pli
faith, F– feıθ
faith-healer 'feıθ hilə(r)
fake feık
fakir 'feıkıə(r) 'fækıə(r) 'fakıə(r)
$ fə'kıər fa- fæ-
falcon 'fɔlkən $ £ 'fælkən
fall fɔl
fallacious fə'leıʃəs
fallacy 'fæləsı
fallen 'fɔlən
fallibility 'fælə'bılətı
fallible 'fæləbl
fall-out 'fɔl aʊt
fallow 'fæləʊ
false fɔls £ fols

false alarm 'fɔls ə`lam £ 'fɔls $ ə`larm
falsehood `fɔlshʊd £ `fol-
false teeth 'fɔls `tiθ £ 'fɔls
falsetto fɔl`setəʊ £ fol-
falsify `fɔlsɪfaɪ £ `fol-
falsity `fɔlsətɪ £ `fol-
Falstaff `fɔlstaf £ `fol- $ -stæf
falter `fɔltə(r) £ `fol-
fame feɪm
familiar fə`mɪlɪə(r)
familiarity fə`mɪlɪ`ærətɪ
familiarize fə`mɪlɪəraɪz
family `fæmļɪ -məlɪ
family man `fæmļɪ mæn -məlɪ
family name `fæmļɪ neɪm -məlɪ
famine `fæmɪn
famish `fæmɪʃ
famous `feɪməs
fan fæn
fanatic fə`nætɪk
fanaticism fə`nætɪsɪzm
fancier `fænsɪə(r)
fanciful `fænsɪfl
fancy `fænsɪ
fancy-free 'fænsɪ `fri
fancy-work `fænsɪwɜk
fanfare `fænfeə(r)
fang fæŋ
fan-light `fæn laɪt
fantasia 'fæntə`zɪə fæn`teɪzɪə
  $ fæn`teɪʒə etc
fantastic fæn`tæstɪk
fantasy `fæntəsɪ -əzɪ
far fa(r)
far-away 'far ə`weɪ
farce fas $ fars
farcical `fasɪkl $ `fars-
fare feə(r)
farewell feə`wel $ feər-
far-fetched 'fa `fetʃt $ 'far
far-flung 'fa `flʌŋ $ 'far
farinaceous `færɪ`neɪʃəs
farm fam $ farm
farm-hand `fam hænd $ `farm
farmhouse `famhaʊs $ `farm-
farmyard `famjad $ `farmjard
far-off 'far `of $ £ `ɔf
farrago fə`ragəʊ
far-reaching 'fa `ritʃɪŋ $ 'far
farrow `færəʊ
farther `faðə(r) $ `farðər
farthest `faðɪst -ðəst $ `far-
farthing `faðɪŋ $ `farðɪŋ

fascia `feɪʃə `fæʃɪə
fascinate `fæsɪneɪt $ £ -sņ-
fascination `fæsɪ`neɪʃn $ £ -sņ-
Fascism `fæʃɪzm
fashion `fæʃn
fashionable `fæʃnəbl -ņ-
fashion-plate `fæʃn pleɪt
fast fast $ fæst
fasten `fasn $ `fæsn
fastener `fasnə(r) $ `fæsnər
fastidious fə`stɪdɪəs $ fæ-
fat fæt
fatal `feɪtl
fatalism `feɪtļɪzm
fatality fə`tælətɪ
fate feɪt
fat-head `fæt hed
father `faðə(r)
fatherhood `faðəhʊd $ `faðər-
father-in-law `faðr ɪn lɔ
fatherland `faðəlænd $ `faðər-
fathom `fæðəm
fatigue fə`tig
fatten `fætn
fatty `fætɪ
fatuous `fætʃʊəs £ -tjʊ-
faucet `fɔsɪt -sət
fault fɔlt £ folt
faun fɔn
fauna `fɔnə
Faust faʊst
Faustus `faʊstəs `fɔstəs
faux pas 'fəʊ `pa
favour($ -or) `feɪvə(r)
favourable($ -or-) `feɪvrəbl
favourite($ -or-) `feɪvrɪt -rət
favouritism($ -or-) `feɪvrɪtɪzm -rət-
fawn fɔn
fay feɪ
FBI 'ef bi `aɪ
fear fɪə(r)
fearsome `fɪəsm $ `fɪərsm
feasibility 'fizə`bɪlətɪ
feasible `fizəbl
feast fist
feat fit
feather `feðə(r)
feather-bed 'feðə `bed $ 'feðər
feather-weight `feðə weɪt $ `feðər
feature `fitʃə(r)
feature film `fitʃə film $ `fitʃər
February `februərɪ -bjʊ- -bŗɪ
  $ `februerɪ -bjʊ-

feces ˈfisiz
feckless ˈfekləs
fecund ˈfikənd ˈfekənd
fecundity fɪˈkʌndətɪ
fed fed
federal ˈfedrl
federate ˈfedəreɪt
federation ˌfedəˈreɪʃn
fee fi
feeble ˈfibl
feeble-minded ˈfibl ˈmaɪndɪd
feed fid
feeding-bottle ˈfidɪŋ botl
feel fil
feet fit
feign feɪn
feint feɪnt
feldspar ˈfeldspɑ(r)
felicitate fəˈlɪsɪteɪt
felicitation fəˌlɪsɪˈteɪʃn
felicitous fəˈlɪsɪtəs
felicity, F– fəˈlɪsətɪ
feline ˈfilaɪn
fell fel
fellow ˈfeləʊ *very colloq in the sense of 'person' only:* ˈfelə
fellow-countryman ˈfeləʊ ˈkʌntrɪmən
fellow-feeling ˈfeləʊ ˈfilɪŋ
fellow-men ˈfeləʊ ˈmen
fellowship ˈfeləʊʃɪp
fellow-traveller ˈfeləʊ ˈtrævlə(r)
felon ˈfelən
felonious fɪˈləʊnɪəs
felony ˈfelənɪ
felt felt
female ˈfimeɪl
feminine ˈfemənɪn
feminism ˈfemɪnɪzm
feminity ˈfeməˈnɪnətɪ
femur ˈfimə(r)
fen fen
fence fens
fend fend
fender ˈfendə(r)
fennel ˈfenl
Ferdinand ˈfɜdɪnənd $ £ -nænd
ferment *n* ˈfɜment
ferment *v* fɜˈment
fern fɜn
ferocious fəˈrəʊʃəs fɪ-
ferocity fəˈrosətɪ fɪ-
ferret ˈferɪt -ət
ferro-concrete ˈferəʊ ˈkoŋkrit

ferrous ˈferəs
ferrule ˈferl -rul
ferry ˈferɪ
ferry-boat ˈferɪ bəʊt
fertile ˈfɜtaɪl $ ˈfɜtl
fertilisation ˌfɜtɪlaɪˈzeɪʃn -tl̩- $ ˈfɜtl̩ˈzeɪʃn
fertilize ˈfɜtɪlaɪz $ £ -tl̩-
fertilizer ˈfɜtɪlaɪzə(r) $ £ -tl̩-
fervent ˈfɜvənt
fervour($ -or) ˈfɜvə(r)
festal ˈfestl
fester ˈfestə(r)
festival ˈfestɪvl
festive ˈfestɪv
festivity feˈstɪvətɪ
festoon feˈstun
fetch fetʃ
fête feɪt
fetid ˈfetɪd ˈfi-
fetish ˈfetɪʃ ˈfi-
fetlock ˈfetlok
fetter ˈfetə(r)
fettle ˈfetl
fetus ˈfitəs
feud fjud
feudal ˈfjudl
fever ˈfivə(r)
few fju
fez fez
fiancé(e) fɪˈ̃ɔseɪ -ˈɔns- -ˈɔns- -ˈ̃ɔs- $ ˈfiɑ̃nˈseɪ ˈfion- ˈfiɔ̃-
fiasco fiˈæskəʊ
fiat ˈfaɪæt -ət $ ˈfiat
Fiat *car* ˈfiət ˈfiæt $ ˈfiat *etc*
fib fɪb
fibre($ -ber) ˈfaɪbə(r)
fibre-glass($ -ber) ˈfaɪbə glas $ ˈfaɪbər glæs
fibrositis ˌfaɪbrəˈsaɪtɪs -təs
fibrous ˈfaɪbrəs
fibula ˈfɪbjʊlə
fickle ˈfɪkl
fiction ˈfɪkʃn
fictitious fɪkˈtɪʃəs
fiddle ˈfɪdl
fiddlesticks ˈfɪdlstɪks
Fidelio fɪˈdeɪlɪəʊ
fidelity fɪˈdelətɪ
fidget ˈfɪdʒɪt -ət
fie faɪ
fief fif
field fild

field-day ˈfild deɪ
field-glasses ˈfild glɑsɪz $ glæsɪz
field-hospital 'fild ˈhospɪtl
field-mouse ˈfild məʊs
fieldwork ˈfildwɜk
fiend find
fierce fɪəs
fiery ˈfaɪərɪ
fiesta fɪˈestə
fife, F– faɪf
fifteen 'fɪfˈtin
fifteenth 'fɪfˈtinθ
fifth fɪfθ
fifth column 'fɪfθ ˈkoləm
fiftieth ˈfɪftɪəθ
fifty ˈfɪftɪ
fifty-fifty 'fɪftɪ ˈfɪftɪ
fifty-one 'fɪftɪ ˈwʌn
fig fɪg
Figaro ˈfɪgərəʊ ˈfi-
fig-leaf ˈfɪg lif
fight faɪt
figment ˈfɪgmənt
figurative ˈfɪgrətɪv $ £ ˈfɪgjərətɪv etc
figure ˈfɪgə(r) $ ˈfɪgjər
figure-head ˈfɪgə hed $ ˈfɪgjər
figure of speech 'fɪgər əv ˈspitʃ
    $ ˈfɪgjər
Fiji fiˈdʒi ˈfidʒi
filament ˈfɪləmənt
filch fɪltʃ
file faɪl
filial ˈfɪlɪəl
filibuster ˈfɪlɪbʌstə(r)
filigree ˈfɪlɪgri
filings ˈfaɪlɪŋz
fill fɪl
fillet ˈfɪlɪt
filling-station ˈfɪlɪŋ steɪʃn
fillip ˈfɪlɪp
filly ˈfɪlɪ
film fɪlm
film-star ˈfɪlm stɑ(r)
film-strip ˈfɪlm strɪp
filter ˈfɪltə(r)
filter-paper ˈfɪltə peɪpə(r) $ ˈfɪltər
filter-tip ˈfɪltə tɪp $ ˈfɪltər
filth fɪlθ
filthy ˈfɪlθɪ
filtrate ˈfɪltreɪt
filtration 'fɪlˈtreɪʃn
fin fɪn
final ˈfaɪnl

finale fɪˈnɑlɪ -leɪ
finalist ˈfaɪnl̩ɪst
finality faɪˈnælətɪ fɪˈn-
finalize ˈfaɪnl̩aɪz
finance ˈfaɪnæns fɪˈnæns faɪˈn-
financial faɪˈnænʃl fɪˈn-
financier faɪˈnænsɪə(r) fɪˈn-
    $ 'faɪnænˈsɪər -nən- 'fɪn-
finch fɪntʃ
find faɪnd
fine faɪn
fine arts 'faɪn ˈats $ ˈarts
finery ˈfaɪnərɪ
finesse fɪˈnes
finger ˈfɪŋgə(r)
finger-bowl ˈfɪŋgə bəʊl $ ˈfɪŋgər
finger-nail ˈfɪŋgə neɪl $ ˈfɪŋgər
finger-print ˈfɪŋgə prɪnt $ ˈfɪŋgər
finger-stall ˈfɪŋgə stɔl $ ˈfɪŋgər
finger-tip ˈfɪŋgə tɪp $ ˈfɪŋgər
finical ˈfɪnɪkl
finicky ˈfɪnɪkɪ
finis ˈfɪnɪs $ ˈfaɪnɪs etc
finish ˈfɪnɪʃ
finite ˈfaɪnaɪt
Finn fɪn
fire ˈfaɪə(r)
fire-alarm ˈfaɪər əlam $ əlarm
fire-arms ˈfaɪər amz $ armz
fire-brand ˈfaɪə brænd $ ˈfaɪər
fire-brick ˈfaɪə brɪk $ ˈfaɪər
fire-brigade ˈfaɪə brɪgeɪd $ ˈfaɪər
fireclay ˈfaɪəkleɪ $ ˈfaɪərkleɪ
fire-cracker ˈfaɪə krækə(r) $ ˈfaɪər
fire-damp ˈfaɪə dæmp $ ˈfaɪər
fire-eater ˈfaɪər itə(r)
fire-engine ˈfaɪər endʒɪn
fire-extinguisher ˈfaɪər ɪkstɪŋgwɪʃə(r)
fire-fighter ˈfaɪə faɪtə(r) $ ˈfaɪər
firefly ˈfaɪəflaɪ $ ˈfaɪər
fire-guard ˈfaɪə gad $ ˈfaɪər gard
fire-hose ˈfaɪə həʊz $ ˈfaɪər
fire-irons ˈfaɪər aɪənz $ aɪərnz
fire-light ˈfaɪə laɪt $ ˈfaɪər
fireman ˈfaɪəmən $ ˈfaɪərmən
fire-place ˈfaɪə pleɪs $ ˈfaɪər
fire-power ˈfaɪə paʊə(r) $ ˈfaɪər
fire-proof ˈfaɪə pruf $ ˈfaɪər
fire-side ˈfaɪə saɪd $ ˈfaɪər
fire-water ˈfaɪə wɔtə(r) $ ˈfaɪər
firewood ˈfaɪəwʊd $ ˈfaɪər-
firework ˈfaɪəwɜk $ ˈfaɪər-
firing-line ˈfaɪərɪŋ laɪn

firm fɜm
firmament ˋfɜməmənt
first fɜst
first-aid 'fɜst ˋeɪd
first-born ˋfɜst bɔn $ ˋbɔrn
first class 'fɜs ˋklɑs $ ˋklæs
first floor 'fɜst ˋflɔ(r)
first-fruits ˋfɜst fruts
first-hand 'fɜst ˋhænd
first name 'fɜst ˋneɪm
first offender 'fɜst əˋfendə(r)
first rate 'fɜst ˋreɪt
first sight, at ət 'fɜst ˋsaɪt
Firth fɜθ
fiscal ˋfɪskl
fish fɪʃ
fish-bone ˋfɪʃ bəʊn
fisherman 'fɪʃəmən $ -ʃər-
fishery ˋfɪʃərɪ
fish-hook ˋfɪʃ hʊk
fishpond ˋfɪʃpond
fishing-tackle ˋfɪʃɪŋ tækl
fish-knife ˋfɪʃ naɪf
fishmonger ˋfɪʃmʌŋgə(r)
fishing-rod ˋfɪʃɪŋ rod
fish-slice ˋfɪʃ slaɪs
fishwife ˋfɪʃwaɪf
fissile ˋfɪsaɪl $ ˋfɪsl
fission ˋfɪʃn
fissiparous fɪˋsɪpərəs
fissure ˋfɪʃə(r)
fist fɪst
fisticuffs ˋfɪstɪkʌfs
fit fɪt
fits and starts 'fɪts n ˋstɑts $ ˋstɑrts
fitful ˋfɪtfl
fitment ˋfɪtmənt
FitzGerald fɪtsˋdʒerld
five faɪv
fivepence ˋfaɪfpəns $ ˋfaɪvpens
fivepenny ˋfaɪfpənɪ $ ˋfaɪvpenɪ
fiver ˋfaɪvə(r)
fix fɪks
fixation fɪkˋseɪʃn
fixture ˋfɪkstʃə(r)
fizz fɪz
fizzle ˋfɪzl
fjord ˋfjɔd fɪˋɔd $ -ɔrd
flabbergast ˋflæbəgɑst $ -bərgæst
flabby ˋflæbɪ
flaccid ˋflæksɪd
flaccidity flækˋsɪdətɪ
flag flæg

flag-day ˋflæg deɪ
flagellation 'flædʒɪˋleɪʃn
flagon ˋflægən
flag-pole ˋflæg pəʊl
flagrant ˋfleɪgrənt
flag ship ˋflæg ʃɪp
flag staff ˋflæg stɑf $ stæf
flail fleɪl
flair fleə(r)
flake fleɪk
flamboyant flæmˋbɔɪənt
flame fleɪm
flamingo fləˋmɪŋgəʊ
flan flæn
flange flændʒ
flank flæŋk
flannel ˋflænl
flannelette 'flænlˋet
flap flæp
flapjack ˋflæpdʒæk
flare fleə(r)
flare-up n ˋfleər ʌp
flash flæʃ
flash-back ˋflæʃ bæk
flash-light ˋflæʃ laɪt
flash-point ˋflæʃ pɔɪnt
flask flɑsk $ flæsk
flat flæt
flat-bottomed 'flæt ˋbotəmd
flat-fish ˋflæt fɪʃ
flat-footed 'flæt ˋfʊtɪd
flatlet ˋflætlət
flat racing ˋflæt reɪsɪŋ
flatten ˋflætn
flatter ˋflætə(r)
flatulence ˋflætjʊləns $ ˋflætʃʊləns
flatulent ˋflætjʊlənt $ ˋflætʃʊlənt
flaunt flɔnt
flautist ˋflɔtɪst
flavour($ -or) ˋfleɪvə(r)
flaw flɔ
flax flæks
flaxen ˋflæksn
flay fleɪ
flea fli
flea-bite ˋfli baɪt
fleck flek
fled fled
fledged fledʒd
fledgeling ˋfledʒlɪŋ
flee fli
fleece flis
fleecy ˋflisɪ

fleet flit
Fleet Street ˋflit strit
Fleming ˋflemɪŋ
Flemish ˋflemɪʃ
flesh fleʃ
flesh and blood 'fleʃ n ˋblʌd
flesh-pot ˋfleʃ pot
flesh-wound ˋfleʃ wund
fleur-de-lis 'flɜ də ˋli
flew flu
flex fleks
flexible ˋfleksəbl
flexibility 'fleksəˋbɪlətɪ
flibbertigibbet 'flɪbətɪˋdʒɪbɪt $ -bərt-
flick flɪk
flicker ˋflɪkə(r)
flight flaɪt
flight-deck ˋflaɪt dek
flimsy ˋflɪmzɪ
flinch flɪntʃ
fling flɪŋ
flint flɪnt
flintstone ˋflɪntstəun
flip flɪp
flippant ˋflɪpənt
flippancy ˋflɪpənsɪ
flip-side ˋflɪp saɪd
flirt flɜt
flirtation flɜˋteɪʃn
flirtatious flɜˋteɪʃəs
flit flɪt
flitch flɪtʃ
float fləut
flock flok
flog flog $ flɔg etc
flood flʌd
flood-gate ˋflʌd geɪt
flood-light ˋflʌd laɪt
flood-lit ˋflʌd lɪt
floor flɔ(r)
floor-cloth ˋflɔ kloθ $ ˋflɔr
floor-show ˋflɔ ʃəu $ ˋflɔr
floor-walker ˋflɔ wɔkə(r) $ ˋflɔr
flop flop
floppy ˋflopɪ
flora, F– ˋflɔrə
floral ˋflɔrl £ ˋflorl
Florence ˋflorns $ ˋflɔrns
florid ˋflorɪd $ ˋflɔrɪd
Florida ˋflorɪdə $ ˋflɔrɪdə
florin ˋflorɪn $ ˋflɔrɪn
florist ˋflorɪst $ ˋflɔrɪst
floss flos

flotilla fləˋtɪlə fləu-
flotsam ˋflotsəm
flounce flauns
flounder ˋflaundə(r)
flour ˋflauə(r)
flourish ˋflʌrɪʃ $ ˋflɜɪʃ
flout flaut
flow fləu
flower ˋflauə(r)
flower-bed ˋflauə bed $ ˋflauər
flower-girl ˋflauə gɜl $ 'flauər
flower-pot ˋflauə pot $ ˋflauər
flown fləun
flu flu
fluctuate ˋflʌktʃueɪt
fluctuation 'flʌktʃuˋeɪʃn
flue flu
fluency ˋfluənsɪ
fluent ˋfluənt
fluff flʌf
fluid ˋfluɪd
fluidity fluˋɪdətɪ
fluke fluk
flummox ˋflʌməks
flung flʌŋ
flunk(e)y ˋflʌŋkɪ
fluorescent fluəˋresnt
flurry ˋflʌrɪ $ ˋflɜɪ
flush flʌʃ
fluster ˋflʌstə(r)
flute flut
flutter ˋflʌtə(r)
fluvial ˋfluvɪəl
flux flʌks
fly flaɪ
fly-blown ˋflaɪ bləun
fly-catcher ˋflaɪ kætʃə(r)
flyer ˋflaɪə(r)
fly-leaf ˋflaɪ lif
fly-over ˋflaɪ əuvə(r)
fly-paper ˋflaɪ peɪpə(r)
fly-swatter ˋflaɪ swotə(r)
fly-trap ˋflaɪ træp
fly-wheel ˋflaɪ wil $ hwil etc
foal fəul
foam fəum
fob fob
focal ˋfəukl
foci ˋfəusaɪ £ ˋfəuki -kaɪ
fo'c'sle ˋfəuksl
focus ˋfəukəs
fodder ˋfodə(r)
foe fəu

foetus ˈfiːtəs
fog fog $ fɔg etc
fog-bank ˈfog bæŋk $ ˈfɔg etc
fog-bound ˈfog baʊnd $ ˈfɔg etc
fogey ˈfəʊgɪ
foggy ˈfogɪ $ ˈfɔgɪ etc
fog-horn ˈfog hɔn $ ˈfɔg etc hɔrn
fog-signal ˈfog sɪgnl $ ˈfɔg etc
foible ˈfɔɪbl
foil fɔɪl
foist fɔɪst
fold fəʊld
-fold suffix fəʊld $ ˈfəʊld
folder ˈfəʊldə(r)
foliage ˈfəʊlɪɪdʒ
folio ˈfəʊlɪəʊ
folk fəʊk
folk-dance ˈfəʊk dɑns $ dæns
folk-lore ˈfəʊk lɔ(r)
folk-song ˈfəʊk soŋ $ sɔŋ
folk-tale ˈfəʊk teɪl
follow ˈfoləʊ
folly ˈfolɪ
foment fəˈment $ £ fəʊˈment
fond fond
fondant ˈfondənt
fondle ˈfondl
font font
food fud
food-stuff ˈfud stʌf
fool ful
foolery ˈfulərɪ
foolhardy ˈfulhadɪ $ -hardɪ
foolish ˈfulɪʃ
fool-proof ˈful pruf
foolscap ˈful-skæp
fool's cap ˈfulz kæp
fool's paradise 'fulz ˈpærədaɪs
foot fʊt
foot-and-mouth disease
  'fʊt n ˈmaʊθ dɪziz
football ˈfʊtbɔl
foot-bridge ˈfʊt brɪdʒ
footfall ˈfʊtfɔl
foot-hills ˈfʊt hɪlz
foothold ˈfʊthəʊld
footing ˈfʊtɪŋ
footlights ˈfʊt laɪts
footman ˈfʊtmən
footnote ˈfʊt nəʊt
foot-pad ˈfʊt pæd
foot-path ˈfʊt pɑθ $ pæθ
foot-plate ˈfʊt pleɪt

footprint ˈfʊtprɪnt
foot-race ˈfʊt reɪs
footsore ˈfʊtsɔ(r)
footstep ˈfʊtstep
footstool ˈfʊtstul
footsure ˈfʊt-ʃʊə(r) £ -ʃɔ(r)
footwear ˈfʊtweə(r)
footwork ˈfʊtwɜk
fop fop
for usual form: fə(r) strong-form: fɔ(r)
forage ˈforɪdʒ $ ˈfɔrɪdʒ
foray ˈforeɪ $ ˈfɔreɪ
forbade fəˈbæd -ˈbeɪd $ fər-
forbear fəˈbeə(r) $ fər-
forbearance fɔˈbeərns $ fɔr-
forbid fəˈbɪd $ fərˈbɪd
forbore fɔˈbɔ(r) $ fɔr-
force fɔs $ fɔrs
forceful ˈfɔsfl $ ˈfɔrsfl
force-meat ˈfɔs mit $ ˈfɔrs
forceps ˈfɔseps $ ˈfɔr-
forcible ˈfɔsəbl $ ˈfɔr-
ford fɔd $ fɔrd
fore fɔ(r)
fore- prefix fɔ(r)
forearm 'fɔram $ ˈfɔrarm
foreboding fɔˈbəʊdɪŋ $ fɔr-
forecast ˈfɔkast $ ˈfɔrkæst
forecastle(= fo'c'sle) ˈfəʊksl
foreclose fɔˈkləʊz $ fɔr-
forecourt ˈfɔkɔt $ ˈfɔrkɔrt
foredoom fɔˈdum $ fɔr-
forefathers ˈfɔfaðəz $ ˈfɔrfaðərz
forefinger ˈfɔfɪŋgə(r) $ ˈfɔr-
forefeet ˈfɔfit $ ˈfɔrfit
forefront ˈfɔfrʌnt $ ˈfɔr-
foregather fɔˈgæðə(r) $ fɔr-
forego fɔˈgəʊ $ fɔr-
foregone fɔˈgon $ fɔrˈgɔn
foreground ˈfɔgraʊnd $ ˈfɔr-
forehand ˈfɔhænd $ ˈfɔr-
forehead ˈforɪd ˈfɔhed $ ˈfɔrhed
foreign ˈforən -ɪn $ ˈfɔr-
foreigner ˈforənə -ɪnə $ ˈfɔr-
foreland ˈfɔlənd $ ˈfɔr-
forelegs ˈfɔlegz $ ˈfɔr-
forelock ˈfɔlok $ ˈfɔr-
foreman ˈfɔmən $ ˈfɔr-
foremast ˈfɔmast $ ˈfɔrmæst
foremost ˈfɔməʊst $ ˈfɔr-
forename ˈfɔneɪm $ ˈfɔr-
forenoon ˈfɔnun $ ˈfɔr-
forensic fəˈrensɪk -zɪk

fox 77

forerunner ˈfɔrʌnə(r)
foresail ˈfɔseɪl ˈfɔsl $ ˈfɔr-
foresee fɔˈsi $ fɔrˈsi
foreshadow fɔˈʃædəʊ $ fɔr-
foreshore ˈfɔʃɔ(r) $ ˈfɔrʃɔr
foreshorten fɔˈʃɔtn $ fɔrˈʃɔrtn
foresight ˈfɔsaɪt $ ˈfɔr-
foreskin ˈfɔskɪn $ ˈfɔr-
forest ˈfɒrɪst $ ˈfɔrɪst etc
forestall fɔˈstɔl $ ˈfɔr-
forestry ˈfɒrɪstrɪ $ ˈfɔr- etc
foretaste ˈfɔteɪst $ ˈfɔr-
foretell fɔˈtel $ fɔr-
forethought ˈfɔθɔt $ ˈfɔr-
foretold fɔˈtəʊld $ ˈfɔr-
forever fəˈrevə(r)
forewarn fɔˈwɔn $ fɔrˈwɔrn
foreword ˈfɔwɜd $ ˈfɔr-
forfeit ˈfɔfɪt $ ˈfɔr-
forgather fɔˈgæðə(r) $ fɔr-
forgave fəˈgeɪv $ fər-
forge fɔdʒ $ fɔrdʒ
forgery ˈfɔdʒərɪ $ ˈfɔr-
forget fəˈget $ fər-
forgetful fəˈgetfl $ fər-
forget-me-not fəˈget mɪ nɒt $ fər-
forgive fəˈgɪv $ fər-
forgiven fəˈgɪvn $ fər-
forgo fɔˈgəʊ $ fɔr-
forgot fəˈgɒt $ fər-
forgotten fəˈgɒtn $ fər-
fork fɔk $ fɔrk
fork-lift ˈfɔk lɪft $ ˈfɔrk
forlorn fəˈlɔn $ fərˈlɔrn
form fɔm $ fɔrm
formal ˈfɔml $ ˈfɔrml
formality fɔˈmælətɪ $ fɔr-
format ˈfɔmæt £ -mə $ ˈfɔr-
formation fɔˈmeɪʃn $ fɔr-
formative ˈfɔmətɪv $ ˈfɔr-
former ˈfɔmə(r) $ ˈfɔr-
formic ˈfɔmɪk $ ˈfɔr-
formidable ˈfɔmɪdəbl £ fəˈmɪdəbl $ ˈfɔr-
Formosa fɔˈməʊsə -zə $ fɔr-
formula ˈfɔmjʊlə $ ˈfɔr-
formulae ˈfɔmjʊli -laɪ $ ˈfɔr-
formulate ˈfɔmjʊleɪt $ ˈfɔr-
formulation ˈfɔmjʊˈleɪʃn $ ˈfɔr-
fornicate ˈfɔnɪkeɪt $ ˈfɔr-
forsake fəˈseɪk $ fər-
forsaken fəˈseɪkən $ fər-
forsooth fəˈsuθ $ fər-
forswear fɔˈsweə(r) $ fɔr-

forsworn fɔˈswɔn $ fɔrˈswɔrn
fort fɔt $ fɔrt
forte ˈfɔteɪ $ ˈfɔrteɪ
forte strong point ˈfɔteɪ $ £ ˈfɔrt etc
forth fɔθ $ fɔrθ
forthcoming fɔθˈkʌmɪŋ $ fɔrθ-
forthright ˈfɔθraɪt $ ˈfɔrθ-
forthwith fɔθˈwɪθ -ˈwɪð $ ˈfɔrθ-
fortieth ˈfɔtɪəθ $ ˈfɔr-
fortification ˈfɔtɪfɪˈkeɪʃn $ ˈfɔr-
fortify ˈfɔtɪfaɪ $ ˈfɔr-
fortissimo fɔˈtɪsɪməʊ $ fɔr-
fortitude ˈfɔtɪtjud $ ˈfɔrtɪtud
fortnight ˈfɔtnaɪt $ ˈfɔrt-
fortress ˈfɔtrɪs -trəs with tr as in 'try'
fortuitous fɔˈtjuɪtəs $ fɔrˈtuɪtəs
fortunate ˈfɔtʃʊnət $ ˈfɔrt-
fortune ˈfɔtʃun -tʃən £ -tjun $ ˈfɔr-
fortune-hunter ˈfɔtʃən hʌntə(r) £ -tʃun $ ˈfɔr-
fortune-teller ˈfɔtʃən telə(r) -tʃun $ ˈfɔr-
forty ˈfɔtɪ $ ˈfɔrtɪ
forty-one ˈfɔtɪ ˈwʌn $ ˈfɔrtɪ
forum ˈfɔrəm
forward(s) ˈfɔwəd(z) £ -wʊd(z) $ ˈfɔr-
fossil ˈfɒsl
fossilize ˈfɒslaɪz
foster ˈfɒstə(r) $ ˈfɔs- etc
foster-child ˈfɒstə tʃaɪld $ ˈfɔstər etc
foster-mother ˈfɒstə mʌðə(r) $ ˈfɔstər etc
fought fɔt
foul faʊl
found faʊnd
foundation faʊnˈdeɪʃn
foundation-stone faʊnˈdeɪʃn stəʊn
foundling ˈfaʊndlɪŋ
foundry ˈfaʊndrɪ
fount faʊnt
fountain ˈfaʊntɪn -tn etc
fountain-pen ˈfaʊntɪn pen $ -tn etc
four fɔ(r)
fourfold ˈfɔfəʊld $ ˈfɔr-
fourpenny ˈfɔpnɪ $ ˈfɔrpenɪ
four-ply ˈfɔ ˈplaɪ $ ˈfɔr
fourscore ˈfɔˈskɔ(r) $ ˈfɔr-
foursome ˈfɔsəm $ ˈfɔrsəm
four-square ˈfɔ ˈskweə(r) $ ˈfɔr
fourteen ˈfɔˈtin $ ˈfɔr-
fourteenth ˈfɔˈtinθ $ ˈfɔr-
fourth fɔθ $ fɔrθ
fowl faʊl
fowler ˈfaʊlə(r)
fox fɒks

fox-glove ˈfoks glʌv
foxhole ˈfokshəʊl
foxhound ˈfokshaʊnd
foxhunt ˈfokshʌnt
fox-terrier ˈfoks ˈterɪə(r)
foxtrot ˈfokstrot
foyer ˈfɔɪeɪ ˈfwajeɪ ˈfwɑɪjeɪ
    $ ˈfɔɪər etc
fracas ˈfrækɑ $ ˈfreɪkəs
fraction ˈfrækʃn
fractious ˈfrækʃəs
fracture ˈfræktʃə(r)
fragile ˈfrædʒaɪl $ ˈfrædʒl
fragment ˈfrægmənt
fragmentary ˈfrægməntrɪ $ -terɪ
fragmentation ˈfrægmənˈteɪʃn
fragrance ˈfreɪgrəns
fragrant ˈfreɪgrənt
frail freɪl
frailty ˈfreɪltɪ
frame freɪm
frame-up ˈfreɪm ʌp
framework ˈfreɪmwɜk
franc fræŋk
France frɑns $ fræns
Frances(-cis) ˈfrɑnsɪs $ ˈfrænsɪs
franchise ˈfræntʃaɪz
Franciscan frænˈsɪskən
Franco- prefix fræŋkəʊ
frank, F– fræŋk
frankfurter ˈfræŋkfɜtə(r)
frankincense ˈfræŋkɪnsens
frantic ˈfræntɪk
fraternal frəˈtɜnl
fraternity frəˈtɜnɪtɪ
fraternize ˈfrætənaɪz $ -tɜrn-
fratricide ˈfrætrɪsaɪd
Frau fraʊ
fraud frɔd
fraudulent ˈfrɔdjʊlənt $ ˈfrɔdʒʊlənt
fraught frɔt
Fräulein ˈfrɔɪlaɪn
fray freɪ
frazzle ˈfræzl
freak frik
freckle ˈfrekl
free fri
free and easy ˈfri ən ˈizɪ
free-booter ˈfri butə(r)
freed frid
freedom ˈfridəm
free-for-all ˈfri fər ɔl ˈfri fər ˈɔl
freehand ˈfrihænd

freehold ˈfrihəʊld
freelance ˈfrilɑns $ -læns
freeman ˈfrimən
freemason ˈfrimeɪsn
freethinker ˈfriˈθɪŋkə(r)
free verse ˈfri ˈvɜs
freeway ˈfriweɪ
freeze friz
freezing-point ˈfrizɪŋ pɔɪnt
freight freɪt
French frentʃ
french horn ˈfrentʃ ˈhɔn $ ˈhɔrn
Frenchman ˈfrentʃmən
french window ˈfrentʃ ˈwɪndəʊ
frenzy ˈfrenzɪ
frequency ˈfrikwənsɪ
frequent adj ˈfrikwənt
frequent v friˈkwent
fresco ˈfreskəʊ
fresh freʃ
freshman ˈfreʃmən
freshwater ˈfreʃwɔtə(r)
fretsaw ˈfretsɔ
fretwork ˈfretwɜk
Freud frɔɪd
friar ˈfraɪə(r)
fricassee ˈfrɪkəˈsi
fricative ˈfrɪkətɪv
friction ˈfrɪkʃn
Friday ˈfraɪdɪ -deɪ
fridge frɪdʒ
fried fraɪd
friend frend
friendly society ˈfrendlɪ səsaɪətɪ
friendship ˈfrendʃɪp
Friesian ˈfrizɪən $ £ ˈfriʒn
frieze friz
frigate ˈfrɪgət -ɪt
fright fraɪt
frighten ˈfraɪtn
frigid ˈfrɪdʒɪd
frill frɪl
fringe frɪndʒ
frippery ˈfrɪpərɪ
Frisian ˈfrɪzɪən $ £ ˈfrɪʒn
frisk frɪsk
fritter ˈfrɪtə(r)
frivolity frɪˈvolətɪ
frivolous ˈfrɪvləs
frizzle ˈfrɪzl
frizzy ˈfrɪzɪ
fro frəʊ
frock frok

frock-coat 'frok `kəut
frog frog $ frɔg etc
frog-march `frog matʃ $ `frɔg etc martʃ
frogman `frogmæn $ `frɔg- etc
frolic `frolɪk
frolicsome `frolɪksm
from usual form: frəm frm
  strong-form: from
frond frond
front frʌnt
frontage `frʌntɪdʒ
frontal `frʌntl
frontier `frʌntɪə(r) $ frʌn`tɪər etc
frontiersman `frʌntɪəzmən
  $ frʌn`tɪər- etc
frontispiece `frʌntɪspis
frost frost $ frɔst
frost-bite `frost baɪt $ `frɔst
froth froθ $ frɔθ etc
frown fraʊn
frowzy `fraʊzɪ
froze frəʊz
frozen `frəʊzn
fructify `frʌktɪfaɪ
frugal `frugl
fruit frut
fruit-cake `frut keɪk
fruiterer `frutərə(r)
fruition fru`ɪʃn
fruit-knife `frut naɪf
fruit-machine `frut məʃin
fruit salad `frut `sæləd
frump frʌmp
frustrate frʌ`streɪt $ `frʌstreɪt
frustration frʌ`streɪʃn
fry fraɪ
frying-pan `fraɪŋ pæn
fuchsia `fjuʃə
fuddle `fʌdl
fudge fʌdʒ
fuel `fjuḷ fjʊəl
fug fʌg
fugitive `fjudʒɪtɪv
fugue fjug
Führer `fjʊərə(r)
-ful adj suffix fl
-ful n suffix -`fʊl
fulcrum `fʌlkrəm $ £ `fʊlkrəm etc
fulfil(l) fʊl`fɪl
full fʊl
full-back 'fʊl `bæk `fʊl bæk
full-blooded 'fʊl `blʌdɪd
full-blown 'fʊl `bləʊn

full-grown 'fʊl `grəʊn
-fully suffix flɪ fəlɪ
fulmar `fʊlmə(r)
fulminate `fʌlmɪneɪt $ `fʊl- etc
fulsome `fʊlsəm
fumble `fʌmbl
fume fjum
fumigate `fjumɪgeɪt
fun fʌn
function `fʌŋkʃn
functional `fʌŋkʃnl
functionary `fʌŋkʃnrɪ $ -ʃnerɪ
fund fʌnd
fundamental 'fʌndə`mentl
funeral `fjunrəl
funereal fju`nɪərɪəl
fungi `fʌŋgaɪ -gi `fʌndʒaɪ
fungoid `fʌŋgɔɪd
fungus `fʌŋgəs
funk fʌŋk
funnel `fʌnl
funnily `fʌnḷɪ
funny `fʌnɪ
fur fɜ(r)
furbish `fɜbɪʃ
furious `fjʊərɪəs
furl fɜl
furlong `fɜloŋ $ `fɜlɔŋ etc
furlough `fɜləʊ
furnace `fɜnɪs
furnish `fɜnɪʃ
furniture `fɜnɪtʃə(r)
furore fjʊ`rɔrɪ $ `fjʊərɔr
furrier n `fʌrɪə(r) $ `fɜɪər
furrow `fʌrəʊ $ `fɜəʊ
furry `fɜrɪ
further `fɜðə(r)
furtherance `fɜðərəns
furthest `fɜðɪst -əst
furtive `fɜtɪv
fury `fjʊərɪ
furze fɜz
fuse fjuz
fuselage `fjuzəlaʒ -dʒ $ `fjusə- -lɪdʒ
fuse-wire `fjuz waɪə(r)
fusilier 'fjuzɪ`lɪə(r)
fusillade `fjuzɪ`leɪd
fusion `fjuʒn
fuss fʌs
fustian `fʌstɪən $ `fʌstʃən
fusty `fʌstɪ
futile `fjutaɪl $ -tl
futility fju`tɪlətɪ

future ˈfjutʃə(r)
futurity fjuˈtjuərətɪ $ -ˈtuər-

fuzz fʌz
fuzzy ˈfʌzɪ

G

G g dʒi
gab gæb
gabble ˈgæbl
gaberdine ˈgæbəˈdin ˈgæbədin $ -bər-
gable ˈgeɪbl
gad gæd
gad-about ˈgæd əbaʊt
gadfly ˈgæd flaɪ
gadget ˈgædʒɪt -ət
Gaelic ˈgeɪlɪk £ ˈgælɪk
gaff gæf
gaffe gæf
gag gæg
ga-ga ˈgæ ga $ £ ˈgɑ gɑ
gage geɪdʒ
gaggle ˈgægl
gaiety ˈgeɪətɪ
gaily ˈgeɪlɪ
gain geɪn
Gainsborough ˈgeɪnzbr̩ə $ -bɜrəʊ
gainsay geɪnˈseɪ
gait geɪt
gaiter ˈgeɪtə(r)
gala ˈgɑlə $ £ ˈgeɪlə
galactic gəˈlæktɪk
galaxy ˈgæləksɪ
gale geɪl
Galilee ˈgælɪli
Galileo ˈgælɪˈleɪəʊ
gall gɔl
gallant brave ˈgælənt
gallant attentive gəˈlænt
gall-bladder ˈgɔl blædə(r)
galleon ˈgælɪən
gallery ˈgælərɪ
galley ˈgælɪ
Gallic ˈgælɪk
Gallicism ˈgælɪsɪzm
gallivant ˈgælɪˈvænt
gallon ˈgælən
gallop ˈgæləp
gallows ˈgæləʊz
gall-stone ˈgɔl stəʊn
Gallup poll ˈgæləp pəʊl
galore gəˈlɔ(r)

galoshes gəˈlɒʃɪz
Galsworthy ˈgɔlzwɜðɪ ˈgæl-
galvanize ˈgælvənaɪz
Gambia ˈgæmbɪə
gambit ˈgæmbɪt
gamble ˈgæmbl
gambling-den ˈgæmblɪŋ den
gambol ˈgæmbl
game geɪm
game-cock ˈgeɪm kɒk
game-keeper ˈgeɪm kipə(r)
games-master ˈgeɪmz mɑstə(r)
   $ mæstər
gamma ˈgæmə
gamma-rays ˈgæmə reɪz
gammon ˈgæmən
gamut ˈgæmət
gander ˈgændə(r)
Gandhi ˈgændɪ ˈgɑn-
gang gæŋ
ganglion ˈgæŋglɪən
gangplank ˈgæŋplæŋk
gangrene ˈgæŋgrin
gangrenous ˈgæŋgrɪnəs
gangster ˈgæŋstə(r)
gangway ˈgæŋweɪ
gannet ˈgænɪt -ət
gantry ˈgæntrɪ
gaol dʒeɪl
gap gæp
gape geɪp
garage ˈgærɑʒ -ɑdʒ -ɪdʒ
   $ gəˈrɑʒ gəˈrɑdʒ
garb gɑb $ gɑrb
garbage ˈgɑbɪdʒ $ ˈgɑr-
garble ˈgɑbl $ ˈgɑrbl
garden ˈgɑdn $ ˈgɑrdn
gardener ˈgɑdnə(r) $ ˈgɑr-
garden city ˈgɑdn ˈsɪtɪ $ ˈgɑrdn
gardenia gɑˈdɪnɪə $ gɑr-
garden party ˈgɑdn pɑtɪ $ ˈgɑrdn pɑrtɪ
gargantuan gɑˈgæntʃʊən £ -tjʊ- $ gɑr-
gargle ˈgɑgl $ ˈgɑrgl
gargoyle ˈgɑgɔɪl $ ˈgɑr-
garish ˈgeərɪʃ

garland ˈgɑlənd $ ˈgɑr-
garlic ˈgɑlɪk $ ˈgɑr-
garment ˈgɑmənt $ ˈgɑr-
garner ˈgɑnə(r) $ ˈgɑrnər
garnish ˈgɑnɪʃ $ ˈgɑrnɪʃ
garret ˈgærət
garrison ˈgærɪsn
gar(r)otte gəˈrot
garrulity gæˈrulətɪ
garrulous ˈgærələs -rjʊl-
garter ˈgɑtə(r) $ ˈgɑrtər
gas gæs
gas-bag ˈgæs bæg
gas chamber ˈgæs tʃeɪmbə(r)
gaseous ˈgæsɪəs £ ˈgeɪsɪəs -zɪəs
gas fire ˈgæs ˈfaɪə(r) ˈgæs faɪə(r)
gas-fitter ˈgæs ˈfɪtə(r)
gash gæʃ
gasket ˈgæskɪt
gaslight ˈgæslaɪt
gas-mask ˈgæs mɑsk $ mæsk
gas-meter ˈgæs mitə(r)
gasolene ˈgæsəlin
gasometer gæˈsomɪtə(r) £ gə-
gas-oven ˈgæs ʌvn
gasp gɑsp $ gæsp
gas poker ˈgæs ˈpəʊkə(r)
gas ring ˈgæs rɪŋ
gas stove ˈgæs stəʊv gæs ˈstəʊv
gastric ˈgæstrɪk
gastritis gæˈstraɪtɪs -təs
gastronomic ˈgæstrəˈnomɪk
gastronomy gæˈstronəmɪ
gas works ˈgæs wɜks
gate geɪt
gate-crash ˈgeɪt kræʃ
gate-legged-table ˈgeɪt ˈlegd ˈteɪbl
gate-post ˈgeɪt pəʊst
gate-way ˈgeɪt weɪ
gather ˈgæðə(r)
Gatwick ˈgætwɪk
gauche gəʊʃ
gaucherie ˈgəʊʃərɪ $ ˈgəʊʃəˈri etc
gaucho ˈgaʊtʃəʊ
gaudy ˈgɔdɪ
gauge geɪdʒ
gaunt gɔnt
gauntlet ˈgɔntlət -lɪt
gauze gɔz
gave geɪv
gavel ˈgævl
gavotte gəˈvot
gawky ˈgɔkɪ

gay geɪ
gaze geɪz
gazelle gəˈzel
gazette gəˈzet
gazetteer ˈgæzəˈtɪə(r)
GB ˈgreɪt ˈbrɪtn
GCE ˈdʒi si ˈi
gear gɪə(r)
gear-box ˈgɪəboks $ ˈgɪər-
gee-gee ˈdʒi dʒi
gee-up ˈdʒi ˈʌp
geese gis
Geiger counter ˈgaɪgə kaʊntə(r)
    $ ˈgaɪgər
geisha girl ˈgeɪʃə gɜl
gelatine ˈdʒelətin $ -tn -tɪn
gelatinous ˈdʒɪˈlætɪnəs $ £ -tṇəs
geld geld
gelignite ˈdʒelɪgnaɪt
gem dʒem
Gemini ˈdʒemɪnɪ -naɪ
gendarme ˈʒondɑm ˈʒɒd- $ -dɑrm
gender ˈdʒendə(r)
gene dʒin
genealogical ˈdʒiːnɪəˈlodʒɪkl
genealogy ˈdʒiːnɪˈælədʒɪ -ˈol-
genera ˈdʒenərə
general ˈdʒenrl
general election ˈdʒenrəl ɪˈlekʃn əˈl-
generalissimo ˈdʒenrəˈlɪsɪməʊ -nər-
generality ˈdʒenəˈrælətɪ
generalization ˈdʒenrəlaɪˈzeɪʃn
    $ -ɪˈzeɪʃn
generalize ˈdʒenrəlaɪz
general knowledge ˈdʒenrl ˈnolɪdʒ
generally ˈdʒenrəlɪ ˈdʒenrlɪ
general practitioner
    ˈdʒenrl prækˈtɪʃṇə(r)
generate ˈdʒenəreɪt
generation ˈdʒenəˈreɪʃn
generative ˈdʒenrətɪv $ ˈdʒenəreɪtɪv
generator ˈdʒenəreɪtə(r)
generic dʒɪˈnerɪk
generosity ˈdʒenəˈrosətɪ
generous ˈdʒenrəs
genesis, G- ˈdʒenɪsɪs
genetics dʒɪˈnetɪks
Geneva dʒɪˈnivə
genial ˈdʒiniəl
genie ˈdʒini
genii ˈdʒiniaɪ
genital ˈdʒenɪtl
genitive ˈdʒenɪtɪv

genius ˈdʒiːnɪəs
Genoa ˈdʒenəʊə dʒɔˈnəʊə
genocide ˈdʒenəsaɪd
genre ʒɒr *with unsyllabic* r
$ £ ˈʒɒnrə
gent dʒent
genteel dʒenˈtiːl
gentian ˈdʒenʃn
gentile ˈdʒentaɪl
gentle ˈdʒentl
gentlefolk ˈdʒentlfəʊk
gentleman ˈdʒentlmən
gentlemen ˈdʒentlmən
gently ˈdʒentlɪ
gentry ˈdʒentrɪ
genuflect ˈdʒenjʊflekt
genuflection ˈdʒenjʊˈflekʃn
genuine ˈdʒenjʊɪn
genus ˈdʒiːnəs
geocentric ˈdʒiːəʊˈsentrɪk
Geoffrey ˈdʒefrɪ
geographical dʒɪəˈgræfɪkl
geography dʒɪˈɒgrəfɪ
geological dʒɪəˈlɒdʒɪkl
geologist dʒɪˈɒlədʒɪst
geometrical dʒɪəˈmetrɪkl
geometry dʒɪˈɒmɪtrɪ -mət-
geophysical ˈdʒiːəʊˈfɪzɪkl
geophysics ˈdʒiːəʊˈfɪzɪks
George ˈdʒɔːdʒ $ ˈdʒɔːrdʒ
georgette, G– dʒɔːˈdʒet $ dʒɔːr-
Georgia ˈdʒɔːdʒə $ ˈdʒɔːr-
Georgian ˈdʒɔːdʒən $ ˈdʒɔːr-
Gerald ˈdʒerld
geranium dʒɪˈreɪnɪəm
geriatrics ˈdʒerɪˈætrɪks
germ dʒɜːm
German ˈdʒɜːmən
germane dʒɜːˈmeɪn
Germanic dʒɜːˈmænɪk $ dʒɜːr-
Germany ˈdʒɜːmənɪ
germicide ˈdʒɜːmɪsaɪd
germinate ˈdʒɜːmɪneɪt
gerontology ˈdʒerɒnˈtɒlədʒɪ
gerrymander ˈdʒerɪˈmændə(r)
gerund ˈdʒerənd
Gestapo geˈstɑːpəʊ
gestation dʒeˈsteɪʃn
gesticulate dʒɪˈstɪkjʊleɪt
gesture ˈdʒestʃə(r)
get get
get-at-able ˈget ˈæt əbl
Gettysburg ˈgetɪzbɜg

geyser ˈgiːzə(r)
Ghana ˈgɑːnə
Ghanaian gɑːˈneɪən
ghastly ˈgɑːstlɪ $ ˈgæstlɪ
gherkin ˈgɜːkɪn
ghetto ˈgetəʊ
ghost gəʊst
ghost-writer ˈgəʊst raɪtə(r)
ghoul guːl
G.I. ˈdʒiː ˈaɪ
giant ˈdʒaɪənt
gibber ˈdʒɪbə(r) ˈgɪbə(r)
gibbet ˈdʒɪbɪt -ət
gibbon ˈgɪbən
giblets ˈdʒɪbləts -lɪts
Gibraltar dʒɪˈbrɔːltə(r) £ -ˈbrɒl-
giddy ˈgɪdɪ
gift gɪft
gig gɪg
gigantic dʒaɪˈgæntɪk
giggle ˈgɪgl
gigolo ˈʒɪgələʊ
Gilbert ˈgɪlbət $ ˈgɪlbərt
gild gɪld
gill *of fish* gɪl
gill *measure* dʒɪl
gilt gɪlt
gimcrack ˈgɪmkræk
gimlet ˈgɪmlət -lɪt
gimmick ˈgɪmɪk
gin dʒɪn
ginger ˈdʒɪndʒə(r)
ginger ale ˈdʒɪndʒər ˈeɪl
gingerbread ˈdʒɪndʒəbred $ -dʒər-
gingerly ˈdʒɪndʒəlɪ $ -dʒərlɪ
gingham ˈgɪŋəm
gipsy ˈdʒɪpsɪ
giraffe dʒɪˈrɑːf $ £ -ˈræf
gird gɜːd
girder ˈgɜːdə(r)
girdle ˈgɜːdl
girl gɜːl
girl-friend ˈgɜːl frend
Girl Guide ˈgɜːl ˈgaɪd
girt gɜːt
girth gɜːθ
gist dʒɪst
give gɪv
given ˈgɪvn
gizzard ˈgɪzəd $ ˈgɪzərd
glacé ˈglæseɪ $ glæˈseɪ
glacial ˈgleɪʃl
glacier ˈglæsɪə(r) $ ˈgleɪʃər

glad glæd
glade gleɪd
gladiator ˈglædɪeɪtə(r)
gladioli ˈglædɪˈəʊlaɪ
gladiolus ˈglædɪˈəʊləs
glad rags ˈglæd rægz
Glamorgan gləˈmɔɡən $ -ˈmɔr-
glamorize ˈglæməraɪz
glamorous ˈglæmərəs
glamour ˈglæmə(r)
glance glɑns $ glæns
gland glænd
glandular ˈglændjʊlə(r) $ -ndʒʊ-
glare gleə(r)
Glasgow ˈglɑzgəʊ $ £ ˈglæz-
glass glɑs $ glæs
glass-house ˈglɑs haʊs $ ˈglæs
glassware ˈglɑsweə(r) $ ˈglæs-
Glaswegian glæzˈwidʒən
glaucoma glɔˈkəʊmə
glaucous ˈglɔkəs
glaze gleɪz
glazier ˈgleɪzɪə(r) $ £ ˈgleɪʒə(r)
gleam glim
glean glin
glee gli
glen glen
glib glɪb
glide glaɪd
glider ˈglaɪdə(r)
glimmer ˈglɪmə(r)
glimpse glɪmps
glint glɪnt
glissade glɪˈsɑd glɪˈseɪd
glisten ˈglɪsn
glitter ˈglɪtə(r)
gloaming ˈgləʊmɪŋ
gloat gləʊt
global ˈgləʊbl
globe gləʊb
globe-fish ˈgləʊb fɪʃ
globe-trotter ˈgləʊb trɒtə(r)
globous ˈgləʊbəs
globular ˈgləʊbjʊlə(r)
globule ˈglɒbjul
glockenspiel ˈglɒkənspil -nʃp-
gloom glum
glorification ˈglɔrɪfɪˈkeɪʃn
glorify ˈglɔrɪfaɪ
glorious ˈglɔrɪəs
glory ˈglɔrɪ
gloss glɒs $ glɔs
glossary ˈglɒsərɪ

glottal ˈglotl
glottis ˈglotɪs
Gloucester ˈglostə(r) $ ˈglɔstər etc
glove glʌv
glow gləʊ
glow-worm ˈgləʊ wɜm
glower ˈglaʊə(r)
glucose ˈglukəʊs
glue glu
glut glʌt
glutinous ˈglutɪnəs $ ˈglutn̩əs
glutton ˈglʌtn
gluttonous ˈglʌtn̩əs -tən-
gluttony ˈglʌtn̩ɪ
glycerin(e) ˈglɪsəˈrin ˈglɪsərin
$ £ ˈglɪsərɪn
Glyndebourne ˈglaɪndbɔn $ -bɔrn
gm. græm
GMT ˈdʒi em ˈti
gnarled nald
gnash næʃ
gnat næt
gnaw nɔ
gnome nəʊm
gnu nu
go gəʊ
goal-keeper ˈgəʊl kipə(r)
go-as-you-please ˈgəʊ əz ju ˈpliz
goat gəʊt
goat-herd ˈgəʊt hɜd
goatskin ˈgəʊtskɪn
go-between ˈgəʊ bɪtwin
gobble ˈgobl
goblet ˈgoblət -lɪt
goblin ˈgoblɪn
go-cart(-kart) ˈgəʊ kat $ kart
god, G– god
godchild ˈgodtʃaɪld
goddaughter ˈgoddɔtə(r)
goddess ˈgodes -ɪs -əs
godfather ˈgodfɑðə(r)
godfearing ˈgodfɪərɪŋ
god-forsaken ˈgod fəseɪkən $ fər-
godhead ˈgodhed
godliness ˈgodlɪnəs
godmother ˈgodmʌðə(r)
godparent ˈgodpeərnt
godsend ˈgodsend
godson ˈgodsʌn
godspeed ˈgodˈspid
Goethe ˈgɜtə
for $ this ə may have no r quality
go-getter ˈgəʊ ˈgetə(r)

goggle ˈgogl
goggle-eyed ˈgogl ˈaɪd
going ˈgəʊɪŋ
going to *familiar forms:* ˈgənə ˈgəʊnə
  before vowels: ˈgənu ˈgəʊnu
goitre($ -ter) ˈgɔɪtə(r)
gold ˈgəʊld
goldbeater ˈgəʊldbitə(r)
gold-digger ˈgəʊld dɪgə(r)
gold-dust ˈgəʊld dʌst
golden ˈgəʊldn
gold-field ˈgəʊld fild
goldfinch ˈgəʊldfɪntʃ
goldfish ˈgəʊldfɪʃ
gold-leaf ˈgəʊld ˈlif
gold-mine ˈgəʊld maɪn
gold plate ˈgəʊld ˈpleɪt
gold-rush ˈgəʊld rʌʃ
goldsmith ˈgəʊldsmɪθ
golf golf $ gɔlf
golf-ball ˈgolf bɔl $ ˈgɔlf
golf-club ˈgolf klʌb $ ˈgɔlf
Goliath gəˈlaɪəθ
Gollancz gəˈlænts
golliwog ˈgolɪwog
golly ˈgolɪ
goloshes gəˈloʃɪz
Gomorrah gəˈmorə $ -ɔrə *etc*
gondola ˈgondələ
gondolier ˈgondəˈlɪə(r)
gone gon $ gɔn *etc*
gong goŋ $ gɔŋ *etc*
gonorrh(o)ea ˈgonəˈrɪə
good gʊd
goodbye *serious* ˈgʊdˈbaɪ
goodbye *routine* gəˈbaɪ
good-for-nothing ˈgʊd fə nʌθɪŋ $ fər
good-humoured ˈgʊd ˈhjuməd $ -mərd
good-looking ˈgʊd ˈlʊkɪŋ
good-natured ˈgʊd ˈneɪtʃəd $ -tʃərd
goodness ˈgʊdnəs
good-tempered ˈgʊd ˈtempəd $ -pərd
goodwill ˈgʊdˈwɪl
goody-goody ˈgʊdɪ ˈgʊdɪ ˈg- g-
go-off gəʊ ˈof $ ˈgəʊ ɔf
goofy ˈgufɪ
goon gun
goose gus
gooseberry ˈgʊzbrɪ $ ˈgusberɪ ˈguz-
goose-flesh ˈgus fleʃ
goose-step ˈgus step
Gordian ˈgodɪən $ ˈgɔr-
gore gɔ(r)

gorge gɔdʒ $ gɔrdʒ
gorgeous ˈgodʒəs $ ˈgɔr-
Gorgon ˈgogən $ ˈgɔr-
Gorgonzola ˈgogənˈzəʊlə $ ˈgɔr-
gorilla gəˈrɪlə
gormandize ˈgoməndaɪz $ ˈgɔr-
gorse gos $ gɔrs
gory ˈgorɪ
gosh goʃ
gosling ˈgozlɪŋ
gospel, G– ˈgospl
gossamer ˈgosəmə(r)
gossip ˈgosɪp
got got
Gothic ˈgoθɪk
gotten ˈgotn
gouge gaʊdʒ
goulash ˈgulæʃ $ -laʃ
gourd gʊəd gɔd $ gɔrd gʊərd
gourmand ˈgʊəmənd $ ˈgʊər-
gourmet ˈgʊəmeɪ ˈgomeɪ $ ˈgʊər-
gout gaʊt
govern ˈgʌvn $ ˈgʌvərn
governess ˈgʌvənɪs -əs $ -vərn-
government ˈgʌvm̩ənt -vəm-
  $ -vərm- *etc*
governmental ˈgʌvnˈmentl $ ˈgʌvərn-
governor ˈgʌvnə(r) $ -vərnər -vn̩-
governor-general ˈgʌvnə ˈdʒenrl
  $ ˈgʌvərnər -vn̩-
gown gaʊn
G.P. ˈdʒi ˈpi
G.P.O. ˈdʒi pi ˈəʊ
grab græb
grace greɪs
graceful ˈgreɪsfl
gracious ˈgreɪʃəs
gradation greɪˈdeɪʃn grə-
grade greɪd
gradient ˈgreɪdɪənt
gradual ˈgrædʒʊəl
graduate *adj, n* ˈgrædʒʊət
graduate *v* ˈgrædʒʊeɪt
graduation ˈgrædʒʊˈeɪʃn
graft grɑft $ ˈgræft
Graham(e) ˈgreɪəm $ græm grɑm
grail greɪl
grain greɪn
grammar ˈgræmə(r)
grammar school ˈgræmə skul $ -mər
grammatical grəˈmætɪkl
gram(me) græm
gramophone ˈgræməfəʊn

granary ˈgrænərɪ
grand grænd
grandchild ˈgrændtʃaɪld
granddad ˈgrændæd
granddaughter ˈgrændɔːtə(r)
grandee grænˈdiː
grandeur ˈgrændʒə(r) -djʊə(r)
grandfather ˈgrændfaðə(r)
grandfather clock ˈgrændfaðə ˈklɒk
   $ -faðər
grandiloquent grænˈdɪləkwənt
grandiose ˈgrændɪəʊs ˈgrændɪˈəʊs -əʊz
grandma ˈgrænma -ndma
grandmother ˈgrændmʌðə(r)
grandpa ˈgrænpa -ndpa
grand piano ˈgrænd pɪˈænəʊ
grandson ˈgrændsʌn -nsʌn
grange ˈgreɪndʒ
granite ˈgrænɪt
grant, G– grant $ grænt
granular ˈgrænjʊlə(r)
granulate ˈgrænjʊleɪt
granule ˈgrænjʊl
grape greɪp
grapefruit ˈgreɪpfruːt
grapevine ˈgreɪpvaɪn
graph græf £ graf
graphic ˈgræfɪk
graphite ˈgræfaɪt
grapple ˈgræpl
grappling-iron ˈgræplɪŋ aɪən $ aɪərn
grasp grasp $ græsp
grass gras $ græs
grasshopper ˈgrashɒpə(r) $ ˈgræs-
grass widow ˈgras ˈwɪdəʊ $ ˈgræs
grate greɪt
grateful ˈgreɪtfl
gratification ˈgrætɪfɪˈkeɪʃn
gratify ˈgrætɪfaɪ
grating ˈgreɪtɪŋ
gratis ˈgrætɪs ˈgreɪtɪs £ ˈgratɪs
gratitude ˈgrætɪtjuːd -tʃud $ -tud
gratuitous grəˈtjuːɪtəs $ -ˈtu-
gratuity grəˈtjuːətɪ $ -ˈtu-
grave greɪv
gravel ˈgrævl
gravestone ˈgreɪvstəʊn
graveyard ˈgreɪvjad $ -jard
gravitate ˈgrævɪteɪt
gravity ˈgrævətɪ
gravy ˈgreɪvɪ
gray greɪ
graze greɪz

grease n gris
grease v gris griz
grease-paint ˈgris peɪnt
greasy ˈgrisɪ ˈgrizɪ
great greɪt
Great Britain ˈgreɪt ˈbrɪtn
greatcoat ˈgreɪtkəʊt
great-grandchild ˈgreɪt ˈgrændtʃaɪld
great-granddaughter
   ˈgreɪt ˈgrændɔːtə(r)
great-grandfather ˈgreɪt ˈgrændfaðə(r)
great-grandmother ˈgreɪt ˈgrændmʌðə(r)
great-grandson ˈgreɪt ˈgrændsʌn
grebe grib
Grecian ˈgriʃn
Greece gris
greed grid
Greek grik
green grin
greenery ˈgrinərɪ
greenfingers ˈgrinfɪŋɡəz $ -ɡərz
greengage ˈgringeɪdʒ
greengrocer ˈgringrəʊsə(r)
greenhouse ˈgrinhaʊs
Greenland ˈgrinlænd -lənd
Greenwich ˈgrenɪtʃ ˈgrɪn- -ɪdʒ
greet grit
gregarious grɪˈgeərɪəs
gremlin ˈgremlɪn
grenade grɪˈneɪd grə-
grenadier ˈgrenəˈdɪə(r)
grew gru
grey greɪ
greyhound ˈgreɪhaʊnd
grid grɪd
griddle ˈgrɪdl
gridiron ˈgrɪdaɪən $ -aɪərn
grief grif
grievance ˈgrivns
grieve griv
grievous ˈgrivəs
griffin ˈgrɪfɪn
grill grɪl
grille gril
grim grɪm
grimace grɪˈmeɪs $ ˈgrɪmɪs etc
grime graɪm
grin grɪn
grind graɪnd
grindstone ˈgraɪndstəʊn
grip grɪp
gripe graɪp
grisly ˈgrɪzlɪ

grist grɪst
gristle ˈgrɪsl
grit grɪt
grizzle ˈgrɪzl
grizzly bear ˈgrɪzlɪ beə(r)
groan grəʊn
groat grəʊt
grocer ˈgrəʊsə(r)
grocery ˈgrəʊsərɪ -srɪ
groggy ˈgrogɪ
groin grɔɪn
groom grum grʊm
groove gruv
grope grəʊp
gross grəʊs
grotesque grəʊˈtesk
grotto ˈgrotəʊ
grouch graʊtʃ
ground graʊnd
ground-crew ˈgraʊnd kru
ground floor ˈgraʊnd ˈflɔ(r)
groundnut ˈgraʊndnʌt
ground-rent ˈgraʊnd rent
groundwork ˈgraʊndwɜk
group grup
grouse graʊs
grove grəʊv
grovel ˈgrovl $ ˈgrʌvl
grow grəʊ
growl graʊl
grown grəʊn
grown up adj ˈgrəʊn ˈʌp
grown-ups ˈgrəʊn ʌps
growth grəʊθ
grub grʌb
grudge grʌdʒ
gruel gruļ grʊəl
gruesome ˈgrusəm with u as in 'use'
   not as in 'grew'
gruff grʌf
grumble ˈgrʌmbl
grumpy ˈgrʌmpɪ
grunt grʌnt
gryphon ˈgrɪfən
Guadeloupe ˈgwadəˈlup $ ˈgwadļup etc
guarantee ˈgærənˈti
guarantor ˈgærənˈtɔ(r) ˈgærəntɔ(r)
   $ ˈgærəntər
guard gad $ gard
guardian ˈgadɪən $ ˈgar-
guard-room ˈgad rum rum
   $ ˈgard rum etc
guardsman ˈgadzmən $ ˈgar-

guava ˈgwavə
gudgeon ˈgʌdʒən
gue(r)rilla gəˈrɪlə
guess ges
guesswork ˈgeswɜk
guest gest
guest-house ˈgest haʊs
guest-room ˈgest rum $ £ rum etc
guest-towel ˈgest taʊļ
guffaw gəˈfɔ
Guiana gaɪˈænə $ gɪ- £ gɪˈanə
guidance ˈgaɪdns
guide gaɪd
guild gɪld
Guild-hall ˈgɪld ˈhɔl $ £ ˈgɪld hɔl
guile gaɪl
guillemot ˈgɪlɪmot
guillotine ˈgɪlətin ˈgɪləˈtin
guilt gɪlt
guinea ˈgɪnɪ
guinea-fowl ˈgɪnɪ faʊl
guinea-pig ˈgɪnɪ pɪg
Guinness ˈgɪnɪs
guise gaɪz
guitar gɪˈta(r)
gulch gʌltʃ
gulf gʌlf
gull gʌl
gullet ˈgʌlɪt
gullible ˈgʌləbl
Gulliver ˈgʌlɪvə(r)
gully ˈgʌlɪ
gulp gʌlp
gum gʌm
gumboil ˈgʌmbɔɪl
gumption ˈgʌmpʃn
gun gʌn
gun-boat ˈgʌn bəʊt
gun-carriage ˈgʌn kærɪdʒ
gun-fire ˈgʌn faɪə(r)
gunman ˈgʌnmən
gunmen ˈgʌnmən ˈgʌnmen
gun-metal ˈgʌn metl
gunner ˈgʌnə(r)
gunpowder ˈgʌnpaʊdə(r)
gun-runner ˈgʌn rʌnə(r)
gunshot ˈgʌn-ʃot
gunsmith ˈgʌn-smɪθ
gunwale ˈgʌnl
gurgle ˈgɜgl
Gurkha ˈgɜkə
guru ˈgʊru
gush gʌʃ

gusset `gʌsɪt
gust gʌst
gusto `gʌstəʊ
gut gʌt
gutter `gʌtə(r)
guttersnipe `gʌtəsnaɪp $ `gʌtər-
guttural `gʌtərl `gʌtrl
guy gaɪ
Guy Fawkes `gaɪ `fɔks $ £ `gaɪ fɔks
guzzle `gʌzl
Gwendoline `gwendəlɪn
gym dʒɪm

gymkhana dʒɪm`kanə $ -`kænə etc
gymnasium dʒɪm`neɪzɪəm
gymnastics dʒɪm`næstɪks
gyn(a)ecologist 'gaɪnɪ`kɔlədʒɪst
gyn(a)ecological 'gaɪnɪkə`lɔdʒɪkl
gyn(a)ecology 'gaɪnɪ`kɔlədʒɪ
gyp dʒɪp
gypsum `dʒɪpsəm
gypsy `dʒɪpsɪ
gyrate dʒaɪ`reɪt $ `dʒaɪreɪt
gyro `dʒaɪərəʊ
gyroscope `dʒaɪərəskəʊp

H

H h eɪtʃ
ha ha or realistic laugh
habeas corpus 'heɪbɪəs `kɔpəs $ `kɔrpəs
haberdasher `hæbədæʃə(r) $ -bər-
habit `hæbɪt
habitat `hæbɪtæt
habitation 'hæbɪ`teɪʃn
habitual hə`bɪtʃʊəl
habituate hə`bɪtʃʊeɪt
hacienda 'hæsɪ`endə $ 'has- 'as-
hack hæk
hack-saw `hæk sɔ
hackles `hæklz
hackney `hæknɪ
had auxiliary verb, usual forms: after
   I, he, she, we, you, they: d
   after a pause: həd otherwise: əd
   strong-form: hæd
had possessed hæd $ weak-form: æd
haddock `hædək $ -dɪk
Hades `heɪdiz
Hadji `hædʒɪ
hadn't `hædnt $ weak-form: ædnt
haemoglobin 'hiːmə`gləʊbɪn
   $ `hemək- `hiːmək-
haemorrhage `hemərɪdʒ
haft haft $ hæft
hag hæg
haggard `hægəd $ `hægərd
haggis `hægɪs
haggle `hægl
ha-ha n `ha ha
ha ha! ha `ha or realistic laughter
hail heɪl
hail-fellow-well-met 'heɪl feləʊ wel `met

hailstone `heɪl-stəʊn
hailstorm `heɪl-stɔm $ -stɔrm
hair heə(r)
hairbrush `heəbrʌʃ $ `heər-
haircut `heəkʌt $ `heər-
hair-do `heə du $ `heər
hairdresser `heədresə(r) $ `heər-
hair-net `heə net $ `heər
hair-oil `heər ɔɪl
hairpin `heəpɪn $ `heər-
hair-raising `heə reɪzɪŋ $ `heər
hair's breadth `heəz bretθ $ `heərz
hair-shirt `heə `ʃɜt $ `heər
hair-spring `heə sprɪŋ $ `heər
hake heɪk
halcyon `hælsɪən
hale heɪl
half haf $ hæf
half-back `haf bæk $ `hæf
half-baked `haf `beɪkt $ `hæf
half-breed `haf brid $ `hæf
half-brother `haf brʌðə(r) $ `hæf
half-caste `haf kast $ `hæf kæst
half-crown `haf `kraʊn $ `hæf
half-hearted `haf `hatɪd $ `hæf `hartɪd
half-holiday `haf `hɔlədɪ $ `hæf -deɪ
half-hourly `haf `aʊəlɪ $ `hæf `aʊərlɪ
half-mast `haf `mast $ `hæf `mæst
half-pay `haf `peɪ $ `hæf
halfpenny `heɪpnɪ $ `hæfpenɪ
halfpennyworth `heɪpəθ `heɪpnɪwзθ
   $ `hæfpenɪwзθ
half-price `haf `praɪs $ `hæf
half-time `haf `taɪm $ `hæf
half-tone `haf `təʊn $ `hæf

half-track 'haf `træk $ 'hæf
half-way 'haf `weɪ $ 'hæf
half-wit 'haf wɪt $ 'hæf
half-witted 'haf `wɪtɪd $ 'hæf
halibut `hælɪbət
halitosis 'hælɪ`təʊsɪs
hall hɔl
hallelujah 'hælɪ`lujə
hallmark `hɔlmak $ -mark
hallo hə`ləʊ
hallow `hæləʊ
Hallowe'en 'hæləʊ`in
hallucination hə'lusɪ`neɪʃn
halo `heɪləʊ
halt hɔlt £ holt
halve hav $ hæv
halves havz $ hævz
halyard `hæljad $ -jard
ham hæm
Hamburg `hæmbɜg
hamburger `hæmbɜgə(r)
ham-handed 'hæm `hændɪd
hamlet, H– `hæmlət -lɪt
hammer `hæmə(r)
hammock `hæmək $ -mɪk
hamper `hæmpə(r)
Hampshire `hæmpʃə(r) $ `hæmpʃɪər etc
Hampstead `hæmpstɪd -sted
hamster `hæmstə(r)
hamstring `hæm-strɪŋ
hamstrung `hæm-strʌŋ
hand hænd
handbag `hændbæg
handbook `hændbʊk
handcart `hændkat $ -kart
handclap `hændklæp
handcuffs `hændkʌfs
hand-grenade `hænd grɪneɪd
handicap `hændɪkæp
handicraft `hændɪkraft $ -kræft
handiwork `hændɪwɜk
handkerchief `hæŋkətʃɪf -tʃif $ -kər-
handle `hændl
hand-luggage `hænd lʌgɪdʒ
hand-made 'hænd `meɪd
hand-maid `hænd meɪd
hand-out `hændaʊt
handrail `hænd-reɪl
handshake `hændʃeɪk
handsome `hænsəm
handstand `hændstænd
handwork `hændwɜk
handwriting `hænd-raɪtɪŋ

handy `hændɪ
hang hæŋ
hangar `hæŋə(r)
hangdog `hæŋdog $ `hæŋdɔg etc
hanger `hæŋə(r)
hanger-on 'hæŋər `on $ `ɔn etc
hangers-on 'hæŋəz `on $ 'hæŋərz `ɔn etc
hanging matter `hæŋɪŋ mætə(r)
hangman `hæŋmən
hangover `hæŋəʊvə(r)
hang-up `hæŋ ʌp
hank hæŋk
hanker `hæŋkə(r)
hanky `hæŋkɪ
hanky-panky 'hæŋkɪ `pæŋkɪ
Hansard `hænsad $ -sard
hansom `hænsəm
haphazard hæp`hæzəd $ -zərd
ha'p'orth `heɪpəθ
happen `hæpn
happily `hæpḷɪ
happy `hæpɪ
happy-go-lucky 'hæpɪ gəʊ `lʌkɪ
hara-kiri 'hærə `kɪrɪ $ `hærɪ kɪrɪ
harangue hə`ræŋ
harass `hærəs $ hə`ræs
harbinger `habɪndʒə(r) $ `har-
harbour($ -or) `habə(r) $ `har-
harbourage($ -or-) `habərɪdʒ $ `har-
hard had $ hard
hardback `hadbæk $ `hard-
hard-bitten 'had `bɪtn $ 'hard
hardboard `hadbɔd $ `hardbɔrd
harden `hadn $ `hardn
hard-headed 'had `hedɪd $ 'hard
hard-hearted 'had `hatɪd
    $ 'hard `hartɪd
hardly `hadlɪ $ `hardlɪ
hardship `hadʃɪp $ `hard-
hardware `hadweə(r) $ `hard-
hardwood `hadwʊd $ `hard-
hardy `hadɪ $ `hardɪ
hare heə(r)
hare-brained 'heə `breɪnd $ 'heər
harelip 'heə`lɪp $ 'heər-
harem `heərəm £ `harim hɑ`rim
    $ hə`rim
haricot `hærɪkəʊ $ -kot
hark hak $ hark
harlequin `haləkwɪn $ `har-
Harlem `haləm $ `har-
harlot `halət $ `har-
harm ham $ harm

harmonic haˈmɒnɪk $ har-
harmonica haˈmɒnɪkə $ har-
harmonious haˈməʊnɪəs $ har-
harmonium haˈməʊnɪəm $ har-
harmonize ˈhaːmənaɪz $ ˈhar-
harmony ˈhaːmənɪ $ ˈhar-
harness ˈhaːnɪs $ ˈharnɪs
Harold ˈhærld
harp haːp $ harp
harpoon haːˈpuːn $ har-
harpsichord ˈhaːpsɪkɔːd $ ˈharpsɪkɔrd
harpy ˈhaːpɪ $ ˈharpɪ
harridan ˈhærɪdən
harrier ˈhærɪə(r)
Harris ˈhærɪs
harrow, H– ˈhærəʊ
harry, H– ˈhærɪ
harsh haːʃ $ harʃ
Harvard ˈhaːvəd $ ˈharvərd
hart haːt $ hart
harum-scarum ˌheərəm ˈskeərəm
harvest ˈhaːvɪst $ ˈhar-
harvest festival ˌhaːvɪst ˈfestɪvl
   $ ˈhar-
has *auxiliary verb, usual forms:* z
   after the 'sibilants' s z ʃ ʒ tʃ dʒ: əz
   after a pause həz *strong-form:* hæz
has *possesses* hæz $ *weak-form:* æz
has-been ˈhæz bɪn $ bɪn
hash hæʃ
hashish ˈhæʃiːʃ -ʃɪʃ
hasn't ˈhæznt $ *weak-form:* ˈæznt
hasp hæsp £ hasp
hassock ˈhæsək -sɪk
haste heɪst
hasten ˈheɪsn
hasty ˈheɪstɪ
hat hæt
hatch hætʃ
hatchet ˈhætʃɪt -ət
hatchway ˈhætʃweɪ
hate heɪt
hath hæθ
hat-pin ˈhæt pɪn
hatred ˈheɪtrɪd -rəd
hat trick ˈhæt trɪk
haughty ˈhɔːtɪ
haul hɔːl
haulage ˈhɔːlɪdʒ
haulier ˈhɔːlɪə(r)
haunch hɔːntʃ
haunt hɔːnt
Havana həˈvænə £ həˈvɑnə

have *auxiliary v, usual form after*
   I, we, you, they*:* v
   usual form after a pause: həv
   usual form elsewhere: əv
   strong-form: hæv
have *possess* have
haven ˈheɪvn
haven't ˈhævnt
haversack ˈhævəsæk $ -vər-
havoc ˈhævək $ -vɪk
Hawaii həˈwaɪi həˈwaɪ $ həˈwaɪə
Hawaiian həˈwaɪən
hawk hɔːk
hawser ˈhɔːzə(r)
hawthorn ˈhɔːθɔn $ -θɔrn
hay heɪ
haycock ˈheɪkɒk
Haydn *composer* ˈhaɪdn
Haydn *name* ˈheɪdn
hay-fever ˈheɪ fiːvə(r)
hay-loft ˈheɪ lɒft
hay-rack ˈheɪ ræk
hay-rick ˈheɪ rɪk
hay-stack ˈheɪ stæk
haywire ˈheɪwaɪə(r)
hazard ˈhæzəd $ -zərd
haze heɪz
hazel ˈheɪzl
H-bomb ˈeɪtʃ bɒm
he *usual form:* i
   after a pause, strong-form: hi
he-man ˈhi mæn
head hed
headache ˈhedeɪk
headdress ˈheddres
headgear ˈhedgɪə(r)
head-hunter ˈhed hʌntə(r)
headland ˈhedlənd -lænd
head-light ˈhed laɪt
headline ˈhedlaɪn
headlong ˈhedlɒŋ $ -lɔŋ *etc*
headman ˈhedmæn
headmaster ˌhedˈmaːstə(r) $ -ˈmæstər
headmistress ˌhedˈmɪstrəs -ɪs
head-on ˌhed ˈon
headphones ˈhedfəʊnz
headquarters ˈhedˈkwɔtəz $ -ˈkwɔrtərz
head-set ˈhed set
headstone ˈhedstəʊn
headstrong ˈhedstrɒŋ $ ˈhedstrɔŋ
headway ˈhedweɪ
headwind ˈhedwɪnd
headword ˈhedwɜd

heal **hil**
health **helθ**
heap **hip**
hear **hɪə(r)**
heard **hɜd**
Hear, hear! **'hɪə 'hɪə $ 'hɪər 'hɪər**
hearing **'hɪərɪŋ**
hearing-aid **'hɪərɪŋ eɪd**
hearken **'hɑkən $ 'hɑrkən**
hearsay **'hɪəseɪ $ 'hɪərseɪ**
hearse **hɜs**
heart **hɑt $ hɑrt**
heart-ache **'hɑt eɪk $ 'hɑrt**
heart-beat **'hɑt bit $ 'hɑrt**
heart-break **'hɑt breɪk $ 'hɑrt**
heart-broken **'hɑt brəʊkən $ 'hɑrt**
heartburn **'hɑtbɜn $ 'hɑrt-**
heartening **'hɑtŋɪŋ $ 'hɑrt-**
heart-failure **'hɑt feɪljə(r) $ 'hɑrt**
heartfelt **'hɑtfelt $ 'hɑrt-**
hearth **hɑθ $ hɑrθ**
hearth-rug **'hɑθ rʌg $ 'hɑrθ**
heart-rending **'hɑt rendɪŋ $ 'hɑrt**
heart-strings **'hɑt strɪŋz $ 'hɑrt**
heat **hit**
heath, H– **hiθ**
heathen **'hiðn**
heather, H– **'heðə(r)**
Heathrow **'hiθ'rəʊ**
heat-spot **'hit spot**
heat-wave **'hit weɪv**
heave **hiv**
heaven **'hevn**
heavily **'hevl̩ɪ**
heavy **'hevɪ**
heavy-handed **'hevɪ 'hændɪd**
heavy-hearted **'hevɪ 'hɑtɪd $ 'hɑrtɪd**
heavy-weight **'hevɪ weɪt**
Hebraic **hi'breɪk**
Hebrew **'hibru**
heckle **'hekl**
hectare **'hektɑ(r) $ 'hekteə(r)**
hectic **'hektɪk**
hectogram(me) **'hektəgræm**
hectometre($ -er) **'hektəmitə(r)**
hector, H– **'hektə(r)**
he'd *usual form:* id
  after a pause, strong-form: hid
hedge **hedʒ**
hedgehog **'hedʒhog $ -hɔg** *etc*
hedgerow **'hedʒrəʊ**
hedonism **'hidənɪzm -dn̩-**
heed **hid**

heehaw **'hihɔ**
heel **hil**
hefty **'heftɪ**
hegemony **hi'gemənɪ 'hedʒɪmənɪ 'hegɪ-**
  $ hɪ'dʒemənɪ 'hedʒɪməʊnɪ
heifer **'hefə(r)**
heigh-ho **'heɪ'həʊ $ 'haɪ 'həʊ** *etc*
height **haɪt**
heighten **'haɪtn**
heinous **'heɪnəs**
Heinz **haɪnz haɪnts**
heir **eə(r)**
heir-apparent **'eər ə'pærnt**
heiress **'eəres -rɪs -rəs**
heirloom **'eəlum $ 'eərlum**
heir-presumptive **'eə prɪ'zʌmptɪv $ 'eər**
held **held**
Helen(a) **helən(ə) -lɪn(ə)**
helicopter **'helɪkoptə(r)**
heliograph **'hilɪəʊgrɑf $ -græf**
heliport **'helɪpɔt $ -pɔrt**
helium **'hilɪəm**
he'll *usual form:* il
  after a pause, strong-form: hil
hell **hel**
Hellenes **'helinz**
Hellenic **he'linɪk $ he'lenɪk**
hello **he'ləʊ hə'ləʊ**
helm **helm**
helmet **'helmɪt -ət**
helmsman **'helmzmən**
helot **'helət**
help **help**
helpmate **'helpmeɪt**
Helsinki **'helsɪŋkɪ hel'sɪŋkɪ**
helter-skelter **'heltə 'skeltə(r)**
  $ 'heltər
Helvetia **hel'viʃə**
hem *in sewing* hem
hem *grunt* hm mhm *etc*
hem-line **'hem laɪn**
hemisphere **'hemɪsfɪə(r)**
hemlock **'hemlok**
hemoglobin **'himə'gləʊbɪn**
  $ 'hemɔg- 'himəg-
hemophilia **'himə'fɪlɪə $ 'hem-**
hemorrhage **'hemərɪdʒ**
hemorrhoids **'hemərɔɪdz**
hemp **hemp**
hemstitch **'hem-stɪtʃ**
hen **hen**
hence **hens**
henceforth **'hens'fɔθ $ 'fɔrθ**

henceforward 'hens'fɔwəd £ -wʊd
$ -'fɔrwərd
henchman 'hentʃmən
hen-coop 'hen kup
hen-house 'hen haʊs
henna 'henə
hen-party 'hen patɪ $ partɪ
hen-pecked 'hen pekt
Henry 'henrɪ
hepatitis 'hepə'taɪtɪs -təs
heptagon 'heptəgən $ -gon
her usual form: ɜ(r) strong-form: hɜ(r)
herald 'herld
heraldic he'rældɪk hɪ-
heraldry 'herldrɪ
herb hɜb $ ɜb etc
herbaceous hɜ'beɪʃəs
herbalist 'hɜbḷɪst
herbivorous hɜ'bɪvərəs
Herbert 'hɜbət $ 'hɜbərt
Herculean 'hɜkjʊ'liən
Hercules 'hɜkjʊliz
herd hɜd
here hɪə(r)
hereabouts 'hɪərə'baʊts 'hɪərəbaʊts
hereafter hɪər'aftə(r) $ -'æftər
hereby hɪə'baɪ $ hɪər-
hereditary hɪ'redɪtrɪ $ -terɪ
heredity hɪ'redətɪ
Hereford 'herɪfəd $ 'hɜfərd 'herɪfərd
heresy 'herəsɪ
heretic 'herətɪk
heretical hɪ'retɪkl
heretofor 'hɪətu'fɔ(r) $ 'hɪər-
herewith hɪə'wɪð $ hɪər- -'wɪθ
heritage 'herɪtɪdʒ
hermaphrodite hɜ'mæfrədaɪt
hermetic hɜ'metɪk
hermit 'hɜmɪt
hernia 'hɜnɪə
hero 'hɪərəʊ $ 'hɪrəʊ
heroic hɪ'rəʊɪk
heroin 'herəʊɪn
heroine 'herəʊɪn
heroism 'herəʊɪzm
heron 'herən
hero-worship 'hɪərəʊ wɜʃɪp
Herr heə(r)
herring 'herɪŋ
herring-bone 'herɪŋ bəʊn
hers hɜz
herself usual form: ɜ'self
    after a pause, strong-form: hɜ'self

he's usual form: iz
    after a pause, strong-form: hiz
hesitant 'hezɪtənt
hesitate 'hezɪteɪt
hesitation 'hezɪ'teɪʃn
hessian 'hesɪən $ 'heʃn
heterodox 'hetərədoks -tr-
heterogeneous 'hetərə'dʒɪnɪəs -rəʊ-
hew hju
hexagon 'heksəgən $ -gon etc
hexagonal heks'ægənl
hexameter heks'æmɪtə(r)
hey! heɪ
heyday 'heɪdeɪ
Hey presto 'heɪ 'prestəʊ
hi! haɪ
hiatus haɪ'eɪtəs
hibernate 'haɪbəneɪt $ -bər-
hibernation 'haɪbə'neɪʃn $ -bər-
hibiscus hɪ'bɪskəs
hiccough 'hɪkʌp
hiccup 'hɪkʌp
hid hɪd
hidden 'hɪdn
hide haɪd
hide-and-seek 'haɪd n 'sik
hide-away 'haɪd əweɪ
hidebound 'haɪdbaʊnd
hideous 'hɪdɪəs
hiding 'haɪdɪŋ
hiding-place 'haɪdɪŋ pleɪs
hierarchy 'haɪərakɪ $ -arkɪ
hieroglyphics 'haɪərəʊ'glɪfɪks
hi-fi n 'haɪ 'faɪ
higgledy-piggledy 'hɪgldɪ 'pɪgldɪ
high haɪ
highball 'haɪbɔl
high-born 'haɪ 'bɔn $ 'bɔrn
high-brow 'haɪ braʊ
high-falutin' 'haɪ fə'lutn -tɪn
high-fidelity 'haɪ fɪ'delətɪ
high-handed 'haɪ 'hændɪd
highlands 'haɪləndz
highlander 'haɪləndə(r)
highlight 'haɪlaɪt
highly-strung 'haɪlɪ 'strʌŋ
high-minded 'haɪ 'maɪndɪd
high-necked 'haɪ 'nekt
highness, H– 'haɪnəs -nɪs
high-pitched 'haɪ 'pɪtʃt
high-powered 'haɪ 'paʊəd $ 'paʊərd
high-spirited 'haɪ 'spɪrɪtɪd
high street 'haɪ strit

high tea 'haɪ 'ti
highway 'haɪweɪ
highway code 'haɪweɪ 'kəʊd
highwayman 'haɪwɪmən $ £ -weɪ-
hijack 'haɪdʒæk
hike haɪk
hilarious hɪ'leərɪəs $ haɪ- -'lær-
hilarity hɪ'lærətɪ
Hilary 'hɪlərɪ
Hilda 'hɪldə
hill hɪl
hillock 'hɪlək
hillside 'hɪl-saɪd
hilt hɪlt
him *usual form:* ɪm *strong-form:* hɪm
himself *usual form:* ɪm'self
    after a pause, strong-form: hɪm'self
hind haɪnd
hinder *v* 'hɪndə(r)
hinder(most) 'haɪndə(məʊst) $ 'haɪndər-
Hindi 'hɪndi
hindmost 'haɪndməʊst
hindrance 'hɪndrns
hindsight 'haɪndsaɪt
Hindu 'hɪn'du
hinge hɪndʒ
hint hɪnt
hinterland 'hɪntəlænd $ 'hɪntər-
hip hɪp
hip-bath 'hɪp baθ $ bæθ
hip-flask 'hɪp flask $ flæsk
hip-pocket 'hɪp 'pokɪt
hippodrome 'hɪpədrəʊm
hippopotamus 'hɪpə'potəməs
hippy 'hɪpɪ
hipster 'hɪpstə(r)
hire 'haɪə(r)
hire purchase 'haɪə 'pɜtʃəs 'pɜtʃɪs
    $ 'haɪər
his *adj usual form:* ɪz *strong-form:* hɪz
his *pron* hɪz
hiss hɪs
historian hɪ'stɔrɪən
historic hɪ'storɪk $ -'stɔr- *etc*
historical hɪ'storɪkl $ -'stɔr- *etc*
history 'hɪstrɪ
histrionic 'hɪstrɪ'onɪk
hit hɪt
hit-and-run 'hɪt n 'rʌn
hitch hɪtʃ
hitch-hike 'hɪtʃ haɪk
hither 'hɪðə(r)
Hitler 'hɪtlə(r)

hive haɪv
H.M.S. 'eɪtʃ em 'es
Ho! həʊ
hoar hɔ(r)
hoard hɔd $ hɔrd
hoar-frost 'hɔ frost $ 'hɔr frɔst
hoarse hɔs $ hɔrs
hoax həʊks
hob hob
hobble 'hobl
hobble-de-hoy 'hobl dɪ 'hɔɪ
hobby 'hobɪ
hobby-horse 'hobɪ hɔs $ hɔrs
hobgoblin hob'goblɪn
hobnailed 'hobneɪld
hobnob hob'nob
hobo 'həʊbəʊ
Hobson 'hobsn
hock hok
hockey 'hokɪ
hocus-pocus 'həʊkəs 'pəʊkəs
hod hod
hodge-podge 'hodʒ podʒ
hoe həʊ
hog hog $ hɔg *etc*
hogmanay 'hogməneɪ
hoi polloi 'hɔɪ 'polɔɪ pə'lɔɪ
hoist hɔɪst
hoity-toity 'hɔɪtɪ 'tɔɪtɪ
Holbein 'holbaɪn
Holborn 'həʊbən $ 'həʊlbɔrn
hold həʊld
hold-up 'həʊld ʌp
hole həʊl
hole-and-corner 'həʊl ən 'kɔnə(r) $ 'kɔr-
holiday 'holədɪ $ £ -deɪ
holiday-camp 'holədɪ kæmp $ -deɪ
holiday-maker 'holədɪ meɪkə(r) $ -deɪ
Holland 'holənd
hollow 'holəʊ
holly, H- 'holɪ
hollyhock 'holɪhok
Hollywood 'holɪwʊd
holocaust 'holəkɔst
holograph 'holəgraf $ £ -græf
holster 'həʊlstə(r)
holy 'həʊlɪ
Holy Land, the ðə 'həʊlɪ 'lænd
    ðə 'həʊlɪ lænd
Holy Week 'həʊlɪ wik
homage 'homɪdʒ
home həʊm
home-coming 'həʊm kʌmɪŋ

home-grown ˈhəʊm ˈgrəʊn
home-made ˈhəʊm ˈmeɪd
Home Office ˈhəʊm ofɪs $ ɔfɪs
homeopathy ˌhəʊmɪˈopəθɪ ˈhom
Homer ˈhəʊmə(r)
homesick ˈhəʊmsɪk
homespun ˈhəʊmspʌn
homestead ˈhəʊmsted
homeward(s) ˈhəʊmwəd(z) £ -wʊd(z)
    $ -wərd(z)
homework ˈhəʊmwɜk
homicidal ˌhomɪˈsaɪdl
homicide ˈhomɪsaɪd
homily ˈhomɪlɪ -əlɪ
homing ˈhəʊmɪŋ
homo ˈhəʊməʊ
homoeopathy ˌhəʊmɪˈopəθɪ ˈhom-
homogeneity ˌhəʊməʊdʒɪˈniːɪtɪ -ˈneɪə- ˈho-
homogeneous ˌhəʊməˈdʒiːnɪəs ˈhom-
homonym ˈhomənɪm
homosexual ˈhəʊməˈsekʃʊəl ˈhom- £ -ksjʊ-
homosexuality ˈhəʊməˈsekʃʊˈælətɪ
    ˈhom- £ -ksjʊ-
Honduras honˈdjʊərəs $ -ˈdʊərəs
honest ˈonɪst
honesty ˈonɪstɪ
honey ˈhʌnɪ
honey-bee ˈhʌnɪ biː
honeycomb ˈhʌnɪkəʊm
honeydew ˈhʌnɪdjuː $ -du
honeymoon ˈhʌnɪmuːn
honey-suckle ˈhʌnɪ sʌkl
Hong Kong ˈhoŋ ˈkoŋ
    $ ˈhoŋ koŋ ˈhoŋ kɔŋ ˈhoŋ ˈkɔŋ etc
honk hoŋk $ hɔŋk etc
Honolulu ˌhonəˈluːluː
honorarium ˌonəˈreərɪəm
honorary ˈonrɪ ˈonərɪ $ ˈonərerɪ
honorific ˌonəˈrɪfɪk
honour($ -or) ˈonə(r)
honourable($ -or-) ˈonrbl -nər-
hood hʊd
-hood suffix hʊd
hoodlum ˈhʊdləm
hoodoo ˈhuːduː
hoodwink ˈhʊdwɪŋk
hooey ˈhuːɪ
hoof huːf $ hʊf etc
hook hʊk
hookah ˈhʊkə
hookey ˈhʊkɪ
hook-nosed ˈhʊk ˈnəʊzd
hook-up ˈhʊk ʌp

hook-worm ˈhʊk wɜm
hooligan ˈhuːlɪgən
hoop huːp
hoop-la ˈhuːp lɑ
hoot huːt
hoover, H– ˈhuːvə(r)
hooves huːvz $ hʊvz etc
hop hop
hope həʊp
hop-field ˈhop fiːld
hop-picking ˈhop pɪkɪŋ
hopscotch ˈhopskotʃ
Horace ˈhorɪs ˈhorəs $ ˈhɔr-
horde hɔd $ hɔrd
horizon həˈraɪzn
horizontal ˌhorɪˈzontl $ ˈhɔr- etc
hormone ˈhɔməʊn $ ˈhɔr-
horn hɔn $ hɔrn
hornbeam ˈhɔnbiːm $ ˈhɔrn-
hornbill ˈhɔnbɪl $ ˈhɔrn-
hornblende ˈhɔnblend $ ˈhɔrn-
hornet ˈhɔnɪt $ ˈhɔrn-
horn-rimmed ˈhɔn ˈrɪmd $ ˈhɔrn
hornpipe ˈhɔnpaɪp $ ˈhɔrn-
horology hɔˈrolədʒɪ ho-
horoscope ˈhorəskəʊp $ ˈhɔr- etc
horrible ˈhorəbl $ ˈhɔrəbl etc
horrid ˈhorɪd $ ˈhɔrɪd etc
horrific hoˈrɪfɪk həˈr- $ hɔˈrɪfɪk etc
horrify ˈhorɪfaɪ $ ˈhɔrɪfaɪ etc
horror ˈhorə(r) $ ˈhɔrər etc
horror-film ˈhorə fɪlm $ ˈhɔrər etc
horror-struck ˈhorə strʌk $ ˈhɔrər etc
hors de combat ˈɔ də ˈkɔ̃ba $ ˈɔr
hors d'oeuvres ɔ ˈdɜvr with unsyllabic r,
    dɜv $ ˈɔr ˈdɜv
horse hɔs $ hɔrs
horseback ˈhɔsbæk $ ˈhɔrs-
horse-box ˈhɔs boks $ ˈhɔrs
horse-chestnut ˈhɔs ˈtʃesnʌt $ ˈhɔrs
horse-flesh ˈhɔs fleʃ $ ˈhɔrs
horse-fly ˈhɔs flaɪ $ ˈhɔrs
horsehair ˈhɔsheə(r) $ ˈhɔrs-
horse-laugh ˈhɔs lɑf $ ˈhɔrs læf
horseman ˈhɔsmən $ ˈhɔrs-
horse-play ˈhɔs pleɪ $ ˈhɔrs
horse-power ˈhɔs paʊə(r) $ ˈhɔrs
horse-racing ˈhɔs reɪsɪŋ $ ˈhɔrs
horse-radish ˈhɔs rædɪʃ $ ˈhɔrs
horse-sense ˈhɔs sens $ ˈhɔrs
horse-shoe ˈhɔʃ ʃu $ ˈhɔrʃ
horse-whip ˈhɔs wɪp $ ˈhɔrs hwɪp wɪp
horsewoman ˈhɔs wʊmən $ ˈhɔrs

horticultural 'hɔtɪˋkʌltʃərl $ 'hɔr-
horticulture ˋhɔtɪkʌltʃə(r) $ ˋhɔr-
hosanna həʊˋzænə
hose həʊz
hose-pipe ˋhəʊz paɪp
hosier ˋhəʊzɪə(r) $ £ ˋhəʊʒə(r)
hosiery ˋhəʊzɪərɪ $ £ ˋhəʊʒərɪ
hospitable hoˋspɪtəbl ˋhospɪtəbl
hospital ˋhospɪtl -ɪdl
hospitality 'hospɪˋtælətɪ
host həʊst
hostage ˋhostɪdʒ
hostel ˋhostl
hostess ˋhəʊstɪs -əs -es
hostile ˋhostaɪl $ ˋhostl
hostility hoˋstɪlətɪ
hot hot
hotbed ˋhotbed
hot-blooded 'hot ˋblʌdɪd
hotchpotch ˋhotʃpotʃ
hot cross bun 'hot kros ˋbʌn $ krɔs
hot dog 'hot ˋdog $ ˋdɔg
hotel həʊˋtel əʊˋtel
hothead ˋhothed
hot-headed 'hot ˋhedɪd
hothouse ˋhothaʊs
hot line ˋhot laɪn
hot-plate ˋhot pleɪt
hotpot ˋhot pot
hot-water-bottle hot ˋwɔtə botl
   $ ˋwɔtər
hound haʊnd
hour ˋaʊə(r)
hour-glass ˋaʊə glas $ ˋaʊər glæs
hour-hand ˋaʊə hænd $ ˋaʊər
house haʊs
house-agent ˋhaʊs eɪdʒənt
house-arrest ˋhaʊs ərest
houseboat ˋhaʊsbəʊt
house-breaker ˋhaʊs breɪkə(r)
house-dog ˋhaʊs dog $ dɔg
house down, bring the ˋhaʊs daʊn
household ˋhaʊshəʊld ˋhaʊsəʊld
housekeeper ˋhaʊs kipə(r)
housemaid ˋhaʊsmeɪd
house-master ˋhaʊs mastə(r) $ mæstər
house on fire, like a ˋhaʊs on faɪə(r)
house-party ˋhaʊs patɪ $ partɪ
house-proud ˋhaʊs praʊd
house-room ˋhaʊs rʊm $ £ rum etc
houses ˋhaʊzɪz
house-surgeon ˋhaʊs sədʒən
house-top ˋhaʊs top

house-trained ˋhaʊs treɪnd
house-warming ˋhaʊs wɔmɪŋ $ wɔr-
housewife person ˋhaʊswaɪf
housewife sewing-case ˋhazɪf
housewifery ˋhaʊswɪfrɪ -waɪfərɪ
housework ˋhaʊswɜk
hove, H– həʊv
hovel ˋhovl $ ˋhʌvl
hover ˋhovə(r) $ ˋhʌvər
hovercraft ˋhovəkraft $ ˋhʌvərkræft
how haʊ
Howard ˋhaʊəd $ ˋhaʊərd
howbeit haʊˋbiɪt
however haʊˋevə(r)
howitzer ˋhaʊɪtsə(r)
howl haʊl
hoyden ˋhɔɪdn
H.P. 'eɪtʃ ˋpi
hub hʌb
hubbub ˋhʌbʌb
Hubert ˋhjubət $ -bərt
huckleberry ˋhʌklbərɪ $ -berɪ
Huddersfield ˋhʌdəzfild $ -dərz-
huddle ˋhʌdl
hue hju
huff hʌf
hug hʌg
huge hjudʒ
Huguenot ˋhjugənəʊ $ £ -not
hula ˋhulə
hula-hoop 'hulə ˋhup
hulk hʌlk
hull, H– hʌl
hullabaloo 'hʌləbəˋlu
hullo həˋləʊ 'hʌˋləʊ
hum hʌm
human ˋhjumən
humane hjuˋmeɪn
humanist ˋhjumənɪst
humanitarian hju'mænɪˋteərɪən
humanity hjuˋmænətɪ
humanize ˋhjumənaɪz
humble ˋhʌmbl
humbug ˋhʌmbʌg
humdrum ˋhʌmdrʌm
humerus ˋhjumərəs
humid ˋhjumɪd
humidity hjuˋmɪdətɪ
humiliate hjuˋmɪlɪeɪt
humiliation hju'mɪlɪˋeɪʃn
humility hjuˋmɪlətɪ
humming-bird ˋhʌmɪŋ bɜd
humorist ˋhjumərɪst $ ˋju-

humorous ˈhjumərəs $ ˈju-
humour($ -or) ˈhjumə(r) $ ˈjumər
hump hʌmp
humpbacked ˈhʌmpˈbækt
humph hʌmpf *realistically a grunt with
   lips closed and then puffed open*
Humphrey ˈhʌmfrɪ
Humpty Dumpty ˈhʌmptɪ ˈdʌmptɪ
humus ˈhjuməs
hunch hʌntʃ
hunchback ˈhʌntʃbæk
hundred ˈhʌndrəd
hundred-and-one ˈhʌndrd n ˈwʌn
hundredth ˈhʌndrədθ -ətθ
hundredweight ˈhʌndrədweɪt
hung hʌŋ
Hungary ˈhʌŋgərɪ
hunger ˈhʌŋgə(r)
hunger-strike ˈhʌŋgə straɪk $ ˈhʌŋgər
hungry ˈhʌŋgrɪ
hunk hʌŋk
hunt hʌnt
Huntingdon ˈhʌntɪŋdən
huntress ˈhʌntrəs -ɪs
huntsman ˈhʌntsmən
hurdle ˈhɜdl
hurdy-gurdy ˈhɜdɪ gɜdɪ ˈh- ˈg-
hurl hɜl
hurly-burly ˈhɜlɪ bɜlɪ ˈh- ˈb-
hurrah huˈra $ həˈrɔ *etc*
hurray huˈreɪ
hurricane ˈhʌrɪkən -keɪn $ ˈhɜɪkeɪn
hurricane-lamp ˈhʌrɪkən læmp
   $ ˈhɜɪkeɪn *etc*
hurry ˈhʌrɪ $ ˈhɜɪ
hurt hɜt
hurtle ˈhɜtl
husband ˈhʌzbənd
husbandry ˈhʌzbəndrɪ
hush hʌʃ
husk hʌsk
husky ˈhʌskɪ
hussar huˈza(r)
hussy ˈhʌzɪ ˈhʌsɪ
hustings ˈhʌstɪŋz
hustle ˈhʌsl
hut hʌt
hutch hʌtʃ
hyacinth ˈhaɪəsɪnθ

hyaena haɪˈinə
hybrid ˈhaɪbrɪd
Hyde Park ˈhaɪd ˈpak $ ˈpark
hydra ˈhaɪdrə
hydrangea haɪˈdreɪndʒə
hydrant ˈhaɪdrənt
hydrate ˈhaɪdreɪt
hydraulic haɪˈdrɔlɪk
hydrocarbon ˈhaɪdrəuˈkabən $ -ˈkar-
hydrochloric ˈhaɪdrəuˈklorɪk $ -ˈklɔrɪk
hydro-electric ˈhaɪdrəu ɪˈlektrɪk
hydrofoil ˈhaɪdrəfɔɪl
hydrogen ˈhaɪdrədʒən -drɪdʒən -dʒɪn
hydrogen-bomb ˈhaɪdrədʒən bom ˈh- ˈb-
hydrophobia ˈhaɪdrəˈfəubɪə
hydroplane ˈhaɪdrəpleɪn
hyena haɪˈinə
hygiene ˈhaɪdʒin
hygienic haɪˈdʒinɪk
   $ -ˈdʒenɪk ˈhaɪdʒɪˈenɪk
hymen ˈhaɪmən -men
hymn hɪm
hymnal ˈhɪmnl
hyper- *prefix* ˈhaɪpə(r)
hyperbola haɪˈpəbələ
hyperbole haɪˈpəbəlɪ
hypercritical ˈhaɪpəˈkrɪtɪkl $ ˈhaɪpər-
hypersensitive ˈhaɪpəˈsensətɪv
   $ ˈhaɪpər-
hyphen ˈhaɪfən
hyphenate ˈhaɪfn̩eɪt -fən-
hypnosis hɪpˈnəusɪs
hypnotic hɪpˈnotɪk
hypnotism ˈhɪpnətɪzm
hypnotize ˈhɪpnətaɪz
hypo- *prefix* ˈhaɪpəu
hypochondria ˈhaɪpəˈkondrɪə ˈhɪp-
hypochondriac ˈhaɪpəˈkondrɪæk ˈhɪp-
hypocrisy hɪˈpokrəsɪ
hypocrite ˈhɪpəkrɪt
hypocritical ˈhɪpəˈkrɪtɪkl
hypodermic ˈhaɪpəˈdəmɪk
hypotenuse haɪˈpotɪnjuz -jus
   $ -tn̩us *etc*
hypothesis haɪˈpoθəsɪs
hypothetical ˈhaɪpəˈθetɪkl
hysteria hɪˈstɪərɪə $ hɪˈsterɪə
hysterical hɪˈsterɪkl
hysterics hɪˈsterɪks

I

I i aɪ
Iago iˋagəʊ
iambic aɪˋæmbɪk
iambus aɪˋæmbəs
Ian ˋiən
Ibadan ɪˋbædn
Iberia aɪˋbɪərɪə
ibex ˋaɪbeks
ibid ˋɪbɪd
ibidem ˋɪbɪdem ɪˋbaɪdem
ibis ˋaɪbɪs
-ible suffix əbl
Ibsen ˋɪbsn ˋɪpsn
-ic suffix ɪk
-ically suffix ɪklɪ
ice aɪs
ice-age ˋaɪs eɪdʒ
ice-axe ˋaɪs æks
iceberg ˋaɪs bɜg
ice-bound ˋaɪs baʊnd
ice-box ˋaɪs boks
ice-breaker ˋaɪs breɪkə(r)
ice-cap ˋaɪs kæp
ice-cream ˋaɪs ˋkrim ˋaɪs krim
Iceland ˋaɪslənd
Icelandic aɪsˋlændɪk
ice-man ˋaɪs mæn
ice-show ˋaɪs ʃəʊ ˋaɪʃ ʃəʊ
ichneumon ɪkˋnjumən
ICI ˈaɪ si ˋaɪ
icicle ˋaɪsɪkl
icing ˋaɪsɪŋ
icon ˋaɪkon
iconoclast aɪˋkonəklæst £ -klɑst
I'd aɪd
Ida ˋaɪdə
Idaho ˋaɪdəhəʊ
-ide suffix aɪd
idea aɪˋdɪə
ideal aɪˋdɪəl aɪˋdiļ
idealism aɪˋdɪəlɪzm
idealist aɪˋdɪəlɪst
idealize aɪˋdɪəlaɪz
idem ˋɪdem ˋaɪdem
identical aɪˋdentɪkl
identification aɪˈdentɪfɪˋkeɪʃn
identify aɪˋdentɪfaɪ
identity aɪˋdentətɪ $ ɪˋd-
identity card aɪˋdentətɪ kad $ kard
ideograph ˋɪdɪəʊgraf $ £ -græf

ideogram ˋɪdɪəʊgræm
ideological ˈaɪdɪəˋlodʒɪkl
ideology ˈaɪdɪˋolədʒɪ
ides aɪdz
idiocy ˋɪdɪəsɪ
idiom ˋɪdɪəm
idiomatic ˈɪdɪəˋmætɪk
idiosyncrasy ˈɪdɪəʊˋsɪŋkrəsɪ -dɪəˋs-
idiot ˋɪdɪət
idiotic ˈɪdɪˋotɪk
idle ˋaɪdl
idler ˋaɪdlə(r)
idly ˋaɪdlɪ
idol ˋaɪdl
idolater aɪˋdolətə(r)
idolatry aɪˋdolətrɪ
idolize ˋaɪdļaɪz
idyll ˋɪdɪl ˋaɪdɪl $ ˋaɪdl
idyllic ɪˋdɪlɪk $ £ aɪˋdɪlɪk
i.e. ˈaɪ ˋi
-ier suffix ɪə(r)
-iest suffix ɪəst ɪɪst
if ɪf
igloo ˋɪglu
igneous ˋɪgnɪəs
ignite ɪgˋnaɪt
ignition ɪgˋnɪʃn
ignoble ɪgˋnəʊbl
ignominious ˈɪgnəˋmɪnɪəs
ignominy ˋɪgnəmɪnɪ
ignoramus ˈɪgnəˋreɪməs
ignorance ˋɪgnərəns
ignorant ˋɪgnərənt
ignore ɪgˋnɔ(r)
iguana ɪˋgwɑnə
ikon ˋaɪkon
ilex ˋaɪleks
ilk ɪlk
I'll aɪl al
ill ɪl
ill-advised ˈɪl ədˋvaɪzd
ill-bred ˈɪl ˋbred
ill-disposed ˈɪl dɪˋspəʊzd
illegal ɪˋligl
illegality ˈɪliˋgælətɪ
illegible ɪˋledʒəbl
illegibility ɪˈledʒəˋbɪlətɪ
illegitimate ˈɪlɪˋdʒɪtɪmət
illegitimacy ˈɪlɪˋdʒɪtɪməsɪ
ill-gotten ˈɪl ˋgotn

illiberal ɪˈlɪbrl
illicit ɪˈlɪsɪt
Illinois ˈɪlɪˈnɔɪ
illiteracy ɪˈlɪtɾəsɪ
illiterate ɪˈlɪtɾət
ill-judged 'ɪl ˈdʒʌdʒd
ill-mannered 'ɪl ˈmænəd $ -nərd
ill-natured 'ɪl ˈneɪtʃəd $ -tʃərd
illogical ɪˈlodʒɪkl
ill-tempered 'ɪl ˈtempəd $ -pərd
ill-timed 'ɪl ˈtaɪmd
ill-treat 'ɪl ˈtrit
illuminate ɪˈlumɪneɪt
illumination ɪˈlumɪˈneɪʃn
illusion ɪˈluʒn
illusory ɪˈlusərɪ £ -ˈlju-
illustrate ˈɪləstreɪt
illustration ˈɪləˈstreɪʃn
illustrative ˈɪləstrətɪv -streɪt-
    $ ɪˈlʌstrətɪv
illustrator ˈɪləstreɪtə(r)
illustrious ɪˈlʌstrɪəs
ill-will 'ɪl ˈwɪl
I'm aɪm
im- prefix ɪm
image ˈɪmɪdʒ
imagery ˈɪmɪdʒrɪ $ -dʒərɪ
imaginable ɪˈmædʒnəbl -dʒn̩-
imaginary ɪˈmædʒɪnɾɪ -dʒn- $ -dʒənerɪ
imagination ɪˈmædʒɪˈneɪʃn
imaginative ɪˈmædʒnətɪv -dʒn̩-
    $ ɪˈmædʒɪneɪtɪv etc
imagine ɪˈmædʒɪn -dʒən
imam ɪˈmam
imbalance ɪmˈbæləns
imbecile ˈɪmbəsil $ -sl̩ $ £ -saɪl
imbecility ˈɪmbəˈsɪlətɪ
imbibe ɪmˈbaɪb
imbroglio ɪmˈbrəʊlɪəʊ
imbue ɪmˈbju
imitate ˈɪmɪteɪt
imitation ˈɪmɪˈteɪʃn
imitative ˈɪmɪtətɪv $ -teɪt-
immaculate ɪˈmækjʊlət
immanence ˈɪmənəns
immanent ˈɪmənənt
immaterial ˈɪməˈtɪərɪəl
immature ˈɪməˈtʃʊə(r) $ ˈɪməˈtʊər
immaturity ˈɪməˈtʃʊərətɪ -tjʊər-
    $ -ˈtʊər-
immeasurable ɪˈmeʒɾəbl
immediate ɪˈmidɪət əˈm- £ -idʒət
immemorial ˈɪməˈmɔrɪəl

immense ɪˈmens
immensity ɪˈmensətɪ
immerse ɪˈmɜs
immersion ɪˈmɜʃn $ ɪˈmɜʒn etc
immigrant ˈɪmɪgrənt
immigrate ˈɪmɪgreɪt
immigration ˈɪmɪˈgreɪʃn
imminent ˈɪmɪnənt
immobile ɪˈməʊbaɪl $ -bl -bɪl
immobility ˈɪməˈbɪlətɪ
immobilization ɪˈməʊblaɪˈzeɪʃn $ -lɪˈz-
immobilize ɪˈməʊblaɪz
immoderate ɪˈmodɾət
immodest ɪˈmodɪst
immolate ˈɪməleɪt
immoral ɪˈmorl $ ɪˈmɔrl
immorality ˈɪməˈrælətɪ
immortal ɪˈmotl $ ɪˈmɔrtl
immortality ˈɪmɔˈtælətɪ $ -mɔr-
immovable ɪˈmuvəbl
immune ɪˈmjun
immunity ɪˈmjunətɪ
immunization ˈɪmjʊnaɪˈzeɪʃn
    $ -nɪˈzeɪʃn etc
immunize ˈɪmjʊnaɪz
immure ɪˈmjʊə(r)
immutable ɪˈmjutəbl
imp ɪmp
impact n ˈɪmpækt
impacted ɪmˈpæktɪd
impair ɪmˈpeə(r)
impale ɪmˈpeɪl
impalpable ɪmˈpælpəbl
impart ɪmˈpat $ ɪmˈpart
impartial ɪmˈpaʃl $ ɪmˈparʃl
impartiality ˈɪmˈpaʃɪˈælətɪ $ -ˈpar-
impassable ɪmˈpasəbl $ -ˈpæs-
impasse ˈæmpas æmˈpas
    $ ɪmˈpæs æm-
impassioned ɪmˈpæʃnd
impassive ɪmˈpæsɪv
impassivity ˈɪmpæˈsɪvətɪ
impatience ɪmˈpeɪʃns
impatient ɪmˈpeɪʃnt
impeach ɪmˈpitʃ
impeachment ɪmˈpitʃmənt
impeccable ɪmˈpekəbl
impecunious ˈɪmpɪˈkjunɪəs
impede ɪmˈpid
impediment ɪmˈpedɪmənt
impel ɪmˈpel
impend ɪmˈpend
impenetrable ɪmˈpenɪtrəbl

impenitent ɪmˈpenɪtənt
imperative ɪmˈperətɪv
imperceptible ˌɪmpəˈseptəbl $ -pər-
imperfect ɪmˈpɜfɪkt
imperfection ˌɪmpəˈfekʃn $ -pər-
imperial ɪmˈpɪərɪəl
imperialist ɪmˈpɪərɪəlɪst
imperil ɪmˈperl
imperious ɪmˈpɪərɪəs
imperishable ɪmˈperɪʃəbl
impermeable ɪmˈpɜmɪəbl
impersonal ɪmˈpɜsnl
impersonate ɪmˈpɜsŋeɪt
impersonation ɪmˈpɜsnˈeɪʃn
impertinent ɪmˈpɜtɪnənt $ £ -tŋənt
imperturbable ˌɪmpəˈtɜbəbl $ ˌɪmpər-
impervious ɪmˈpɜvɪəs
impetigo ˌɪmpɪˈtaɪɡəʊ
impetuosity ɪmˈpetʃʊˈosətɪ
impetuous ɪmˈpetʃʊəs
impetus ˈɪmpɪtəs
impiety ɪmˈpaɪətɪ
impinge ɪmˈpɪndʒ
impious ˈɪmpɪəs $ ˈɪmˈpaɪəs
implacable ɪmˈplækəbl
implant ɪmˈplant $ ɪmˈplænt
implement n ˈɪmplɪmənt
implement v ˈɪmplɪment
implicate ˈɪmplɪkeɪt
implication ˈɪmplɪˈkeɪʃn
implicit ɪmˈplɪsɪt
implore ɪmˈplɔ(r)
imply ɪmˈplaɪ
impolite ˌɪmpəˈlaɪt
impolitic ɪmˈpolətɪk
imponderable ɪmˈpondrəbl
import n ˈɪmpɔt $ ˈɪmpɔrt
import v ɪmˈpɔt $ ɪmˈpɔrt
importance ɪmˈpɔtns $ -ˈpɔr-
important ɪmˈpɔtnt $ -ˈpɔr-
importation ˈɪmpɔˈteɪʃn $ -pər-
importunate adj ɪmˈpɔtjʊnət
  $ ɪmˈpɔrtʃʊnət
importunate v ɪmˈpɔtjʊneɪt
  $ ɪmˈpɔrtʃʊneɪt
importune ˈɪmpɔtjun ɪmˈpɔtjun -tʃun
  $ ˈɪmpɔrˈtun -pər- -ˈtjun -ˈpɔrtʃən
importunity ˈɪmpɔˈtjunətɪ -pə- $ -pɔr-
impose ɪmˈpəʊz
imposition ˈɪmpəˈzɪʃn
impossible ɪmˈposəbl
impossibility ɪmˈposəˈbɪlətɪ
impost ˈɪmpəʊst

impostor ɪmˈpostə(r)
imposture ɪmˈpostʃə(r)
impotence ˈɪmpətəns
impotent ˈɪmpətənt
impound ɪmˈpaʊnd
impoverish ɪmˈpovərɪʃ
impracticable ɪmˈpræktɪkəbl
imprecate ˈɪmprɪkeɪt -rək-
imprecation ˈɪmprɪˈkeɪʃn -rəˈk-
impregnable ɪmˈpregnəbl
impregnate ˈɪmpregneɪt $ £ ɪmˈpregneɪt
impres(s)ario ˈɪmprɪˈzarɪəʊ $ £ -ˈsa-
impress n ˈɪmpres
impress v ɪmˈpres
impression ɪmˈpreʃn
impressionist ɪmˈpreʃŋɪst
impressionable ɪmˈpreʃŋəbl
impressive ɪmˈpresɪv
imprint n ˈɪmprɪnt
imprint v ɪmˈprɪnt
imprison ɪmˈprɪzn
imprisonment ɪmˈprɪznmənt
improbable ɪmˈprobəbl
improbability ɪmˈprobəˈbɪlətɪ
impromptu ɪmˈpromptju $ -tu
improper ɪmˈpropə(r)
impropriety ˈɪmprəˈpraɪətɪ
improve ɪmˈpruv
improvement ɪmˈpruvmənt
improvident ɪmˈprovɪdənt
improvisation ˈɪmprəvaɪˈzeɪʃn
  $ -ˈprovɪˈz-
improvise ˈɪmprəvaɪz
imprudent ɪmˈprudnt
impudent ˈɪmpjʊdənt
impugn ɪmˈpjun
impulse ˈɪmpʌls
impulsive ɪmˈpʌlsɪv
impunity ɪmˈpjunətɪ
impure ɪmˈpjʊə(r)
impurity ɪmˈpjʊərətɪ
imputation ˈɪmpjʊˈteɪʃn
impute ɪmˈpjut
in ɪn
inability ˈɪnəˈbɪlətɪ
inaccessible ˈɪnækˈsesəbl
inaccessibility ˈɪnækˈsesəˈbɪlətɪ
inaccuracy ɪnˈækjərəsɪ
inaccurate ɪnˈækjərət -ɪt
inaction ɪnˈækʃn
inactive ɪnˈæktɪv
inactivity ˈɪnækˈtɪvətɪ
inadequacy ɪnˈædɪkwəsɪ

inadequate ɪnˈædɪkwət
inadmissible ˈɪnədˈmɪsəbl
inadvertent ˈɪnədˈvɜtnt
inalienable ɪnˈeɪlɪənəbl
inamorata ˈɪnˈæməˈrɑtə
inane ɪˈneɪn
inanimate ɪnˈænɪmət
inanition ˈɪnəˈnɪʃn
inanity ɪnˈænətɪ -ˈeɪn-
inapplicable ɪnˈæplɪkəbl ˈɪnəˈp-
inappreciable ˈɪnəˈpriʃəbl
inappropriate ˈɪnəˈprəʊprɪət
inapt ɪnˈæpt
inaptitude ɪnˈæptɪtjud -tʃud $ -tud
inarticulate ˈɪnɑˈtɪkjʊlət $ ˈɪnɑr-
inasmuch ˈɪnəzˈmʌtʃ
inattention ˈɪnəˈtenʃn
inattentive ˈɪnəˈtentɪv
inaugural ɪˈnɔgjʊrl
inaugurate ɪˈnɔgjʊreɪt
inborn ˈɪnˈbɔn $ ˈɪnˈbɔrn
inbred ˈɪnˈbred
inbreeding ˈɪnˈbridɪŋ $ £ ˈɪnbridɪŋ
Inc. ɪnˈkɔpəreɪtɪd $ -ˈkɔr- joc ɪŋk
incalculable ɪnˈkælkjʊləbl
incandescent ˈɪnkənˈdesnt -kæn-
incantation ˈɪnkænˈteɪʃn
incapability ˈɪnˈkeɪpəˈbɪlətɪ
incapable ɪnˈkeɪpəbl
incapacitate ˈɪnkəˈpæsəteɪt -sɪteɪt
incapacity ˈɪnkəˈpæsətɪ
incarcerate ɪnˈkɑsəreɪt $ -ˈkɑr-
incarnate ɪnˈkɑnət -neɪt $ -ˈkɑr-
incarnation ˈɪnkɑˈneɪʃn $ -kɑr-
incendiarism ɪnˈsendɪərɪzm $ -dɪer-
incendiary ɪnˈsendɪərɪ -dɪerɪ
incense n ˈɪnsens
incense v ɪnˈsens
incentive ɪnˈsentɪv
inception ɪnˈsepʃn
incertitude ɪnˈsɜtɪtjud $ -tud etc
incessant ɪnˈsesnt
incest ˈɪnsest
incestuous ɪnˈsestʃʊəs £ -tjʊəs
inch ɪntʃ
inchoate ɪnˈkəʊeɪt ˈɪnkəʊeɪt
inchoative ɪnˈkəʊətɪv
incidence ˈɪnsɪdəns
incident ˈɪnsɪdənt
incidental ˈɪnsɪˈdentl
incidentally ˈɪnsɪˈdentlɪ -tʃlɪ
incinerate ɪnˈsɪnəreɪt
incinerator ɪnˈsɪnəreɪtə(r)

incipient ɪnˈsɪpɪənt
incise ɪnˈsaɪs
incision ɪnˈsɪʒn
incisive ɪnˈsaɪsɪv
incisor ɪnˈsaɪzə(r)
incite ɪnˈsaɪt
incivility ˈɪnsɪˈvɪlətɪ
inclemency ɪnˈklemənsɪ
inclination ˈɪnklɪˈneɪʃn -klə-
incline n ˈɪnklaɪn
incline v ɪnˈklaɪn
inclose ɪnˈkləʊz
inclosure ɪnˈkləʊʒə(r)
include ɪnˈklud
inclusion ɪnˈkluʒn
inclusive ɪnˈklusɪv
incognito ˈɪnkogˈnitəʊ ɪnˈkognɪtəʊ
incoherent ˈɪnkəʊˈhɪərnt
income ˈɪnkʌm -kəm
income-tax ˈɪnkəm tæks
incoming ɪnˈkʌmɪŋ
incommensurate ˈɪnkəˈmenʃərət
incommode ˈɪnkəˈməʊd
incommunicado ˈɪnkəˈmjunɪˈkɑdəʊ
incomparability ˈɪnˈkomprəˈbɪlətɪ
incomparable ɪnˈkomprəbl
incompetence ɪnˈkompətəns -pɪt-
incompetent ɪnˈkompətənt -pɪt-
incomplete ˈɪnkəmˈplit
incomprehensible ˈɪnˈkomprɪˈhensəbl
incomprehension ˈɪnˈkomprɪˈhenʃn
incompressible ˈɪnkəmˈpresəbl
inconceivable ˈɪnkənˈsivəbl
inconclusive ˈɪnkənˈklusɪv
incongruity ˈɪnkoŋˈgruətɪ
incongruous ˈɪnˈkoŋgruəs
inconsequent ɪnˈkonsɪkwənt
inconsequential ˈɪnˈkonsɪˈkwenʃl
inconsiderable ˈɪnkənˈsɪdrəbl
inconsiderate ˈɪnkənˈsɪdrət -dɾət
inconsistency ˈɪnkənˈsɪstənsɪ
inconsistent ˈɪnkənˈsɪstənt
inconsolable ˈɪnkənˈsəʊləbl
inconspicuous ˈɪnkənˈspɪkjuəs
inconstant ɪnˈkonstənt
incontestable ˈɪnkənˈtestəbl
incontinent ɪnˈkontɪnənt
incontravertible ˈɪnˈkontrəˈvɜtəbl
inconvenience ˈɪnkənˈvinɪəns
inconvenient ˈɪnkənˈvinɪənt
inconvertibility ˈɪnkənˈvɜtəˈbɪlətɪ
inconvertible ˈɪnkənˈvɜtəbl
incorporate adj ɪnˈkɔpərət $ -ˈkɔr-

incorporate v ɪnˈkɔːpəreɪt $ -ˈkɔr-
incorrect ˈɪnkəˈrekt
incorrigible ɪnˈkɒrɪdʒəbl $ -ˈkɔr- etc
incorruptible ˈɪnkəˈrʌptəbl
increase n ˈɪnkriːs
increase v ɪnˈkriːs
incredibility ɪnˈkredəˈbɪlətɪ
incredible ɪnˈkredəbl
incredulity ˈɪnkrɪˈdjuːlətɪ $ -ˈduː-
incredulous ɪnˈkredjʊləs $ -dʒʊl-
increment ˈɪnkrəmənt
incriminate ɪnˈkrɪmɪneɪt
incrustation ˈɪnkrʌˈsteɪʃn
incubate ˈɪnkjʊbeɪt
incubator ˈɪnkjʊbeɪtə(r)
incubus ˈɪnkjʊbəs
inculcate ˈɪnkʌlkeɪt $ ɪnˈkʌlkeɪt etc
inculpate ˈɪnkʌlpeɪt $ ɪnˈkʌlpeɪt etc
incumbent ɪnˈkʌmbənt
incur ɪnˈkɜː(r)
incurable ɪnˈkjʊərəbl
incursion ɪnˈkɜːʃn $ ɪnˈkɜːʒn
indebted ɪnˈdetɪd
indecency ɪnˈdiːsnsɪ
indecent ɪnˈdiːsnt
indecipherable ˈɪndɪˈsaɪfrəbl
indecision ˈɪndɪˈsɪʒn
indecisive ˈɪndɪˈsaɪsɪv
indecorous ɪnˈdekərəs
indecorum ˈɪndɪˈkɔːrəm
indeed ɪnˈdiːd
indefatigable ˈɪndɪˈfætɪgəbl
indefensible ˈɪndɪˈfensəbl
indefinable ˈɪndɪˈfaɪnəbl
indefinite ɪnˈdefɪnɪt -ŋət -fɪn-
indelible ɪnˈdeləbl
indelicate ɪnˈdelɪkət
indemnify ɪnˈdemnɪfaɪ
indemnity ɪnˈdemnətɪ
indent n ˈɪndent
indent v ɪnˈdent
indentation ˈɪndenˈteɪʃn
indenture ɪnˈdentʃə(r)
independence ˈɪndɪˈpendəns
Independence Day ˈɪndɪˈpendəns deɪ
independent ˈɪndɪˈpendənt
indescribable ˈɪndɪˈskraɪbəbl
indestructible ˈɪndɪˈstrʌktəbl
indeterminacy ˈɪndɪˈtɜːmɪnəsɪ
indeterminate ˈɪndɪˈtɜːmɪnət
index ˈɪndeks
index finger ˈɪndeks fɪŋgə(r)
index number ˈɪndeks nʌmbə(r)

India ˈɪndɪə
Indian ˈɪndɪən
Indiana ˈɪndɪˈænə £ -ˈɑnə
Indian ink ˈɪndɪən ˈɪnk
Indian summer ˈɪndɪən ˈsʌmə(r)
India-rubber ˈɪndɪə ˈrʌbə(r)
indicate ˈɪndɪkeɪt
indication ˈɪndɪˈkeɪʃn
indicative ɪnˈdɪkətɪv
indicator ˈɪndɪkeɪtə(r)
indices ˈɪndɪsiːz
indict ɪnˈdaɪt
indictable ɪnˈdaɪtəbl
indictment ɪnˈdaɪtmənt
indifference ɪnˈdɪfrns
indifferent ɪnˈdɪfrnt
indigenous ɪnˈdɪdʒɪnəs
indigent ˈɪndɪdʒənt
indigestible ˈɪndɪˈdʒestəbl
indigestion ˈɪndɪˈdʒestʃən
indignant ɪnˈdɪgnənt
indignation ˈɪndɪgˈneɪʃn
indignity ɪnˈdɪgnətɪ
indigo ˈɪndɪgəʊ
indirect ˈɪndɪˈrekt ˈɪndaɪˈrekt
indiscipline ɪnˈdɪsəplɪn
indiscreet ˈɪndɪˈskriːt
indiscretion ˈɪndɪˈskreʃn
indiscriminate ˈɪndɪˈskrɪmɪnət
indispensable ˈɪndɪˈspensəbl
indisposed ˈɪndɪˈspəʊzd
indisposition ˈɪnˈdɪspəˈzɪʃn
indisputable ˈɪndɪˈspjuːtəbl
indissoluble ˈɪndɪˈsɒljʊbl
indistinct ˈɪndɪˈstɪŋkt
indite ɪnˈdaɪt
individual ˈɪndɪˈvɪdʒʊəl
individualist ˈɪndɪˈvɪdʒʊəlɪst
individualistic ˈɪndɪˈvɪdʒʊəˈlɪstɪk
individuality ˈɪndɪˈvɪdʒʊˈælətɪ
indivisible ˈɪndɪˈvɪzəbl
Indo-China ˈɪndəʊ ˈtʃaɪnə
indoctrinate ɪnˈdɒktrɪneɪt
indoctrination ɪnˈdɒktrɪˈneɪʃn
Indo-European ˈɪndəʊ ˈjʊərəˈpɪən
indolence ˈɪndələns
indolent ˈɪndələnt
indomitable ɪnˈdɒmɪtəbl
Indonesia ˈɪndəˈniːzɪə -iʃə $ £ -iʒə etc
indoor(s) ɪnˈdɔː(z) $ ɪnˈdɔr(z)
indubitable ɪnˈdjuːbɪtəbl $ -ˈduː-
induce ɪnˈdjuːs $ ɪnˈduːs
induct ɪnˈdʌkt

induction ɪnˈdʌkʃn
inductive ɪnˈdʌktɪv
indulge ɪnˈdʌldʒ
indulgence ɪnˈdʌldʒəns
industrial ɪnˈdʌstrɪəl
industrious ɪnˈdʌstrɪəs
industry ˈɪndəstrɪ $ -dʌs-
inebriate adj ɪˈnibrɪət
inebriate v ɪˈnibrɪeɪt
inebriety ˈɪniˈbraɪətɪ
inedible ɪnˈedəbl
ineffable ɪnˈefəbl
ineffective ˈɪnɪˈfektɪv
ineffectual ˈɪnɪˈfektʃuəl
inefficiency ˈɪnɪˈfɪʃnsɪ
inefficient ˈɪnɪˈfɪʃnt
inelegant ɪnˈelɪgənt
ineligibility ˈɪnˈelɪdʒəˈbɪlətɪ
ineligible ɪnˈelɪdʒəbl
ineluctable ˈɪnɪˈlʌktəbl
inept ɪnˈept
ineptitude ɪnˈeptɪtjud -tʃud $ -tud
inequality ˈɪnɪˈkwolətɪ
inequitable ɪnˈekwɪtəbl
ineradicable ˈɪnɪˈrædɪkəbl
inert ɪˈnɜt
inertia ɪˈnɜʃə
inescapable ˈɪnɪˈskeɪpəbl
inestimable ɪnˈestɪməbl
inevitable ɪnˈevɪtəbl
inexact ˈɪnɪgˈzækt
inexcusable ˈɪnɪkˈskjuzəbl
inexhaustible ˈɪnɪgˈzɔstəbl
inexorable ɪˈnegzərəbl ɪˈneksərəbl
inexpediency ˈɪnɪkˈspidɪənsɪ
inexpedient ˈɪnɪkˈspidɪənt
inexpensive ˈɪnɪkˈspensɪv
inexperience ˈɪnɪkˈspɪərɪəns
inexpert ˈɪnˈekspɜt
inexpiable ɪnˈekspɪəbl
inexplicable ˈɪnɪkˈsplɪkəbl
inexpressible ˈɪnɪkˈspresəbl
inextinguishable ˈɪnɪkˈstɪŋgwɪʃəbl
inextricable ɪnˈekstrɪkəbl
infallibility ˈɪnˈfæləˈbɪlətɪ
infallible ɪnˈfæləbl
infamous ˈɪnfəməs
infamy ˈɪnfəmɪ
infancy ˈɪnfənsɪ
infant ˈɪnfənt
infanticide ɪnˈfæntɪsaɪd
infantile ˈɪnfəntaɪl $ -tl
infantry ˈɪnfəntrɪ

infantryman ˈɪnfəntrɪmən
infatuate ɪnˈfætʃueɪt
infatuation ɪnˈfætʃuˈeɪʃn
infect ɪnˈfekt
infection ɪnˈfekʃn
infectious ɪnˈfekʃəs
infer ɪnˈfɜ(r)
inference ˈɪnfərəns
inferior ɪnˈfɪərɪə(r)
inferiority ˈɪnˈfɪərɪˈorətɪ $ -ˈɔr-
inferiority complex
   ˈɪnˈfɪərɪˈorətɪ kompleks $ -ˈɔr-
infernal ɪnˈfɜnl
inferno ɪnˈfɜnəʊ
infest ɪnˈfest
infidel ˈɪnfɪdl ˈɪnfɪdel
infidelity ˈɪnfɪˈdelətɪ
infield ˈɪnfild
in-fighting ˈɪn faɪtɪŋ
infiltrate ˈɪnfɪltreɪt $ ɪnˈfɪltreɪt
infiltration ˈɪnfɪlˈtreɪʃn
infinite ˈɪnfənɪt -fɪn-
infinitesimal ˈɪnˈfɪnɪˈtesɪml
infinitive ɪnˈfɪnɪtɪv
infinity ɪnˈfɪnətɪ
infirmary ɪnˈfɜmərɪ
infirmity ɪnˈfɜmətɪ
inflame ɪnˈfleɪm
inflammable ɪnˈflæməbl
inflammation ˈɪnfləˈmeɪʃn
inflammatory ɪnˈflæmətrɪ $ -tɔrɪ
inflate ɪnˈfleɪt
inflation ɪnˈfleɪʃn
inflationary ɪnˈfleɪʃnrɪ $ -ŋerɪ
inflect ɪnˈflekt
inflection ɪnˈflekʃn
inflexion ɪnˈflekʃn
inflict ɪnˈflɪct
infliction ɪnˈflɪkʃn
inflorescence ˈɪnfləˈresns
inflow ˈɪnfləʊ
influence ˈɪnfluəns
influential ˈɪnfluˈenʃl
influenza ˈɪnfluˈenzə
influx ˈɪnflʌks
inform ɪnˈfɔm $ ɪnˈfɔrm
informal ɪnˈfɔml $ ɪnˈfɔrml
informality ˈɪnfɔˈmælətɪ $ -fɔr-
informant ɪnˈfɔmənt $ -ˈfɔr-
information ˈɪnfəˈmeɪʃn $ -fɔr-
informative ɪnˈfɔmətɪv $ -ˈfɔr-
infra dig ˈɪnfrə ˈdɪg
infra-red ˈɪnfrə ˈred

infraction ɪnˈfrækʃn
infra-structure ˈɪnfrə strʌktʃə(r)
infrequency ɪnˈfrikwənsɪ
infrequent ɪnˈfrikwənt
infringe ɪnˈfrɪndʒ
infringement ɪnˈfrɪndʒmənt
infuriate ɪnˈfjʊərɪeɪt
infuse ɪnˈfjuz
infusion ɪnˈfuʒn
-ing suffix ɪŋ
ingenious ɪnˈdʒɪnɪəs
ingénue ˈæʒeɪˈnju ˈæn- $ ˈændʒənu
ingenuity ˈɪndʒɪˈnjuətɪ $ -ˈnu-
ingenuous ɪnˈdʒenjʊəs
ingot ˈɪŋgot $ £ ˈɪŋgət
ingrained ɪnˈgreɪnd
ingratiate ɪnˈgreɪʃɪeɪt
ingratitude ɪnˈgrætɪtjud -tʃud $ -tud
ingredient ɪnˈgridɪənt
ingress ˈɪngres
ingrowing ˈɪnˈgrəʊɪŋ
inhabit ɪnˈhæbɪt
inhabitable ɪnˈhæbɪtəbl
inhabitant ɪnˈhæbɪtənt
inhale ɪnˈheɪl
inhere ɪnˈhɪə(r)
inherent ɪnˈhɪərnt
inherit ɪnˈherɪt
inheritance ɪnˈherɪtəns
inhibit ɪnˈhɪbɪt
inhibition ˈɪnɪˈbɪʃn -nhɪ-
inhospitable ˈɪnhoˈspɪtəbl ɪnˈhospɪtəbl
inhuman ɪnˈhjumən
inimical ɪˈnɪmɪkl
inimitable ɪˈnɪmɪtəbl
iniquitous ɪˈnɪkwɪtəs
initial ɪˈnɪʃl
initiate n ɪˈnɪʃɪeɪt -ʃɪət
initiate v ɪˈnɪʃɪeɪt
initiative ɪˈnɪʃətɪv
inject ɪnˈdʒekt
injection ɪnˈdʒekʃn
injudicious ˈɪndʒuˈdɪʃəs
injunction ɪnˈdʒʌŋkʃn
injure ˈɪndʒə(r)
injurious ɪnˈdʒʊərɪəs
injury ˈɪndʒərɪ
injustice ɪnˈdʒʌstɪs
ink ɪŋk
ink-bottle ˈɪŋk botl
inkling ˈɪŋklɪŋ
ink-pot ˈɪŋk pot
ink-well ˈɪŋk wel

inland adj ˈɪnlənd
inland adv ɪnˈlænd
inland revenue ˈɪnlənd ˈrevnju
in-law(s) ˈɪn lɔ(z) ɪn ˈlɔ(z)
inlay ˈɪnleɪ
inlet ˈɪnlet ˈɪnlət
inmate ˈɪnmeɪt
inmost ˈɪnməʊst
inn ɪn
innards ˈɪnədz $ ˈɪnərdz
innate ɪˈneɪt
inner ˈɪnə(r)
innermost ˈɪnəməʊst $ ˈɪnər-
innings ˈɪnɪŋz
inn-keeper ˈɪn kipə(r)
innocence ˈɪnəsns
innocent ˈɪnəsnt
innocuous ɪˈnokjʊəs
innovate ˈɪnəveɪt
innovation ˈɪnəˈveɪʃn
innuendo ˈɪnjuˈendəʊ
innumerable ɪˈnjumrəbl $ ɪˈnu-
inoculate ɪˈnokjʊleɪt
inoculation ɪˈnokjʊˈleɪʃn
inoffensive ˈɪnəˈfensɪv
inopportune ɪnˈopətjun $ -pərtun
inordinate ɪˈnɔdɪnət $ £ -dṇət $ ɪˈnɔr-
inorganic̆ ˈɪnɔˈgænɪk $ ˈɪnɔr-
in-patient ˈɪn peɪʃnt
input ˈɪnpʊt
inquest ˈɪnkwest
inquietude ɪnˈkwaɪətjud $ -tud
inquire ɪnˈkwaɪə(r)
inquiry ɪnˈkwaɪərɪ $ ˈɪnkwaɪərɪ -kwərɪ
inquisition ˈɪnkwɪˈzɪʃn
inquisitive ɪnˈkwɪzətɪv
inquisitor ɪnˈkwɪzɪtə(r)
inquisitorial ɪnˈkwɪzɪˈtɔrɪəl
inroad ˈɪnrəʊd
insane ɪnˈseɪn
insanitary ɪnˈsænɪtrɪ $ -terɪ
insanity ɪnˈsænətɪ
insatiable ɪnˈseɪʃəbl
insatiate ɪnˈseɪʃɪət
inscribe ɪnˈskraɪb
inscrutable ɪnˈskrutəbl
insect ˈɪnsekt
insecticide ɪnˈsektɪsaɪd
insectivorous ˈɪnsekˈtɪvərəs
insecure ˈɪnsɪˈkjʊə(r)
insecurity ˈɪnsɪˈkjʊərətɪ
inseminate ɪnˈsemɪneɪt
insensate ɪnˈsenseɪt

insensibility 'ɪn'sensə'bɪlətɪ

insensible ɪn'sensəbl

insensitive 'ɪn'sensətɪv

insensitivity 'ɪn'sensə'tɪvətɪ

inseparable ɪn'seprəbl

insert ɪn'sɜt

insertion ɪn'sɜʃn

inset 'ɪnset

inshore 'ɪn'ʃɔ(r)

inside ɪn'saɪd

inside-out 'ɪnsaɪd 'aʊt

insidious ɪn'sɪdɪəs

insight 'ɪnsaɪt

insignia ɪn'sɪgnɪə

insignificant 'ɪnsɪg'nɪfɪkənt

insincere 'ɪnsɪn'sɪə(r)

insincerity 'ɪnsɪn'serətɪ

insinuate ɪn'sɪnjʊeɪt

insipid ɪn'sɪpɪd

insipidity 'ɪnsɪ'pɪdətɪ

insist ɪn'sɪst

insistent ɪn'sɪstənt

insole 'ɪnsəʊl

insolent 'ɪnsələnt

insoluble ɪn'soljʊbl

insolvent ɪn'solvənt

insomnia ɪn'somnɪə

insomuch 'ɪnsəʊ'mʌtʃ

insouciance ɪn'suːsɪəns $ ɪn'suːʃns

inspan 'ɪnspæn

inspect ɪn'spekt

inspection ɪn'spekʃn

inspector ɪn'spektə(r)

inspectorate ɪn'spektərət

inspiration 'ɪnspə'reɪʃn

inspire ɪn'spaɪə(r)

inspirit ɪn'spɪrɪt

Inst. 'ɪnstɪtjut -tʃut $ -tut

instability 'ɪnstə'bɪlətɪ

install ɪn'stɔl

installation 'ɪnstə'leɪʃn

instalment ɪn'stɔlmənt

instalment plan ɪn'stɔlmənt plæn

instance 'ɪnstəns

instant 'ɪnstənt

instantaneous 'ɪnstən'teɪnɪəs

instead ɪn'sted

instep 'ɪnstep

instigate 'ɪnstɪgeɪt

instigation 'ɪnstɪ'geɪʃn

instill ɪn'stɪl

instinct adj ɪn'stɪŋkt

instinct n 'ɪnstɪŋkt

instinctive ɪn'stɪŋktɪv

institute 'ɪnstɪtjut -tʃut $ -tut

institution 'ɪnstɪ'tjuʃn -'tʃuʃn $ -'tuʃn

institutional 'ɪnstɪ'tjuʃnl -'tʃu- $ -'tuʃnl

instruct ɪn'strʌkt

instruction ɪn'strʌkʃn

instructive ɪn'strʌktɪv

instructor ɪn'strʌktə(r)

instructress ɪn'strʌktrəs -ɪs

instrument 'ɪnstrʊmənt

instrumental 'ɪnstrʊ'mentl

instrumentation 'ɪnstrʊmen'teɪʃn

insubordination 'ɪnsə'bɔdɪ'neɪʃn

　　 $ 'ɪnsə'bɔrdn'eɪʃn

insufferable ɪn'sʌfrəbl

insufficient 'ɪnsə'fɪʃnt

insular 'ɪnsjʊlə(r) $ 'ɪnsələr

insularity 'ɪnsjʊ'lærətɪ $ -sə'l-

insulate 'ɪnsjʊleɪt £ -səl-

insulation 'ɪnsjʊ'leɪʃn $ £ -sə'l-

insulator 'ɪnsjʊleɪtə(r) $ £ -səl-

insulin 'ɪnsjʊlɪn $ 'ɪnsəlɪn

insult n 'ɪnsʌlt

insult v ɪn'sʌlt

insuperable ɪn'sjuprəbl $ £ -'sup-

insupportable 'ɪnsə'pɔtəbl $ -'pɔr-

insurance ɪn'ʃʊərns £ -'ʃɔr-

insurance policy ɪn'ʃʊərns pɔləsɪ £ -'ʃɔr-

insure ɪn'ʃʊə(r) £ -ʃɔ(r)

insurgent ɪn'sɜdʒənt

insurmountable 'ɪnsə'maʊntəbl $ -sər-

insurrection 'ɪnsə'rekʃn

intact ɪn'tækt

intake 'ɪnteɪk

intangible ɪn'tændʒəbl

integer 'ɪntɪdʒə(r) 'ɪntɪgə(r)

integral 'ɪntɪgrəl £ ɪn'tegrl

integrate 'ɪntɪgreɪt

integrity ɪn'tegrətɪ

integument ɪn'tegjʊmənt

intellect 'ɪntəlekt

intellectual 'ɪntə'lektʃʊəl

intelligence ɪn'telɪdʒəns

intelligent ɪn'telɪdʒənt

intelligentsia ɪn'telɪ'dʒentsɪə

intelligibility ɪn'telɪdʒə'bɪlətɪ

intelligible ɪn'telɪdʒəbl

intemperance ɪn'tempərns

intemperate ɪn'tempərət

intend ɪn'tend

intense ɪn'tens

intensification ɪn'tensɪfɪ'keɪʃn

intensify ɪn'tensɪfaɪ

intensity ɪnˈtensətɪ
intensive ɪnˈtensɪv
intent ɪnˈtent
intentional ɪnˈtenʃnl
inter ɪnˈtɜ(r)
interact ˈɪntərˈækt
interbreed ˈɪntəˈbrid $ ˈɪntər-
intercede ˈɪntəˈsid $ ˈɪntər-
intercession ˈɪntəˈseʃn $ ˈɪntər-
intercept ˈɪntəˈsept $ ˈɪntər-
interceptor ˈɪntəˈseptə(r) $ ˈɪntər-
interchange _n_ ˈɪntətʃeɪndʒ $ ˈɪntər-
interchange _v_ ˈɪntəˈtʃeɪndʒ $ ˈɪntər-
intercollegiate ˈɪntəkəˈlidʒət $ ˈɪntər-
intercolonial ˈɪntəkəˈləʊnɪəl $ ˈɪntər-
intercom ˈɪntəkom $ ˈɪntər-
intercommunication ˈɪntəkəˈmjunɪˈkeɪʃn
   $ ˈɪntər-
inter-continental ˈɪntəˈkontɪˈnentl
   $ ˈɪntər- -tn̩ˈentl
intercourse ˈɪntəkɔs $ ˈɪntərkɔrs
interdependent ˈɪntədɪˈpendənt
   $ ˈɪntər-
interdict _n_ ˈɪntədɪkt ˈɪntəˈdɪkt $ -tər-
interest ˈɪntrəst -rest -tərest
interfere ˈɪntəˈfɪə(r) $ ˈɪntər-
interference ˈɪntəˈfɪərns $ ˈɪntər-
interim ˈɪntərɪm
interior ɪnˈtɪərɪə(r)
interject ˈɪntəˈdʒekt $ ˈɪntər-
interjection ˈɪntəˈdʒekʃn $ ˈɪntər-
interlace ˈɪntəˈleɪs $ ˈɪntər-
interleave ˈɪntəˈliv $ ˈɪntər-
interline ˈɪntəˈlaɪn $ ˈɪntər-
interlinear ˈɪntəˈlɪnɪə(r) $ ˈɪntər-
interlink ˈɪntəˈlɪŋk $ ˈɪntər-
interlock ˈɪntəˈlok $ ˈɪntər-
interlocutor ˈɪntəˈlokjʊtə(r) $ ˈɪntər-
interloper ˈɪntələʊpə(r)
   $ ˈɪntərˈləʊpər _etc_
interlude ˈɪntəlud £ -ljud $ ˈɪntər-
intermarriage ˈɪntəˈmærɪdʒ $ ˈɪntər-
intermarry ˈɪntəˈmærɪ $ ˈɪntər-
intermediary ˈɪntəˈmidɪərɪ
   $ ˈɪntərˈmidɪerɪ
intermediate ˈɪntəˈmidɪət $ ˈɪntər-
interment ɪnˈtɜmənt
intermezzo ˈɪntəˈmetsəʊ $ ˈɪntər-
interminable ɪnˈtɜmɪnəbl -mn-
intermingle ˈɪntəˈmɪŋgl $ ˈɪntər-
intermission ˈɪntəˈmɪʃn $ ˈɪntər-
intermittent ˈɪntəˈmɪtnt $ ˈɪntər-
intermix ˈɪntəˈmɪks $ ˈɪntər-

intern _n_ ˈɪntɜn
intern _v_ ɪnˈtɜn
internal ɪnˈtɜnl
international ˈɪntəˈnæʃnl $ ˈɪntər-
internecine ˈɪntəˈnisaɪn
   $ ˈɪntərˈnesin -sn _etc_
interpellate ɪnˈtɜpɪleɪt $ ˈɪntərˈpeleɪt _etc_
interpellation ɪnˈtɜpɪˈleɪʃn -pəl-
   $ ˈɪntərˈpeˈleɪʃn _etc_
interplanetary ˈɪntəˈplænɪtrɪ
   $ ˈɪntərˈplænɪterɪ
interplay ˈɪntəpleɪ $ ˈɪntər-
interpolate ɪnˈtɜpəleɪt
interpose ˈɪntəˈpəʊz $ ˈɪntər-
interposition ˈɪntəpəˈzɪʃn $ ˈɪntər-
interpret ɪnˈtɜprɪt -rət
interpretation ɪnˈtɜprɪˈteɪʃn -rəˈt-
interracial ˈɪntəˈreɪʃl
interregnum ˈɪntəˈregnəm
interrelationship ˈɪntərɪˈleɪʃnʃɪp
interrogate ɪnˈterəgeɪt
interrogation ɪnˈterəˈgeɪʃn
interrogative ˈɪntəˈrogətɪv
interrupt ˈɪntəˈrʌpt
interruption ˈɪntəˈrʌpʃn
intersect ˈɪntəˈsekt $ ˈɪntər-
intersection ˈɪntəˈsekʃn $ ˈɪntər-
intersperse ˈɪntəˈspɜs $ ˈɪntər-
interstate ˈɪntəˈsteɪt $ ˈɪntər-
interstellar ˈɪntəˈstelə(r) ˈɪntər-
intertribal ˈɪntəˈtraɪbl $ ˈɪntər-
intertwine ˈɪntəˈtwaɪn $ ˈɪntər-
interval ˈɪntəvl $ ˈɪntərvl
intervene ˈɪntəˈvin $ ˈɪntər-
intervention ˈɪntəˈvenʃn $ ˈɪntər-
interview ˈɪntəvju $ ˈɪntər-
interweave ˈɪntəˈwiv $ ˈɪntər-
intestate ɪnˈtesteɪt ɪnˈtestɪt
intestinal ɪnˈtestɪnl £ ˈɪnteˈstaɪnl
intestine ɪnˈtestɪn
intimacy ˈɪntɪməsɪ
intimate _n_ ˈɪntɪmət
intimate _v_ ˈɪntɪmeɪt
intimation ˈɪntɪˈmeɪʃn
intimidate ɪnˈtɪmɪdeɪt
intimidation ɪnˈtɪmɪˈdeɪʃn
into _usual form:_ ˈɪntə _strong-form:_ ˈɪntu
intolerable ɪnˈtolɾəbl
intolerance ɪnˈtolərns
intolerant ɪnˈtolərnt
intonation ˈɪntəˈneɪʃn
intone ɪnˈtəʊn
intoxicant ɪnˈtoksɪkənt

intoxicate ɪnˈtɒksɪkeɪt
intra- *prefix* ˈɪntrə
intractable ɪnˈtræktəbl
intramural ˈɪntrəˈmjʊərl
intransigent ɪnˈtrænsɪdʒənt -nzɪ-
intransitive ɪnˈtrænsɪtɪv -nzɪ- £ -ˈtrans-
intrench ɪnˈtrentʃ
intrepid ɪnˈtrepɪd
intrepidity ˈɪntrɪˈpɪdətɪ
intricate ˈɪntrɪkət
intricacy ˈɪntrɪkəsɪ
intrigue ɪnˈtrig
intrinsic ɪnˈtrɪnsɪk -nzɪk
introduce ˈɪntrəˈdjus $ -ˈdus
introduction ˈɪntrəˈdʌkʃn
introductory ˈɪntrəˈdʌktrɪ
introspection ˈɪntrəˈspekʃn
introspective ˈɪntrəˈspektɪv
introvert ˈɪntrəvɜt
intrude ɪnˈtrud
intruder ɪnˈtrudə(r)
intrusion ɪnˈtruʒn
intrusive ɪnˈtrusɪv
intuition ˈɪntjuˈɪʃn $ -tu-
intuitive ɪnˈtjuɪtɪv $ -ˈtu-
inundate ˈɪnʌndeɪt -nən-
inundation ˈɪnʌnˈdeɪʃn -nən-
inure ɪˈnjʊə(r) $ ɪˈnuər *etc*
invade ɪnˈveɪd
invalid *adj* ɪnˈvælɪd
invalid *n* ˈɪnvəlid $ £ -lɪd
invalidate ɪnˈvælɪdeɪt
invaluable ɪnˈvæljʊbl
invariable ɪnˈveərɪəbl
invasion ɪnˈveɪʒn
invective ɪnˈvektɪv
inveigh ɪnˈveɪ
inveigle ɪnˈvigl $ £ ɪnˈveɪgl *etc*
invent ɪnˈvent
invention ɪnˈvenʃn
inventive ɪnˈventɪv
inventory ˈɪnvəntrɪ $ -tɔrɪ
Inverness ˈɪnvəˈnes $ ˈɪnvərˈnes
inverse ˈɪnˈvɜs
inversion ɪnˈvɜʃn $ ɪnˈvɜʒn *etc*
invert ɪnˈvɜt
invertebrate ɪnˈvɜtəbreɪt -brət -brɪt
invest ɪnˈvest
investigate ɪnˈvestɪgeɪt
investigation ɪnˈvestɪˈgeɪʃn
investigator ɪnˈvestɪgeɪtə(r)
investiture ɪnˈvestɪtʃə(r) $ -tʃʊər *etc*
inveterate ɪnˈvetərət -trət

invidious ɪnˈvɪdɪəs
invigilate ɪnˈvɪdʒɪleɪt
invigilator ɪnˈvɪdʒɪleɪtə(r)
invigorate ɪnˈvɪgəreɪt
invincible ɪnˈvɪnsəbl
inviolable ɪnˈvaɪələbl
inviolate ɪnˈvaɪələt -leɪt
invisible ɪnˈvɪzəbl
invitation ˈɪnvɪˈteɪʃn
invite ɪnˈvaɪt
invocation ˈɪnvəˈkeɪʃn
invoice ˈɪnvɔɪs
invoke ɪnˈvəʊk
involuntary ɪnˈvɒləntrɪ $ -terɪ
involve ɪnˈvɒlv
invulnerable ɪnˈvʌlnərəbl
inward(s) *adv* ˈɪnwəd(z) £ -wʊd(z)
    $ ˈɪnwərd(z)
inwards *n* ˈɪnədz $ ˈɪnərdz
iodine ˈaɪədin $ £ -daɪn -dɪn *etc*
ion ˈaɪən
-ion *suffix* ɪən
Ionic aɪˈɒnɪk
iota aɪˈəʊtə
IOU ˈaɪ əʊ ˈju
-ious *suffix* ɪəs
Iowa ˈaɪəwə $ -weɪ
ipso facto ˈɪpsəʊ ˈfæktəʊ
IQ ˈaɪ ˈkju
irascible ɪˈræsəbl
Iran ɪˈran $ ɪˈræn ɪˈran *etc*
Iranian ɪˈranɪən $ £ ɪˈreɪnɪən
Iraq ɪˈrak $ ɪˈræk
Iraqi ɪˈrakɪ $ ɪˈrækɪ
irate aɪˈreɪt $ ˈaɪreɪt
Irene ˈaɪərin aɪəˈrin aɪəˈrinɪ
Ireland ˈaɪələnd $ ˈaɪərlənd
iridescent ˈɪrɪˈdesnt
iris, I- ˈaɪərɪs
Irish ˈaɪərɪʃ
Irishman ˈaɪərɪʃmən
irk ɜk
irksome ˈɜksəm
iron ˈaɪən $ ˈaɪərn
iron-grey ˈaɪən ˈgreɪ $ ˈaɪərn
ironic aɪˈrɒnɪk
ironing-board ˈaɪənɪŋ bɔd
    $ ˈaɪərnɪŋ bɔrd
ironmonger ˈaɪənmʌŋgə(r) $ ˈaɪərn-
ironmongery ˈaɪənmʌŋgrɪ $ ˈaɪərn-
ironmould($ -mold) ˈaɪənməʊld
    $ ˈaɪərn-
ironwork(s) ˈaɪənwɜk(s) $ ˈaɪərn-

irony ˈaɪərənɪ
irradiate ɪˈreɪdɪeɪt
irrational ɪˈræʃnl
irreconcilable ɪˈrekənˈsaɪləbl
irrecoverable ˈɪrɪˈkʌvɽəbl
irredeemable ˈɪrɪˈdiməbl
irreducible ˈɪrɪˈdjusəbl $ -ˈdus-
irrefragable ɪˈrefrəgəbl
irrefutable ˈɪrɪˈfjutəbl ˈɪˈrefjutəbl
irregular ɪˈregjʊlə(r)
irregularity ˈɪˈregjʊˈlærətɪ
irrelevance ɪˈreləvəns
irrelevant ɪˈreləvənt
irregligious ˈɪrɪˈlɪdʒəs
irremediable ˈɪrɪˈmidɪəbl
irremovable ˈɪrɪˈmuvəbl
irreparable ɪˈrepɽəbl
irreplaceable ˈɪrɪˈpleɪsəbl
irrepressible ˈɪrɪˈpresəbl
irreproachable ˈɪrɪˈprəʊtʃəbl
irresistible ˈɪrɪˈzɪstəbl
irresolute ɪˈrezəlut £ -ljut
irrespective ˈɪrɪˈspektɪv
irresponsibility ˈɪrɪˈsponsəˈbɪlətɪ
irresponsible ˈɪrɪˈsponsəbl
irretrievable ˈɪrɪˈtrivəbl
irreverence ɪˈrevɽəns
irreverent ɪˈrevɽənt
irreversible ˈɪrɪˈvɜsəbl
irrevocable ɪˈrevəkəbl
irrigate ˈɪrɪgeɪt
irrigation ˈɪrɪˈgeɪʃn
irritability ˈɪrɪtəˈbɪlətɪ
irritable ˈɪrɪtəbl
irritant ˈɪrɪtənt
irritate ˈɪrɪteɪt
irritation ˈɪrɪˈteɪʃn
irruption ɪˈrʌpʃn
is *usual forms:* z, *after* p, t, k, f, θ: s
   strong-form: ɪz
Isabel ˈɪzəbel
Isaiah aɪˈzaɪə
-isation *suffix* aɪˈzeɪʃn $ £ ɪˈzeɪʃn
-ish *suffix* ɪʃ

Islam ɪzˈlɑm
island ˈaɪlənd
isle aɪl
Isle of Wight ˈaɪl əv ˈwaɪt
ism *n*, -ism *suffix* ˈɪzm ɪzm
isn't ˈɪznt
isobar ˈaɪsəba(r)
isolate ˈaɪsəleɪt
isolation ˈaɪsəˈleɪʃn
isosceles aɪˈsosļiz
isotherm ˈaɪsəθɜm
isotope ˈaɪsətəʊp
Israel ˈɪzreɪl $ £ ˈɪzrɪəl
Israeli ɪzˈreɪlɪ
Israelite ˈɪzrəlaɪt
issue ˈɪʃu ˈɪʃju £ ˈɪsju
Istanbul ˈɪstænˈbʊl -bul $ ˈɪstanˈbʊl *etc*
isthmus ˈɪsməs
   ˈɪsθməs *with* sθ *combined*
-ist *suffix* ɪst
it ɪt
Italian ɪˈtælɪən
italic ɪˈtælɪk
italicize ɪˈtælɪsaɪz
Italy ˈɪtəlɪ $ £ ˈɪtļɪ
itch ɪtʃ
it'd ɪtd
item ˈaɪtəm
iterate ˈɪtəreɪt
itinerant aɪˈtɪnərənt ɪˈt-
itinerary aɪˈtɪnərərɪ ɪˈt- $ -rerɪ
it is ɪˈtɪz ˈtɪz $ ɪt ˈɪz *etc*
it isn't ɪˈtɪznt ˈtɪznt $ ɪt ˈɪznt *etc*
it'll ɪtl
its, it's ɪts
itself ɪtˈself
-ity *suffix* ətɪ
ivory ˈaɪvɽɪ
Ivan ˈaɪvən *of Russians:* ɪˈvɑn
I've aɪv
-ive *suffix* ɪv
Ivor ˈaɪvə(r)
ivy, I– ˈaɪvɪ
-ization aɪˈzeɪʃn $ ɪˈzeɪʃn
-ize *suffix* aɪz

J

J j dʒeɪ
jab dʒæb
jabber ˈdʒæbə(r)

jabot ˈʒæbəʊ
jack, J– dʒæk
jackal ˈdʒækɔl $ ˈdʒækl

jackass ˈdʒækæs
jackboot ˈdʒækbut
jackdaw ˈdʒækdɔ
jacket ˈdʒækɪt
jack-in-the-box ˈdʒæk ɪn ðə boks
jack-knife ˈdʒæk naɪf
Jack of all trades ˈdʒæk əv ˈɔl treɪdz
jackpot ˈdʒækpot
jack-rabbit ˈdʒæk ræbɪt
Jacob ˈdʒeɪkəb
Jacobean ˈdʒækəˈbɪən
Jacobin ˈdʒækəbɪn
Jacobite ˈdʒækəbaɪt
Jacqueline ˈdʒækl̩ɪn -lin ˌʒæk-
    $ ˈdʒækwəlɪn -lin
jade dʒeɪd
jag dʒæg
jagged ˈdʒægɪd
jaguar, J– ˈdʒægjʊə(r)
    $ ˈdʒægwar -gjuar
jail dʒeɪl
jaloppy dʒəˈlopɪ
jam dʒæm
Jamaica dʒəˈmeɪkə
jamb dʒæm
jamboree ˈdʒæmbəˈri
James dʒeɪmz
jam-jar ˈdʒæm dʒɑ(r)
jam-pot ˈdʒæm pot
Jane dʒeɪn
Janet ˈdʒænɪt -ət
jangle ˈdʒæŋgl
janitor ˈdʒænɪtə(r)
January ˈdʒænjʊərɪ $ -jʊerɪ
Janus ˈdʒeɪnəs
japan, J– dʒəˈpæn
Japanese ˈdʒæpəˈniz
japonica dʒəˈponɪkə
jar dʒɑ(r)
jargon ˈdʒɑgən $ ˈdʒɑrgən
jasmin(e) ˈdʒæzmɪn
jasper, J– ˈdʒæspə(r)
jaundice ˈdʒɔndɪs
jaunt dʒɔnt
Java ˈdʒɑvə $ ˈdʒævə
Javanese ˈdʒɑvəˈniz $ ˈdʒæv-
javelin ˈdʒævl̩ɪn
jaw dʒɔ
jaw-bone ˈdʒɔ bəun
jaw-breaker ˈdʒɔ breɪkə(r)
jay dʒeɪ
jay-walker ˈdʒeɪ wɔkə(r)
jazz dʒæz

jazz band ˈdʒæz bænd
jealous ˈdʒeləs
jealousy ˈdʒeləsɪ
jean, J– dʒin
Jeanette dʒəˈnet ʒə-
jeep dʒip
jeer dʒɪə(r)
Jeffrey ˈdʒefrɪ
Jehovah dʒɪˈhəuvə
Jehu ˈdʒihju
jejune dʒɪˈdʒun
jell dʒel
jelly ˈdʒelɪ
jelly-fish ˈdʒelɪ fɪʃ
jemmy ˈdʒemɪ
Jennifer ˈdʒenɪfə(r)
jenny, J– ˈdʒenɪ
jeopardize ˈdʒepədaɪz $ -pərd-
jeopardy ˈdʒepədɪ $ -pərdɪ
Jeremiah ˈdʒerɪˈmaɪə
Jeremy ˈdʒerəmɪ
Jericho ˈdʒerɪkəu
jerimiad ˈdʒerɪˈmaɪæd
jerk dʒɜk
jerkin ˈdʒɜkɪn
Jerome dʒəˈrəum
jerry, J– ˈdʒerɪ
jerry-builder ˈdʒerɪ bɪldə(r)
jersey, J– ˈdʒɜzɪ
Jessie ˈdʒesɪ
jest dʒest
Jesuit ˈdʒezjuɪt $ £ ˈdʒeʒuɪt etc
Jesu ˈdʒizju $ ˈdʒizu
Jesus ˈdʒizəs -zəz
jet dʒet
jet-black ˈdʒet ˈblæk
jet-propelled ˈdʒet prəˈpeld
jetsam ˈdʒetsm
jettison ˈdʒetɪsn -ɪzn
jetty ˈdʒetɪ
Jew dʒu
jewel ˈdʒuḷ
jewellery ˈdʒuḷrɪ
jewelry ˈdʒuḷrɪ
Jewess dʒuˈes £ ˈdʒuɪs
Jewish ˈdʒuɪʃ
Jezebel ˈdʒezəbl -zɪb- $ £ -bel
jib dʒɪb
jibe dʒaɪb
jiffy ˈdʒɪfɪ
jig dʒɪg
jigger ˈdʒɪgə(r)
jiggery-pokery ˈdʒɪgərɪ ˈpəukərɪ

jigsaw ˈdʒɪgsɔ
jigsaw puzzle ˈdʒɪgsɔ pʌzl
Jill dʒɪl
jilt dʒɪlt
Jim dʒɪm
jingle ˈdʒɪŋgl
jingo ˈdʒɪŋgəʊ
jingoistic ˌdʒɪŋgəʊˈɪstɪk
jinks dʒɪŋks
jinn dʒɪn
jinricksha(w) dʒɪnˈrɪkʃɔ
jinx dʒɪŋks
jitter ˈdʒɪtə(r)
jitter-bug ˈdʒɪtə bʌg $ ˈdʒɪtər
jiu-jitsu dʒu ˈdʒɪtsu
jive dʒaɪv
Jnr ˈdʒunɪə(r)
Joan dʒəʊn
job dʒob
Job dʒəʊb
jockey ˈdʒokɪ
Jockey Club ˈdʒokɪ klʌb
jocose dʒəʊˈkəʊs
jocosity dʒəʊˈkosətɪ
jocular ˈdʒokjʊlə(r)
jocularity ˌdʒokjʊˈlærətɪ
jocund ˈdʒokənd
jocundity dʒəʊˈkʌndətɪ
jodhpurs ˈdʒodʒpəz £ -puəz $ -pərz
Jodrell ˈdʒodrl
Joe dʒəʊ
jog dʒog
joggle ˈdʒogl
Johannesburg dʒəˈhænɪsbəg
  dʒəʊˈh- -ɪzb-
John dʒon
Johnson ˈdʒonsn
joie de vivre ˈʒwɑ də ˈvivr *with*
  unsyllabic r ˈviv
join dʒɔɪn
joint dʒɔɪnt
jointure ˈdʒɔɪntʃə(r)
joist dʒɔɪst
joke dʒəʊk
jollification ˌdʒolɪfɪˈkeɪʃn
jollity ˈdʒolətɪ
jolly ˈdʒolɪ
jolt dʒəʊlt
Jonah ˈdʒəʊnə
Jonathan ˈdʒonəθən
Jones dʒəʊnz
jonquil ˈdʒoŋkwɪl
Jordan ˈdʒɔdn $ ˈdʒɔrdn

Jordanian dʒɔˈdeɪnɪən $ dʒɔr-
Joseph ˈdʒəʊzɪf -sɪf -əf
Josephine ˈdʒəʊzɪfin -sɪf -əf-
Joshua ˈdʒoʃʊə
joss dʒos
joss-house ˈdʒos haʊs
joss-stick ˈdʒos stɪk
jostle ˈdʒosl
jot dʒot
journal ˈdʒɜnl
journalese ˌdʒɜnlˈiz
journalism ˈdʒɜnlɪzm
journalist ˈdʒɜnlɪst
journey ˈdʒɜnɪ
joust dʒaʊst
Jove dʒəʊv
jovial ˈdʒəʊvɪəl
jowl dʒaʊl
joy, J– dʒɔɪ
Joyce dʒɔɪs
joy-ride ˈdʒɔɪ raɪd
joy-stick ˈdʒɔɪ stɪk
JP ˈdʒeɪ ˈpi
Jr ˈdʒunɪə(r)
jubilant ˈdʒubɪlənt
jubilation ˌdʒubɪˈleɪʃn
jubilee ˈdʒubɪli -bļi
judge dʒʌdʒ
judgement ˈdʒʌdʒmənt
judicature ˈdʒudɪkətʃə(r)
  dʒuˈdɪkətʃə(r) -tʃʊə(r)
judicial dʒuˈdɪʃl
judiciary dʒuˈdɪʃərɪ $ -ʃɪerɪ *etc*
judicious dʒuˈdɪʃəs
Judith ˈdʒudɪθ
judo ˈdʒudəʊ
jug dʒʌg
Juggernaut ˈdʒʌgənɔt $ -gər-
juggle ˈdʒʌgl
Jugoslav ˈjugəʊslav -slæv
Jugoslavia ˌjugəʊˈslavɪə
jugular ˈdʒʌgjʊlə(r)
juice dʒus
ju-jitsu dʒu ˈdʒɪtsu
juke-box ˈdʒuk boks
julep ˈdʒuləp -lɪp £ -lep
Julia ˈdʒulɪə
Julian ˈdʒulɪən
Juliet ˈdʒulɪət -ɪet ˈdʒulɪˈet
Julius ˈdʒulɪəs
July dʒuˈlaɪ
jumble ˈdʒʌmbl
jump dʒʌmp

jumper `dʒʌmpə(r)
junction `dʒʌŋkʃn
juncture `dʒʌŋktʃə(r)
June dʒun
jungle `dʒʌŋgl
junior `dʒunɪə(r)
juniper `dʒunɪpə(r)
junk dʒʌŋk
junket `dʒʌŋkɪt
Juno `dʒunəʊ
Junoesque 'dʒunəʊ`esk
junta `dʒʌntə
Jupiter `dʒupɪtə(r)
juridical dʒʊ`rɪdɪkl
jurisdiction 'dʒʊərɪs`dɪkʃn
jurisprudence 'dʒʊərɪs`prudns
jurist `dʒʊərɪst

juror `dʒʊərə(r)
jury `dʒʊərɪ
jury-box `dʒʊərɪ bɒks
juryman `dʒʊərɪmən
just adj dʒʌst
just adv dʒʌst dʒəst dʒest $ dʒɪst
justice `dʒʌstɪs
justifiable 'dʒʌstɪ`faɪəbl `dʒʌstɪfaɪəbl
justification 'dʒʌstɪfɪ`keɪʃn
justify `dʒʌstɪfaɪ
jut dʒʌt
Jutland `dʒʌtlənd
jute dʒut
juvenile `dʒuvənaɪl $ -nl
juxtapose 'dʒʌkstə`pəʊz
juxtaposition 'dʒʌkstəpə`zɪʃn

K

K k keɪ
Kaffir `kæfə(r)
Kaiser `kaɪzə(r)
kaleidoscope kə`laɪdəskəʊp
kaleidoscopic kə`laɪdə`skɒpɪk
kangaroo 'kæŋgə`ru
Kansas `kænzəs £ -nsəs
kaolin `keɪəlɪn
kapok `keɪpɒk
Karachi kə`ratʃɪ
karate kə`ratɪ
Kashmir kæʃ`mɪə(r) $ `kæʃmɪər -æʒm-
Kate keɪt
Katherine `kæθrɪn
kayak `kaɪæk
Keats kits
kedgeree `kedʒərɪ 'kedʒə`ri
keel kil
keen kin
keen-sighted 'kin `saɪtɪd
keep kip
keepsake `kipseɪk
keg keg
Keith kiθ
kelp kelp
ken, K- ken
Kennedy `kenədɪ
kennel `kenl
Kenneth `kenɪθ -əθ
Kensington `kenzɪŋtən

Kentucky ken`tʌkɪ $ kɪn- etc
Kenya `kenjə $ £ `kinjə
kept kept
kerb kɜb
kerbstone `kɜbstəʊn
kerchief `kɜtʃɪf -tʃif
kernel `kɜnl
kerosene `kerəsin 'kerə`sin
kestrel `kestrəl
ketch ketʃ
ketchup `ketʃəp
kettle `ketl
kettle-drum `ketl drʌm
kettle of fish, a pretty ə `prɪtɪ ketl əv fɪʃ
key ki
keyboard `kibɔd $ -bɔrd
keyhole `kihəʊl
key-money `ki mʌnɪ
keynote `kinəʊt
key-ring `ki rɪŋ
keystone `ki-stəʊn
khaki `kakɪ $ `kækɪ
khan kan kæn
kibbutz kɪ`buts kɪ`bʊts
kibbutzim 'kɪbʊt`sim
kick kɪk
kick-off `kɪk ɒf $ ɔf
kick-starter `kɪk statə(r) $ startər
kid kɪd
kid-glove 'kɪd `glʌv

kidnap `kɪdnæp
kidney `kɪdnɪ
kidney-bean 'kɪdnɪ `bin
kill kɪl
killjoy `kɪldʒɔɪ
kiln kɪln $ kɪl
kilo `kiləʊ
kilo- *prefix* `kɪlə-
kilocycle `kɪləsaɪkl
kilogram(me) `kɪləgræm
kilometer `kɪləmɪtə(r) $ £ kɪ`lomɪtə(r)
kilowatt `kɪləwot
kilt kɪlt
kimono kɪ`məʊnəʊ $ kɪ`məʊnə *etc*
kin kɪn
-kin *suffix* kɪn
kind kaɪnd
kindergarten `kɪndəgatn $ -dərgartn
kind-hearted 'kaɪnd `hatɪd $ `har-
kindle `kɪndl
kindling `kɪndlɪŋ
kindred `kɪndrəd -ɪd
kinetic kɪ`netɪk kaɪ`n-
king kɪŋ
kingdom `kɪŋdəm
kingfisher `kɪŋfɪʃə(r)
king-size 'kɪŋ `saɪz
Kingston `kɪŋstən
kink kɪŋk
Kinross kɪn`ros
kinsfolk `kɪnzfəʊk
kinship `kɪn-ʃɪp
kinsman `kɪnzmən
kiosk `kiosk $ `kaɪosk
kipper `kɪpə(r)
kirk, K– kɜk
Kirkcudbright kə`kubrɪ
kismet `kɪzmet `kɪs-
kiss kɪs
kit kɪt
kit-bag `kɪt bæg
kitchen `kɪtʃɪn -ən
kitchenette 'kɪtʃɪ`net
kitchen-maid `kɪtʃɪn meɪd -ən
kite kaɪt
kith and kin 'kɪθ ən `kɪn
kitten `kɪtn
kitty, K– `kɪtɪ
kiwi `kiwi
kleptomania 'kleptə`meɪnɪə
kleptomaniac 'kleptə`meɪnɪæk
knack næk
knap næp

knapsack `næpsæk
knave neɪv
knavery `neɪvərɪ
knead nid
knee ni
knee-breeches `ni brɪtʃɪz
kneecap `ni-kæp
knee-deep 'ni `dip
knee-high 'ni `haɪ
kneel nil
knell nel
knelt nelt
knew nju $ nu
knickerbockers `nɪkəbokəz
    $ `nɪkərbokərz
knickers `nɪkəz $ `nɪkərz
knick-knack `nɪk næk
knife naɪf
knife-edge `naɪf edʒ
knight naɪt
knight-errant 'naɪt `erənt
knighthood `naɪthʊd
knit nɪt
knitting-needle `nɪtɪŋ nidl
knitwear `nɪtweə(r)
knives naɪvz
knob nob
knock nok
knock-about `nok əbaʊt
knock-kneed 'nok `nid
knock-out `nok aʊt
knoll nəʊl nol
knot not
know nəʊ
know-all `nəʊ ɔl
know-how `nəʊ haʊ
knowledge `nolɪdʒ
knowledgeable `nolɪdʒəbl
known nəʊn
knuckle `nʌkl
koala kəʊ`alə
Kodak `kəʊdæk
kopek `kəʊpek
Koran kə`ran kɔ`r- $ kəʊ`ræn *etc*
Korea kə`rɪə
Korean kə`rɪən
kosher `kəʊʃə(r)
kow-tow 'kaʊ`taʊ
kraal kral krɔl
km `kɪləmɪtə(r) $ £ kɪ`lomɪtə(r)
Kremlin `kremlɪn
krone `krəʊnə
kudos `kjudos $ `ku- -dəʊs

Kuala·Lumpur 'kwɑlə 'lʊmpʊə(r)
  'kwɒl- 'lʌm- -pə(r)
Ku-Klux-Klan 'ku 'klʌks 'klæn

Kuwait kʊ'weɪt $ kʊ'waɪt *etc*
Kuweit kʊ'weɪt $ kʊ'waɪt *etc*

L

L l el
la lɑ
lab læb
label 'leɪbl
labial 'leɪbɪəl
laboratory lə'bɒrətrɪ $ 'læbrətɔrɪ
laborious lə'bɔrɪəs
labour($ -or) 'leɪbə(r)
labourite 'leɪbərɑɪt
Labour Party 'leɪbə pɑtɪ $ -bər pɑrtɪ
labour($ -or)-saving 'leɪbə seɪvɪŋ $ -bər
labrador, L– 'læbrədɔ(r)
laburnum lə'bɜnəm
labyrinth 'læbərɪnθ
labyrinthine 'læbə'rɪnθɑɪn $ -θɪn -θɪn
lace leɪs
lacerate 'læsəreɪt
lachrymose 'lækrɪməʊs
lack læk
lack-lustre($ -ter) 'læk lʌstə(r)
lackadaisical 'lækə'deɪzɪkl
lackey 'lækɪ
laconic lə'kɒnɪk
lacquer 'lækə(r)
lacrosse lə'krɒs $ -krɔs
lactic 'læktɪk
lacuna lə'kjunə
lad læd
ladder 'lædə(r)
ladder-proof 'lædə pruf $ 'lædər
laden 'leɪdn
ladies' man 'leɪdɪz mæn
la-di-da 'lɑ dɪ 'dɑ
lading 'leɪdɪŋ
ladle 'leɪdl
lady 'leɪdɪ
ladybird 'leɪdɪbɜd
lady-chapel 'leɪdɪ tʃæpl
lady-in-waiting 'leɪdɪ ɪn weɪtɪŋ
lady-killer 'leɪdɪ kɪlə(r)
ladyship 'leɪdɪʃɪp
lady's maid 'leɪdɪz meɪd
lag læg
lager 'lɑgə(r)

laggard 'lægəd $ 'lægərd
lagoon lə'gun
Lagos 'leɪgɒs $ 'lɑgəʊs
laid leɪd
lain leɪn
lair leə(r)
laird leəd $ leərd
laissez-faire 'leɪseɪ 'feə(r)
laity 'leɪətɪ
lake leɪk
Lake District 'leɪk dɪstrɪkt
lama 'lɑmə
lamb læm
lambaste læm'beɪst
lambent 'læmbənt
lambkin 'læmkɪn
lambskin 'læm-skɪn
lame leɪm
lament lə'ment
lamentable 'læməntəbl
lamentation 'læmen'teɪʃn
laminate 'læmɪneɪt
lamp læmp
lamp-light 'læmp lɑɪt
lamp-oil 'læmp ɔɪl
lamp-post 'læmp pəʊst
lamp-shade 'læmp ʃeɪd
lampoon læm'pun
Lanark 'lænək -nak $ -nɜrk -nark
Lancashire 'læŋkəʃə(r) -kɪʃ- $ -ʃɪər *etc*
Lancaster 'læŋkəstə -kɪs-
lance lɑns $ læns
lance-corporal 'lɑns 'kɔprl
    $ 'læns 'kɔrprl
lancet 'lɑnsɪt $ 'lænsɪt
land lænd
land-agent 'lænd eɪdʒənt
landing-field 'lændɪŋ fild
landing-stage 'lændɪŋ steɪdʒ
landing-strip 'lændɪŋ strɪp
landlady 'lændleɪdɪ
landlocked 'lændlɒkt
landlord 'lændlɒd $ -lɔrd
land-lubber 'lænd lʌbə(r)

landmark ˈlændmɑk $ -mark
landmine ˈlændmaɪn
landowner ˈlændəʊnə(r)
landscape ˈlændskeɪp
landslide ˈlændslaɪd
landslip ˈlændslɪp
lane leɪn
language ˈlæŋgwɪdʒ -ŋw-
language laboratory
  ˈlæŋgwɪdʒ ləbɔrətrɪ $ læbrətɔrɪ
languid ˈlæŋgwɪd
languish ˈlæŋgwɪʃ
languor ˈlæŋgə(r)
lank læŋk
lanolin ˈlænəlɪn -lin
lanoline ˈlænəlin -lɪn
lantern ˈlæntən $ -tərn
lanyard ˈlænjad $ -jard
Laos ˈlɑ-ʊs laʊs
Laotian ˈlaʊʃn leɪˈəʊʃn
lap, L– læp
lap-dog ˈlæp dog $ dɔg
lapel ləˈpel
lapidary ˈlæpɪdərɪ $ -derɪ
lapis lazuli 'læpɪs ˈlæzjʊlɪ -laɪ $ -æʒʊ-
Lapland ˈlæplænd
lapse læps
lapwing ˈlæpwɪŋ
larceny ˈlasn̩ɪ $ ˈlar-
larch lɑtʃ $ lɑrtʃ
lard lad $ lard
large ladʒ $ lardʒ
large-scale 'ladʒ ˈskeɪl $ 'lardʒ
largesse laˈdʒes ˈladʒes laˈʒes $ -ar-
largo ˈlagəʊ $ ˈlargəʊ
lark lak $ lark
larkspur ˈlakspə $ ˈlark-
larva ˈlavə $ ˈlarvə
larvae ˈlavi -vaɪ $ ˈlar-
laryngitis 'lærɪnˈdʒaɪtɪs -təs
larynx ˈlærɪŋks
lascivious ləˈsɪvɪəs
lash læʃ
Las Palmas læs ˈpælməs $ las ˈpal-
lass læs
lassitude ˈlæsɪtjud $ -tud
lasso læˈsu ˈlæsəʊ $ ˈlæsu
last last $ læst
Las Vegas læs ˈveɪgəs $ las
latch lætʃ
late leɪt
latent ˈleɪtnt

lateral ˈlætrl -tərl
laterite ˈlætəraɪt
latex ˈleɪteks
lath lɑθ $ læθ
lathe leɪð
lather ˈlɑðə(r) $ £ ˈlæðər
Latin ˈlætɪn $ ˈlætn etc
latitude ˈlætɪtjud -tʃud $ -tud
latrine ləˈtrin
latter ˈlætə(r)
lattice ˈlætɪs
lattice-work ˈlætɪs wɜk
Latvia ˈlætvɪə
laud lɔd
laudanum ˈlɔdn̩əm £ ˈlodnəm
laugh laf $ læf
laughing-gas ˈlafɪŋ gæs $ ˈlæf-
laughing-stock ˈlafɪŋ stok $ ˈlæf-
laughter ˈlaftə(r) $ ˈlæftər
launch lɔntʃ
launching-pad ˈlɔntʃɪŋ pæd
launder ˈlɔndə(r)
launderette ˈlɔndəˈret lɔnˈdret
laundress ˈlɔndrəs -ɪs
laundry ˈlɔndrɪ
laundryman ˈlɔndrɪmæn -mən
laureate ˈlɔrɪət -ɪeɪt
laurel ˈlorl $ ˈbrl etc
Laurence ˈlorns $ ˈlɔrns etc
lava ˈlavə $ ˈlævə
lavatory ˈlævətrɪ $ -tɔrɪ
lavender ˈlævɪndə(r) -vndə(r)
lavish ˈlævɪʃ
law lɔ
law-abiding ˈlɔ əbaɪdɪŋ £ ˈlɔr
law-breaker ˈlɔ breɪkə(r)
law-court ˈlɔ kɔt $ kɔrt
lawn lɔn
lawn-mower ˈlɔn məʊə(r)
lawn-tennis ˈlɔn ˈtenɪs
Lawrence ˈlorns $ ˈlɔrns etc
lawsuit ˈlɔsut £ -sjut
lawyer ˈlɔjə(r) ˈlɔɪə(r)
lax læks
laxative ˈlæksətɪv
lay leɪ
layabout ˈleɪəbaut
lay-by ˈleɪ baɪ
layer ˈleɪə(r)
layette leɪˈet
layman ˈleɪmən
lay-out ˈleɪ aut
Lazarus ˈlæzərəs

laze leɪz
lazy ˈleɪzɪ
lazy-bones ˈleɪzɪ bəʊnz
lb. paʊnd(z)
leach liːtʃ
lead *metal* led
lead *direct* liːd
leaden ˈledn
lead-in ˈliːd ɪn
lead poisoning ˈled ˈpɔɪznɪŋ
leaf liːf
leaflet ˈliːflət
league liːg
leak liːk
leakage ˈliːkɪdʒ
lean liːn
lean-to ˈliːn tuː
leant lent
leap liːp
leap-frog ˈliːp frɒg $ frɔːg
leapt lept
leap-year ˈliːp jɜː(r) $ jɪər
learn lɜːn
learned *adj* ˈlɜːnɪd *pp* lɜːnd
learnt lɜːnt
lease liːs
leasehold ˈliːshəʊld
leash liːʃ
least liːst
leastways ˈliːstweɪz
leather ˈleðə(r)
leather-jacket ˈleðə dʒækɪt $ ˈleðər
leather-neck ˈleðə nek $ ˈleðər
leavened ˈlevnd
leaves liːvz
Lebanese ˌlebəˈniːz
Lebanon ˈlebənən $ -nɒn
lecherous ˈletʃərəs
lechery ˈletʃərɪ
lectern ˈlektən $ -tɜːrn
lecture ˈlektʃə(r)
lecturer ˈlektʃərə(r)
led led
ledge ledʒ
lee liː
leech liːtʃ
leek liːk
leer lɪə(r)
lees liːz
leeward ˈliːwəd $ ˈliːwərd
 nautical ˈluːəd $ ˈluːərd
left left
left-handed ˌleft ˈhændɪd

leg leg
legacy ˈlegəsɪ
legal ˈliːgl
legality liˈgælətɪ
legate ˈlegət -ɪt
legatee ˌlegəˈtiː
legation lɪˈgeɪʃn
legato lɪˈgɑːtəʊ
legend ˈledʒənd
legendary ˈledʒəndrɪ $ -derɪ
legibility ˌledʒɪˈbɪlətɪ
legible ˈledʒəbl
legion ˈliːdʒən
legionary ˈliːdʒənrɪ $ -nerɪ
legislate ˈledʒɪsleɪt
legislation ˌledʒɪsˈleɪʃn
legislative ˈledʒɪslətɪv $ -leɪt- *etc*
legislator ˈledʒɪsleɪtə(r)
legislature ˈledʒɪsleɪtʃə(r) £ -lətʃə(r)
legitimacy lɪˈdʒɪtɪməsɪ
legitimate lɪˈdʒɪtɪmət
legitimatize lɪˈdʒɪtɪmətaɪz
leg-pull ˈleg pʊl
leguminous lɪˈgjuːmɪnəs
Leicester ˈlestə(r)
Leigh liː
Leipzig ˈlaɪpsɪg -zɪg
leisure ˈleʒə(r) $ ˈliːʒər *etc*
lemming ˈlemɪŋ
lemon ˈlemən
lemonade ˌleməˈneɪd
lemon-squash ˈlemən ˈskwɒʃ
lemon-squeezer ˈlemən skwiːzə(r)
lemur ˈliːmə(r)
lend lend
lending-library ˈlendɪŋ laɪbrərɪ $ -rerɪ
length leŋθ leŋkθ
leniency ˈliːnɪənsɪ
lenient ˈliːnɪənt
Lenin ˈlenɪn
Leningrad ˈlenɪngræd
lens lenz
lent, L– lent
Lenten ˈlentən
lentil ˈlentl
lento ˈlentəʊ
Leonard ˈlenəd $ ˈlenərd
Leonardo ˌlɪəˈnɑːdəʊ ˌleɪə- $ -ɑːrdəʊ
leonine ˈliːənaɪn
leopard ˈlepəd $ ˈlepərd
leopardess ˌlepəˈdes ˈlepədes -ɪs
 $ ˈlepərdɪs
leper ˈlepə(r)

leprechaun ˋleprəkɔn
leprosy ˋleprəsɪ
lesbian ˋlezbɪən
lese-majesty 'liz ˋmædʒəstɪ £ 'leɪz-
lesion ˋliʒn
Leslie, Lesley ˋlezlɪ $ ˋleslɪ
Lesotho ləˋsəutəu £ ləˋsutəu
less les *suffix* ləs
lessee leˋsi
lessen ˋlesn
lesser ˋlesə(r)
lesson ˋlesn
lessor ˋlesɔ(r) 'leˋsɔ(r)
lest lest
let let
lethal ˋliθl
lethargic lɪˋθɑdʒɪk $ -ˋθɑr-
lethargy ˋleθədʒɪ $ -θər-
Lethe ˋliθɪ
letter ˋletə(r)
letter-box ˋletə bɒks $ ˋletər
letter-head ˋletə hed $ ˋletər
lettering ˋletrɪŋ $ £ ˋletərɪŋ
letter-press ˋletə pres $ ˋletər
lettuce ˋletɪs
leukaemia luˋkimɪə £ lju-
Levant lɪˋvænt
levee ˋlevi
level ˋlevl
level-headed 'levl ˋhedɪd
lever ˋlivə(r) $ ˋlevər *etc*
leveret ˋlevərɪt -ət
leviathan lɪˋvaɪəθən
levitate ˋlevɪteɪt
levity ˋlevətɪ
levy ˋlevɪ
lewd lud £ ljud
Lewis ˋluɪs
lexical ˋleksɪkl
lexicography 'leksɪˋkogrəfɪ
lexicon ˋleksɪkən $ -kon *etc*
liability 'laɪəˋbɪlətɪ
liable ˋlaɪəbl
liaison lɪˋeɪzn -zõ $ ˋlɪəzon ˋlieɪzon
liar ˋlaɪə(r)
libation laɪˋbeɪʃn
libel ˋlaɪbl
libellous($ -elous) ˋlaɪbləs
liberal ˋlɪbrl
liberality 'lɪbəˋrælətɪ
Liberal Party ˋlɪbrl pɑtɪ $ pɑrtɪ
liberate ˋlɪbəreɪt
liberation 'lɪbəˋreɪʃn

Liberia laɪˋbɪərɪə
libertine ˋlɪbətin $ -bər-
liberty ˋlɪbətɪ $ -bər-
libidinous lɪˋbɪdɪnəs $ -dṇəs
librarian laɪˋbreərɪən
library ˋlaɪbrɪ $ -rerɪ *etc*
library book ˋlaɪbrɪ buk $ -rerɪ
librettist lɪˋbretɪst
libretto lɪˋbretəu
Libya ˋlɪbɪə
Libyan ˋlɪbɪən
lice laɪs
licence ˋlaɪsns
license ˋlaɪsns
licensee 'laɪsnˋsi
licentiate laɪˋsenʃɪət -ɪeɪt
licentious laɪˋsenʃəs
lichen ˋlaɪkən £ ˋlɪtʃən -ɪn
lick lɪk
licorice ˋlɪkərɪs $ £ -ɪʃ
lid lɪd
lido ˋlidəu
lie laɪ
lieder ˋlidə(r)
lie-down laɪ ˋdaun
liege lidʒ liʒ
lie-in laɪ ˋɪn
lieu lu £ lju
lieutenant 'lefˋtenənt $ 'luˋtenənt
    British Navy 'leˋtenənt lə-
life laɪf
life-belt ˋlaɪf belt
life-blood ˋlaɪf blʌd
life-boat ˋlaɪf bəut
life-buoy ˋlaɪf bɔɪ
life-guard ˋlaɪf gɑd $ gɑrd
life-interest 'laɪf ˋɪntrəst -est
life-jacket ˋlaɪf dʒækɪt
life-like ˋlaɪf laɪk
life-line ˋlaɪf laɪn
life-long ˋlaɪf lɒŋ $ lɔŋ
life-saver ˋlaɪf seɪvə(r)
life-size 'laɪf ˋsaɪz
life sentence ˋlaɪf sentəns
lifetime ˋlaɪftaɪm
life-work 'laɪf ˋwɜk
lift lɪft
lift-man ˋlɪft mæn
ligament ˋlɪgəmənt
ligature ˋlɪgətʃə(r) -tʃuə(r)
light laɪt
lighten ˋlaɪtn
light-fingered 'laɪt ˋfɪŋgəd $ -gərd

light-headed ˈlaɪt ˈhedɪd
light-hearted ˈlaɪt ˈhɑːtɪd $ ˈhɑːrtɪd
light-house ˈlaɪt haʊs
lighting-up-time ˈlaɪtɪŋ ˈʌp taɪm
lightning ˈlaɪtnɪŋ
light-weight ˈlaɪt weɪt
light year ˈlaɪt jɜː(r) $ jɪər
ligneous ˈlɪɡnɪəs
like laɪk
-like suffix laɪk
likelihood ˈlaɪklɪhʊd
liken ˈlaɪkən
likewise ˈlaɪkwaɪz
lilac ˈlaɪlək $ ˈlaɪlæk -lok
Lilian ˈlɪlɪən
Lilliput ˈlɪlɪpʌt -pət -pʊt
Lilliputian ˌlɪlɪˈpjuːʃn
lilt lɪlt
lily ˈlɪlɪ
lily-livered ˈlɪlɪ lɪvəd $ -vərd
lily-white ˈlɪlɪ ˈwaɪt $ ˈhwaɪt etc
limb lɪm
limber ˈlɪmbə(r)
limbo ˈlɪmbəʊ
lime laɪm
lime-juice ˈlaɪm dʒuːs
limekiln ˈlaɪmkɪln $ -kɪl
limelight ˈlaɪmlaɪt
limerick, L– ˈlɪmərɪk
limestone ˈlaɪmstəʊn
limit ˈlɪmɪt
limousine ˈlɪməziːn
limp lɪmp
limpet ˈlɪmpɪt
limpid ˈlɪmpɪd
linchpin ˈlɪntʃpɪn
Lincoln ˈlɪŋkən
linden ˈlɪndən
line laɪn
lineage ˈlɪnɪɪdʒ
lineal ˈlɪnɪəl
linear ˈlɪnɪə(r)
lineman ˈlaɪnmən
linen ˈlɪnɪn
linesman ˈlaɪnzmən
line-up ˈlaɪn ʌp
ling lɪŋ
-ling suffix lɪŋ
linger ˈlɪŋɡə(r)
lingerie ˈlõːʒəri ˈlæ- -rɪ $ ˌlõːʒəˈriː -ˈreɪ etc
lingo ˈlɪŋɡəʊ
lingua franca ˌlɪŋɡwə ˈfræŋkə
lingual ˈlɪŋɡwl

linguist ˈlɪŋɡwɪst
linguistic lɪŋˈɡwɪstɪk
linguistician ˌlɪŋɡwɪˈstɪʃn
liniment ˈlɪnɪmənt -nəm-
link lɪŋk
linkman ˈlɪŋkmæn
linnet ˈlɪnɪt
lino ˈlaɪnəʊ
lino-cut ˈlaɪnəʊ kʌt
linoleum lɪˈnəʊlɪəm
linseed ˈlɪnsiːd
linseed oil ˈlɪnsiːd ɔɪl
lint lɪnt
lintel ˈlɪntl
lion ˈlaɪən
Lionel ˈlaɪənl
lion-hunter ˈlaɪən hʌntə(r)
lip lɪp
lip-reading ˈlɪp riːdɪŋ
lip-service ˈlɪp sɜːvɪs
lip-stick ˈlɪp stɪk
liquefaction ˌlɪkwɪˈfækʃn
liquefy ˈlɪkwɪfaɪ
liqueur lɪˈkjʊə(r) $ £ lɪˈkɜː(r)
liquid ˈlɪkwɪd
liquidate ˈlɪkwɪdeɪt
liquidation ˌlɪkwɪˈdeɪʃn
liquor ˈlɪkə(r)
liquorice ˈlɪkərɪs $ £ ˈlɪkərɪʃ
lira ˈlɪərə
lire ˈlɪəreɪ
lisle laɪl
lisp lɪsp
lissom(e) ˈlɪsəm
list lɪst
listen ˈlɪsn
lit lɪt
litany ˈlɪtənɪ
literacy ˈlɪtrəsɪ -tər-
literal ˈlɪtrl
liter ˈliːtə(r)
literary ˈlɪtrɪ -rərɪ $ ˈlɪtəreri
literate ˈlɪtərət ˈlɪtrət
literature ˈlɪtrətʃə(r) $ ˈlɪtrətʃʊə(r) etc
lithe laɪð $ laɪθ
lithograph ˈlɪθəɡrɑːf $ -ɡræf
lithography lɪˈθɒɡrəfɪ
litigant ˈlɪtɪɡənt
litigate ˈlɪtɪɡeɪt
litigation ˌlɪtɪˈɡeɪʃn
litigious lɪˈtɪdʒəs $ -dʒɪəs
litmus ˈlɪtməs
litmus-paper ˈlɪtməs peɪpə(r)

litotes ˈlaɪtətiz -təut-
litre($ -er) ˈliːtə(r)
litter ˈlɪtə(r)
litter-basket ˈlɪtə baskɪt $ ˈlɪtər bæskɪt
litter-bin ˈlɪtə bɪn $ ˈlɪtər
little ˈlɪtl
littoral ˈlɪtərl
liturgical lɪˈtɜːdʒɪkl
liturgy ˈlɪtədʒɪ $ -ərdʒɪ
live adj laɪv
live v lɪv
livelihood ˈlaɪvlɪhʊd
livelong ˈlɪvlɒŋ ˈlaɪv- $ -lɔːŋ
lively ˈlaɪvlɪ
liven ˈlaɪvn
liver ˈlɪvə(r)
Liverpool ˈlɪvəpuːl $ -vər-
livery ˈlɪvərɪ
livestock ˈlaɪvstok
livid ˈlɪvɪd
living-room ˈlɪvɪŋ rʊm $ £ rum etc
lizard ˈlɪzəd $ ˈlɪzərd
llama ˈlaːmə $ ˈjaːmə
Llandudno læŋˈdɪdnəʊ θlæn- hlæn-
$ £ lænˈdʌdnəʊ
Llanelly lænˈeθlɪ θlæ- hlæn- $ lænˈelɪ
Llangollen læŋˈgoθlən θlæ- $ lænˈgolɪn
Llewellyn ləˈwelɪn
Lloyd lɔɪd
lo ləʊ
load ləʊd
loaf ləʊf
loaf-sugar ˈləʊf ʃʊgə(r)
loam ləʊm
loath ləʊθ
loathe ləʊð
loathsome ˈləʊðsəm
loaves ləʊvz
lob lob
lobby ˈlobɪ
lobe ləʊb
lobelia ləʊˈbiːlɪə
lobster ˈlobstə(r)
lobster-pot ˈlobstə pot $ -stər
local ˈləʊkl
locality ləʊˈkælətɪ
localize ˈləʊkəlaɪz
locate ləʊˈkeɪt $ ˈləʊkeɪt
location ləʊˈkeɪʃn
loch lok this k is often replaced with
x, the corresponding 'scraping'
(fricative) sound as in Scottish usage
lock lok

locket ˈlokɪt
locksmith ˈloksmɪθ
locomotion ˈləʊkəˈməʊʃn
locomotive ˈləʊkəˈməʊtɪv
locum tenens ˈləʊkəm ˈtiːnənz ˈten- -enz
locust ˈləʊkəst
locution ləʊˈkjuːʃn £ ləˈk-
lodestar ˈləʊdstɑː(r)
lodestone ˈləʊdstəʊn
lodge lodʒ
lodging-house ˈlodʒɪŋ haʊs
loess ˈləʊɪs lɜːs
loft loft $ lɔːft etc
log log $ lɔːg etc
loganberry ˈləʊgənberɪ £ -brɪ
logarithm ˈlogərɪðm -rɪθm $ ˈlɔːg- etc
log-cabin ˈlog ˈkæbɪn $ ˈlɔːg
loggerheads ˈlogəhedz $ -gər-
loggia ˈlodʒɪə
logic ˈlodʒɪk
logician loˈdʒɪʃn lə- ləʊ-
logistics ləˈdʒɪstɪks ləʊ-
-log(ue) suffix log $ lɔːg
loin(s) lɔɪn(z)
loin-cloth ˈlɔɪn kloθ $ klɔːθ
loiter ˈlɔɪtə(r)
loll lol
lollipop ˈlolɪpop
lollop ˈloləp
lolly ˈlolɪ
London ˈlʌndən
Londonderry ˈlʌndənˈderɪ
lone ləʊn
lonely ˈləʊnlɪ
lonesome ˈləʊnsəm
long loŋ $ lɔːŋ etc
longboat ˈloŋbəʊt $ ˈlɔːŋ-
longbow ˈloŋbəʊ $ ˈlɔːŋ-
long-drawn-out ˈloŋ drɔːn ˈaʊt $ ˈlɔːŋ
longevity lonˈdʒevətɪ
longhand ˈloŋhænd $ ˈlɔːŋ-
longitude ˈlondʒɪtjuːd £ ˈloŋgɪ-
$ ˈlɔːŋgdʒɪtud
longitudinal ˈlondʒɪˈtjuːdɪnl
£ ˈloŋgɪ- -dnl $ ˈlɔːŋgdʒɪˈtudnl
long-shoreman ˈloŋ ʃomən $ ˈlɔːŋ ʃɔr-
long-sighted ˈloŋ ˈsaɪtɪd $ ˈlɔːŋ
long-standing ˈloŋ ˈstændɪŋ $ ˈlɔːŋ
long stop ˈloŋ stop $ ˈlɔːŋ
long-suffering ˈloŋ ˈsʌfrɪŋ $ ˈlɔː ŋ
longways ˈloŋweɪz $ ˈlɔːŋ-
long winded ˈloŋ ˈwɪndɪd $ ˈlɔːŋ
loofah ˈluːfə

look lʊk
looking-glass ˈlʊkɪŋ glɑs $ glæs
loom lum
loon lun
loop lup
loop-hole ˈlup həʊl
loose lus
loose-limbed ˈlus ˈlɪmd
loosen ˈlusn
loot lut
lop lop
lop-eared ˈlop ɪəd $ ɪərd
lop-sided lop ˈsaɪdɪd
lope ləʊp
loquacious ləʊˈkweɪʃəs ləˈk-
loquacity ləʊˈkwæsətɪ lə-
lord, L– lɔd $ lɔrd
lordship ˈlɔdʃɪp $ ˈlɔr-
lore lɔ(r)
lorgnette lɔˈnjet $ lɔr-
lorn lɔn $ lɔrn
lorry ˈlorɪ $ ˈlɔrɪ
Los Angeles ˈlos ˈændʒəliz -lɪz -lɪs $ ˈlɔs
lose luz
loss los $ lɔs
lost lost $ ˈlɔst
lot lot
loth ləʊθ
lotion ˈləʊʃn
lottery ˈlotərɪ
lotus ˈləʊtəs
lotus-eater ˈləʊtəs itə(r)
loud laʊd
loud-hailer ˈlaʊd ˈheɪlə(r)
loudspeaker ˈlaʊdˈspikə(r) ˈl- s-
lough lok *with fricative 'k'*: lox
Loughborough ˈlʌfbərə $ -bərəʊ
Louis ˈluɪ ˈluɪs
Louise luˈiz
Louisiana luˈizɪˈænə £ -ˈɑnə
lounge laʊndʒ
lounge-suit ˈlaʊndʒ sut £ sjut
lour ˈlaʊə(r)
louse *n* laʊs *v* laʊz
lousy ˈlaʊzɪ
lout laʊt
Louvre, the luvr *with unsyllabic* r
lovable ˈlʌvəbl
love lʌv
love-affair ˈlʌv əfeə(r)
lovebird ˈlʌvbɜd
love-letter ˈlʌv letə(r)
lovelorn ˈlʌvlɔn $ -lɔrn

lovesick ˈlʌvsɪk
love-song ˈlʌv soŋ $ sɔŋ
love-story ˈlʌv stɔrɪ
loving-cup ˈlʌvɪŋ kʌp
loving-kindness ˈlʌvɪŋ ˈkaɪndnəs
low ləʊ
low-brow ˈləʊbraʊ
Low Countries ˈləʊ kʌntrɪz
low-down ˈləʊ daʊn
lower case ˈləʊə ˈkeɪs $ ˈləʊər
lowland ˈləʊlənd $ -lænd *etc*
lowly ˈləʊlɪ
low-spirited ˈləʊ ˈspɪrɪtɪd
low-water mark ləʊ ˈwɔtə mak
   $ ˈwɔtər mark
loyal ˈlɔɪl
loyalty ˈlɔɪltɪ
lozenge ˈlozɪndʒ
LP ˈel ˈpi
£.s.d ˈel es ˈdi
LSD ˈel es ˈdi
Ltd ˈlɪmɪtɪd
lubricant ˈlubrɪkənt £ ˈljub-
lubricate ˈlubrɪkeɪt £ ˈljub-
Lucerne luˈsɜn
lucid ˈlusɪd £ ˈlju-
lucidity luˈsɪdətɪ £ lju-
Lucifer ˈlusɪfə(r)
luck lʌk
luckily ˈlʌkɪlɪ ˈlʌkəlɪ
Lucknow ˈlʌknaʊ
lucky-dip ˈlʌkɪ ˈdɪp
lucrative ˈlukrətɪv
lucre ˈlukə(r)
lucubration ˈlukjʊˈbreɪʃn
Lucy ˈlusɪ
ludicrous ˈludɪkrəs
ludo ˈludəʊ
lug lʌg
luggage ˈlʌgɪdʒ
luggage-rack ˈlʌgɪdʒ ræk
luggage-van ˈlʌgɪdʒ væn
lugger ˈlʌgə(r)
lugubrious luˈgubrɪəs luˈg- -ˈgju-
lukewarm ˈlukˈwɔm $ -ˈwɔrm
lull lʌl
lullaby ˈlʌləbaɪ
lumbago lʌmˈbeɪgəʊ
lumbar ˈlʌmbə(r) $ ˈlʌmbɑr
lumber ˈlʌmbə(r)
lumber-jack ˈlʌmbə dʒæk $ -bər
lumber-room ˈlʌmbə rum rum
   $ ˈlʌmbər rum rʊm

luminary ˈluːmɪnərɪ £ ˈljuː- $ -nerɪ
luminosity ˈluːmɪˈnɒsətɪ £ ˈljuː-
luminous ˈluːmɪnəs £ ˈljuː-
lump lʌmp
lunacy ˈluːnəsɪ
lunar ˈluːnə(r)
lunatic ˈluːnətɪk
lunatic asylum ˈluːnətɪk əsaɪləm
lunch lʌntʃ
luncheon ˈlʌntʃən
lung lʌŋ
lunge lʌndʒ
lung-fish ˈlʌŋ fɪʃ
lupin ˈluːpɪn
lurch lɜːtʃ
lure lʊə(r) £ ljʊə(r)
lurid ˈlʊərɪd £ ˈljʊərɪd
lurk lɜːk
Lusaka luˈsaːkə
luscious ˈlʌʃəs
lush lʌʃ

lust lʌst
lustre($ -ter) ˈlʌstə(r)
lustrous ˈlʌstrəs
lutanist ˈluːtənɪst
lute luːt
Luther ˈluːθə(r) £ ˈljuːθə(r)
Lutheran ˈluːθərən £ ˈljuː-
Luxemburg ˈlʌksmbɜɡ
luxuriant lʌɡˈʒʊərɪənt ləɡ- -ˈzjʊə-
luxuriate lʌɡˈʒʊərɪeɪt ləɡ- -ˈzjʊə-
luxurious lʌɡˈʒʊərɪəs ləɡ- -ˈzjʊə-
luxury ˈlʌkʃərɪ -ʃrɪ
-ly *suffix* lɪ
lyceum laɪˈsɪəm
lying ˈlaɪɪŋ
lymph lɪmf $ lɪmpf
lynch lɪntʃ
lynx lɪŋks
lynx-eyed ˈlɪŋks ˈaɪd
Lyons ˈlɪõ ˈlaɪənz
lyre ˈlaɪə(r)
lyric ˈlɪrɪk

M

M m em
ma maː
MA ˈem ˈeɪ
ma'am mæm mɑm
Mabel ˈmeɪbl
macabre məˈkaːbr *with unsyllabic* r
  mæ- -bə(r) $ -brə *etc*
macadam məˈkædəm
macaroni ˈmækəˈrəʊnɪ
macaroon ˈmækəˈruːn
macaw məˈkɔː
Macbeth mækˈbeθ
mace meɪs
mace-bearer ˈmeɪs beərə(r)
macerate ˈmæsəreɪt
Mach maːk £ mæk
machete məˈtʃeɪtɪ $ məˈʃetɪ
Machiavelli ˈmækɪəˈvelɪ
machiavellian ˈmækɪəˈvelɪən
machination ˈmækɪˈneɪʃn ˈmæʃɪ-
machine məˈʃiːn
machinery məˈʃiːnrɪ
machinist məˈʃiːnɪst
mac(k) mæk
mackerel ˈmækrl
mackintosh ˈmækɪntɒʃ

MacMillan məkˈmɪlən mæk-
macrobiotic ˈmækrəʊbaɪˈɒtɪk
macrocosm ˈmækrəʊkozm
mad mæd
Madagascar ˈmædəˈɡæskə(r)
madam ˈmædəm
Madame ˈmædəm mæˈdæm
madcap ˈmædkæp
madder ˈmædə(r)
made meɪd
Madeira məˈdɪərə
Madeira cake məˈdɪərə keɪk
Madeleine ˈmædleɪn -lɪn
mademoiselle ˈmædəməˈzel
  -dəmwɑ- ˈmæmˈzel
madhouse ˈmædhaʊs
madman ˈmædmən
Madonna məˈdonə
Madras məˈdrɑs $ £ məˈdræs
  $ ˈmædrəs
Madrid məˈdrɪd
madrigal ˈmædrɪgl
Maecenas miˈsiːnæs mɪ- maɪ- $ £ -nəs
maelstrom ˈmeɪlstrəm -əʊm
maestro ˈmaɪstrəʊ
magazine ˈmægəˈziːn $ ˈmægəzin *etc*

magenta mə'dʒentə

maggot 'mægət

Magi 'meɪdʒaɪ

magic 'mædʒɪk

magical 'mædʒɪkl

magician mə'dʒɪʃn

magisterial 'mædʒɪ'stɪərɪəl

magistrate 'mædʒɪstreɪt -ɪt -ət

Magna Carta 'mægnə 'katə $ 'kartə

magnanimity 'mægnə'nɪmətɪ

magnanimous mæg'nænɪməs

magnate 'mægneɪt

magnesia mæg'niʃə -niʒə

magnesium mæg'niziəm $ -nizm

magnet 'mægnɪt -ət

magnetic mæg'netɪk

magnetism 'mægnɪtɪzm

magneto mæg'nitəʊ

magnificat mæg'nɪfɪkæt

magnification 'mægnɪfɪ'keɪʃn

magnificent mæg'nɪfɪsnt

magnify 'mægnɪfaɪ

magnifying-glass 'mægnɪfaɪɪŋ glas $ -æs

magniloquent mæg'nɪləkwənt

magnitude 'mægnɪtjud $ -tud

magnolia mæg'nəʊlɪə

magnum 'mægnəm

magnum opus 'mægnəm 'əʊpəs

magpie 'mægpaɪ

Magyar 'mægja(r)

Maharaja(h) 'maə'radʒə 'mahə-

Maharanee 'maə'rani 'mahə-

Mahatma mə'hætmə -'hat-

mah-jong(g) 'ma 'dʒɒŋ $ 'dʒɔŋ etc

mahogany mə'hɒgənɪ

Mahomet mə'hɒmɪt -ət

Mahommed mə'hɒmɪd

Mahommedan mə'hɒmɪdən

maid meɪd

maiden 'meɪdn

maidenhead, M– 'meɪdnhed

maidenhood 'meɪdnhʊd

maid-of-honour 'meɪd əv 'ɒnə(r)

mail meɪl

mailbag 'meɪlbæg

mailbox 'meɪlbɒks

mail-order 'meɪl 'ɔdə(r) $ 'ɔrdər

mailing-list 'meɪlɪŋ lɪst

mailman 'meɪlmæn

maim meɪm

main meɪn

mainland 'meɪnlænd -lənd

mainmast 'meɪnmast $ -mæst

mainspring 'meɪn-sprɪŋ

mainstay 'meɪn-steɪ

maintain meɪn'teɪn mən-

maintenance 'meɪntɪnəns

maisonette 'meɪzə'net $ -zəʊ'net

maize meɪz

majestic mə'dʒestɪk

majesty 'mædʒɪstɪ

majolica mə'dʒɒlɪkə

major 'meɪdʒə(r)

Majorca maɪ'jɔkə mə'jɔkə mə'dʒɔkə $ mə'dʒɔrkə

major-general 'meɪdʒə 'dʒenrl $ -dʒər

majority mə'dʒɒrətɪ $ mə'dʒɔrətɪ etc

make meɪk

make-believe 'meɪk bɪliv

makeshift 'meɪkʃɪft

make-up 'meɪk ʌp

make-weight 'meɪk weɪt

malachite 'mæləkaɪt

maladjusted 'mælə'dʒʌstɪd

maladjustment 'mælə'dʒʌstmənt

maladroit 'mælə'drɔɪt

malady 'mælədɪ

malaise mæ'leɪz

malapert 'mæləpət

malapropism 'mæləpropɪzm

malapropos 'mæl'æprə'pəʊ -'æprəpəʊ

malaria mə'leərɪə

Malay mə'leɪ

Malaya mə'leɪə

Malayalam 'mælə'jaləm -leɪ'ja-

Malaysia meɪ'leɪzɪə $ -eɪʒə -eɪʃə

Malawi mə'lawɪ

malcontent 'mælkəntent

male meɪl

malediction 'mælɪ'dɪkʃn

malefactor 'mælɪfæktə(r)

maleficent mə'lefɪsnt

malevolent mə'levələnt

malformation 'mælfɔ'meɪʃn $ -fɔr-

malformed 'mæl'fɔmd $ -'fɔr-

Mali 'malɪ

malice 'mælɪs

malicious mə'lɪʃəs

malign mə'laɪn

malignant mə'lɪgnənt

malignity mə'lɪgnətɪ

malinger mə'lɪŋgə(r)

mallard 'mæləd -lad $ -lərd -lard

malleable 'mælɪəbl

mallet 'mælɪt -ət

mallow 'mæləʊ

malnutrition 'mælnjuˈtrɪʃn $ -nu-
malodorous mælˈəudərəs
malpractice mælˈpræktɪs
malt mɔlt £ molt
Malta ˈmɔltə £ ˈmoltə
Maltese mɔlˈtiz £ molˈtiz
Malthusian mælˈθjuzɪən $ -uʒn etc
maltreat mælˈtrit
Malvern ˈmɔlvən £ ˈmol- ˈmælvərn
mamba ˈmæmbə
mamma məˈma $ ˈmamə
mammal ˈmæml
mammon ˈmæmən
mammoth ˈmæməθ
mammy ˈmæmɪ
man, M– mæn
manacle ˈmænəkl
manage ˈmænɪdʒ
manageable ˈmænɪdʒəbl
management ˈmænɪdʒmənt
manager ˈmænɪdʒə(r)
managerial 'mænəˈdʒɪərɪəl
Manchester ˈmæntʃɪstə(r) -tʃəs- $ -tʃes-
Manchuria mænˈtʃuərɪə
Mandalay 'mændəˈleɪ $ ˈmændəleɪ
mandarin, M– ˈmændərɪn
mandate ˈmændeɪt
mandatory ˈmændətrɪ $ -tɔrɪ
mandible ˈmændɪbl
mandolin ˈmændəlɪn 'mændəˈlɪn
mandrake ˈmæn-dreɪk
mandrill ˈmæn-drɪl
mane meɪn
maneuver məˈnuvə(r)
manganate ˈmæŋgəneɪt
manganese ˈmæŋgəˈniz $ ˈmæŋgəniz
mange meɪndʒ
mangel-wurzel ˈmæŋgl wɜzl
manger ˈmeɪndʒə(r)
mangle ˈmæŋgl
mango ˈmæŋgəu
mangrove ˈmæŋgrəuv
mangy ˈmeɪndʒɪ
manhandle ˈmænhændl
Manhattan mænˈhætn
manhole ˈmænhəul
manhood ˈmænhud
man-hour ˈmæn auə(r)
mania n, suffix ˈmeɪnɪə
maniac ˈmeɪnɪæk
maniacal məˈnaɪəkl
manicure ˈmænɪkjuə(r)
manicurist ˈmænɪkjuərɪst

manifest ˈmænɪfest
manifestation 'mænɪfeˈsteɪʃn
manifesto 'mænɪˈfestəu
manifold ˈmænɪfəuld
manikin ˈmænɪkɪn
manil(l)a, M– məˈnɪlə
manipulate məˈnɪpjuleɪt
Manitoba 'mænɪˈtəubə
mankind mænˈkaɪnd
manna ˈmænə
mannequin ˈmænəkɪn
manner ˈmænə(r)
mannerism ˈmænərɪzm
manoeuvre məˈnuvə(r)
manoeuvrable məˈnuvrəbl
manor ˈmænə(r)
manorial məˈnɔrɪəl
manpower ˈmænpauə(r)
manse mæns
manservant ˈmæn-sɜvənt
mansion ˈmænʃn
Mansion-house, the ˈmænʃn haus
man-sized ˈmæn saɪzd
manslaughter ˈmæn-slɔtə(r)
mantel ˈmæntl
mantel-piece ˈmæntl pis
mantilla mænˈtɪlə
mantis ˈmæntɪs
mantle ˈmæntl
mantlepiece ˈmæntlpis
mantrap ˈmæntræp
manual ˈmænjuəl
manufacture 'mænjuˈfæktʃə(r) -nəˈf-
manure məˈnjuə(r) $ məˈnuər
manuscript ˈmænjuskrɪpt
Manx mæŋks
many ˈmenɪ
many-sided 'menɪ ˈsaɪdɪd
Maoist ˈmauɪst
Maori ˈmaurɪ ˈma-urɪ
map mæp
maple ˈmeɪpl
maple-syrup 'meɪpl ˈsɪrəp
maquis ˈmækɪ $ £ ˈmaki
mar ma(r)
marabou ˈmærəbu
Marathon ˈmærəθən $ -θon etc
maraud məˈrɔd
marble ˈmabl $ ˈmarbl
Marcel(le) maˈsel $ mar-
march, M– matʃ $ martʃ
marching orders ˈmatʃɪŋ ɔdəz
  $ ˈmartʃɪŋ ɔrdərz

marchioness 'maʃə'nes `maʃɲɪs
$ `marʃɲɪs
Mardi gras 'madɪ `gra $ 'mar-
mare meə(r)
Margaret `magrət -ɪt $ `mar-
margarine 'madʒə'rin 'magə-
$ `mardʒərɪn -in
margin `madʒɪn $ `mardʒɪn
marginal `madʒɪnl $ `mar-
marguerite 'magə'rit $ `mar-
Maria mə`rɪə mə`raɪə
Marie `marɪ mə`ri
marigold `mærɪgəʊld
marihuana 'mærɪ'wanə -`hwa-
Marilyn `mærɫɪn
marinade 'mærɪ'neɪd
marine mə`rin
mariner `mærɪnə(r)
marionette 'mærɪə'net
marital `mærɪtl £ mə`raɪtl
maritime `mærɪtaɪm
marjoram `madʒərəm $ `mar-
Marjorie `madʒərɪ $ `mar-
mark, M– mak $ mark
market `makɪt $ `markɪt
market-day `makɪt deɪ $ `markɪt
market-garden 'makɪt `gadn
$ 'markɪt `gardn
market-place `makɪt pleɪs $ `markɪt
market-town `makɪt taʊn $ `markɪt
marking-ink `makɪŋ ɪŋk $ `markɪŋ
marksman `maksmən $ `marksmən
Marlborough `mɔlbrə `mal-
$ `marlbərəʊ -bərə
marmalade `maməleɪd $ `mar-
marmot `mamət $ `marmət
maroon mə`run
marquee ma`ki $ mar-
marquess `makwɪs $ `mar-
marquis `makwɪs $ `mar-
marriage `mærɪdʒ
marriage lines `mærɪdʒ laɪnz
marrow `mærəʊ
marrowbone `mærəʊbəʊn
marry `mærɪ
Mars maz $ marz
Marsala ma`salə $ mar-
Marseillaise, la la 'masə`leɪz -seɪ`eɪz
-seɪ`eəz $ 'mar-
Marseilles ma`seɪ -`seɪlz $ mar-
marsh maʃ $ marʃ
marshal `maʃl $ `marʃl
marsh-mallow `maʃ mæləʊ $ `marʃ

marsupial ma`sjupɪəl $ mar`supɪəl
mart mat $ mart
Martha `maθə $ `marθə
martial `maʃl $ `marʃl
Martian `maʃn $ `marʃn
martin, M– `matɪn $ `martn
martinet 'matɪ`net $ `martɲet etc
martini ma`tinɪ $ mar-
Martinique 'matɪ`nik $ `martn`ik
Martinmas `matɪnməs -mæs $ `martn-
martyr `matə(r) $ `mar-
martyrdom `matədəm $ `martərdəm
marvel `mavl $ `marvl
marvellous($ -elous) `mavɫəs $ `mar-
Marx maks $ marks
Marxian `maksɪən $ `mark-
Marxist `maksɪst $ `mark-
Mary `meərɪ
Maryland `meərɪlənd £ -lænd
marzipan 'mazɪ`pæn
$ `marzəpæn `martsəpan -pæn etc
mascara mæ`skarə $ mæ`skærə etc
mascot `mæskot -ət
masculine `mæskjʊlɪn £ `mas-
masculinity 'mæskjʊ`lɪnətɪ £ 'mas-
mash mæʃ
mashie `mæʃɪ
mask mask $ mæsk
masochism `mæsəkɪzm
masochist `mæsəkɪst
mason, M– `meɪsn
masonic mə`sonɪk
masonry `meɪsnrɪ
masque mask $ £ mæsk
masquerade 'mæskə`reɪd £ 'ma-
mass, M– mæs
Massachusetts 'mæsə`tʃusɪts $ -zɪts
massacre `mæsəkə(r)
massage `mæsaʒ $ mə`saʒ -adʒ
masseur mæ`sɜ(r) $ mə`sɜ
masseuse mæ`sɜz $ -`suz mə-
this ʒ may have no r *quality*
massif mæ`sif
massive `mæsɪv
mast mast $ mæst
master `mastə(r) $ `mæstər
master-key `mastə ki $ `mæstər
masterpiece `mastəpis $ `mæstər-
mastery `mastərɪ $ `mæstərɪ
mast-head `mast hed $ `mæst
masticate `mæstɪkeɪt
mastiff `mæstɪf £ `mastɪf
mastodon `mæstədon -dən

mastoid ˈmæstɔɪd
masturbate ˈmæstəbeɪt $ -tɜːb-
masturbation ˌmæstəˈbeɪʃn $ -tərˈb-
mat mæt
matador ˈmætədɔ(r)
match mætʃ
matchbox ˈmætʃbɒks
matchet ˈmætʃɪt mæˈtʃet
matchmaker ˈmætʃmeɪkə(r)
matchwood ˈmætʃwʊd
mate meɪt
mater ˈmeɪtə(r)
material məˈtɪərɪəl
materialistic məˌtɪərɪəˈlɪstɪk
maternal məˈtɜːnl
maternity məˈtɜːnətɪ
matey ˈmeɪtɪ
math mæθ
mathematician ˌmæθəməˈtɪʃn -θm-
mathematics ˌmæθəˈmætɪks -θˈm-
maths mæθs
Matilda məˈtɪldə
matinée ˈmætɪneɪ $ ˌmætnˈeɪ
matins ˈmætɪnz
matriarch ˈmeɪtrɪɑk $ -ɑrk
matriarchal ˌmeɪtrɪˈɑkl ˈmæt- $ -ˈɑrkl
matriarchy ˈmeɪtrɪɑkɪ $ -ɑrkɪ
matrices ˈmeɪtrɪsiz
matricide ˈmætrɪsaɪd ˈmeɪ-
matriculate məˈtrɪkjʊleɪt
matriculation məˌtrɪkjʊˈleɪʃn
matrimonial ˌmætrɪˈməʊnɪəl
matrimony ˈmætrɪmənɪ $ -məʊnɪ
matrix ˈmeɪtrɪks
matron ˈmeɪtrən
matt mæt
matter ˈmætə(r)
Matthew ˈmæθju
matting ˈmætɪŋ
mattins ˈmætɪnz
mattock ˈmætək
mattress ˈmætrəs -ɪs
mature məˈtʃʊə(r) -ˈtjʊə(r) $ məˈtʊər etc
maturity məˈtʃʊərətɪ -ˈtjʊə- $ -ˈtʊərətɪ etc
matutinal məˈtjutɪnl ˈmætjʊˈtaɪnl
    $ məˈtutn̩ ˈmætʃʊˈtaɪnl
Maud mɔd
maudlin ˈmɔdlɪn
Maugham mɔm
maul mɔl
maunder ˈmɔndə(r)
Maundy ˈmɔndɪ
Mauretania ˌmɒrɪˈteɪnɪə $ ˈmɔr-

Maurice ˈmɒrɪs $ ˈmɔrɪs məˈris
Mauritius məˈrɪʃəs $ mɔˈrɪʃəs
mausoleum ˌmɔsəˈlɪəm
mauve məʊv
maverick ˈmævərɪk
mawkish ˈmɔkɪʃ
maxim, M– ˈmæksɪm
maximum ˈmæksɪməm
may, M– meɪ
maybe ˈmeɪbi
mayday, M– D– ˈmeɪ deɪ
Mayfair ˈmeɪfeə(r)
mayflower, M– ˈmeɪflaʊə(r)
mayfly ˈmeɪflaɪ
mayhem ˈmeɪhem $ ˈmeɪəm
mayn't meɪnt ˈmeɪənt
mayonnaise ˌmeɪəˈneɪz $ ˈmeɪəneɪz etc
mayor meə(r) $ ˈmeɪər etc
mayoralty ˈmeərltɪ $ ˈmeɪərltɪ etc
mayoress meəˈres ˈmeəres $ £ ˈmeərəs -ɪs
maypole ˈmeɪpəʊl
May Queen ˈmeɪ kwin
maze meɪz
mazurka məˈzɜkə
me mi
mead mid
meadow ˈmedəʊ
meagre($ -er) ˈmigə(r)
meal mil
mealtime ˈmil-taɪm
mealy-mouthed ˌmilɪ ˈmaʊðd $ ˈmaʊθt
mean min
meander mɪˈændə(r)
meaning ˈminɪŋ
means-test ˈminz test
meant ment
meantime ˈmin-taɪm ˈminˈtaɪm
meanwhile ˈminˈwaɪl ˈminwaɪl $ -ˈhw- etc
measles ˈmizlz
measly ˈmizlɪ
measurable ˈmeʒr̩bl
measure ˈmeʒə(r) $ ˈmeɪʒər
measurement ˈmeʒəmənt $ -ʒər- ˈmeɪ-
meat mit
meat-safe ˈmit seɪf
Mecca ˈmekə
mechanic mɪˈkænɪk
mechanism ˈmekənɪzm
mechanize ˈmekənaɪz
medal ˈmedl
medalist ˈmedl̩ɪst
medallion mɪˈdælɪən
medallist ˈmedl̩ɪst

meddle ˈmedl
meddlesome ˈmedlsm
media ˈmidɪə
mediaeval ˈmedɪˈivl
$ ˈmidɪˈivl meˈdivl mi- mɪ- etc
medial ˈmidɪəl
median ˈmidɪən
mediate ˈmidɪeɪt
mediator ˈmidɪeɪtə(r)
medical ˈmedɪkl
medicament mɪˈdɪkəmənt mə- me-
ˈmedɪkəmənt
Medicare ˈmedɪkeə(r)
medicated ˈmedɪkeɪtɪd
medicinal mɪˈdɪsɪnl
medicine ˈmedsn £ ˈmedɪsn
medicine-ball ˈmedsn bɔl $ -dɪsn
medicine-chest ˈmedsn tʃest $ -dɪsn
medicine-man ˈmedsn mæn $ -dɪsn
medico ˈmedɪkəʊ
medieval ˈmedɪˈivl
$ ˈmidɪˈivl meˈdivl mi- mɪ- etc
mediocre ˈmidɪˈəʊkə(r)
mediocrity ˈmidɪˈokrətɪ
meditate ˈmedɪteɪt
meditation ˈmedɪˈteɪʃn
meditative ˈmedɪtətɪv $ -teɪtɪv
Mediterranean ˈmedɪtəˈreɪnɪən
medium ˈmidɪəm
medlar ˈmedlə(r)
medley ˈmedlɪ
meek mik
meet mit
meeting-place ˈmitɪŋ pleɪs
megacycle ˈmegəsaɪkl
megalith ˈmegəlɪθ
megalomania ˈmegələˈmeɪnɪə -ləʊ-
megalomaniac ˈmegələˈmeɪnɪæk -ləʊ-
megaphone ˈmegəfəʊn
melancholia ˈmelənˈkəʊlɪə
melancholy ˈmelənkolɪ £ -kəlɪ
mélange ˈmeɪlõʒ $ meɪˈlõʒ -ˈlondʒ
melba toast ˈmelbə ˈtəʊst
Melbourne ˈmelbən -bən $ -bərn -bɔrn
mêlée ˈmeleɪ $ meɪˈleɪ ˈmeɪleɪ etc
mellifluous meˈlɪfluəs
mellow ˈmeləʊ
melodic məˈlodɪk
melodious məˈləʊdɪəs
melodrama ˈmelədrɑmə -ləʊ- $ -dræmə
melodramatic ˈmelədrəˈmætɪk -ləʊ-
melody ˈmelədɪ
melon ˈmelən

melt melt
melting-point ˈmeltɪŋ pɔɪnt
melting-pot ˈmeltɪŋ pot
member ˈmembə(r)
membership ˈmembəʃɪp $ ˈmembər-
membrane ˈmembreɪn
membraneous memˈbreɪnɪəs
memento məˈmentəʊ mɪ-
memo ˈmeməʊ ˈmi-
memoir ˈmemwɑ(r)
memorable ˈmemrəbl
memorandum ˈmeməˈrændəm
memorial məˈmɔrɪəl mɪ-
Memorial Day məˈmɔrɪəl deɪ mɪ-
memorize ˈmeməraɪz
memory ˈmemərɪ -mrɪ
Memphis ˈmemfɪs
mem-sahib ˈmem sɑb sɑ-ɪb sɑhɪb
men men
menace ˈmenəs -ɪs
ménage ˈmeɪnɑʒ ˈmen- $ meɪˈnɑʒ
menagerie məˈnædʒərɪ
mend mend
mendacious menˈdeɪʃəs
mendacity menˈdæsətɪ
Mendelssohn ˈmendlsn -səʊn
mendicant ˈmendɪkənt
menfolk ˈmen-fəʊk
menial ˈminɪəl
meningitis ˈmenɪnˈdʒaɪtɪs -təs
menopause ˈmenəpɔz
menstrual ˈmenstruəl
menstruate ˈmenstrueɪt
menstruation ˈmenstruˈeɪʃn
mensurable ˈmenʃurəbl $ -nsər- etc
mensuration ˈmensjuˈreɪʃn
$ -nsəˈr- -nʃuˈr-
-ment n, suffix mənt v ment
mental ˈmentl
mental home ˈmentl həʊm
mental hospital ˈmentl hospɪtl
mentality menˈtælətɪ
mental patient ˈmentl peɪʃnt
mental specialist ˈmentl speʃlɪst
mental test ˈmentl test
menthol ˈmenθol -θl $ ˈmenθɔl -θəʊl
mention ˈmenʃn
mentor ˈmentə(r) $ ˈmentər
menu ˈmenju
Mephistophelean ˈmefɪstəˈfilɪən
Mephistopheles ˈmefɪˈstofliz
mercantile ˈmɜkəntaɪl $ -til -tɪl etc
mercenary ˈmɜsnrɪ -ɲərɪ $ -ɲerɪ

mercerize ˈmɜsəraɪz
merchandise ˈmɜtʃəndaɪz $ -aɪs
merchant ˈmɜtʃənt
merchantman ˈmɜtʃəntmən
merchant-seaman ˈmɜtʃənt ˈsimən
merchant ship ˈmɜtʃənt ʃɪp
merciful ˈmɜsɪfl
mercurial məˈkjʊərɪəl
mercury ˈmɜkjʊrɪ -jərɪ $ -kərɪ
mercy ˈmɜsɪ
mere mɪə(r)
merely ˈmɪəlɪ $ ˈmɪərlɪ
meretricious ˈmerəˈtrɪʃəs
merge mɜdʒ
merger ˈmɜdʒə(r)
meridian məˈrɪdɪən
meridional məˈrɪdɪənl
Merioneth ˈmerɪˈonɪθ -əθ
meringue məˈræŋ
merino məˈrinəʊ
merino-sheep məˈrinəʊ ʃip
merit ˈmerɪt
meritorious ˈmerɪˈtɔrɪəs
mermaid ˈmɜmeɪd
merman ˈmɜmæn
merriment ˈmerɪmənt
merry ˈmerɪ
merry-go-round ˈmerɪ gəʊ raʊnd
merry-making ˈmerɪ-meɪkɪŋ
mésalliance meɪˈzælɪəns meˈz-
    $ ˈmeɪzælˈjɑs ˈmeɪzəˈlɪəns ˈmez-
mesdames meɪˈdɑm -ˈdæm
mesh meʃ
mesmeric mezˈmerɪk
mesmerism ˈmezmərɪzm
mesmerize ˈmezməraɪz
Mesopotamia ˈmesəpəˈteɪmɪə
mess mes
message ˈmesɪdʒ
messenger ˈmesɪndʒə(r)
Messiah məˈsaɪə
Messina məˈsinə
mess-mate ˈmes meɪt
Messrs ˈmesəz $ ˈmesərz
messuage ˈmesjʊɪdʒ
mess-up ˈmes ʌp
met met
metabolism mɪˈtæbəlɪzm
metal ˈmetl
metalled ˈmetld
metallic məˈtælɪk
metallurgical ˈmetəˈlɜdʒɪkl
metallurgist mɪˈtælədʒɪst $ £ ˈmetʃədʒɪst

metallurgy mɪˈtælədʒɪ $ £ ˈmetʃədʒɪ
metal-worker ˈmetl wɜkə(r)
metamorphose ˈmetəˈmɔfəʊz $ -ˈmɔr-
metamorphoses pl ˈmetəˈmɔfəsiz
    $ -ˈmɔr-
metamorphosis ˈmetəˈmɔfəsɪs $ -ˈmɔr-
metaphor ˈmetəfə(r) -fɔ(r)
metaphorical ˈmetəˈforɪkl $ -ˈfɔr-
metaphysical ˈmetəˈfɪzɪkl
metaphysics ˈmetəfɪzɪks
mete mit
meteor ˈmitɪə(r) ˈmitɪɔ(r)
meteoric ˈmitɪˈorɪk $ -ˈɔr-
meteorite ˈmitɪəraɪt
meteorological ˈmitrəˈlodʒɪkl -tɪər-
    $ -tɪɔr- etc
meteorologist ˈmitɪəˈrolədʒɪst $ -tɪɔˈr- etc
meteorology ˈmitɪəˈrolədʒɪ $ -tɪɔˈr- etc
meter ˈmitə(r)
-meter suffix mɪtə(r)
methane ˈmiθeɪn $ £ ˈmeθeɪn
method ˈmeθəd
methodical məˈθodɪkl mɪ-
Methodism ˈmeθədɪzm
methodology ˈmeθəˈdolədʒɪ
Methuselah mɪˈθjuzələ -θu- mə-
meths meθs
methyl ˈmeθl -θɪl £ chemists: ˈmiθaɪl
methylated ˈmeθ]eɪtɪd
meticulous mɪˈtɪkjʊləs
métier ˈmeɪtɪeɪ $ meɪˈtjeɪ etc
metre($ -ter) ˈmitə(r)
metric ˈmetrɪk
metrical ˈmetrɪkl
metrication ˈmetrɪˈkeɪʃn
Metro ˈmetrəʊ ˈmeɪ-
metronome ˈmetrənəʊm
metropolis məˈtropəlɪs
metropolitan ˈmetrəˈpolɪtən
mettle ˈmetl
mew mju
Mexican ˈmeksɪkən
Mexico ˈmeksɪkəʊ
mezzanine ˈmetsənin $ £ ˈmezə-
mezzo ˈmetsəʊ
mezzo-soprano ˈmetsəʊ səˈprɑnəʊ
    $ səˈprænəʊ etc
mezzotint ˈmetsəʊtɪnt
M.I.5. ˈem aɪ ˈfaɪv
Miami maɪˈæmɪ
miaow miˈaʊ as if by cat: miˈɑ-ʊ
mica ˈmaɪkə
mice maɪs

Michael ˈmaɪkl
Michaelmas ˈmɪklməs
Michelangelo ˈmaɪklˈændʒələʊ
Michigan ˈmɪʃɪgən -ɪtʃɪ-
microbe ˈmaɪkrəʊb
microcosm ˈmaɪkrəʊkozm
microfilm ˈmaɪkrəʊfɪlm
micrometer maɪˈkromɪtə(r)
microphone ˈmaɪkrəfəʊn
microscope ˈmaɪkrəskəʊp
microscopic ˈmaɪkrəˈskopɪk
microwave ˈmaɪkrəʊweɪv
mid adj, prefix mɪd
midday mɪdˈdeɪ
midden ˈmɪdn
middle ˈmɪdl
middle-aged ˈmɪdl ˈeɪdʒd
middle-class ˈmɪdl ˈklɑs $ ˈklæs
middleman ˈmɪdlmæn
middle-of-the-road ˈmɪdl əv ðə ˈrəʊd
Middlesex ˈmɪdlseks
middle-weight ˈmɪdl weɪt
middling ˈmɪdlɪŋ
midge mɪdʒ
midget ˈmɪdʒɪt
midland ˈmɪdlənd
Midlands, the ˈmɪdləndz
Midlothian mɪdˈləʊðɪən
midnight ˈmɪdnaɪt
mid-off ˈmɪd ˈof $ £ ˈɔf
mid-on ˈmɪd ˈon $ ˈɔn
midriff ˈmɪdrɪf
midshipman ˈmɪdʃɪpmən
midst mɪdst mɪtst
midsummer ˈmɪdˈsʌmə(r)
midway ˈmɪdˈweɪ
Mid West ˈmɪd ˈwest
midwife ˈmɪdwaɪf
midwifery ˈmɪdwɪfrɪ $ -waɪfərɪ
midwinter ˈmɪd ˈwɪntə(r)
mien min
might maɪt
mightn't ˈmaɪtnt
mignonette ˈmɪnjəˈnet
migraine ˈmigreɪn $ £ ˈmaɪ-
migrant ˈmaɪgrənt
migrate maɪˈgreɪt $ ˈmaɪgreɪt
migration maɪˈgreɪʃn
migratory ˈmaɪgrətərɪ $ -tɔrɪ
mikado mɪˈkɑdəʊ
milady mɪˈleɪdɪ
milage ˈmaɪlɪdʒ
Milan mɪˈlæn $ mɪˈlɑn

milch mɪltʃ
mild maɪld
mildew ˈmɪldju $ -du
Mildred ˈmɪldrɪd -rəd
mile maɪl
mileage ˈmaɪlɪdʒ
milestone ˈmaɪlstəʊn
milieu ˈmilɪɜ $ ˈmilɪˈɜ this ɜ may have no r quality ˈmilɪˈu
militant ˈmɪlɪtənt
militarism ˈmɪlɪtərɪzm
military ˈmɪlɪtrɪ $ -terɪ
militate ˈmɪlɪteɪt
militia mɪˈlɪʃə
militiaman mɪˈlɪʃəmən
milk mɪlk
milk-bar ˈmɪlk bɑ(r)
milk-churn ˈmɪlk tʃɜn
milk-maid ˈmɪlk meɪd
milkman ˈmɪlkmən
milk-powder ˈmɪlk paʊdə(r)
milk-shake ˈmɪlk ʃeɪk ˈm- ˈʃ-
milksop ˈmɪlksop
milk-tooth ˈmɪlk tuθ
milk-white ˈmɪlk ˈwaɪt $ ˈhwaɪt etc
mill mɪl
millboard ˈmɪlbɔd $ -bɔrd
millenium mɪˈlenɪəm
millepede ˈmɪlɪpid
millet ˈmɪlɪt
mill-girl ˈmɪl gɜl
mill-hand ˈmɪl hænd
milli- prefix mɪlɪ
milliard ˈmɪlɪɑd $ -ɑrd
Millicent ˈmɪlɪsnt
milliner ˈmɪlɪnə(r)
million ˈmɪlɪən
millionaire ˈmɪlɪəˈneə(r)
millionth ˈmɪlɪənθ
millipede ˈmɪlɪpid
millpond ˈmɪl pond
millstone ˈmɪl stəʊn
mill-wheel ˈmɪl wil $ hwil etc
millwright ˈmɪlraɪt
milord mɪˈlɔd $ mɪˈlɔrd
milt mɪlt
Milton ˈmɪltən
Milwaukee mɪlˈwɔkɪ
mime maɪm
mimeograph ˈmɪmɪəʊgrɑf $ £ -græf
mimetic mɪˈmetɪk maɪ-
mimic ˈmɪmɪk
mimicry ˈmɪmɪkrɪ

mimosa **mɪˋməʊzə $ mɪˋməʊsə** *etc*
minaret **ˈmɪnəˋret** $ ˋmɪnəret
minatory **ˋmɪnətərɪ $ -tɔrɪ**
mince **mɪns**
mince matters, not **ˋmɪns mætəz $ -tərz**
mincemeat **ˋmɪnsmit**
mince-pie **ˈmɪns ˋpɑɪ**
mind **mɑɪnd**
mind, to my **tə ˋmɑɪ mɑɪnd**
Mind you! **ˈmɑɪnd ˋju**
mine **mɑɪn**
minefield **ˋmɑɪn-fild**
miner **ˋmɑɪnə(r)**
mineral **ˋmɪnrl**
mineralogy **ˈmɪnəˋrælədʒɪ** -ˋrol-
mineral water **ˋmɪnrl wɔtə(r)**
minestrone **ˈmɪnɪˋstrəʊnɪ**
mine-sweeper **ˋmɑɪn swipə(r)**
mingle **ˋmɪŋgl**
mingy **ˋmɪndʒɪ**
miniature **ˋmɪnɪtʃə(r)** -nɪətʃ- **$ -tʃʊər** *etc*
mini- *prefix* **mɪnɪ**
minim **ˋmɪnɪm**
minimize **ˋmɪnɪmɑɪz**
minimum **ˋmɪnɪməm**
minion **ˋmɪnɪən**
mini-skirt **ˋmɪnɪ skɜt**
minister **ˋmɪnɪstə(r)**
ministerial **ˈmɪnɪˋstɪərɪəl**
ministration **ˈmɪnɪˋstreɪʃn**
ministry **ˋmɪnɪstrɪ**
mink **mɪŋk**
Minneapolis **ˈmɪnɪˋæpəlɪs**
Minnesota **ˈmɪnɪˋsəʊtə**
minnow **ˋmɪnəʊ**
minor **ˋmɑɪnə(r)**
minority **mɪˋnorətɪ** mɑɪˋn- **$ -ˋnɔr-**
minority report **mɪˋnorətɪ rɪpɔt $ -ˋnɔr-**
Minotaur **ˋmɑɪnətɔ(r)**
minster **ˋmɪnstə(r)**
minstrel **ˋmɪnstrəl**
mint **mɪnt**
minuet **ˈmɪnjʊˋet**
minus **ˋmɑɪnəs**
minute *adj* **mɑɪˋnjut $ mɑɪˋnut** mɪ-
minute *n* **ˋmɪnɪt**
minute-book **ˋmɪnɪt bʊk**
minute-hand **ˋmɪnɪt hænd**
minutiae **mɑɪˋnjuʃii** mɪ- **$ mɪˋnuʃii** *etc*
minx **mɪŋks**
miracle **ˋmɪrəkl** -rɪkl
miracle play **ˋmɪrəkl pleɪ**
miraculous **mɪˋrækjʊləs**

mirage **ˋmɪrɑʒ $ mɪˋrɑʒ**
mire **ˋmɑɪə(r)**
Miriam **ˋmɪrɪəm**
mirror **ˋmɪrə(r)**
mirth **mɜθ**
mis- *prefix* **mɪs**
misadventure **ˈmɪsədˋventʃə(r)**
misalliance **ˈmɪsəˋlɑɪəns**
misanthrope **ˋmɪsnθrəʊp**
misanthropic **ˈmɪsnˋθropɪk**
misapplication **ˈmɪsˈæplɪˋkeɪʃn**
misapply **ˈmɪsəˋplɑɪ**
misapprehend **ˈmɪsˈæprɪˋhend**
misapprehension **ˈmɪsˈæprɪˋhenʃn**
misappropriate **ˈmɪsəˋprəʊprɪeɪt**
misbegotten **ˈmɪsbɪˋgotn**
misbehave **ˈmɪsbɪˋheɪv**
misbehaviour **ˈmɪsbɪˋheɪvɪə(r)**
misbeliever **ˈmɪsbɪˋlivə(r)**
miscalculate **ˈmɪsˋkælkjʊleɪt**
miscall **mɪsˋkɔl**
miscarriage **mɪsˋkærɪdʒ** ˋmɪskærɪdʒ
miscarry **mɪsˋkærɪ**
miscast **mɪsˋkɑst $ mɪsˋkæst**
miscegenation **ˈmɪsɪdʒɪˋneɪʃn**
miscellaneous **ˈmɪsəˋleɪnɪəs**
miscellany **mɪˋselənɪ $ ˋmɪsḷeɪnɪ**
mischance **mɪsˋtʃɑns $ mɪsˋtʃæns**
mischief **ˋmɪstʃɪf**
mischief-maker **ˋmɪstʃɪf meɪkə(r)**
mischievous **ˋmɪstʃɪvəs**
misconceive **ˈmɪskənˋsiv**
misconception **ˈmɪskənˋsepʃn**
misconduct *n* **mɪsˋkondʌkt**
misconduct *v* **ˈmɪskənˋdʌkt**
misconstrue **ˈmɪskənˋstru**
miscount **mɪsˋkaʊnt**
miscreant **ˋmɪskrɪənt**
misdeal **mɪsˋdil**
misdeed **mɪsˋdid**
misdemeanour($ -or) **ˈmɪsdɪˋminə(r)**
misdirect **ˈmɪsdɑɪˋrekt** -dɪr-
misdoing **mɪsˋduɪŋ**
mise-en-scène **ˈmiz õ ˋseən**
$ £ ˋseɪn ˋsen
miser **ˋmɑɪzə(r)**
miserable **ˋmɪzr̩əbl**
misery **ˋmɪzərɪ**
misfire **mɪsˋfɑɪə(r)**
misfit **ˋmɪsfɪt**
misfortune **mɪsˋfɔtʃun** -tʃən **$ -ˋfɔr-**
misgivings **mɪsˋgɪvɪŋz**
misgovern **mɪsˋgʌvn $ -ˋgʌvərn**

misguide mɪsˋgaɪd
mishandle mɪsˋhændl
mishap ˋmɪshæp mɪsˋhæp
misinform ˈmɪsɪnˋfɔm $ -ˋfɔrm
misinterpret ˈmɪsɪnˋtɜprət -ɪt
misjudge mɪsˋdʒʌdʒ
mislay mɪsˋleɪ
mislead mɪsˋlid
misled mɪsˋled
mismanage mɪsˋmænɪdʒ
misname mɪsˋneɪm
misnomer mɪsˋnəʊmə(r)
misogynist mɪˋsodʒɪnɪst maɪˋs-
misplace mɪsˋpleɪs
misprint n ˋmɪsprɪnt
misprint v mɪsˋprɪnt
mispronounce ˈmɪsprəˋnaʊns
mispronunciation ˈmɪsprəˋnʌnsɪˋeɪʃn
misquote mɪsˋkwəʊt
misread pp mɪsˋred
misread v mɪsˋrid
misrepresent ˈmɪsˋreprɪˋzent
misrule mɪsˋrul
miss, M– mɪs
missal ˋmɪsl
misshapen mɪsˋʃeɪpən mɪʃˋʃ-
missile ˋmɪsaɪl $ ˋmɪsl
mission ˋmɪʃn
missionary ˋmɪʃnrɪ $ -ɳerɪ
Mississippi ˈmɪsɪˋsɪpɪ
missive ˋmɪsɪv
Missouri mɪˋzʊərɪ $ -rə
mis-spell mɪs ˋspel
mis-spent mɪs ˋspent
mis-state mɪs ˋsteɪt
missus ˋmɪsɪz
missy ˋmɪsɪ
mist mɪst
mistake mɪˋsteɪk
mistaken mɪˋsteɪkən
mister ˋmɪstə(r)
mistime ˈmɪsˋtaɪm
mistletoe ˋmɪsltəʊ
mistook mɪˋstʊk
mistress ˋmɪstrəs -ɪs
mistrial mɪsˋtraɪəl
mistrust ˈmɪsˋtrʌst
misty ˋmɪstɪ
misunderstand ˈmɪsˋʌndəˋstænd $ -dər-
misunderstood ˈmɪsˋʌndəˋstʊd $ -dər-
misuse n mɪsˋjus mɪʃˋjus
misuse v mɪsˋjuz mɪʃˋjuz
mite maɪt

mitigate ˋmɪtɪgeɪt
mitre($ -ter) ˋmaɪtə(r)
mitt mɪt
mitten ˋmɪtn
mix mɪks
mixture ˋmɪkstʃə(r)
mix-up ˋmɪks ʌp
miz(z)en ˋmɪzn
miz(z)en-mast ˋmɪzn mast $ mæst
mm. ˋmɪlɪmitə(r)
mnemonic niˋmonɪk nɪˋm-
moan məʊn
moat məʊt
mob mob
mobile ˋməʊbaɪl $ ˋməʊbl
mobility məʊˋbɪlətɪ məˋb-
mobilize ˋməʊbḷaɪz
mobster ˋmobstə(r)
moccasin ˋmokəsɪn
mocha ˋmokə $ £ ˋməʊkə
mock mok
mockery ˋmokərɪ
mocking-bird ˋmokɪŋ bɜd
mock-up ˋmok ʌp
modal ˋməʊdl
mod. cons. ˋmod ˋkonz
mode məʊd
model ˋmodl
modelling($ -eling) ˋmodḷɪŋ
moderate v ˋmodəreɪt
moderate adj, n ˋmodrət -ɪt
moderation ˈmodəˋreɪʃn
moderator ˋmodəreɪtə(r)
modern ˋmodn -dən $ -dərn
modernity məˋdɜnətɪ
modernize ˋmodɳaɪz $ ˋmodərnaɪz
modest ˋmodɪst -əst
modesty ˋmodɪstɪ -əstɪ
modicum ˋmodɪkəm
modification ˈmodɪfɪˋkeɪʃn
modify ˋmodɪfaɪ
modish ˋməʊdɪʃ
modulate ˋmodjʊleɪt $ ˋmodʊleɪt
module ˋmodjul $ ˋmodʒul
modus operandi ˈməʊdəs ˋopəˋrændɪ
   -ndi $ £ -daɪ
mohair ˋməʊheə(r)
Mohammedan məˋhomɪdən
   $ £ məʊˋhæmɪdən
moiety ˋmɔɪətɪ
moil mɔɪl
moist mɔɪst
moisten ˋmɔɪsn

moisture ˈmɔɪstʃə(r)
molar ˈməʊlə(r)
molasses məˈlæsɪz
mold(y) məʊld(ɪ)
molder ˈməʊldə(r)
mole məʊl
molecular məˈlekjʊlə(r)
molecule ˈmolɪkjul
mole-hill ˈməʊl hɪl
molest məˈlest
molestation ˌmolɪˈsteɪʃn
Molière ˈmolɪeə(r) ˈmolɪˈeə(r)
    $ ˈməʊlɪˈeər
moll, M– mol
mollify ˈmolɪfaɪ
mollusc ˈmoləsk
Molly ˈmolɪ
molly-coddle ˈmolɪ kodl
molt məʊlt
molten ˈməʊltən
molto ˈmoltəʊ $ ˈməʊltəʊ
moment ˈməʊmənt
momentary ˈməʊməntrɪ $ -terɪ
momentarily ˈməʊmənˈterlɪ
    £ ˈməʊməntrəlɪ
momentous məʊˈmentəs məˈm-
momentum məʊˈmentəm məˈm-
Monaco ˈmonəkəʊ
monarch ˈmonək -nak $ -nərk -nark
monarchic məˈnakɪk $ -ˈnar-
monarchist ˈmonəkɪst $ -nər-
monarchy ˈmonəkɪ $ -nər-
monastery ˈmonəstrɪ $ ˈmonəsterɪ
monastic məˈnæstɪk
monasticism məˈnæstɪsɪzm
monaural ˈmonˈɔrl $ ˈməʊnˈɔrl
Monday ˈmʌndɪ -deɪ
monetary ˈmʌnɪtrɪ ˈmon- $ -terɪ
money ˈmʌnɪ
money-box ˈmʌnɪ boks
moneyed ˈmʌnɪd
money-grubber ˈmʌnɪ grʌbə(r)
money-lender ˈmʌnɪ lendə(r)
money-market ˈmʌnɪ makɪt $ markɪt
money-order ˈmʌnɪ ɔdə(r) $ ɔrdər
money-spinner ˈmʌnɪ spɪnə(r)
-monger suffix mʌŋgə(r)
Mongol ˈmoŋgl $ -gəʊl
Mongolia moŋˈgəʊlɪə
mongoloid ˈmoŋglɔɪd
mongoose ˈmoŋgus
mongrel ˈmʌŋgrəl $ ˈmoŋgrəl
Monica ˈmonɪkə

monitor ˈmonɪtə(r)
monk mʌŋk
monkey ˈmʌŋkɪ
monkey-nut ˈmʌŋkɪ nʌt
monkey-wrench ˈmʌŋkɪ rentʃ
Monmouth ˈmonməθ ˈmʌn-
mono ˈmonəʊ
mono opp. 'stereo' ˈmonəʊ
    type ˈməʊnəʊ etc
mono- prefix monəʊ
monochrome ˈmonəkrəʊm
monocle ˈmonəkl
monocotyledon ˈmonəʊˈkotɪˈlidn
monogamist məˈnogəmɪst
monogamous məˈnogəməs
monogamy məˈnogəmɪ
monogram ˈmonəgræm
monograph ˈmonəgraf $ £ -græf
monolith ˈmonəlɪθ
monologue ˈmonəlog $ -lɔg etc
monomania ˈmonəʊˈmeɪnɪə
monomaniac ˈmonəʊˈmeɪnɪæk
monoplane ˈmonəpleɪn
monopolist məˈnopəlɪst
monopolize məˈnopəlaɪz
monopoly məˈnopəlɪ
monosyllabic ˈmonəʊsɪˈlæbɪk
monosyllable ˈmonəsɪləbl
monotheism ˈmonəʊθiɪzm
monotheist ˈmonəʊθiɪst
monotone ˈmonətəʊn
monotonous məˈnotənəs -tnəs
monotony məˈnotənɪ
monotype ˈmonətaɪp
monoxide moˈnoksaɪd
monsieur məˈsjɜ(r) məˈsɪə(r)
    $ məˈsʊər məˈʃʊər
monsoon monˈsun
monster ˈmonstə(r)
monstrance ˈmonstrəns
monstrosity monˈstrosətɪ
monstrous ˈmonstrəs
montage ˈmontaʒ
Montana monˈtænə £ -tanə
Mont Blanc ˈmõ ˈblõ $ £ ˈmont $ ˈblæŋk
Monte Carlo ˈmontɪ ˈkaləʊ $ ˈkar-
Montenegro ˈmontɪˈnigrəʊ
Montevideo ˈmontɪvɪˈdeɪəʊ
Montgomery məntˈgʌmrɪ -ˈgom-
    $ £ mont-
Montreal ˈmontrɪˈɔl
month mʌnθ
months ˈmʌnθs mʌns

monument ˈmɒnjʊmənt
monumental ˌmɒnjʊˈmentl
moo mu
moo-cow ˈmu kaʊ
mooch mutʃ
mood mud
moon mun
moonbeam ˈmunbim
moonlight ˈmunlaɪt
moonshine ˈmun-ʃaɪn
moor, M– mʊə(r) mɔ(r)
moorhen ˈmʊəhen ˈmɔ- $ ˈmʊər-
moorings ˈmʊərɪŋz ˈmɔ-
Moorish ˈmʊərɪʃ ˈmɔ-
moorland ˈmʊələnd ˈmɔ- $ ˈmʊər-
moose mus
moot mut
mop mop
mope məʊp
moped ˈməʊ-ped
moraine mɒˈreɪn $ mɔˈreɪn
moral ˈmɒrl $ ˈmɔrl etc
morale məˈrɑl mɒˈrɑl $ məˈræl mɔˈræl
moralist ˈmɒrlɪst $ ˈmɔrlɪst etc
morality məˈrælətɪ
moralize ˈmɒrlaɪz $ ˈmɔrlaɪz etc
morass məˈræs
moratorium ˌmɒrəˈtɔrɪəm $ £ ˈmɔr-
Moray ˈmʌrɪ $ ˈmɜɪ
morbid ˈmɒbɪd $ ˈmɔrbɪd
mordant ˈmɔdnt $ ˈmɔrdnt
more mɔ(r)
morello məˈreləʊ
moreover mɔˈrəʊvə(r)
morganatic ˌmɔgəˈnætɪk $ ˈmɔr-
morgue mɔg $ mɔrg
moribund ˈmɒrɪbənd $ ˈmɔrɪbʌnd etc
Mormon ˈmɔmən $ ˈmɔrmən
morning ˈmɔnɪŋ $ ˈmɔrnɪŋ
morning-glory ˈmɔnɪŋ ˈglɔrɪ $ ˈmɔr- g-
morning-room ˈmɔnɪŋ rʊm rum
    $ ˈmɔrnɪŋ rum rʊm
morocco, M– məˈrɒkəʊ
moron ˈmɔron £ -ən
moronic məˈronɪk
morose məˈrəʊs
Morpheus ˈmɔfɪəs ˈmɔfjus $ ˈmɔr-
morphia ˈmɔfɪə $ ˈmɔr-
morphine ˈmɔfin $ ˈmɔr-
morphology mɔˈfolədʒɪ $ mɔr-
morris dance ˈmɒrɪs dɑns
    $ ˈmɔrɪs etc dæns
morrow ˈmɒrəʊ $ ˈmɔrəʊ

Morse Code ˈmɔs kəʊd $ ˈmɔrs
morsel ˈmɔsl $ ˈmɔrsl
mortal ˈmɔtl $ ˈmɔrtl
mortality mɔˈtælətɪ $ mɔr-
mortally ˈmɔtlɪ $ ˈmɔrtlɪ
mortar ˈmɔtə(r) $ ˈmɔrtər
mortar-board ˈmɔtə bɔd $ ˈmɔrtər bɔrd
mortgage ˈmɔgɪdʒ $ ˈmɔrgɪdʒ
mortgagee ˌmɔgɪˈdʒi $ ˌmɔr-
mortgagor ˌmɔgɪˈdʒɔ(r)
    $ ˈmɔrgɪdʒər etc
mortice ˈmɔtɪs $ ˈmɔrtɪs
mortician mɔˈtɪʃn $ mɔr-
mortification ˌmɔtɪfɪˈkeɪʃn $ ˌmɔr-
mortify ˈmɔtɪfaɪ $ ˈmɔr-
mortise ˈmɔtɪs $ ˈmɔrtɪs
mortuary ˈmɔtʃʊərɪ $ ˈmɔrtʃʊerɪ
mosaic, M– məʊˈzeɪɪk
Moscow ˈmoskəʊ $ ˈmoskaʊ etc
Moselle məʊˈzel məˈzel
Moses ˈməʊzɪz
Moslem ˈmozləm -lem
mosque mosk
mosquito məˈskitəʊ £ moˈs-
mosquito-net məˈskitəʊ net
moss mos $ mɔs etc
most məʊst
-most suffix məʊst
mostly ˈməʊstlɪ
most part, for the ˈməʊst pɑt $ pɑrt
mote məʊt
motel məʊˈtel
moth moθ $ mɔθ $ pl məðz
moth-ball ˈmoθ bɔl $ ˈmɔθ
moth-eaten ˈmoθ itn $ ˈmɔθ
mother ˈmʌðə(r)
mother country ˈmʌðə kʌntrɪ $ ˈmʌðər
motherhood ˈmʌðəhʊd $ ˈmʌðər-
mother-in-law ˈmʌðr ɪn lɔ
mother-of-pearl ˈmʌðər ə ˈpɜl əv ˈpɜl
mother tongue ˈmʌðə ˈtʌŋ $ ˈmʌðər
moth-proof ˈmoθ pruf $ ˈmɔθ
motif məʊˈtif
motion ˈməʊʃn
motion-study ˈməʊʃn stʌdɪ
motivate ˈməʊtɪveɪt
motive ˈməʊtɪv
motivation ˌməʊtɪˈveɪʃn
motley ˈmotlɪ
motor ˈməʊtə(r)
motor-assisted ˈməʊtər əˈsɪstɪd
motorbike ˈməʊtəbaɪk $ -tər-
motorboat ˈməʊtəbəʊt $ -tər-

motorcade 'məʊtə`keɪd $ -tər-
motorcar `məʊtəka(r) $ -tər-
motorcycle `məʊtəsaɪkl $ -tər-
motorist `məʊtərɪst -trɪst
motorize `məʊtəraɪz
motor nerve `məʊtə nɜv $ -tər
motor-scooter `məʊtə skutə(r) $ -tər
motorway `məʊtəweɪ $ -tər-
mottle `mɒtl
motto `mɒtəʊ
mould məʊld
moulder `məʊldə(r)
mouldy `məʊldɪ
moult məʊlt
mound maʊnd
mount maʊnt
mountain `maʊntɪn $ -ntn etc
mountaineer 'maʊntɪ`nɪə(r) $ -tn`ɪər
mountainous `maʊntɪnəs $ -tnəs
mountebank `maʊntɪbæŋk
mourn mɔn £ mʊən $ mɔrn
mourning `mɔnɪŋ `mʊənɪŋ $ `mɔr-
mouse n maʊs
mouse v maʊs maʊz
mouse-trap `maʊs træp
mousse mus
moustache mə`staʃ $ `mʌstæʃ mə`stæʃ
mouth n maʊθ
mouth v maʊð
mouth-organ `maʊθ ɔgən $ ɔrgən
movable `muvəbl
move muv
movement `muvmənt
movies `muvɪz
mow məʊ
Mozambique 'məʊzæm`bik
Mozart `məʊtsat $ `məʊzart etc
MP 'em `pi
Mr `mɪstə(r)
Mrs `mɪsɪz
MS 'em `es `mænjʊskrɪpt
MSc 'em es `si
mu (μ) mju $ mu
much mʌtʃ
muck mʌk
mucous `mjukəs
mud mʌd
mud-bath `mʌd baθ $ bæθ
muddle `mʌdl
mud-guard `mʌd gad $ gard
muezzin mu`ezɪn $ £ mju- etc $ -zn
muff mʌf
muffin `mʌfɪn

muffle `mʌfl
muffler `mʌflə(r)
mufti `mʌftɪ
mug mʌg
mugwump `mʌgwʌmp
Muhammad mə`hæmɪd -məd
mulatto mju`lætəʊ $ mə`lætəʊ etc
mulberry `mʌlbrɪ $ -berɪ
mulct mʌlkt
mule mjul
muleteer 'mjulɪ`tɪə(r)
mull mʌl
mullah `mʌlə `mʊlə
mullet `mʌlɪt -ət
mulligatawny 'mʌlɪgə`tɔnɪ
mullion `mʌlɪən
multi- prefix mʌltɪ
multi-coloured($ -or-) 'mʌltɪ `kʌləd $ -ərd
multifarious 'mʌltɪ`feərɪəs
multiform `mʌltɪfɔm $ -fɔrm
multilateral 'mʌltɪ`lætrl
multi-millionaire 'mʌltɪ`mɪlɪə`neə(r)
multiple `mʌltɪpl
multiplex `mʌltɪpleks
multiplication 'mʌltɪplɪ`keɪʃn
multiplication table 'mʌltɪplɪ`keɪʃn teɪbl
multiplicity 'mʌltɪ`plɪsətɪ
multiply `mʌltɪplaɪ
multi-racial 'mʌltɪ `reɪʃl
multitude `mʌltɪtjud -tʃud $ -tud
multitudinous 'mʌltɪ`tjudɪnəs $ -`tudn̩əs
multi-stage 'mʌltɪ `steɪdʒ
multum in parvo 'mʌltəm ɪn `pavəʊ
$ `parvəʊ
mum mʌm
mumble `mʌmbl
mumbo jumbo 'mʌmbəʊ `dʒʌmbəʊ
mummify `mʌmɪfaɪ
mummy `mʌmɪ
mumps mʌmps
munch mʌntʃ
mundane `mʌndeɪn mʌn`deɪn
Munich `mjunɪk
municipal mju`nɪsɪpl
municipality mju`nɪsɪ`pælətɪ
munificent mju`nɪfɪsnt
munitions mju`nɪʃnz
mural `mjʊərl
murder `mɜdə(r)
murderer `mɜdərə(r) -drə(r)
murderess `mɜdərəs -ɪs -es
murderous `mɜdrəs -dər-
Muriel `mjʊərɪəl

murky ˈmɜkɪ
murmur ˈmɜmə(r)
murrain ˈmʌreɪn -rɪn $ ˈmɜɪn
Murray ˈmʌrɪ $ ˈmɜɪ
muscatel ˈmʌskəˈtel
muscle ˈmʌsl
muscle-bound ˈmʌsl baʊnd
Muscovite ˈmʌskəvaɪt
muscular ˈmʌskjʊlə(r)
muse mjuz
museum mjuˈzɪəm
mush mʌʃ
mushroom ˈmʌʃrʊm $ £ -rum
music ˈmjuzɪk
musical ˈmjuzɪkl
musical-box ˈmjuzɪkl bɒks
music-box ˈmjuzɪk bɒks
music-hall ˈmjuzɪk hɔl
musician mjuˈzɪʃn
music-stand ˈmjuzɪk stænd
music-stool ˈmjuzɪk stul
musk mʌsk
musket ˈmʌskɪt
musketeer ˈmʌskɪˈtɪə(r)
musk-rat ˈmʌsk ræt
musk-rose ˈmʌsk rəʊz
Muslim ˈmʊzlɪm ˈmʌz- -sl-
muslin ˈmʌzlɪn
musquash ˈmʌskwɒʃ
muss mʌs
mussel ˈmʌsl
Mussolini ˈmʊsəˈlinɪ ˈmʌs-
Mussulman ˈmʌslmən
must mʌst
mustache məˈstaʃ $ ˈmʌstæʃ məˈstæʃ
mustang, M– ˈmʌstæŋ
mustard ˈmʌstəd $ ˈmʌstərd
mustard plaster ˈmʌstəd plastə(r)
 $ ˈmʌstərd plæstər
muster ˈmʌstə(r)
mustn't ˈmʌsnt

musty ˈmʌstɪ
mutable ˈmjutəbl
mutation mjuˈteɪʃn
mutatis mutandis muˈtɑtɪs muˈtændɪs
 mjuˈt- mjuˈtɑtɪs mutændɪs
 $ -ˈtɑn- muˈtætɪs muˈtændɪs
mute mjut
mutilate ˈmjutɪleɪt $ -tʃeɪt
mutilation ˈmjutɪˈleɪʃn $ -tʃˈeɪʃn
mutineer mjutɪˈnɪə(r) $ £ -tnˈɪər
mutinous ˈmjutɪnəs $ £ -tnəs
mutiny ˈmjutɪnɪ $ £ -tn̩ɪ
mutt mʌt
mutter ˈmʌtə(r)
mutton ˈmʌtn
mutton chop ˈmʌtn ˈtʃɒp
mutual ˈmjutʃʊəl
muzzle ˈmʌzl
muzzle-loading ˈmʌzl ləʊdɪŋ
muzzy ˈmʌzɪ
my maɪ
Mycenaean ˈmaɪsɪˈniən
mycology maɪˈkɒlədʒɪ
myopia maɪˈəʊpɪə
myopic maɪˈopɪk maɪˈəʊpɪk
myriad ˈmɪrɪəd
myrrh mɜ(r)
myrtle ˈmɜtl
myself maɪˈself *familiarly:* mɪ- mə-
mysterious mɪˈstɪərɪəs
mystery ˈmɪstrɪ -tərɪ
mystery play ˈmɪstrɪ pleɪ
mystic ˈmɪstɪk
mystical ˈmɪstɪkl
mysticism ˈmɪstɪsɪzm
mystify ˈmɪstɪfaɪ
mystique mɪˈstik
myth mɪθ
mythical ˈmɪθɪkl
mythological ˈmɪθəˈlodʒɪkl
mythology mɪˈθɒlədʒɪ
myxomatosis ˈmɪksəməˈtəʊsɪs

N

N n en
NAAFI ˈnæfɪ
nab næb
nadir ˈnædɪə(r) $ £ ˈneɪ-
nag næg
naked ˈneɪkɪd

naiad ˈnaɪæd
nail neɪl
nail-brush ˈneɪl brʌʃ
nail-scissors ˈneɪl sɪzəz $ -zərz
nail-varnish ˈneɪl vanɪʃ $ varn-
Nairn neən $ neərn

Nairobi naɪˈrəʊbɪ
naïve naɪˈiv naˈiv
naïvete naɪˈivteɪ naˈiv-
$ 'naɪvˈteɪ -vəˈteɪ
namby-pamby 'næmbɪ ˈpæmbɪ
name neɪm
name-day ˈneɪm deɪ
namely ˈneɪmlɪ
name-part ˈneɪm pat $ part
namesake ˈneɪmseɪk
Nancy ˈnænsɪ
nankeen nænˈkin
nanny ˈnænɪ
nanny-goat ˈnænɪ gəʊt
Naomi ˈneɪəmɪ $ -maɪ etc neɪˈəʊm-
nap næp
napalm ˈneɪpam
nape neɪp
napkin ˈnæpkɪn
napkin-ring ˈnæpkɪn rɪŋ
Naples ˈneɪplz
Napoleon nəˈpəʊlɪən
Napoleonic nəˈpəʊlɪˈɒnɪk
nappy ˈnæpɪ
narcissi naˈsɪsaɪ $ nar-
narcissism ˈnasɪsɪzm $ ˈnar-
narcissus naˈsɪsəs $ nar-
narcotic naˈkɒtɪk $ nar-
nark nak $ nark
narrate nəˈreɪt næˈr- $ ˈnæreɪt
narration næˈreɪʃn nəˈr-
narrative ˈnærətɪv
narrator næˈreɪtə(r) nəˈr- $ ˈnær-
narrow ˈnærəʊ
narrow-minded 'nærəʊ ˈmaɪndɪd
nasal ˈneɪzl
nasalize ˈneɪzḷaɪz
nascent ˈnæsnt ˈneɪsnt
nasturtium nəˈstəʃəm $ næˈst- etc
nasty ˈnastɪ $ ˈnæstɪ
natal ˈneɪtl
Natal nəˈtæl
natation nəˈteɪʃn neɪˈt-
nation ˈneɪʃn
national ˈnæʃnl
nationalism ˈnæʃnḷɪzm
nationalist ˈnæʃnḷɪst
nationality 'næʃnˈælətɪ
nationalization 'næʃnḷaɪˈzeɪʃn $ -ḷɪˈzeɪʃn
nationalize ˈnæʃṇəlaɪz
native ˈneɪtɪv
nativity nəˈtɪvətɪ
NATO ˈneɪtəʊ

natter ˈnætə(r)
natty ˈnætɪ
natural ˈnætʃərl ˈnætʃrl
naturalistic 'nætʃrlˈɪstɪk
naturalize ˈnætʃrḷaɪz
naturally ˈnætʃrḷɪ
nature ˈneɪtʃə(r)
naught nɔt
naughty ˈnɔtɪ
nausea ˈnɔsɪə -zɪə -ʃɪə $ -ʃə -ʒə etc
nauseate ˈnɔsɪeɪt -zɪeɪt -ʃɪeɪt $ -ʒɪeɪt etc
nauseous ˈnɔsɪəs -zɪəs $ ˈnɔʃəs -ʒəs etc
nautical ˈnɔtɪkl
naval ˈneɪvl
nave neɪv
navel ˈneɪvl
navel orange ˈneɪvl ɒrɪndʒ $ ɔrɪndʒ
navigability 'nævɪgəˈbɪlətɪ
navigable ˈnævɪgəbl
navigate ˈnævɪgeɪt
navigation 'nævɪˈgeɪʃn
navigator ˈnævɪgeɪtə(r)
navvy ˈnævɪ
navy ˈneɪvɪ
nay neɪ
Nazi ˈnatsɪ $ ˈnætsɪ
Neapolitan nɪəˈpɒlɪtən
near nɪə(r)
nearby nɪəˈbaɪ $ nɪər-
nearly ˈnɪəlɪ $ ˈnɪərlɪ
nearside ˈnɪəsaɪd $ ˈnɪər-
near-sighted 'nɪə ˈsaɪtɪd $ ˈnɪər
neat nit
Nebraska nɪˈbræskə
nebula ˈnebjʊlə
nebulae ˈnebjʊli -laɪ
nebulous ˈnebjʊləs
necessarily 'nesəˈserəlɪ £ ˈnesəsṛlɪ
necessary ˈnesəsrɪ -sɪs- $ £ -əserɪ
necessitate nɪˈsesɪteɪt
necessity nɪˈsesətɪ
neck nek
neckband ˈnekbænd
neckerchief ˈnekətʃɪf -tʃif $ -kər-
necklace ˈnekləs -lɪs
necklet ˈneklət
necktie ˈnektaɪ
necromancy ˈnekrəmænsɪ
necropolis nɪˈkrɒpəlɪs
nectar ˈnektə(r)
nectarine ˈnektərɪn
née neɪ
need nid

needle `nidl
needle-woman `nidl wʊmən
needlework `nidlwɜk
ne'er neə(r)
ne'er-do-well `neə du wel $ `neər
nefarious nɪ`feərɪəs
negate nɪ`geɪt
negation nɪ`geɪʃn
negative `negətɪv
neglect nɪ`glekt
négligé `neglɪʒeɪ $ 'neglɪ`ʒeɪ etc
negligence `neglɪdʒəns
negligent `neglɪdʒənt
negligible `neglɪdʒəbl
negotiable nɪ`gəʊʃəbl
negotiation nɪ'gəʊʃɪ`eɪʃn -əʊsɪ-
negotiate nɪ`gəʊʃɪeɪt -əʊsɪeɪt
Negress `nigrəs -ɪs -es
Negro `nigrəʊ $ `nɪgrəʊ `nigrə
negroid `nigrɔɪd
negus `nigəs
Nehru `neəru $ £ `neɪru
neigh neɪ
neighbour($ -bor) `neɪbə(r)
neighbourhood($ -bor-) `neɪbəhʊd $ -ər-
neither `naɪðə(r) $ `niðər
Nelly `nelɪ
Nelson `nelsn
nem. con. 'nem `kon
nemesis `neməsɪs
neo- prefix niəʊ
neolithic niə`lɪθɪk
neologism ni`olədʒɪzm
neon `nion
neon light `nion laɪt
neon sign `nion saɪn
Nepal ne`pɔl nɪ-
nephew `nevju $ `nefju
nepotism `nepətɪzm
Neptune `neptjun -tʃun $ -tun
Nero `nɪərəʊ
nerve nɜv
nerve-racking `nɜv rækɪŋ
nervous `nɜvəs
nervy `nɜvɪ
ness nes
-ness suffix nəs
nest nest
nest-egg `nest eg
nestle `nesl
nestling `neslɪŋ
net net
netball `netbɔl

nether `neðə(r)
Netherlands `neðələndz $ `neðər-
netting `netɪŋ
nettle `netl
nettle-rash `netl ræʃ
network `netwɜk
neural `njʊərl $ `nʊərl
neuralgia njʊə`rældʒə $ nʊə`r- etc
neurasthenia 'njʊərəs`θinɪə $ 'nʊər- etc
neuritis njʊə`raɪtɪs -təs $ nʊə`r- etc
neurology njʊə`rolədʒɪ $ nʊə`r- etc
neurosis njʊə`rəʊsɪs $ nʊə`r- etc
neurotic njʊə`rotɪk $ nʊə`r- etc
neuter `njutə(r) $ `nutər etc
neutral `njutrl $ `nutrl etc
neutrality nju`trælətɪ $ nu`t- etc
neutralize `njutrəlaɪz $ `nu- etc
neutron `njutron -trən $ `nu- etc
Nevada nɪ`vadə $ nɪ`vædə etc
never `nevə(r)
nevertheless 'nevəðə`les $ 'nevər-
Neville `nevl
new nju $ nu etc
Newcastle `njukasl $ `nukæsl `nju-
newel `njuḷ $ `nuḷ etc
newfangled 'nju`fæŋgld $ 'nu- etc
Newfoundland 'njufənd`lænd
    nju`faʊndlənd `njufəndlənd
    $ `nufəndlənd 'nu- nu`f- etc
New Hampshire nju `hæmpʃə(r) $ nu
Newhaven nju`heɪvn $ nu- etc
newly-wed `njulɪ wed $ `nu- etc
Newmarket `njumakɪt $ `numar- etc
New Mexico nju `meksɪkəʊ $ nu etc
New Orleans 'nju ɔ`lɪənz `ɔlɪənz
    $ nu `ɔrlɪənz -lɪnz nju
Newport `njupɔt $ `nupɔrt
news njuz $ nuz etc
news-agent `njuz eɪdʒənt $ `nuz etc
New South Wales 'nju saʊθ `weɪlz $ 'nu
newspaper `njuspeɪpə(r) $ `nus- -uz- etc
newsprint `njuzprɪnt $ `nuz- etc
newsreel `njuzril $ `nuz- etc
news-stand `njuz stænd $ `nuz etc
newsvendor `njuzvendə(r) $ `nuz- etc
newt njut $ nut etc
Newton `njutn $ `nutn etc
New York 'nju `jɔk $ 'nu `jɔrk etc
New Zealand 'nju `zilənd $ 'nju etc
next nekst
next door 'neks `dɔ(r)
nexus `neksəs
Niagara naɪ`ægrə

nib nɪb
nibble ˈnɪbl
niblick ˈnɪblɪk
Nicaragua ˈnɪkəˈrægjuə $ £ -ˈragwə
nice naɪs
Nice niːs
nice and ... ˈnaɪs n
nicety ˈnaɪsətɪ
niche nɪtʃ niːʃ
Nicholas ˈnɪkləs
nick nɪk
nickel ˈnɪkl
nick-nack ˈnɪk-næk
nickname ˈnɪkneɪm
nicotine ˈnɪkətiːn
niece niːs
niff nɪf
nifty ˈnɪftɪ
Niger ˈnaɪdʒə(r)
Nigeria naɪˈdʒɪərɪə
niggardly ˈnɪgədlɪ $ ˈnɪgərdlɪ
nigger-brown ˈnɪgə ˈbraʊn $ ˈnɪgər
niggling ˈnɪglɪŋ
nigh naɪ
night naɪt
night-bird ˈnaɪt bɜd
nightcap ˈnaɪt kæp
night-club ˈnaɪt klʌb
nightdress ˈnaɪt dres
nightfall ˈnaɪtfɔl
nightgown ˈnaɪtgaʊn
nightie ˈnaɪtɪ
nightingale ˈnaɪtɪŋgeɪl $ -tng- etc
nightlight ˈnaɪtlaɪt
nightmare ˈnaɪtmeə(r)
night-porter ˈnaɪt pɔtə(r) $ pɔrtər
nightschool ˈnaɪtskuːl
nightshade ˈnaɪt-ʃeɪd
night-shift ˈnaɪt ʃɪft
nightshirt ˈnaɪt-ʃɜt
night-time ˈnaɪt taɪm
night-watchman naɪt ˈwotʃmən
night-work ˈnaɪt wɜk
nihilism ˈnaɪhɪlɪzm ˈnaɪɪl- $ ˈnɪhɪl-
nil nɪl
Nile naɪl
nimble ˈnɪmbl
nimbus ˈnɪmbəs
niminy-piminy ˈnɪmɪnɪ ˈpɪmɪnɪ
nincompoop ˈnɪŋkəmpuːp
nine naɪn
ninepence ˈnaɪnpəns
ninepenny ˈnaɪnpənɪ $ -penɪ

ninepins ˈnaɪn-pɪnz
nineteen ˈnaɪnˈtiːn
nineteenth ˈnaɪnˈtiːnθ
ninetieth ˈnaɪntɪəθ
ninety ˈnaɪntɪ
ninety-one ˈnaɪntɪ ˈwʌn
ninny ˈnɪnɪ
ninth naɪnθ
nip nɪp
nipper ˈnɪpə(r)
nipple ˈnɪpl
nippy ˈnɪpɪ
nirvana nɪəˈvanə $ nɪər- -ˈvænə
nisi ˈnaɪsaɪ $ ˈniːsiː
Nissen hut ˈnɪsn hʌt
nit nɪt
nitrate ˈnaɪtreɪt
nitre($ -ter) ˈnaɪtə(r)
nitric ˈnaɪtrɪk
nitrogen ˈnaɪtrədʒən -dʒɪn
nitro-glycerine ˈnaɪtrəʊ ˈglɪsəˈriːn
  ˈglɪsəriːn $ £ ˈglɪsərɪn
nitrous ˈnaɪtrəs
nitwit ˈnɪtwɪt
no nəʊ
No. ˈnʌmbə(r)
Noah ˈnəʊə
nob nob
nobble ˈnobl
nobility nəˈbɪlətɪ nəʊ-
noble ˈnəʊbl
nobleman ˈnəʊblmən
noble-minded ˈnəʊbl ˈmaɪndɪd
noblesse oblige nəʊˈbles əʊˈbliːʒ
nobody ˈnəʊbədɪ -bodɪ
nocturnal nokˈtɜnl
nocturne ˈnoktɜn
nod nod
node nəʊd
nodule ˈnodjuːl $ ˈnodʒuːl
Noel Christmas nəʊˈel
Noel person ˈnəʊl ˈnəʊel
noise nɔɪz
noisome ˈnɔɪsəm the ɔɪ is short as in
  'choice', not long as in 'joy-stick'
noisy ˈnɔɪzɪ
nomad ˈnəʊmæd
nomadic nəʊˈmædɪk
no man's land ˈnəʊ mænz lænd
nom de plume ˈnom də ˈpluːm nɔ̃
nomenclature ˈnəʊmənkleɪtʃə(r)
  £ nəʊˈmenklətʃə(r)
nominal ˈnomɪnl

nominate ˈnɒmɪneɪt
nomination ˈnɒmɪˈneɪʃn
nominative ˈnɒmnətɪv -mɪn-
nominee ˈnɒmɪˈni
non non
non- prefix non
nonagenarian ˈnɒnədʒɪˈneərɪən
nonce nɒns
nonce-word ˈnɒnswɜd
nonchalant ˈnɒnʃələnt $ ˈnɒnʃəˈlɒnt etc
non-commissioned ˈnɒn kəˈmɪʃnd
non compos mentis
  ˈnɒn ˈkɒmpəs ˈmentɪs -pɒs
non-conformist ˈnɒn kənˈfɔmɪst
  $ -ˈfɔrm-
nondescript ˈnɒndɪskrɪpt
none nʌn
nonentity nɒnˈentətɪ
nonpareil ˈnɒnprl ˈnɒnpəˈreɪl
  $ ˈnɒnpəˈrel
nonplus nɒnˈplʌs
non-resident ˈnɒn ˈrezɪdənt
nonsense ˈnɒnsns $ -sens etc
nonsensical nɒnˈsensɪkl
non sequitur ˈnɒn ˈsekwɪtə(r)
non-stop ˈnɒn ˈstɒp
noodle ˈnudl
noonday ˈnundeɪ
nook nʊk
noon nun
noose nus
nor nɔ(r)
Nora ˈnɔrə
Nordic ˈnɒdɪk $ ˈnɔrdɪk
Norfolk ˈnɒfək $ ˈnɔrfək
norm nɒm $ nɔrm
normal ˈnɒml $ ˈnɔrml
normality nɔˈmælətɪ $ nɔr-
Norman ˈnɒmən $ ˈnɔrmən
Normandy ˈnɒməndɪ $ ˈnɔr-
normative ˈnɒmətɪv $ ˈnɔrm-
Norse nɔs $ nɔrs
north nɔθ $ nɔrθ
Northampton nɔˈθæmptən nɔθˈhæ-
  $ nɔrˈθæmptən
northeast nɔθˈist $ nɔrθ-
northeastern nɔθˈistən $ nɔrθˈistərn
northern ˈnɒðən $ ˈnɔrðərn
north-northeast ˈnɒθ nɔθˈist
  $ ˈnɔrθ nɔrθˈist
northwards ˈnɒθwədz £ -wʊdz
  $ ˈnɔrθwərdz
northwest ˈnɒθˈwest $ ˈnɔrθ-

northwestern ˈnɒθˈwestən $ ˈnɔrθ-
Norway ˈnɔweɪ $ ˈnɔrweɪ
Norwegian nɔˈwɪdʒən $ nɔr-
Norwich ˈnɒrɪdʒ -ɪtʃ $ ˈnɔrwɪtʃ
nose nəʊz
nosedive ˈnəʊzdaɪv
nosegay ˈnəʊzgeɪ
nosey ˈnəʊzɪ
nostalgia nɒˈstældʒə
nostril ˈnɒstrɪl -trl
not nɒt
notability ˈnəʊtəˈbɪlətɪ
notable ˈnəʊtəbl
notary ˈnəʊtərɪ
notation nəʊˈteɪʃn
notch nɒtʃ
note nəʊt
notebook ˈnəʊtbʊk
note-paper ˈnəʊt peɪpə(r)
nothing ˈnʌθɪŋ
notice ˈnəʊtɪs
notice-board ˈnəʊtɪs bɔd $ bɔrd
notifiable ˈnəʊtɪˈfaɪəbl ˈnəʊtɪfaɪəbl
notification ˈnəʊtɪfɪˈkeɪʃn
notify ˈnəʊtɪfaɪ
notion ˈnəʊʃn
notoriety ˈnəʊtəˈraɪətɪ
notorious nəʊˈtɔrɪəs nə-
Notre Dame ˈnɒtrə ˈdam $ ˈnəʊtər ˈdeɪm
Nottingham ˈnɒtɪŋəm $ -ŋhæm
notwithstanding ˈnɒtwɪðˈstændɪŋ $ -wɪθ-
nougat ˈnugɑ ˈnʌgət $ ˈnugət etc
nought nɔt
noun naʊn
nourish ˈnʌrɪʃ $ ˈnɜɪʃ
nous naʊs
nouveau riche ˈnuvəʊ ˈriʃ
Nova Scotia ˈnəʊvə ˈskəʊʃə
novel ˈnɒvl
novelette ˈnɒvlˈet
novelist ˈnɒvlɪst
novelty ˈnɒvltɪ
November nəʊˈvembə(r) nə-
novice ˈnɒvɪs
now naʊ
nowadays ˈnaʊədeɪz
nowhere ˈnəʊweə(r) $ -hweər etc
noxious ˈnɒkʃəs
nozzle ˈnɒzl
nuance ˈnjuɑns ˈnjuɒ̃s njuˈɒ̃s
  $ nuˈɑns ˈnuɑns
nub nʌb
nubile ˈnjubaɪl $ ˈnubļ ˈnjubļ

nuclear ˈnjuklɪə(r) $ ˈnu- etc
nucleus ˈnjuklɪəs $ ˈnuklɪəs etc
nude njud $ nud etc
nudism ˈnjud-ɪzm as two words $ ˈnud-
nudist ˈnjudɪst $ ˈnudɪst etc
nudge nʌdʒ
nugget ˈnʌgɪt -ət
nuisance ˈnjusns $ ˈnusns etc
null nʌl
nullify ˈnʌlɪfaɪ
nullity ˈnʌlətɪ
numb nʌm
number ˈnʌmbə(r)
numeral ˈnjumərl $ ˈnumərl etc
numerate ˈnjuməreɪt $ ˈnu- etc
numerical njuˈmerɪkl $ nu- etc
numerous ˈnjumrəs $ ˈnu- etc
numismatics ˌnjumɪzˈmætɪks $ ˌnu- etc
numismatist njuˈmɪzmətɪst $ nu- etc
numskull ˈnʌm-skʌl
nun nʌn
nuncio ˈnʌnsɪəʊ

nunnery ˈnʌnərɪ
nuptial ˈnʌpʃl
nurse nɜs
nursemaid ˈnɜsmeɪd
nursery ˈnɜsrɪ
nursing-home ˈnɜsɪŋ həʊm
nurture ˈnɜtʃə(r)
nut nʌt
nut-brown ˈnʌt ˈbraʊn
nutcracker ˈnʌtkrækə(r)
nutmeg ˈnʌtmeg
nutshell ˈnʌt-ʃel
nutrient ˈnjutrɪənt $ ˈnu- etc
nutriment ˈnjutrɪmənt $ ˈnu- etc
nutrition njuˈtrɪʃn $ nu- etc
nutritious njuˈtrɪʃəs $ nu- etc
nutritive ˈnjutrɪtɪv $ ˈnu- etc
nuzzle ˈnʌzl
nylon ˈnaɪlon £ -lən
nymph nɪmf
nymphomania ˌnɪmfəˈmeɪnɪə
nymphomaniac ˌnɪmfəˈmeɪnɪæk

O

O o əʊ
oaf əʊf
oafish ˈəʊfɪʃ
oak əʊk
oaken ˈəʊkən
oar ɔ(r)
oarsman ˈɔzmən $ ˈɔrz-
oases əʊˈeɪsiz $ ˈəʊəsiz
oasis əʊˈeɪsɪs $ ˈəʊəsɪs
oast əʊst
oat əʊt
oatmeal ˈəʊtmil
oath əʊθ
oaths əʊðz
obbligato ˌoblɪˈgatəʊ
obduracy ˈobdjʊərəsɪ $ -dərəsɪ etc
obdurate ˈobdjʊərət $ -dərət etc
OBE ˈəʊ bi ˈi
obedience əˈbidɪəns $ əʊˈb-
obedient əˈbidɪənt $ əʊˈb-
obeisance əʊˈbeɪsns £ əʊˈbisns
obelisk ˈobəlɪsk -bɪl-
obese əʊˈbis
obesity əʊˈbisətɪ
obey əˈbeɪ $ əʊˈbeɪ etc

obfuscate ˈobfʌskeɪt -fəs-
obituary əˈbɪtʃʊərɪ $ -ʊerɪ əʊ-
object n ˈobdʒɪkt
object v əbˈdʒekt
objection əbˈdʒekʃn
objective əbˈdʒektɪv
objectivity ˌobdʒekˈtɪvətɪ
object-lesson ˈobdʒɪkt lesn
objurgate ˈobdʒɜgeɪt
obligate ˈoblɪgeɪt
obligation ˌoblɪˈgeɪʃn
obligatory əˈblɪgətrɪ $ -tɔrɪ ˈoblɪgə-
oblige əˈblaɪdʒ
oblique əˈblik
obliterate əˈblɪtəreɪt
obliteration əˌblɪtəˈreɪʃn
oblivion əˈblɪvɪən
oblivious əˈblɪvɪəs
oblong ˈoblɒŋ $ ˈoblɔŋ
obloquy ˈobləkwɪ
obnoxious əbˈnokʃəs ob-
oboe ˈəʊbəʊ
obscene əbˈsin ob-
obscenity əbˈsenətɪ -ˈsin- ob-
obscure əbˈskjʊə(r)

obscurity əbˈskjʊərətɪ
obsequies ˈobsɪkwɪz
obsequious əbˈsikwɪəs
observance əbˈzɜvəns
observant əbˈzɜvənt
observation ˈobzəˈveɪʃn $ -zər-
observation-car ˈobzəˈveɪʃn kɑ(r) $ -zər-
observation-post ˈobzəˈveɪʃn pəʊst $ -zər-
observatory əbˈzɜvətrɪ $ -tɔrɪ
observe əbˈzɜv
obsess əbˈses
obsession əbˈseʃn
obsolescent ˈobsəˈlesnt
obsolete ˈobsəlit $ ˈobsəˈlit etc
obstacle ˈobstəkl
obstacle race ˈobstəkl reɪs
obstetric obˈstetrɪk əb-
obstetrician ˈobstɪˈtrɪʃn
obstetrics obˈstetrɪks əb-
obstinacy ˈobstɪnəsɪ
obstinate ˈobstɪnət -nɪt
obstreperous əbˈstrepərəs ob-
obstruct əbˈstrʌkt
obstruction əbˈstrʌkʃn
obstructive əbˈstrʌktɪv
obtain əbˈteɪn
obtrude əbˈtrud
obtrusive əbˈtrusɪv
obtuse əbˈtjus $ əbˈtus ob-
obverse ˈobvɜs
obviate ˈobvɪeɪt
obvious ˈobvɪəs
occasion əˈkeɪʒn
occasional əˈkeɪʒnl
occasionally əˈkeɪʒnˌlɪ -nəlɪ
Occident ˈoksɪdənt
Occidental ˈoksɪˈdentl
occult oˈkʌlt $ £ əˈkʌlt
occupancy ˈokjʊpənsɪ
occupant ˈokjʊpənt
occupation ˈokjʊˈpeɪʃn
occupier ˈokjʊpaɪə(r)
occupy ˈokjʊpaɪ
occur əˈkɜ
occurrence əˈkʌrns $ əˈkɜns
ocean ˈəʊʃn
Oceania ˈəʊʃɪˈeɪnɪə $ -ˈænɪə etc
oceanic ˈəʊʃɪˈænɪk
ocelot ˈəʊsɪlot $ ˈosɪlot
ochre($ -er) ˈəʊkə(r)
o'clock ˈəˈklok
octagon ˈoktəgən $ -gon etc
octagonal okˈtægənl

octane ˈokteɪn
octave ˈoktɪv
Octavia okˈteɪvɪə
octavo okˈteɪvəʊ
octet okˈtet
October okˈtəʊbə(r)
octogenarian ˈoktədʒɪˈneərɪən
octopus ˈoktəpəs
octoroon ˈoktəˈrun
ocular ˈokjʊlə(r)
oculist ˈokjʊlɪst
odd od
oddity ˈodətɪ
odd-job man od ˈdʒob mæn
odds and ends ˈodz n ˈendz
ode əʊd
odious ˈəʊdɪəs
odium ˈəʊdɪəm
odoriferous ˈəʊdəˈrɪfərəs
odorous ˈəʊdərəs
odour ˈəʊdə(r)
Odyssey ˈodɪsɪ
oecumenical ˈikjuˈmenɪkl $ ˈek-
Oedipus ˈidɪpəs $ ˈed- etc
o'er ɔ(r) ˈəʊə(r)
oesophagus iˈsofəgəs $ ɪˈs-
of usual form: əv
    strong-form: ov $ ʌv
off of $ £ ɔf
offal ˈofl $ ˈɔfl
off-beat ˈof bit $ £ ˈɔf
offence əˈfens
offend əˈfend
offense əˈfens
offensive əˈfensɪv
offer ˈofə(r) $ ˈɔfər
offertory ˈofətrɪ $ ˈɔfərtɔrɪ
off-hand of ˈhænd $ £ ɔf
office ˈofɪs $ ˈɔfɪs
office-block ˈofɪs blok $ ˈɔfɪs
office-boy ˈofɪs bɔɪ $ ˈɔfɪs
officer ˈofɪsə(r) $ ˈɔfɪsər
official əˈfɪʃl
officiate əˈfɪʃɪeɪt
officious əˈfɪʃəs
offing ˈofɪŋ $ ˈɔfɪŋ
offish ˈofɪʃ $ £ ˈɔfɪʃ
off-licence ˈof laɪsns $ £ ˈɔf
off-peak ˈof pik $ £ ˈɔf
off-print ˈof prɪnt $ £ ˈɔf
offset ˈofset $ £ ˈɔfset
offshoot ˈofʃut $ £ ˈɔfʃut
off-shore ˈof ˈʃɔ(r) $ £ ˈɔf

off-side ˈof ˈsaɪd $ £ ˈɔf
offspring ˈofsprɪŋ $ £ ˈɔfsprɪŋ
off-stage ˈof ˈsteɪdʒ $ £ ˈɔf
oft oft $ ɔft
often ˈofn ˈoftən $ ˈɔf-
ogle ˈəʊgl
ogre ˈəʊgə(r)
ogreish ˈəʊgərɪʃ
oh əʊ
Ohio əʊˈhaɪəʊ
ohm əʊm
oho! əʊˈhəʊ
-oid suffix ɔɪd
oil ɔɪl
oil-can ˈɔɪl kæn
oilcloth ˈɔɪlklɒθ $ -klɔθ
oil-colours ˈɔɪl kʌləz $ kʌlərz
oil-field ˈɔɪl fild
oil-painting ˈɔɪl ˈpeɪntɪŋ
oil-skin ˈɔɪl skɪn
oil-tanker ˈɔɪl tæŋkə(r)
oil-well ˈɔɪl wel
oily ˈɔɪlɪ
ointment ˈɔɪntmənt
O.K., okay ˈəʊˈkeɪ
Oklahoma ˈəʊkləˈhəʊmə
old əʊld
olden ˈəʊldn
old-fashioned ˈəʊld ˈfæʃnd
old-timer ˈəʊld ˈtaɪmə(r)
old-world ˈəʊld ˈwɜld
oleaginous ˈəʊlɪˈædʒɪnəs
olfactory olˈfæktərɪ
oligarchy ˈolɪgakɪ $ -garkɪ
olive, O– ˈolɪv
Oliver ˈolɪvə(r)
Olympiad əʊˈlɪmpɪæd £ əˈl-
Olympian əʊˈlɪmpɪən £ əˈl-
Olympic əˈlɪmpɪk $ əʊˈl- etc
Oman əʊˈman
ombudsman ˈombʊdzmæn -mən
omega (Ω) ˈəʊmɪgə ˈomɪgə -meg-
   $ əʊˈmegə -ˈmɪgə -ˈmeɪgə etc
omelet(te) ˈomlət -lɪt
omen ˈəʊmen $ £ ˈəʊmən
ominous ˈomɪnəs
omission əˈmɪʃn əʊˈmɪʃn
omit əˈmɪt əʊˈmɪt
omnibus ˈomnɪbəs $ -bʌs
omnipotent omˈnɪpətənt
omniscient omˈnɪʃnt £ omˈnɪsɪənt
omnivorous omˈnɪvərəs
on on $ ɔn

once wʌns
one wʌn
one another wʌn əˈnʌðə(r)
one-armed ˈwʌn ˈamd $ ˈarmd
one-eyed ˈwʌn ˈaɪd
O'Neill əʊˈnil
one-off ˈwʌn ˈof $ ˈɔf
onerous ˈonərəs ˈəʊnərəs
one-sided ˈwʌn ˈsaɪdɪd
one-track ˈwʌn ˈtræk
one-way ˈwʌn ˈweɪ
onion ˈʌnɪən
onlooker ˈonlʊkə(r) $ ˈɔn-
only ˈəʊnlɪ except finally: ˈəʊnɪ
onomatopoeia əˈnoˈmætəˈpɪə
   $ £ ˈonəˈmætəˈpɪə
onrush ˈonrʌʃ $ ˈɔn-
onset ˈon-set $ ˈɔn-
onslaught ˈon-slɔt $ ˈɔn-
Ontario onˈteərɪəʊ $ -ˈtar-
onto usual form: ˈontə $ ˈɔntə
   strong-form: ˈontu $ ˈɔntu
ontology onˈtolədʒɪ
onus ˈəʊnəs
onward(s) ˈonwəd(z) £ -wʊd(z)
   $ -wərd(z) ˈɔn-
onyx ˈonɪks ˈəʊnɪks
oodles ˈudlz
oof uf
ooze uz
opacity əʊˈpæsətɪ əˈp-
opal ˈəʊpl
opalescent ˈəʊpəˈlesnt
opaque əʊˈpeɪk £ əˈpeɪk
open ˈəʊpən
open-air ˈəʊpən ˈeə(r)
opencast ˈəʊpənkast $ -kæst
open-eyed ˈəʊpən ˈaɪd
open-handed ˈəʊpən ˈhændɪd
opening ˈəʊpnɪŋ
open-minded ˈəʊpən ˈmaɪndɪd
open-mouthed ˈəʊpən ˈmaʊðd
open season ˈəʊpən sizn
opera ˈoprə ˈopərə
opera-glasses ˈoprə glasɪz $ glæsɪz
opera-house ˈoprə haʊs
operate ˈopəreɪt
operatic ˈopəˈrætɪk
operating-table ˈopreɪtɪŋ teɪbl
operating-theatre($ -ter)
   ˈopreɪtɪŋ θɪətə(r)
operation ˈopəˈreɪʃn
operational ˈopəˈreɪʃnl

operative ˈɒprətɪv $ ˈɒpəreɪtɪv
operator ˈɒpəreɪtə(r)
operetta ˌɒpəˈretə
Ophelia əˈfiːlɪə əʊ-
ophthalmia ofˈθælmɪə op-
ophthalmic ofˈθælmɪk op-
opiate ˈəʊpɪət -ɪeɪt
opine əʊˈpaɪn
opinion əˈpɪnɪən
opinionated əˈpɪnɪəneɪtɪd
opinion-poll əˈpɪnɪən pəʊl
opium ˈəʊpɪəm
Oporto əˈpɔːtəʊ əʊ- $ -ˈpɔːr-
opossum əˈpɒsəm
opponent əˈpəʊnənt
opportune ˈɒpətjuːn $ ˈɒpərtuːn
opportunism ˈɒpətjuːnɪzm $ -ərˈtuːn-
opportunist ˈɒpətjuːnɪst $ -ərˈtuːn-
opportunity ˌɒpəˈtjuːnətɪ -ˈtʃuːnətɪ
  $ ˌɒpərˈtuːnətɪ
oppose əˈpəʊz
opposite ˈɒpəzɪt -sɪt
opposition ˌɒpəˈzɪʃn
oppress əˈpres
oppression əˈpreʃn
oppressive əˈpresɪv
oppressor əˈpresə(r)
opprobrious əˈprəʊbrɪəs
opprobrium əˈprəʊbrɪəm
oppugn əˈpjuːn
opt opt
optative ˈɒptətɪv
optic ˈɒptɪk
optical ˈɒptɪkl
optician opˈtɪʃn
optimism ˈɒptɪmɪzm
optimist ˈɒptɪmɪst
optimistic ˌɒptɪˈmɪstɪk
optimum ˈɒptɪməm
option ˈɒpʃn
optional ˈɒpʃnl
opulence ˈɒpjʊləns
opulent ˈɒpjʊlənt
opus ˈəʊpəs £ ˈɒpəs
or ɔː(r)
oracle ˈɒrəkl $ ˈɔːrəkl etc
oracular əˈrækjʊlə(r)
oral ˈɔːrl $ ˈɒrl
orange ˈɒrɪndʒ $ ˈɔːrɪndʒ etc
orangeade ˌɒrɪnˈdʒeɪd $ ˈɔːr- etc
orange-peel ˈɒrɪndʒ piːl $ ˈɔːr- etc
orang-(o)utan(g) ɔːˈræŋ uˈtæŋ ˈɔːræŋ ˈuːtæn
  -rəŋ -tæŋ $ əˈræŋ əˈtæŋ -æn etc

oration ɔːˈreɪʃn o-
orator ˈɒrətə(r) $ ˈɔːr- etc
oratorio ˌɒrəˈtɔːrɪəʊ $ £ ˈɔːr- etc
oratorical ˌɒrəˈtorɪkl $ ˌɔːrəˈtɔːr- etc
oratory ˈɒrətrɪ $ ˈɔːrətɔrɪ ˈɒr-
orb ɔb $ ɔrb
orbit ˈɒbɪt $ ˈɔrbɪt
orchard ˈɒtʃəd $ ˈɔrtʃərd
orchestra ˈɔkɪstrə $ ˈɔrk-
orchestral ɔˈkestrl $ ɔr-
orchestrate ˈɔkɪstreɪt $ ˈɔrk-
orchestration ˌɔkɪˈstreɪʃn $ ˈɔrk-
orchid ˈɔkɪd $ ˈɔrk-
ordain ɔˈdeɪn $ ɔr-
ordeal ɔˈdiːl ˈɔdiːl $ ɔrˈdiːl ˈɔr-
order ˈɔdə(r) $ ˈɔrdər
order-book ˈɔdə bʊk $ ˈɔrdər
order-form ˈɔdə fɔm $ ˈɔrdər fɔrm
orderly ˈɔdəlɪ $ ˈɔrdərlɪ
orderly-room ˈɔdəlɪ rʊm $ ˈɔrdərlɪ rʊm
ordinal ˈɔdɪnl $ ˈɔrdnl
ordinance ˈɔdnəns ˈɔdɪnəns $ ˈɔrd-
ordinand ˈɔdɪˈnænd $ ˈɔrdn̩ænd
ordinarily ˈɔdnrɪlɪ $ ˈɔrdn̩erlɪ
  ˌɔrdn̩ˈerlɪ
ordinary ˈɔdnrɪ $ ˈɔrdn̩erɪ
ordination ˌɔdɪˈneɪʃn $ ˈɔrdn̩eɪʃn
ordnance ˈɔdnəns $ ˈɔrdnəns
ordure ˈɔdjʊə(r) $ ˈɔrdʒər etc
ore ɔː(r)
Oregon ˈɒrɪgən $ ˈɔːrɪgən -gon
organ ˈɔgən $ ˈɔrgən
organdie, -dy ɔˈgændɪ $ ɔr-
organ-grinder ˈɔgən graɪndə(r) $ ˈɔrg-
organic ɔˈgænɪk $ ɔr-
organisation ˌɔgənaɪˈzeɪʃn $ ˈɔrgənɪ-
organism ˈɔgənɪzm $ ˈɔrg-
organist ˈɔgənɪst $ ˈɔrgənɪst
organize ˈɔgənaɪz $ ˈɔrg-
orgasm ˈɔgæzm $ ˈɔrg-
orgiastic ˌɔdʒɪˈæstɪk $ ˌɔrdʒɪ-
orgy ˈɔdʒɪ $ ˈɔrdʒɪ
oriel ˈɔːrɪəl
orient ˈɔːrɪent
oriental ˌɔːrɪˈentl
orientate ˈɔːrɪənteɪt
orientation ˌɔːrɪenˈteɪʃn ˌɔːrɪən-
orifice ˈɒrɪfɪs $ ˈɔːrəfɪs etc
origin ˈɒrədʒɪn $ ˈɔːrədʒɪn etc
original əˈrɪdʒnl
originality əˌrɪdʒəˈnælətɪ
originally əˈrɪdʒn̩əlɪ
originate əˈrɪdʒɪneɪt

originator ɔˈrɪdʒɪneɪtə(r)
oriole ˈɔrɪəʊl
orison ˈɔrɪzn $ ˈɔrɪzn -ɪsn *etc*
Orkneys ˈɔknɪz $ ˈɔrk-
ormolu ˈɔməlu $ ˈɔrm-
ornament *n* ˈɔnəmənt $ ˈɔrn-
ornament *v* ˈɔnəmənt $ ˈɔrn-
ornamental ˈɔnəˈmentl $ ˈɔrnə-
ornamentation ˈɔnəmenˈteɪʃn $ ˈɔrn-
ornate ɔˈneɪt $ ɔr-
ornithology ˈɔnɪˈθɒlədʒɪ $ ˈɔrnɪ-
orotund ˈɔrəʊtʌnd ˈor- -rət-
orphan ˈɔfən $ ˈɔrfən
orphanage ˈɔfənɪdʒ $ ˈɔrf-
orthodox ˈɔθədoks $ ˈɔrθ-
orthographic ˈɔθəˈgræfɪk $ ˈɔrθə-
orthography ɔˈθogrəfɪ $ ɔr-
orthop(a)edic ˈɔθəˈpidɪk $ ˈɔr-
Osbert ˈozbət $ ˈozbərt
Oscar ˈoskə(r)
oscillate ˈosɪleɪt
oscillation ˈosɪˈleɪʃn
oscillograph əˈsɪləgraf $ £ -græf
osculate ˈoskjʊleɪt
osier ˈəʊzɪə(r) $ £ ˈəʊʒə(r)
Oslo ˈozləʊ
osprey oˈspreɪ $ £ ˈosprɪ *etc*
osseous ˈosɪəs
ossification ˈosɪfɪˈkeɪʃn
ossify ˈosɪfaɪ
Ostend oˈstend
ostensible oˈstensəbl
ostentatious ˈostenˈteɪʃəs
osteopath ˈostɪəpæθ
osteopathy ˈostɪˈopəθɪ
ostler ˈoslə(r)
ostracize ˈostrəsaɪz
ostrich ˈostrɪtʃ -ɪdʒ $ ˈos-
ostriches ˈostrɪdʒɪz -ɪtʃɪz $ ˈos-
Oswald ˈozwld
Othello əˈθeləʊ o- $ əʊˈθeləʊ *etc*
other ˈʌðə(r)
otherwise ˈʌðəwaɪz $ ˈʌðər-
otiose ˈəʊʃɪəʊs ˈəʊtɪəʊs
otter ˈotə(r)
ottoman ˈotəmən
oubliette ˈublɪˈet
ought ɔt
oughtn't ˈɔtnt
ouija ˈwidʒə £ ˈwidʒa
ounce aʊns
our ˈaʊə(r) *weak-form:* a(r)
ours ˈaʊəz $ ˈaʊərz

ourselves aˈselvz $ ar-
-ous *suffix* əs
oust aʊst
out aʊt
out- *prefix* aʊt
out and out ˈaʊt ən ˈaʊt
outback ˈaʊtbæk
outbalance aʊtˈbæləns
outbid aʊtˈbɪd
outboard ˈaʊtbɔd $ -bɔrd
outbound ˈaʊtbaʊnd
outbrave aʊtˈbreɪv
outbreak ˈaʊtbreɪk
outbuilding ˈaʊtbɪldɪŋ
outburst ˈaʊtbɜst
outcast ˈaʊtkast $ -kæst
outclass aʊtˈklas $ -ˈklæs
outcome ˈaʊtkʌm
outcrop ˈaʊtkrop
outcry ˈaʊtkraɪ
outdated aʊtˈdeɪtɪd
outdistance aʊtˈdɪstəns
outdo aʊtˈdu
outdone aʊtˈdʌn
outdoor aʊtˈdɔ(r)
outer ˈaʊtə(r)
outermost ˈaʊtəməʊst $ ˈaʊtər-
outface aʊtˈfeɪs
outfall ˈaʊtfɔl
outfield ˈaʊtfild
outfighting ˈaʊtfaɪtɪŋ
outfit ˈaʊtfɪt
outflank aʊtˈflæŋk
outflow ˈaʊtfləʊ
outgeneral aʊtˈdʒenrl
outgoing aʊtˈgəʊɪŋ
outgrow aʊtˈgrəʊ
outhouse ˈaʊthaʊs
outing ˈaʊtɪŋ
outlandish aʊtˈlændɪʃ
outlast aʊtˈlast $ -ˈlæst
outlaw ˈaʊtlɔ
outlay ˈaʊtleɪ
outlet ˈaʊtlet -lət
outline ˈaʊtlaɪn
outlive aʊtˈlɪv
outlook ˈaʊtlʊk
outlying ˈaʊtlaɪɪŋ
outmaneuver ˈaʊtməˈnuvə(r)
outmanoevre ˈaʊtməˈnuvə(r)
outmatch aʊˈtmætʃ
outmoded aʊtˈməʊdɪd
outmost ˈaʊtməʊst

outnumber aʊtˈnʌmbə(r)
out-of-the-way ˈaʊt əv ðə ˈweɪ
outpatient ˈaʊtpeɪʃnt
outplay aʊtˈpleɪ
outpoint aʊtˈpɔɪnt
outpost ˈaʊtpəʊst
outpouring ˈaʊtpɔːrɪŋ
output ˈaʊtpʊt
outrage n ˈaʊt-reɪdʒ
outrage v aʊtˈreɪdʒ
outrageous aʊtˈreɪdʒəs
outré ˈuːtreɪ $ uˈtreɪ
outrider ˈaʊt-raɪdə(r)
outrigger ˈaʊt-rɪɡə(r)
outright adj ˈaʊt-raɪt
outright adv aʊtˈraɪt
outrival aʊtˈraɪvl
outrun aʊtˈrʌn
outset ˈaʊtset
outshine aʊtˈʃaɪn
outside aʊtˈsaɪd
outsider aʊtˈsaɪdə(r)
outsize aʊtˈsaɪz
outskirts ˈaʊtskɜːts
outsmart aʊtˈsmat $ -ˈsmart
outspan ˈaʊtspæn
outspoken aʊtˈspəʊkən
outspokenness aʊtˈspəʊkənnəs
outspread aʊtˈspred
outstanding aʊtˈstændɪŋ
outstay aʊtˈsteɪ
outstretched aʊtˈstretʃt
outstrip aʊtˈstrɪp
outvote aʊtˈvəʊt
outward(s) ˈaʊtwəd(z) £ -wʊd(z)
   $ -wərd(z)
outwear aʊtˈweə(r)
outweigh aʊtˈweɪ
outwit aʊtˈwɪt
outworn aʊtˈwɔn $ -ˈwɔrn
ouzo ˈuːzəʊ
ova ˈəʊvə
oval ˈəʊvl
ovary ˈəʊvərɪ
ovation əʊˈveɪʃn
oven ˈʌvn
over ˈəʊvə(r)
over- prefix əʊvə(r)
overact ˌəʊvərˈækt
overall adj, adv ˌəʊvərˈɔl
overall n ˈəʊvərɔl
overarm ˈəʊvəram $ -arm
overawe ˌəʊvərˈɔ

overbalance ˌəʊvəˈbæləns $ ˌəʊvər-
overbear ˌəʊvəˈbeə(r) $ ˌəʊvər-
overbid ˌəʊvəˈbɪd $ ˌəʊvər-
overblown ˌəʊvəˈbləʊn $ ˌəʊvər-
overboard ˈəʊvəbɔd $ ˈəʊvərbɔrd
overburden ˌəʊvəˈbɜdn $ ˌəʊvər-
overcast ˌəʊvəˈkast $ ˌəʊvərˈkæst
overcharge ˌəʊvəˈtʃadʒ $ ˌəʊvərˈtʃardʒ
overcloud ˌəʊvəˈklaʊd $ ˌəʊvər-
overcoat ˈəʊvəkəʊt $ ˈəʊvər-
overcome ˌəʊvəˈkʌm $ ˌəʊvər-
overcrowd ˌəʊvəˈkraʊd $ ˌəʊvər-
overdo ˌəʊvəˈdu $ ˌəʊvər-
overdraft ˈəʊvədraft $ ˈəʊvərdræft
overdraw ˌəʊvəˈdrɔ ˌəʊvər-
overdress ˌəʊvəˈdres $ ˌəʊvər-
overdrive ˈəʊvədraɪv $ ˈəʊvər-
overdue ˌəʊvəˈdju $ ˌəʊvərˈdu
overflow n ˈəʊvəfləʊ $ ˌəʊvər-
overflow v ˌəʊvəˈfləʊ $ ˌəʊvər-
overgrown ˌəʊvəˈɡrəʊn $ ˌəʊvər-
overhand adj, adv ˌəʊvəˈhænd $ ˌəʊvər-
overhand n ˈəʊvəhænd $ ˈəʊvər-
overhanging ˌəʊvəˈhæŋɪŋ $ ˌəʊvər-
overhaul n ˈəʊvəhɔl $ ˈəʊvər-
overhaul v ˌəʊvəˈhɔl $ ˌəʊvər-
overhead adj, adv ˌəʊvəˈhed $ ˌəʊvər-
overhead n ˈəʊvəhed $ ˈəʊvər-
overhear ˌəʊvəˈhɪə(r) $ ˌəʊvər-
overjoyed ˌəʊvəˈdʒɔɪd $ ˌəʊvər-
overland adj ˈəʊvəlænd $ ˈəʊvər-
overland adv ˌəʊvəˈlænd $ ˌəʊvər-
overlap n ˈəʊvəlæp $ ˈəʊvər-
overlap v ˌəʊvəˈlæp $ ˌəʊvər-
overlay n ˈəʊvəleɪ $ ˈəʊvər-
overlay v ˌəʊvəˈleɪ $ ˌəʊvər-
overleaf ˌəʊvəˈlif $ ˌəʊvər-
overlook ˌəʊvəˈlʊk $ ˌəʊvər-
overlord ˈəʊvəlɔd $ ˈəʊvərlɔrd
overmaster ˌəʊvəmastə(r)
   $ ˈəʊvərmæstər
overmuch ˌəʊvəˈmʌtʃ $ ˌəʊvər-
overnight ˌəʊvəˈnaɪt $ ˌəʊvər-
overpaid ˌəʊvəˈpeɪd $ ˌəʊvər-
overpower ˌəʊvəˈpaʊə(r) $ ˌəʊvər-
overprint ˌəʊvəˈprɪnt $ ˌəʊvər-
overrate ˌəʊvəˈreɪt
overreach ˌəʊvəˈritʃ
override ˌəʊvəˈraɪd
overrule ˌəʊvəˈrul
overrun ˌəʊvəˈrʌn
oversea ˌəʊvəˈsi $ ˌəʊvər-
overseas ˌəʊvəˈsiz $ ˌəʊvər-

overseer ˈəʊvəsɪə(r) $ ˈəʊvər-
overshadow ˈəʊvəˈʃædəʊ $ ˈəʊvər-
overshoe ˈəʊvəʃu $ ˈəʊvər-
overshoot ˈəʊvəˈʃut $ ˈəʊvər-
overshot ˈəʊvəˈʃot $ ˈəʊvər-
oversight ˈəʊvəsaɪt $ ˈəʊvər-
oversleep ˈəʊvəˈslip $ ˈəʊvər-
overspill n ˈəʊvəspɪl $ ˈəʊvər-
overspill v ˈəʊvəˈspɪl $ ˈəʊvər-
overstate ˈəʊvəˈsteɪt $ ˈəʊvər-
overstatement ˈəʊvəsteɪtmənt $ ˈəʊvər-
overstay ˈəʊvəˈsteɪ $ ˈəʊvər-
overstep ˈəʊvəˈstep $ ˈəʊvər-
overstock ˈəʊvəˈstok $ ˈəʊvər-
overt ˈəʊvɜt $ £ əʊˈvɜt etc
overtake ˈəʊvəˈteɪk $ ˈəʊvər-
overtax ˈəʊvəˈtæks $ ˈəʊvər-
overthrow n ˈəʊvəθrəʊ $ ˈəʊvər-
overthrow v ˈəʊvəˈθrəʊ $ ˈəʊvər-
overtime ˈəʊvətaɪm $ ˈəʊvər-
overtone ˈəʊvətəʊn $ ˈəʊvər-
overture ˈəʊvətʃə(r) -tʃʊə(r) $ ˈəʊvər-
overturn ˈəʊvəˈtɜn $ ˈəʊvər-
overweight adj ˈəʊvəˈweɪt $ ˈəʊvər-
overweight n ˈəʊvəweɪt $ ˈəʊvər-
overwhelm ˈəʊvəˈwelm
  $ ˈəʊvərˈhwelm -ˈwelm
overwork ˈəʊvəˈwɜk $ ˈəʊvər-

overwrought ˈəʊvəˈrɔt
oviparous əʊˈvɪpərəs
ovoid ˈəʊvɔɪd
ovum ˈəʊvəm
owe əʊ
owing ˈəʊɪŋ
owl aʊl
owlet ˈaʊlət
own əʊn
owner-occupied ˈəʊnər ˈokjupaɪd
owner-occupier ˈəʊnər ˈokjupaɪə(r)
ox oks
ox-cart ˈoks kat $ kart
ox-tail n ˈoks teɪl
Oxbridge ˈoksbrɪdʒ
Oxford ˈoksfəd $ ˈoksfərd
oxide ˈoksaɪd
oxidize ˈoksɪdaɪz
Oxon ˈoksn
Oxonian okˈsəʊnɪən
oxy-acetylene ˈoksɪ əˈsetəlin -lɪn
oxygen ˈoksɪdʒən -dʒɪn
oxygen mask ˈoksɪdʒən mask $ mæsk
oxygen tent ˈoksɪdʒən tent
oyez əʊˈjez əʊˈjes
oyster ˈɔɪstə(r)
oyster-bed ˈɔɪstə bed $ ˈɔɪstər
ozone əʊˈzəʊn ˈəʊzəʊn

P

P p pi
p British currency pens
pa pɑ
P.A. ˈpi ˈeɪ
pace peɪs
pace-maker ˈpeɪs meɪkə(r)
pachyderm ˈpækɪdɜm
pacific, P– pəˈsɪfɪk
pacifism ˈpæsɪfɪzm
pacifist ˈpæsɪfɪst
pacify ˈpæsɪfaɪ
pack pæk
package ˈpækɪdʒ
packet ˈpækɪt
pack-horse ˈpæk hɔs $ hɔrs
packing-case ˈpækɪŋ keɪs
pact pækt
pad pæd
paddle ˈpædl

paddle-steamer ˈpædl stimə(r)
paddock ˈpædək $ -dɪk
paddy, P– ˈpædɪ
paddy-field ˈpædɪ fild
padlock ˈpædlok
padre ˈpɑdreɪ -drɪ
paean ˈpiən
paederasty ˈpedəræstɪ ˈpid-
paediatrician ˈpidɪəˈtrɪʃn
paediatrics ˈpidɪˈætrɪks
pagan ˈpeɪgən
Paganini ˈpægəˈnini $ ˈpagə-
page peɪdʒ
pageant ˈpædʒənt
pageantry ˈpædʒəntrɪ
pagination ˈpædʒɪˈneɪʃn ˈpeɪdʒ-
pagoda pəˈgəʊdə
pah! pɑ or realistic vocal eruption
paid peɪd

pail peɪl
paillasse ˋpælɪæs $ £ ˈpælɪˋæs
pain peɪn
pain-killer ˋpeɪn kɪlə(r)
painstaking ˋpeɪnzteɪkɪŋ
paint peɪnt
paint-brush ˋpeɪnt brʌʃ
pair peə(r)
Paisley ˋpeɪzlɪ
pajamas pəˋdʒaməz $ -ˋdʒæm- etc
Pakistan ˈpɑkɪˋstɑn
$ £ ˈpæk- $ -ˋstæn etc
Pakistani ˈpɑkɪˋstɑnɪ
$ £ ˈpæk- $ -ˋstænɪ etc
pal pæl
palace ˋpælɪs -əs
palaeolithic ˈpælɪəʊˋlɪθɪk $ £ ˈpeɪl-
palaeontology ˈpælɪonˋtolədʒɪ $ £ ˈpeɪl-
palanquin, palankeen ˈpælənˋkin
palatable ˋpælətəbl
palatal ˋpælətəl
palate ˋpælət -ɪt
palatial pəˋleɪʃl
palatinate pəˋlætɪnət $ -tŋeɪt
palaver pəˋlɑvə(r) $ -ˋlævər etc
pale peɪl
pale-face ˋpeɪl feɪs
paleolithic ˈpælɪəʊˋlɪθɪk $ £ ˈpeɪl-
paleontology ˈpælɪonˋtolədʒɪ $ £ ˈpeɪl-
Palestine ˋpælɪstaɪn
Palestinian ˈpælɪˋstɪnɪən
palette ˋpælɪt -ət -et
palfrey ˋpolfrɪ
palindrome ˋpælɪndrəʊm
paling ˋpeɪlɪŋ
palisade ˋpælɪseɪd
pall pol
palladium, P– pəˋleɪdɪəm
pall-bearer ˋpol beərə(r)
pallet ˋpælɪt -ət
palliasse ˋpælɪæs $ £ ˈpælɪˋæs etc
palliate ˋpælɪeɪt
palliative ˋpælɪətɪv $ -ɪeɪtɪv etc
pallid ˋpælɪd
Pall Mall ˈpæl ˋmæl ˈpel ˋmel
pallor ˋpælə(r)
pally ˋpælɪ
palm pɑm
palmist ˋpɑmɪst
palm-oil ˋpɑm oɪl
Palm Sunday ˈpɑm ˋsʌndɪ
palmy ˋpɑmɪ
palpable ˋpælpəbl

palpitate ˋpælpɪteɪt
palpitation ˈpælpɪˋteɪʃn
palsy ˋpolzɪ
palter ˋpoltə(r)
paltry ˋpoltrɪ
Pamela ˋpæmlə
pampas ˋpæmpəs $ ˋpæmpəz etc
pamper ˋpæmpə(r)
pamphlet ˋpæmflət -lɪt
pamphleteer ˈpæmfləˋtɪə(r)
pan pæn
pan- prefix pæn
PanAm ˋpænˋæm
panacea ˈpænəˋsɪə
panache pæˋnæʃ $ £ pəˋnæʃ -ˋnɑʃ
Panama ˈpænəˋmɑ $ ˋpænəmɑ etc
pancake ˋpænkeɪk
panchromatic ˈpænkrəˋmætɪk
$ -krəʊˋm- etc
pancreas ˋpænkrɪəs
pancreatic ˈpænkrɪˋætɪk
panda ˋpændə
pandemic pænˋdemɪk
pandemonium ˈpændɪˋməʊnɪəm
pander ˋpændə(r)
pane peɪn
panegyric ˈpænɪˋdʒɪrɪk
panel ˋpænl
panelling ˋpænlɪŋ
panga ˋpæŋgə
panic ˋpænɪk
panicky ˋpænɪkɪ
pannier ˋpænɪə(r)
panoply ˋpænəplɪ
panoptic pænˋoptɪk
panorama ˈpænəˋrɑmə $ -ˋræmə etc
panoramic ˈpænəˋræmɪk
pan-pipes ˋpænpaɪps
pansy ˋpænzɪ
pant pænt
pantaloon ˈpæntəˋlun
pantechnicon pænˋteknɪkən $ -kon etc
pantheism ˋpænθiɪzm
pantheistic ˈpænθiˋɪstɪc
pantheon, P– ˋpænθɪən $ -θɪon etc
panther ˋpænθə(r)
panties ˋpæntɪz
pantile ˋpæntaɪl
panto ˋpæntəʊ
pantograph ˋpæntəgrɑf $ £ -græf
pantomime ˋpæntəmaɪm
pantry ˋpæntrɪ
pants pænts

pap pæp
papa pə`pɑ $ `pɑpə
papacy `peɪpəsɪ
papal `peɪpl
papaw pə`pɔ $ £ `pɔpɔ
paper `peɪpə(r)
paper-back `peɪpə bæk $ `peɪpər
paper-chase `peɪpə tʃeɪs $ `peɪpər
paper-clip `peɪpə klɪp $ `peɪpər
paper-hanger `peɪpə hæŋə(r) $ `peɪpər
paper-knife `peɪpə naɪf $ `peɪpər
paper-weight `peɪpə weɪt $ `peɪpər
papier-mâché `pæpɪeɪ `mæʃeɪ `mɑʃ-
   $ 'peɪpər mə`ʃeɪ mæ`ʃeɪ
papist `peɪpɪst
papoose pə`pus $ pæ`pus etc
paprika `pæprɪkə $ pə`prikə pæ- pa-
Papua `pæpjʊə
papyrus pə`paɪərəs
par pɑ(r)
parable `pærəbl
parabola pə`ræbələ
parachute `pærəʃut £ 'pærə`ʃut
parachutist `pærəʃutɪst £ 'pærə`ʃutɪst
parade pə`reɪd
paradigm `pærədaɪm $ -dɪm
paradigmatic 'pærədɪg`mætɪk
paradise `pærədaɪs
paradox `pærədoks
paradoxical 'pærə`doksɪkl
paraffin `pærəfɪn £ -fin
paragon `pærəgən $ -gon etc
paragraph `pærəgrɑf $ -græf
Paraguay `pærəgwaɪ $ -gweɪ
parakeet `pærəkit 'pærə`kit
parallel `pærəlel
parallelogram 'pærə`leləgræm
paralyse($ -yze) `pærəlaɪz
paralysis pə`ræləsɪs
paralytic 'pærə`lɪtɪk
paralyze `pærəlaɪz
parameter pə`ræmɪtə(r)
paramount, P– `pærəmaʊnt
paramour `pærəmɔ(r) -mʊə(r)
paranoia 'pærə`nɔɪə
paranoiac 'pærə`nɔɪæk
parapet `pærəpɪt .-et
paraphernalia 'pærəfə`neɪlɪə $ -fər-
paraphrase `pærəfreɪz
paraplegic 'pærə`plidʒɪk
parasite `pærəsaɪt
parasitic 'pærə`sɪtɪk
parasol `pærəsol $ -sɔl etc

paratroops `pærətrups
paratyphoid 'pærə`taɪfɔɪd
parboil `pabɔɪl $ `par-
parcel `pasl $ `parsl
parcel post `pasl pəʊst $ `parsl
parch patʃ $ partʃ
parchment `patʃmənt $ `partʃ-
pardon `padn $ `pardn
pardonable `padnəbl $ `pard-
pardoner `padnə(r) $ `par-
pare peə(r)
paregoric 'pærɪ`gorɪk $ -`gɔrɪk etc
parent `peərnt
parental pə`rentl
parentheses pə`renθəsiz
parenthesis pə`renθəsɪs
parenthetic 'pærən`θetɪk
par excellence 'par `eksə`lõs
   $ 'par 'eksə`lõs -`lons etc
pariah `pærɪə $ pə`raɪə etc
parings `peərɪŋz
Paris `pærɪs
parish `pærɪʃ
parishioner pə`rɪʃnə(r)
Parisian pə`rɪzɪən $ -`rɪʒn etc
parity `pærətɪ
park pak $ park
parking lot `pakɪŋ lot $ `park-
parking meter `pakɪŋ mitə(r) $ `park-
Parkinson `pakɪnsn $ `park-
parlance `paləns $ `par-
parley `palɪ $ `parlɪ
parliament `paləmənt $ `parl-
parliamentarian 'paləmen`teərɪən $ -arl-
parliamentary 'palə`mentrɪ $ `parl-
parlour `palə(r) $ `parlər
parlour-maid `palə meɪd $ `parlər
parlous `paləs $ `parləs
Parmesan 'pamɪ`zæn $ `parmɪzæn -zən
parochial pə`rəʊkɪəl
parody `pærədɪ
parole pə`rəʊl
paroxysm `pærəksɪzm
parquet `pakeɪ -kɪ $ par`keɪ -`ket
parricide `pærɪsaɪd
parrot `pærət
parry `pærɪ
parse paz $ pars parz
Parsee pa`si $ par`si
parsimonious 'pasɪ`məʊnɪəs $ 'parsɪ-
parsimony `pasɪmənɪ $ `parsɪməʊnɪ
parsley `paslɪ $ `parslɪ
parsnip `pasnɪp $ `parsnɪp

parson ˈpɑsn $ ˈpɑrsn
parsonage ˈpɑsn̩dʒ $ ˈpɑr-
part pɑt $ pɑrt
partake pɑˈteɪk $ pɑr-
parterre pɑˈteə(r) $ pɑr-
parthenogenesis ˈpɑθɪnəʊˈdʒenɪsɪs $ ˈpɑr-
Parthenon ˈpɑθɪnən $ ˈpɑrθɪnon
partial ˈpɑʃl $ ˈpɑrʃl
partiality ˈpɑʃɪˈælətɪ $ ˈpɑrʃɪ-
participant pɑˈtɪsɪpənt $ pɑr-
participate pɑˈtɪsɪpeɪt $ pɑr-
participation pɑˈtɪsɪˈpeɪʃn $ pɑr-
participial ˈpɑtɪˈsɪpɪəl $ ˈpɑrtɪ-
participle ˈpɑtspl -səpl -tɪsəpl
  $ ˈpɑrtəsɪpl
particle ˈpɑtɪkl $ ˈpɑr-
particoloured($ -lor-) ˈpɑtɪkʌləd
  $ ˈpɑrtɪkʌlərd
particular pəˈtɪkjʊlə(r) $ pər- pəˈt-
particularity pəˈtɪkjʊˈlærətɪ $ pər- pəˈt-
particularize pəˈtɪkjʊləraɪz $ pər- pəˈt-
parting ˈpɑtɪŋ $ ˈpɑr-
partisan ˈpɑtɪˈzæn $ ˈpɑrtɪzn -ɪsn
partition pɑˈtɪʃn $ pɑr-
partitive ˈpɑtɪtɪv $ ˈpɑr-
partner ˈpɑtnə(r) $ ˈpɑr-
partnership ˈpɑtnəʃɪp $ ˈpɑrtnər-
partook pɑˈtʊk $ pɑr-
partridge ˈpɑ-trɪdʒ $ ˈpɑr-
parturition ˈpɑtjʊˈrɪʃn $ -ˈpɑrtʃʊˈ -təˈr-
party ˈpɑtɪ $ ˈpɑrtɪ
party-spirit ˈpɑtɪ ˈspɪrɪt $ ˈpɑrtɪ
parvenu ˈpɑvənju $ ˈpɑrvənu etc
Pasadena ˈpæsəˈdinə
paschal ˈpæskl £ ˈpɑs-
pas de deux ˈpɑ də ˈdɜ
  $ this ɜ may have no r quality
pasha ˈpɑʃə pəˈʃɑ $ ˈpæʃə etc
pass pɑs $ pæs
passacaglia ˈpæsəˈkɑlɪə
passage ˈpæsɪdʒ
passé ˈpɑseɪ ˈpæseɪ $ pæˈseɪ
passenger ˈpæsndʒə(r) -sɪn-
passe partout ˈpæs pɑˈtu $ pɑrˈtu £ ˈpɑs
passer-by ˈpɑsəˈbaɪ $ ˈpæsər-
passing-out parade ˈpɑsɪŋ ˈaʊt pəreɪd
  $ ˈpæsɪŋ
passim ˈpæsɪm
passion ˈpæʃn
passionate ˈpæʃn̩ət
passion-flower ˈpæʃn flaʊə(r)
Passion-play ˈpæʃn pleɪ
Passion Sunday ˈpæʃn ˈsʌndɪ -deɪ

Passion Week ˈpæʃn wik
passive ˈpæsɪv
passive resistance ˈpæsɪv rɪˈzɪstəns
passivity pæˈsɪvətɪ pəˈs-
Passover ˈpɑsəʊvə(r) $ ˈpæs-
passport ˈpɑspɔt $ ˈpæspɔrt
password ˈpɑswɜd $ ˈpæswɜd
past pɑst $ pæst
paste peɪst
pasteboard ˈpeɪstbɔd $ -bɔrd
pastel ˈpæstl $ pæˈstel
pastern ˈpæstən $ -tərn
Pasteur pæˈstɜ(r) pɑˈs-
pasteurize ˈpæstʃəraɪz -stə- £ ˈpɑs-
pastiche pæˈstiʃ
pastille ˈpæstɪl -stl $ pæˈstil -ˈstɪl
pastime ˈpɑs-taɪm $ ˈpæs-
pastor ˈpɑstə(r) $ ˈpæstər
pastoral ˈpɑstərl $ ˈpæs-
pastry ˈpeɪstrɪ
pastry-cook ˈpeɪstrɪ kʊk
pasture ˈpɑstʃə(r) $ ˈpæstʃər
pasty adj ˈpeɪstɪ
pasty n ˈpæstɪ
pat pæt
patch pætʃ
patchwork ˈpætʃwɜk
pate peɪt
pâté ˈpæteɪ ˈpɑ- $ pɑˈteɪ
patent ˈpeɪtnt exc. in 'P-Office' and
  'letters p-' ˈpætnt $ ˈpætnt
Patent Office ˈpætnt ofɪs $ ɔfɪs
pater ˈpeɪtə(r)
paterfamilias ˈpeɪtəfəˈmɪlɪæs -ɪəs
  $ ˈpeɪtərf- ˈpɑt- ˈpæt-
paternal pəˈtɜnl
paternity pəˈtɜnətɪ
pater noster ˈpætəˈnostə(r) $ ˈpætər n- etc
path pɑθ $ pæθ
pathfinder ˈpɑθfaɪndə(r) $ ˈpæθ-
pathetic pəˈθetɪk
pathological ˈpæθəˈlodʒɪkl
pathologist pəˈθolədʒɪst
pathology pəˈθolədʒɪ
pathos ˈpeɪθos
pathway ˈpɑθweɪ $ ˈpæθ-
patience ˈpeɪʃns
patient ˈpeɪʃnt
patina ˈpætɪnə $ pəˈtinə
patio ˈpætɪəʊ
patna ˈpætnə
patois ˈpætwɑ
patriarch ˈpeɪtrɪɑk $ -ɑrk

patriarchal ˈpeɪtrɪˈɑːkl $ -ˈɑːrkl
Patricia pəˈtrɪʃə
patrician pəˈtrɪʃn
patricide ˈpætrɪsaɪd
Patrick ˈpætrɪk
patrimonial ˈpætrɪˈməʊnɪəl
patrimony ˈpætrɪmənɪ $ -məʊnɪ
patriot ˈpeɪtrɪət £ ˈpæt- $ -ɪot
patriotic ˈpætrɪˈotɪk $ ˈpeɪt-
patriotism ˈpætrɪətɪzm $ ˈpeɪt-
patrol pəˈtrəʊl
patrolman pəˈtrəʊlmən
patron ˈpeɪtrən
patronage ˈpætrənɪdʒ $ ˈpeɪt- etc
patronize ˈpætrənaɪz $ ˈpeɪt-
patronymic ˈpætrəˈnɪmɪk
patter ˈpætə(r)
pattern ˈpætn $ ˈpætərn
Patterson ˈpætəsn $ ˈpætərsn
patty ˈpætɪ
paucity ˈpɔːsətɪ
Paul pɔːl
Pauline pɔːˈliːn ˈpɔːlin
paunch pɔːntʃ
pauper ˈpɔːpə(r)
pause pɔːz
pave peɪv
pavement ˈpeɪvmənt
pavement artist ˈpeɪvmənt ɑːtɪst $ ɑːr-
pavilion pəˈvɪlɪən
paving-stone ˈpeɪvɪŋ stəʊn
paw pɔː
pawky ˈpɔːkɪ
pawl pɔːl
pawn pɔːn
pawnbroker ˈpɔːnbrəʊkə(r)
pawnshop ˈpɔːnʃop
pawn-ticket ˈpɔːn tɪkɪt
pawpaw pəˈpɔː $ £ ˈpɔːpɔː
pax pæks
pay peɪ
pay-as-you-earn ˈpeɪ əz ju ˈɜːn
pay-day ˈpeɪ deɪ
payee peɪˈiː
payload ˈpeɪləʊd
pay-master ˈpeɪ mɑːstə(r) $ mæstər
payment ˈpeɪmənt
pay-packet ˈpeɪ pækɪt
pay-roll ˈpeɪ rəʊl
pay-sheet ˈpeɪ ʃiːt
P.E. ˈpiː ˈiː
pea piː
peace piːs

peaceable ˈpiːsəbl
peaceful ˈpiːsfl
peacemaker ˈpiːsmeɪkə(r)
peace-offering ˈpiːs ofrɪŋ $ ɔfrɪŋ
peach piːtʃ
peacock ˈpiːkok with i short as in 'peak',
　　not as in 'pea'
peafowl ˈpiːfaʊl
pea-green ˈpiː ˈgriːn
peahen ˈpiːhen
peak piːk
peal piːl
peanut ˈpiːnʌt $ ˈpiːnət
pear peə(r)
pearl pɜːl
pearl-barley ˈpɜːl ˈbɑːlɪ $ ˈbɑːrlɪ
pearl-diver ˈpɜːl daɪvə(r)
pearl-fisher ˈpɜːl fɪʃə(r)
peasant ˈpeznt
pease-pudding ˈpiːz pʊdɪŋ
pea-shooter ˈpiː ʃuːtə(r)
pea-soup ˈpiː ˈsuːp
peat piːt
pebble ˈpebl
pecan prˈkæn $ prˈkɑːn ˈpiː- etc
peccable ˈpekəbl
peccadillo ˈpekəˈdɪləʊ
peccary ˈpekərɪ
peck pek
pectin ˈpektɪn
pectoral ˈpektərl
peculate ˈpekjʊleɪt
peculiar prˈkjuːlɪə(r)
peculiarity prˈkjuːlɪˈærətɪ
pecuniary prˈkjuːnɪərɪ $ -nɪerɪ
pedagogical ˈpedəˈgodʒɪkl -ˈgəʊdʒ-
pedagogue ˈpedəgog $ -gɔːg
pedagogy ˈpedəgodʒɪ -gəʊdʒɪ
pedal ˈpedl
pedant ˈpednt
pedantic prˈdæntɪk
peddle ˈpedl
pederasty ˈpedəræstɪ ˈpiːd-
pedestal ˈpedɪstl
pedestrian prˈdestrɪən
pediatrician ˈpiːdɪəˈtrɪʃn ˈped-
pediatrics ˈpiːdɪˈætrɪks ˈped-
pedicab ˈpedɪkæb
pedicure ˈpedɪkjʊə(r)
pedigree ˈpedɪgriː
pediment ˈpedɪmənt
pedlar ˈpedlə(r)
peek piːk

peel pil
peep pip
peep-hole ˈpip həʊl
peep-show ˈpip ʃəʊ
peer pɪə(r)
peerage ˈpɪərɪdʒ
peeress ˈpɪərəs -es -ɪs
peeved pivd
peevish ˈpivɪʃ
peewit ˈpiwɪt
peg peg
Pegasus ˈpegəsəs
Peggy ˈpegɪ
peignoir ˈpeɪnwɑ(r) $ peɪnˈwar
pejorative pɪˈdʒɒrətɪv ˈpidʒərətɪv
  $ ˈpidʒəreɪtɪv ˈpedʒ- etc
peke pik
Pekin ˈpiˈkɪn
pekinese ˈpikɪˈniz
Peking ˈpiˈkɪŋ $ ˈpikɪŋ
pekoe ˈpikəʊ
pelf pelf
pelican ˈpelɪkən
pellet ˈpelɪt -ət
pell-mell ˈpel ˈmel
pellucid peˈlusɪd £ -ˈlju-
pelmet ˈpelmɪt -mət
pelt pelt
pelvis ˈpelvɪs
Pembroke ˈpembrʊk -brəʊk
pemmican ˈpemɪkən
pen pen
penal ˈpinl
penalise ˈpinlaɪz $ ˈpen-
penalty ˈpenltɪ
penance ˈpenəns
pence pens
penchant ˈpõʃõ $ ˈpentʃənt
pencil ˈpensl
pendant ˈpendənt
pendent ˈpendənt
pending ˈpendɪŋ
pendulous ˈpendjʊləs $ ˈpendʒʊləs
pendulum ˈpendjʊləm $ ˈpendʒʊləm
Penelope pəˈneləpɪ
penetrable ˈpenɪtrəbl
penetrate ˈpenɪtreɪt
penetration ˈpenɪˈtreɪʃn
pen-friend ˈpen frend
penguin ˈpeŋgwɪn
penicillin ˈpenɪˈsɪlɪn
peninsula pəˈnɪnsjʊlə $ -ɪnsələ -ɪnʃələ
peninsular pəˈnɪnsjʊlə(r) $ -ɪnsə- -ɪnʃə-

penis ˈpinɪs
penitence ˈpenɪtəns
penitent ˈpenɪtənt
penitentiary ˈpenɪˈtenʃərɪ
pen-knife ˈpen naɪf
penmanship ˈpenmənʃɪp
pen-name ˈpen neɪm
pennant ˈpenənt
penniless ˈpenɪləs
pennon ˈpenən
penn'orth ˈpenəθ
Pennsylvania ˈpenslˈveɪnɪə
penny ˈpenɪ
pennyweight ˈpenɪweɪt
pennyworth ˈpenɪwɜθ £ ˈpenəθ
penology piˈnɒlədʒɪ
pen-pal ˈpen pæl
pen-pusher ˈpen pʊʃə(r)
pension ˈpenʃn
pension boarding-house ˈpõsɪõ
pensionable ˈpenʃnəbl
pensioner ˈpenʃənə(r)
pensive ˈpensɪv
pent pent
pentagon ˈpentəgən $ -gon
pentagonal penˈtægənl
pentameter penˈtæmɪtə(r)
Pentateuch ˈpentətjuk $ -tuk
pentathlon penˈtæθlən $ -lon
Pentecost ˈpentɪkost $ -kɔst etc
penthouse ˈpenthaʊs
penultimate penˈʌltɪmət
penumbra pɪnˈʌmbrə pen-
penurious pɪˈnjʊərɪəs peˈn- $ pɪˈnʊ-
penury ˈpenjʊrɪ
peon ˈpiən of India: pjun
peony ˈpiənɪ
people ˈpipl
pep pep
pepper ˈpepə(r)
pepper-and-salt ˈpepər ən ˈsɔlt
peppercorn ˈpepəkən $ ˈpepərkɔrn
pepper-mill ˈpepə mɪl $ ˈpepər
peppermint ˈpepəmɪnt $ ˈpepər-
pepper-pot ˈpepə pot $ ˈpepər
pepsin ˈpepsɪn
pep-talk ˈpep tɔk
Pepys pips
per pɜ(r)
peradventure ˈperədˈventʃə(r) $ £ ˈpɜr-
perambulate pəˈræmbjʊleɪt
perambulator pəˈræmbjʊleɪtə(r)
perceive pəˈsiv $ pər-

percent pəˋsent $ pər-
percentage pəˋsentɪdʒ $ pər-
perceptible pəˋseptəbl $ pər-
perception pəˋsepʃn $ pər-
perceptive pəˋseptɪv $ pər-
perch pɜtʃ
perchance pəˋtʃɑns $ pərˋtʃæns
percipient pəˋsɪpɪənt $ pər-
percolate ˋpɜkəleɪt
percolator ˋpɜkəleɪtə(r)
percussion pəˋkʌʃn $ pər-
percussion cap pəˋkʌʃn kæp $ pər-
Percy ˋpɜsɪ
perdition pəˋdɪʃn $ pər-
peregrination ˌperəgrɪˋneɪʃn
peremptory pəˋremptərɪ ˋperəmptərɪ
   $ ˋperəm̃ptərɪ
perennial pəˋrenɪəl
perfect adj ˋpɜfɪkt
perfect v pəˋfekt $ pər-
perfection pəˋfekʃn $ pər-
perfectionist pəˋfekʃn̩ɪst $ pər-
perfidious pəˋfɪdɪəs $ pər-
perfidy ˋpɜfɪdɪ
perforate ˋpɜfəreɪt
perforation ˌpɜfəˋreɪʃn
perforce pəˋfɔs $ pəˋfɔrs
perform pəˋfɔm $ pərˋfɔrm pəˋf-
performance pəˋfɔmən s $ pərˋfɔrm- pəˋf-
perfume n ˋpɜfjum $ pərˋfjum
perfume v pəˋfjum $ pər- $ £ ˋpɜfjum
perfumer pəˋfjumə(r) $ pərˋfjumər
perfunctory pəˋfʌŋktərɪ $ pər-
pergola ˋpɜgələ
perhaps pəˋhæps præps
   $ pərˋhæps pəˋræps præps
peri ˋpɪərɪ
peri- prefix perɪ
Pericles ˋperɪkliz
perihelion ˌperɪˋhilɪən
peril ˋperl
perilous ˋperl̩əs
perimeter pəˋrɪmɪtə(r)
period ˋpɪərɪəd
periodical ˌpɪərɪˋodɪkl
peripatetic ˌperɪpəˋtetɪk
periphery pəˋrɪfərɪ
periphrasis pəˋrɪfrəsɪs
periphrastic ˌperɪˋfræstɪk
periscope ˋperɪskəʊp
perish ˋperɪʃ
peristyle ˋperɪstaɪl
peritonitis ˌperɪtəˋnaɪtɪs -təs

periwig ˋperɪwɪg
periwinkle ˋperɪwɪŋkl
perjure ˋpɜdʒə(r)
perjurer ˋpɜdʒərə(r)
perjury ˋpɜdʒərɪ
perk pɜk
perm pɜm
permanence ˋpɜmənəns
permanent ˋpɜmənənt
permanganate pəˋmæŋgəneɪt $ pər-
permeate ˋpɜmɪeɪt
permeation ˌpɜmɪˋeɪʃn
permeable ˋpɜmɪəbl
permissible pəˋmɪsəbl $ pər-
permission pəˋmɪʃn $ pər-
permissive pəˋmɪsɪv $ pər-
permissive society, the
   ðə pəˈmɪsɪv səˋsaɪətɪ $ pər-
permit n ˋpɜmɪt $ pərˋmɪt
permit v pəˋmɪt $ pər-
permutation ˌpɜmjʊˋteɪʃn
pernicious pəˋnɪʃəs $ pər-
pernickety pəˋnɪkətɪ $ pər-
peroration ˌperəˋreɪʃn
peroxide pəˋroksaɪd
perpendicular ˌpɜpənˋdɪkjʊlə(r)
perpetrate ˋpɜpɪtreɪt
perpetration ˌpɜpɪˋtreɪʃn
perpetrator ˋpɜpɪtreɪtə(r)
perpetual pəˋpetʃʊəl $ pər-
perpetuate pəˋpetʃʊeɪt $ pər-
perpetuity ˌpɜpɪˋtjuətɪ $ -ˋtuətɪ
perplex pəˋpleks $ pər-
perlexity pəˋpleksətɪ $ pər-
perquisite ˋpɜkwɪzɪt
perry ˋperɪ
persecute ˋpɜsɪkjut
persecution ˌpɜsɪˋkjuʃn
persecutor ˋpɜsɪkjutə(r)
perseverance ˌpɜsɪˋvɪərəns
persevere ˌpɜsɪˋvɪə(r)
Persia ˋpɜʃə $ £ ˋpɜʒə etc
Persian ˋpɜʃn $ £ ˋpɜʒn etc
persist pəˋsɪst $ pər-
persistence pəˋsɪstəns $ pər-
persistent pəˋsɪstənt $ pər-
person ˋpɜsn
personable ˋpɜsnəbl
personage ˋpɜsn̩ɪdʒ
personal ˋpɜsnl
personality ˌpɜsəˋnælətɪ -sn̩ˋæ-
personification pəˈsonɪfɪˋkeɪʃn $ pər-
personify pəˋsonɪfaɪ $ pər-

personnel ˈpɜːsəˈnel ˈpɜːsn̩ˈel
perspective pəˈspektɪv $ pər-
perspex ˈpɜːspeks
perspicacious ˈpɜːspɪˈkeɪʃəs
perspicacity ˈpɜːspɪˈkæsətɪ
perspicuity ˈpɜːspɪˈkjuːətɪ
perspicuous pəˈspɪkjuəs $ pər-
perspiration ˈpɜːspəˈreɪʃn
perspire pəˈspaɪə(r) $ pər-
persuade pəˈsweɪd $ pər-
persuasion pəˈsweɪʒn $ pər-
persuasive pəˈsweɪsɪv -zɪv $ pər-
pert pɜːt
pertain pəˈteɪn $ pər-
Perth pɜːθ
pertinacious ˈpɜːtɪˈneɪʃəs $ -tn̩ˈeɪʃəs
pertinacity ˈpɜːtɪˈnæsətɪ
pertinence ˈpɜːtɪnəns $ ˈpɜːtn̩əns
pertinent ˈpɜːtɪnənt $ ˈpɜːtn̩ənt
perturb pəˈtɜːb $ pər-
perturbation ˈpɜːtəˈbeɪʃn $ -tərˈb-
Peru pəˈruː
peruke pəˈruːk
perusal pəˈruːzl
peruse pəˈruːz
Peruvian pəˈruːvɪən
pervade pəˈveɪd $ pər-
pervasion pəˈveɪʒn $ pər-
pervasive pəˈveɪsɪv -zɪv $ pər-
perverse pəˈvɜːs pɜː- $ pər-
perversion pəˈvɜːʃn pɜː- $ pər- $ £ -ˈvɜːʒn
perversity pəˈvɜːsətɪ pɜː- $ pər-
pervert n ˈpɜːvɜːt
pervert v pəˈvɜːt pɜː- $ pər-
pervious ˈpɜːvɪəs
peseta pəˈseɪtə pəˈseɪtə
peso ˈpeɪsəʊ
pessimism ˈpesɪmɪzm ˈpezɪm-
pessimist ˈpesɪmɪst ˈpezɪ-
pessimistic ˈpesɪˈmɪstɪk ˈpezɪ-
pest pest
pester ˈpestə(r)
pesticide ˈpestɪsaɪd
pestiferous peˈstɪfərəs
pestilence ˈpestɪləns
pestilential ˈpestɪˈlenʃl
pestle ˈpesl ˈpestl
pet pet
petal ˈpetl
petard peˈtɑːd $ peˈtɑːrd
Peter ˈpiːtə(r)
Peterborough ˈpiːtəbərə $ ˈpiːtər- -bɜːəʊ
petersham ˈpiːtəʃəm $ ˈpiːtərʃəm

petite pəˈtiːt
petition prˈtɪʃn
Petrarch ˈpetrɑːk $ ˈpiːtrɑːrk
petrel ˈpetrl
petrifaction ˈpetrɪˈfækʃn
petrify ˈpetrɪfaɪ
petrol ˈpetrl $ ˈpetrol
petroleum prˈtrəʊlɪəm
petticoat ˈpetɪkəʊt
pettifogging ˈpetɪfogɪŋ
pettish ˈpetɪʃ
petty ˈpetɪ
Petula pəˈtjuːlə $ -ˈtu-
petulance ˈpetjʊləns $ -tʃəl-
petulant ˈpetjʊlənt $ -tʃəl-
petunia prˈtjuːnɪə $ -ˈtun-
Peugeot ˈpɜːʒəʊ $ pɜːˈʒəʊ this ʒ may
   have no r quality
pew pjuː
pewit piwɪt
pewter ˈpjuːtə(r)
phaeton ˈfeɪtn $ ˈfeɪətən
phagocyte ˈfægəsaɪt
phalanx ˈfælæŋks $ ˈfeɪlæŋks
phallic ˈfælɪk
phallus ˈfæləs
phantasm ˈfæntæzm
phantasmagoria ˈfæntæzməˈgɔːrɪə
phantasmal fænˈtæzml
phantasy ˈfæntəsɪ -əzɪ
phantom ˈfæntəm
Pharaoh ˈfeərəʊ
pharisaical ˈfærɪˈseɪɪkl -ˈzeɪ-
Pharisee ˈfærɪsiː
pharmaceutical ˈfɑːməˈsjuːtɪkl -ˈsuːt-
   -ˈkjuːt- $ ˈfɑːrməˈsuːtɪkl
pharmacist ˈfɑːməsɪst $ ˈfɑːrm-
pharmacologist ˈfɑːməˈkɒlədʒɪst $ ˈfɑːr-
pharmacology ˈfɑːməˈkɒlədʒɪ $ ˈfɑːrmə-
pharmacopoeia ˈfɑːməkəˈpiːə $ ˈfɑːrmə-
pharmacy ˈfɑːməsɪ $ ˈfɑːrməsɪ
pharyngitis ˈfærɪnˈdʒaɪtɪs -təs
pharynx ˈfærɪŋks
phase feɪz
Ph.D. ˈpiː eɪtʃ ˈdiː
pheasant ˈfeznt
phenobarbitone ˈfiːnəʊˈbɑːbɪtəʊn $ -ˈbɑːr-
phenomena frˈnɒmɪnə
phenomenal frˈnɒmɪnl
phenomenon frˈnɒmɪnən $ -non
phew fjuː realistically a 'puffing' noise
phi faɪ
phial ˈfaɪəl

Philadelphia ˈfɪləˈdelfɪə
philander fɪˈlændə(r)
philanthropic ˈfɪlənˈθrɒpɪk
philanthropist fɪˈlænθrəpɪst
philanthropy fɪˈlænθrəpɪ
philatelist fɪˈlætəlɪst
philately fɪˈlætəlɪ
philharmonic ˈfɪləˈmɒnɪk
$ -lər- -lar- -lhar-
philhellenic ˈfɪlheˈlinɪk
Philip ˈfɪlɪp
Philippines ˈfɪlɪpinz
philistine ˈfɪlɪstaɪn $ -stɪn -stin *etc*
philological ˈfɪləˈlɒdʒɪkl
philologist fɪˈlɒlədʒɪst
philology fɪˈlɒlədʒɪ
philosopher fɪˈlɒsəfə(r)
philosophical ˈfɪləˈsɒfɪkl
philosophize fɪˈlɒsəfaɪz
philosophy fɪˈlɒsəfɪ
philtre($ -er) ˈfɪltə(r)
phlebitis flɪˈbaɪtɪs -təs
phlegm flem
phlegmatic flegˈmætɪk
phlox flɒks
phobia ˈfəʊbɪə
-phobia *suffix* fəʊbɪə
Phoebe ˈfibɪ
Phoenician fɪˈnɪʃn
phoenix, P– ˈfinɪks
phone fəʊn
phoneme ˈfəʊnim
phonemic fəˈnimɪk fəʊ-
phonetic fəˈnetɪk fəʊ-
phonetician ˈfəʊnɪˈtɪʃn
phoney ˈfəʊnɪ
phonic ˈfəʊnɪk ˈfɒnɪk
phonograph ˈfəʊnəgrɑf $ -græf
phonology fəˈnɒlədʒɪ
phosphate ˈfɒsfeɪt
phosphorescent ˈfɒsfəˈresnt
phosphoric fosˈfɒrɪk
phosphorous ˈfɒsfərəs
phosphorus ˈfɒsfərəs
photo ˈfəʊtəʊ
photocopy ˈfəʊtəʊkɒpɪ
photo-electric ˈfəʊtəʊ ɪˈlektrɪk
photofinish ˈfəʊtəʊˈfɪnɪʃ
photogenic ˈfəʊtəˈdʒenɪk -dʒin-
photograph ˈfəʊtəgrɑf $ £ -græf
photographer fəˈtɒgrəfə(r)
photographic ˈfəʊtəˈgræfɪk
photography fəˈtɒgrəfɪ

photogravure ˈfəʊtəgrəˈvjʊə(r)
photostat ˈfəʊtəstæt
phrasal ˈfreɪzl
phrase freɪz
phrase-book ˈfreɪz bʊk
phraseology ˈfreɪzɪˈɒlədʒɪ
phrenetic frɪˈnetɪk
phrenology frɪˈnɒlədʒɪ
phthisis ˈθaɪsɪs ˈtaɪsɪs ˈfθaɪsɪs
phut fʌt
Phyllis ˈfɪlɪs
physic ˈfɪzɪk
physical ˈfɪzɪkl
physician fɪˈzɪʃn
physicist ˈfɪzɪsɪst
physiognomy ˈfɪzɪˈɒnəmɪ $ -ˈɒgn- *etc*
physiological ˈfɪzɪəˈlɒdʒɪkl
physiologist ˈfɪzɪˈɒlədʒɪst
physiology ˈfɪzɪˈɒlədʒɪ
physiotherapist ˈfɪzɪəʊˈθerəpɪst
physiotherapy ˈfɪzɪəʊˈθerəpɪ
physique fɪˈzik
pi (π) paɪ
pianissimo pɪəˈnɪsɪməʊ
pianist ˈpɪənɪst pɪˈænɪst
piano *adj* pɪˈɑnəʊ
piano *n* pɪˈænəʊ
pianoforte pɪˈænəʊˈfɔtɪ -teɪ
$ pɪˈænəfɔrt pɪˈænəˈf- -tɪ -teɪ
pianola pɪəˈnəʊlə
piastre(-ter) pɪˈæstə(r)
piazza pɪˈætsə $ pɪˈæzə
of Italy: pɪˈætsə
picador ˈpɪkədɔ(r)
picaresque ˈpɪkəˈresk
Picasso pɪˈkæsəʊ
Piccadilly ˈpɪkəˈdɪlɪ
piccalilli ˈpɪkəˈlɪlɪ ˈpɪkəlɪlɪ
piccaninny ˈpɪkəˈnɪnɪ
piccolo ˈpɪkələʊ
pick pɪk
pick-a-back ˈpɪk ə bæk
pickaxe ˈpɪkæks
picket ˈpɪkɪt
pickle ˈpɪkl
pick-me-up ˈpɪk mɪ ʌp
pickpocket ˈpɪkpokɪt
Pickwick ˈpɪkwɪk
picnic ˈpɪknɪk
picnicker ˈpɪknɪkə(r)
pictorial pɪkˈtɔrɪəl
picture ˈpɪktʃə(r)
picture-book ˈpɪktʃə bʊk $ ˈpɪktʃər

picture-gallery ˈpɪktʃə gælərɪ $ -tʃər
picturesque ˌpɪktʃəˈresk
piddle ˈpɪdl
piddling ˈpɪd‖ɪŋ
pidgin ˈpɪdʒən £ -dʒɪn
pie paɪ
piebald ˈpaɪbɔld
piece pis
piecemeal ˈpismil
piece-work ˈpis wɜk
pie-crust ˈpaɪ krʌst
pied paɪd
pied à terre pɪˈeɪd ɑ ˈteə(r) ˈpjeɪd
pier pɪə(r)
pierce pɪəs $ pɪərs
piercing ˈpɪəsɪŋ $ ˈpɪərsɪŋ
pierrot ˈpɪərəʊ $ pɪəˈrəʊ
pietà ˌpɪeɪˈta pjeɪˈta
piety ˈpaɪətɪ
piffling ˈpɪf‖ɪŋ
pig pɪg
pigeon ˈpɪdʒən £ ˈpɪdʒɪn
pigeon-chested ˌpɪdʒən ˈtʃestɪd £ -dʒɪn
pigeon-hole ˈpɪdʒən həʊl £ -dʒɪn
pigeon-toed ˈpɪdʒən ˈtəʊd £ -dʒɪn
piggery ˈpɪgərɪ
piggish ˈpɪgɪʃ
pig-headed ˈpɪg ˈhedɪd
pig-iron ˈpɪg aɪən $ aɪərn
pigment ˈpɪgmənt
pigmy ˈpɪgmɪ
pigskin ˈpɪgskɪn
pigsty ˈpɪgstaɪ
pigtail ˈpɪgteɪl
pike paɪk
pikestaff ˈpaɪkstaf $ -stæf
pilaff pɪˈlæf ˈpɪlæf $ pɪˈlaf pi- etc
pilaster pɪˈlæstə(r)
pilau pɪˈlaʊ pɪˈla-ʊ
pilchard ˈpɪltʃəd $ ˈpɪltʃərd
pile paɪl
pile-driver ˈpaɪl draɪvə(r)
pilfer ˈpɪlfə(r)
pilgrim ˈpɪlgrɪm
pilgrimage ˈpɪlgrɪmɪdʒ
pill pɪl
pillage ˈpɪlɪdʒ
pillar ˈpɪlə(r)
pillar-box ˈpɪlə boks $ ˈpɪlər
pillion ˈpɪlɪən
pillory ˈpɪlərɪ
pillow ˈpɪləʊ
pillow-case ˈpɪləʊ keɪs

pillow-slip ˈpɪləʊ slɪp
pilot ˈpaɪlət
pilot-light ˈpaɪlət laɪt
Pilot Officer ˈpaɪlət ofɪsə(r) $ ɔf-
pimento pɪˈmentəʊ
pimp pɪmp
pimpernel ˈpɪmpənel -nl $ -pərn-
pimple ˈpɪmpl
pin pɪn
pinafore ˈpɪnəfɔ(r)
pince-nez ˈpæs neɪ ˈpæs ˈneɪ
    $ £ ˈpæns neɪ ˈp- ˈneɪ ˈpɪns etc
pincers ˈpɪnsəz $ ˈpɪnsərz
pinch pɪntʃ
pinchbeck ˈpɪntʃbek
pincushion ˈpɪnkʊʃn -ʃɪn
pine paɪn
pineapple ˈpaɪnæpl
ping pɪŋ
ping-pong ˈpɪŋ poŋ
pinion ˈpɪnɪən
pink pɪŋk
pin-money ˈpɪn mʌnɪ
pinnacle ˈpɪnəkl ˈpɪnɪkl
pinnate ˈpɪneɪt -ət
pinny ˈpɪnɪ
pin-point ˈpɪn pɔɪnt
pin-prick ˈpɪn prɪk
pint paɪnt
pin-table ˈpɪn teɪbl
pin-up ˈpɪn ʌp
pioneer ˌpaɪəˈnɪə(r)
pious ˈpaɪəs
pip pɪp
pipe paɪp
pipeclay ˈpaɪpkleɪ
pipe-dream ˈpaɪp drim
pipette pɪˈpet
pipe-rack ˈpaɪp ræk
pippin ˈpɪpɪn
pip-squeak ˈpɪp skwik
piquancy ˈpikənsɪ
piquant ˈpikənt
pique pik
piqué ˈpikeɪ $ pɪˈkeɪ
piquet pɪˈket
piracy ˈpaɪərəsɪ
pirate ˈpaɪərət -rɪt
piratical ˌpaɪəˈrætɪkl
pirouette ˌpɪrʊˈet
Pisa ˈpizə
piscatorial ˌpɪskəˈtɔrɪəl
Pisces ˈpaɪsiz

pish pɪʃ
pistachio pɪˈstatʃɪəʊ $ £ -æʃɪəʊ -aʃ-
pistil ˈpɪstl
pistol ˈpɪstl
piston ˈpɪstən
pit pɪt
pit-a-pat ˈpɪt ə ˈpæt
pitch pɪtʃ
pitch-and-toss ˈpɪtʃ ən ˈtos $ ˈtɔs etc
pitch-black ˈpɪtʃ ˈblæk
pitchblende ˈpɪtʃblend
pitch dark ˈpɪtʃ ˈdak $ ˈdark
pitcher ˈpɪtʃə(r)
pitch pine ˈpɪtʃ paɪn
piteous ˈpɪtɪəs
pitfall ˈpɪtfɔl
pith pɪθ
pitiable ˈpɪtɪəbl
pitiful ˈpɪtɪfl
pitiless ˈpɪtɪləs
pit pony ˈpɪt pəʊnɪ
pittance ˈpɪtns
Pittsburg(h) ˈpɪtsbəg
pituitary pɪˈtjuətərɪ $ pɪˈtuəterɪ
pity ˈpɪtɪ
pivot ˈpɪvət
pivotal ˈpɪvətl
pixie ˈpɪksɪ
pixilated ˈpɪksɪleɪtɪd
pizza ˈpitsə
pizzicato ˈpɪtsɪˈkatəʊ
placard ˈplækad $ -kard
placate pləˈkeɪt $ ˈpleɪkeɪt ˈplæk-
place pleɪs
place-bet ˈpleɪs bet
place-kick ˈpleɪs kɪk
placid ˈplæsɪd
placket ˈplækɪt
plagiarism ˈpleɪdʒərɪzm
plagiarist ˈpleɪdʒərɪst
plagiarize ˈpleɪdʒəraɪz
plague pleɪg
plaice pleɪs
plaid plæd
plain pleɪn
plainsong ˈpleɪnsoŋ $ -sɔŋ
plain-spoken ˈpleɪn ˈspəʊkən
plaint pleɪnt
plaintiff ˈpleɪntɪf
plaintive ˈpleɪntɪv
plait plæt $ pleɪt
plan plæn
planchette plɔˈʃet plonˈʃet $ plænˈʃet

plane pleɪn
planet ˈplænɪt
planetarium ˈplænɪˈteərɪəm
plane-tree ˈpleɪn tri
plangent ˈplændʒənt
plank plæŋk
plankton ˈplæŋktən -ton
plant plant $ plænt
plantain ˈplæntɪn £ ˈplan- -teɪn
plantation plænˈteɪʃn £ plan-
plaque plak $ £ plæk
plash plæʃ
plasma ˈplæzmə
plaster ˈplastə(r) $ ˈplæstər
plasterboard ˈplastəbɔd $ ˈplæstərbɔrd
plaster-cast ˈplastə kast $ ˈplæstər kæst
plastic ˈplæstɪk £ plastɪk
plasticine ˈplæstɪsin £ ˈplas-
plasticity plæˈstɪsətɪ £ plaˈs-
plate pleɪt
plateau ˈplætəʊ $ plæˈtəʊ
plateaux ˈplætəʊz $ plæˈtəʊz
plate-glass ˈpleɪt ˈglas $ ˈglæs
plate-layer ˈpleɪt leɪə(r)
plate-rack ˈpleɪt ræk
platform ˈplætfəm $ -fɔrm
platinum ˈplætɪnəm -tɪn-
platitude ˈplætɪtjud -tʃud $ -tud
platitudinous ˈplætɪˈtjudɪnəs $ -ˈtudn̩əs
Plato ˈpleɪtəʊ
Platonic pləˈtonɪk
platoon pləˈtun
platter ˈplætə(r)
platypus ˈplætɪpəs
plaudit ˈplɔdɪt
plausible ˈplɔzəbl
play pleɪ
play-acting ˈpleɪ æktɪŋ
play-back ˈpleɪ bæk
playbill ˈpleɪbɪl
play-boy ˈpleɪ bɔɪ
playfellow ˈpleɪ-feləʊ
playgoer ˈpleɪgəʊə(r)
playground ˈpleɪgraʊnd
playhouse ˈpleɪhaʊs
playing-field ˈpleɪŋ fild
playlet ˈpleɪlət
playmate ˈpleɪmeɪt
play-pen ˈpleɪ pen
plaything ˈpleɪ-θɪŋ
play-time ˈpleɪ taɪm
playwright ˈpleɪraɪt
plaza ˈplazə $ ˈplæzə etc

plea pli
pleach plitʃ
plead plid
pleasant `pleznt
pleasantry `plezntrɪ
please pliz
pleasurable `pleʒrəbl
pleasure `pleʒə(r) $ `pleɪʒər
pleat plit
pleb pleb
plebeian plɪ`biən
plebiscite `plebɪsɪt $ £ -saɪt
plectrum `plektrəm
pledge pledʒ
plenary `plinərɪ
plenipotentiary 'plenɪpə`tenʃərɪ
plenteous `plentɪəs
plentiful `plentɪfl
plentitude `plentɪtjud $ -tud
plenty `plentɪ
pleonasm `plɪənæzm
plethora `pleθərə
pleurisy `plʊərɪsɪ
plexus `pleksəs
pliability 'plaɪə`bɪlətɪ
pliable `plaɪəbl
pliant `plaɪənt
pliers `plaɪəz $ `plaɪərz
plight plaɪt
plimsoll `plɪmsl $ -sol -səl
plinth plɪnθ
plod plod
plonk ploŋk
plop plop
plosive `pləʊsɪv `pləʊzɪv
plot plot
plough plaʊ
plough-boy `plaʊ bɔɪ
ploughman `plaʊmən
ploughshare `plaʊ-ʃeə(r)
plover `plʌvə(r) $ `pləʊvər
plow plaʊ
ploy plɔɪ
pluck plʌk
plug plʌg
plum plʌm
plumage `plumɪdʒ
plumb plʌm
plumbago plʌm`beɪgəʊ
plumber `plʌmə(r)
plumbing `plʌmɪŋ
plumb-line `plʌm laɪn
plume plum

plummet `plʌmɪt
plummy `plʌmɪ
plump plʌmp
plum(-)pudding 'plʌm `pʊdɪŋ
plunder `plʌndə(r)
plunge plʌndʒ
pluperfect 'plu`pəfɪkt
plural `plʊərl
plurality plʊə`rælətɪ
plus plʌs
plus-fours 'plʌs `fɔz $ `fɔrz
plush plʌʃ
plutocracy plu`tokrəsɪ
plutocrat `plutəkræt
plutocratic 'plutə`krætɪk
plutonium plu`təʊnɪəm
ply plaɪ
Plymouth `plɪməθ
plywood `plaɪwʊd
p.m. 'pi `em
pneumatic nju`mætɪk $ nu- etc
pneumonia nju`məʊnɪə $ nu- etc
poach pəʊtʃ
pock pok
pock-marked `pok makt $ markt
pocket `pokɪt
pocket-book `pokɪt bʊk
pocket-handkerchief 'pokɪt `hæŋkətʃɪf
    -tʃif $ -kərtʃɪf
pocket-knife `pokɪt naɪf
pocket-money `pokɪt mʌnɪ
pod pod
podgy `podʒɪ
podium `pəʊdɪəm
poem `pəʊɪm
poet `pəʊɪt
poetess `pəʊɪtes -ɪs 'pəʊɪ`tes
poetic pəʊ`etɪk
poetry `pəʊɪtrɪ
pogrom `pogrəm -rom
poignancy `pɔɪnjənsɪ `pɔɪnənsɪ
poignant `pɔɪnjənt `pɔɪnənt
poinsettia pɔɪn`setɪə
point pɔɪnt
point-blank 'pɔɪnt `blæŋk
point-duty `pɔɪnt djutɪ $ dutɪ
pointsman `pɔɪntsmən
point-to-point 'pɔɪnt tə `pɔɪnt
poise pɔɪz
poison `pɔɪzn
poison-gas 'pɔɪzn `gæs
poison-ivy 'pɔɪzn `aɪvɪ
poisonous `pɔɪznəs

poke pəʊk
poker ˈpəʊkə(r)
poker-face ˈpəʊkə feɪs $ ˈpəʊkər
poky ˈpəʊkɪ
Poland ˈpəʊlənd
polar ˈpəʊlə(r)
Polaris pəʊˈlɑːrɪs -ˈlærɪs pəˈl- $ -ˈleərɪs
polarity pəˈlærətɪ pəʊ-
pole, P– pəʊl
pole-axe ˈpəʊlæks
polecat ˈpəʊlkæt
polemic pəˈlemɪk pəʊ-
pole-star ˈpəʊl stɑː(r)
pole-vault ˈpəʊl vɔlt £ volt
police pəˈlis
police constable pəˈlis ˈkʌnstəbl $ ˈkɒn-
police-court pəˈlis kɔt $ kɔrt
policeman pəˈlismən ˈplismən
police-officer pəˈlis ɒfɪsə(r) $ ɔf-
police-station pəˈlis steɪʃn
policy ˈpɒləsɪ
polio ˈpəʊlɪəʊ
polio-myelitis ˈpəʊlɪəʊ ˈmaɪəˈlaɪtɪs -təs
polish ˈpɒlɪʃ
Polish ˈpəʊlɪʃ
polite pəˈlaɪt
politic ˈpɒlətɪk
political pəˈlɪtɪkl
politician ˈpɒləˈtɪʃn
polka ˈpɒlkə $ £ ˈpəʊlkə ˈpəʊkə
poll pəʊl
pollen ˈpɒlən
pollinate ˈpɒlɪneɪt
pollination ˈpɒlɪˈneɪʃn
polling-booth ˈpəʊlɪŋ buð $ £ buθ
polling-day ˈpəʊlɪŋ deɪ
polling-station ˈpəʊlɪŋ steɪʃn
pollster ˈpəʊlstə(r)
poll-tax ˈpəʊl tæks
pollute pəˈlut £ -ˈljut
pollution pəˈluʃn £ -ˈljuʃn
polo ˈpəʊləʊ
polonaise ˈpɒləˈneɪz
polony pəˈləʊnɪ
polyandrous ˈpɒlɪˈændrəs
polyandry ˈpɒlɪændrɪ
polyanthus ˈpɒlɪˈænθəs
polygamist pəˈlɪgəmɪst
polygamous pəˈlɪgəməs
polygamy pəˈlɪgəmɪ
polyglot ˈpɒlɪglot
polygon ˈpɒlɪgən $ -gon
Polynesia ˈpɒlɪˈnizɪə $ £ -iʒə -iʃə

polyphonic ˈpɒlɪˈfonɪk
polyphony pəˈlɪfənɪ
polypus ˈpɒlɪpəs
polysyllabic ˈpɒlɪsɪˈlæbɪk
polytechnic ˈpɒlɪˈteknɪk
polytheism ˈpɒlɪˈθiɪzm
polythene ˈpɒlɪθin
pomade pəˈmad $ pəʊˈmeɪd
pomegranate ˈpomɪgrænət -mg-
Pomeranian ˈpoməˈreɪnɪən
pommel ˈpʌml
pomp pomp
Pompeii pomˈpeɪi £ ˈpompɪaɪ pomˈpiaɪ
pompom ˈpompom
pompon ˈpõpõ $ £ ˈpompon
pomposity pomˈposətɪ
pompous ˈpompəs
ponce pons
poncho ˈpontʃəʊ
pond pond
ponder ˈpondə(r)
ponderous ˈpondərəs
pontiff ˈpontɪf
pontifical ponˈtɪfɪkl
pontificate ponˈtɪfɪkeɪt
Pontius Pilate ˈponʃəs ˈpaɪlət
pontoon ponˈtun
pony ˈpəʊnɪ
pony-tail ˈpəʊnɪ teɪl
poodle ˈpudl
pooh pu
pooh-pooh pu ˈpu
pool pul
pool-room ˈpul rom $ £ rum
poop pup
poor pʊə(r)
poor-house ˈpʊə haus ˈpɔ $ ˈpʊər
poorly ˈpʊəlɪ ˈpɔlɪ $ ˈpʊərlɪ
pop pop
Pope pəʊp
popgun ˈpopgʌn
popinjay ˈpopɪndʒeɪ
poplar ˈpoplə(r)
poplin ˈpoplɪn
pop-music ˈpop mjuzɪk
poppa ˈpopə
poppers ˈpopəz $ ˈpopərz
poppet ˈpopɪt
poppy ˈpopɪ
poppycock ˈpopɪkok
pop-star ˈpop stɑː(r)
popsy ˈpopsɪ
populace ˈpopjʊləs

popular ˈpɒpjʊlə(r)
popularity ˌpɒpjʊˈlærətɪ
popularize ˈpɒpjʊləraɪz
populate ˈpɒpjʊleɪt
population ˌpɒpjʊˈleɪʃn
populous ˈpɒpjʊləs
porcelain ˈpɒslɪn -lem $ ˈpɔrs-
porch pɔtʃ $ pɔrtʃ
porcupine ˈpɒkjʊpaɪn $ ˈpɔr-
pore pɔ(r)
pork pɔk $ pɔrk
pornographic ˌpɒnəˈgræfɪk $ ˌpɔrnə-
pornography pɔˈnɒgrəfɪ $ pɔr-
porous ˈpɔrəs
porpoise ˈpɔpəs $ ˈpɔrpəs
porridge ˈpɒrɪdʒ $ ˈpɔr- etc
porringer ˈpɒrɪndʒə(r) $ ˈpɔr- etc
Porsche ˈpɔʃə $ ˈpɔrʃə
port pɔt $ pɔrt
portable ˈpɔtəbl $ ˈpɔrt-
portage ˈpɔtɪdʒ $ ˈpɔrt-
portal ˈpɔtl $ ˈpɔrtl
portcullis pɔtˈkʌlɪs $ pɔrt-
portend pɔˈtend $ pɔr-
portent ˈpɔtent $ pɔr-
portentous pɔˈtentəs $ pɔr-
porter ˈpɔtə(r) $ ˈpɔrtər
porterhouse ˈpɔtəhaʊs $ ˈpɔrtər-
portfolio pɔtˈfəʊlɪəʊ $ ˈpɔrt-
porthole ˈpɔthəʊl $ ˈpɔrt-
portico ˈpɔtɪkəʊ $ ˈpɔrt-
portion ˈpɔʃn $ ˈpɔrʃn
Portland ˈpɔtlənd $ ˈpɔrt-
portly ˈpɔtlɪ $ ˈpɔrtlɪ
portmanteau pɔtˈmæntəʊ $ pɔrt-
portrait ˈpɔtrɪt -ət -eɪt $ ˈpɔrt-
portraiture ˈpɔtrɪtʃə(r) $ ˈpɔrt-
portray pɔˈtreɪ $ pɔr-
Portsmouth ˈpɔtsməθ $ ˈpɔrts-
Portugal ˈpɔtʃʊgl $ ˈpɔrtʃ-
Portuguese ˌpɔtʃʊˈgiz $ ˈpɔrtʃ-
pose pəʊz
poseur pəʊˈzɜ(r)
posh pɒʃ
position pəˈzɪʃn
positive ˈpɒzətɪv
posse ˈpɒsɪ
possess pəˈzes
possession pəˈzeʃn
possessive pəˈzesɪv
possessor pəˈzesə(r)
posset ˈpɒsɪt
possibility ˌpɒsəˈbɪlətɪ

possible ˈpɒsəbl
possum ˈpɒsəm
post pəʊst
post- prefix pəʊst
postage ˈpəʊstɪdʒ
postage stamp ˈpəʊstɪdʒ stæmp
postal ˈpəʊstl
postal order ˈpəʊstl ɔdə(r) $ ɔrdər
post-bag ˈpəʊstbæg
postcard ˈpəʊskad $ -kard
post-date ˌpəʊst ˈdeɪt
poster ˈpəʊstə(r)
poste restante ˌpəʊst ˈrestɒt -tɔ̃t -tɔnt
    $ reˈstant
posterior pɒˈstɪərɪə(r)
posterity pɒˈsterətɪ
postern ˈpɒstən ˈpəʊs- $ -tərn
post-free ˌpəʊst ˈfri
post-graduate pəʊstˈgrædʒʊət
post-haste pəʊstˈheɪst
posthumous ˈpɒstjʊməs $ -tʃʊ-
postil(l)ion pɒˈstɪlɪən pəˈst- pəʊˈst-
postman ˈpəʊsmən -stmən
postmark ˈpəʊstmak $ -mark
postmaster ˈpəʊstmastə(r) $ -mæstər
postmistress ˈpəʊstmɪstrəs
post mortem pəʊst ˈmɔtəm -em $ ˈmɔrt-
post office ˈpəʊst ɒfɪs $ ɔfɪs
post-paid ˌpəʊst ˈpeɪd
postpone pəˈspəʊn pəʊˈspəʊn
postprandial pəʊstˈprændɪəl
postscript ˈpəʊsskrɪpt
postulate n ˈpɒstʃʊlət -eɪt
postulate v ˈpɒstʃʊleɪt
posture ˈpɒstʃə(r)
post-war ˌpəʊst ˈwɔ(r)
posy ˈpəʊzɪ
pot pɒt
potash ˈpɒtæʃ
potassium pəˈtæsɪəm
potato pəˈteɪtəʊ $ pəˈteɪtə
pot-bellied ˌpɒt ˈbelɪd
pot-boiler ˌpɒt ˈbɔɪlə(r)
potency ˈpəʊtnsɪ
potent ˈpəʊtnt
potentate ˈpəʊtnteɪt
potential pəˈtenʃl
pot-hole ˈpɒt həʊl
potion ˈpəʊʃn
pot-pourri pəʊ ˈpʊərɪ $ ˈpəʊpəˈri
potsherd ˈpɒt-ʃəd
pot-shot ˈpɒt ʃɒt
pottage ˈpɒtɪdʒ

potter ˋpotə(r)
pottery ˋpotərɪ
potty ˋpotɪ
pouch paʊtʃ
pouf(fe) puf
poulterer ˋpəʊltərə(r)
poultice ˋpəʊltɪs
poultry ˋpəʊltrɪ
pounce paʊns
pound paʊnd
poundage ˋpaʊndɪdʒ
pour pɔ(r)
pout paʊt
poverty ˋpovətɪ $ ˋpovərtɪ
poverty-stricken ˋpovətɪ strɪkən $ -vər-
powder ˋpaʊdə(r)
powder-magazine ˋpaʊdə mægəzin $ -dər
powder-puff ˋpaʊdə pʌf $ ˋpaʊdər
powder-room ˋpaʊdə rʊm $ -dər
　$ £ rum etc
Powell ˋpaʊḷ ˋpəʊḷ
power ˋpaʊə(r)
power-dive ˋpaʊə daɪv $ ˋpaʊər
powerful ˋpaʊəfḷ $ ˋpaʊərfḷ
power-house ˋpaʊə haʊs $ ˋpaʊər
power-lathe ˋpaʊə leɪð $ ˋpaʊər
powwow ˋpaʊwaʊ
pox poks
practicable ˋpræktɪkəbl
practical ˋpræktɪkl
practically ˋpræktɪklɪ
practice ˋpræktɪs
practise ˋpræktɪs
practitioner præk̀tɪʃṇə(r)
praesidium prɪˋsɪdɪəm -ˋzɪd-
praetor ˋpritə(r) -tɔ(r)
praetorian prɪˋtɔrɪən
pragmatic prægˋmætɪk
pragmatism ˋprægmətɪzm
pragmatist ˋprægmətɪst
Prague prɑg
prairie ˋpreərɪ
praise preɪz
praiseworthy ˋpreɪzwɜðɪ
pram præm
prance prɑns $ præns
prank præŋk
prate preɪt
prattle ˋprætl
prawn prɔn
pray preɪ
prayer person ˋpreɪə(r)
prayer thing preə(r)

prayer book ˋpreə bʊk $ ˋpreər
prayer-mat ˋpreə mæt $ ˋpreər
prayer-meeting ˋpreə mitɪŋ $ ˋpreər
preach pritʃ
preamble prɪˋæmbl
precarious prɪˋkeərɪəs
precaution prɪˋkɔʃn
precautionary prɪˋkɔʃnrɪ $ -ŋerɪ
precede prɪˋsid
precedence ˋpresɪdəns prɪˋsidns
precedent ˋpresɪdənt prɪˋsidnt
precentor prɪˋsentə(r)
precept ˋprisept
precession prɪˋseʃn
precinct ˋprisɪŋkt
preciosity ˌpreʃɪˋosətɪ ˌpresɪ-
precious ˋpreʃəs
precipice ˋpresəpɪs
precipitate adj, n prəˋsɪpɪtət
precipitate v, n prəˋsɪpɪteɪt
precipitation prəˌsɪpɪˋteɪʃn
precipitous prəˋsɪpɪtəs
précis sing n ˋpreɪsɪ $ preɪˋsi etc
précis pl n ˋpreɪsiz $ preɪˋsiz etc
precise prɪˋsaɪs
precision prɪˋsɪʒn
preclude prɪˋklud
precocious prɪˋkəʊʃəs
precocity prɪˋkosətɪ
preconceived ˌprikənˋsivd
preconception ˌprikənˋsepʃn
preconcerted ˌprikənˋsɜtɪd
precursor priˋkɜsə(r)
predatory ˋpredətərɪ $ -tɔrɪ
predecessor ˋpridɪsesə(r) $ ˋpredɪˋsesər
predestination ˌpriˌdestɪˋneɪʃn
predestined priˋdestɪnd
predetermined ˌpridɪˋtɜmɪnd
predicament prɪˋdɪkəmənt
predicate n ˋpredɪkət -eɪt
predicate v ˋpredɪkeɪt
predicative prɪˋdɪkətɪv
predict prɪˋdɪkt
prediction prɪˋdɪkʃn
predilection ˌpridɪˋlekʃn
predispose ˌpridɪˋspəʊz
predisposition ˌpriˌdɪspəˋzɪʃn
predominance prɪˋdomɪnəns
predominant prɪˋdomɪnənt
predominate prɪˋdomɪneɪt
pre-eminent priˋemɪnənt
pre-empt priˋempt
pre-emption priˋempʃn

pre-emptive prıˈemptıv
preen prin
pre-existence ˈpriːgˈzıstəns
prefab ˈpriːfæb \$ £ ˈpriˈfæb
prefabricate priˈfæbrıkeıt
prefabrication ˈpriːˈfæbrıˈkeıʃn
preface ˈprefıs
prefatory ˈprefətərı \$ -tɔrı
prefect ˈpriːfekt
prefecture ˈpriːfektjʊə(r)
   \$ £ -tʃə(r) -tʃʊə(r)
prefer prıˈfɜ(r)
preferable ˈprefrəbl
preference ˈprefrəns
preferential ˈprefəˈrenʃl
preferment prıˈfɜmənt
prefigure priˈfıgə(r) \$ priˈfıgjər
prefix n ˈpriːfıks
prefix v priˈfıks
pregnancy ˈpregnənsı
pregnant ˈpregnənt
prehensile prıˈhensaıl \$ -sl
prehistoric ˈpriːˈstorık -ihı- \$ -ˈstɔr-
prehistory priːˈhıstrı
prejudge ˈpriːˈdʒʌdʒ
prejudice ˈpredʒədıs -dʒʊ-
prejudicial ˈpredʒʊˈdıʃl
prelate ˈprelət -lıt
preliminary prıˈlımınərı -mınrı \$ -nerı
prelude ˈpreljud \$ ˈpriː- -lud
premature ˈpremətʃə(r) -tʃʊə(r)
   \$ ˈpriːmətʊər -tʃʊər
premeditated priːˈmedıteıtıd
premeditation ˈpriːˈmedıˈteıʃn
premier ˈpremıə(r) \$ ˈpriːmıər prıˈmıər
première ˈpremıeə(r) ˈprəmıeə(r)
   \$ prıˈmıər ˈpriːmıˈeər etc
premise ˈpremıs
premium ˈpriːmıəm
premonition ˈpreməˈnıʃn
premonitory prıˈmonıtrı \$ -tɔrı
prentice ˈprentıs
preoccupation ˈpriːokjʊˈpeıʃn
preoccupied priːˈokjʊpaıd
preordain ˈpriːɔˈdeın \$ -ɔrˈd-
prep prep
preparation ˈprepəˈreıʃn
preparative prıˈpærətıv
preparatory prıˈpærətrı \$ -tɔrı
preparatory school prıˈpærətrı skul \$ -tɔrı
prepare prıˈpeə(r)
preparedness prıˈpeədnəs -ˈpeərıd-
   \$ prıˈpeərdnəs etc

prepay ˈpriːˈpeı
preponderance prıˈpondrəns
preponderate prıˈpondəreıt
preposition ˈprepəˈzıʃn
prepossessing ˈpriːpəˈzesıŋ
preposterous prıˈpostərəs
Pre-Raphaelite ˈpriːˈræflaıt
   \$ £ -fıəlaıt \$ -ˈreıf-
pre-record ˈpriː rıˈkɔd \$ rıˈkɔrd
pre-requisite priː ˈrekwızıt
prerogative prıˈrogətıv
Pres. ˈprezıdənt
presage n ˈpresıdʒ
presage v ˈpresıdʒ prıˈseıdʒ
presbyterian ˈprezbıˈtıərıən
presbytery ˈprezbıtrı \$ -terı
prescient ˈpresıənt \$ ˈpriː-
prescribe prıˈskraıb
prescription prıˈskrıpʃn
prescriptive prıˈskrıptıv
presence ˈprezns
present adj, n ˈpreznt
present v prıˈzent
presentable prıˈzentəbl
presentation ˈpreznˈteıʃn
   \$ ˈprizenˈteıʃn -zn- etc
presentiment prıˈzentımənt
preservation ˈprezəˈveıʃn \$ -zər-
preservative prıˈzɜvətıv
preserve prıˈzɜv
preside prıˈzaıd
presidency ˈprezıdənsı
president ˈprezıdənt
presidential ˈprezıˈdenʃl
presidium prıˈsıdıəm -ˈzıd-
press pres
press-agent ˈpres eıdʒənt
press-conference ˈpres konfrns
press-cutting ˈpres kʌtıŋ
press-gang ˈpres gæŋ
press-photographer ˈpres fətogrəfə(r)
pressure ˈpreʃə(r)
pressure-cooker ˈpreʃə kʊkə(r) \$ ˈpreʃər
pressure-gauge ˈpreʃə geıdʒ \$ ˈpreʃər
pressure group ˈpreʃə grup \$ ˈpreʃər
pressurized ˈpreʃəraızd
prestidigitator ˈprestıˈdıdʒıteıtə(r)
prestige preˈstiːʒ
prestigious preˈstıdʒəs
prestissimo preˈstısıməʊ
presto ˈprestəʊ
pre-stressed ˈpriː ˈstrest
presumably prıˈzuməblı £ -ˈzju-

presume prɪˈzum £ -ˈzju-
presumption prɪˈzʌmpʃn
presumptive prɪˈzʌmptɪv
presumptuous prɪˈzʌmptʃʊəs
presuppose ˈprisəˈpəʊz
presupposition ˈpriˌsʌpəˈzɪʃn
pretence prɪˈtens
pretend prɪˈtend
pretense prɪˈtens
pretension prɪˈtenʃn
pretentious prɪˈtenʃəs
preterit(e) ˈpretərɪt
preternatural ˈpritəˈnætʃərl $ ˈpritər-
pretext ˈpritekst
Pretoria prɪˈtɔrɪə
pretty ˈprɪtɪ
pretzel ˈpretsl
prevail prɪˈveɪl
prevalence ˈprevələns
prevalent ˈprevələnt
prevaricate prɪˈværɪkeɪt
prevarication prɪˈværɪˈkeɪʃn
prevent prɪˈvent
preventative prɪˈventətɪv
prevention prɪˈvenʃn
preventive prɪˈventɪv
preview ˈprivju
previous ˈprivɪəs
pre-war ˈpri ˈwɔ(r)
prey preɪ
price praɪs
price-list ˈpraɪs lɪst
prick prɪk
prickle ˈprɪkl
pride praɪd
priest prist
priesthood ˈpristhʊd
prig prɪg
prim prɪm
prima ballerina ˈprimə ˈbæləˈrinə
prima donna ˈprimə ˈdɒnə ˈprimə
prima facie ˈpraɪmə ˈfeɪʃɪ ˈfeɪʃɪ ˈfeɪsɪ
primal ˈpraɪml
primarily ˈpraɪmrlɪ
    $ ˈpraɪmerˌlɪ praɪˈmerəlɪ
primary ˈpraɪmrɪ -mərɪ $ ˈpraɪmerɪ etc
primary school ˈpraɪmrɪ skul $ -merɪ
primate ˈpraɪmeɪt ˈpraɪmɪt
primates apes praɪˈmeɪtiz ˈpraɪmeɪts
prime praɪm
prime minister praɪm ˈmɪnɪstə(r)
primer ˈpraɪmə(r)
primeval praɪˈmivl

primitive ˈprɪmɪtɪv
primogeniture ˈpraɪməʊˈdʒenɪtʃə(r)
    $ -ˈdʒenɪtʃʊər etc
primordial praɪˈmɔdɪəl $ -ˈmɔrd-
primrose ˈprɪmrəʊz
primula ˈprɪmjʊlə
primus stove ˈpraɪməs stəʊv
prince prɪns
princedom ˈprɪnsdəm
princess ˈprɪnˈses $ £ ˈprɪnses -ɪs etc
Princeton ˈprɪnstən
principal ˈprɪnsəpl -əbl
principality ˈprɪnsəˈpælətɪ
principle ˈprɪnsəpl -əbl
prink prɪŋk
print prɪnt
printing-ink ˈprɪntɪŋ ɪŋk
printing-press ˈprɪntɪŋ pres
print-out ˈprɪnt aʊt
prior ˈpraɪə(r)
prioress ˈpraɪərɪs -es
priority praɪˈɒrətɪ $ -ˈɔrətɪ
Priscilla prɪˈsɪlə
prise praɪz
prism ˈprɪzm
prismatic prɪzˈmætɪk
prison ˈprɪzn
prisoner ˈprɪzṇə(r)
pristine ˈprɪstin ˈprɪstaɪn
prithee ˈprɪðɪ ˈprɪðɪ
privacy ˈprɪvəsɪ $ £ ˈpraɪvəsɪ
private ˈpraɪvɪt
privateer ˈpraɪvɪˈtɪə(r)
privation praɪˈveɪʃn
privet ˈprɪvɪt
privilege ˈprɪvḷɪdʒ
privy ˈprɪvɪ
prize praɪz
prize-fight ˈpraɪz faɪt
prize-money ˈpraɪz mʌnɪ
probability ˈprɒbəˈbɪlətɪ
probable ˈprɒbəbl
probably ˈprɒbəblɪ
probate ˈprəʊbeɪt -ət
probation prəˈbeɪʃn $ prəʊˈb-
probationary prəˈbeɪʃnrɪ $ prəʊˈbeɪʃṇerɪ
probation officer prəˈbeɪʃn ɒfɪsə(r)
    $ prəʊˈbeɪʃn ɔfisər
probe prəʊb
probity ˈprəʊbətɪ
problem ˈprɒbləm
problematic ˈprɒbləˈmætɪk
problem child ˈprɒbləm tʃaɪld

proboscis prəʊˈbɒsɪs £ prəˈb-
procedure prəˈsidʒə(r)
proceed prəˈsid
proceeds n ˈprəʊsidz
process ˈprəʊses $ ˈproses etc
procession prəˈseʃn
processional prəˈseʃnl
proclamation ˈprɒkləˈmeɪʃn
proclaim prəˈkleɪm $ prəʊˈk-
proclivity prəʊˈklɪvətɪ £ prəˈk-
proconsul ˈprəʊˈkɒnsl
proconsular ˈprəʊˈkɒnsjʊlə(r)
procrastinate prəʊˈkræstɪneɪt prə-
procrastination prəʊˈkræstɪˈneɪʃn prə-
procreate ˈprəʊkrɪeɪt
procreation ˈprəʊkrɪˈeɪʃn
proctor ˈprɒktə(r)
procurator ˈprɒkjʊreɪtə(r)
procure prəˈkjʊə(r) $ prəʊ-
procurer prəˈkjʊərə(r) $ prəʊ-
prod prod
prodigal ˈprɒdɪgl
prodigality ˈprɒdɪˈgælətɪ
prodigious prəˈdɪdʒəs
prodigy ˈprɒdɪdʒɪ
produce n ˈprɒdjus $ -dus ˈprəʊ-
produce v prəˈdjus $ -ˈdus prəʊ-
product ˈprɒdʌkt
production prəˈdʌkʃn
productivity ˈprɒdəkˈtɪvətɪ
profane prəˈfeɪn $ prəʊ- etc
profanity prəˈfænətɪ $ prəʊ- etc
profess prəˈfes
professedly prəˈfesɪdlɪ
profession prəˈfeʃn
professional prəˈfeʃnl
professor prəˈfesə(r)
professorial ˈprɒfɪˈsɔrɪəl $ ˈprəʊ-
proffer ˈprɒfə(r)
proficiency prəˈfɪʃnsɪ
proficient prəˈfɪʃnt
profile ˈprəʊfaɪl
profit ˈprɒfɪt
profitable ˈprɒfɪtəbl
profiteer ˈprɒfɪˈtɪə(r)
profit-sharing ˈprɒfɪt ʃeərɪŋ
profligacy ˈprɒflɪgəsɪ
profligate ˈprɒflɪgət -geɪt
profound prəˈfaʊnd $ prəʊ-
profundity prəˈfʌndətɪ $ prəʊ-
profuse prəˈfjus $ prəʊ-
profusion prəˈfjuʒn $ prəʊ-
progenitor prəʊˈdʒenɪtə(r)

progeny ˈprɒdʒɪnɪ
prognosis progˈnəʊsɪs
prognosticate progˈnɒstɪkeɪt
prognostication ˈprogˈnɒstɪˈkeɪʃn
program(me) ˈprəʊgræm $ -grəm
progress n ˈprəʊgres
  $ ˈprogres -grɪs etc
progress v prəˈgres $ prəʊ-
progression prəˈgreʃn $ prəʊ-
progressive prəˈgresɪv $ prəʊ-
prohibit prəˈhɪbɪt $ £ prəʊ-
prohibition ˈprəʊɪˈbɪʃn -əʊhɪ-
prohibitive prəˈhɪbətɪv $ prəʊ-
project n ˈprɒdʒekt ˈprəʊdʒekt
project v prəˈdʒekt prəʊ-
projectile prəˈdʒektaɪl prəʊ- $ -tl etc
projection prəˈdʒekʃn
projector prəˈdʒektə(r)
prolapse n ˈprəʊlæps
prolapse v prəʊˈlæps
prolegomena ˈprəʊlɪˈgomɪnə
proletarian ˈprəʊlɪˈteərɪən
proletariat ˈprəʊlɪˈteərɪət -ɪæt
proliferate prəˈlɪfəreɪt $ prəʊ-
proliferation prəˈlɪfəˈreɪʃn $ prəʊ-
prolific prəˈlɪfɪk prəʊ-
prolix ˈprəʊlɪks $ £ prəʊˈlɪks
prolog(ue) ˈprəʊlog $ -lɔg
prolong prəˈlɒŋ $ prəˈlɔŋ
prolongation ˈprəʊlɒŋˈgeɪʃn $ -lɔŋ-
promenade ˈproməˈnad $ -ˈneɪd etc
prominence ˈprɒmɪnəns
prominent ˈprɒmɪnənt
promiscuity ˈprɒmɪˈskjuətɪ
promiscuous prəˈmɪskjʊəs
promise ˈprɒmɪs
promising ˈprɒmɪsɪŋ
promissory ˈprɒmɪsrɪ $ -sɔrɪ
promontory ˈprɒməntrɪ $ -tɔrɪ
promote prəˈməʊt
promotion prəˈməʊʃn
prompt prompt
prompt-box ˈprompt boks
promptitude ˈpromptɪtjud $ -tud
promulgate ˈprɒmlgeɪt
  $ prəˈmʌlgeɪt prəʊ- etc
prone prəʊn
prong proŋ $ prɔŋ etc
pronominal prəʊˈnomɪnl prə-
pronoun ˈprəʊnaʊn
pronounce prəˈnaʊns
pronouncement prəˈnaʊnsmənt
pronunciation prəˈnʌnsɪˈeɪʃn

proof pruf
-proof *suffix* pruf
proof-reader ˈpruf ridə(r)
prop prop
propaganda ˈpropəˈgændə
propagate ˈpropəgeɪt
propagation ˈpropəˈgeɪʃn
propel prəˈpel
propellent prəˈpelənt
propeller prəˈpelə(r)
propensity prəˈpensətɪ
proper ˈpropə(r)
property ˈpropətɪ $ ˈpropərtɪ
prophecy ˈprofɪsɪ
prophesy ˈprofɪsaɪ
prophet ˈprofɪt
prophetess ˈprofɪtes $ £ -tɪs
prophetic prəˈfetɪk
prophylactic ˈprofɪˈlæktɪk
prophylaxis ˈprofɪˈlæksɪs
propinquity prəˈpɪŋkwətɪ $ prəʊ-
propitiate prəˈpɪʃɪeɪt -ɪsɪ- $ prəʊ-
propitiation prəˈpɪʃɪˈeɪʃn -ɪsɪ- $ prəʊ-
propitiatory prəˈpɪʃətərɪ $ prəʊˈpɪʃɪətərɪ
propitious prəˈpɪʃəs $ prəʊ-
proportion prəˈpɔʃn $ prəˈpɔrʃn
proportional prəˈpɔʃnl $ prəˈpɔrʃnl
proportionate prəˈpɔʃŋət $ -ˈpɔr-
proposal prəˈpəʊzl
propose prəˈpəʊz
proposition ˈpropəˈzɪʃn
propound prəˈpaʊnd
proprietary prəˈpraɪətrɪ $ -terɪ
proprietor prəˈpraɪətə(r)
proprietress prəˈpraɪətrəs -ɪs
propriety prəˈpraɪətɪ
props props
propulsion prəˈpʌlʃn
pro rata prəʊ ˈratə $ £ ˈreɪtə $ ˈrætə
prorogation ˈprəʊrəˈgeɪʃn
prosaic prəˈzeɪɪk $ prəʊ-
proscenium prəˈsiniəm $ prəʊ-
proscribe prəʊˈskraɪb
proscription prəʊˈskrɪpʃn
prose prəʊz
prosecute ˈprosɪkjut
prosecution ˈprosɪˈkjuʃn
prosecutor ˈprosɪkjutə(r)
proselyte ˈprosəlaɪt
proselytize ˈprosḷɪtaɪz
prosody ˈprosədɪ
prospect *n* ˈprospekt
prospect *v* prəˈspekt $ ˈprospekt

prospector prəˈspektə(r) $ ˈprospektər
prospective prəˈspektɪv
prospectus prəˈspektəs
prosper ˈprospə(r)
prosperity proˈsperətɪ
prosperous ˈprospərəs
prostitute ˈprostɪtjut -tʃut $ -tut *etc*
prostitution ˈprostɪˈtjuʃn $ -ˈtuʃn *etc*
prostrate *adj* ˈprostreɪt
prostrate *v* proˈstreɪt
prosy ˈprəʊzɪ
protagonist prəʊˈtægənɪst
protean ˈprəʊtɪən prəʊˈtiən
protect prəˈtekt
protection prəˈtekʃn
protective prəˈtektɪv
protectorate prəˈtektərət
protégé ˈprotɪʒeɪ ˈprəʊt- $ ˈprəʊtɪˈʒeɪ
protein ˈprəʊtin
pro tem ˈprəʊ ˈtem
protest *n* ˈprəʊtest
protest *v* prəˈtest $ ˈprəʊtest
protestant, P– ˈprotɪstənt
Protestantism ˈprotɪstəntɪzm
protestation ˈprotɪˈsteɪʃn
Proteus ˈprəʊtɪəs ˈprəʊtjus
protocol ˈprəʊtəkol
proton ˈprəʊton
protoplasm ˈprəʊtəplæzm
prototype ˈprəʊtətaɪp
protozoa ˈprəʊtəˈzəʊə
protract prəˈtrækt $ prəʊ- *etc*
protraction prəˈtrækʃn $ prəʊ- *etc*
protractor prəˈtræktə(r) $ prəʊ- *etc*
protrude prəˈtrud $ prəʊ-
protrusion prəˈtruʒn $ prəʊ-
protrusive prəˈtrusɪv $ prəʊ-
protuberance prəˈtjubərəns $ prəʊˈtu-
protuberant prəˈtjubərənt $ prəʊˈtu-
proud praʊd
prove pruv
proven ˈpruvn
provenance ˈprovənəns
Provençal ˈprovõˈsal $ ˈprəʊvənˈsal ˈpro-
provender ˈprovɪndə(r)
proverb ˈprovɜb
proverbial prəˈvɜbɪəl
provide prəˈvaɪd
providence ˈprovɪdns
providential ˈprovɪˈdenʃl
province ˈprovɪns
provincial prəˈvɪnʃl
provision prəˈvɪʒn

provisional prə'vɪʒnl
proviso prə'vaɪzəʊ
provocation 'prɒvə'keɪʃn
provocative prə'vɒkətɪv
provoke prə'vəʊk
provost 'prɒvəst
   $ 'prəʊvɒst 'prəʊvəʊst etc
provost marshal prə'vəʊ 'maʃl
   $ 'prəʊvəʊ 'marʃl etc
prow praʊ
prowess 'praʊɪs -es
prowl praʊl
proximate 'prɒksɪmət
proximity prɒk'sɪmətɪ
proximo 'prɒksɪməʊ
proxy 'prɒksɪ
prude prud
prudery 'prudərɪ
prudent 'prudnt
prudential pru'denʃl
prune prun
prurient 'prʊərɪənt
Prussia 'prʌʃə
Prussian 'prʌʃn
prussic 'prʌsɪk
pry praɪ
P.S. 'pi 'es
psalm sam
psalmody 'samədɪ 'sælmədɪ
psalter 'sɒltə(r) £ 'sɒltə(r)
psephology se'fɒlədʒɪ ps- $ sɪ'f-
pseudo- prefix 'sjudəʊ $ £ 'sudəʊ
pseudonym 'sjudənɪm $ 'sudn̩ɪm
pseudonymous sju'dɒnɪməs $ su-
pshaw pʃə or similar vocal eruption
   to indicate contempt
psyche, P– 'saɪkɪ
psychedelic 'saɪkɪ'delɪk
psychiatrist saɪ'kaɪətrɪst $ sɪ'kaɪ- etc
psychiatry saɪ'kaɪətrɪ $ sɪ'kaɪ- etc
psychic 'saɪkɪk
psychical 'saɪkɪkl
psycho- prefix saɪkəʊ
psycho-analyse 'saɪkəʊ 'ænəlaɪz
psycho-analysis 'saɪkəʊ ə'næləsɪs
psycho-analyst 'saɪkəʊ 'ænəlɪst
psycho-analytic 'saɪkəʊ 'ænə'lɪtɪk
psychological 'saɪkə'lɒdʒɪkl
psychologist saɪ'kɒlədʒɪst
psychology saɪ'kɒlədʒɪ
psychopath 'saɪkəʊpæθ
psychopathic 'saɪkəʊ'pæθɪk
psychosis saɪ'kəʊsɪs

psychotherapy 'saɪkəʊ'θerəpɪ
P.T. 'pi 'ti
ptarmigan 'tamɪgən $ 'tarmɪgən
Pte 'praɪvɪt
pterodactyl 'terə'dæktɪl
ptomaine 'təʊmeɪn təʊ'meɪn
pub pʌb
puberty 'pjubətɪ $ 'pjubərtɪ
public 'pʌblɪk
publican 'pʌblɪkən
publication 'pʌblɪ'keɪʃn
public house 'pʌblɪk 'haʊs
publicise 'pʌblɪsaɪz
publicist 'pʌblɪsɪst
publicity pʌb'lɪsətɪ
publicity campaign pʌb'lɪsətɪ kæmpeɪn
publicity stunt pʌb'lɪsətɪ stʌnt
public-spirited 'pʌblɪk 'spɪrɪtɪd
publish 'pʌblɪʃ
Puccini pʊ'tʃinɪ
puce pjus
puck pʌk
pucker 'pʌkə(r)
pudding 'pʊdɪŋ
puddle 'pʌdl
pudgy 'pʌdʒɪ
pueblo 'pwebləʊ
puerile 'pjʊəraɪl $ 'pjʊərl etc
puerperal pju'əpərəl
Puerto Rico 'pweətə 'rikəʊ
   'pwɜtə $ 'pweərtə
puff pʌf
puff-adder 'pʌf ædə(r)
puffin 'pʌfɪn
pug pʌg
pugilist 'pjudʒɪlɪst
pugnacious pʌg'neɪʃəs
pugnacity pʌg'næsətɪ
pug-nose 'pʌg nəʊz
puissant 'pjuɪsnt 'pwɪsnt
puke pjuk
pull pʊl
pullet 'pʊlɪt
pulley 'pʊlɪ
Pullman car 'pʊlmən ka(r)
pull-over 'pʊl əʊvə(r)
pull-up 'pʊl ʌp
pulmonary 'pʌlmənərɪ $ -nerɪ 'pʊl-
pulp pʌlp
pulpit 'pʊlpɪt
pulsar 'pʌlsa(r)
pulsate pʌl'seɪt $ 'pʌlseɪt
pulse pʌls

pulverise ˈpʌlvəraɪz
puma ˈpjumə $ ˈpumə
pumice-stone ˈpʌmɪs stəʊn
pummel ˈpʌml
pump pʌmp
pumpernickel ˈpʌmpənɪkl $ -pər-
pumpkin ˈpʌmpkɪn $ ˈpʌŋkɪn
pump-room ˈpʌmp rʊm $ £ rum *etc*
pun pʌn
punch, P– pʌntʃ
punch-ball ˈpʌntʃ bɔl
punch-bowl ˈpʌntʃ bəʊl
punch-drunk ˈpʌntʃ ˈdrʌŋk $ ˈpʌntʃ drʌŋk
punctilious pʌŋkˈtɪlɪəs
punctual ˈpʌŋktʃʊəl
punctuate ˈpʌŋktʃʊeɪt
punctuation ˈpʌŋktʃʊˈeɪʃn
puncture ˈpʌŋktʃə(r)
pundit ˈpʌndɪt
pungency ˈpʌndʒənsɪ
pungent ˈpʌndʒənt
Punic ˈpjunɪk
punish ˈpʌnɪʃ
punishment ˈpʌnɪʃmənt
punitive ˈpjunɪtɪv
Punjab pʌnˈdʒab $ £ ˈpʌndʒab *etc*
punk pʌŋk
punnet ˈpʌnɪt
punt pʌnt
puny ˈpjunɪ
pup pʌp
pupa ˈpjupə
pupae ˈpjupi ˈpjupaɪ
pupil ˈpjupl
puppet ˈpʌpɪt
puppet-show ˈpʌpɪt ʃəʊ
puppy ˈpʌpɪ
Purcell ˈpɜsl pɜˈsel
purchase ˈpɜtʃəs -tʃɪs
purchase tax ˈpɜtʃəs tæks
purdah ˈpɜdə
pure pjʊə(r)
purée ˈpjʊəreɪ $ pjʊəˈreɪ
purgation pɜˈgeɪʃn
purgative ˈpɜgətɪv
purgatorial ˈpɜgəˈtɔrɪəl
purgatory ˈpɜgətrɪ $ -tɔrɪ
purge pɜdʒ
purification ˈpjʊərɪfɪˈkeɪʃn
purify ˈpjʊərɪfaɪ
purist ˈpjʊərɪst
puritan, P– ˈpjʊərɪtən
puritanical ˈpjʊərɪˈtænɪkl

purity ˈpjʊərətɪ
purl pɜl
purloin pɜˈlɔɪn
purple ˈpɜpl
purplish ˈpɜplɪʃ
purport *n* ˈpɜpət $ ˈpɜpɔrt
purport *v* ˈpɜpət pəˈpɔt $ pərˈpɔrt
purpose ˈpɜpəs
purposive ˈpɜpəsɪv
purr pɜ(r)
purse pɜs
purser ˈpɜsə(r)
purse-strings ˈpɜs strɪŋz
pursuance pəˈsjuəns $ £ -ˈsu- $ pər-
pursuant pəˈsjuənt $ £ -ˈsu- $ pər-
pursue pəˈsju $ £ -ˈsu $ pər-
pursuer pəˈsjuə(r) $ £ -ˈsuə(r) $ pər-
pursuit pəˈsjut $ £ -ˈsut $ pər-
purulent ˈpjʊərələnt
purvey pɜˈveɪ $ pərˈveɪ
purveyance pɜˈveɪəns
purview ˈpɜvju
pus pʌs
push pʊʃ
push-bike ˈpʊʃ baɪk
pusher ˈpʊʃə(r)
pusillanimity ˈpjusɪləˈnɪmətɪ
pusillanimous ˈpjusɪˈlænɪməs
puss pʊs
pussy-cat ˈpʊsɪ kæt
pussy-willow ˈpʊsɪ wɪləʊ
pustule ˈpʌstjul $ ˈpʌstʃul
put *golf* pʌt
put *place* pʊt
putative ˈpjutətɪv
putrefaction ˈpjutrɪˈfækʃn
putrefy ˈpjutrɪfaɪ
putrescent pjuˈtresnt
putrid ˈpjutrɪd
putsch pʊtʃ
putt pʌt
putting-green ˈpʌtɪŋ grin
puttee ˈpʌtɪ
putty ˈpʌtɪ
put-up job ˈpʊt ʌp ˈdʒob
put up with pʊt ˈʌp wɪð
puzzle ˈpʌzl
Pvt ˈpraɪvɪt
PX ˈpi ˈeks
Pygmalion pɪgˈmeɪlɪən
pygmy ˈpɪgmɪ
pyjamas pəˈdʒaməz $ -ˈdʒæm- *etc*
pylon ˈpaɪlən $ £ -lon

pyorrhoea ˈpaɪəˈrɪə
pyramid ˈpɪrəmɪd
pyramidal pɪˈræmɪdl
pyre ˈpaɪə(r)
Pyrenees ˈpɪrəˈniz
pyrites ˈpaɪəˈraɪtiz $ pɪˈraɪtiz

pyrotechnic ˈpaɪərəʊˈteknɪk
Pyrrhic ˈpɪrɪk
Pythagoras paɪˈθægərəs $ pɪˈθ-
python ˈpaɪθən $ -θon
pyx pɪks

Q

Q q kju
Q.C. ˈkju ˈsi
qua kweɪ kwɑ
quack kwæk
quad kwod
quadrangle ˈkwodræŋgl *with* dr *as in*
   'dry', *not as in* 'cod-roe'
quadrangular kwoˈdræŋgjʊlə(r)
quadrant ˈkwodrənt
quadrate n, adj ˈkwodreɪt -rət
quadrate v kwoˈdreɪt $ ˈkwodreɪt
quadratic kwəˈdrætɪk kwo-
quadrilateral ˈkwodrɪˈlætərl
quadrille kwəˈdrɪl
   $ kwoˈdrɪl kəˈdrɪl *etc*
quadrillion kwoˈdrɪlɪən
quadroon kwoˈdrun kwə-
quadruped ˈkwodrʊped
quadruple ˈkwodrupl
   $ kwoˈdrupl *etc*
quadruplets ˈkwodruplɪts
   $ £ kwoˈdruplɪts $ -ˈdrʌp-
quadruplicate n kwoˈdruplɪkət
quadruplicate v kwoˈdruplɪkeɪt
quaff kwof £ kwɑf $ kwæf *etc*
quagmire ˈkwægmaɪə(r) $ ˈkwog-
Quai D'Orsai ˈkeɪ dɔˈseɪ $ dɔrˈseɪ
quail kweɪl
quaint kweɪnt
quake kweɪk
Quaker ˈkweɪkə(r)
qualification ˈkwolɪfɪˈkeɪʃn
qualify ˈkwolɪfaɪ
qualitative ˈkwolɪtətɪv $ -teɪtɪv
quality ˈkwolətɪ
qualm kwɑm kwɔm
quandary ˈkwondərɪ
quanta ˈkwontə
quantify ˈkwontɪfaɪ
quantitative ˈkwontɪtətɪv $ -teɪtɪv
quantity ˈkwontətɪ

quantum ˈkwontəm
quarantine ˈkworəntin
   $ ˈkwɔr- ˈkwɔrənˈtin *etc*
quarrel ˈkworl $ ˈkwɔrl *etc*
quarrelsome ˈkworlsəm $ ˈkwɔr- *etc*
quarry ˈkworɪ $ ˈkwɔrɪ *etc*
quart kwɔt $ kwɔrt
quarter ˈkwɔtə(r) $ ˈkwɔrtər
quarter-day ˈkwɔtə deɪ $ ˈkwɔrtər
·quarter-deck ˈkwɔtə dek $ ˈkwɔrtər
quarter master ˈkwɔtə mɑstə(r)
   $ ˈkwɔrtər mæstər
quarter-sessions ˈkwɔtə seʃnz $ -ɔrtər
quartet(te) kwɔˈtet $ kwɔr-
quarto ˈkwɔtəʊ $ ˈkwɔrtəʊ
quartz ˈkwɔts $ ˈkwɔrts
quash kwoʃ $ kwɔʃ
quasi- *prefix* ˈkweɪsaɪ -zaɪ ˈkwɑzɪ
quassia ˈkwoʃə -ʃɪə
quatercentenary ˈkwætəsenˈtinərɪ ˈkweɪt-
   ˈkwot- $ ˈkwotərˈsentṇerɪ ˈkweɪt-
quaternary kwəˈtɜnərɪ $ ˈkwotərnerɪ
quatrain ˈkwotreɪn
quaver ˈkweɪvə(r)
quay ki
queasy ˈkwizɪ
Quebec kwɪˈbek
queen kwin
Queensbury ˈkwinzbrɪ -bərɪ $ -berɪ
Queensland ˈkwinzlənd
queer kwɪə(r)
quell kwel
quench kwentʃ
querulous ˈkwerjələs ˈkwerələs
query ˈkwɪərɪ
quest kwest
question ˈkwestʃən
question-mark ˈkwestʃən mak $ mark
question-master ˈkwestʃən mɑstə(r)
   $ mæstər
questionnaire ˈkwestʃəˈneə(r)

queue kju
quibble ˈkwɪbl
quick kwɪk
quick-change (artist) ˈkwɪk ˈtʃeɪndʒ
quicken ˈkwɪkən
quick-frozen ˈkwɪk ˈfrəʊzn
quickie ˈkwɪkɪ
quicklime ˈkwɪk-laɪm
quicksand ˈkwɪksænd
quickset ˈkwɪkset
quick-sighted ˈkwɪk ˈsaɪtɪd
quicksilver ˈkwɪksɪlvə(r)
quick-step ˈkwɪkstep
quick-tempered ˈkwɪk ˈtempəd $ -pərd
quick-witted ˈkwɪk ˈwɪtɪd
quid kwɪd
quid pro quo ˈkwɪd prəʊ ˈkwəʊ
quiesence kwaɪˈesns kwɪ-
quiescent kwaɪˈesnt kwɪ-
quiet ˈkwaɪət
quieten ˈkwaɪətn
quietism ˈkwaɪətɪzm
quietude ˈkwaɪətjud $ -tud etc
quietus kwaɪˈitəs
quill kwɪl
quilt kwɪlt
quince kwɪns
quinine kwɪˈnin ˈkwɪnin $ ˈkwaɪnaɪn
Quinquagesima ˈkwɪŋkwəˈdʒesɪmə

quins kwɪnz
quinsy ˈkwɪnzɪ
quintessence kwɪnˈtesns
quintet(te) kwɪnˈtet
quintuplets ˈkwɪntjuplɪts kwɪnˈtjuplɪts
   $ kwɪnˈtuplɪts -ˈtʌp-
quip kwɪp
quire ˈkwaɪə(r)
quirk kwɜk
quisling ˈkwɪzlɪŋ
quit kwɪt
quite kwaɪt
quiver ˈkwɪvə(r)
qui vive ˈki ˈviv
Quixote ˈkwɪksəʊt -sət $ kiˈhəʊtɪ etc
quixotic kwɪkˈsotɪk
quiz kwɪz
quiz-master ˈkwɪz mastə(r) $ mæstər
quizzical ˈkwɪzɪkl
quoit kɔɪt $ kwɔɪt
quondam ˈkwondəm ˈkwondæm
quorum ˈkwɔrəm
quota ˈkwəʊtə
quotation kwəʊˈteɪʃn
quote kwəʊt
quoth kwəʊθ
quotidian kwəʊˈtɪdɪən
quotient ˈkwəʊʃnt
q.v. ˈkju ˈvi ˈkwod ˈvaɪdɪ ˈvideɪ

R

R r ɑ(r)
rabbi ˈræbaɪ
rabbit ˈræbɪt
rabbit-hole ˈræbɪt həʊl
rabbit-burrow ˈræbɪt bʌrəʊ $ bɜəʊ
rabbit-hutch ˈræbɪt hʌtʃ
rabbit-warren ˈræbɪt worən
   $ ˈwɔrən etc
rabble ˈræbl
Rabelais ˈræbəleɪ
Rabelaisian ˈræbəˈleɪzɪən $ -ˈleɪʒn etc
rabid ˈræbɪd
rabies ˈreɪbiz
raccoon rəˈkun $ ræˈkun
race reɪs
race-course ˈreɪs kɔs $ kɔrs
race-horse ˈreɪs hɔs $ hɔrs
race-meeting ˈreɪs mitɪŋ

Rachel ˈreɪtʃl
Rachmaninoff rækˈmænɪnof
   $ rakˈmanɪnof etc £ $ instead of k
   many use the corresponding fricative x
racial ˈreɪʃl
racialist reɪʃlɪst
Racine author ræˈsin
Racine place rəˈsin
rack ræk
racket ˈrækɪt
racketeer ˈrækɪˈtɪə(r)
raconteur ˈrækonˈtɜ(r)
racoon rəˈkun $ ræˈkun
racquet ˈrækɪt
racy ˈreɪsɪ
RADA ˈrɑdə
radar ˈreɪdɑ(r)
radar screen ˈreɪdɑ skrin $ ˈreɪdɑr

radial 'reɪdɪəl
radiance 'reɪdɪəns
radiant 'reɪdɪənt
radiate 'reɪdɪeɪt
radiation 'reɪdɪ'eɪʃn
radiator 'reɪdɪeɪtə(r)
radical 'rædɪkl
radii 'reɪdɪaɪ
radio 'reɪdɪəʊ
radio-active 'reɪdɪəʊ 'æktɪv
radiogram 'reɪdɪəʊgræm
radiography 'reɪdɪ'ɒgrəfɪ
radio-isotope 'reɪdɪəʊ 'aɪsətəʊp
radio-telescope 'reɪdɪəʊ 'telɪskəʊp
radio-therapy 'reɪdɪəʊ 'θerəpɪ
radish 'rædɪʃ
radium 'reɪdɪəm
radius 'reɪdɪəs
RAF 'ɑr eɪ 'ef informal: 'ræf
raffia 'ræfɪə
raffish 'ræfɪʃ
raffle 'ræg
raft rɑft $ ræft
rafter 'rɑftə(r) $ ræftər
rag ræg
ragamuffin 'rægəmʌfɪn
rage reɪdʒ
ragged adj 'rægɪd
raglan 'ræglən
ragout 'rægu $ ræ'gu
ragtag and bobtail 'rægtæg ən 'bobteɪl
ragtime 'rægtaɪm
raid reɪd
rail reɪl
railhead 'reɪlhed
railing 'reɪlɪŋ
raillery 'reɪlərɪ
railroad 'reɪlrəʊd
railway 'reɪlweɪ
raiment 'reɪmənt
rain reɪn
rainbow 'reɪnbəʊ
raincoat 'reɪnkəʊt
raindrop 'reɪndrop
rainfall 'reɪnfɔl
rain-gauge 'reɪn geɪdʒ
rainproof 'reɪnpruf
rainwater 'reɪnwɔtə(r) $ -wɔtər
raise reɪz
raisin 'reɪzn
raison d'être 'reɪzõ 'deətr with
   unsyllabic r 'reɪzon 'deɪtrə
   $ 'reɪzəʊn 'detrə -zõ 'det

raj rɑdʒ
rajah 'rɑdʒə
rake reɪk
rake-off 'reɪk of $ £ ɔf
rakish 'reɪkɪʃ
Raleigh 'rɔlɪ bicycle: 'rælɪ
rallentando 'rælən'tændəʊ
rally 'rælɪ
Ralph rælf £ reɪf
ram ræm
Ramadan 'ræmə'dan -'dæn 'ræməd-
ramble 'ræmbl
ramification 'ræmɪfɪ'keɪʃn
ramify 'ræmɪfaɪ
ramp ræmp
rampage n 'ræmpeɪdʒ
rampage v ræm'peɪdʒ
rampant 'ræmpənt
rampart 'ræmpɑt $ -pɑrt
ramrod 'ræmrod
ramshackle 'ræmʃækl
ran ræn
ranch 'rɑntʃ $ ræntʃ
rancid 'rænsɪd
rancorous 'ræŋkərəs
rancour($ -or) 'ræŋkə(r)
Randolph 'rændolf
randy 'rændɪ
ranee rɑ'ni
rang ræŋ
range reɪndʒ
range-finder 'reɪndʒ faɪndə(r)
rank ræŋk
rankle 'ræŋkl
ransack 'rænsæk $ 'ræn'sæk etc
ransom 'rænsəm
rant rænt
rap ræp
rapacious rə'peɪʃəs
rapacity rə'pæsətɪ
rape reɪp
Raphael 'ræfeɪl $ 'ræfɪəl 'reɪfɪəl
rapid 'ræpɪd
rapidity rə'pɪdətɪ
rapier 'reɪpɪə(r)
rapine 'ræpaɪn $ £ 'ræpɪn
rapport ræ'pɔ(r) $ ræ'pɔrt
rapprochement ræ'proʃmõ
   $ 'ræprəʊʃmõ
rapscallion ræp'skælɪən
rapt ræpt
rapture 'ræptʃə(r)
rapturous 'ræptʃərəs

rare reə(r)
rarebit ˈreəbɪt ˈræbɪt $ ˈreərbɪt
rarefaction ˈreərɪˈfækʃn
rarefy ˈreərɪfaɪ
rarity ˈreərətɪ
rascal ˈrɑːskl $ ˈræskl
rash ræʃ
rasher ˈræʃə(r)
rasp rɑːsp $ ræsp
raspberry ˈrɑːzbrɪ $ ˈræzberɪ
rat ræt
ratability ˈreɪtəbɪlətɪ
ratable ˈreɪtəbl
rat-a-tat ˈræt ə ˈtæt
ratchet ˈrætʃɪt
rate reɪt
rate, at any əˈtenɪ reɪt
rate, at that/this ət ˈðæt/ˈðɪs reɪt
rateability ˈreɪtəˈbɪlətɪ
rateable ˈreɪtəbl
rate-payer ˈreɪt peɪə(r)
rather ˈrɑːðə(r) $ ˈræðər; colloq in
   the sense ˈcertainly' only £ ˈrɑːˈðə(r)
ratification ˈrætɪfɪˈkeɪʃn
ratify ˈrætɪfaɪ
ratio ˈreɪʃɪəʊ -ʃəʊ
ratiocination ˈrætɪˈosɪˈneɪʃn $ ˈræʃɪ-
ration ˈræʃn $ ˈreɪʃn
rational ˈræʃnl
rationale ˈræʃəˈnɑːl -ɑːlɪ $ -ˈnæl
rationalist ˈræʃṇəlɪst
rationalistic ˈræʃnlˈɪstɪk
rationalize ˈræʃṇəlaɪz
ration book ˈræʃn bʊk
rat-tat ˈræt ˈtæt
rattle ˈrætl
rattlesnake ˈrætlsneɪk
raucous ˈrɔːkəs
ravage ˈrævɪdʒ
rave reɪv
ravel rævl
Ravel rəˈvel ræ-
raven ˈreɪvn
ravenous ˈrævṇəs
ravine rəˈviːn
ravish ˈrævɪʃ
raw rɔː
raw-boned ˈrɔː ˈbəʊnd
rawhide ˈrɔːhaɪd
ray, R– reɪ
Raymond ˈreɪmənd
rayon ˈreɪon -ən
raze reɪz

razor ˈreɪzə(r)
razor-back ˈreɪzə bæk $ ˈreɪzər
razor blade ˈreɪzə bleɪd $ ˈreɪzər
razzle ˈræzl
Rd rəʊd
re riː
reach riːtʃ
react riˈækt
reaction riˈækʃn
reactor riˈæktə(r)
read riːd
read pp red
re-address ˈriː əˈdres
Reading ˈredɪŋ
reading-glasses ˈriːdɪŋ glɑːsɪz $ glæs-
reading-lamp ˈriːdɪŋ læmp
reading-room ˈriːdɪŋ rʊm $ £ rum etc
readjust ˈriːəˈdʒʌst
ready ˈredɪ
ready-made ˈredɪ ˈmeɪd
ready-reckoner ˈredɪ ˈreknə(r) -kən
reaffirm ˈriːəˈfɜːm
reagent riːˈeɪdʒənt
real rɪəl riːl
realism ˈrɪəl-ɪzm as two words
realistic rɪəˈlɪstɪk
readmission ˈriːədˈmɪʃn
readmit ˈriːədˈmɪt
reality riːˈælətɪ
realization ˈrɪəlaɪˈzeɪʃn $ -lɪˈz-
realize ˈrɪəlaɪz
really ˈrɪəlɪ
realm ˈrelm
ream riːm
reanimate riːˈænɪmeɪt
reap riːp
reappear ˈriːəˈpɪə(r)
reapply ˈriːəˈplaɪ
reappraisal ˈriːəˈpreɪzl
rear rɪə(r)
rear-admiral ˈrɪər ˈædmṛl
rearguard ˈrɪəgɑːd $ ˈrɪərgɑːrd
rearm riːˈɑːm $ riːˈɑːrm
rearmament riːˈɑːməmənt $ -ˈɑːrm-
rearmost ˈrɪəməʊst $ ˈrɪər-
reason ˈriːzn
reasonable ˈriːznəbl
reassurance ˈriːəˈʃʊərns £ -ˈʃɔːr-
reassure ˈriːəˈʃʊə(r) £ -ˈʃɔː(r)
rebate ˈriːbeɪt
Rebecca rəˈbekə rɪ-
rebel n ˈrebl
rebel v rɪˈbel

rebellion rɪˈbelɪən
rebellious rɪˈbelɪəs
rebind ˈriˈbaɪnd
rebirth ˈriˈbɜθ
reborn ˈriˈbɔn $ ˈriˈbɔrn
rebound n ˈribaʊnd
rebound v riˈbaʊnd
rebuff rɪˈbʌf
rebuild ˈriˈbɪld
rebuke rɪˈbjuk
rebus ˈribəs
rebut rɪˈbʌt
rebuttal rɪˈbʌtl
recalcitrant rɪˈkælsɪtrənt
recall rɪˈkɔl $ n ˈrikɔl
recant rɪˈkænt
recantation ˈrikænˈteɪʃn
recap n ˈrikæp
recap v ˈriˈkæp
recapitulate ˈri-kəˈpɪtʃuleɪt ˈrikə
recast ˈriˈkast $ ˈriˈkæst
recede rɪˈsid
receipt rɪˈsit
receipt-book rɪˈsit bʊk
receive rɪˈsiv
recent ˈrisnt
receptacle rɪˈseptəkl
reception rɪˈsepʃn
reception clerk rɪˈsepʃn klak $ klɜk
reception desk rɪˈsepʃn desk
receptionist rɪˈsepʃnɪst
receptive rɪˈseptɪv
recess rɪˈses ˈrises
recession rɪˈseʃn
recessional rɪˈseʃnl
recessive rɪˈsesɪv
recherché rəˈʃeəʃeɪ $ -ˈʃeər- ˈrəʃeərˈʃeɪ
recidivist rɪˈsɪdəvɪst
recipe ˈresəpɪ -sɪpɪ
recipient rɪˈsɪpɪənt
reciprocal rɪˈsɪprəkl
reciprocate rɪˈsɪprəkeɪt
reciprocity ˈresɪˈprosətɪ
recital rɪˈsaɪtl
recitation ˈresɪˈteɪʃn
recitative n ˈresɪtəˈtiv
recite rɪˈsaɪt
reckless ˈrekləs
reckon ˈrekən
reclaim rɪˈkleɪm
recline rɪˈklaɪn
recluse rɪˈklus
recognition ˈrekəgˈnɪʃn

recognizance rɪˈkognɪzns
recognizable ˈrekəgnaɪzəbl ˈrekəgˈnaɪzəbl
recognize ˈrekəgnaɪz
recoil rɪˈkɔɪl
recoilless rɪˈkɔɪlləs
recollect ˈrekəˈlekt
re-collect ˈri kəˈlekt
recollection ˈrekəˈlekʃn
recommend ˈrekəˈmend
recommendation ˈrekəmenˈdeɪʃn
recompense ˈrekəmpens
reconcilable ˈrekənˈsaɪləbl ˈrekənsaɪləbl
reconcile ˈrekənsaɪl $ ˈrekənˈsaɪl
reconciliation ˈrekənˈsɪlɪˈeɪʃn
recondite ˈrekəndaɪt rɪˈkondaɪt
recondition ˈrikənˈdɪʃn
reconnaissance rɪˈkonɪsns
reconnoitre($ -ter) ˈrekəˈnɔɪtə(r)
reconstruct ˈrikənˈstrʌkt
reconstruction ˈrikənˈstrʌkʃn
record n ˈrekɔd $ ˈrekərd ˈrekɔrd
record v rɪˈkɔd $ rɪˈkɔrd
record-player ˈrekɔd pleɪə(r) $ ˈrekərd
recount rɪkaʊnt
re-count n ˈri kaʊnt
re-count v ˈri ˈkaʊnt
recoup rɪˈkup
recourse rɪˈkɔs $ rɪˈkɔrs ˈrikɔrs
recover rɪˈkʌvə(r)
re-cover ˈri ˈkʌvə(r)
recovery rɪˈkʌvɽɪ
recreant ˈrekrɪənt
recreation ˈrekrɪˈeɪʃn
re-creation ˈri krɪˈeɪʃn
recreation ground ˈrekrɪˈeɪʃn graʊnd
recrimination rɪˈkrɪmɪˈneɪʃn
recriminate rɪˈkrɪmɪneɪt
recrudescence ˈrikruˈdesns £ ˈrek-
recruit rɪˈkrut
rectangle ˈrektæŋgl with t as in 'tangle', not as in 'correct angle'
rectangular rekˈtæŋgjʊlə(r)
rectification ˈrektɪfɪˈkeɪʃn
rectify ˈrektɪfaɪ
rectilinear ˈrektɪˈlɪnɪə(r)
rectitude ˈrektɪtjud $ -tud etc
rector ˈrektə(r)
rectory ˈrektərɪ
rectum ˈrektəm
recumbent rɪˈkʌmbənt
recuperate rɪˈkjupəreɪt -ˈkup-
recur rɪˈkɜ(r)

recurrence rɪˈkʌrns $ rɪˈkɜːns
recurrent rɪˈkʌrnt $ rɪˈkɜːnt
recurring rɪˈkɜːrɪŋ
recusant ˈrekjʊznt
red red
redbreast ˈredbrest
Redbrick ˈredˈbrɪk
redcap ˈredkæp
redcoat ˈredkəʊt
redden ˈredn
redeem rɪˈdiːm
redemption rɪˈdempʃn
redeploy ˈriːdɪˈplɔɪ
rediffusion ˈriːdɪˈfjuːʒn
red-handed ˈred ˈhændɪd
redhead ˈredhed
red-letter day ˈred ˈletə deɪ $ ˈletər
redo ˈriːˈduː
redolent ˈredələnt
redouble rɪˈdʌbl
redoubt rɪˈdaʊt
redoubtable rɪˈdaʊtəbl
redound rɪˈdaʊnd
redraw ˈriːˈdrɔː
redress rɪˈdres
redskin ˈredskɪn
reduce rɪˈdjuːs $ rɪˈduːs
reduction rɪˈdʌkʃn
redundancy rɪˈdʌndənsɪ
redundant rɪˈdʌndənt
reduplicate rɪˈdjuːplɪkeɪt $ rɪˈduːp-
re-echo riː ˈekəʊ
reed riːd
reef riːf
reef-knot ˈriːf nɒt
reek riːk
reel riːl
re-entry riː ˈentrɪ
reeve riːv
refectory rɪˈfektərɪ
refer rɪˈfɜː(r)
referee ˈrefəˈriː
reference ˈrefrns
reference book ˈrefrns bʊk
reference library ˈrefrns laɪbrɪ $ -brerɪ *etc*
referendum ˈrefəˈrendəm
refill *n* ˈriːfɪl
refill *v* riːˈfɪl
refine rɪˈfaɪn
refinement rɪˈfaɪnmənt
refinery rɪˈfaɪnrɪ
refit *n* ˈriːfɪt
refit *v* ˈriːˈfɪt

reflation riːˈfleɪʃn
reflect rɪˈflekt
reflection rɪˈflekʃn
reflective rɪˈflektɪv
reflector rɪˈflektə(r)
reflex ˈriːfleks
reflexive rɪˈfleksɪv
refloat riːˈfləʊt
reform rɪˈfɔm $ rɪˈfɔrm
re-form ˈriːˈfɔm $ ˈriːˈfɔrm
reformation ˈrefəˈmeɪʃn $ -fər-
reformatory rɪˈfɔmətrɪ $ rɪˈfɔrmətɔrɪ
Reform Bill rɪˈfɔm bɪl $ rɪˈfɔrm
refract rɪˈfrækt
refraction rɪˈfrækʃn
refractory rɪˈfræktərɪ
refrain rɪˈfreɪn
refresh rɪˈfreʃ
refresher course rɪˈfreʃə kɔs $ -ʃər kɔrs
refreshment rɪˈfreʃmənt
refrigerate rɪˈfrɪdʒəreɪt
refrigerator rɪˈfrɪdʒəreɪtə(r)
refuge ˈrefjuːdʒ
refugee ˈrefjʊˈdʒiː $ ˈrefjʊdʒiː *etc*
refulgent rɪˈfʌldʒənt
refund *n* ˈriːfʌnd
refund *v* riːˈfʌnd
refusal rɪˈfjuːzl
refuse *n* ˈrefjuːs
refuse *v* rɪˈfjuːz
refutation ˈrefjuːˈteɪʃn
refute rɪˈfjuːt
regain rɪˈgeɪn
regal ˈriːgl
regale rɪˈgeɪl
regalia rɪˈgeɪlɪə
regard rɪˈgad $ rɪˈgard
regatta rɪˈgætə
regency ˈriːdʒənsɪ
regenerate *adj* rɪˈdʒenərət
regenerate *v* rɪˈdʒenəreɪt
regent ˈriːdʒənt
regicide ˈredʒɪsaɪd
regime reɪˈʒiːm £ ˈreɪʒiːm $ rɪˈʒiːm
regimen ˈredʒɪmən -men
regiment ˈredʒɪmənt ˈredʒmənt
regimental ˈredʒɪˈmentl
regimentation ˈredʒɪmenˈteɪʃn
Regina rɪˈdʒaɪnə
Reginald ˈredʒɪnld
region ˈriːdʒən
regional ˈriːdʒənl
register ˈredʒɪstə(r)

registrar ˈredʒɪˌstra(r) ˌredʒɪstrɑ(r)
registration ˌredʒɪˈstreɪʃn
registry ˈredʒɪstrɪ
registry office ˈredʒɪstrɪ ofɪs $ ɔfɪs
Regius ˈridʒɪəs £ ˈridʒəs
regnant ˈregnənt
regression rɪˈgreʃn
regret rɪˈgret
regular ˈregjələ(r) -jʊ-
regularity ˌregjəˈlærətɪ -jʊ-
regularize ˈregjələraɪz -jʊ-
regulate ˈregjəleɪt -jʊ-
regulations ˌregjəˈleɪʃnz -jʊ-
regurgitate rɪˈgədʒɪteɪt rɪ-
rehabilitate ˌriəˈbɪlɪteɪt ˈrihə-
rehabilitation ˌriəˌbɪlɪˈteɪʃn ˈrihə-
rehash n ˈrihæʃ
rehash v ˈriˈhæʃ
rehearsal rɪˈhəsl
rehearse rɪˈhəs
rehouse ˈriˈhaʊz
reign reɪn
reimburse ˈriɪmˈbəs
rein reɪn
reincarnate adj ˈriɪnˈkanət $ -ˈkarneɪt
reincarnate v ˈriɪnˈkaneɪt $ -ˈkar-
reincarnation ˈriɪnkaˈneɪʃn $ -kar-
reindeer ˈreɪndɪə(r)
reinforce ˈriɪnˈfɔs $ -ˈfɔrs
reinstate ˈriɪnˈsteɪt
reinsurance ˈriɪnˈʃʊərns £ -ˈʃɔr-
reissue ˈriˈɪʃu £ ˈriˈɪsju
reiterate riˈɪtəreɪt
reiteration ˈriˈɪtəˈreɪʃn
reject n ˈridʒekt
reject v rɪˈdʒekt
rejection rɪˈdʒekʃn
rejoice rɪˈdʒɔɪs
rejoin answer rɪˈdʒɔɪn
rejoin join again ˈriˈdʒɔɪn
rejoinder rɪˈdʒɔɪndə(r)
rejuvenate rɪˈdʒuvəneɪt
rekindle ˈriˈkɪndl
relapse rɪˈlæps
relate rɪˈleɪt
relation rɪˈleɪʃn
relationship rɪˈleɪʃnʃɪp
relative ˈrelətɪv
relativity ˈreləˈtɪvətɪ
relax rɪˈlæks
relaxation ˈrilækˈseɪʃn
relay n ˈrileɪ rɪˈleɪ
relay v rɪˈleɪ

relay race ˈrileɪ reɪs
release rɪˈlis
relegate ˈreləgeɪt
relegation ˈreləˈgeɪʃn
relent rɪˈlent
relevance ˈreləvəns
relevant ˈreləvənt
reliability rɪˈlaɪəˈbɪlətɪ
reliable rɪˈlaɪəbl
reliance rɪˈlaɪəns
reliant rɪˈlaɪənt
relic ˈrelɪk
relict ˈrelɪkt
relief rɪˈlif
relieve rɪˈliv
religion rɪˈlɪdʒən
religious rɪˈlɪdʒəs
relinquish rɪˈlɪŋkwɪʃ
relish ˈrelɪʃ
relocation ˈriləʊˈkeɪʃn
reluctance rɪˈlʌktəns
reluctant rɪˈlʌktənt
rely rɪˈlaɪ
remain rɪˈmeɪn
remainder rɪˈmeɪndə(r)
remand rɪˈmand $ rɪˈmænd
remand home rɪˈmand həʊm $ -ænd
remark rɪˈmak $ rɪˈmark
remarkable rɪˈmakəbl $ -ˈmar-
remarry ˈriˈmærɪ
Rembrandt ˈrembrænt -brant
remedial rɪˈmidɪəl
remedy ˈremədɪ
remember rɪˈmembə(r)
remembrance rɪˈmembrns
Remembrance Day rɪˈmembrns deɪ
remind rɪˈmaɪnd
reminder rɪˈmaɪndə(r)
Remington ˈremɪŋtən
reminisce ˈremɪˈnɪs
reminiscence ˈremɪˈnɪsns
remiss rɪˈmɪs
remission rɪˈmɪʃn
remit rɪˈmɪt
remittance rɪˈmɪtns
remnant ˈremnənt
remonstrance rɪˈmonstrəns
remonstrate ˈremənstreɪt $ £ rɪˈmons-
remorse rɪˈmɔs $ rɪˈmɔrs
remote rɪˈməʊt
remount n ˈriˈmaʊnt ˈrimaʊnt
remount v ˈriˈmaʊnt
removal rɪˈmuvl

remove rɪˋmuv
remunerate rɪˋmjunəreɪt
remunerative rɪˋmjunɾ̣ətɪv $ -reɪtɪv *etc*
Remus ˋriməs
renaissance, R– rɪˋneɪsns -sɔ̃s
  $ ˋrenəsans ˈrenəˋsans
rename 'riˋneɪm
renascence rɪˋnæsns
Renault *car* ˋrenəʊ ˈrənəʊ
rend rend
render ˋrendə(r)
rendering ˋrendɾ̣ɪŋ
rendezvous ˋrondɪvu -deɪvu ˋrõd-
rendition renˋdɪʃn
René(e) ˋrəneɪ ˋreneɪ $ reˋneɪ rə-
renegade ˋrenɪgeɪd
reneg(u)e rɪˋnig
renew rɪˋnju $ rɪˋnu *etc*
renewal rɪˋnjuḷ $ rɪˋnuḷ *etc*
Renfrew ˋrenfru
rennet ˋrenɪt
Renoir ˋrənwɑ(r) ˋren- $ £ rəˋnwɑ(r)
renounce rɪˋnaʊns
renovate ˋrenəveɪt
renown rɪˋnaʊn
rent rent
rental ˋrentl
rent-collector ˋrent kəlektə(r)
rent-free 'rent ˋfri
rentier ˋrõtɪeɪ ˋrontɪeɪ $ rɑ̃ˋtjeɪ
renunciation rɪˋnʌnsɪˋeɪʃn
reopen 'riˋəʊpən
rep rep
repair rɪˋpeə(r)
reparable ˋrepɾ̣əbl
reparation 'repəˋreɪʃn
repartee 'repɑˋti $ -pɑr-
repast rɪˋpɑst $ rɪˋpæst
repatriate *v* rɪˋpætrɪeɪt $ ˋ-peɪt-
re-pay, repay *pay again* 'ri ˋpeɪ
repay *pay back* riˋpɔɪ rɪ-
repeal rɪˋpil
repeat rɪˋpit
repel rɪˋpel
repellent rɪˋpelənt
repent rɪˋpent
repentant rɪˋpentənt
repercussion 'ripəˋkʌʃn $ -pər-
repertoire ˋrepətwɑ(r) $ -pər-
repertory ˋrepətrɪ $ ˋrepərtɔrɪ
repertory theatre ˋrepətrɪ θɪətə(r)
  $ ˋrepərtɔrɪ
repetition 'repəˋtɪʃn

repetitive rɪˋpetətɪv
repine rɪˋpaɪn
replace rɪˋpleɪs
replay *n* ˋripleɪ
replay *v* riˋpleɪ
replenish rɪˋplenɪʃ
replete rɪˋplit
repletion rɪˋpliʃn
replica ˋreplɪkə
reply rɪˋplaɪ
repoint 'riˋpɔɪnt
report rɪˋpɔt $ rɪˋpɔrt
reportage rɪˋpɔtɪdʒ $ -ˋpɔr-
repose rɪˋpəʊz
repository rɪˋpozɪtrɪ $ -tɔrɪ
reprehend 'reprɪˋhend
reprehensible 'reprɪˋhensəbl
represent 'reprɪˋzent
re-present 'ri prɪˋzent
representation 'reprɪzenˋteɪʃn
representative 'reprɪˋzentətɪv
repress rɪˋpres
repression rɪˋpreʃn
repressive rɪˋpresɪv
reprieve rɪˋpriv
reprimand *n* ˋreprɪmɑnd $ -mænd
reprimand *v* ˋreprɪˋmɑnd
  $ -ˋmænd ˋreprɪmænd
reprint *n* ˋri-prɪnt
reprint *v* riˋprɪnt
reprisal rɪˋpraɪzl
reproach rɪˋprəʊtʃ
reprobate ˋreprəbeɪt
reproduce 'riprəˋdjus $ -ˋdus
reproduction 'riprəˋdʌkʃn
reproductive 'riprəˋdʌktɪv
reproof rɪˋpruf
reproval rɪˋpruvl
reprove rɪˋpruv
reptile ˋreptaɪl $ ˋreptəl *etc*
republic rɪˋpʌblɪk
republican, R– rɪˋpʌblɪkən
Republican Party rɪˋpʌblɪkən pɑtɪ $ pɑr-
repudiate rɪˋpjudɪeɪt
repugnant rɪˋpʌgnənt
repulse rɪˋpʌls
repulsion rɪˋpʌlʃn
repulsive rɪˋpʌlsɪv
reputable ˋrepjʊtəbl
reputation 'repjʊˋteɪʃn
repute rɪˋpjut
request rɪˋkwest
requiem ˋrekwɪəm -wɪem

require rɪˈkwaɪə(r)
requisite ˈrekwɪzɪt
requisition ˈrekwɪˈzɪʃn
requital rɪˈkwaɪtl
requite rɪˈkwaɪt
reredos ˈrɪədos $ £ ˈreərədos ˈrɪərə- etc
rescind rɪˈsɪnd
rescue ˈreskju
rescuer ˈreskjuə(r)
research rɪˈsɜtʃ $ £ ˈrisɜtʃ etc
resemblance rɪˈzembləns
resemble rɪˈzembl
resent rɪˈzent
resentment rɪˈzentmənt
reservation ˈrezəˈveɪʃn $ -zər-
reserve rɪˈzɜv
reservoir ˈrezəvwa(r)
  $ -zərv- -zəv- -vɔr
reset ˈriˈset
resettle ˈriˈsetl
reshuffle ˈriˈʃʌfl
reside rɪˈzaɪd
residence ˈrezɪdəns
residency ˈrezɪdənsɪ
resident ˈrezɪdənt
residential ˈrezɪˈdenʃl
residual rɪˈzɪdjuəl $ £ rɪˈzɪdʒuəl
residuary rɪˈzɪdjuərɪ $ rɪˈzɪdʒuerɪ
residue ˈrezɪdju $ -du
resign rɪˈzaɪn
resignation ˈrezɪgˈneɪʃn
resignedly rɪˈzaɪnɪdlɪ
resilient rɪˈzɪlɪənt
resin ˈrezɪn $ ˈrezn
resist rɪˈzɪst
resistance rɪˈzɪstəns
resistance movement rɪˈzɪstəns muvmənt
resistant rɪˈzɪstənt
resole ˈriˈsəʊl
resolute ˈrezəlut £ -ljut
resolution ˈrezəˈluʃn
resolve rɪˈzolv
resonance ˈrezənəns
resonant ˈrezənənt
resort rɪˈzɔt $ rɪˈzɔrt
resound rɪˈzaʊnd
resources rɪˈsɔsɪz rɪˈzɔsɪz $ -ɔrs-
respect rɪˈspekt
respectability rɪˈspektəˈbɪlətɪ
respectable rɪˈspektəbl
respective rɪˈspektɪv
respiration ˈrespəˈreɪʃn
respirator ˈrespəreɪtə(r)

respire rɪˈspaɪə(r)
respite ˈrespaɪt $ ˈrespɪt
resplendent rɪˈsplendənt
respond rɪˈspond
respondent rɪˈspondənt
response rɪˈspons
responsibility rɪˈsponsəˈbɪlətɪ
responsible rɪˈsponsəbl
responsive rɪˈsponsɪv
rest rest
restate ˈriˈsteɪt
restaurant ˈrestrɔ̃ -rõ -rɒnt -ront
  $ ˈrestərənt -rant -tr-
rest-cure ˈresk kjʊə(r)
rest-day ˈrest deɪ
rest-house ˈrest haʊs
restitution ˈrestɪˈtjuʃn $ -ˈtuʃn
restive ˈrestɪv
restock ˈriˈstok
restoration, R– ˈrestəˈreɪʃn
restorative rɪˈstɔrətɪv
restore rɪˈstɔ(r)
restrain rɪˈstreɪn
restraint rɪˈstreɪnt
restrict rɪˈstrɪkt
restriction rɪˈstrɪkʃn
result rɪˈzʌlt
resultant rɪˈzʌltənt
resume rɪˈzjum $ £ rɪˈzum
résumé ˈrezʊmeɪ -zjʊ- $ ˈrezʊˈmeɪ
resumption rɪˈzʌmpʃn
resurface ˈriˈsɜfɪs
resurgent rɪˈsɜdʒənt
resurrect ˈrezəˈrekt
resurrection, R– ˈrezəˈrekʃn
resuscitate rɪˈsʌsɪteɪt
resuscitation rɪˈsʌsɪˈteɪʃn
retail adj ˈriteɪl
retail v rɪˈteɪl
retain rɪˈteɪn
retaliate rɪˈtælɪeɪt
retaliation rɪˈtælɪˈeɪʃn
retaliatory rɪˈtælɪətrɪ $ -tɔrɪ
retard rɪˈtad $ rɪˈtard
retch retʃ £ rɪtʃ
retell ˈriˈtel
retention rɪˈtenʃn
retentive rɪˈtentɪv
rethink ˈriˈθɪŋk
reticent ˈretɪsnt
reticulate adj rɪˈtɪkjʊlət
reticulate v rɪˈtɪkjʊleɪt
reticule ˈretɪkjul

retina ˈretɪnə
retinue ˈretɪnju ˈretn̩ju -nu
retire rɪˈtaɪər
retirement rɪˈtaɪəmənt $ -ˈtaɪər-
retirement pension rɪˈtaɪəmənt penʃn
 $ -ˈtaɪər-
retool ˈriˈtul
retort rɪˈtɔt $ rɪˈtɔrt
retouch ˈriˈtʌtʃ
retrace riˈtreɪs
retract rɪˈtrækt
retraction rɪˈtrækʃn
retread n ˈritred ˈriˈtred
retread v ˈriˈtred
retreat rɪˈtrit
retrench rɪˈtrentʃ
retrial ˈriˈtraɪl̩
retribution ˈretrɪˈbjuʃn
retributive rɪˈtrɪbjʊtɪv
retrieval rɪˈtrivl
retrieve rɪˈtriv
retroactive ˈretrəʊˈæktɪv
retrograde ˈretrəgreɪd -trəʊg-
retrogression ˈretrəˈgreʃn -trəʊg-
retro-rocket ˈretrəʊ rokɪt
retrospect ˈretrəspekt
retrospective ˈretrəˈspektɪv
retroussé rəˈtruseɪ $ ˈretrʊˈseɪ -tru- ˈrə-
return rɪˈtɜn
returning officer rɪˈtɜnɪŋ ˈofɪsə(r) $ ˈɔf-
reunion ˈriˈjunɪən
reunite ˈrijuˈnaɪt
Reuter ˈrɔɪtə(r)
rev rev
Rev. ˈrevərənd
revaluation ˈriˈvæljʊˈeɪʃn
revalue riˈvælju
revamp ˈriˈvæmp
reveal rɪˈvil
reveille rɪˈvælɪ $ ˈrevəlɪ
revel ˈrevl
revelation ˈrevəˈleɪʃn
revenge rɪˈvendʒ
revenue ˈrevənju $ -nu
reverberate rɪˈvɜbəreɪt
revere rɪˈvɪə(r)
reverence ˈrevərəns
reverend ˈrevərənd
reverent ˈrevərənt
reverential ˈrevəˈrenʃl
reverie ˈrevərɪ
revers plural rɪˈvɪəz $ rɪˈvɪərz
revers sing rɪˈvɪə(r)

reverse rɪˈvɜs
reversible rɪˈvɜsəbl
reversion rɪˈvɜʃn $ rɪˈvɜʒn etc
revert rɪˈvɜt
review rɪˈvju
revile rɪˈvaɪl
revise rɪˈvaɪz
revival rɪˈvaɪvl
revive rɪˈvaɪv
revocable ˈrevəkəbl rɪˈvəʊkəbl
revoke rɪˈvəʊk
revolt rɪˈvəʊlt
revolution ˈrevəˈluʃn
revolutionary ˈrevəˈluʃnrɪ $ -nerɪ
revolve rɪˈvolv
revue rɪˈvju
revulsion rɪˈvʌlʃn
reward rɪˈwɔd $ rɪˈwɔrd
reword ˈriˈwɜd
rewrite ˈriˈraɪt
rex, R- reks
rhapsodize ˈræpsədaɪz
rhapsody ˈræpsədɪ
Rheims rimz
Rhenish ˈrenɪʃ ˈrinɪʃ
rheostat ˈrɪəstæt
rhesus ˈrisəs
rhetoric ˈretərɪk
rhetorical rɪˈtorɪkl
rhetorician ˈretəˈrɪʃn
rheum rum
rheumatic ruˈmætɪk
rheumatism ˈrumətɪzm
rheumatoid ˈrumətɔɪd
Rhine raɪn
Rhinestone ˈraɪn-stəʊn
rhino ˈraɪnəʊ
rhinosceros raɪˈnosərəs
Rhode Island ˈrəʊd ˈaɪlənd
Rhodesia rəʊˈdiʃə -ˈdizɪə -ˈdiʒə
rhododendron ˈrəʊdəˈdendrən
rhombus ˈrombəs
rhubarb ˈrubab $ ˈrubarb
rhyme raɪm
rhythm ˈrɪðm
rhythmical ˈrɪðmɪkl
rib rɪb
ribald ˈrɪbld
ribaldry ˈrɪbldrɪ
ribbon ˈrɪbən
ribbon development ˈrɪbən dɪveləpmənt
rice raɪs
rich rɪtʃ

Richard ˈrɪtʃəd $ ˈrɪtʃərd
riches ˈrɪtʃɪz
rick rɪk
rickets ˈrɪkɪts
rickety ˈrɪkɪtɪ
rickshaw ˈrɪkʃɔ
ricochet ˈrɪkəʃeɪ $ ˈrɪkəˈʃeɪ
rid rɪd
riddance ˈrɪdns
ridden ˈrɪdn
riddle ˈrɪdl
ride raɪd
ridge rɪdʒ
ridicule ˈrɪdɪkjul
ridiculous rɪˈdɪkjələs
riding-breeches ˈraɪdɪŋ brɪtʃɪz
riding-habit ˈraɪdɪŋ hæbɪt
rife raɪf
rifle ˈraɪfl
rifle-range ˈraɪfl reɪndʒ
rifle-shot ˈraɪfl ʃot
rift rɪft
rig rɪg
right raɪt
right-about turn ˈraɪt əbaʊt ˈtɜn
right-angled ˈraɪt æŋgld
righteous ˈraɪtʃəs
rightful ˈraɪtfl
right-hand ˈraɪt ˈhænd
right-handed ˈraɪt ˈhændɪd
right-minded ˈraɪt ˈmaɪndɪd
rigid ˈrɪdʒɪd
rigidity rɪˈdʒɪdətɪ
rigmarole ˈrɪgmərəʊl
Rigoletto ˈrɪgəˈletəʊ
rigor mortis ˈraɪgɔ ˈmɔtɪs ˈrɪgə
  $ ˈrɪgər ˈmɔrtɪs
rigorous ˈrɪgərəs
rigour($ -gor) ˈrɪgə(r)
rile raɪl
rill rɪl
rim rɪm
rime raɪm
Rimsky-Korsakov ˈrɪmskɪ ˈkɔsəkof -ov
  $ ˈkɔrsəkɔf
rind raɪnd
ring rɪŋ
ring-finger ˈrɪŋ fɪŋgə(r)
ring-leader ˈrɪŋ lidə(r)
ringlet ˈrɪŋlət
ring-road ˈrɪŋ rəʊd
ringside ˈrɪŋsaɪd
ringworm ˈrɪŋwɜm

rink rɪŋk
rinse rɪns
Rio Grande ˈriəʊ ˈgrænd
Rio de Janeiro ˈriəʊ dɪ dʒəˈneərəʊ -ˈnɪər-
riot ˈraɪət
riotous ˈraɪətəs
rip rɪp
rip-cord ˈrɪpkɔd $ ˈrɪpkɔrd
ripe raɪp
riposte rɪˈpəʊst -post
ripple ˈrɪpl
Rip Van Winkle ˈrɪp ˈvæn ˈwɪŋkl væn
rise raɪz
risen ˈrɪzn
risible ˈrɪzəbl
risk rɪsk
risotto rɪˈzotəʊ $ -ˈso- rɪˈsotəʊ -ˈzɔ-
risqué ˈriskeɪ $ rɪˈskeɪ
rissole ˈrɪsəʊl
Rita ˈritə
rite raɪt
ritual ˈrɪtʃʊəl
rival ˈraɪvl
rivalry ˈraɪvlrɪ
rive raɪv
river ˈrɪvə(r)
riverside ˈrɪvəsaɪd $ ˈrɪvər-
rivet ˈrɪvɪt
riviera ˈrɪvɪˈeərə
rivulet ˈrɪvjʊlət -let
roach rəʊtʃ
road rəʊd
road-block ˈrəʊd blok
road-hog ˈrəʊd hog $ hɔg etc
road-house ˈrəʊd haʊs
road-sense ˈrəʊd sens
roadside ˈrəʊdsaɪd
roadway ˈrəʊdweɪ
roam rəʊm
roan rəʊn
roar rɔ(r)
roast rəʊst
rob rob
robbery ˈrobərɪ
robe rəʊb
Robert ˈrobət $ ˈrobərt
robin ˈrobɪn
robot ˈrəʊbot $ ˈrəʊbət
robust rəʊˈbʌst rəˈbʌst $ ˈrəʊbʌst
rock rok
rock-bottom ˈrok ˈbotəm
rock-cake ˈrok keɪk
rock-climbing ˈrok klaɪmɪŋ

Rockefeller ˈrɒkəfelə(r)
rockery ˈrɒkərɪ
rocket ˈrɒkɪt
rocket-range ˈrɒkɪt reɪndʒ
rock-garden ˈrɒk ɡɑdn $ ɡɑrdn
Rockies ˈrɒkɪz
rocking-chair ˈrɒkɪŋ tʃeə(r)
rocking-horse ˈrɒkɪŋ hɔs $ hɔrs
rock-salmon ˈrɒk ˈsæmən
rock-salt ˈrɒk ˈsɔlt £ ˈsolt
rocky ˈrɒkɪ
rococo rəˈkəʊkəʊ rəʊ-
rod rɒd
rode rəʊd
rodent ˈrəʊdnt
rodeo rəʊˈdeɪəʊ $ ˈrəʊdɪəʊ etc
Roderick ˈrɒdərɪk
Rodney ˈrɒdnɪ
roe rəʊ
Roentgen see ‘Rontgen’ below
rogation rəʊˈɡeɪʃn
Roger ˈrɒdʒə(r)
rogue rəʊɡ
roguery ˈrəʊɡərɪ
roguish ˈrəʊɡɪʃ
roisterer ˈrɔɪstərə(r)
Roland ˈrəʊlənd
rôle rəʊl
roll rəʊl
roll-call ˈrəʊl kɔl
roller-skates ˈrəʊlə skeɪts $ ˈrəʊlər
rollicking ˈrɒlɪkɪŋ
rolling-pin ˈrəʊlɪŋ pɪn
rolling-stock ˈrəʊlɪŋ stɒk
roll-on ˈrəʊl ɒn
roll-top desk ˈrəʊl tɒp ˈdesk
Rolls Royce ˈrəʊlz ˈrɔɪs
roly-poly ˈrəʊlɪ ˈpəʊlɪ
Roman ˈrəʊmən
romance, R– rəˈmæns $ ˈrəʊmæns
Romanesque ˈrəʊməˈnesk
Romania rəʊˈmeɪnɪə
romantic rəˈmæntɪk $ £ rəʊ-
romanticize rəˈmæntɪsaɪz
Romany ˈrɒmənɪ £ ˈrəʊmənɪ
Romeo ˈrəʊmɪəʊ
romp rɒmp
Ronald ˈrɒnld
rondo ˈrɒndəʊ
Roneo ˈrəʊnɪəʊ
Röntgen ˈrɒntjən -ntɡən ˈrʌn- ˈrɜn-
 $ ˈrentɡən ˈrʌn- -tjən
rood-screen ˈrudskrin

roof ruf $ rʊf
roof-garden ˈruf ɡɑdn $ ɡɑrdn ˈrʊf
rook rʊk
rookery rʊkərɪ
room rʊm $ £ rum etc
room-mate ˈrʊm meɪt $ £ rum etc
Roosevelt ˈrəʊzəvelt -zv-
roost rust
root rut $ rʊt
root-crop ˈrut krɒp $ rʊt
rootle ˈrutl
rope rəʊp
rope-ladder ˈrəʊp ˈlædə(r) ˈrəʊp lædə(r)
rope-trick ˈrəʊp trɪk
Rosalind ˈrɒzəlɪnd
rosary ˈrəʊzərɪ
rose, R– rəʊz
roseate ˈrəʊzɪət -zɪɪt -zɪeɪt
rosebud ˈrəʊzbʌd
roseleaf ˈrəʊzlif
rosemary, R– ˈrəʊzmərɪ -mrɪ $ -merɪ etc
rosette rəˈzet $ £ rəʊˈzet
rose-water ˈrəʊz wɔtə(r)
rose window ˈrəʊz wɪndəʊ
rosewood ˈrəʊzwʊd
rosin ˈrɒzɪn $ ˈrɒzn etc
Rossetti rəˈzetɪ rəˈsetɪ ro-
Rossini rəˈsini ro- $ rɒ- etc
roster ˈrɒstə(r)
rostrum ˈrɒstrəm
rosy ˈrəʊzɪ
rot rɒt
rota ˈrəʊtə
Rotarian rəʊˈteərɪən
rotary ˈrəʊtərɪ
rotate rəʊˈteɪt $ ˈrəʊteɪt
rotation rəʊˈteɪʃn
rotatory ˈrəʊtətərɪ rəʊˈteɪtərɪ $ -tɔrɪ
rote rəʊt
rot-gut ˈrɒt ɡʌt
rotor ˈrəʊtə(r)
rotten ˈrɒtn
rotter ˈrɒtə(r)
Rotterdam ˈrɒtədæm $ ˈrɒtər-
rotund rəʊˈtʌnd
rotunda rəʊˈtʌndə
rotundity rəʊˈtʌndətɪ
rouble ˈrubl
roué ˈrueɪ $ ruˈeɪ
Rouen ˈruɒ̃ $ ruˈɒ̃ ruˈɑn
rouge ruʒ
rough rʌf
roughage ˈrʌfɪdʒ

rough-and-tumble 'rʌf n 'tʌmbl
rough-cast 'rʌf kɑst $ kæst
rough-hew 'rʌf 'hju
rough house 'rʌf haʊs
rough-neck 'rʌf nek
rough-rider 'rʌf raɪdə(r)
roughshod adv 'rʌfʃod
rough-spoken 'rʌf 'spəʊkən
roulette ru'let
roulette wheel ru'let wil $ hwil etc
Roumania ru'meɪnɪə
round raʊnd
roundabout adj, n 'raʊndəbaʊt
round about adv, prep 'raʊnd ə'baʊt
roundelay 'raʊndɪleɪ
rounders 'raʊndəz $ -dərz
round-eyed 'raʊnd 'aɪd
roundhead 'raʊndhed
round-shouldered 'raʊnd 'ʃəʊldəd $ -ərd
roundsman 'raʊndzmən
round-the-clock 'raʊnd ðə 'klok
rouse raʊz
Rousseau 'rusəʊ $ ru'səʊ
rout raʊt
route rut $ raʊt
route-march 'rut mɑtʃ $ mɑrtʃ
routine ru'tin
rove rəʊv
rover 'rəʊvə(r)
row a line; propel a boat rəʊ
row noise raʊ
rowan 'raʊən 'rəʊən
rowdy 'raʊdɪ
rowel 'raʊəl
rowing-boat 'rəʊɪŋ bəʊt
rowlock 'rolək 'rʌl- $ 'rəʊlok etc
Roxburgh 'roksbərə $ -bʌrə etc
royal 'rɔɪəl 'rɔɪl
royalty 'rɔɪəltɪ 'rɔɪltɪ
r.s.v.p. 'ɑr es vi 'pi
Rt. Hon. 'raɪt 'onrbl
rub rʌb
rub-a-dub 'rʌb ə 'dʌb
rubber 'rʌbə(r)
rubber-neck 'rʌbə nek $ 'rʌbər
rubber-stamp 'rʌbə 'stæmp $ 'rʌbər
rubbish 'rʌbɪʃ
rubble 'rʌbl
rub-down 'rʌb daʊn
Rubens 'rubɪn -ənz
Rubicon 'rubɪkən $ -kon
rubicund 'rubɪkənd
rubric 'rubrɪk

ruby 'rubɪ
ruck rʌk
rucksack 'rʌksæk 'rʊksæk
ructions 'rʌkʃnz
rudder 'rʌdə(r)
ruddy 'rʌdɪ
rude rud
rudimentary 'rudɪ'mentrɪ
rudiments 'rudɪmənts
Rudolph 'rudolf
rue ru
rueful 'rufl with u as in 'too', not
    shortened as in 'roof'
ruff rʌf
ruffian 'rʌfɪən
ruffle 'rʌfl
rug rʌg
Rugby 'rʌgbɪ
rugged 'rʌgɪd
rugger 'rʌgə(r)
ruin 'ruɪn
ruination 'ruɪ'neɪʃn
ruinous 'ruɪnəs
rule rul
ruler 'rulə(r)
rum rʌm
Rumania ru'meɪnɪə
rumble 'rʌmbl
ruminant 'rumɪnənt
ruminate 'rumɪneɪt
rumination 'rumɪ'neɪʃn
rummage 'rʌmɪdʒ
rummy 'rʌmɪ
rumour($ -or) 'rumə(r)
rump rʌmp
rumple 'rʌmpl
rump-steak 'rʌmp steɪk 'rʌmp 'steɪk
rumpus 'rʌmpəs
run rʌn
run-about n 'rʌn əbaʊt
runaway 'rʌnəweɪ
rune run
runic 'runɪk
rung rʌŋ
runner-up 'rʌnər 'ʌp
running-board 'rʌnɪŋ bɔd $ bɔrd
running knot 'rʌnɪŋ not
Runnymede 'rʌnɪmid
runt rʌnt
rupee ru'pi
Rupert 'rupət $ 'rupərt
rupture 'rʌptʃə(r)
rural 'ruərl

ruse ruz $ rus *etc*
rush rʌʃ
rush-hour 'rʌʃ aʊə(r)
rusk rʌsk
Russell 'rʌsl
russet 'rʌsɪt
Russia 'rʌʃə
Russian 'rʌʃn
rust rʌst

rustic 'rʌstɪk
rusticate 'rʌstɪkeɪt
rustle 'rʌsl
rut rʌt
Ruth ruθ
ruthless 'ruθləs
Rwanda ru'ændə $ ru'andə
rye raɪ
rye-bread 'raɪ bred

S

S s es
s. *old British currency* 'ʃɪlɪŋ(z)
sabbatarian 'sæbə'teərɪən
Sabbath 'sæbəθ
sabbatical sə'bætɪkl
sable 'seɪbl
sabot 'sæbəʊ
sabotage 'sæbətaʒ $ 'sæbə'taʒ
sabre($ -er) 'seɪbə(r)
sac sæk
saccharin 'sækərɪn
saccharine 'sækərin -rɪn
sacerdotal 'sæsə'dəʊtl $ -sər-
sachet 'sæʃeɪ $ sæ'ʃeɪ
sack sæk
sackcloth 'sækkloθ $ 'sækklɔθ
sack-race 'sæk reɪs
sacrament 'sækrəmənt
Sacramento 'sækrə'mentəʊ
sacred 'seɪkrəd -rɪd
sacrifice 'sækrɪfaɪs
sacrificial 'sækrɪ'fɪʃl
sacrilege 'sækrɪlɪdʒ
sacrilegious 'sækrɪ'lɪdʒəs $ -'lɪdʒəs
sacristan 'sækrɪstən
sacristy 'sækrɪstɪ
sacrosanct 'sækrəʊsæŋkt
sad sæd
sadden 'sædn
saddle-bag 'sædl bæg
saddler 'sædlə(r)
Sadie seɪdɪ
sadism 'sæd-ɪzm 'seɪd- *as two words*
sadist 'sædɪst 'seɪd-
sadistic sə'dɪstɪk
safari sə'farɪ
safe seɪf
safe-conduct 'seɪf 'kondʌkt

safe-deposit 'seɪf dɪpozɪt
safeguard 'seɪf gad $ gard
safe-keeping 'seɪf 'kipɪŋ
safety 'seɪftɪ
safety-curtain 'seɪftɪ kɜtn
safety-lamp 'seɪftɪ læmp
safety-match 'seɪftɪ mætʃ
safety-pin 'seɪftɪ pɪn
safety-razor 'seɪftɪ reɪzə(r)
safety-valve 'seɪftɪ vælv
saffron 'sæfrən
sag sæg
saga 'sagə
sagacious sə'geɪʃəs
sagacity sə'gæsətɪ
sage seɪdʒ
sage-green 'seɪdʒ 'grin
Sagittarius 'sædʒɪ'teərɪəs
sago 'seɪgəʊ
Sahara sə'harə $ sə'hærə sə'heərə *etc*
Sahib sab 'sa-ɪb 'sahɪb
said sed
sail seɪl
sail-cloth 'seɪl kloθ $ klɔθ
sailing-boat 'seɪlɪŋ bəʊt
sailing-ship 'seɪlɪŋ ʃɪp
sailor 'seɪlə(r)
sailor suit 'seɪlə sut £ sjut $ 'seɪlər
saint seɪnt *before names:* snt $ seɪnt
St Albans snt 'ɔlbənz $ 'seɪnt
St Bernard snt 'bɜnəd $ 'seɪnt bər'nard
St Louis snt 'luɪ $ 'seɪnt 'luɪs
St Pancras snt 'pæŋkrəs $ seɪnt
St Valentine's Day snt 'væləntaɪnz deɪ
    $ 'seɪnt
saith seθ
sake seɪk
saké 'sakɪ

salaam sə'lɑm
salable 'seɪləbl
salacious sə'leɪʃəs
salacity sə'læsətɪ
salad 'sæləd
salad-days 'sæləd deɪz
salad-dressing 'sæləd 'dresɪŋ
salad-oil 'sæləd ɔɪl
salamander 'sæləmændə(r)
salami sə'lɑmɪ
salaried 'sælərɪd
salary 'sælərɪ
sale seɪl
Salem 'seɪləm
salesman 'seɪlzmən
sales resistance 'seɪlz rɪzɪstəns
sales tax 'seɪlz tæks
salient 'seɪlɪənt
saline 'seɪlaɪn $ 'seɪlin etc
salinity sə'lɪnətɪ
Salisbury 'sɔlzbrɪ £ 'sɒl- $ -berɪ
saliva sə'laɪvə
salivary 'sælɪvərɪ sə'laɪvərɪ $ 'sælɪverɪ
sallow 'sæləʊ $ 'sælə
sally, S– 'sælɪ
salmon 'sæmən
Salome sə'ləʊmɪ
salon 'sælɒ̃ $ 'sælɔ̃ sə'lɒn sæ'lɒn
Salonica sə'lɒnɪkə
saloon sə'lun
salt sɔlt £ sɒlt
salt-cellar 'sɔlt selə(r) £ sɒlt
saltpetre($ -ter) sɔlt'pitə(r) £ sɒlt-
salubrious sə'lubrɪəs
salutary 'sæljʊtrɪ $ -terɪ
salutation 'sælju'teɪʃn
salute sə'lut
Salvador, El el 'sælvədə(r)
salvage 'sælvɪdʒ
salvation sæl'veɪʃn
salve ointment sɑv sælv $ sæv
salve save sælv
salver 'sælvə(r)
salvo 'sælvəʊ
sal volatile 'sæl və'lætəlɪ
Samaritan sə'mærɪtən
same seɪm
samovar 'sæməvɑ(r)
sampan 'sæmpæn
sample 'sɑmpl $ 'sæmpl
sampler 'sɑmplə(r) $ 'sæmplər
Samson 'sæmsn
Samuel 'sæmjʊəl

sanatorium 'sænə'tɔrɪəm
sanctify 'sæŋktɪfaɪ
sanctimonious 'sæŋktɪ'məʊnɪəs
sanction 'sæŋkʃn
sanctity 'sæŋktətɪ
sanctuary 'sæŋktʃʊərɪ $ -tʃuerɪ
sanctum 'sæŋktəm
sand sænd
sandal 'sændl
sandal-wood 'sændl wʊd
sand-bag 'sænd bæg
sandfly 'sændflaɪ
Sandhurst 'sændhɜst
sandpaper 'sændpeɪpə(r)
Sandra 'sændrə £ 'sɑndrə
sandstone 'sændstəʊn
sand-storm 'sænd stɔm $ stɔrm
sandwich 'sænwɪdʒ 'sænd- $ £ -wɪtʃ
sandwich-boards 'sænwɪdʒ bɔdz
   $ 'sænwɪtʃ bɔrdz
sandwich-man 'sænwɪdʒ mæn $ -wɪtʃ
sane seɪn
San Francisco 'sæn frən'sɪskəʊ £ fræn-
sang sæŋ
sang froid 'sɒŋ 'frwɑ 'sɔ̃ $ 'sæŋ
sanguinary 'sæŋgwɪnərɪ -nrɪ $ -nerɪ
sanguine 'sæŋgwɪn
sanitarium 'sænɪ'teərɪəm
sanitary 'sænɪtrɪ $ -terɪ
sanitary inspector 'sænɪtrɪ ɪnspektə(r)
   $ -terɪ
sanitary napkin 'sænɪtrɪ næpkɪn $ -terɪ
sanitary towel 'sænɪtrɪ taʊl $ -terɪ
sanitation 'sænɪ'teɪʃn
sanity 'sænətɪ
sank sæŋk
sans sænz
Sanskrit 'sænskrɪt
Santa Claus 'sæntə 'klɔz $ £ 'sæntə klɔz
Santiago 'sæntɪ'ɑgəʊ
sap sæp
sapient 'seɪpɪənt $ 'sæpɪənt
sapling 'sæplɪŋ
Sapphic 'sæfɪk
sapphire 'sæfaɪə(r)
Sara 'seərə £ 'sɑrə
saraband 'særəbænd
Saracen 'særəsn
Sarah 'seərə
Saratoga 'særə'təʊgə
Sarawak sə'rɑwək -wə $ -wɑk -wɑ etc
sarcasm 'sɑkæzm $ 'sɑr-
sarcastic sɑ'kæstɪk $ sɑr-

sarcophagus saˋkofəgəs $ sar-
sardine saˋdin $ sar-
Sardinia saˋdınıə $ sar-
sardonic saˋdonık $ sar-
sari ˋsarı
sarong səˋroŋ $ səˋrɔŋ etc
sarsaparilla ˋsaspəˋrılə -səp-
  $ ˋsæs- -relə
sartorial saˋtɔrıəl $ sar-
sash sæʃ
sash-cord ˋsæʃ kɔd $ kɔrd
Saskatchewan səsˋkætʃəwən
  $ £ -won $ sæs-
sat sæt
Satan ˋseitn
satanic səˋtænık $ £ seiˋtænık
satchel ˋsætʃl
sate seit
sateen sæˋtin səˋtin
satellite ˋsætəlait ˋsætlait
satiate ˋseiʃieit
satiety səˋtaıətı
satin ˋsætın $ ˋsætn etc
satinwood ˋsætınwʊd $ -tn- etc
satire ˋsætaıə(r)
satirical səˋtırıkl
satirist ˋsætərıst
satirize ˋsætəraız
satisfaction ˋsætısˋfækʃn
satisfactory ˋsætısˋfæktrı
satisfy ˋsætısfaı
saturate ˋsætʃəreit
saturation ˋsætʃəˋreiʃn
saturation point ˋsætʃəˋreiʃn pɔint
Saturday ˋsætədı -dei $ -tər-
Saturn ˋsætən $ ˋsætərn
saturnine ˋsætənaın $ -tər-
satyr ˋsætə(r) ˋseitə(r)
sauce sɔs $ sauciness sæs
saucepan ˋsɔspən $ -pæn etc
saucer ˋsɔsə(r)
saucer-eyed ˋsɔsər ˋaid
Saudi Arabia ˋsaudı əˋreibıə
sauerkraut ˋsauəkraut $ ˋsauər-
sauna ˋsaunə ˋsɔnə
saunter ˋsɔntə(r)
sausage ˋsosıdʒ $ ˋsɔsıdʒ
sausage-meat ˋsosıdʒ mit $ ˋsɔs-
sausage-roll ˋsosıdʒ ˋrəul $ ˋsɔs-
sauté ˋsautei $ səuˋtei etc
savage ˋsævıdʒ
savagery ˋsævıdʒrı
savanna(h) səˋvænə

savant ˋsævõ ˋsævənt
  $ sæˋvant səˋv- -ˋvã -ˋvænt etc
save seiv
saveloy ˋsævəlɔı
Savile Row ˋsævl ˋrəu
savings bank ˋseivıŋz bæŋk
saviour, S- ˋseivıə(r)
savoir faire ˋsævwa ˋfeə(r) $ -war
savour($ -vor) ˋseivə(r)
savoury($ -vory) ˋseivərı
savoy səˋvɔı
savvy ˋsævı
saw sɔ
sawdust ˋsɔdʌst
sawmill ˋsɔmıl
sawn sɔn
sawyer ˋsɔjə(r)
Saxon ˋsæksn
saxophone ˋsæksəfəun
say sei
says sez
scab skæb
scabbard ˋskæbəd $ -bərd
scabies ˋskeibiz
scabrous ˋskeibrəs $ ˋskæb-
scaffolding ˋskæfldıŋ -fəul-
scalawag ˋskæləwæg
scald skɔld
scale skeil
scallop ˋskoləp ˋskæləp
scallop-shell ˋskoləp ʃel
scallywag ˋskælıwæg
scalp skælp
scalpel ˋskælpl $ skælˋpel
scamp skæmp
scamper ˋskæmpə(r)
scampi ˋskæmpı -pi
scan skæn
scandal ˋskændl
scandalize ˋskændəlaız
scandalmonger ˋskændlmʌŋgə(r)
scandalous ˋskændələs
Scandinavia ˋskændıˋneivıə
Scandinavian ˋskændıˋneiviən
scansion ˋskænʃn
scant skænt
scapegoat ˋskeipgəut
scapula ˋskæpjulə
scar ska(r)
Scarborough ˋskabrə $ ˋskarbərə
scarab ˋskærəb
scarce skeəs $ skeərs
scarcity ˋskeəsətı $ ˋskeərsətı

scare skeə(r)
scarecrow ˈskeəkrəu $ ˈskeər-
scarf skaf $ skarf
scarf-pin ˈskaf pɪn $ ˈskarf
scarify ˈskærɪfaɪ ˈskeər-
scarlet ˈskalət -lɪt $ ˈskar-
scarves skavz $ skarvz
scathing ˈskeɪðɪŋ
scatter ˈskætə(r)
scatterbrain ˈskætəbreɪn $ -tər-
scavenger ˈskævɪndʒə(r)
scenario sɪˈnariəu $ sɪˈnæriəu etc
scene sin
scene-painter ˈsin peɪntə(r)
scenery ˈsinərɪ
scene-shifter ˈsin ʃɪftə(r)
scenic ˈsinɪk
scent sent
sceptic ˈskeptɪk
sceptical ˈskeptɪkl
scepticism ˈskeptɪsɪzm
sceptre($ -ter) ˈseptə(r)
Sch. skul
schedule ˈʃedjul $ ˈskedʒl -dʒul
schematic skɪˈmætɪk skiˈm-
scheme skim
scherzo ˈskeətsəu $ ˈskeər-
schism ˈsɪzm ˈʃɪzm £ ˈskɪzm
schizophrenia ˈskɪtsəuˈfrɪnɪə
schizophrenic ˈskɪtsəuˈfrenɪk
schnap(p)s ʃnæps
schnorkel ˈʃnɔkl $ ˈʃnɔrkl
scholar ˈskolə(r)
scholarship ˈskoləʃɪp $ -lər-
scholastic skəˈlæstɪk
Scholasticism skəˈlæstɪsɪzm
school skul
school age ˈskul eɪdʒ
school-book ˈskul bʊk
schoolboy ˈskulbɔɪ
school-days ˈskul deɪz
school-fellow ˈskul feləu
schoolgirl ˈskulgəl
schoolhouse ˈskulhaʊs
school-ma(')am(-marm) ˈskul mam
$ marm·mæm
schoolmaster ˈskulmastə(r) $ -mæstər
schoolmate ˈskulmeɪt
schoolmistress ˈskulmɪstrəs -rɪs
school-teacher ˈskul titʃə(r)
school-time ˈskul taɪm
schooner ˈskunə(r)
Schubert ˈʃubət $ ˈʃubərt

Schumann ˈʃumæn -mən $ £ ˈʃuman
sciatica saɪˈætɪkə
science ˈsaɪəns
scientific ˈsaɪənˈtɪfɪk
scientist ˈsaɪəntɪst
scimitar ˈsɪmɪtə(r) -tə(r)
scintillate ˈsɪntɪleɪt $ ˈsɪntʃeɪt
scion ˈsaɪən
scissors ˈsɪzəz $ ˈsɪzərz
sclerosis skləˈrəusɪs sklɪə-
scoff skof $ skɔf
scold skəuld
scollop ˈskoləp
sconce skons
scone skon $ £ skəun
scoop skup
scoot skut
scooter ˈskutə(r)
scope skəup
scorch skɔtʃ $ skɔrtʃ
score skɔ(r)
score-board ˈskɔ bɔd $ ˈskɔr bɔrd
score-card ˈskɔ kad $ ˈskɔr kard
scorn skɔn $ skɔrn
Scorpio ˈskɔpɪəu $ ˈskɔrpɪəu
scorpion ˈskɔpɪən $ ˈskɔrpɪən
scot, S- skot
scotch, S- skotʃ
Scotchman ˈskotʃmən
scot-free ˈskot ˈfri
Scotland ˈskotlənd
Scotsman ˈskotsmən
Scottish ˈskotɪʃ
scoundrel ˈskaundrl
scour ˈskauə(r)
scourge skədʒ
scout skaut
scoutmaster ˈskautmastə(r) $ -mæstər
scow skau
scowl skaul
scrabble ˈskræbl
scrag skræg
scraggy ˈskrægɪ
scram skræm
scramble ˈskræmbl
scrap skræp
scrap-book ˈskræp bʊk
scrape skreɪp
scrap-heap ˈskræp hip
scratch skrætʃ
scratch-race ˈskrætʃ reɪs
scrawl skrɔl
scrawny ˈskrɔnɪ

scream skrim
scree skri
screech skritʃ
screech-owl ˋskritʃ aʊl
screed skrid
screen skrin
screen play ˋskrin pleɪ
screw skru
screw-driver ˋskru draɪvə(r)
screw-topped ˈskru ˋtopt
scribble ˋskrɪbl
scribe skraɪb
scrimmage ˋskrɪmɪdʒ
scrimp skrɪmp
scrip skrɪp
script skrɪpt
script-writer ˋskrɪpt raɪtə(r)
scriptural ˋskrɪptʃərl
scripture ˋskrɪptʃə(r)
scrivener ˋskrɪvn̩ə(r)
scrofula ˋskrofjʊlə $ ˋskrɔfjʊlə etc
scroll skrəʊl
scrounge skraʊndʒ
scrub skrʌb
scrubbing-brush ˋskrʌbɪŋ brʌʃ
scruff skrʌf
scrum skrʌm
scrummage ˋskrʌmɪdʒ
scrumptious ˋskrʌmpʃəs
scruple ˋskrupl
scrupulous ˋskrupjələs
scrutineer ˋskrutɪˋnɪə(r) $ -tn̩ˋɪər
scrutinize ˋskrutɪnaɪz $ -tn̩aɪz
scrutiny ˋskrutɪnɪ $ -tn̩ɪ
scud skʌd
scuff skʌf
scuffle ˋskʌfl
scull skʌl
scullery ˋskʌlərɪ
scullery-maid ˋskʌlərɪ meɪd
scullion ˋskʌlɪən
sculptor ˋskʌlptə(r)
sculptress ˋskʌlptrəs
sculpture ˋskʌlptʃə(r)
scum skʌm
scupper ˋskʌpə(r)
scurf skɜf
scurrilous ˋskʌrɪləs $ ˋskɜ̩ləs
scurry ˋskʌrɪ $ ˋskɜɪ
scurvy ˋskɜvɪ
scut skʌt
scutcheon ˋskʌtʃən
scuttle ˋskʌtl

Scylla and Charybdis ˈsɪlər ən kəˋrɪbdɪs
$ £ -lə ən-
scythe saɪð
sea si
sea-anemone ˋsi ənemənɪ
sea-bathing ˋsi beɪðɪŋ
seaboard ˋsibɔd $ ˋsibɔrd
sea-borne ˋsi bɔn $ bɔrn
sea-dog ˋsi dog $ dɔg
sea-faring ˋsi feərɪŋ
sea-front ˋsi frʌnt
sea-going ˋsi gəʊɪŋ
sea-green ˋsi ˋgrin
sea-gull ˋsi gʌl
sea-horse ˋsi hɔs $ hɔrs
seal sil
sea-legs ˋsi legz
sea-level ˋsi levl
sealing-wax ˋsilɪŋ wæks
sea-lion ˋsi laɪən
Sea Lord ˋsi lɔd $ lɔrd
sealskin ˋsil-skɪn
seam sim
seaman ˋsimən
Sean ʃon
séance ˋseɪɔ̃s ˋseɪɔns ˋseɪɒns
seaplane ˋsi-pleɪn
seaport ˋsi-pɔt $ -pɔrt
sea-power ˋsi paʊə(r)
sear sɪə(r)
search sɜtʃ
searchlight ˋsɜtʃlaɪt
search-party ˋsɜtʃ patɪ $ partɪ
search-warrant ˋsɜtʃ wornt $ wɔr- etc
sea-rover ˋsi rəʊvə(r)
seascape ˋsi-skeɪp
seashore ˋsi-ʃɔ(r)
seasick ˋsi-sɪk
seaside ˋsi-saɪd
season ˋsizn
seasonable ˋsiznəbl
seasonal ˋsiznl
seasoning ˋsizn̩ɪŋ
season-ticket ˋsizn tɪkɪt
seat sit
seat-belt ˋsit belt
SEATO ˋsitəʊ
sea-urchin ˋsi ɜtʃɪn
sea-wall ˈsi ˋwɔl
sea-water ˋsi wɔtə(r)
seaweed ˋsiwid
seaworthy ˋsiwɜðɪ
Sebastian sɪˋbæstɪən $ -stʃən

secateurs ˈsekətɜz
secede sɪˈsid
secession sɪˈseʃn
seclude sɪˈklud
seclusion sɪˈkluʒn
second ˈsekənd $ ˈsekənt
second transfer sɪˈkond $ ˈsekənd -nt
secondary ˈsekəndrɪ $ -derɪ
secondary school ˈsekəndrɪ skul $ -derɪ
second-best ˈsekənd ˈbest
second-class ˈsekənd ˈklas $ ˈklæs
second-hand ˈsekənd ˈhænd
second-rate ˈsekənd ˈreɪt
secrecy ˈsikrəsɪ
secret ˈsikrət -rɪt
secretariat(e) ˈsekrəˈteərɪæt -ɪət
secretarial ˈsekrəˈteərɪəl
secretary ˈsekrətrɪ -tərɪ $ £ -terɪ
secrete sɪˈkrit
secretion sɪˈkriʃn
secretive causing secretion sɪˈkritɪv
secretive having secrets ˈsikrətɪv
sect sekt
sectarian sekˈteərɪən
section ˈsekʃn
sectional ˈsekʃnl
sector ˈsektə(r)
secular ˈsekjʊlə(r)
secularize ˈsekjʊləraɪz
secure sɪˈkjʊə(r)
security sɪˈkjʊərətɪ
Security Council sɪˈkjʊərətɪ kaʊnsl
security police sɪˈkjʊərətɪ pəlis
security risk sɪˈkjʊərətɪ rɪsk
sedan-chair sɪˈdæn ˈtʃeə(r)
sedate sɪˈdeɪt
sedative ˈsedətɪv
sedentary ˈsedntrɪ $ -terɪ
sedge sedʒ
sediment ˈsedɪmənt
sedimentary ˈsedɪˈmentrɪ
sedition sɪˈdɪʃn
seditious sɪˈdɪʃəs
seduce sɪˈdjus $ sɪˈdus
seduction sɪˈdʌkʃn
seductive sɪˈdʌktɪv
sedulous ˈsedjʊləs $ ˈsedʒʊləs
see si
seed sid
seed-bed ˈsid bed
seed-cake ˈsid keɪk
seed-pearl ˈsid pɜl
seed-potato ˈsid pəteɪtəʊ

seedsman ˈsidzmən
seedy ˈsidɪ
seek sik
seem sim
seemly ˈsimlɪ
seen sin
seep sip
seer sɪə(r)
seersucker ˈsɪəsʌkə(r) $ ˈsɪərsʌkər
seesaw ˈsi-sɔ
seethe sið
see-through ˈsi θru
segment ˈsegmənt
segmentation ˈsegmenˈteɪʃn
segregate ˈsegrɪgeɪt
segregation ˈsegrɪˈgeɪʃn
Seine seɪn
seismic ˈsaɪzmɪk
seismograph ˈsaɪzməgraf $ £ -græf
seismology saɪzˈmolədʒɪ
seize siz
seizure ˈsiʒə(r)
seldom ˈseldəm
select sɪˈlekt
selection sɪˈlekʃn
selection committee sɪˈlekʃn kəmɪtɪ
selective sɪˈlektɪv
selectivity ˈselekˈtɪvətɪ sɪˈlek-
selector sɪˈlektə(r)
self self
self- prefix self
self-assertion ˈself əˈsɜʃn
self-conscious ˈself ˈkonʃəs
self-confidence ˈself ˈkonfɪdəns
self-control ˈself kənˈtrəʊl
self-defence ˈself dɪˈfens
self-denial ˈself dɪˈnaɪəl
self-educated ˈself ˈedʒʊkeɪtɪd £ ˈedjʊ-
self-employed ˈself ɪmˈplɔɪd
self-evident ˈself ˈevɪdənt
selfish ˈselfɪʃ
self-righteous ˈself ˈraɪtʃəs
self-sacrifice ˈself ˈsækrɪfaɪs
self-same ˈself ˈseɪm ...
self-starter ˈself ˈstatə(r) $ ˈstartər
self-sufficient ˈself səˈfɪʃnt
self-supporting ˈself səˈpɔtɪŋ $ -ˈpɔr-
Selkirk ˈselkɜk
sell sel
sell-out ˈsel aʊt
selvage, -vedge ˈselvɪdʒ
semantic sɪˈmæntɪk
semaphore ˈseməfɔ(r)

semblance ˈsembləns
semen ˈsiːmən ˈsiːmen
semester səˈmestə(r)
semi- *prefix* ˈsemɪ $ ˈsemaɪ
semibreve ˈsemɪbriːv
semicircle ˈsemɪsɜːkl
semi-colon ˈsemɪ ˈkəʊlən $ ˈsemɪ k-
semi-detached ˈsemɪ dɪˈtætʃt
semi-final ˈsemɪ ˈfaɪnl
seminal ˈseminl
seminar ˈseminɑː(r)
seminary ˈseminəri $ -neri
semi-quaver ˈsemɪ kweɪvə(r)
Semite ˈsiːmaɪt ˈsem-
Semitic sɪˈmɪtɪk
semitone ˈsemɪtəʊn
semolina ˌseməˈliːnə
sempstress ˈsempstrəs -ɪs
senate, S– ˈsenət ˈsenɪt
senator ˈsenətə(r)
senatorial ˌsenəˈtɔːriəl
send send
send-off ˈsend ɒf $ £ ɔːf
Senegal ˈsenɪˈgɔːl
seneschal ˈsenɪʃl
senile ˈsiːnaɪl $ ˈsiːnl
senility sɪˈnɪlətɪ
senior ˈsiːniə(r)
seniority ˈsiːnɪˈɒrətɪ $ -ˈɔːrətɪ
senna ˈsenə
senna-pod ˈsenə pɒd
señor senˈjɔː(r)
Señor *before names* ˈsenjɔː(r)
señora senˈjɔːrə
señorita ˈsenjəˈriːtə -jɔːˈr-
sensation senˈseɪʃn
sensational senˈseɪʃnl
sensationalist senˈseɪʃnḷɪst
sense sens
sense-organ ˈsens ɔːgən $ ɔːgən
sensibility ˌsensəˈbɪlətɪ
sensible ˈsensəbl
sensitive ˈsensətɪv -sɪt-
sensitize ˈsensətaɪz -sɪt-
sensory ˈsensərɪ
sensual ˈsenʃʊəl £ ˈsensjʊəl
sensuality ˈsensʃʊˈælətɪ £ -nsjʊ-
sensuous ˈsensʃʊəs £ ˈsensjʊəs
sent sent
sentence ˈsentəns $ -tns
sententious senˈtenʃəs
sentient ˈsenʃənt -ʃɪənt
sentiment ˈsentɪmənt

sentimental ˈsentɪˈmentl
sentinel ˈsentɪnl $ -tn̩əl
sentry ˈsentrɪ
sentry-box ˈsentrɪ bɒks
sentry-go ˈsentrɪ gəʊ
separable ˈsepṛəbl
separate *adj, n* ˈsepṛət
separate *v* ˈsepəreɪt
separatist ˈsepṛətɪst
separation ˈsepəˈreɪʃn
separator ˈsepəreɪtə(r)
sepia ˈsiːpɪə
sepoy ˈsiːpɔɪ
sepsis ˈsepsɪs
septic ˈseptɪk
September sepˈtembə(r) səp-
septet sepˈtet
septuagenarian ˈseptjʊədʒɪˈneəriən $ £ -tʃʊə- *etc*
Septuagint ˈseptjʊədʒɪnt $ £ -tʃʊə- *etc*
sepulchral sɪˈpʌlkrl
sepulchre($ -cher) ˈseplkə(r)
sequel ˈsiːkwl
sequence ˈsiːkwəns
sequential sɪˈkwenʃl
sequester sɪˈkwestə(r)
sequestrate sɪˈkwestreɪt ˈsiːkwɪstreɪt
sequin ˈsiːkwɪn
sequoia sɪˈkwɔɪə
seraph ˈserəf
seraphic sɪˈræfɪk
seraphim ˈserəfɪm
Serbia ˈsɜːbɪə
Serbo-Croat ˈsɜːbəʊ ˈkrəʊæt
sere sɪə(r)
serenade ˈserəˈneɪd $ ˈserəneɪd
serene sɪˈriːn
serenity sɪˈrenətɪ
serf sɜːf
serfdom ˈsɜːfdəm
serge sɜːdʒ
sergeant ˈsɑːdʒənt $ ˈsɑːrdʒənt
sergeant-major ˈsɑːdʒm ˈmeɪdʒə(r) -dʒənt ˈm- £ ˈsɑːmp ˈmeɪdʒə(r) $ ˈsɑːr-
serial ˈsɪəriəl
seriatim ˈsɪərɪˈeɪtɪm
series ˈsɪəriːz $ £ ˈsɪərɪz
serio-comic ˈsɪərɪəʊ ˈkɒmɪk
serious ˈsɪəriəs
serjeant ˈsɑːdʒənt $ ˈsɑːrdʒənt
sermon ˈsɜːmən
serpent ˈsɜːpənt
serpentine ˈsɜːpəntaɪn $ -tiːn *etc*

serrated seˈreɪtɪd $ ˈsereɪtɪd
serried ˈserɪd
serum ˈsɪərəm
servant ˈsɜvənt
serve sɜv
service ˈsɜvɪs
serviette ˈsɜvɪˈet
servile ˈsɜvaɪl $ ˈsɜvḷ
servility sɜˈvɪlətɪ
servitude ˈsɜvɪtjud $ -tud *etc*
servo-assisted ˈsɜvəʊ əˈsɪstɪd
sesame ˈsesəmɪ
session ˈseʃn
set set
set-back ˈset bæk
set-square ˈset skweə(r)
set-to ˈset ˈtu
settee seˈti
setter ˈsetə(r)
setting ˈsetɪŋ
settle ˈsetl
settlement ˈsetlmənt
seven ˈsevn
sevenfold ˈsevnfəʊld
seventeen ˈsevnˈtin
seventh ˈsevnθ
seventieth ˈsevntɪəθ
seventy ˈsevntɪ
seventy-one ˈsevntɪ ˈwʌn
sever ˈsevə(r)
severance ˈsevərəns
several ˈsevrl
severe səˈvɪə(r)
severity səˈverətɪ
Seville səˈvɪl ˈsevl
sew səʊ
sewage ˈsuɪdʒ £ ˈsjuɪdʒ
sewage-farm ˈsuɪdʒ fam $ farm
sewer ˈsuə(r) £ ˈsjuə(r)
sewer-rat ˈsuə ræt £ ˈsjuə $ ˈsuər
sewing-machine ˈsəʊɪŋ məʃin
sewn səʊn
sex seks
sex-appeal ˈseks əpil
sexagenarian ˈseksədʒɪˈneərɪən
sextant ˈsekstənt
sextet(te) seksˈtet
sexton ˈsekstən
sexual ˈsekʃʊəl £ ˈseksjʊəl
sexuality ˈsekʃʊˈælətɪ £ ˈseksju-
shabby ˈʃæbɪ
shack ʃæk
shackle ˈʃækl

shade ʃeɪd
shadow ˈʃædəʊ $ ˈʃædə
shaft ˈʃaft $ ʃæft
shag ʃæg
shaggy ˈʃægɪ
shagreen ʃəˈgrin
shake ʃeɪk
shake-down ˈʃeɪk daʊn
shake-up ˈʃeɪk ʌp
Shakespeare ˈʃeɪkspɪə(r)
Shakespearian ʃeɪkˈspɪərɪən
shaky ˈʃeɪkɪ
shale ʃeɪl
shall *usual forms:* ʃl ʃəl
    strong-form: ʃæl
shallop ˈʃæləp
shallot ʃəˈlot
shallow ˈʃæləʊ $ ˈʃælə
shalt ʃælt
sham ʃæm
shamble ˈʃæmbl
shame ʃeɪm
shamefaced ˈʃeɪmfeɪst
shamefacedly ˈʃeɪmfeɪstlɪ ʃeɪmˈfeɪsɪdlɪ
shammy ˈʃæmɪ
shampoo ʃæmˈpu
shamrock ˈʃæmrok
shandy ˈʃændɪ
shanghai, S– ʃæŋˈhaɪ
shank ʃæŋk
shan't ʃant $ ʃænt
shantung ˈʃænˈtʌŋ
shanty ˈʃæntɪ
shape ʃeɪp
shapely ˈʃeɪplɪ
shard ʃad $ ʃard
share ʃeə(r)
share-cropper ˈʃeə kropə(r) $ ˈʃeər
share-holder ˈʃeə həʊldə(r) $ ˈʃeər
shark ʃak $ ʃark
sharkskin ˈʃakskɪn $ ˈʃark-
sharp ʃap $ ʃarp
sharpener ˈʃapnə(r) $ ˈʃar-
sharp-shooter ˈʃap ʃutə(r) $ ˈʃarp
sharp-witted ˈʃap ˈwɪtɪd $ ˈʃarp
shatter ˈʃætə(r)
shave ʃeɪv
shaving-brush ˈʃeɪvɪŋ brʌʃ
Shavian ˈʃeɪvɪən
shaw, S– ʃɔ
shawl ʃɔl
she ʃi
sheaf ʃif

shear ʃɪə(r)
sheath ʃiθ
sheathe ʃið
sheath-knife ˈʃiθ naɪf
sheaves ʃivz
shed ʃed
she'd ʃid
sheen ʃin
sheep ʃip
sheep-dog ˈʃip dɒg $ dɔg
sheep-fold ˈʃip fəʊld
sheep-run ˈʃip rʌn
sheepskin ˈʃipskɪn
sheer ʃɪə(r)
sheet ʃit
sheet-anchor ˈʃit æŋkə(r)
sheet-lightning ˈʃit ˈlaɪtnɪŋ
Sheffield ˈʃefild
sheik(h) ʃeɪk $ £ ʃik
shekel ˈʃekl
shelf ʃelf
shell ʃel
she'll ʃil
shellac ʃeˈlæk ʃəˈlæk
shellfish ˈʃelfɪʃ
shell-shock ˈʃel ʃok
shelter ˈʃeltə(r)
shelve ʃelv
shelves ʃelvz
shepherd ˈʃepəd $ ˈʃepərd
shepherdess ˈʃepədes -ɪs $ -pər-
shepherd's pie ˈʃepədz ˈpaɪ $ -pərdz
sherbet ˈʃabət
Sheridan ˈʃerɪdən
sherriff ˈʃerɪf
sherry ˈʃerɪ
she's ʃiz
Shetland ˈʃetlənd
shew ˈʃəʊ
shibboleth ˈʃɪbəleθ
shield ʃild
shift ʃɪft
shilling ˈʃɪlɪŋ
shilling's-worth ˈʃɪlɪŋz wɜθ
shilly-shally ˈʃɪlɪ ˈʃælɪ ˈʃɪlɪ ʃælɪ
shimmer ˈʃɪmə(r)
shin ˈʃɪn
shin-bone ˈʃɪn bəʊn
shindy ˈʃɪndɪ
shine ʃaɪn
shingle ˈʃɪŋgl
ship ʃɪp
-ship suffix ʃɪp

shipboard ˈʃɪpbɒd $ -bɔrd
shipbuilding ˈʃɪpbɪldɪŋ
ship-canal ˈʃɪp kənæl
ship-chandler ˈʃɪp tʃandlə(r) $ tʃæn-
shipload ˈʃɪp-ləʊd
shipmate ˈʃɪpmeɪt
shipment ˈʃɪpmənt
shipping-agent ˈʃɪpɪŋ eɪdʒənt
shipping-office ˈʃɪpɪŋ ofɪs $ ɔfɪs
shipshape ˈʃɪpʃeɪp
shipwreck ˈʃɪp-rek
shipwright ˈʃɪp-raɪt
shipyard ˈʃɪp-jad $ -jard
Shiraz ʃɪˈraz $ ʃɪˈræz
shire ˈʃaɪə(r)
-shire suffix ʃə(r) for Scottish
    counties: ʃaɪə(r) $ ʃɪər etc
shirk ʃak
Shirley ˈʃalɪ
shirt ʃat
shirt-front ˈʃat frʌnt
shirt-sleeves ˈʃat slivz
shiver ˈʃɪvə(r)
shoal ʃəʊl
shock ʃok
shock-absorber ˈʃok əbsɔbə(r) $ -sɔr-
shock-tactics ˈʃok tæktɪks
shock treatment ˈʃok tritmənt
shock troops ˈʃok trups
shock wave ˈʃok weɪv
shod ʃod
shoddy ˈʃodɪ
shoe ʃu
shoe-horn ˈʃu hɔn $ hɔrn
shoe-lace ˈʃu leɪs
shoe-leather ˈʃu leðə(r)
shoemaker ˈʃumeɪkə(r)
shoe shine ˈʃu ʃaɪn
shoe-string ˈʃu strɪŋ
shone ʃon $ ʃəʊn etc
shoo ʃu
shook ʃʊk
shoot ʃut
shooting-brake ˈʃutɪŋ breɪk
shooting-gallery ˈʃutɪŋ gælərɪ
shooting-range ˈʃutɪŋ reɪndʒ
shop ʃop
shop-assistant ˈʃop əsɪstənt
shopkeeper ˈʃopkipə(r)
shop-lifter ˈʃop lɪftə(r)
shop-soiled ˈʃop sɔɪld
shop-steward ʃop ˈstjuəd $ ˈstuərd
shop-walker ˈʃop wɔkə(r)

shop-window 'ʃop ˎwɪndəʊ
shore ʃɔ(r)
shorn ʃɔn $ ʃɔrn
short ʃɔt $ ʃɔrt
shortage 'ʃɔtɪdʒ $ 'ʃɔrtɪdʒ
shortbread 'ʃɔtbred $ 'ʃɔrt-
shortcake 'ʃɔtkeɪk $ 'ʃɔrt-
short-circuit 'ʃɔt ˎsɜkɪt $ 'ʃɔrt
shortcomings 'ʃɔtkʌmɪŋz $ 'ʃɔrt-
short-cut 'ʃɔt ˎkʌt $ 'ʃɔrt kʌt
shorten 'ʃɔtn $ 'ʃɔrtn
shorthand 'ʃɔthænd $ 'ʃɔrt-
shorthanded 'ʃɔt'hændɪd $ 'ʃɔrt-
shorthorn 'ʃɔthɔn $ 'ʃɔrthɔrn
short-lived 'ʃɔt 'lɪvd $ 'ʃɔrt 'laɪvd etc
short-list 'ʃɔt lɪst $ 'ʃɔrt
short-sighted 'ʃɔt ˎsaɪtɪd $ 'ʃɔrt
short story 'ʃɔt ˎstɔrɪ $ 'ʃɔrt 'ʃ- s-
short-tempered 'ʃɔt ˎtempəd $ 'ʃɔrt -ərd
short-term 'ʃɔt tɜm $ 'ʃɔrt
short-winded 'ʃɔt ˎwɪndɪd $ 'ʃɔtr
shot ʃot
shot-gun 'ʃot gʌn
shot-tower 'ʃot taʊə(r)
should ʃʊd weak-forms: ʃəd ʃd
shoulder 'ʃəʊldə(r)
shoulder-blade 'ʃəʊldə bleɪd $ -dər
shoulder-strap 'ʃəʊldə stræp $ -dər
shouldn't 'ʃʊdnt
shout ʃaʊt
shove ʃʌv
shovel 'ʃʌvl
show ʃəʊ
show-boat 'ʃəʊ bəʊt
show-case 'ʃəʊ keɪs
show-down 'ʃəʊ daʊn
shower 'ʃaʊə(r)
shower-bath 'ʃaʊə baθ $ 'ʃaʊər bæθ
showman 'ʃəʊmən
shown ʃəʊn
show-off 'ʃəʊ of $ £ ɔf
show-piece 'ʃəʊ pis
show-place 'ʃəʊ pleɪs
show-room 'ʃəʊ rʊm $ £ rum etc
shrank ʃræŋk
shrapnel 'ʃræpnl
shred ʃred
shrew ʃru
shrewd ʃrud
Shrewsbury 'ʃrəʊzbrɪ 'ʃruz-
   $ 'ʃruzberɪ etc
shriek ʃrik
shrift ʃrɪft

shrike ʃraɪk
shrill ʃrɪl
shrimp ʃrɪmp
shrine ʃraɪn
shrink ʃrɪŋk
shrive ʃraɪv
shrivel 'ʃrɪvl
shriven 'ʃrɪvn
Shropshire 'ʃropʃə(r) $ -ʃɪər etc
shroud ʃraʊd
shrove ʃrəʊv
Shrove Tuesday 'ʃrəʊv 'tjuzdɪ $ 'tu-
shrub ʃrʌb
shrubbery 'ʃrʌbərɪ
shrug ʃrʌg
shrunk ʃrʌŋk
shrunken 'ʃrʌŋkən
shuck ʃʌk
shudder 'ʃʌdə(r)
shuffle 'ʃʌfl
shuffle-board 'ʃʌfl bɔd $ bɔrd
shun ʃʌn
shunt ʃʌnt
shut ʃʌt
shutter 'ʃʌtə(r)
shuttle 'ʃʌtl
shuttle-cock 'ʃʌtl kok
shuttle service 'ʃʌtl sɜvɪs
shy ʃaɪ
Shylock 'ʃaɪlok
shyster 'ʃaɪstə(r) with aɪ as in 'mice'
Siam saɪ'æm
Siamese 'saɪə'miz
sibling 'sɪblɪŋ
Siberia saɪ'bɪərɪə
Siberian saɪ'bɪərɪən
sibilant 'sɪbələnt
sibyl, S– 'sɪbl
sibylline 'sɪblaɪn
sic sɪk
Sicilian sɪ'sɪlɪən
Sicily 'sɪsl̩ɪ
sick sɪk
sick-bay 'sɪk beɪ
sick-bed 'sɪk bed
sick-berth 'sɪk bɜθ
sicken 'sɪkən
sickening 'sɪkn̩ɪŋ
sickle 'sɪkl
sick-leave 'sɪk liv
sick-list 'sɪk lɪst
sickly 'sɪklɪ
sick-room 'sɪk rʊm $ £ rum etc

side saɪd *with adjectives of degree e.g. 'high', 'dear', 'thick' etc in phrases like 'on the — side', 'side' is usually unstressed*
sideboard ˈsaɪdbɔd $ -bɔrd
sideburns ˈsaɪdbɜnz
side-car ˈsaɪd ka(r)
side-drum ˈsaɪd drʌm
side-issue ˈsaɪd ɪʃu £ ɪsju
side line ˈsaɪd laɪn
sidelong ˈsaɪdlɒŋ $ -lɔŋ
sidereal saɪˈdɪərɪəl
side-road ˈsaɪd rəud
side-saddle ˈsaɪd sædl
side-show ˈsaɪd ʃəu
sidesman ˈsaɪdzmən
sidestep ˈsaɪdstep
side-stroke ˈsaɪd strəuk
side-track ˈsaɪd træk
sidewalk ˈsaɪdwɔk
sideways ˈsaɪdweɪz
sidewhiskers ˈsaɪdwɪskəz $ -hwɪskərz
siding ˈsaɪdɪŋ
sidle ˈsaɪdl
Sidney ˈsɪdnɪ
siege sidʒ
sienna sɪˈenə
sierra sɪˈerə
Sierra Leone sɪˈerə liˈəun
siesta sɪˈestə
sieve sɪv
sift sɪft
sigh saɪ
sight saɪt
sight, by a long baɪ ə ˈlɒŋ saɪt $ ˈlɔŋ
sightseeing ˈsaɪtsiɪŋ
sightseer ˈsaɪtsiə(r)
sigma ˈsɪgmə
sign saɪn
signal ˈsɪgnl
signal-box ˈsɪgnl boks
signalman ˈsɪgnlmən
signalize ˈsɪgnlaɪz
signatory ˈsɪgnətrɪ $ -tɔrɪ
signature ˈsɪgnətʃə(r) -nɪtʃə(r) $ -tʃʊər
signature tune ˈsɪgnətʃə tjun $ -tʃər tun
signet-ring ˈsɪgnɪt rɪŋ
significance sɪgˈnɪfɪkəns
significant sɪgˈnɪfɪkənt
signification ˈsɪgnɪfɪˈkeɪʃn
signify ˈsɪgnɪfaɪ
Signor *before names* ˈsinjɔ(r)
Signora sɪˈnjɔrə

Signorina ˈsinjɔˈrinə
signpost ˈsaɪnpəust
Sikh sik
silage ˈsaɪlɪdʒ
silence ˈsaɪləns
silent ˈsaɪlənt
Silesia saɪˈlizɪə $ £ -iʒə
silhouette ˈsɪluˈet
silica ˈsɪlɪkə
silicate ˈsɪlɪkət -keɪt
silicon ˈsɪlɪkən $ -kon
silicone ˈsɪlɪkəun
silicosis ˈsɪlɪˈkəusɪs
silk sɪlk
silken ˈsɪlkən
silkworm ˈsɪlkwɜm
sill sɪl
sillabub ˈsɪləbʌb
silly ˈsɪlɪ
silo ˈsaɪləu
silt sɪlt
silvan ˈsɪlvən
silver ˈsɪlvə(r)
silver-fish ˈsɪlvə fɪʃ $ ˈsɪlvər
silverside ˈsɪlvəsaɪd $ ˈsɪlvər-
silversmith ˈsɪlvəsmɪθ $ ˈsɪlvər-
Simeon ˈsɪmɪən
simian ˈsɪmɪən
similar ˈsɪmlə(r) -mələ(r)
similarity sɪməˈlærətɪ
simile ˈsɪmlɪ
similitude sɪˈmɪlɪtjud $ -tud
simmer ˈsɪmə(r)
Simon ˈsaɪmən
simony ˈsɪmənɪ ˈsaɪmənɪ
simper ˈsɪmpə(r)
simple ˈsɪmpl
simple-minded ˈsɪmpl ˈmaɪndɪd
simpleton ˈsɪmpltən
simplicity sɪmˈplɪsətɪ
simplification ˈsɪmplɪfɪˈkeɪʃn
simplify ˈsɪmplɪfaɪ
simulacrum ˈsɪmjuˈleɪkrəm
simulate ˈsɪmjuleɪt
simultaneity ˈsɪmltəˈniətɪ -ˈneɪətɪ
   $ ˈsaɪmltəˈniətɪ -ˈneɪətɪ
simultaneous ˈsɪmlˈteɪnɪəs $ ˈsaɪml- *etc*
sin sɪn
since sɪns
sincere sɪnˈsɪə(r)
Sindbad ˈsɪnbæd
sine saɪn
sinecure ˈsaɪnɪkjuə(r) ˈsɪn-

sine qua non ˈsɪnɪ ˈkweɪ ˈnon
   $ £ ˈsɪneɪ ˈkwɑ ˈnəʊn
sinew ˈsɪnju
sing sɪŋ
Singapore ˈsɪŋgəˈpɔ(r) ˈsɪŋə- $ ˈsɪŋgəp
single ˈsɪŋgl
single-breasted ˈsɪŋgl ˈbrestɪd
single-handed ˈsɪŋgl ˈhændɪd
single-minded ˈsɪŋgl ˈmaɪndɪd
singlet ˈsɪŋglət
singsong ˈsɪŋsoŋ $ ˈsɪŋsɔŋ
singular ˈsɪŋgjʊlə(r) -gjələ(r)
Sinhalese ˈsɪnhəˈliz £ ˈsɪŋə- ˈsɪnə-
sinister ˈsɪnɪstə(r)
sink sɪŋk
Sino- prefix ˈsaɪnəʊ
sinuous ˈsɪnjʊəs
sinus ˈsaɪnəs
sip sɪp
siphon ˈsaɪfən
sir, S— sɜ(r) weak-form: sə(r)
sire ˈsaɪə(r)
siren ˈsaɪərən
sirloin ˈsɜlɔɪn
sirocco sɪˈrokəʊ
sirrah ˈsɪrə
sisal ˈsaɪsl ˈsaɪzl
sissy ˈsɪsɪ
sister ˈsɪstə(r)
sisterhood ˈsɪstəhʊd $ ˈsɪstər-
sister-in-law ˈsɪstr̩ ɪn lɔ
sit sɪt
site saɪt
sitting-room ˈsɪtɪŋ rʊm $ £ rum etc
situated ˈsɪtʃʊeɪtɪd
situation ˈsɪtʃʊˈeɪʃn
six sɪks
sixpence ˈsɪkspəns $ ˈsɪkspens etc
sixpenny ˈsɪkspənɪ $ ˈsɪkspenɪ etc
six-shooter ˈsɪkʃ ʃutə(r) ˈsɪkʃutə(r)
sixteen ˈsɪkˈstin
sixth ˈsɪksθ with the final s and θ
   usually made simultaneously
sixtieth ˈsɪkstɪəθ
sixty ˈsɪkstɪ
sixty-one ˈsɪkstɪ ˈwʌn
sizable ˈsaɪzəbl
size saɪz
sizzle ˈsɪzl
skate skeɪt
skating-rink ˈskeɪtɪŋ rɪŋk
skedaddle skɪˈdædl
skein skeɪn

skeleton ˈskelɪtən -lətən
skep skep
skeptic ˈskeptɪk
skeptical ˈskeptɪkl
skepticism ˈskeptɪsɪzm
sketch sketʃ
sketch-book ˈsketʃ bʊk
sketch-map ˈsketʃ mæp
skew-whiff ˈskju ˈwɪf $ ˈhwɪf etc
skewer ˈskjuə(r)
ski ski
skid skɪd
skies skaɪz
skiff skɪf
skiing ˈskiɪŋ
ski-jump ˈski dʒʌmp
skilful ˈskɪlfl
ski-lift ˈski lɪft
skill skɪl
skil(l)ful ˈskɪlfl
skillet ˈskɪlɪt
skim skɪm
skimp skɪmp
skin skɪn
skin-deep ˈskɪn ˈdip
skin-diving ˈskɪn daɪvɪŋ
skinflint ˈskɪnflɪnt
skinhead ˈskɪnhed
skinny ˈskɪnɪ
skin-tight ˈskɪn ˈtaɪt
skip skɪp
skipper ˈskɪpə(r)
skipping-rope ˈskɪpɪŋ rəʊp
skirl skɜl
skirmish ˈskɜmɪʃ
skirt skɜt
skirting-board ˈskɜtɪŋ bɔd $ bɔrd
skit skɪt
skittish ˈskɪtɪʃ
skittles ˈskɪtlz
skulk skʌlk
skull skʌl
skull-cap ˈskʌl kæp
skunk skʌŋk
sky skaɪ
sky-blue ˈskaɪ ˈblu
sky-high ˈskaɪ ˈhaɪ
skylark ˈskaɪlɑk $ -lark
sky-line ˈskaɪ laɪn
sky-rocket ˈskaɪ rokɪt
sky-scraper ˈskaɪ skreɪpə(r)
sky-writing ˈskaɪ raɪtɪŋ
slab slæb

slack slæk
slacken 'slækən
slag slæg
slag-heap 'slæg hip
slain sleın
slake sleık
slalom 'slaləm
slam slæm
slander 'slandə(r) $ 'slændər
slanderous 'slandərəs $ 'slændərəs
slang slæŋ
slant slant $ slænt
slap slæp
slap-bang 'slæp 'bæŋ
slapdash 'slæpdæʃ 'slæp'dæʃ
slapstick 'slæpstık
slash slæʃ
slat slæt
slate sleıt
slattern 'slætən $ 'slætərn
slaughter-house 'slɔtə haʊs $ -tər
Slav slav slæv
slave sleıv
slave-driver 'sleıv draıvə(r)
slavery 'sleıvərı
slave-trade 'sleıv treıd
slavish 'sleıvıʃ
slaver n 'sleıvə(r)
slaver v 'slævə(r)
Slavonic slə'vonık
slay sleı
sleazy 'slizı
sled sled
sledge sledʒ
sledge-hammer 'sledʒ hæmə(r)
sleek slik
sleep slip
sleeping-bag 'slipıŋ bæg
sleeping-car 'slipıŋ ka(r)
sleeping-pill 'slipıŋ pıl
sleeping-sickness 'slipıŋ sıknəs
sleepy-head 'slipı hed
sleet slit
sleeve sliv
sleigh sleı
sleight of hand 'slaıt əv 'hænd
slender 'slendə(r)
slept slept
sleuth sluθ
slew slu
slice slaıs
slick slık
slide slaıd

slight slaıt
slim slım
slime slaım
sling slıŋ
slink slıŋk
slip slıp
slip-coach 'slıp kəʊtʃ
slip-knot 'slıp not
slippery 'slıprı
slip-road 'slıp rəʊd
slipshod 'slıpʃod
slip-stream 'slıp strim
slip-up 'slıp ʌp
slip-way 'slıp weı
slit slıt
slither 'slıðə(r)
sliver 'slıvə(r) 'slaıvə(r)
slobber 'slobə(r)
sloe sləʊ
slog slog $ slɔg
slogan 'sləʊgən
sloop slup
slop slop
slop-basin 'slop beısn
slope sləʊp
slop-pail 'slop peıl
sloppy 'slopı
slosh sloʃ
slot slot
sloth sləʊθ $ slɔθ
slot-machine 'slot məʃin
slouch slaʊtʃ
slough, S– slaʊ $ slu
slough v slʌf
slovenly 'slʌvnlı
slow sləʊ
slowcoach 'sləʊ kəʊtʃ
slow-moving 'sləʊ 'muvıŋ
slow-spoken 'sləʊ 'spəʊkən
slowworm 'sləʊwɜm
sludge slʌdʒ
slug slʌg
sluggard 'slʌgəd $ 'slʌgərd
sluggish 'slʌgıʃ
sluice slus
sluice-gate 'slus geıt
slum slʌm
slumber 'slʌmbə(r)
slump slʌmp
slung slʌŋ
slunk slʌŋk
slur slɜ(r)
slush slʌʃ

slut slʌt
sluttish ˈslʌtɪʃ
sly slaɪ
smack smæk
small smɔl
small-arms ˈsmɔl amz $ armz
small fry ˈsmɔl fraɪ
small-holding ˈsmɔl həʊldɪŋ
small hours 'smɔl ˈaʊəz $ ˈaʊərz
smallpox ˈsmɔlpoks
small talk ˈsmɔl tɔk
smalltime ˈsmɔltaɪm
smarmy ˈsmamɪ $ ˈsmarmɪ
smart smat $ smart
smash smæʃ
smash-and-grab raid 'smæʃ ŋ ˈgræb reɪd
smash-up ˈsmæʃ ʌp
smattering ˈsmætrɪŋ
smear smɪə(r)
smell smel
smelling-salts ˈsmelɪŋ sɔlts £ solts
smelt smelt
smile smaɪl
smirch smɜtʃ
smirk smɜk
smite smaɪt
smith, S– smɪθ
smithereens 'smɪðəˈrinz
smithy ˈsmɪðɪ
smitten ˈsmɪtn
smock smok
smocking ˈsmokɪŋ
smog smog $ smɔg
smoke sməʊk
smoke-screen ˈsməʊk skrin
smoking-compartment
  ˈsməʊkɪŋ kəmpatmənt $ -par-
smooth smuð
smooth-bore 'smuð ˈbɔ(r)
smoothing-iron ˈsmuðɪŋ aɪən $ aɪərn
smolder ˈsməʊldə(r)
smote sməʊt
smother ˈsmʌðə(r)
smoulder ˈsməʊldə(r)
smudge smʌdʒ
smug smʌg
smuggle ˈsmʌgl
smut smʌt
Sn. ˈsinɪə(r)
snack snæk
snack-bar ˈsnæk ba(r)
snaffle ˈsnæfl
snag snæg

snail sneɪl
snail's pace ˈsneɪlz peɪs
snake sneɪk
snake-charmer ˈsneɪk tʃamə(r) $ tʃar-
snap snæp
snapdragon ˈsnæpdrægən
snapshot ˈsnæpʃot
snare sneə(r)
snarl snal $ snarl
snatch snætʃ
sneak snik
sneaker ˈsnikə(r)
sneak-thief ˈsnik θif
sneer snɪə(r)
sneeze sniz
snicker ˈsnɪkə(r)
sniff snɪf
sniffle ˈsnɪfl
snigger ˈsnɪgə(r)
snip snɪp
snipe snaɪp
snippet ˈsnɪpɪt
snivel ˈsnɪvl
snob snob
snob appeal ˈsnob əpil
snobbery ˈsnobərɪ
snobbish ˈsnobɪʃ
snood snud
snook snuk
snooker ˈsnukə(r)
snoop snup
snooty ˈsnutɪ
snooze snuz
snore snɔ(r)
snorkel ˈsnɔkl $ ˈsnɔrkl
snort snɔt $ snɔrt
snot snot
snout snaʊt
snow snəʊ
snowball ˈsnəʊbɔl
snowblind ˈsnəʊblaɪnd
snow-bound ˈsnəʊ baʊnd
snow-capped ˈsnəʊ kæpt
Snowdon ˈsnəʊdn
snow-drift ˈsnəʊ drɪft
snowdrop ˈsnəʊdrop
snowfall ˈsnəʊfɔl
snow-field ˈsnəʊ fild
snowflake ˈsnəʊfleɪk
snow-line ˈsnəʊlaɪn
snowman ˈsnəʊmæn
snow-plough($ -plow) ˈsnəʊ plaʊ
snow-shoes ˈsnəʊ ʃuz

snow-storm ˈsnəʊ stɔːm $ stɔːrm
snow-white ˈsnəʊ ˈwaɪt $ ˈhwaɪt *etc*
Snr. ˈsiːnɪə(r)
snub snʌb
snub-nosed ˈsnʌb ˈnəʊzd ˈsnʌb nəʊzd
snuff snʌf
snuff-box ˈsnʌf bɒks
snuff-coloured($ -lor-) ˈsnʌf kʌləd $ -ərd
snuffle ˈsnʌfl
snug snʌg
snuggery ˈsnʌgərɪ
snuggle ˈsnʌgl
so səʊ
soak səʊk
so-and-so ˈsəʊ n səʊ ən
soap səʊp
soap-box ˈsəʊp bɒks
soap-bubble ˈsəʊp bʌbl
soap-opera ˈsəʊp ɒprə
soap-suds ˈsəʊp sʌdz
soar sɔː(r)
sob sɒb
sober ˈsəʊbə(r)
sobriety səˈbraɪətɪ səʊ-
sobriquet ˈsəʊbrɪkeɪ $ ˈsəʊbrɪˈkeɪ
sob-sister ˈsɒb sɪstə(r)
sob-stuff ˈsɒb stʌf
Soc. səˈsaɪətɪ *informally:* sɒk
soccer ˈsɒkə(r)
sociable ˈsəʊʃəbl
social ˈsəʊʃl
social club ˈsəʊʃl klʌb
socialism ˈsəʊʃlɪzm
socialist, S– ˈsəʊʃlɪst
socialite ˈsəʊʃlaɪt
socialize ˈsəʊʃlaɪz
society səˈsaɪətɪ
sociological ˈsəʊsɪəˈlɒdʒɪkl ˈsəʊʃə- -ʃɪə-
sociology ˈsəʊsɪˈɒlədʒɪ ˈsəʊʃɪ-
sock sɒk
socket ˈsɒkɪt
Socrates ˈsɒkrətiz
Socratic səˈkrætɪk $ £ səʊ-
sod sɒd
soda ˈsəʊdə
soda-fountain ˈsəʊdə faʊntɪn $ -tn
soda-water ˈsəʊdə wɔːtə(r)
sodden ˈsɒdn
sodium ˈsəʊdɪəm
sodomite ˈsɒdəmaɪt
sodomy ˈsɒdəmɪ
-soever *suffix* səʊˈevə(r)
sofa ˈsəʊfə

Sofia ˈsəʊfɪə
soft sɒft $ sɔːft
soft-boiled ˈsɒft ˈbɔɪld $ ˈsɔːft
soften ˈsɒfn $ ˈsɔːfn
soft-hearted ˈsɒft ˈhɑːtɪd $ ˈsɔːft ˈhɑːrtɪd
soft-pedal ˈsɒft ˈpedl $ ˈsɔːft
soft soap ˈsɒft səʊp $ ˈsɔːft
softwear ˈsɒftweə(r) $ ˈsɔːft-
soft-witted ˈsɒft ˈwɪtɪd $ ˈsɔːft
softwood ˈsɒftwʊd $ ˈsɔːft-
soggy ˈsɒgɪ $ ˈsɔːgɪ
Soho ˈsəʊhəʊ
soil sɔɪl
soil-pipe ˈsɔɪl paɪp
soirée ˈswɑːreɪ $ ˈswɑːˈreɪ
sojourn ˈsɒdʒən ˈsʌ- -dʒɜːn
  $ səʊˈdʒɜːn ˈsəʊdʒɜːn
solace ˈsɒlɪs -əs
solar ˈsəʊlə(r)
solarium səʊˈleərɪəm
solar-system ˈsəʊlə sɪstəm $ -lər
sold səʊld
solder ˈsɒldə(r) ˈsəʊldə(r)
  $ ˈsɒdər ˈsɔːdər
soldering-iron ˈsɒldrɪŋ aɪən
  $ ˈsɒdərɪŋ aɪərn
soldier ˈsəʊldʒə(r)
sole səʊl
solecism ˈsɒlɪsɪzm
solely ˈsəʊllɪ
solemn ˈsɒləm
solemnity səˈlemnətɪ
solemnize ˈsɒləmnaɪz
Solent ˈsəʊlənt
sol-fa ˈsɒl ˈfɑː $ ˈsəʊl
solicit səˈlɪsɪt
solicitation səˈlɪsɪˈteɪʃn
solicitor səˈlɪsɪtə(r)
Solicitor General səˈlɪsɪtə ˈdʒenrl $ -tər
solicitous səˈlɪsɪtəs
solicitude səˈlɪsɪtjuːd $ -tuːd
solid ˈsɒlɪd
solidarity ˈsɒlɪˈdærətɪ
solidify səˈlɪdɪfaɪ
solidity səˈlɪdətɪ
soliloquize səˈlɪləkwaɪz
soliloquy səˈlɪləkwɪ
solitaire ˈsɒlɪˈteə(r) $ ˈsɒliteər *etc*
solitary ˈsɒlɪtrɪ $ -terɪ
solitude ˈsɒlɪtjuːd $ -tuːd *etc*
solo ˈsəʊləʊ
soloist ˈsəʊləʊɪst
Solomon ˈsɒləmən

solstice ˈsɒlstɪs $ ˈsɔːlstɪs
soluble ˈsɒljʊbl
solution səˈluːʃn
solve sɒlv
solvency ˈsɒlvənsɪ
solvent ˈsɒlvənt
Somalia səˈmɑːlɪə $ £ səʊ-
Somaliland səˈmɑːlɪlænd $ £ səʊ-
sombre($ -ber) ˈsɒmbə(r)
sombrero sɒmˈbreərəʊ
some *In adjectival use as 'consisting of*
  an undefined amount or number of'
  normally sm səm
  other senses and strong-form sʌm
-some *suffix* səm
somebody ˈsʌmbədɪ -bodɪ
somehow ˈsʌmhaʊ
someone ˈsʌmwʌn *weak-form:* -wən
someplace ˈsʌm-pleɪs
somersault ˈsʌməsɔːlt £ -sɒlt $ -mər-
Somerset ˈsʌməset -sɪt $ -mər-
something ˈsʌmθɪŋ
sometime ˈsʌmtaɪm
sometimes ˈsʌmtaɪmz
somewhat ˈsʌmwɒt $ ˈsʌmhwɒt *etc*
somewhere ˈsʌmweə(r) $ ˈsʌmhweər *etc*
somnambulism sɒmˈnæmbjʊlɪzm
somnolent ˈsɒmnələnt
son sʌn
sonata səˈnɑːtə
son et lumière ˈsɒn eɪ ˈluːmɪeə(r) sɔ̃
  $ £ ˈluːmɪˈeə(r)
song sɒŋ $ sɔːŋ
song-bird ˈsɒŋ bɜːd $ ˈsɔːŋ
song-book ˈsɒŋ bʊk $ ˈsɔːŋ
songster ˈsɒŋstə(r) $ ˈsɔːŋ-
songstress ˈsɒŋstrəs -rɪs $ ˈsɔːŋ-
Sonia ˈsəʊnɪə ˈsɒnɪə
sonic ˈsɒnɪk ˈsəʊnɪk
son-in-law ˈsʌn ɪn lɔː
sonnet ˈsɒnɪt
sonneteer ˈsɒnɪˈtɪə(r)
sonny ˈsʌnɪ
sonorous səˈnɔːrəs ˈsɒnərəs
soon suːn
soot sʊt
soothe suːð
soothsayer ˈsuːθseɪə(r)
sop sɒp
sophism ˈsɒf-ɪzm *as two words*
sophisticated səˈfɪstɪkeɪtɪd
sophistication səˈfɪstɪˈkeɪʃn
sophistry ˈsɒfɪstrɪ

Sophocles ˈsɒfəkliːz
sophomore ˈsɒfəmɔː(r)
soporific ˈsɒpəˈrɪfɪk $ ˈsəʊp-
soppy ˈsɒpɪ
soprano səˈprɑːnəʊ $ səˈprænəʊ *etc*
Sorbonne sɔːˈbɒn $ sɔrˈbɒn
sorcerer ˈsɔːsərə(r) $ ˈsɔːr-
sorceress ˈsɔːsərəs -rɪs $ ˈsɔːr-
sorcery ˈsɔːsərɪ $ ˈsɔːr-
sordid ˈsɔːdɪd $ ˈsɔːrdɪd
sore sɔː(r)
sorority səˈrɒrətɪ $ səˈrɔːrətɪ *etc*
sorrel ˈsɒrl $ ˈsɔːrl
sorrow ˈsɒrəʊ $ ˈsɔːrəʊ -rə
sorry ˈsɒrɪ $ ˈsɔːrɪ
sort sɔːt $ sɔrt
sortie ˈsɔːtɪ $ ˈsɔːrtɪ
SOS ˈes əʊ ˈes
so-so ˈsəʊ səʊ
sot sɒt
sottish ˈsɒtɪʃ
sotto voce ˈsɒtəʊ ˈvəʊtʃɪ -tʃeɪ
sou suː
soufflé ˈsuːfleɪ $ suːˈfleɪ
sough sʌf $ saʊ *etc*
sought sɔːt
soul səʊl
soul-destroying ˈsəʊl dɪstrɔɪɪŋ
soul-stirring ˈsəʊl stɜːrɪŋ
sound saʊnd
sound effects ˈsaʊnd ɪfekts əf-
sounding-board ˈsaʊndɪŋ bɔːd $ bɔːrd
sound-proof ˈsaʊnd pruːf
sound-track ˈsaʊnd træk
sound-wave ˈsaʊnd weɪv
soup suːp
soup-kitchen ˈsuːp kɪtʃɪn
sour ˈsaʊə(r)
source sɔːs $ sɔːrs
souse saʊs
south saʊθ
Southampton saʊˈθæmptən saʊθˈhæ-
south-east saʊθˈiːst
south-easterly saʊθˈiːstəlɪ $ -tərlɪ
southerly ˈsʌðəlɪ $ ˈsʌðərlɪ
southern ˈsʌðən $ ˈsʌðərn
southernmost ˈsʌðnməʊst $ ˈsʌðərn-
south-south-east ˈsaʊθ saʊθ ˈiːst
south-south-west ˈsaʊθ saʊθ ˈwest
southward(s) ˈsaʊθwəd(z) £ -wʊd(z)
  $ -wərd(z)
south-west saʊθˈwest
souvenir ˈsuːvəˈnɪə(r) $ £ ˈsuːvənɪə(r)

sou'wester saʊ'westə(r)
sovereign 'sovrɪn
sovereignty 'sovrəntɪ
soviet 'səʊvɪət 'səʊvɪet 'sov-
Soviet Union 'səʊvɪət 'junɪən
sow *of seed* səʊ
sow *pig* saʊ
sown səʊn
soy sɔɪ
soya-bean 'sɔɪə bin
sozzled 'sozld
spa spɑ
space speɪs
space-bar 'speɪs bɑ(r)
space capsule 'speɪs kæpsjul $ kæpsl
space-craft 'speɪs krɑft $ kræft
space-heater 'speɪs hitə(r)
spaceship 'speɪʃʃɪp
spacesuit 'speɪssut £ -sjut
spacious 'speɪʃəs
spade speɪd
spade-work 'speɪd wɜk
spaghetti spə'getɪ
Spain speɪn
spake speɪk
spam spæm
span spæn
spangle 'spæŋgl
Spaniard 'spænɪəd $ 'spænɪərd
spaniel 'spænɪəl
Spanish 'spænɪʃ
spank spæŋk
spanner 'spænə(r)
spar spɑ(r)
spare speə(r)
spark spak $ spark
sparking-plug 'spakɪŋ plʌg $ 'spar-
sparkle 'spakl $ 'sparkl
spark-plug 'spak plʌg $ 'spark
sparring-partner 'sparɪŋ patnə(r) $ par-
sparrow 'spærəʊ $ 'spærə
sparse spas $ spars
sparsity 'spasətɪ $ 'sparsətɪ
Spartan 'spatn $ 'spartn
spasm 'spæzm
spasmodic spæz'modɪk
spastic 'spæstɪk
spat spæt
spate speɪt
spatial 'speɪʃl
spatter 'spætə(r)
spatula 'spætjʊlə $ £ 'spætʃʊlə
spawn spɔn

speak spik
speak-easy 'spik izɪ
spear spɪə(r)
spear-head 'spɪə hed $ 'spɪər
spec spek
special 'speʃl
specialist 'speʃlɪst
speciality 'speʃɪ'ælətɪ
specialize 'speʃlaɪz
specialty 'speʃltɪ
species 'spiʃiz -ʃɪz
specific spə'sɪfɪk
specification 'spesɪfɪ'keɪʃn
specify 'spesɪfaɪ
specimen 'spesɪmən 'spesəmɪn
specious 'spiʃəs
speck spek
speckle 'spekl
specs speks
spectacle 'spektəkl
spectacular spek'tækjʊlə(r)
spectator spek'teɪtə(r) $ 'spekteɪtər *etc*
spectra 'spektrə
spectral 'spektrəl
spectre($ -ter) 'spektə(r)
spectroscope 'spektrəskəʊp
spectrum 'spektrəm
speculate 'spekjʊleɪt
speculative 'spekjʊlətɪv $ -leɪtɪv
speculator 'spekjʊleɪtə(r)
sped sped
speech spitʃ
speech-day 'spitʃ deɪ
speechify 'spitʃɪfaɪ
speed spid
speed-boat 'spid bəʊt
speed-limit 'spid lɪmɪt
speedometer spi'domɪtə(r)
speedway 'spidweɪ
speedwell 'spidwel
spell spel
spellbinder 'spelbaɪndə(r)
spellbound 'spelbaʊnd
spelling 'spelɪŋ
spelling pronunciation
    'spelɪŋ prənʌnsɪeɪʃn
spelt spelt
spend spend
spendthrift 'spendθrɪft
Spenser 'spensə(r)
Spenserian spen'sɪərɪən
spent spent
sperm spɜm

spermaceti ˈspɜːməˈsetɪ
spew spju
sphere sfɪə(r)
spherical ˈsferɪkl
spheroid ˈsfɪərɔɪd
sphinx sfɪŋks
spice spaɪs
spick and span ˈspɪk ən ˈspæn
spider ˈspaɪdə(r)
spied spaɪd
spike spaɪk
spill spɪl
spilt spɪlt
spin spɪn
spinach ˈspɪnɪdʒ $ £ ˈspɪnɪtʃ etc
spinal ˈspaɪnl
spindle ˈspɪndl
spin-drier ˈspɪn ˈdraɪə(r)
spindrift ˈspɪndrɪft
spine spaɪn
spinet spɪˈnet $ £ ˈspɪnɪt
spinnaker ˈspɪnəkə(r)
spinney ˈspɪnɪ
Spinoza spɪˈnəʊzə
spinning-jenny ˈspɪnɪŋ dʒenɪ
spinning-wheel ˈspɪnɪŋ wil $ hwil etc
spinster ˈspɪnstə(r)
spiraea spaɪˈrɪə
spiral ˈspaɪərl
spire ˈspaɪə(r)
spirit ˈspɪrɪt
spirit-lamp ˈspɪrɪt læmp
spirit-level ˈspɪrɪt levl
spiritual ˈspɪrɪtʃʊəl
spiritualism ˈspɪrɪtʃʊlɪzm
spiritualist ˈspɪrɪtʃʊlɪst
spirituous ˈspɪrɪtjʊəs $ -tʃʊəs
spirt spɜːt
spit spɪt
spite spaɪt
spitfire ˈspɪtfaɪə(r)
spittle ˈspɪtl
spittoon spɪˈtun
spiv spɪv
splash splæʃ
splash-down ˈsplæʃ daʊn
splay spleɪ
splay-footed ˈspleɪ ˈfʊtɪd
spleen splin
splendid ˈsplendɪd
splendour($ -or) ˈsplendə(r)
splenetic spliˈnetɪk
splice splaɪs

splint splɪnt
splinter ˈsplɪntə(r)
split splɪt
splodge splodʒ
splosh sploʃ
splotch splotʃ
splurge splɜːdʒ
splutter ˈsplʌtə(r)
spoil spɔɪl
spoil-sport ˈspɔɪl spɔt $ spɔrt
spoilt spɔɪlt
spoke spəʊk
spoken ˈspəʊkən
spokesman ˈspəʊksmən
spoliation ˈspəʊlɪˈeɪʃn
spondee ˈspondi
sponge spʌndʒ
sponge-cake ˈspʌndʒ-keɪk
spongy ˈspʌndʒɪ
sponsor ˈsponsə(r)
spontaneity ˈspontəˈnɪətɪ -ˈneɪətɪ
spontaneous sponˈteɪnɪəs
spoof spuf
spook spuk
spool spul
spoon spun
spoonerism ˈspunərɪzm
spoon-fed ˈspun-fed
spoor spɔ(r)
sporadic spəˈrædɪk
spore spɔ(r)
sporran ˈsporən
sport spɔt $ spɔrt
sportive ˈspɔtɪv $ ˈspɔrtɪv
sports-car ˈspɔts ka(r) $ ˈspɔrts
sports-coat ˈspɔts kəʊt $ ˈspɔrts
sports-editor ˈspɔts edɪtə(r) $ ˈspɔrts
sports-jacket ˈspɔts dʒækɪt $ ˈspɔrts
sportsman ˈspɔtsmən $ ˈspɔrtsmən
sports model ˈspɔts modl $ ˈspɔrts
spot spot
spotlight ˈspotlaɪt
spouse spaʊz $ £ spaʊs etc
spout spaʊt
sprain spreɪn
sprang spræŋ
sprat spræt
sprawl sprɔl
spray spreɪ
spray-gun ˈspreɪ gʌn
spread spred
spread-eagle spred ˈigl
spree spri

sprig sprɪg
sprightly ˈspraɪtlɪ
spring sprɪŋ
spring-balance ˈsprɪŋ ˈbæləns
spring-board ˈsprɪŋ bɔd $ bɔrd
springbok ˈsprɪŋbok
spring-mattress ˈsprɪŋ ˈmætrəs -rɪs
springtide ˈsprɪŋtaɪd
springtime ˈsprɪŋtaɪm
sprinkle ˈsprɪŋkl
sprinkling ˈsprɪŋklɪŋ
sprint sprɪnt
sprite spraɪt
sprocket ˈsprokɪt
sprout spraʊt
spruce sprus
sprung sprʌŋ
spry spraɪ
spud spʌd
spume spjum
spun spʌn
spunk spʌŋk
spur spɜ(r)
spurious ˈspjʊərɪəs
spurn spɜn
spurt spɜt
sputnik ˈspʊtnɪk ˈsputnɪk
sputter ˈspʌtə(r)
sputum ˈspjutəm
spy spaɪ
spy-glass ˈspaɪ glas $ glæs
squab skwob $ skwɔb
squabble ˈskwobl $ ˈskwɔbl
squad skwod $ skwɔd
squadron ˈskwodrən $ ˈskwɔdrən
squadron-leader ˈskwodrən lidə(r) $ -wɔ-
squalid ˈskwolɪd $ ˈskwɔlɪd
squalor ˈskwolə(r) $ ˈskwɔlər
squall skwɔl
squander ˈskwondə(r) $ ˈskwɔndər
square skweə $ skweər
square-dance ˈskweə dans $ -eər dæns
square-shouldered ˈskweə ˈʃəʊldəd
    $ ˈskweər ˈʃəʊldərd
squash skwoʃ $ skwɔʃ
squash-racket ˈskwoʃ rækɪt $ ˈskwɔʃ
squat skwot $ skwɔt
squatter ˈskwotə(r) $ ˈskwɔtər
squaw skwɔ
squawk skwɔk
squeak skwik
squeal skwil
squeamish ˈskwimɪʃ

squeegee ˈskwiˈdʒi $ ˈskwidʒi
squeeze skwiz
squelch skweltʃ
squib skwɪb
squid skwɪd
squiffy ˈskwɪfɪ
squiggle ˈskwɪgl
squint skwɪnt
squint-eyed ˈskwɪnt ˈaɪd
squire ˈskwaɪə(r)
squirearchy ˈskwaɪərakɪ $ -arkɪ
squirm skwɜm
squirrel ˈskwɪrl $ ˈskwɜ̩l etc
squirt skwɜt
St prefix Saint snt $ seɪnt
St suffix Street strit not stressed
stab stæb
stability stəˈbɪlətɪ
stabilize ˈsteɪblaɪz
stable ˈsteɪbl
stable-boy ˈsteɪbl bɔɪ
staccato stəˈkatəʊ
stack stæk
stadium ˈsteɪdɪəm
staff staf $ stæf
Stafford ˈstæfəd $ -fərd
stag stæg
stage steɪdʒ
stage-coach ˈsteɪdʒ kəʊtʃ
stage-craft ˈsteɪdʒ kraft $ kræft
stage directions ˈsteɪdʒ dɪrekʃnz
stage fright ˈsteɪdʒ fraɪt
stage-struck ˈsteɪdʒ strʌk
stage whisper ˈsteɪdʒ wɪspə(r) $ hw- etc
stagger ˈstægə(r)
stagnant ˈstægnənt
stagnate stægˈneɪt $ ˈstægneɪt
staid steɪd
stain steɪn
stair steə(r)
stair-carpet ˈsteə kapɪt $ ˈsteər karpɪt
staircase ˈsteəkeɪs $ ˈsteər-
stair-rod ˈsteə rod $ ˈsteər
stairway ˈsteəweɪ $ ˈsteər-
stake steɪk
stake-holder ˈsteɪk həʊldə(r)
stalactite ˈstæləktaɪt $ stəˈlæktaɪt etc
stalagmite ˈstæləgmaɪt $ stəˈlægmaɪt etc
St Albans snt ˈɔlbənz $ ˈseɪnt
stale steɪl
stalemate ˈsteɪlmeɪt
Stalin ˈstalɪn
Stalingrad ˈstalɪngræd

stalk stɔk
stall stɔl
stallion ˈstælɪən
stalwart ˈstɔlwət $ -wərt
stamen ˈsteɪmən
stamina ˈstæmɪnə
stammer ˈstæmə(r)
stamp stæmp
stamp-album ˈstæmp ælbəm
stamp-collector ˈstæmp kəlektə(r)
stamp-dealer ˈstæmp dilə(r)
stamp-duty ˈstæmp djutɪ $ dutɪ
stampede stæmˈpid
stance stæns £ stɑns
stanchion ˈstɑntʃən $ ˈstæntʃən
stand stænd
standard ˈstændəd $ -dərd
standard-bearer ˈstændəd beərə(r) $ -dərd
standardize ˈstændədaɪz $ -dərd-
standardization ˈstændədaɪˈzeɪʃn -ərdɪˈz-
stand-by ˈstænd baɪ
stand-in ˈstænd ɪn
stand-offish stænd ˈofɪʃ $ ˈɔfɪʃ
stand-point ˈstænd pɔɪnt
standstill ˈstænd stɪl
stand-to stænd ˈtu
stand-up ˈstænd ʌp
stank stæŋk
Stanley ˈstænlɪ
stanza ˈstænzə
staple ˈsteɪpl
stapling-machine ˈsteɪplɪŋ məʃin
star stɑ(r)
starboard ˈstɑbɔd $ ˈstɑrbɔrd
starch stɑtʃ $ stɑrtʃ
stare steə(r)
starfish ˈstɑfɪʃ $ ˈstɑrfɪʃ
stargazer ˈstɑgeɪzə(r) $ ˈstɑr-
stark stɑk $ stɑrk
starlet ˈstɑlət $ ˈstɑrlət
starlight ˈstɑlaɪt $ ˈstɑrlaɪt
starling ˈstɑlɪŋ $ ˈstɑrlɪŋ
starlit ˈstɑlɪt $ ˈstɑrlɪt
starry ˈstɑrɪ
starry-eyed ˈstɑrɪ ˈaɪd
start stɑt $ stɑrt
starting-point ˈstɑtɪŋ pɔɪnt $ ˈstɑr-
starting-price ˈstɑtɪŋ praɪs $ ˈstɑr-
startle ˈstɑtl $ ˈstɑrtl
starvation stɑˈveɪʃn $ stɑrˈveɪʃn
starve stɑv $ stɑrv
starveling ˈstɑvlɪŋ $ ˈstɑrvlɪŋ
state steɪt

statecraft ˈsteɪtkrɑft $ -kræft
stateroom ˈsteɪt-rum $ £ -rum etc
statesman ˈsteɪtsmən
static ˈstætɪk
station ˈsteɪʃn
stationary ˈsteɪʃnrɪ $ ˈsteɪʃṇerɪ
stationer ˈsteɪʃnə(r)
stationery ˈsteɪʃnrɪ $ ˈsteɪʃṇerɪ
station-master ˈsteɪʃn mɑstə(r) $ mæstər
station-wagon ˈsteɪʃn wægən
statistical stəˈtɪstɪkl
statistician ˈstætɪˈstɪʃn
statistics stəˈtɪstɪks
statuary ˈstætʃuərɪ £ -tju- $ -ʊerɪ
statue ˈstætʃu £ ˈstætju
statuesque ˈstætʃuˈesk £ -tju-
statuette ˈstætʃuˈet £ -tju-
stature ˈstætʃə(r)
status ˈsteɪtəs $ ˈstætəs
status quo ˈsteɪtəs ˈkwəʊ $ ˈstætəs
statute ˈstætʃut £ ˈstætjut
statute-book ˈstætʃut bʊk £ ˈstætjut
statutory ˈstætʃutrɪ $ ˈstætʃutɔrɪ
staunch stɔntʃ
Stavanger stəˈvæŋə(r)
stave steɪv
stay steɪ
stay-at-home ˈsteɪ ət həʊm
stead sted
steadfast ˈstedfəst $ -fæst
steady ˈstedɪ
steak steɪk
steal stil
stealth stelθ
steam stim
steamboat ˈstimbəʊt
steam coal ˈstim kəʊl
steam-engine ˈstim endʒɪn
steamer ˈstimə(r)
steam-hammer ˈstim hæmə(r)
steam-roller ˈstim rəʊlə(r)
steamship ˈstimʃɪp
steed stid
steel stil
steel-plated ˈstil ˈpleɪtɪd
steel-works ˈstil wɜks
steelyard ˈstiljad £ ˈstɪljəd $ -jard
steep stip
steeple ˈstipl
steeplechase ˈstipl tʃeɪs
steeplejack ˈstipl dʒæk
steer ˈstɪə(r)
steerage ˈstɪərɪdʒ

steering-wheel ˈstɪərɪŋ wil $ hwil *etc*
steersman ˈstɪəzmən $ ˈstɪərz-
Stella ˈstelə
stellar ˈstelə(r)
stem stem
stench stentʃ
stencil ˈstensl
stenographer stəˈnogrəfə(r) stɪ-
stenography stəˈnogrəfɪ stɪ-
step step
step-brother ˈstep brʌðə(r)
step-child ˈstep tʃaɪld
step-daughter ˈstep dɔtə(r)
step-father ˈstep faðə(r)
Stephanie ˈstefənɪ
Stephen ˈstivn
step-ladder ˈstep lædə(r)
step-mother ˈstep mʌðə(r)
steppes steps
stepping-stone ˈstepɪŋ stəʊn
stereo ˈstɪərɪəʊ $ £ ˈsterɪəʊ
stereophonic ˈstɪərɪəˈfonɪk $ £ ˈster-
stereophony ˈstɪərɪˈofənɪ $ £ ˈsterɪ-
stereoscope ˈstɪərɪəskəʊp $ £ ˈster-
stereoscopic ˈstɪərɪəˈskopɪk $ £ ˈster-
stereotype ˈstɪərɪətaɪp $ £ ˈster-
sterile ˈsteraɪl $ ˈsterl
sterility stəˈrɪlətɪ
sterilization ˈsterɪlaɪˈzeɪʃn $ -lɪˈz-
sterilize ˈsterɪlaɪz
sterling ˈstɜlɪŋ
stern stɜn
stertorous ˈstɜtərəs
stethoscope ˈsteθəskəʊp
stevedore ˈstivədɔ(r)
Steven ˈstivn
stew stju $ stu
steward ˈstjuəd $ ˈstuərd
stewardess ˈstjuəˈdes $ ˈstuərdɪs
stick stɪk
sticking-plaster ˈstɪkɪŋ plastə(r) $ plæstər
stick-in-the-mud ˈstɪk ɪn ðə mʌd
stickler ˈstɪklə(r)
stick-on ˈstɪk on
stick-up ˈstɪk ʌp
stiff stɪf
stiff-necked ˈstɪf ˈnekt
stifle ˈstaɪfl
stigma ˈstɪgmə
sitgmata stɪgmatə ˈstɪgmətə
stigmatize ˈstɪgmətaɪz
stile staɪl
stiletto stɪˈletəʊ

still stɪl
still-born ˈstɪl bɔn ˈs- ˈb- $ ˈs- ˈbɔrn
still-life ˈstɪl ˈlaɪf
stilt stɪlt
stimulant ˈstɪmjʊlənt
stimulate ˈstɪmjʊleɪt
stimulus ˈstɪmjʊləs
sting stɪŋ
stingy *miserly* ˈstɪndʒɪ
stink stɪŋk
stint stɪnt
stipend ˈstaɪpend
stipple ˈstɪpl
stipulate ˈstɪpjʊleɪt
stipulation ˈstɪpjʊˈleɪʃn
stir stɜ(r)
Stirling ˈstɜlɪŋ
stirrup ˈstɪrəp $ ˈstɜəp
stirrup-cup ˈstɪrəp kʌp $ ˈstɜəp
stirrup-pump ˈstɪrəp pʌmp $ ˈstɜəp
stitch stɪtʃ
stoat stəʊt
stock stok
stockade stoˈkeɪd
stock-breeder ˈstok bridə(r)
stockbroker ˈstokbrəʊkə(r)
stock-car *racing* ˈstok ˈka(r)
stock-car *railroad* ˈstok ka(r)
stock company ˈstok kʌmpənɪ
stock exchange ˈstok ɪkstʃeɪndʒ
stockinet ˈstokɪˈnet
stocking ˈstokɪŋ
stock-in-trade ˈstok ɪn ˈtreɪd
stock-jobber ˈstok dʒobə(r)
stock-piling ˈstok paɪlɪŋ
stock-pot ˈstok pot
stock-still ˈstok ˈstɪl
stock-taking ˈstok teɪkɪŋ
stockyard ˈstokjad $ -jard
stodgy ˈstodʒɪ
stoep stup
stoic ˈstəʊɪk
stoical ˈstəʊɪkl
stoicism ˈstəʊɪsɪzm
stoke stəʊk
stole stəʊl
stolen ˈstəʊlən
stolid ˈstolɪd
stomach ˈstʌmək $ -mɪk
stomach ache ˈstʌmək eɪk $ -mɪk
stone stəʊn
Stone Age, the ˈstəʊn eɪdʒ
stone-cold ˈstəʊn ˈkəʊld

stone-dead ˈstəʊn ˈded
stone-deaf ˈstəʊn ˈdef
Stonehenge ˈstəʊnˈhendʒ $ ˈstəʊnh-
stonemason ˈstəʊnmeɪsn
stone's throw ˈstəʊnz θrəʊ
stone-wall ˈstəʊn ˈwɔl $ ˈstəʊn wɔl
stoneware ˈstəʊnweə(r)
stonework ˈstəʊnwɜk
stony ˈstəʊnɪ
stood stʊd
stooge studʒ
stool stul
stool-pigeon ˈstul pɪdʒən
stoop stup
stop stop
stop-cock ˈstop kok
stop-gap ˈstop gæp
stop-over ˈstop əʊvə(r)
stoppage ˈstopɪdʒ
stop-press ˈstop ˈpres
stop-watch ˈstop wotʃ $ wɔtʃ
storage ˈstɔrɪdʒ
store stɔ(r)
store-room ˈstɔ rʊm $ ˈstɔr $ £ rʊm
storey ˈstɔrɪ
-storied *suffix* ˈstɔrɪd
stork stɔk $ stɔrk
storm stɔm $ stɔrm
stormbound ˈstɔmbaʊnd $ ˈstɔrm-
storm-centre($ -ter) ˈstɔm sentə(r) $ -ɔrm
storm-cloud ˈstɔm klaʊd $ ˈstɔrm
storm-proof ˈstɔm pruf $ ˈstɔrm
storm-trooper ˈstɔm trupə(r) $ ˈstɔrm
story ˈstɔrɪ
story-teller ˈstɔrɪ telə(r)
stoup stup
stout staʊt
stout-hearted ˈstaʊt ˈhatɪd $ ˈhartɪd
stove stəʊv
stove-pipe ˈstəʊv paɪp
stow stəʊ
stow-away ˈstəʊ əweɪ
straddle ˈstrædl
Stradivarius ˈstrædɪˈveərɪəs
strafe straf $ streɪf
straggle ˈstrægl
straight streɪt
straightaway ˈstreɪtəˈweɪ
straighten ˈstreɪtn
straightforward streɪtˈfɔwəd £ -wʊd
$ streɪtˈfɔrwərd
strain streɪn
strait streɪt

straitened ˈstreɪtnd
strait-jacket ˈstreɪt dʒækɪt
strait-laced ˈstreɪt ˈleɪst
strand strænd
strange streɪndʒ
stranger ˈstreɪndʒə(r)
strangle ˈstræŋgl
strangle-hold ˈstræŋgl həʊld
strangulation ˈstræŋgjʊˈleɪʃn
strap stræp
strap-hanger ˈstræp hæŋə(r)
strata ˈstratə $ £ ˈstreɪtə $ ˈstrætə
stratagem ˈstrætədʒəm
strategic strəˈtidʒɪk
strategy ˈstrætɪdʒɪ -tədʒɪ
Stratford-on-Avon ˈstrætfəd on ˈeɪvn
$ ˈstrætfərd on ˈeɪvon
stratification ˈstrætɪfɪˈkeɪʃn
stratify ˈstrætɪfaɪ
stratosphere ˈstrætəsfɪə(r)
stratum ˈstratəm
$ £ ˈstreɪtəm $ ˈstrætəm *etc*
Strauss straʊs
Stravinsky strəˈvɪnskɪ
straw strɔ
strawberry ˈstrɔbrɪ $ -berɪ
strawboard ˈstrɔbɔd $ -bɔrd
stray streɪ
streak strik
stream strim
stream-lined ˈstrim laɪnd
street strit
street-car ˈstrit ka(r)
street door ˈstrit dɔ(r)
street-walker ˈstrit wɔkə(r)
strength ˈstreŋθ ˈstreŋkθ
strengthen ˈstreŋθn ˈstreŋkθn
strenuous ˈstrenjʊəs
streptococci ˈstreptəˈkokaɪ $ £ -ˈkoksaɪ
streptococcus ˈstreptəˈkokəs
stress stres
stress-mark ˈstres mak $ mark
stretch stretʃ
stretcher ˈstretʃə(r)
stretcher-bearer ˈstretʃə beərə(r) $ -tʃər
strew stru
strewn strun
striated straɪˈeɪtɪd
stricken ˈstrɪkən
strict strɪkt
stricture ˈstrɪktʃə(r)
stride ˈstraɪd
strident ˈstraɪdnt

strife straɪf
strike straɪk
strike-bound ˈstraɪk baʊnd
strike-breaker ˈstraɪk breɪkə(r)
strike-leader ˈstraɪk lidə(r)
strike-pay ˈstraɪk peɪ
striking distance ˈstraɪkɪŋ dɪstəns
striking force ˈstraɪkɪŋ fɔs $ fɔrs
Strindberg ˈstrɪndbəg
string strɪŋ
stringent ˈstrɪndʒənt
strip strɪp
strip-cartoon ˈstrɪp katun $ kar-
stripe straɪp
stripling ˈstrɪplɪŋ
strip-tease ˈstrɪp ˈtiz $ ˈstrɪp tiz
strive straɪv
striven ˈstrɪvn
strode strəʊd
stroke strəʊk
stroll strəʊl
strong strɒŋ $ strɔŋ etc
strong-box ˈstrɒŋ bɒks $ ˈstrɔŋ etc
strong-hold ˈstrɒŋ həʊld $ ˈstrɔŋ etc
strong-minded ˈstrɒŋ ˈmaɪndɪd $ ˈstrɔŋ
strong-room ˈstrɒŋ rʊm $ £ rum etc
　　$ ˈstrɔŋ etc
strontium ˈstrɒnʃɪəm ˈstrɒntɪəm
strop strɒp
strove strəʊv
St Swithin(-un) snt ˈswɪðɪn -ən $ ˈseɪnt
struck strʌk
structural ˈstrʌktʃərl
structure ˈstrʌktʃə(r)
struggle ˈstrʌgl
strum strʌm
strumpet ˈstrʌmpɪt
strung strʌŋ
strut strʌt
strychnine ˈstrɪknin $ -naɪn -nɪn
stub stʌb
stubble ˈstʌbl
stubborn ˈstʌbən $ ˈstʌbərn
stubby ˈstʌbɪ
stucco ˈstʌkəʊ
stuck stʌk
stuck-up ˈstʌk ˈʌp
stud stʌd
student ˈstjudnt $ ˈstudnt
stud-farm ˈstʌd fam $ farm
stud-horse ˈstʌd hɔs $ hɔrs
studio ˈstjudɪəʊ $ ˈstudɪəʊ
studious ˈstjudɪəs $ ˈstudɪəs

study ˈstʌdɪ
stuff stʌf
stuffy ˈstʌfɪ
stultify ˈstʌltɪfaɪ
stumble ˈstʌmbl
stumbling-block ˈstʌmblɪŋ blɒk
stump stʌmp
stun stʌn
stung stʌŋ
stunk stʌŋk
stunt stʌnt
stupefaction ˈstjupɪˈfækʃn $ ˈstu-
stupefy ˈstjupɪfaɪ $ ˈstu-
stupendous stjuˈpendəs $ stu-
stupid ˈstjupɪd $ ˈstupɪd
stupidity stjuˈpɪdətɪ $ stu-
stupor ˈstjupə(r) $ ˈstu-
sturdy ˈstɜdɪ
sturgeon ˈstɜdʒən
stutter ˈstʌtə(r)
sty staɪ
stye staɪ
Stygian ˈstɪdʒɪən
style staɪl
stylise ˈstaɪlaɪz
stylist ˈstaɪlɪst -ḷ-
stylograph ˈstaɪləgraf $ -græf
stylus ˈstaɪləs
stymie ˈstaɪmɪ
Styx stɪks
suave swav
suavity ˈswavətɪ
subaltern ˈsʌbltən $ səˈbɔltərn
sub-committee ˈsʌb kəmɪtɪ
subconscious ˈsʌbˈkɒnʃəs
subcontinent ˈsʌbˈkɒntɪnənt $ -tṇənt etc
subcontractor ˈsʌbkənˈtræktə(r)
　　$ ˈsʌnˈkɒntræktər
subcutaneous ˈsʌbkjuˈteɪnɪəs
subdivide ˈsʌbdɪˈvaɪd
subdivision ˈsʌbdɪˈvɪʒn ˈsʌbdɪvɪʒn
subdue səbˈdju $ səbˈdu
subheading ˈsʌbhedɪŋ
subhuman ˈsʌbˈhjumən
subject n ˈsʌbdʒɪkt
subject v səbˈdʒekt
subjective səbˈdʒektɪv
subjectivity ˈsʌbdʒekˈtɪvətɪ
subjection səbˈdʒekʃn
subject matter ˈsʌbdʒɪkt mætə(r)
subjoin sʌbˈdʒɔɪn
sub judice ˈsʌb ˈdʒudɪsɪ ˈjudɪkeɪ
subjugate ˈsʌbdʒʊgeɪt

subjunctive səbˈdʒʌŋktɪv
sublimate ˈsʌblɪmeɪt
sublimation ˌsʌblɪˈmeɪʃn
sublime səˈblaɪm
subliminal sʌbˈlɪmɪnl
submarine adj ˈsʌbməˈriːn
submarine n ˈsʌbməˈriːn $ £ ˈsʌbmərin
submerge səbˈmɜːdʒ
submersion səbˈmɜːʃn $ £ səbˈmɜːʒn
submission səbˈmɪʃn
submissive səbˈmɪsɪv
submit səbˈmɪt
subnormal ˈsʌbˈnɔːml $ -ˈnɔːrml
sub-orbital ˈsʌb ˈɔːbɪtl $ ˈɔːrb-
subordinate səˈbɔːdɪnət -dn̩- $ -ˈbɔːrd-
subordinate v səˈbɔːdɪneɪt $ -ˈbɔːrdn̩eɪt
subordination səˈbɔːdɪˈneɪʃn $ -ˈbɔːrdn̩ˈeɪʃn
suborn səˈbɔːn $ səˈbɔːrn
subp(o)ena səˈpiːnə səbˈp-
subscribe səbˈskraɪb
subscription səbˈskrɪpʃn
subsequent ˈsʌbsɪkwənt
subservient səbˈsɜːvɪənt
subside səbˈsaɪd
subsidence səbˈsaɪdns ˈsʌbsɪdəns
subsidiary səbˈsɪdɪəri $ səbˈsɪdɪeri
subsidize ˈsʌbsɪdaɪz
subsidy ˈsʌbsɪdi
subsist səbˈsɪst
subsoil ˈsʌbsɔɪl
subsonic ˈsʌbˈsɒnɪk
substance ˈsʌbstəns
substantial səbˈstænʃl
substantiate səbˈstænʃɪeɪt
substantival ˈsʌbstənˈtaɪvl
substantive səbˈstæntɪv
substation ˈsʌbsteɪʃn
substitute ˈsʌbstɪtjuːt -tʃuːt $ -tuːt
substitution ˈsʌbstɪˈtjuːʃn -tʃuː- $ -ˈtuːʃn
substratum ˈsʌbˈstraːtəm $ -reɪt- -ræt-
subsume səbˈsjuːm $ sʌbˈsuːm
subtend səbˈtend
subterfuge ˈsʌbtəfjuːdʒ $ -tər-
subterranean ˈsʌbtəˈreɪnɪən
subtitle ˈsʌbtaɪtl
subtle ˈsʌtl
subtlety ˈsʌtlti
subtly ˈsʌtl̩i ˈsʌtli
subtopia sʌbˈtəupɪə
subtract səbˈtrækt
subtraction səbˈtrækʃn
subtropical ˈsʌbˈtrɒpɪkl
suburb ˈsʌbɜːb

suburban səˈbɜːbən
suburbia səˈbɜːbɪə
subvention sʌbˈvenʃn
subversion səbˈvɜːʃn $ £ səbˈvɜːʒn
subversive səbˈvɜːsɪv
subvert sʌbˈvɜːt
subway ˈsʌbweɪ
succeed səkˈsiːd
success səkˈses
succession səkˈseʃn
successive səkˈsesɪv
successor səkˈsesə(r)
succinct səkˈsɪŋkt
succour ˈsʌkə(r)
succulent ˈsʌkjʊlənt
succumb səˈkʌm
such sʌtʃ
suchlike ˈsʌtʃlaɪk
suck sʌk
sucking-pig ˈsʌkɪŋ pɪg
suckle ˈsʌkl
suckling n ˈsʌklɪŋ
suction ˈsʌkʃn
suction pump ˈsʌkʃn pʌmp
Sudan suˈdæn -ˈdɑːn
Sudanese ˈsudəˈniːz
sudden ˈsʌdn
suds sʌdz
sue su £ sjuː
suede sweɪd
suet ˈsuːɪt ˈsjuːɪt
Suez ˈsuːɪz $ ˈsuez suˈez £ ˈsjuːɪz
suffer ˈsʌfə(r)
sufferable ˈsʌfrəbl
sufferance ˈsʌfrəns
suffice səˈfaɪs
sufficiency səˈfɪʃnsi
sufficient səˈfɪʃnt
suffix ˈsʌfɪks
suffocate ˈsʌfəkeɪt
Suffolk ˈsʌfək
suffragan ˈsʌfrəgən
suffrage ˈsʌfrɪdʒ
suffragette ˈsʌfrəˈdʒet
suffuse səˈfjuːz
suffusion səˈfjuːʒn
sugar ˈʃʊgə(r)
sugar-beet ˈʃʊgə biːt $ ˈʃʊgər
sugar-cane ˈʃʊgə keɪn $ ˈʃʊgər
sugar-loaf ˈʃʊgə ləuf $ ˈʃʊgər
sugar-tongs ˈʃʊgə tɒŋz $ ˈʃʊgər
sugar-refinery ˈʃʊgə rɪfaɪnəri $ ˈʃʊgər
suggest səˈdʒest $ səgˈdʒest etc

suggestion səˈdʒestʃən $ səgˈdʒ- etc
suggestive səˈdʒestɪv $ səgˈdʒ- etc
suicidal suɪˈsaɪdl £ sju-
suicide ˈsuɪsaɪd £ ˈsju-
suit sut £ sjut
suitability ˈsutəˈbɪlətɪ £ ˈsju-
suitable ˈsutəbl £ ˈsju-
suitcase ˈsutkeɪs £ ˈsju-
suite swit
suitor ˈsutə(r) £ ˈsjutə(r)
sulf- see 'sulph-' on this page
sulk sʌlk
sullen ˈsʌlən
Sullivan ˈsʌlɪvən
sully ˈsʌlɪ
sulpha($ sulf-) ˈsʌlfə
sulphate($ sulf-) ˈsʌlfeɪt
sulphide($ sulf-) ˈsʌlfaɪd
sulphonomide($ sulf-) sʌlˈfonəmaɪd
sulphur($ sulf-) ˈsʌlfə(r)
sulphuric($ sulf-) sʌlˈfjʊərɪk
sulphurous($ sulf-) ˈsʌlfərəs -fjʊrəs
sultan ˈsʌltən
sultana slˈtanə sʌl- $ slˈtænə
sultanate ˈsʌltəneɪt
sultry ˈsʌltrɪ
sum sʌm
Sumatra suˈmatrə
summarize ˈsʌmɹaɪz -mər-
summary ˈsʌmɹɪ -mərɪ
summer ˈsʌmə(r)
summer-house ˈsʌmə haʊs $ ˈsʌmər
summer school ˈsʌmə skul $ ˈsʌmər
summertime ˈsʌmətaɪm $ ˈsʌmər-
summing-up ˈsʌmɪŋ ˈʌp
summit ˈsʌmɪt
summon ˈsʌmən
sump sʌmp
sumptuary ˈsʌmptjʊərɪ $ ˈsʌmptʃʊerɪ
sumptuous ˈsʌmptʃʊəs £ -tjʊəs
sun sʌn
sun-bathe ˈsʌn beɪð
sun-beam ˈsʌn bim
sun-blind ˈsʌn blaɪnd
sunburn ˈsʌnbən
sundae ˈsʌndeɪ ˈsʌndɪ
Sunday ˈsʌndɪ ˈsʌndeɪ
Sunday school ˈsʌndɪ skul
sunder ˈsʌndə(r)
Sunderland ˈsʌndələnd $ -dər-
sun-dial ˈsʌn daɪl̩
sundown ˈsʌndaʊn
sundowner ˈsʌndaʊnə(r)

sundry ˈsʌndrɪ
sunflower ˈsʌnflaʊə(r)
sung sʌŋ
sun-glasses ˈsʌn glasɪz $ glæsɪz
sun-god ˈsʌn god
sun-hat ˈsʌn hæt
sun-helmet ˈsʌn helmɪt -mət
sunk sʌŋk
sunken ˈsʌŋkən
sun-lamp ˈsʌn læmp
sunlight ˈsʌnlaɪt
sunlit ˈsʌnlɪt
sunny ˈsʌnɪ
sunrise ˈsʌnraɪz
sunset ˈsʌnset
sunshade ˈsʌnʃeɪd
sunshine ˈsʌnʃaɪn
sun-spot ˈsʌn spot
sunstroke ˈsʌnstrəʊk
sun-up ˈsʌn ʌp
sun-worship ˈsʌn wɜʃɪp
sup sʌp
super informal adj and n ˈsupə(r)
super- prefix ˈsupə(r) £ ˈsjupə(r)
superabundant ˈsupərəˈbʌndənt £ ˈsju-
superannuate ˈsupərˈænjʊeɪt £ ˈsju-
superannuation ˈsupərˈænjʊˈeɪʃn £ ˈsju-
superb suˈpəb £ sju-
supercargo ˈsupəkagəʊ £ ˈsju-
    $ ˈsupərkargəʊ
supercede ˈsupəˈsid £ ˈsju- $ ˈsupər-
supercharger ˈsupətʃadʒə(r) £ ˈsju-
    $ ˈsupərtʃardʒər
supercilious ˈsupəˈsɪlɪəs £ ˈsju- $ -pər-
supererogation ˈsupərˈerəˈgeɪʃn £ ˈsju-
superficial ˈsupəˈfɪʃl £ ˈsju- $ ˈsupər-
superfine ˈsupəfaɪn £ ˈsju- $ ˈsupər-
superfluity ˈsupəˈfluətɪ £ ˈsju- $ ˈsupər-
superfluous suˈpəfluəs səˈp- £ sju-
superhuman ˈsupəˈhjumən £ ˈsju- -pər-
superimpose ˈsupɹɪmˈpəʊz £ ˈsju-
superintend ˈsupɹɪnˈtend £ ˈsju-
superintendent ˈsupɹɪnˈtendənt £ ˈsju-
superior səˈpɪərɪə(r) £ su- sju-
superiority səˈpɪərɪˈorətɪ £ su̇ˈp- sjuˈp-
    $ səˈpɪərɪˈorətɪ
superlative suˈpələtɪv sə- £ sju-
superman ˈsupəmæn £ ˈsju- $ ˈsupər-
supermarket ˈsupəmakɪt £ ˈsju- $ -ərmar-
supernatural ˈsupəˈnætʃərl £ ˈsju- $ -pər-
supernumerary ˈsupəˈnjumərərɪ £ ˈsju-
    $ ˈsupərˈnumərerɪ -ˈnju-
superpower ˈsupəpaʊə(r) £ ˈsju- $ -pər-

superscription ˈsupəskrɪpʃn £ ˈsjuː- $ -pər-
supersede ˈsupəˈsid £ ˈsjuː- $ ˈsupər-
supersonic ˈsupəˈsɒnɪk £ ˈsjuː- $ ˈsupər-
superstition ˈsupəˈstɪʃn £ ˈsjuː- $ ˈsupər-
superstitious ˈsupəˈstɪʃəs £ ˈsjuː- $ ˈsupər-
superstructure ˈsupəstrʌktʃə(r) £ ˈsjuː-
 $ ˈsupərstrʌktʃər
supertax ˈsupətæks £ ˈsjuː- $ ˈsupər-
supervene ˈsupəˈvin £ ˈsjuː- $ ˈsupər-
supervise ˈsupəvaɪz £ ˈsjuː- $ ˈsupər-
supervision ˈsupəˈvɪʒn £ ˈsjuː- $ ˈsupər-
supervisor ˈsupəvaɪzə(r) £ ˈsjuː- $ -pər-
supervisory ˈsupəˈvaɪzərɪ £ ˈsjuː- $ -pər-
supine adj ˈsupaɪn ˈsjuː- $ səˈpaɪn su-
supine n ˈsupaɪn £ ˈsjupaɪn
supper ˈsʌpə(r)
supplant səˈplant $ səˈplænt
supple ˈsʌpl
supplement n ˈsʌplɪmənt
supplement v ˈsʌplɪment
supplementary ˈsʌplɪˈmentrɪ
suppliant ˈsʌplɪənt
supplicant ˈsʌplɪkənt
supplicate ˈsʌplɪkeɪt
supplication ˈsʌplɪˈkeɪʃn
supply səˈplaɪ
support səˈpɔt $ səˈpɔrt
suppose səˈpəuz
supposed before ʻtoʼ səˈpəuz -zd -əus
supposedly səˈpəuzɪdlɪ
supposition ˈsʌpəˈzɪʃn
suppository səˈpɒzɪtrɪ $ -tɔrɪ
suppress səˈpres
suppression səˈpreʃn
suppressive səˈpresɪv
suppressor səˈpresə(r)
suppurate ˈsʌpjʊreɪt
supra-national ˈsuprəˈnæʃnl £ ˈsjuː-
supremacy səˈpreməsɪ su- £ sjuː-
supreme səˈprim su- £ sjuː-
surcharge ˈsɜtʃɑdʒ $ ˈsɜrtʃɑrdʒ
sure ʃuə(r) £ ʃɔ(r)
sure-footed ˈʃuə ˈfutɪd £ ˈʃɔ $ ˈʃuər
surely ˈʃuəlɪ £ ˈʃɔlɪ $ ˈʃuərlɪ
surety ˈʃuərətɪ £ ˈʃɔrətɪ ˈʃuətɪ $ ˈʃuərtɪ etc
surf sɜf
surface ˈsɜfɪs
surf-board ˈsɜf bɔd $ bɔrd
surfeit ˈsɜfɪt
surf-riding ˈsɜf raɪdɪŋ
surge sɜdʒ
surgeon ˈsɜdʒən
surgery ˈsɜdʒərɪ

surgical ˈsɜdʒɪkl
surly ˈsɜlɪ
surmise n ˈsɜmaɪz sɜˈmaɪz $ sərˈmaɪz
surmise v sɜˈmaɪz sə- $ sərˈmaɪz
surmount səˈmaunt $ sər-
surmountable səˈmauntəbl $ sər-
surname ˈsɜneɪm
surpass səˈpas $ sərˈpæs
surplice ˈsɜplɪs
surplus ˈsɜpləs
surprise səˈpraɪz $ sərˈpraɪz səˈp-
surrealism səˈrɪəlɪzm su- $ ˈsɜrɪəlɪzm
surrealist səˈrɪəlɪst su- $ ˈsɜrɪəlɪst
surrealistic səˈrɪəˈlɪstɪk su- ˈsɜrɪə-
surreptitious ˈsʌrəpˈtɪʃəs $ ˈsɜəp-
Surrey ˈsʌrɪ $ ˈsɜɪ
surrogate ˈsʌrəgeɪt -gət $ ˈsɜəgeɪt
surround səˈraund
surtax ˈsɜtæks
surveillance sɜˈveɪləns
survey n ˈsɜveɪ
survey v sɜˈveɪ sə- $ sər- $ and in
 sense of ʻmeasure and mapʼ £ ˈsɜveɪ
survival səˈvaɪvl $ sər-
survive səˈvaɪv $ sər-
survivor səˈvaɪvə(r) $ sər-
Susan ˈsuzn
Susanna(h) suˈzænə
susceptibility səˈseptəˈbɪlətɪ
susceptible səˈseptəbl
suspect n ˈsʌspekt
suspect v səˈspekt
suspend səˈspend
suspense səˈspens
suspension səˈspenʃn
suspension bridge səˈspenʃn brɪdʒ
suspicion səˈspɪʃn
suspicious səˈspɪʃəs
Sussex ˈsʌsɪks
sustain səˈsteɪn
sustenance ˈsʌstɪnəns
Sutherland ˈsʌðələnd $ -ðər-
suture ˈsutʃə(r)
suzerain ˈsuzəreɪn $ -rɪn etc
svelte svelt
swab swɒb $ swɔb
swaddle ˈswɒdl $ ˈswɔdl
swaddling-clothes ˈswɒdlɪŋ kləuðz
 $ kləuz etc $ ˈswɔdlɪŋ
swag swæg
swagger ˈswægə(r)
Swahili swaˈhilɪ £ swəˈhilɪ
swain sweɪn

swallow ˈswɔləʊ $ ˈswɔləʊ -lə
swallow-dive ˈswɔləʊ daɪv $ ˈswɔ-
swallow-tailed ˈswɔləʊ teɪld $ ˈswɔ-
swam swæm
swamp swɒmp $ swɔmp
swan swɒn $ swɔn
Swanee ˈswɒnɪ $ ˈswɔnɪ
swank swæŋk
swan's-down ˈswɒnz daʊn $ ˈswɔnz
Swansea ˈswɒnzɪ
swan-song ˈswɒn sɒŋ $ sɔŋ ˈswɔn
swap swɒp $ swɔp
sward swɔd $ swɔrd
swarm swɔm $ swɔrm
swart swɔt $ swɔrt
swarthy ˈswɔðɪ $ ˈswɔrðɪ
swashbuckler ˈswɒʃbʌklə(r) $ ˈswɔʃ-
swastika ˈswɒstɪkə
swat swɒt $ swɔt
swathe sweɪð
sway sweɪ
Swaziland ˈswɑzɪlænd
swear sweə(r)
swear-word ˈsweəwɜd $ ˈsweər-
sweat swet
sweater ˈswetə(r)
sweat-shirt ˈswet ʃɜt
sweat-shop ˈswet ʃɒp
swede, S– swid
Sweden ˈswidn
Swedish ˈswidɪʃ
sweep swip
sweepstake ˈswipsteɪk
sweet swit
sweetbread ˈswitbred
sweetening ˈswitnɪŋ
sweetheart ˈswithɑt $ -hɑrt
sweetmeat ˈswitmit
sweet pea ˈswit ˈpi
sweet-scented ˈswit ˈsentɪd
sweet-william ˈswit ˈwɪlɪəm
swell swel
swelter ˈsweltə(r)
swept swept
swerve swɜv
swift swɪft
swig swɪg
swill swɪl
swim swɪm
swimming-baths ˈswɪmɪŋ bɑðz $ bæðz
swimming-pool ˈswɪmɪŋ pul
swimsuit ˈswɪmsut £ -sjut
swindle ˈswɪndl

swine swaɪn
swineherd ˈswaɪnhɜd
swing swɪŋ
swipe swaɪp
swirl swɜl
swish swɪʃ
Swiss swɪs
switch swɪtʃ
switchboard ˈswɪtʃbɔd $ -bɔrd
Switzerland ˈswɪtsələnd $ -sərl-
swivel ˈswɪvl
swollen ˈswəʊlən
swoon swun
swoop swup
swop swɒp $ swɔp
sword sɔd $ sɔrd
sword-dance ˈsɔd dɑns $ ˈsɔrd dæns
sword-fish ˈsɔd fɪʃ $ ˈsɔrd
swordplay ˈsɔdpleɪ $ ˈsɔrdpleɪ
swordsman ˈsɔdzmən $ ˈsɔrdzmən
swore swɔ(r)
sworn swɔn $ swɔrn
swot swɒt $ swɔt
swum swʌm
swung swʌŋ
sybarite ˈsɪbəraɪt
sybaritic ˈsɪbəˈrɪtɪk
Sybil ˈsɪbl
sycamore ˈsɪkəmɔ(r)
sycophant ˈsɪkəfənt -fænt
syllabary ˈsɪləbərɪ $ -berɪ
syllabic sɪˈlæbɪk
syllabification sɪˈlæbɪfɪˈkeɪʃn
syllable ˈsɪləbl
syllogism ˈsɪlədʒɪzm
syllogistic ˈsɪləˈdʒɪstɪk
sylph sɪlf
sylph-like ˈsɪlf laɪk
sylvan ˈsɪlvən
Sylvia ˈsɪlvɪə
symbol ˈsɪmbl
symbolic sɪmˈbɒlɪk
symbolism ˈsɪmblɪzm
symbolize ˈsɪmblaɪz
symmetrical sɪˈmetrɪkl
symmetry ˈsɪmɪtrɪ -ətrɪ
sympathetic ˈsɪmpəˈθetɪk
sympathize ˈsɪmpəθaɪz
sympathy ˈsɪmpəθɪ
symphonic sɪmˈfɒnɪk
symphony ˈsɪmfənɪ
symposium sɪmˈpəʊzɪəm
symptom ˈsɪmptəm

symptomatic ˈsɪmptəˈmætɪk
synagogue ˈsɪnəgog $ -gɔg
synchroflash ˈsɪŋkrəʊˈflæʃ
synchromesh ˈsɪŋkrəʊˈmeʃ
synchronic sɪnˈkronɪk
synchronize ˈsɪŋkrənaɪz
syncopate ˈsɪŋkəpeɪt
syncopation ˈsɪŋkəˈpeɪʃn
syncope ˈsɪŋkəpɪ
syndicalism ˈsɪndɪkļɪzm
syndicalist ˈsɪndɪkļɪst
syndicate n ˈsɪndɪkət
syndicate v ˈsɪndɪkeɪt
synod ˈsɪnəd ˈsɪnod
synonym ˈsɪnənɪm
synonymous sɪˈnonɪməs
synopsis sɪˈnopsɪs

synoptic sɪˈnoptɪk
syntactical sɪnˈtæktɪkl
syntax ˈsɪntæks
syntheses ˈsɪnθəsiz
synthesis ˈsɪnθəsɪs
synthetic sɪnˈθetɪk
syphilis ˈsɪfļɪs -fəl-
syphilitic ˈsɪfļˈɪtɪk
syphon ˈsaɪfən
Syracuse ˈsaɪərəkjuz $ ˈsɪrəkjus -uz
Syria ˈsɪrɪə
Syrian ˈsɪrɪən
syringe sɪˈrɪndʒ ˈsɪrɪndʒ
syrup ˈsɪrəp $ ˈsɜəp etc
system ˈsɪstəm
systematic ˈsɪstəˈmætɪk
systematize ˈsɪstəmətaɪz

T

T t ti
ta tɑ
tab tæb
tabby ˈtæbɪ
tabby-cat ˈtæbɪ kæt
tabernacle, T– ˈtæbənækl $ -bɜrn-
table ˈteɪbl
tableau ˈtæbləʊ $ tæˈbləʊ
table d'hôte ˈtabl ˈdəʊt -blə $ ˈtæbl
table-cloth ˈteɪbl kloθ $ klɔθ etc
table-knife ˈteɪbl naɪf pl naɪvz
table-land ˈteɪbl lænd
table-linen ˈteɪbl lɪnɪn
tablespoon ˈteɪblspun
tablet ˈtæblət -lɪt
table-talk ˈteɪbl tɔk
table-tennis ˈteɪbl tenɪs ˈteɪbl ˈtenɪs
tabloid ˈtæblɔɪd
taboo təˈbu $ tæˈbu
tabor ˈteɪbə(r) -bɔ(r)
tabular ˈtæbjʊlə(r)
tabulate ˈtæbjʊleɪt
tabulator ˈtæbjʊleɪtə(r)
tacit ˈtæsɪt
taciturn ˈtæsɪtɜn
taciturnity ˈtæsɪˈtɜnətɪ
tack tæk
tackle ˈtækl
tact tækt
tactical ˈtæktɪkl

tactics ˈtæktɪks
tactile ˈtæktaɪl $ ˈtæktəl etc
tactual ˈtæktʃʊəl £ -tjʊəl
tadpole ˈtædpəʊl
taffeta ˈtæfɪtə
tag tæg
Tahiti tɑˈhitɪ $ £ təˈhitɪ
tail teɪl
tail-board ˈteɪl bɔd $ bɔrd
tail-coat ˈteɪl kəʊt
tail-end teɪl ˈend
tail light ˈteɪl laɪt
tailor ˈteɪlə(r)
tailor-made ˈteɪlə ˈmeɪd $ ˈteɪlər
tailpiece ˈteɪlpis
tailspin ˈteɪlspɪn
taint ˈteɪnt
Taj Mahal ˈtadʒ məˈhal ˈtaʒ
take teɪk
taken ˈteɪkən
take-off ˈteɪk of $ £ ɔf
take-over bid ˈteɪk əʊvə bɪd $ əʊvər
talc tælk
talcum ˈtælkəm
talcum-powder ˈtælkəm paʊdə(r)
tale teɪl
talent ˈtælənt
talisman ˈtælɪzmən $ £ ˈtælɪsmən etc
talk tɔk
talkative ˈtɔkətɪv

talkies ˈtɔkɪz
talking point ˈtɔkɪŋ pɔɪnt
talking-to ˈtɔkɪŋ tu
tall tɔl
Tallahassee ˈtæləˈhæsɪ
tallboy ˈtɔlbɔɪ
tallow ˈtæləʊ ˈtælə
tally ˈtælɪ
tally-clerk ˈtælɪ klɑk $ klɜk
tally-ho ˈtælɪ ˈhəʊ
Talmud ˈtælmʊd $ £ ˈtal- ˈtælməd etc
talon ˈtælən
tamarind ˈtæmərɪnd
tamarisk ˈtæmərɪsk
tambourine ˈtæmbəˈrin $ ˈtæmbərin
tame teɪm
Tamil ˈtæml -mɪl $ ˈtaml ˈtʌml
Tammany ˈtæmənɪ
tam o'shanter ˈtæm ə ˈʃæntə(r)
tamper ˈtæmpə(r)
tan tæn
tandem ˈtændəm
tang tæŋ
Tanganyika ˈtæŋgəˈnjikə -ˈnikə
tangent ˈtændʒənt
tangerine ˈtændʒəˈrin $ ˈtændʒərin etc
tangible ˈtændʒəbl
Tangier tænˈdʒɪə(r)
tangle ˈtæŋgl
tango ˈtæŋgəʊ
tank tæŋk
tankard ˈtæŋkəd $ -kərd
tanker ˈtæŋkə(r)
tannery ˈtænərɪ
Tannhäuser ˈtænhɔɪzə(r)
tannic ˈtænɪk
tannin ˈtænɪn
tansy ˈtænzɪ
tantalize ˈtæntəlaɪz $ ˈtæntḷaɪz
tantamount ˈtæntəmaʊnt
tantrums ˈtæntrəmz
Tanzania ˈtænzəˈnɪə
tap tæp
tap-dancing ˈtæp dɑnsɪŋ $ dænsɪŋ
tape teɪp
tape-measure ˈteɪp meʒə(r)
tape-recorder ˈteɪp rɪkɔdə(r) $ -kɔr-
tapestry ˈtæpɪstrɪ
tapeworm ˈteɪpwɜm
tapioca ˈtæpɪˈəʊkə
tapir ˈteɪpə(r) -pɪə(r)
tap-room ˈtæp rʊm $ £ rum etc
tap-root ˈtæp rut $ rʊt

tapster ˈtæpstə(r)
tar tɑ(r)
tarantula təˈræntjʊlə $ -tʃʊlə -tlə
tardy ˈtadɪ $ ˈtardɪ
tare teə(r)
target ˈtagɪt $ ˈtargɪt
target-practice ˈtagɪt præktɪs $ ˈtar-
tariff ˈtærɪf
tarmac ˈtamæk $ ˈtarmæk
tarn tan $ tarn
tarnish ˈtanɪʃ $ ˈtarnɪʃ
tarpaulin taˈpɔlɪn $ tar- ˈtarpəlɪn
tarragon ˈtærəgən $ -gon etc
tarry adj ˈtarɪ
tarry v ˈtærɪ
tart tat $ tart
tartan ˈtatn $ ˈtartn
tartar ˈtatə(r) $ ˈtartər
tartaric taˈtærɪk $ tar-
Tarzan ˈtazn -zæn $ ˈtar-
task task $ tæsk
task-force ˈtask fɔs $ ˈtæsk fɔrs
task-master ˈtask mastə(r) $ ˈtæsk mæs-
Tasmania tæzˈmeɪnɪə
tassel ˈtæsl
taste teɪst
tat tæt
ta-ta ˈtæ ˈta
tatters ˈtætəz $ ˈtætərz
tattle ˈtætl
tattoo təˈtu $ £ tæˈtu
tatty ˈtætɪ
taught tɔt
taunt tɔnt
Taurus ˈtɔrəs
taut tɔt
tautological ˈtɔtəˈlodʒɪkl
tautology tɔˈtolədʒɪ
tavern ˈtævn $ ˈtævərn
tawdry ˈtɔdrɪ
tawny ˈtɔnɪ
tax tæks
taxation tækˈseɪʃn
tax-collector ˈtæks kəlektə(r)
tax-free ˈtæks ˈfri
taxi ˈtæksɪ
taxidermist ˈtæksɪdəmɪst
　£ tækˈsɪdəmɪst
taxidermy ˈtæksɪdəmɪ
taximeter ˈtæksɪmitə(r)
tax-payer ˈtæks peɪə(r)
Taylor ˈteɪlə(r)
TB ˈti ˈbi

Tchaikovsky(-owsky) tʃaɪˈkovskɪ
$ £ -ˈkofskɪ
tea ti
tea-break ˈti breɪk
tea-caddy ˈti kædɪ
tea-cake ˈti keɪk
teach titʃ
tea-chest ˈti tʃest
tea-cloth ˈti kloθ $ klɔθ
teacup ˈti kʌp *with short i as in 'weak'*
tea-dance ˈti dɑns $ dæns
tea-house ˈti haʊs
teak tik
tea-kettle ˈti ketl
teal til
tea-leaf ˈti lif
team tim
teamster ˈtimstə(r)
team-work ˈtimwɜk
tea-party ˈti pɑtɪ $ pɑrtɪ
teapot ˈtipot *with short i as in 'keep'*
tear *rip* teə(r)
tear *eye fluid* tɪə(r)
tear-drop ˈtɪə drop $ ˈtɪər
tear-gas ˈtɪə gæs $ ˈtɪər
tea-room ˈti rʊm $ £ rum *etc*
tease tiz
teasel ˈtizl
tea-service ˈti sɜvɪs
tea-set ˈti set
teaspoon ˈtispun
tea-strainer ˈti streɪnə(r)
teat tit
tea-table ˈti teɪbl
tea-things ˈti θɪŋz
tea-time ˈtitaɪm *with i short as in 'beat'*
tea-tray ˈti treɪ
tea-trolley ˈti trolɪ
tea-urn ˈti ɜn
tea-wagon ˈti wægən
'tec tek
technic ˈteknɪk $ tekˈnik
technical ˈteknɪkl
technicality ˈteknɪˈkælətɪ
technician tekˈnɪʃn
Technicolor ˈteknɪkʌlə(r)
technique tekˈnik
technocracy tekˈnokrəsɪ
technocrat ˈteknəkræt
technological ˈteknəˈlodʒɪkl
technologist tekˈnolədʒɪst
technology tekˈnolədʒɪ
teddy-bear ˈtedɪ beə(r)

teddy boy ˈtedɪ bɔɪ
Te Deum ˈteɪ ˈdeɪəm ˈti ˈdiəm
tedious ˈtidɪəs $ ˈtidʒəs
tedium ˈtidɪəm
tee ti
teem tim
teenage ˈtineɪdʒ
teenager ˈtineɪdʒə(r)
teens tinz
teeny ˈtinɪ
teeter ˈtitə(r)
teeth tiθ
teethe tið
teething troubles ˈtiðɪŋ trʌblz
teetotal tiˈtəʊtl
teetotaller tiˈtəʊtlə(r)
teetotum tiˈtəʊtəm
Teh(e)ran teəˈrɑn $ teəˈræn
telecast ˈtelɪkɑst $ -kæst
telecommunications ˈtelɪkəˈmjunɪˈkeɪʃnz
telegram ˈtelɪgræm
telegraph ˈtelɪgrɑf $ £ -græf
telegrapher tɪˈlegrəfə(r) tə-
telegraphese ˈtelɪgrɑˈfiz -grə- $ £ -græˈf-
telegraphic telɪˈgræfɪk
telegraphist tɪˈlegrəfɪst tə-
telegraph-line ˈtelɪgrɑf laɪn $ £ -græf
telegraph-pole ˈtelɪgrɑf pəʊl $ £ -græf
teleological ˈtelɪəˈlodʒɪkl
teleology ˈtelɪˈolədʒɪ
telepathic ˈtelɪˈpæθɪk
telepathist tɪˈlepəθɪst tə-
telepathy tɪˈlepəθɪ tə-
telephone ˈteləfəʊn -lɪf-
telephony tɪˈlefənɪ tə-
telephoto ˈtelɪˈfəʊtəʊ
teleprinter ˈtelɪprɪntə(r)
telescope ˈtelɪskəʊp
telescopic ˈtelɪˈskopɪk
televise ˈtelɪvaɪz -ləv-
television ˈtelɪvɪʒn ˈtelɪˈvɪʒn -ləv-
tell tel
telltale ˈtelteɪl
temerity tɪˈmerətɪ
temper ˈtempə(r)
tempera ˈtempərə
temperament ˈtemprəmənt
temperamental ˈtemprəˈmentl
temperance ˈtemprəns
temperance society ˈtemprəns səsaɪətɪ
temperate ˈtempṛət
temperature ˈtempṛətʃə(r) -rɪtʃ- -rtʃ-
$ ˈtempərtʃʊər -pətʃ- -tʃər *etc*

tempest, T– ˈtempɪst
tempestuous temˈpestʃʊəs
template ˈtemplət -pleɪt
temple ˈtempl
templet ˈtemplət -lɪt
tempo ˈtempəʊ
temporal ˈtempərl
temporarily ˈtempr̩lɪ -prəlɪ -prɪlɪ
  $ ˈtempəˈrerəlɪ ˈtempərerlɪ
temporary ˈtempr̩ɪ ˈtemprərɪ -pərɪ
  -prɪ̩ $ ˈtempərerɪ
temporize ˈtempəraɪz
tempt tempt
temptation tempˈteɪʃn -mˈt-
ten ten
tenable ˈtenəbl
tenacious təˈneɪʃəs tɪˈn-
tenacity təˈnæsətɪ tɪˈn-
tenancy ˈtenənsɪ
tenant ˈtenənt
tenantry ˈtenəntrɪ
tench tentʃ
tend tend
tendency ˈtendənsɪ
tendentious tenˈdenʃəs
tender ˈtendə(r)
tenderfoot ˈtendəfʊt $ ˈtendərfʊt
tender-hearted ˈtendəˈhɑtɪd $ -dər ˈhar-
tenderloin ˈtendələɪn $ ˈtendərləɪn
tendon ˈtendən
tendril ˈtendrɪl $ £ ˈtendrəl
tenement ˈtenəmənt
tenement-house ˈtenəmənt haʊs
Tenerif(fe) ˈtenəˈrif $ -ˈrɪf
tenet ˈtenet ˈtinet $ £ ˈtenɪt
tenner ˈtenə(r)
Tennessee ˈtenəˈsi
tennis ˈtenɪs
tennis arm ˈtenɪs ˈɑm $ ˈarm
tennis-ball ˈtenɪs bɔl
tennis-court ˈtenɪs kɔt $ kɔrt
tennis elbow ˈtenɪs ˈelbəʊ
tennis-racquet ˈtenɪs rækɪt
Tennyson ˈtenɪsn
tenon ˈtenən
tenor ˈtenə(r)
tenpence ˈtenpəns $ ˈtenpens
tenpins ˈtenpɪnz
tense tens
tensile ˈtensaɪl $ ˈtensl etc
tension ˈtenʃn
tent tent
tentacle ˈtentəkl

tentative ˈtentətɪv
tenterhooks ˈtentəhʊks $ -tər-
tenth tenθ
tent-peg ˈtent peg
tenuity tɪˈnjuətɪ $ teˈnuətɪ etc
tenuous ˈtenjʊəs
tenure ˈtenjʊə(r) $ ˈtenjər etc
tepee ˈtipi
tepid ˈtepɪd
tercentenary ˈtɜsenˈtinərɪ -ˈten-
  $ tɜˈsentn̩erɪ etc
tercentennial ˈtɜsenˈtenɪəl
Terence ˈterns
Teresa təˈreɪzə təˈrizə $ təˈrisə etc
term tɜm
termagant ˈtɜməgənt
terminable ˈtɜmɪnəbl
terminal ˈtɜmɪnl
terminate ˈtɜmɪneɪt
termini ˈtɜmɪnaɪ
terminological ˈtɜmɪnəˈlodʒɪkl
terminology ˈtɜmɪˈnolədʒɪ
terminus ˈtɜmɪnəs
termite ˈtɜmaɪt
tern tɜn
terrace ˈterəs -rɪs
terra-cotta ˈterə ˈkotə
terra firma ˈterə ˈfɜmə
terrain teˈreɪn ˈtereɪn $ £ təˈreɪn etc
terra incognita ˈterə ɪnˈkognɪtə £ ˈtɜrər
terrapin ˈterəpɪn
terrestrial təˈrestrɪəl
terrible ˈterəbl
terrier ˈterɪə(r)
terrific təˈrɪfɪk
terrify ˈterɪfaɪ
territorial ˈterɪˈtɔrɪəl
territory ˈterɪtrɪ $ -tɔrɪ
terror ˈterə(r)
terrorise ˈterəraɪz ˈterr̩aɪz
terrorism ˈterərɪzm ˈterr̩ɪzm
terrorist ˈterərɪst ˈterr̩ɪst
terror-stricken ˈterə strɪkən $ ˈterər
terse tɜs
tertian ˈtɜʃn
tertiary ˈtɜʃərɪ $ ˈtɜʃɪerɪ etc
terylene ˈterl̩in
tessellated ˈtesl̩eɪtɪd
test test
testament ˈtestəmənt
testate ˈtesteɪt ˈtestɪt
testator teˈsteɪtə(r) $ ˈtesteɪtər etc
testatrix teˈsteɪtrɪks

testicle ˈtestɪkl
testify ˈtestɪfaɪ
testimonial ˌtestɪˈməʊnɪəl
testimony ˈtestɪmənɪ $ -məʊnɪ
test-match ˈtest mætʃ
test pilot ˈtest paɪlət
test-tube ˈtest tjub $ tub
testy ˈtestɪ
tetanus ˈtetnəs £ ˈtetənəs
tetchy ˈtetʃɪ
tête-à-tête ˈteɪt ɑ ˈteɪt ˈteɪt ə ˈteɪt
tether ˈteðə(r)
tetrahedron ˌtetrəˈhidrən $ -ron
Teuton ˈtjutn $ ˈtutn
Teutonic tjuˈtonɪk $ tu-
Texan ˈteksn
Texas ˈteksəs
text tekst
textbook ˈteksbʊk -stb-
textile ˈtekstaɪl $ -təl
textual ˈtekstʃʊəl
texture ˈtekstʃə(r)
Thackeray ˈθækəreɪ -rɪ
Thai taɪ
Thailand ˈtaɪlænd
thalidomide θəˈlɪdəmaɪd
Thames temz
than usual form: ðən
    rarely used strong-form: ðæn
thank θæŋk
thank-offering ˈθæŋk ˈofrɪŋ $ ˈɔfrɪŋ
thanksgiving θæŋksˈgɪvɪŋ ˈθæŋksgɪvɪŋ
Thanksgiving Day θæŋksˈgɪvɪŋ deɪ
that demonstr adj, pron, adv ðæt
that rel pron, conj, usual form: ðət
    rarely used strong-form: ðæt
thatch θætʃ
thaw θɔ
the before consonant-sounds: ðə
    before vowel-sounds, strong-form: ði
theatre($ -ter) ˈθɪətə(r) £ θɪˈetə(r)
theatre-goer ˈθɪətə gəʊə(r) $ ˈθɪətər
theatrical θɪˈætrɪkl
thee ði
theft θeft
their ðeə(r)
theirs ðeəz $ ðeərz
theism ˈθi-ɪzm as two words
theist ˈθiɪst
theistic θiˈɪstɪk
them usual forms: ðm ðəm
    strong-form: ðem $ colloq and £
    familiar weak-form: əm

theme θim
theme-song ˈθim soŋ $ sɔŋ
themselves ðmˈselvz ðəm-
then ðen
thence ðens $ θens
thenceforth ðensˈfɔθ $ ðensˈfɔrθ θe-
thenceforward ðensˈfɔwəd £ -wʊd
    $ ðensˈfɔrwərd
Theobald ˈθɪəbɔld
theocracy θiˈokrəsɪ
theodolite θiˈodəlaɪt $ £ -dļaɪt
Theodore ˈθɪədɔ(r)
theologian ˌθɪəˈləʊdʒən
theological θɪəˈlodʒɪkl
theology θiˈolədʒɪ
theorem ˈθɪərəm
theoretical θɪəˈretɪkl
theorist ˈθɪərɪst
theorize ˈθɪəraɪz
theory ˈθɪərɪ
theosophical θɪəˈsofɪkl
theosophy θiˈosəfɪ
therapeutic ˌθerəˈpjutɪk
therapy ˈθerəpɪ
there ðeə(r) weak-form: ðə(r)
thereabouts ˈðeərəbaʊts ˈðeərəˈbaʊts
thereafter ðeərˈaftə(r) $ -ˈæftər
thereby ðeəˈbaɪ $ ðeərˈbaɪ
therefore ˈðeəfɔ(r) $ ˈðeərfɔr
therein ðeərˈɪn
thereinafter ˈðeərɪnˈaftə(r) $ -ˈæftər
thereof ðeərˈov
Theresa təˈreɪzə təˈrizə $ təˈrisə etc
thereto ðeəˈtu $ ðeərˈtu
thereunder ðeərˈʌndə(r)
thereupon ˈðeərəˈpon $ -ˈpɔn
therewithal ˈðeəwɪðl ˈðeəwɪðˈɔl
    $ -eər- -wɪθ-
therm θɜm
thermal ˈθɜml
thermodynamics ˈθɜməʊdaɪˈnæmɪks
thermometer θəˈmomɪtə(r) $ θər- θəˈm-
thermoplastic ˈθɜməʊˈplæstɪk
thermostat ˈθɜməstæt
thermostatic ˈθɜməˈstætɪk
thermos ˈθɜmos -məs
thesaurus θɪˈsɔrəs
these ðiz
these'd ˈðizəd
these'll ˈðizl
these're ˈðizə(r)
theses ˈθisiz
these've ˈðizəv

thesis ˈθisɪs
Thespian ˈθespɪən
theta (θ) ˈθitə $ ˈθeɪtə *etc*
thews θjuz
they ðeɪ
they'd ðeɪd
they'll ðeɪl
they're ðeə(r)
they've ðeɪv
thick θɪk
thicken ˈθɪkən
thicket ˈθɪkɪt
thick-headed ˈθɪk ˈhedɪd
thickset ˈθɪkˈset
thick-skinned ˈθɪk ˈskɪnd
thief θif
thieves θivz
thievish ˈθivɪʃ
thigh θaɪ
thigh-bone ˈθaɪ bəʊn
thimble ˈθɪmbl
thin θɪn
thine ðaɪn
thing θɪŋ
thingummy, thingamy ˈθɪŋəmɪ
think θɪŋk
thinking-cap ˈθɪŋkɪŋ kæp
thin-skinned ˈθɪn ˈskɪnd
third θɜd
third-rate ˈθɜd ˈreɪt
thirst θɜst
thirteen ˈθɜˈtin
thirteenth ˈθɜˈtinθ
thirtieth ˈθɜtɪəθ
thirty ˈθɜtɪ
thirty-one ˈθɜtɪ ˈwʌn
this ðɪs
thistle ˈθɪsl
thither ˈðɪðə(r) $ ˈθɪðər *etc*
tho' ðəʊ
Thomas ˈtoməs
thong θoŋ $ ˈθɔŋ *etc*
thorax ˈθɔræks
thorn θɔn $ θɔrn
thorough ˈθʌrə $ ˈθɜəʊ ˈθɜə
thoroughbred ˈθʌrəbred $ ˈθɜəʊ- *etc*
thoroughfare ˈθʌrəfeə(r) $ ˈθɜəʊ- *etc*
thorough-going ˈθʌrə ˈgəʊɪŋ $ ˈθɜəʊ *etc*
thorough-paced ˈθʌrəpeɪst $ ˈθɜəʊ- *etc*
those ðəʊz
those'd ˈðəʊzəd
those'll ˈðəʊzl
those're ˈðəʊzə(r)

those've ˈðəʊzəv
thou ðaʊ
though ðəʊ
thought θɔt
thought-reader ˈθɔt ridə(r)
thousand ˈθaʊznd
thousandfold ˈθaʊzndfəʊld -znf-
thousandth ˈθaʊznθ
thrall θrɔl
thrash θræʃ
thread θred
threadbare ˈθredbeə(r)
threat θret
threaten ˈθretn
three θri
three-cornered ˈθri ˈkɔnəd $ ˈkɔrnərd
three-D ˈθri ˈdi
three-dimensional ˈθri daɪˈmenʃnl dɪ-
threefold ˈθri-fəʊld
three-legged ˈθri ˈlegɪd ˈlegd
threepence ˈθrəpəns ˈθre- ˈθrʌ- ˈθrʊ-
$ ˈθri-pens
threepenny ˈθrəpnɪ ˈθre- ˈθrʌ- ˈθrʊ-
$ ˈθri-peni
three-ply ˈθri ˈplaɪ
three-quarter ˈθri ˈkwɔtə(r) $ ˈkwɔrtər
three-score ˈθri ˈskɔ(r)
threesome ˈθrisəm
three-storey ˈθri ˈstɔrɪ
three-wheeled ˈθri ˈwild $ ˈhwild *etc*
threnody ˈθrenədɪ
thresh θreʃ
threshing-floor ˈθreʃɪŋ flɔ(r)
threshing-machine ˈθreʃɪŋ məʃin
threshold ˈθreʃhəʊld ˈθreʃəʊld
threw θru
thrice θraɪs
thrift θrɪft
thrifty ˈθrɪftɪ
thrill θrɪl
thrive θraɪv
thriven ˈθrɪvən
thro' θru
throat θrəʊt
throb θrob
throes θrəʊz
thrombosis θromˈbəʊsɪs
throne θrəʊn
throng θroŋ $ θrɔŋ *etc*
throstle ˈθrosl
throttle ˈθrotl
through θru
throughout θruˈaʊt

throve θrəʊv
throw θrəʊ
throwback ˈθrəʊbæk
thrown θrəʊn
thru θru
thrum θrʌm
thrush θrʌʃ
thrust θrʌst
thud θʌd
thug θʌg
thumb θʌm
thumbnail ˈθʌmneɪl
thumbscrew ˈθʌmskru
thump θʌmp
thunder ˈθʌndə(r)
thunder-bolt ˈθʌndə bəʊlt $ -dər-
thunder-clap ˈθʌndə klæp $ -dər-
thunderous ˈθʌndərəs -dr̩-
thunder-storm ˈθʌndə stɔm $ -dər stɔrm
thunder-struck ˈθʌndə strʌk $ -dər
Thursday ˈθɜzdɪ -deɪ
thus ðʌs
thwack θwæk
thwart θwɔt $ θwɔrt
thy ðaɪ
thyself ðaɪˈself
thyme taɪm
thyroid ˈθaɪrɔɪd
tiara tɪˈɑrə $ tɪˈærə tɪˈeərə etc
Tibet tɪˈbet
Tibetan tɪˈbetn -tən
tibia ˈtɪbɪə
tick tɪk
ticker-tape ˈtɪkə teɪp $ ˈtɪkər
ticket ˈtɪkɪt
ticking ˈtɪkɪŋ
tickle ˈtɪkl
ticklish ˈtɪkl̩ɪʃ
tidal ˈtaɪdl
tidal wave ˈtaɪdl weɪv
tidbit ˈtɪdbɪt
tiddl(e)y ˈtɪdl̩ɪ
tiddly-winks ˈtɪdlɪ wɪŋks
tide taɪd
tideway ˈtaɪdweɪ
tidings ˈtaɪdɪŋz
tidy ˈtaɪdɪ
tie taɪ
tier tɪə(r)
tie-on ˈtaɪ ˈon $ ˈɔn
tie-up ˈtaɪ ʌp
tiff tɪf
tiffin ˈtɪfɪn

tiger ˈtaɪgə(r)
tigerish ˈtaɪgərɪʃ
tiger-lily ˈtaɪgə lɪlɪ $ ˈtaɪgər
tiger moth ˈtaɪgə mɒθ $ ˈtaɪgər mɔθ
tight taɪt
tight-fisted ˈtaɪt ˈfɪstɪd
tight-lipped ˈtaɪt ˈlɪpt
tight-rope ˈtaɪt rəʊp
tigress ˈtaɪgrəs -ɪs -es
tike taɪk
tilde tɪld $ £ ˈtɪldə -dɪ -deɪ
tile taɪl
till conj, prep tɪl weak-form: tl
till n, v tɪl
tillage ˈtɪlɪdʒ
tilt tɪlt
timber ˈtɪmbə(r)
timbre ˈtæbr with unsyllabic r
ˈtæmbə(r) $ ˈtɪmbər etc
timbrel ˈtɪmbrəl
time taɪm
time, (in) no ɪn ˈnəʊ taɪm
time-bomb ˈtaɪm bom
time-exposure ˈtaɪm ɪkspəʊʒə(r)
time-fuse ˈtaɪm fjuz
time-honoured($ -ored) ˈtaɪm onəd $ -ərd
time-keeper ˈtaɪm kipə(r)
time-lag ˈtaɪm læg
time-limit ˈtaɪm lɪmɪt
timely ˈtaɪmlɪ
timepiece ˈtaɪmpis
times, at the best of ət ðə ˈbest əv taɪmz
time-saving ˈtaɪm seɪvɪŋ
time-table ˈtaɪm teɪbl
timid ˈtɪmɪd
timidity tɪˈmɪdətɪ
Timothy ˈtɪməθɪ
tin ˈtɪn
tincture ˈtɪŋktʃə(r)
tinder ˈtɪndə(r)
tinder-box ˈtɪndə boks $ ˈtɪndər
tine taɪn
tin-foil ˈtɪn fɔɪl
ting tɪŋ
tinge tɪndʒ
tingle ˈtɪŋgl
tinker ˈtɪŋkə(r)
tinkle ˈtɪŋkl
tinny ˈtɪnɪ
tin-opener ˈtɪn əʊpṇə(r)
tin-plate ˈtɪn pleɪt
tinsel ˈtɪnsl
tint tɪnt

tintinnabulation ˌtɪntɪˈnæbjʊˈleɪʃn
tiny ˈtaɪnɪ
-tion *suffix* ʃn
tip tɪp
tip-off ˈtɪp ɒf $ £ ɔf
tippet ˈtɪpɪt
tipple tɪpl
tipstaff ˈtɪpstɑf $ ˈtɪpstæf
tipster ˈtɪpstə(r)
tipsy ˈtɪpsɪ
tiptoe ˈtɪptəʊ
tip-top ˈtɪp ˈtop
tip-up ˈtɪp ʌp
tirade taɪˈreɪd tɪˈrɑd
tire ˈtaɪə(r)
tiresome ˈtaɪəsm $ ˈtaɪərsm
tiro ˈtaɪərəʊ
tissue ˈtɪʃu £ ˈtɪsju
tissue paper ˈtɪʃu peɪpə(r) £ ˈtɪsju
'tis tɪz *always stressed after pause*
'tisn't ˈtɪznt
tit tɪt
Titan ˈtaɪtn
titanic taɪˈtænɪk
titanium tɪˈteɪnɪəm taɪ-
titbit ˈtɪtbɪt
tithe taɪð
Titian ˈtɪʃn
titillate ˈtɪtɪleɪt $ ˈtɪtḷeɪt
titivate ˈtɪtɪveɪt
title ˈtaɪtl
title-deed ˈtaɪtl did
title-page ˈtaɪtl peɪdʒ
title-role ˈtaɪtl rəʊl
titmice ˈtɪtmaɪs
titmouse ˈtɪtmaʊs
titter ˈtɪtə(r)
tittle ˈtɪtl
tittle-tattle ˈtɪtl tætl
titular ˈtɪtjʊlə(r) $ ˈtɪtʃʊlər
TNT ˈti en ˈti
to *usual form before consonants:* tə
  before vowels and strong-form: tu
toad təʊd
toadstool ˈtəʊdstul
toady ˈtəʊdɪ
toast təʊst
toasting-fork ˈtəʊstɪŋ fɔk $ fɔrk
toast-master ˈtəʊst mɑstə(r) $ mæstər
tobacco təˈbækəʊ
tobacconist təˈbækənɪst
Tobago təˈbeɪgəʊ $ £ ˈtəʊ-
toboggan təˈbogən

tocsin ˈtoksɪn
today təˈdeɪ
toddle ˈtodl
toddy ˈtodɪ
to-do tə ˈdu
toe təʊ
toe-cap ˈtəʊ kæp
toe-hold ˈtəʊ həʊld
toe-nail ˈtəʊ neɪl
toff tof $ tɔf
toffee ˈtofɪ $ ˈtɔfɪ
tog tog $ tɔg
toga ˈtəʊgə
together təˈgeðə(r)
toggle ˈtogl
Togo ˈtəʊgəʊ
toil tɔɪl
toilet ˈtɔɪlət
toilet-paper ˈtɔɪlət peɪpə(r)
toilet-roll ˈtɔɪlət rəʊl
toilet-table ˈtɔɪlət teɪbl
token ˈtəʊkən
Tokyo(-iyo) ˈtəʊkɪəʊ
told təʊld
tolerable ˈtolṛəbl
tolerance ˈtolərəns
tolerant ˈtolərənt
tolerate ˈtoləreɪt
toll təʊl
toll call ˈtəʊl kɔl
toll-gate ˈtəʊl geɪt
Tolstoy ˈtolstɔɪ $ ˈtɔlstɔɪ *etc*
tomahawk ˈtoməhɔk
tomato təˈmatəʊ $ təˈmeɪtəʊ -tə
tomb tum
tombola tomˈbəʊlə ˈtombələ
tomboy ˈtombɔɪ
tombstone ˈtumstəʊn
tomcat ˈtomkæt
tome təʊm
tomfoolery tomˈfulərɪ
tommy-gun ˈtomɪ gʌn
tommyrot ˈtomɪˈrot $ ˈtomɪrot
tomorrow təˈmorəʊ $ təˈmɔrəʊ -rə
tomtom ˈtomtom
ton tʌn
tonal ˈtəʊnl
tonality təˈnælətɪ təʊˈn-
tone təʊn
tonga, T– ˈtongə -ŋə $ ˈtoŋ-
tongs toŋz $ tɔŋz
tongue tʌŋ
tongue-tied ˈtʌŋ taɪd

tongue-twister `tʌŋ twɪstə(r)
tonic `tonɪk
tonic sol-fa 'tonɪk 'sol `fa $ 'soʊl
tonic water `tonɪk wɔtə(r)
tonight tə`naɪt
tonnage `tʌnɪdʒ
tonsil `tonsl
tonsil(l)itis 'tonsl`aɪtɪs -təs
tonsorial ton`sɔrɪəl
tonsure `tonʃə(r)
too tu
took tʊk
tool tul
toot tut
tooth tuθ
toothache `tuθeɪk
toothbrush `tuθbrʌʃ
tooth-comb `tuθ kəʊm
tooth-paste `tuθ peɪst
toothpick `tuθpɪk
tootle `tutl
top top
topaz `təʊpæz
top-coat `top kəʊt
top-dressing 'top `dresɪŋ $ £ `top dresɪŋ
tope təʊp
topee `təʊpɪ $ £ təʊ`pi
top-gallant `top gælənt  nautical tə `g-
top-heavy top `hevɪ
top-hole top `həʊl
topi `təʊpɪ $ £ təʊ`pi etc
topiary `təʊpɪərɪ $ -ɪerɪ
topic `topɪk
topical `topɪkl
top-knot `top not
topmast `topmast $ -mæst
topmost `topməʊst
topographical 'topə`græfɪkl $ `təʊp-
topography tə`pogrəfɪ $ təʊ-
topper `topə(r)
topple `topl
top-ranking 'top `ræŋkɪŋ
topsail `topsl -seɪl
topsy-turvy 'topsɪ `tɜvɪ
toque təʊk
tor tɔ(r)
torch tɔtʃ $ tɔrtʃ
torchlight `tɔtʃlaɪt $ `tɔr-
torch-song `tɔtʃ soŋ $ `tɔrtʃ sɔŋ
tore tɔ(r)
toreador `torɪədɔ(r) $ `tɔr-
torment n `tɔment $ `tɔr-
torment v tɔ`ment $ tɔr-

tormentor tɔ`mentə(r) $ tɔr-
torn tɔn $ tɔrn
tornado tɔ`neɪdəʊ $ tɔr-
torpedo tɔ`pidəʊ $ tɔr-
torpedo-boat tɔ`pidəʊ bəʊt $ tɔr-
torpid `tɔpɪd $ `tɔrpɪd
torpor `tɔpə(r) $ `tɔrpər
torque tɔk $ tɔrk
Toronto tə`rontəʊ
torrent `torənt $ `tɔrənt etc
torrential tə`renʃl
torrid `torɪd $ `tɔrɪd etc
torsion `tɔʃn $ `tɔrʃn
torso `tɔsəʊ $ `tɔrsəʊ
tort tɔt $ tɔrt
tortoise `tɔtəs $ `tɔrtəs
tortoise-shell `tɔtə ʃel -təʃ ʃel $ `tɔr-
tortuous `tɔtʃʊəs $ `tɔr-
torture `tɔtʃə(r) $ `tɔr-
Tory `tɔrɪ
Toryism `tɔrɪɪzm
Tosca, La la `toskə
Toscanini 'toskə`ninɪ
tosh toʃ
toss tos $ tɔs etc
toss-up `tos ʌp $ `tɔs ʌp etc
tot tot
total `təʊtl
totalitarian 'təʊ'tælɪ`teərɪən
totalizator `təʊtl|aɪzeɪtə(r) $ -|ɪz-
tote təʊt
totem `təʊtəm
totter `totə(r)
toucan `tukæn
touch tʌtʃ
touch-and-go 'tʌtʃ ən `gəʊ əŋ
touch-line `tʌtʃ laɪn
touchstone `tʌtʃstəʊn
touchy `tʌtʃɪ
tough tʌf
toughen `tʌfn
tough guy `tʌf gaɪ
toupee `tupeɪ $ tu`peɪ
tour tʊə(r) £ tɔ(r)
tour de force 'tʊə də `fɔs
  $ 'tʊər də `fɔrs
tourist `tʊərɪst £ `tɔrɪst
tournament `tʊənəmənt £ `tɔn-
  $ £ `tɑnəmənt `tʊərn-
tourniquet `tʊənɪkeɪ £ `tɔn-
  $ `tɜnɪkɪt `tʊərn-
tousle `taʊzl
tout taʊt

tow təʊ
toward(s) tʊˈwɔd(z) $ £ tɔrd(z)
  in £ often as the strong-form and
  weak-form respectively
towel ˈtaʊḷ
towel-rail ˈtaʊḷ reɪl
tower ˈtaʊə(r)
town taʊn
townee taʊˈni
township ˈtaʊnʃɪp
townsfolk ˈtaʊnzfəʊk
townsman ˈtaʊnzmən
townspeople ˈtaʊnzpipl
tox(a)emia tokˈsimɪə
toxic ˈtoksɪk
toxicology ˈtoksɪˈkolədʒɪ
toxin ˈtoksɪn
toy tɔɪ
toyshop ˈtɔɪ-ʃop
trace treɪs
tracery ˈtreɪsərɪ
trachea trəˈkiə $ ˈtreɪkɪə
trachoma trəˈkəʊmə
tracing-paper ˈtreɪsɪŋ peɪpə(r)
track træk
tract trækt
tractable ˈtræktəbl
traction ˈtrækʃn
traction-engine ˈtrækʃn endʒɪn
tractor ˈtræktə(r)
Tracy ˈtreɪsɪ
trade treɪd
trademark ˈtreɪdmak $ -mark
trade name ˈtreɪd neɪm
trade show ˈtreɪd ʃəʊ
tradesman ˈtreɪdzmən
tradespeople ˈtreɪdzpipl
trade(s) union treɪd(z) ˈjunɪən
trade-wind ˈtreɪdwɪnd
trading-estate ˈtreɪdɪŋ ɪsteɪt
tradition trəˈdɪʃn
traditional trəˈdɪʃnl
traditionalist trəˈdɪʃnḷɪst
traduce trəˈdjus $ -ˈdus
Trafalgar trəˈfælgə $ -gər
traffic ˈtræfɪk
trafficators ˈtræfɪkeɪtəz $ -tərz
traffic-jam ˈtræfɪk dʒæm
trafficker ˈtræfɪkə(r)
traffic-light ˈtræfɪk laɪt
traffic warden ˈtræfɪk wɔdn $ wɔrdn
tragedian trəˈdʒidɪən
tragedienne trəˈdʒɪdɪˈen

tragedy ˈtrædʒədɪ
tragic ˈtrædʒɪk
tragically ˈtrædʒɪklɪ
tragi-comedy ˈtrædʒɪ ˈkomədɪ
trail treɪl
train treɪn
train-bearer ˈtreɪn beərə(r)
trainee treɪˈni
training-college ˈtreɪnɪŋ kolɪdʒ
training-establishment
  ˈtreɪnɪŋ ɪstæblɪʃmənt
training-ship ˈtreɪnɪŋ ʃɪp
traipse treɪps
trait treɪt £ treɪ
traitor ˈtreɪtə(r)
traitorous ˈtreɪtərəs
traitress ˈtreɪtrəs -rɪs
trajectory trəˈdʒektərɪ £ ˈtrædʒɪktərɪ
tram træm
tram-car ˈtræm ka(r)
tram-lines ˈtræm laɪnz
trammel ˈtræml
tramp ˈtræmp
trample ˈtræmpl
tramp steamer ˈtræmp stimə(r)
trance trans $ træns
tranquil ˈtræŋkwɪl
tranquil(l)ity træŋˈkwɪlətɪ
tranquil(l)izer ˈtræŋkwɪlaɪzə(r)
trans- *prefix* trænz træns £ tran-
transact trænˈzækt -ˈsæ- £ tran-
transaction trænˈzækʃn -ˈsæ- £ tran-
transalpine trænˈzælpaɪn -ˈsæ- £ tran-
transatlantic ˈtrænzətˈlæntɪk -nsət-
  £ ˈtran-
transcend trænˈsend £ tran-
transcendency trænˈsendənsɪ £ tran-
transcendent trænˈsendənt £ tran-
transcendental ˈtrænsenˈdentl £ ˈtran-
transcendentalism ˈtrænsenˈdentḷɪzm
  £ ˈtran-
transcontinental ˈtrænzˈkontɪˈnentl -ns-
  £ ˈtran-
transcribe trænˈskraɪb £ tran-
transcript ˈtrænskrɪpt £ ˈtran-
transcription trænˈskrɪpʃn £ tran-
transept ˈtrænsept -nz- £ ˈtran-
transfer *n* ˈtrænsfɜ(r) -nz- £ ˈtran-
transfer *v* trænsˈfɜ(r) -nz- £ tran-
transference ˈtrænsfərəns -nzf-
  $ £ trænsˈfɜrəns £ trans-
transfiguration ˈtrænsˈfɪgəˈreɪʃn -nz-
  $ -gjər- £ ˈtran-

transfigure træns`fɪgə(r) -nz- $ -gjər
£ tran-

transfix træns`fɪks -nz- £ tran-

transform n `trænsfɔm -nz- £ `tran-
$ -fɔrm

transform v træns`fɔm -nz- £ tran-
$ -fɔrm

transformation `trænsfə`meɪʃn -nz-
£ `tran- $ -fər-

transfuse træns`fjuz -nz- £ tran-

transfusion træns`fjuʒn -nz- £ tran-

transgress trænz`gres £ tran-

transgression trænz`greʃn £ tran-

transient `trænzɪənt -ns- £ `tran-
$ `trænʃnt

transistor træn`zɪstə(r) -n`sɪ- £ tran-

transistorized træn`zɪstəraɪzd -n`sɪ-
£ tran-

transit `trænsɪt -nzɪt £ `tran-

transit camp `trænsɪt kæmp -nzɪt

transition træn`zɪʃn -`sɪ- £ tran- -`sɪʒn

transitive `trænsətɪv -nz- £ `tran-

transitory `trænsɪtrɪ -nz-
$ -ɪtɔrɪ £ `tran-

Transjordan trænz`dʒɔdn $ -ɔr- £ tran-

translate trænz`leɪt -ns`l- £ tran-
$ `trænsleɪt

translation trænz`leɪʃn -ns`l- £ tran-

translator trænz`leɪtə(r) -ns`l-
£ tran- $ `trænsleɪtər

transliterate trænz`lɪtəreɪt -ns- £ tran-

transliteration trænz`lɪtə`reɪʃn -ns`l-
£ tran-

translucent trænz`lusnt -ns`l- £ tran-

transmigration `trænzmaɪ`greɪʃn
-nsm- £ `tran-

transmission trænz`mɪʃn -ns`m- £ tran-

transmit trænz`mɪt -ns`m- £ tran-

transmitter trænz`mɪtə(r) £ tran-

transmogrify trænz`mogrɪfaɪ
-ns`m- £ tran-

transmutation `trænzmju`teɪʃn -ns`m-
£ `tran-

transmute trænz`mjut -ns`m- £ tran-

transoceanic `trænz`əʊʃɪ`ænɪk -ns- £ `tran-

transom `trænsəm

transparency træn`spærənsɪ $ -pær- etc

transparent træn`speərnt -pær-

transpire træn`spaɪə(r) £ tran-

transplant n `trænsplant -nz- £ `trans-
$ -plænt

transplant v træns`plant -nz-
$ -`plænt £ tran-

transplantation `trænsplan`teɪʃn -nz-
$ -plæn- £ `tran-

transport n `transpɔt
$ £ `træns- -nz- $ -pɔrt

transport v træn`spɔt £ tran- $ -`spɔrt

transportation `trænspɔ`teɪʃn £ `tran-
$ -pɔr-

transpose træn`spəʊz £ tran-

transposition `trænspə`zɪʃn £ `tran-

transubstantiation
`trænsəb`stænʃɪ`eɪʃn -nsɪ`eɪʃn

transverse trænz`vɜs -ns- £ tran-

trap træp

trap-door træp`dɔ(r)

trapes treɪps

trapeze trə`piz $ træ`piz

trapezium trə`pizɪəm $ træ`pizɪəm

trappings `træpɪŋz

Trappist `træpɪst

trash træʃ

trash-can `træʃ kæn

trauma `trɔmə $ £ `traʊmə

traumatic trɔ`mætɪk traʊ-

travail `træveɪl

travel `trævl

travel(l)er `trævlə(r)

travelogue($ -log) `trævlog $ -lɔg etc

traverse `trævɜs

travesty `trævɪstɪ -əstɪ

trawler `trɔlə(r)

trawl-net `trɔl net

tray treɪ

treacherous `tretʃərəs

treachery `tretʃərɪ

treacle `trikl

treacly `triklɪ

tread tred

treadle `tredl

tread-mill `tred mɪl

treason `trizn

treasonable `triznəbl

treasure `treʒə(r) $ `treɪʒər

treasurer `treʒrə(r) $ `treɪʒrər

treasure trove `treʒə `trəʊv £ `t- t
$ `treʒər `treɪʒər

treasury `treʒrɪ $ `treɪʒrɪ

treasury bill `treʒrɪ bɪl $ `treɪʒrɪ

treasury note `treʒrɪ nəʊt $ `treɪʒrɪ

treat trit

treatise `tritɪz $ £ `tritɪs

treatment `tritmənt

treaty `tritɪ

treble `trebl

treble clef 'trebl ˏklef
tree tri
tree-fern ˈtri fɜn
trefoil trɪˈfɔɪl
trek trek
trellis ˈtrelɪs
tremble ˈtrembl
tremendous trɪˈmendəs
tremolo ˈtremə ləʊ
tremor ˈtremə(r)
tremulous ˈtremjʊləs
trench trentʃ
trenchant ˈtrentʃənt
trencherman ˈtrentʃəmən $ -tʃər-
trend trend
trepidation ˌtrepɪˈdeɪʃn
trespass ˈtrespəs $ ˈtrespæs
trespasser ˈtrespəsə(r) $ -pæsər
tress tres
trestle ˈtresl
trestle-table ˈtresl teɪbl
Trevor ˈtrevə(r)
tri- prefix traɪ
triad ˈtraɪæd
trial ˈtraɪļ
triangle ˈtraɪæŋgl
triangular traɪˈæŋgjʊlə(r)
tribal ˈtraɪbl
tribalism ˈtraɪbļɪzm
tribe traɪb
tribesman ˈtraɪbzmən
tribulation ˌtrɪbjʊˈleɪʃn
tribunal traɪˈbjunl trɪˈb-
tribune ˈtrɪbjun $ trɪˈbjun
tributary ˈtrɪbjʊtərɪ $ -terɪ
tribute ˈtrɪbjut
trice traɪs
trick trɪk
trickery ˈtrɪkərɪ
trickle ˈtrɪkl
trickster ˈtrɪkstə(r)
tricolo(u)r ˈtrɪkələ(r) $ ˈtraɪkʌlər
tricycle ˈtraɪsɪkl
trident ˈtraɪdnt
tried traɪd
triennial traɪˈenɪəl
trier ˈtraɪə(r)
Trieste triˈest trɪˈesteɪ
trifle ˈtraɪfl
trifling ˈtraɪflɪŋ
trigger ˈtrɪgə(r)
trigonometry ˌtrɪgəˈnomɪtrɪ
trilateral traɪˈlætərl

trilby ˈtrɪlbɪ
trill trɪl
trillion ˈtrɪlɪən
trilogy ˈtrɪlədʒɪ
trim trɪm
trimaran ˈtraɪməræn
Trinidad ˈtrɪnɪdæd
trinitrotoluene ˌtraɪˈnaɪtrəʊˈtoljuin
trinity ˈtrɪnətɪ
trinket ˈtrɪŋkɪt
trio ˈtriəʊ
triolet ˈtriəʊlet
trip trɪp
tripartite traɪˈpataɪt $ -ˈpar-
tripe traɪp
triplane ˈtraɪ-pleɪn
triple ˈtrɪpl
triplet ˈtrɪplɪt -lət
triplex ˈtrɪpleks
triplicate ˈtrɪplɪkət
tripod ˈtraɪpod
Tripoli ˈtrɪpəlɪ
tripos ˈtraɪpos
triptych ˈtrɪptɪk
trisect traɪˈsekt
trite traɪt
triumph ˈtraɪʌmf ˈtraɪəmf
triumphal traɪˈʌmfl
triumphant traɪˈʌmfnt
triumvir traɪˈʌmvə(r) -vɜ(r)
triumvirate traɪˈʌmvɪrət -reɪt
trivet ˈtrɪvɪt
trivial ˈtrɪvɪəl
triviality ˌtrɪvɪˈælətɪ
trochaic trəʊˈkeɪk trəˈk-
trochee ˈtrəʊki
trod trod
trodden ˈtrodn
troglodyte ˈtroglədaɪt
Troilus ˈtrɔɪləs ˈtrəʊɪləs
Trojan ˈtrəʊdʒən
troll trol $ £ trəʊl
trolley ˈtrolɪ
trolley-bus ˈtrolɪ bʌs
trolley-table ˈtrolɪ teɪbl
trollop ˈtroləp
trombone tromˈbəʊn
　$ ˈtrombəʊn trəmˈbəʊn
trombonist tromˈbəʊnɪst trəm-
troop trup
troop-carrier ˈtrup kærɪə(r)
troopship ˈtrupʃɪp
troop-train ˈtrup treɪn

trope trəʊp
trophy ˋtrəʊfɪ
tropic ˋtropɪk
tropical ˋtropɪkl
trot trot
troth trəʊθ troθ $ trɔθ etc
troubadour ˋtrubədɔ(r)
trouble ˋtrʌbl
troublesome ˋtrʌblsəm
troublous ˋtrʌbləs
trough trof $ trɔf
trounce traʊns
troupe trup
trousers ˋtraʊzəz $ ˋtraʊzərz
trousseau ˋtrusəʊ $ truˋsəʊ
trout traʊt
trove trəʊv
trow trəʊ traʊ
trowel ˋtraʊḷ
troy, T– trɔɪ
truant ˋtruənt
truce trus
truck trʌk
truckle ˋtrʌkl
truckle-bed ˋtrʌkl bed
truculent ˋtrʌkjʊlənt
trudge trʌdʒ
true tru
true-blue ˈtru ˋblu
truffle ˋtrʌfl
truism ˋtruɪzm
truly ˋtrulɪ
trump trʌmp
trumpery ˋtrʌmpərɪ
trumpet ˋtrʌmpɪt
truncate trʌŋˋkeɪt $ ˋtrʌŋkeɪt
truncheon ˋtrʌntʃən
trundle ˋtrʌndl
trunk trʌŋk
trunk-call ˋtrʌŋk kɔl
trunk-road ˋtrʌŋk rəʊd
truss trʌs
trust trʌst
trustee trʌˋsti
trusteeship trʌˋsti-ʃɪp
trustworthy ˋtrʌst-wɜðɪ
truth truθ
truths truðz truθs
try traɪ
try-on ˋtraɪ on $ ɔn
tryst trɪst
Tsar zɑ(r)
Tsarina zɑˋrinə

tsetse ˋsetsɪ ˋtsetsɪ ˋtetsɪ
tsetse-fly ˋsetsɪ flaɪ ˋtse- ˋte-
T-shirt ˋti ʃət
T-square ˋti skweə(r)
tub tʌb
tuba ˋtjubə $ ˋtubə
tube tjub $ tub
tuber ˋtjubə(r) $ ˋtubər
tubercular tjuˋbəkjʊlə(r) $ tu-
tuberculosis tjuˋbəkjuˋləʊsɪs $ tu-
tuberculous tjuˋbəkjʊləs $ tu-
tubular ˋtjubjʊlə(r) $ ˋtu-
TUC ˈti ju ˋsi
tuck tʌk
tuck-shop ˋtʌk ʃop
Tudor ˋtjudə(r) $ ˋtudər
Tuesday ˋtjuzdɪ -deɪ $ ˋtuz-
tuft tʌft
tug tʌg
tug-of-war ˈtʌg əv ˋwɔ(r) £ ə ˋwɔ(r)
tuition tjuˋɪʃn $ tuˋɪʃn
tulip ˋtjulɪp $ ˋtulɪp
tulle tjul $ tul
tumble ˋtʌmbl
tumble-down ˋtʌmbl daʊn
tumbler ˋtʌmblə(r)
tumbrel ˋtʌmbrəl
tumbril ˋtʌmbrɪl
tumescent tjuˋmesnt $ tu-
tumid ˋtjumɪd $ ˋtumɪd
tummy ˋtʌmɪ
tumour($ -or) ˋtjumə(r) $ ˋtumər
tumult ˋtjumʌlt $ ˋtu-
tumultuous tjuˋmʌltʃʊəs £ -tjʊəs $ tu-
tumulus ˋtjumjʊləs $ ˋtum-
tun tʌn
tuna ˋtjunə $ £ ˋtunə
tundra ˋtʌndrə
tune tjun $ tun
tungsten ˋtʌŋstən
tunic ˋtjunɪk $ ˋtunɪk
tuning-fork ˋtjunɪŋ fɔk $ ˋtu-
Tunis ˋtjunɪs $ ˋtunɪs
Tunisia tjuˋnɪzɪə $ tuˋniʒə -ˋnɪʒə -ˋnɪʃə
tunnel ˋtʌnl
tunny ˋtʌnɪ
tuppence ˋtʌpns -pms $ £ ˋtʌpəns
tuppenny ˋtʌpnɪ $ £ ˋtʌpənɪ
tu quoque ˈtju ˋkwəʊkwɪ
    $ £ ˈtu ˋkwəʊkweɪ
turban ˋtəbən
turbid ˋtəbɪd
turbine ˋtəbaɪn -bɪn

turbo-jet ˈtɜbəʊ ˈdʒet $ £ ˈˈtɜbəʊ dʒet
turbo-prop ˈtɜbəʊ ˈprop $ ˈtɜbəʊ prop
turbot ˈtɜbət
turbulent ˈtɜbjʊlənt
tureen tjʊˈrin təˈrin $ tʊˈrin *etc*
turf tɜf
turgid ˈtɜdʒɪd
Turk tɜk
turkey, T– ˈtɜkɪ
turmeric ˈtɜmərɪk
turmoil ˈtɜmɔɪl
turn tɜn
turncoat ˈtɜnkəʊt
turnip ˈtɜnɪp
turning-point ˈtɜnɪŋ pɔɪnt
turn-out ˈtɜn aʊt
turnover ˈtɜnəʊvə(r)
turnpike ˈtɜnpaɪk
turn-round ˈtɜn raʊnd
turnstile ˈtɜnstaɪl
turn-table ˈtɜn teɪbl
turpentine ˈtɜpəntaɪn $ ˈtɜpmtaɪn
turpitude ˈtɜpɪtjud $ -tud *etc*
turps tɜps
turquoise ˈtɜkwɔɪz £ -kwɑz $ -kɔɪz
turret ˈtʌrət $ ˈtɜət *etc*
turtle ˈtɜtl
turtle-dove ˈtɜtl ˈdʌv $ £ ˈtɜtl dʌv
tush tʌʃ
tusk tʌsk
Tussaud's, Madame ˈmædəm təˈsɔdz
  təˈsəʊz
tussle ˈtʌsl
tussock ˈtʌsək
tut *this spelling is used to suggest
  a sound actually made by 'clicking'
  the tongue against or just behind
  the upper teeth. It is often read
  aloud, quoted, etc as* tʌt
tutelage ˈtjutlɪdʒ $ ˈtu-
tutelary ˈtjutlərɪ $ ˈtutlerɪ
tutor ˈtjutə(r) $ ˈtutər *etc*
tutorial tjuˈtɔrɪəl $ tu- *etc*
tuxedo tʌkˈsidəʊ
TV ˈti ˈvi
TWA ˈti dʌbljuˈeɪ
twaddle ˈtwodl $ ˈtwɔdl
twain tweɪn
twang twæŋ
'twas twəz
tweak twik
tweed twid
tween twin

tweeny ˈtwinɪ
tweet twit
tweezers ˈtwizəz $ ˈtwizərz
twelfth twelfθ *with* f *and* θ
  usually made simultaneously
Twelfth Night ˈtwelfθ ˈnaɪt
  $ ˈtwelfθ naɪt *etc*
twelve twelv
twelvemonth ˈtwelvmʌnθ
twentieth ˈtwentɪəθ
twenty ˈtwentɪ
twenty-one ˈtwentɪ ˈwʌn
twerp twɜp
twice twaɪs
twice-told ˈtwaɪs ˈtəʊld
twiddle ˈtwɪdl
twig twɪg
twilight ˈtwaɪlaɪt
twill, 'twill twɪl
twin twɪn
twine twaɪn
twinge twɪndʒ
twinkle ˈtwɪŋkl
twirl twɜl
twirp twɜp
twist twɪst
twit twɪt
twitch twɪtʃ
twitter ˈtwɪtə(r)
'twixt twɪkst
two tu
two-dimensional ˈtu daɪˈmenʃnl dɪ-
two-edged ˈtu ˈedʒd
two-faced ˈtu ˈfeɪst
twofold ˈtu-fəʊld
two-handed ˈtu ˈhændɪd
'twont twəʊnt
twopence ˈtʌpns -pəns -pms $ ˈtu-pens
twopenny ˈtʌpnɪ $ ˈtu-penɪ
two-piece ˈtu ˈpis
two-seater ˈtu ˈsitə(r)
two-step ˈtu step
'twould twʊd
two-way ˈtu ˈweɪ
tycoon taɪˈkun
tying ˈtaɪɪŋ
tyke taɪk
Tyne taɪn
type taɪp
-type *suffix* taɪp
type-setter ˈtaɪp setə(r)
typewriter ˈtaɪp-raɪtə(r)
typhoid ˈtaɪfɔɪd

typhoon taɪˈfun
typhus ˈtaɪfəs
typical ˈtɪpɪkl
typify ˈtɪpɪfaɪ
typist ˈtaɪpɪst
typographical ˌtaɪpəˈgræfɪkl
typography taɪˈpogrəfɪ
tyrannical tɪˈrænɪkl taɪ-
tyrannize ˈtɪrənaɪz
tyrannous ˈtɪrənəs

tyranny ˈtɪrənɪ
tyrant ˈtaɪərənt
tyre ˈtaɪə(r)
tyro ˈtaɪərəʊ
Tyrol tɪˈrəʊl ˈtɪrəl
Tyrolean ˌtɪrəˈliən $ tɪˈrəʊliən
Tyrone tɪˈrəʊn
tzar zɑ(r)
tzarina zɑˈrinə
tzetze ˈsetsɪ ˈtsetsɪ ˈtetsɪ

U

U u ju
UAR ˈju eɪ ˈɑ(r)
ubiquitous juˈbɪkwətəs -wɪtəs
ubiquity juˈbɪkwətɪ
U-boat ˈju bəʊt
udder ˈʌdə(r)
Uganda juˈgændə
ugh *this usually suggests a sound like*
   ɜ *but with very strongly spread or*
   rounded lips as when pulling a face
ugly ˈʌglɪ
uh-huh ˈʌ ˈhʌ
ukelele ˌjukəˈleɪlɪ
UK ˈju ˈkeɪ
Ukraine juˈkreɪn
ukulele ˌjukəˈleɪlɪ
ulcer ˈʌlsə(r)
ulna ˈʌlnə
Ulster ˈʌlstə(r)
ulterior ʌlˈtɪərɪə(r)
ultimate ˈʌltɪmət
ultimatum ˌʌltɪˈmeɪtəm
ultimo ˈʌltɪməʊ
ultra- *prefix* ˈʌltrə
ultramarine ˌʌltrəməˈrin
ultrasonic ˌʌltrəˈsonɪk
ultraviolet ˌʌltrəˈvaɪələt
ululate ˈjuljʊleɪt $ ˈʌljʊleɪt *etc*
Ulysses juˈlɪsiz ˈjulɪsiz
umber ˈʌmbə(r)
umbilical ʌmˈbɪlɪkl ˌʌmbɪˈlaɪkl
umbrage ˈʌmbrɪdʒ
umbrella ʌmˈbrelə
umlaut ˈʊmlaʊt
umpire ˈʌmpaɪə(r)
umpteen ˈʌmpˈtin
umpteenth ˈʌmpˈtinθ

un- *prefix* ʌn
'un ən *after* t, d, s, z *usu:* n̩
UN ˈju ˈen
unabashed ˌʌnəˈbæʃt
unabated ˌʌnəˈbeɪtɪd
unable ʌnˈeɪbl
unaccountable ˌʌnəˈkaʊntəbl
unaccustomed ˌʌnəˈkʌstəmd
unadopted ˌʌnəˈdoptɪd
unadvised ˌʌnədˈvaɪzd
unaffected ˌʌnəˈfektɪd
unalloyed ˌʌnəˈlɔɪd
unalterably ʌnˈɔltərəblɪ £ -ˈol-
un-American ˌʌn əˈmerɪkən
unanimity ˌjunəˈnɪmətɪ
unanimous juˈnænɪməs
unannounced ˌʌnəˈnaʊnst
unanswerable ʌnˈansrəbl $ -ˈæns-
unapproachable ˌʌnəˈprəʊtʃəbl
unarmed ʌnˈamd $ ʌnˈarmd
unasked ʌnˈaskt -st $ -ˈæs-
unassuming ˌʌnəˈsjumɪŋ $ -ˈsu-
unattached ˌʌnəˈtætʃt
unattended ˌʌnəˈtendɪd
unavailing ˌʌnəˈveɪlɪŋ
unavoidable ˌʌnəˈvɔɪdəbl
unaware(s) ˌʌnəˈweə(z) $ -ˈweər(z)
unbalanced ʌnˈbælənst
unbearable ʌnˈbeərəbl
unbeaten ʌnˈbitn
unbecoming ˌʌnbɪˈkʌmɪŋ
unbeknownst ˌʌnbɪˈnəʊnst
unbend ʌnˈbend
unbias(s)ed ʌnˈbaɪəst
unbridled ʌnˈbraɪdld
unbroken ʌnˈbrəʊkən
unburden ʌnˈbɜdn

unbutton ʌnˈbʌtn
uncalled-for ʌnˈkɔld fɔ(r)
uncanny ʌnˈkænɪ
uncared-for ʌnˈkeəd fɔ(r) $ -ˈkeərd
uncertain ʌnˈsɜtn
uncertainty ʌnˈsɜtntɪ
uncharitable ʌnˈtʃærɪtəbl
uncharted ʌnˈtʃɑtɪd $ -ˈtʃɑr-
unchristian ʌnˈkrɪstʃən -stɪən
uncle ˈʌŋkl
unclean ʌnˈklin
un-come-at-able ˈʌn kʌm ˈæt əbl
uncommitted ˈʌnkəˈmɪtɪd
uncommon ʌnˈkomən
uncompromising ʌnˈkomprəmaɪzɪŋ
unconcerned ˈʌnkənˈsɜnd
unconditional ˈʌnkənˈdɪʃnl
unconscionable ʌnˈkonʃnəbl -ʃn̩-
unconscious ʌnˈkonʃəs
uncouth ʌnˈkuθ
uncover ʌnˈkʌvə(r)
unction ˈʌŋkʃn
unctuous ˈʌŋktjuəs $ £ ˈʌŋktʃuəs
undaunted ʌnˈdɔntɪd
undecided ˈʌndɪˈsaɪdɪd
undefended ˈʌndɪˈfendɪd
undeniable ˈʌndɪˈnaɪəbl
undenominational ˈʌndɪˈnomɪˈneɪʃnl
under ˈʌndə(r)
underarm ˈʌndərɑm $ -ɑrm
undercarriage ˈʌndəkærɪdʒ $ ˈʌndər-
underclothes ˈʌndəkləuðz £ -kləuz
  $ ˈʌndərkləuz etc
underclothing ˈʌndəkləuðɪŋ $ ˈʌndər-
undercoat ˈʌndəkəut $ ˈʌndər-
undercurrent ˈʌndəkʌrənt $ ˈʌndərkɜənt
undercut n ˈʌndəkʌt $ ˈʌndər-
undercut v ˈʌndəˈkʌt $ ˈʌndər-
underdeveloped ˈʌndədɪˈveləpt $ ˈʌndər-
underdog ˈʌndədog $ ˈʌndərdɔg
underdone ˈʌndəˈdʌn $ ˈʌndər-
underestimate n ˈʌndərˈestɪmət
underestimate v ˈʌndərˈestɪmeɪt
underfoot ˈʌndəˈfut $ ˈʌndər-
undergarment ˈʌndəgɑmənt $ -ərgɑr-
undergo ˈʌndəˈgəu $ ˈʌndər-
undergraduate ˈʌndəˈgrædʒuət $ ˈʌndər-
underground adj ˈʌndəˈgraund $ ˈʌndər-
underground n ˈʌndəgraund $ ˈʌndər-
undergrowth ˈʌndəgrəuθ $ ˈʌndər-
underhand ˈʌndəˈhænd $ ˈʌndər-
underhanded ˈʌndəˈhændɪd $ ˈʌndər-
underlie ˈʌndəˈlaɪ $ ˈʌndər-

underline ˈʌndəˈlaɪn $ ˈʌndər-
underling ˈʌndəlɪŋ $ ˈʌndər-
undermentioned ˈʌndəˈmenʃnd $ ˈʌndər-
undermine ˈʌndəˈmaɪn $ ˈʌndər-
underneath ˈʌndəˈniθ $ ˈʌndər-
underpass n ˈʌndəpɑs $ ˈʌndərpæs
underpay ˈʌndəˈpeɪ $ ˈʌndər-
underrate ˈʌndəˈreɪt
undersigned ˈʌndəˈsaɪnd ˈʌndəsaɪnd
  $ ˈʌndərˈsaɪnd ˈʌndərsaɪnd
understand ˈʌndəˈstænd $ ˈʌndər-
understanding ˈʌndəˈstændɪŋ $ ˈʌndər-
understate ˈʌndəˈsteɪt $ ˈʌndər-
understock ˈʌndəˈstok $ ˈʌndər-
understood ˈʌndəˈstud $ ˈʌndər-
understudy ˈʌndəstʌdɪ $ ˈʌndər-
undertake ˈʌndəˈteɪk $ ˈʌndər-
undertaker ˈʌndəteɪkə(r) $ ˈʌndər-
undertone ˈʌndətəun $ ˈʌndər-
undertow ˈʌndətəu $ ˈʌndər-
undervalue ˈʌndəˈvælju $ ˈʌndər-
undervest ˈʌndəvest $ ˈʌndər-
underwear ˈʌndəweə(r) $ ˈʌndər-
underwent ˈʌndəˈwent $ ˈʌndər-
underworld ˈʌndəwɜld $ ˈʌndər-
underwriter ˈʌndəraɪtə(r)
undesirable ˈʌndɪˈzaɪərəbl
undid ʌnˈdɪd
undies ˈʌndɪz
undo ˈʌnˈdu
undone ˈʌnˈdʌn
undue ʌnˈdju $ ʌnˈdu etc
undulate ˈʌndjuleɪt $ ˈʌndʒuleɪt
unduly ʌnˈdjulɪ $ ʌnˈdulɪ etc
undying ʌnˈdaɪɪŋ
unearthly ʌnˈɜθlɪ
uneasy ʌnˈizɪ
unemployed ˈʌnɪmˈplɔɪd
unemployment ˈʌnɪmˈplɔɪmənt
unerring ʌnˈɜɪŋ $ ʌnˈeərɪŋ
UNESCO juˈneskəu
unfaithful ʌnˈfeɪθfl
unfamiliar ˈʌnfəˈmɪlɪə(r)
unfathomable ʌnˈfæðəməbl -ðm-
unfit ʌnˈfɪt
unfold ʌnˈfəuld
unforeseen ˈʌnfɔˈsin -fə- $ -fɔr-
unfounded ʌnˈfaundɪd
unfrock ˈʌnˈfrok
unfurnished ʌnˈfɜnɪʃt
ungovernable ʌnˈgʌvn̩əbl $ -vərn-
unguarded ʌnˈgɑdɪd $ -ˈgɑr-
unguent ˈʌŋgwənt

unheard-of ʌn'hɜd ov
UNICEF 'juːnɪsef
unicorn 'juːnɪkɔn $ -kɔrn
unification ˌjuːnɪfɪ'keɪʃn
uniform 'juːnɪfɔm $ -fɔrm
unify 'juːnɪfaɪ
unilateral ˌjuːnɪ'lætrl
uninformed ˌʌnɪn'fɔmd $ -'fɔrmd
union 'juːnɪən
Union Jack 'juːnɪən 'dʒæk
unite juˈnaɪt
United Kingdom juˈnaɪtɪd 'kɪŋdəm
United Nations juˈnaɪtɪd 'neɪʃnz
United States of America
   juˈnaɪtɪd 'steɪts əv ə'merɪkə
unity 'juːnətɪ
universal ˌjuːnɪ'vɜsl
universality ˌjuːnɪvɜ'sælətɪ
universe 'juːnɪvɜs
university ˌjuːnɪ'vɜsətɪ -stɪ
university student ˌjuːnɪ'vɜsətɪ stjudnt
   $ studnt
unkempt ʌn'kempt
unleavened ʌn'levnd
unless ən'les ʌn'les
unload ʌn'ləʊd
unlooked-for ʌn'lʊkt fɔ(r)
unmentionable ʌn'menʃnəbl
unmistakable ˌʌnmɪ'steɪkəbl
unmistakably ˌʌnmɪ'steɪkəblɪ
unnatural ʌn'nætʃərl
unincumbered ˌʌnɪn'kʌmbəd $ -bərd
UNO 'ju en 'əʊ 'juːnəʊ
unpack ʌn'pæk
unparalleled ʌn'pærəleld
unpleasant ʌn'pleznt
unprecedented ʌn'presɪdentɪd
unpretentious ˌʌnprɪ'tenʃəs
unqualified ʌn'kwɒlɪfaɪd
unquestionable ʌn'kwestʃənəbl
unquote ʌn'kwəʊt
unravel ʌn'rævl
unreal ʌn'rɪəl
unreservedly ˌʌnrɪ'zɜvɪdlɪ
unrestricted ˌʌnrɪ'strɪktɪd
unscathed ʌn'skeɪðd
unscrupulous ʌn'skruːpjələs
unseat ʌn'sit
unseemly ʌn'simlɪ
unseen ʌn'sin
unsettled ʌn'setld
unsightly ʌn'saɪtlɪ
unsound ʌn'saʊnd

unstuck ʌn'stʌk
unsung ʌn'sʌŋ
unthinkable ʌn'θɪŋkəbl
until ʌn'tɪl ən'tɪl
untiring ʌn'taɪərɪŋ
unto 'ʌntu as weak-form only: 'ʌntə
untoward ˌʌntʊ'wɔd ʌn'təʊəd
   $ ˌʌntə'wɔrd ʌn'təʊərd
unvarnished ʌn'vɑnɪʃt $ -'vɑr-
unwritten ʌn'rɪtn
up ʌp
up-and-coming 'ʌp ən 'kʌmɪŋ
upbraid ʌp'breɪd
upbringing 'ʌpbrɪŋɪŋ
upcountry 'ʌp'kʌntrɪ
upheaval ʌp'hivl
upheld ʌp'held
uphill 'ʌp'hɪl
uphold ʌp'həʊld
upholster ʌp'həʊlstə(r)
upkeep 'ʌpkip
upland 'ʌplənd
uplift n 'ʌplɪft
uplift v ʌp'lɪft
upmost 'ʌpməʊst
upon ə'pon as a weak-form only: əpən
upper 'ʌpə(r)
upper-cut 'ʌpə kʌt $ 'ʌpər
uppermost 'ʌpəməʊst $ 'ʌpər-
uppish 'ʌpɪʃ
uppity 'ʌpətɪ
upright 'ʌp-raɪt
uprising 'ʌp'raɪzɪŋ ʌp-raɪzɪŋ
uproar 'ʌp-rɔ(r)
uproarious ʌp'rɔrɪəs
uproot ʌp'rut
upset n 'ʌpset
upset v 'ʌp'set
upshot 'ʌpʃot
upside-down 'ʌpsaɪd 'daʊn
upstage 'ʌp'steɪdʒ
upstairs 'ʌp'steəz $ 'ʌp'steərz
upstart 'ʌpstat $ 'ʌpstart
upsurge 'ʌpsɜdʒ
uptake 'ʌpteɪk
up-tight 'ʌp 'taɪt
up-to-date 'ʌp tə 'deɪt
up-to-the-minute 'ʌp tə ðə 'mɪnɪt
uptown 'ʌp'taʊn
upturn 'ʌptɜn
upward(s) 'ʌpwəd(z) £ 'ʌpwʊd(z)
   $ 'ʌpwərd(z)
uranium juˈreɪnɪəm

Uranus ˈjʊərənəs jʊˈreɪnəs
urban ˈɜbən
urbane ɜˈbeɪn
urbanity ɜˈbænətɪ
urbanize ˈɜbənaɪz
urchin ˈɜtʃɪn
Urdu ˈʊədu ˈɜdu $ ˈʊərdu etc
urge ɜdʒ
urgency ˈɜdʒənsɪ
urgent ˈɜdʒənt
uric ˈjʊərɪk
urinal ˈjʊərɪnl £ jʊˈraɪnl
urinary ˈjʊərɪnərɪ $ -nerɪ
urinate ˈjʊərɪneɪt
urine ˈjʊərɪn
urn ɜn
Urquhart ˈɜkət $ ˈɜkərt
Ursula ˈɜsjʊlə
Uruguay ˈjʊərəgwaɪ ˈʊr- $ -gweɪ
us usual form: əs strong-form: ʌs
    weak-form after 'let' in invitations: s
US ˈju ˈes
USA ˈju es ˈeɪ
usage ˈjuzɪdʒ $ £ ˈjusɪdʒ
USAID ˈju es ˈeɪd
use n jus
use v juz
used accustomed ˈjust

used employed ˈjuzd
usedn't ˈjusnt
usher ˈʌʃə(r)
usherette ˈʌʃəˈret
USSR ˈju es es ˈɑ(r)
usual ˈjuʒʊəl ˈjuʒl ˈjuʒʊl
usually ˈjuʒlɪ ˈjuʒʊlɪ
usurer ˈjuʒərə(r)
usurp juˈzɜp juˈsɜp
usurpation ˈjuzɜˈpeɪʃn ˈjusɜ-
usury ˈjuʒərɪ
Utah ˈjutɔ -tɑ
utensil juˈtensl
uterus ˈjutərəs
utilitarian juˈtɪlɪˈteərɪən
utility juˈtɪlətɪ
utilize ˈjutəlaɪz ˈjutˌlaɪz -tɪl-
utmost ˈʌtməʊst
Utopia juˈtəʊpɪə
Utopian juˈtəʊpɪən
Utrecht ˈjutrekt juˈtrekt
U-turn ˈju ˈtɜn
utter ˈʌtə(r)
utterance ˈʌtərəns ˈʌtrəns
uttermost ˈʌtəməʊst $ ˈʌtər-
uvula ˈjuvjʊlə -jələ
uvular ˈjuvjʊlə(r) -jələ(r)
uxorious ʌkˈsɔrɪəs ʌgˈzɔrɪəs

V

V v vi
vac væk
vacancy ˈveɪkənsɪ
vacant ˈveɪkənt
vacate vəˈkeɪt veɪˈkeɪt $ ˈveɪkeɪt
vacation vəˈkeɪʃn £ veɪˈkeɪʃn
vaccinate ˈvæksɪneɪt
vaccination ˈvæksɪˈneɪʃn
vaccine ˈvæksin
vacillate ˈvæsəleɪt -səl-
vacuity vəˈkjuətɪ
vacuous ˈvækjʊəs
vacuum ˈvækjʊəm -jʊm $ ˈvækjum etc
vacuum cleaner ˈvækjʊm klinə(r) $ -jum
vacuum flask ˈvækjʊm flask £ -jum $ flæsk
vacuum pump ˈvækjʊm pʌmp $ £ -jum
vagabond ˈvægəbond
vagary ˈveɪgərɪ $ £ vəˈgeərɪ $ veɪ-
vagina vəˈdʒaɪnə

vaginal vəˈdʒaɪnl ˈvædʒɪnl
vagrancy ˈveɪgrənsɪ
vagrant ˈveɪgrənt
vague veɪg
vain veɪn
vainglorious veɪnˈglɔrɪəs
vainglory ˈveɪnglɔrɪ
valance ˈvæləns
vale veɪl
valediction ˈvælɪˈdɪkʃn
valedictory ˈvælɪˈdɪktərɪ
Valencia vəˈlensɪə $ vəˈlenʃə etc
valentine, V- ˈvæləntaɪn
valerian vəˈlɪərɪən
Valerie ˈvælərɪ
valet ˈvælɪt ˈvæleɪ $ væˈleɪ
valetudinarian ˈvælɪˈtjudɪˈneərɪən
    $ ˈvælɪˈtudn̩ˈeərɪən
valiant ˈvælɪənt

valid ˈvælɪd
validate ˈvælɪdeɪt
validity vəˈlɪdətɪ
valise vəˈliz $ £ vəˈlis
valley ˈvælɪ
valour ($ -or) ˈvælə(r)
valuable ˈvæljʊbl ˈvæljəbl
valuation ˈvæljuˈeɪʃn
value ˈvælju
valve vælv
valvular ˈvælvjʊlə(r)
vamoose væˈmus vəˈmus
vamp væmp
vampire ˈvæmpaɪə(r)
van væn
vanadium vəˈneɪdɪəm
Vanbrugh ˈvænbrə $ vænˈbru etc
Vancouver vænˈkuvə(r)
vandal ˈvændl
vandalism ˈvændḷɪzm
Van Dyck, Dyke væn ˈdaɪk
vane veɪn
Vanessa vəˈnesə
vanguard ˈvængad $ -gard
Van Gogh væn ˈgof $ ˈgəʊ $ £ ˈgox
   x is the fricative corresponding to k
vanguard ˈvængad $ -gard
vanilla vəˈnɪlə
vanish ˈvænɪʃ
vanishing cream ˈvænɪʃɪŋ krim
vanishing point ˈvænɪʃɪŋ pɔɪnt
vanity ˈvænətɪ
vanquish ˈvæŋkwɪʃ
vantage ˈvantɪdʒ $ ˈvæntɪdʒ
vantage point ˈvantɪdʒ pɔɪnt $ ˈvæn-
vapid ˈvæpɪd ˈveɪpɪd
vaporize ˈveɪpəraɪz
vapour($ -or) ˈveɪpə(r)
vapo(u)r-bath ˈveɪpə baθ $ ˈveɪpər bæθ
vapo(u)r-trail ˈveɪpə treɪl $ ˈveɪpər treɪl
variability ˈveərɪəˈbɪlətɪ $ ˈvær-
variable ˈveərɪəbl $ ˈvær-
variance ˈveərɪəns $ ˈvær-
variant ˈveərɪənt $ ˈvær-
variation ˈveərɪˈeɪʃn $ ˈvær-
varicose ˈværɪkəʊs £ -kəs $ ˈveər-
varied ˈveərɪd $ ˈværɪd
variegated ˈveərɪgeɪtɪd -rɪəg- $ ˈvær-
variety vəˈraɪətɪ
variety show vəˈraɪətɪ ʃəʊ
variform ˈveərɪfɔm $ ˈværɪfɔrm
various ˈveərɪəs $ ˈværɪəs
varlet ˈvalət $ ˈvarlɪt

varnish ˈvanɪʃ $ ˈvarnɪʃ
varsity ˈvasətɪ $ ˈvarsətɪ
vary ˈvəerɪ $ ˈværɪ
vascular ˈvæskjʊlə(r)
vase vaz $ veɪs veɪz
vaseline ˈvæsḷin ˈvæz- ˈvæsəˈlin
   $ ˈvæsəlɪn
vassal ˈvæsl
vast vast $ væst
vat væt
Vatican ˈvætɪkən
vaudeville ˈvɔdəvɪl ˈvəʊdəvɪl
Vaughan vɔn
vault vɔlt £ volt
vaunt vɔnt
Vauxhall ˈvoksɔl ˈvɔk- $ £ ˈvɔkshɔl
VD ˈvi ˈdi
V-day ˈvi deɪ
veal vil
veer vɪə(r)
vegetable ˈvedʒtəbl
vegetarian ˈvedʒɪˈteərɪən
vegetate ˈvedʒɪteɪt
vegetation ˈvedʒɪˈteɪʃn
vehement ˈviəmənt
vehicle ˈviɪkl
vehicular viˈhɪkjʊlə(r)
veil veɪl
vein veɪn
Velasquez vəˈlæskwɪz
veld(t) veld velt felt
vellum ˈveləm
velocipede vəˈlosɪpid
velocity vəˈlosətɪ
velour(s) vəˈlʊə(r) $ vəˈlʊər
velum ˈviləm
velvet ˈvelvɪt
velveteen ˈvelvɪˈtin
venal ˈvinl
venality viˈnælətɪ
vend vend
vendee venˈdi
vendetta venˈdetə
vendor ˈvendə(r)
veneer vɪˈnɪə(r)
venerable ˈvenɾəbl
venerate ˈvenəreɪt
veneration ˈvenəˈreɪʃn
venereal vɪˈnɪərɪəl
Venetian vɪˈniʃn
Venezuela ˈvenɪˈzweɪlə $ -ˈzwilə
vengeance ˈvendʒəns
vengeful ˈvendʒfl -fʊl

venial ˈviːnɪəl
Venice ˈvenɪs
venison ˈvenɪsn -nɪzn
venom ˈvenəm
venomous ˈvenəməs
venous ˈviːnəs
vent vent
ventilate ˈventɪleɪt $ -tl̩-
ventilation ˌventɪˈleɪʃn $ -tl̩ˈeɪʃn
ventilator ˈventɪleɪtə(r) $ -tl̩-
ventricle ˈventrɪkl
ventriloquism venˈtrɪləkwɪzm
ventriloquist venˈtrɪləkwɪst
venture ˈventʃə(r)
venturesome ˈventʃəsəm $ -tʃəsəm
venturous ˈventʃərəs
venue ˈvenju $ ˈvenu
Venus ˈviːnəs
Vera ˈvɪərə
veracious vəˈreɪʃəs
veracity vəˈræsətɪ
veranda(h) vəˈrændə
verb vɜːb
verbal ˈvɜːbl
verbatim vɜːˈbeɪtɪm
verbiage ˈvɜːbɪɪdʒ
verbose vɜːˈbəʊs
verbosity vɜːˈbosətɪ
verdant ˈvɜːdnt
Verdi ˈveədɪ $ ˈveədɪ
verdict ˈvɜːdɪkt
verdure ˈvɜːdʒə(r)
verge vɜːdʒ
verger ˈvɜːdʒə(r)
verification ˌverɪfɪˈkeɪʃn
verify ˈverɪfaɪ
verily ˈverɪlɪ verl̩ɪ
verisimilitude ˌverɪsɪˈmɪlɪtjud $ -tud etc
veritable ˈverɪtəbl
verity ˈverətɪ
vermicelli ˌvɜːmɪˈselɪ -ˈtʃelɪ
vermiform ˈvɜːmɪfɔːm $ -fɔːrm
vermilion vəˈmɪlɪən $ vər-
vermin ˈvɜːmɪn
verminous ˈvɜːmɪnəs
Vermont vəˈmont $ vər-
vermouth ˈvɜːməθ $ vərˈmuːθ
vernacular vəˈnækjʊlə(r) $ vər-
vernal ˈvɜːnl
veronica, V– vəˈronɪkə
Versailles veəˈsaɪ $ veərˈsaɪ
versatile ˈvɜːsətaɪl $ ˈvɜːsətl̩ -tɪl
versatility ˌvɜːsəˈtɪlətɪ

verse vɜːs
versification ˌvɜːsɪfɪˈkeɪʃn
versify ˈvɜːsɪfaɪ
version ˈvɜːʃn $ £ ˈvɜːʒn
verso ˈvɜːsəʊ
versus ˈvɜːsəs
vertebra ˈvɜːtɪbrə
vertebrae ˈvɜːtɪbri -breɪ -braɪ
vertebrate ˈvɜːtɪbreɪt
vertex ˈvɜːteks
vertical ˈvɜːtɪkl
vertices ˈvɜːtɪsiz
vertiginous vɜːˈtɪdʒɪnəs
vertigo ˈvɜːtɪgəʊ
verve vɜːv veəv $ veərv
very ˈverɪ
vespers ˈvespəz $ ˈvespərz
vessel ˈvesl
vest vest
vestal ˈvestl
vestibule ˈvestɪbjul
vestige ˈvestɪdʒ
vestigial veˈstɪdʒɪəl
vestment ˈvestmənt
vestry ˈvestrɪ
vesture ˈvestʃə(r)
Vesuvius vɪˈsuvɪəs və-
vet vet
vetch vetʃ
veteran ˈvetərən ˈvetrən
veterinary ˈvetrɪnər £ ˈvetnrɪ ˈvetrnərɪ
    $ -nerɪ ˈvetr̩nerɪ ˈvetn̩erɪ ˈvetər̩nerɪ
veto ˈviːtəʊ
vex veks
vexatious vekˈseɪʃəs
vexation vekˈseɪʃn
VHF ˈviː eɪtʃ ˈef
via ˈvaɪə
viability ˌvaɪəˈbɪlətɪ
viable ˈvaɪəbl
viaduct ˈvaɪədʌkt
vial ˈvaɪəl
viands ˈvaɪəndz ˈvɪəndz
vibrant ˈvaɪbrənt
vibraphone ˈvaɪbrəfəʊn
vibrate vaɪˈbreɪt $ ˈvaɪbreɪt
vibration vaɪˈbreɪʃn
vicar ˈvɪkə(r)
vicarage ˈvɪkərɪdʒ ˈvɪkr̩ɪdʒ
vicarious vɪˈkeərɪəs $ £ vaɪˈkeərɪəs
vice vaɪs
vice- prefix vaɪs
vice-admiral vaɪs ˈædmr̩l

vice-chairman vaɪs ˈtʃeəmən $ ˈtʃeər-
vice-chancellor vaɪs ˈtʃɑːnslə(r) $ ˈtʃæns-
vice-president vaɪs ˈprezɪdnt
vice-principal vaɪs ˈprɪnsəpl
viceregal vaɪsˈriːgl
vicereine vaɪsˈreɪn $ £ ˈvaɪsreɪn
viceroy ˈvaɪsrɔɪ
vice versa ˈvaɪsɪ ˈvɜːsə
vicinity vɪˈsɪnətɪ
vicious ˈvɪʃəs
vicissitude vɪˈsɪsɪtjuːd £ vaɪ- $ -tuːd
victim ˈvɪktɪm
victimization ˈvɪktɪmaɪˈzeɪʃn
victor, V- ˈvɪktə(r)
Victoria vɪkˈtɔːrɪə
Victorian vɪkˈtɔːrɪən
victorious vɪkˈtɔːrɪəs
victory ˈvɪktrɪ -tərɪ
victualler ˈvɪtlə(r)
victuals ˈvɪtlz
vicuña vɪˈkjuːnə vaɪ- -ˈkuː- -unjə
vide ˈvaɪdɪ ˈviːdeɪ ˈviːdeɪ
videlicet vɪˈdiːlɪset $ £ -ˈdel-
video ˈvɪdɪəʊ
video-recorder ˈvɪdɪəʊ rɪkɔːdə(r) $ -kɔːr-
video-tape ˈvɪdɪəʊ teɪp
vie vaɪ
Vienna vɪˈenə
Vietnam vɪetˈnæm vɪetˈnɑːm
Vietnamese vɪˈetnəˈmiːz
view vjuː
view-finder ˈvjuː faɪndə(r)
view-point ˈvjuː pɔɪnt
vigil ˈvɪdʒɪl
vigilant ˈvɪdʒɪlənt
vigilance ˈvɪdʒɪləns
vigilante ˈvɪdʒɪˈlæntɪ
vignette vɪˈnjet vɪ-
vigour($ -or) ˈvɪgə(r)
vigorous ˈvɪgərəs
viking ˈvaɪkɪŋ
vile vaɪl
vilification ˈvɪlɪfɪˈkeɪʃn
vilify ˈvɪlɪfaɪ
villa ˈvɪlə
village ˈvɪlɪdʒ
villager ˈvɪlɪdʒə(r)
villain ˈvɪlən
villainous ˈvɪlənəs
villein ˈvɪleɪn $ ˈvɪlən vɪˈleɪn
villeinage ˈvɪlɪnɪdʒ
vim vɪm
Vincent ˈvɪnsnt

vindicate ˈvɪndɪkeɪt
vindictive vɪnˈdɪktɪv
vine vaɪn
vinegar ˈvɪnɪgə(r)
vineyard ˈvɪnjəd $ -jərd £ -jɑd $ -jɑrd
vinous ˈvaɪnəs
vintage ˈvɪntɪdʒ
vintner ˈvɪntnə(r)
viol ˈvaɪəl
viola instrument vɪˈəʊlə
viola plant, V- ˈvaɪələ
violate ˈvaɪəleɪt
violation ˈvaɪəˈleɪʃn
violence ˈvaɪələns
violent ˈvaɪələnt
violet ˈvaɪələt
violin ˈvaɪəˈlɪn
violinist ˈvaɪəˈlɪnɪst
violoncello ˈvaɪələnˈtʃeləʊ $ ˈvɪəl- etc
VIP ˈviː aɪ ˈpiː
viper ˈvaɪpə(r)
virago vɪˈrɑːgəʊ $ vɪˈreɪgəʊ
Virgil ˈvɜːdʒɪl
virgin ˈvɜːdʒɪn
virginal ˈvɜːdʒɪnl
virginia, V- vəˈdʒɪnɪə $ vər-
virginity vəˈdʒɪnətɪ $ vər-
virile ˈvɪraɪl $ ˈvɪrl
virility vɪˈrɪlətɪ
virtual ˈvɜːtʃʊəl
virtue ˈvɜːtʃuː £ ˈvɜːtju
virtuosity ˈvɜːtʃʊˈɒsətɪ
virtuoso ˈvɜːtʃʊˈəʊzəʊ $ £ -ˈəʊsəʊ
virtuous ˈvɜːtʃʊəs
virulent ˈvɪrələnt -rjʊ-
virus ˈvaɪərəs
visa ˈviːzə
visaed ˈviːzəd
visage ˈvɪzɪdʒ
vis à vis ˈviːz ɑ ˈviː $ £ ˈviːz ə ˈviː
viscera ˈvɪsərə
visceral ˈvɪsərl
viscid ˈvɪsɪd
viscosity vɪsˈkɒsətɪ
viscous ˈvɪskəs
viscount ˈvaɪkaʊnt
viscountess ˈvaɪkaʊntes -ɪs -əs
visibility ˈvɪzəˈbɪlətɪ
visible ˈvɪzəbl
visibly ˈvɪzəblɪ
vision ˈvɪʒn
visionary ˈvɪʒnrɪ $ ˈvɪʒŋerɪ
visit ˈvɪzɪt

visitation 'vɪzɪ'teɪʃn
visting-card 'vɪzɪtɪŋ kad -zt- $ kard
visitor 'vɪzɪtə(r)
visor 'vaɪzə(r)
vista 'vɪstə
visual 'vɪʒuəl
visualize 'vɪʒuəlaɪz
vital 'vaɪtl
vitality vaɪ'tælətɪ
vitalize 'vaɪtlaɪz
vitamin 'vɪtəmɪn $ £ 'vaɪtəmɪn
vitiate 'vɪʃɪeɪt
vitreous 'vɪtrɪəs
vitrify 'vɪtrɪfaɪ
vitriol 'vɪtrɪəl
vitriolic 'vɪtrɪ'olɪk
vituperate vɪ'tjupəreɪt
$ £ vaɪ- $ -'tu- etc
vituperation vɪ'tjupə'reɪʃn
$ £ vaɪ- $ -'tu- etc
vituperative vɪ'tjupərətɪv
$ £ vaɪ- $ -'tupəreɪtɪv etc
viva Long live —! 'vivə
vivacious vɪ'veɪʃəs vaɪ'veɪʃəs
vivacity vɪ'væsətɪ vaɪ'væsətɪ
viva voce 'vaɪvə 'vəʊsɪ
Vivian 'vɪvɪən
vivid 'vɪvɪd
Vivien 'vɪvɪən
Vivienne 'vɪvɪ'en 'vɪvɪən
vivisection 'vɪvɪ'sekʃn
vivisectionist 'vɪvɪ'sekʃṇɪst
vixen 'vɪksn
viz 'neɪmlɪ vɪz vɪ'dɪlɪset
vizier vɪ'zɪə(r) 'vɪzɪə(r)
vocabulary və'kæbjʊlərɪ -lɽɪ $ -lerɪ
vocal 'vəʊkl
vocalist 'vəʊkḷɪst
vocation vəʊ'keɪʃn £ və'keɪʃn
vocative 'vokətɪv
vociferate və'sɪfəreɪt $ £ vəʊ-
vociferous və'sɪfərəs $ £ vəʊ-
vodka 'vodkə
vogue vəʊg
voice vɔɪs
void vɔɪd
volatile 'volətaɪl $ -tl
volcanic vol'kænɪk
volcano vol'keɪnəʊ

vole vəʊl
volition və'lɪʃn $ vəʊ'lɪʃn
Volkswagen 'folksvagən 'vol-
$ 'vəʊlkswægən
volley 'volɪ
volley-ball 'volɪ bɔl
volt vəʊlt
voltage 'vəʊltɪdʒ
Voltaire vol'teə(r) 'volteə(r)
volte-face 'volt 'fas 'fæs
voluble 'voljʊbl
volume 'voljum -jʊm $ 'voljəm
volume-control 'voljum kəntrəʊl $ -jəm
voluminous və'lumɪnəs £ -'lju-
voluntarily 'voləntɽḷɪ -tərəlɪ
$ 'volənterḷɪ 'volən'terḷɪ
voluntary 'voləntrɪ $ -terɪ
volunteer 'volən'tɪə(r)
voluptuary və'lʌptʃʊərɪ $ -ʊerɪ
voluptuous və'lʌptʃʊəs
vomit 'vomɪt
voodoo 'vudu
voracious və'reɪʃəs £ vo'r- $ vɔ'r- etc
voracity və'ræsətɪ £ vo'r- $ vɔ'r- etc
vortex 'voteks $ 'vorteks
vortices 'votɪsiz $ 'vortɪsiz
votary 'vəʊtərɪ
vote vəʊt
votive 'vəʊtɪv
vouch vaʊtʃ
voucher 'vaʊtʃə(r)
vouchsafe vaʊtʃ'seɪf
vow vaʊ
vowel 'vaʊḷ
vox voks
vox populi 'voks 'popjʊlaɪ -li
voyage 'vɔɪdʒ 'vɔɪɪdʒ
voyager 'vɔɪədʒə(r)
vulcanite 'vʌlkənaɪt
vulcanize 'vʌlkənaɪz
vulgar 'vʌlgə(r)
vulgarian vʌl'geərɪən
vulgarism 'vʌlgərɪzm
vulgarize 'vʌlgəraɪz
Vulgate 'vʌlgeɪt -gɪt
vulnerable 'vʌlnɽəbl
vulpine 'vʌlpaɪn
vulture 'vʌltʃə(r)
vying 'vaɪɪŋ

W

W w `dʌblju $ `dʌbljə
WAAC wæk
WAAF wæf
wad wod
WAC wæk
wadding `wodɪŋ $ `wɔdɪŋ
waddle `wodl $ `wɔdl
wade weɪd
wadi `wodɪ
wafer `weɪfə(r)
waffle `wofl $ `wɔfl
waft woft wɑft $ wæft wɔft etc
wag wæg
wage weɪdʒ
wage-earner `weɪdʒ ɜnə(r)
wager `weɪdʒə(r)
waggle `wægl
wag(g)on `wægən
wagon-lit 'vægɔ̃ 'li `vægõ
Wagner `wægnə(r) composer `vagnə(r)
wagtail `wægteɪl
waif weɪf
wail weɪl
wain weɪn
wainscot `weɪnskət $ -kot
waist weɪst
waist-band `weɪstbænd
waistcoat `weɪstkəʊt -sk- $ `weskət
waist-deep 'weɪst `dip
waist-line `weɪstlaɪn
wait weɪt
waiting-room `weɪtɪŋ rʊm $ £ rum etc
waitress `weɪtrəs
waive weɪv
wake weɪk
waken `weɪkən
Wales weɪlz
walk wɔk
walkie-talkie 'wɔkɪ `tɔkɪ
walking-stick `wɔkɪŋ stɪk
walking-tour `wɔkɪŋ tʊə(r) £ tɔ(r)
walk-out `wɔk aʊt
walk-over `wɔk əʊvə(r)
wall wɔl
wallaby `woləbɪ $ `wɔl-
Wallace `wolɪs
wallah `wolə $ `wɔlə
wallet `wolɪt $ `wɔlɪt
wall-flower `wɔl flaʊə(r)
wallop `woləp $ `wɔləp

wallow `woləʊ $ `wɔləʊ $ -lə
wall-painting `wɔl peɪntɪŋ
wallpaper `wɔlpeɪpə(r)
Wall Street `wɔl strit
walnut `wɔlnʌt
Walpole `wɔlpəʊl £ `wol-
walrus `wɔlrəs £ `wol-
Walter `wɔltə(r) £ `wol-
Walton `wɔltən £ `wol-
waltz wɔls £ wols $ £ wɔltz
wan won $ wɔn
wand wond $ wɔnd
wander `wondə(r) $ `wɔndər
wanderlust `wondəlʌst $ -dər- `wɔn-
wane weɪn
wangle `wæŋgl
want wont $ wɔnt etc
want-ad `wont æd $ `wɔnt æd etc
wanton `wontən $ `wɔntn `wontn etc
war wɔ(r)
war-baby `wɔ beɪbɪ $ `wɔr
warble `wɔbl $ `wɔrbl
warbler `wɔblə(r) $ `wɔrblər
war-bride `wɔ braɪd $ `wɔr
war-clouds `wɔ klaʊdz $ `wɔr
war-cry `wɔ kraɪ $ `wɔr
ward wɔd $ wɔrd
-ward(s) suffix wəd(z) £ wʊd(z)
  $ wərd(z)
war-damage `wɔ dæmɪdʒ $ `wɔr
war-dance `wɔ dɑns $ `wɔr dæns
warden `wɔdn $ `wɔrdn
warder `wɔdə(r) $ `wɔrdər
wardress `wɔdrəs $ `wɔrdrəs
wardrobe `wɔ-drəʊb $ `wɔr-
wardroom `wɔdrʊm
  $ £ rum etc $ `wɔr-
ware weə(r)
warehouse `weəhaʊs $ `weər-
warfare `wɔfeə(r) $ `wɔrfeər
war-god `wɔ god $ `wɔr god
warhead `wɔhed $ `wɔrhed
war-horse `wɔ hɔs $ `wɔr hɔrs
warily `weərɪlɪ
war-like `wɔ laɪk $ `wɔr
war-lord `wɔ lɔd $ `wɔr lɔrd
warm wɔm $ wɔrm
warm-blooded 'wɔm `blʌdɪd $ 'wɔrm
warm-hearted 'wɔm `hɑtɪd
  $ 'wɔrm `hɑrtɪd

warming-pan ˈwɔmɪŋ pæn $ ˈwɔr-
warmth wɔmθ $ wɔrmθ
warn wɔn $ wɔrn
War Office ˈwɔr ofɪs $ ɔfɪs
warp wɔp $ wɔrp
war-paint ˈwɔ peɪnt $ ˈwɔr
war-path ˈwɔ paθ $ ˈwɔr pæθ
warrant ˈworənt $ ˈwɔrənt etc
warrantee ˌworənˈti $ ˈwɔr- etc
warrant officer ˈworənt ofɪsə $ ˈwɔr- ɔf-
warrantor ˈworəntɔ(r) -tə(r) $ ˈwɔr- etc
warranty ˈworəntɪ $ ˈwɔr- etc
warren ˈworən $ ˈwɔrən etc
warrior ˈworɪə(r) $ ˈwɔr- etc
Warsaw ˈwɔsɔ $ ˈwɔrsɔ
warship ˈwɔʃɪp $ ˈwɔrʃɪp
wart wɔt $ wɔrt
wart-hog ˈwɔt hog $ wɔrt hɔg etc
wartime ˈwɔtaɪm $ ˈwɔrtaɪm etc
Warwick £ ˈworɪk $ ˈworɪk
   of USA ˈwɔrwɪk
war-widow ˈwɔ wɪdəʊ $ ˈwɔr
wary ˈweərɪ
was *usual forms:* wəz wz
   strong-forms: woz $ wʌz wɔz *etc*
wash woʃ $ wɔʃ *etc*
wash-basin ˈwoʃ beɪsn $ ˈwɔʃ *etc*
wash-board ˈwoʃ bɔd $ ˈwɔʃ *etc* bɔrd
wash-bowl ˈwoʃ bəʊl $ ˈwɔʃ *etc*
washday ˈwoʃdeɪ $ ˈwɔʃdeɪ *etc*
washer ˈwoʃə(r) $ ˈwɔʃər *etc*
washer-woman ˈwoʃə wʊmən $ ˈwɔʃər
wash-house ˈwoʃ haʊs $ ˈwɔʃ *etc*
washing-day ˈwoʃɪŋ deɪ $ ˈwɔʃ- *etc*
washing-machine ˈwoʃɪŋ məʃin $ ˈwɔʃ-
washing-soda ˈwoʃɪŋ səʊdə $ ˈwɔʃ- *etc*
Washington ˈwoʃŋtən $ ˈwɔʃ- *etc*
washing-up ˌwoʃɪŋ ˈʌp $ ˈwɔʃ- *etc*
wash-out ˈwoʃ aʊt $ ˈwɔʃ *etc*
wash-stand ˈwoʃ stænd $ ˈwɔʃ *etc*
wash-tub ˈwoʃ tʌb $ ˈwɔʃ *etc*
washy ˈwoʃɪ $ ˈwɔʃɪ *etc*
wasn't ˈwoznt $ ˈwʌznt ˈwɔznt *etc*
wasp wosp $ wɔsp
wassail ˈwoseɪl ˈwæs- -sl $ ˈwɔs-
wastage ˈweɪstɪdʒ
waste weɪst
waste paper ˌweɪst ˈpeɪpə(r) $ ˈweɪst peɪpər
waste-paper-basket weɪst ˈpeɪpə baskɪt
   $ ˈweɪst peɪpər bæskɪt
waste-pipe ˈweɪstpaɪp -sp-
wastrel ˈweɪstrəl
watch wotʃ $ wɔtʃ

watch-chain ˈwotʃ tʃeɪn $ ˈwɔtʃ
watch-dog ˈwotʃ dog $ dɔg ˈwɔtʃ
watch-maker ˈwotʃ meɪkə(r) $ ˈwɔtʃ
watchman ˈwotʃmən $ ˈwɔtʃ-
watch-tower ˈwotʃ taʊə(r) $ ˈwɔtʃ
watchword ˈwotʃwɜd $ ˈwɔtʃ-
water ˈwotə(r)
water-biscuit ˈwotə bɪskɪt $ ˈwɔtər
water-borne ˈwotə bɔn $ ˈwɔtər bɔrn
water-bottle ˈwotə botl $ ˈwɔtər
water-buffalo ˈwotə bʌfələʊ $ ˈwɔtər
water-cart ˈwotə kat $ ˈwɔtər kart
water-closet ˈwotə klozɪt $ ˈwɔtər
water-colour($ -or) ˈwotə kʌlə(r) $ ˈwɔtər
watercourse ˈwotə kɔs $ ˈwɔtər kɔrs
watercress ˈwotə kres $ ˈwɔtər kres
water-diviner ˈwotə dɪvaɪnə(r) $ ˈwɔtər
waterfall ˈwotəfɔl $ ˈwɔtərfɔl
waterfront ˈwotəfrʌnt $ ˈwɔtər-
water-glass ˈwotə glas $ ˈwɔtər glæs
water-hole ˈwotə həʊl $ ˈwɔtər
watering-can ˈwotrɪŋ kæn
watering-place ˈwotrɪŋ pleɪs
water-level ˈwotə levl $ ˈwɔtər
water-lily ˈwotə lɪlɪ $ ˈwɔtər
water-line ˈwotə laɪn $ ˈwɔtər
waterlogged ˈwotə logd $ ˈwɔtər lɔgd
Waterloo ˌwotəˈlu $ ˌwɔtərˈlu
water-main ˈwotə meɪn $ ˈwɔtər
watermark ˈwotəmak $ ˈwɔtərmark
water-melon ˈwotə melən $ ˈwɔtər
water-mill ˈwotə mɪl $ ˈwɔtər
water-nymph ˈwotə nɪmf $ ˈwɔtər
water-polo ˈwotə pəʊləʊ $ ˈwɔtər
water-power ˈwotə paʊə $ ˈwɔtər paʊər
waterproof ˈwotəpruf $ ˈwɔtər-
water-rat ˈwotə ræt $ ˈwɔtər
water-rate ˈwotə reɪt $ ˈwɔtər
watershed ˈwotəʃed $ ˈwɔtər-
waterside ˈwotəsaɪd $ ˈwɔtər-
water-spaniel ˈwotə spænɪəl $ ˈwɔtər
waterspout ˈwotə spaʊt $ ˈwɔtər
water-supply ˈwotə səplaɪ $ ˈwɔtər
water-tight ˈwotə taɪt $ ˈwɔtər
water-wag(g)on ˈwotə wægən $ ˈwɔtər
waterway ˈwotəweɪ $ ˈwɔtərweɪ
water-wheel ˈwotə wil $ ˈwɔtər hwil etc
water-wings ˈwotə wɪŋz $ ˈwɔtər
waterworks ˈwotəwɜks $ ˈwɔtər-
watery ˈwotərɪ
watt wot $ wɔt
wattage ˈwotɪdʒ $ ˈwɔtɪdʒ
wattle ˈwotl $ ˈwɔtl

Waugh wɔ
wave weɪv
wave-length ˋweɪv leŋθ
waver ˋweɪvə(r)
wax wæks
wax-works ˋwæks wɜks
way weɪ
way-bill ˋweɪ bɪl
wayfarer ˋweɪfeərə(r)
waylay weɪˋleɪ $ ˋweɪleɪ
wayside ˋweɪ-saɪd
wayward ˋweɪwəd £ -wʊd $ -wərd
WC 'dʌbļju ˋsi $ 'dʌbļjə
we wi
weak wik
weaken ˋwikən
weak-headed 'wik ˋhedɪd
weak-kneed 'wik ˋnid
weakling ˋwiklɪŋ
weak-minded 'wik ˋmaɪndɪd
weak-sighted 'wik ˋsaɪtɪd
weal wil
wealth welθ
wean win
weapon ˋwepən
wear weə(r)
wearisome ˋwɪərɪsəm
weary ˋwɪərɪ
weasel ˋwizl
weather ˋweðə(r)
weather-beaten ˋweðə bitn $ ˋweðər
weather-board ˋweðə bɔd $ ˋweðər bɔrd
weather-bound ˋweðə baʊnd $ ˋweðər
weather-bureau ˋweðə bjʊərəʊ $ ˋweðər
weather-chart ˋweðə tʃat $ ˋweðər tʃart
weathercock ˋweðəkok $ ˋweðər-
weather-proof ˋweðə pruf $ ˋweðər
weather-ship ˋweðə ʃɪp $ ˋweðər
weather-vane ˋweðə veɪn $ ˋweðər
weave wiv
web web
webbing ˋwebɪŋ
web-footed 'web ˋfʊtɪd
wed wed
we'd wid
wedding ˋwedɪŋ
wedding-cake ˋwedɪŋ keɪk
wedding-day ˋwedɪŋ deɪ
wedding-ring ˋwedɪŋ rɪŋ
wedge wedʒ
Wedgewood ˋwedʒwʊd
wedlock ˋwedlok
Wednesday ˋwenzdɪ -deɪ

wee wi
weed wid
weed-killer ˋwid kɪlə(r)
week wik
week-day ˋwik deɪ
weekend wik ˋend ˋwik end
ween win
weep wip
weevil ˋwivl
weft weft
weigh weɪ
weighbridge ˋweɪbrɪdʒ
weighing-machine ˋweɪŋ məʃin
weight weɪt
weight-lifting ˋweɪt lɪftɪŋ
weighty ˋweɪtɪ
weir wɪə(r) $ weər
weird wɪəd $ wɪərd
welcome ˋwelkəm
weld weld
welfare ˋwelfeə(r)
well adv wel
well interj wel weak-form: wl
we'll wil
well-advised 'wel ədˋvaɪzd
well-born 'wel ˋbɔn $ ˋbɔrn
well-connected 'wel kəˋnektɪd
well-disposed 'wel dɪˋspəʊzd
well-informed 'wel ɪnˋfɔmd $ ɪnˋfɔrmd
wellington, W– ˋwelɪŋtən
well-knit 'wel ˋnɪt
well-known 'wel ˋnəʊn
well-meant 'wel ˋment
well-nigh 'wel ˋnaɪ . . .
well-read 'wel ˋred
well-spoken 'wel ˋspəʊkən
well-timed 'wel ˋtaɪmd
well-to-do 'wel tə ˋdu
well-wisher ˋwel wɪʃə(r)
Welsh welʃ
welt welt
welter ˋweltə(r)
welter-weight ˋweltə weɪt $ ˋweltər
wen wen
wench wentʃ
wend wend
went went
wept wept
were usual form: wə(r) strong-form: wɜ(r)
we're wɪə(r) weə(r)
weren't wɜnt
wer(e)wolf ˋwɜwʊlf ˋwɪə- ˋweə-
    $ ˋwɪərwʊlf ˋweər- ˋwɜ-

228 wert

wert wɜt
Wesleyan ˈwezlɪən ˈweslɪən
west west
west-end west ˈend
west country, the ˈwest kʌntrɪ
westerly ˈwestəlɪ $ ˈwestərlɪ
western ˈwestən $ ˈwestərn
westernize ˈwestənaɪz $ -tər-
westernmost ˈwestənməʊst $ -tər-
Westminster ˈwestmɪnstə(r)
westward(s) ˈwestwəd(z) £ -wʊd(z)
$ -wərd(z)
wet wet
wet-nurse ˈwet nɜs
wether ˈweðə(r)
we've wiv
whack wæk $ hwæk etc
whacking-great ˈwækɪŋ ˈgreɪt . . .
$ ˈhw- etc
whale weɪl $ hweɪl etc
whalebone ˈweɪlbəʊn $ ˈhweɪl- etc
whaler ˈweɪlə(r) $ ˈhweɪlər etc
whaling-ship ˈweɪlɪŋ ʃɪp $ ˈhw- etc
whang wæŋ $ hwæŋ etc
wharf wɔf $ hwɔrf etc
wharfage ˈwɔfɪdʒ $ ˈhwɔrfɪdʒ etc
wharves wɔvz $ hwɔrvz etc
what wot $ hwot hwʌt hwɔt etc
whate'er wotˈeə(r) $ hwot- etc
whatever wotˈevə(r) $ hwot- etc
what-d'you-call-it ˈwot ʃʊ kɔl ɪt ʃə
$ ˈhwot etc ʃɪ
what-not ˈwot not $ ˈhwot etc
what's-her-name ˈwots ə neɪm
$ ˈhwots etc ər
what's-his-name ˈwots ɪz neɪm
$ ˈhwots etc
what's-the-name ˈwots ə neɪm
$ ˈhwots etc
whatsoever ˈwotsəʊˈevə(r) $ ˈhwot- etc
wheat wit $ hwit etc
wheedle ˈwidl $ ˈhwidl etc
wheel wil $ hwil etc
wheel-barrow ˈwil bærəʊ $ ˈhwil etc
wheel-wright ˈwil raɪt $ ˈhwil etc
wheeze wiz $ hwiz etc
wheezy ˈwizɪ $ ˈhwizɪ etc
whelk welk $ hwelk etc
whelp welp $ hwelp etc
when wen $ hwen etc weak-form: whən
whence wens $ hwens etc
whenever wenˈevə(r) $ hwen- etc
where weə(r) $ hweər etc

whereabouts adv ˈweərəˈbaʊts
ˈweərəbaʊts $ ˈhw- ˈhw- etc
whereabouts n ˈweərəbaʊts $ ˈhw- etc
whereas weərˈæz $ hweərˈæz etc
whereat weərˈæt $ hweərˈæt etc
whereby weəˈbaɪ $ hweərˈbaɪ etc
wherefore ˈweəfɔ(r) $ ˈhweərfɔr etc
wherein weərˈɪn $ hweərˈɪn etc
whereof weərˈov $ hweərˈov etc
whereon weərˈon $ hweərˈon etc
whereupon ˈweərəˈpon ˈweərəpon
$ ˈhw- etc
wherever weərˈevə(r) $ hweər- etc
wherewith weəˈwɪð $ hweər- -ˈwɪθ etc
wherewithal ˈweəwɪðɔl
$ ˈhweər- -wɪθ etc
whet wet $ hwet etc
whether ˈweðə(r) $ ˈhweðər etc
whetstone ˈwetstəʊn $ hwet- etc
whew conventional spelling of sound
'gesture' usually made either by
'blowing open' one's lips (p)fju or
by roughly 'whistling' hju hwju
whey weɪ $ hweɪ etc
which wɪtʃ $ hwɪtʃ etc
whichever wɪtʃˈevə(r) $ hwɪtʃ- etc
whiff wɪf $ hwɪf etc
Whig wɪg $ hwɪg etc
while waɪl $ hwaɪl etc
whilst waɪlst $ hwaɪlst etc
whim wɪm $ hwɪm etc
whimper ˈwɪmpə(r) $ ˈhwɪmpər etc
whimsical ˈwɪmzɪkl -msɪ- $ ˈhw- etc
whimsy ˈwɪmzɪ $ ˈhwɪmzɪ etc
whine waɪn $ hwaɪn etc
whinny ˈwɪnɪ $ ˈhwɪnɪ etc
whip wɪp $ hwɪp etc
whip-cord ˈwɪp kɔd $ ˈhwɪp kɔrd etc
whippet ˈwɪpɪt $ ˈhwɪpɪt etc
whipping-boy ˈwɪpɪŋ bɔɪ $ ˈhw- etc
whipping-top ˈwɪpɪŋ top $ ˈhw- etc
whip-poor-will ˈwɪp pʊə ˈwɪl £ pɔ
$ ˈhwɪ pər ˈwɪl pʊər
whip-round ˈwɪp raʊnd $ ˈhw- etc
whir(r) wɜ(r) $ hwɜ etc
whirl wɜl $ hwɜl etc
whirligig ˈwɜlɪgɪg $ ˈhw- etc
whirlpool ˈwɜlpul $ ˈhw- etc
whirlwind ˈwɜlwɪnd $ ˈhw- etc
whisk wɪsk $ hwɪsk etc
whiskers ˈwɪskəz $ ˈhwɪskərz etc
whisk(e)y ˈwɪskɪ $ ˈhwɪskɪ etc
whisper ˈwɪspə(r) $ ˈhwɪspər etc

whist wɪst $ hwɪst etc
whist-drive ˈwɪst draɪv ˈwɪs $ ˈhw- etc
whistle ˈwɪsl $ ˈhwɪsl etc
whistle-stop ˈwɪsl stop $ ˈhwɪsl etc
whit, W– $ hwɪt etc
white waɪt $ hwaɪt etc
whitebait ˈwaɪtbeɪt $ ˈhwaɪt- etc
white-collar ˈwaɪt ˈkolə(r) $ ˈhwaɪt etc
white-hot ˈwaɪt ˈhot $ ˈhwaɪt etc
Whitehall waɪtˈhɔl $ hwaɪt- etc
White House, the ˈwaɪt haʊs $ ˈhwaɪt
whiteman ˈwaɪtmæn $ ˈhwaɪt- etc
whiten ˈwaɪtn $ ˈhwaɪtn etc
whitening ˈwaɪtn̩ɪŋ $ ˈhwaɪtn̩ɪŋ etc
white-thorn ˈwaɪt θɔn $ ˈhwaɪt θɔrn etc
whitewash ˈwaɪtwoʃ $ ˈhwaɪtwɔʃ etc
whither ˈwɪðə(r) $ ˈhwɪðər etc
whithersoever ˈwɪðəsəʊˈevə(r) $ ˈhwɪðər-
whiting ˈwaɪtɪŋ $ ˈhwaɪtɪŋ etc
whitlow ˈwɪtləʊ $ ˈhwɪtləʊ etc
Whitman ˈwɪtmən $ ˈhwɪtmən
Whitsun ˈwɪtsn $ ˈhwɪtsn etc
Whitsunday ˈwɪtˈsʌndɪ ˈwɪtsn̩ˈdeɪ $ ˈhw-
Whitsuntide ˈwɪtsntaɪd $ ˈhwɪt- etc
whittle ˈwɪtl $ ˈhwɪtl etc
whiz(z) wɪz $ hwɪz etc
who hu weak-form: u
WHO ˈdublju eitʃ ˈəʊ $ ˈdʌbljə
whoa wəʊ $ hwəʊ hɔʊ
who'd hud weak-form: ud
whodun(n)it huˈdʌnɪt
whoever huˈevə(r)
whole həʊl
whole-heartedly həʊl ˈhatɪdlɪ $ ˈhar-
wholemeal ˈhəʊlmil
wholesale ˈhəʊl-seɪl
wholesome ˈhəʊl-səm
who'll hul weak-form: ul
wholly ˈhəʊllɪ ˈhəʊlɪ
whom hum
whoop cough hup $ hʊp
whoop (it up) wup $ hwʊp etc
whoopee interj ˈwʊˈpi
whoopee n ˈwʊpi
whooping-cough ˈhupɪŋ kof $ ˈkɔf etc
whoops interj wʊps wups wəps
whopping ˈwopɪŋ $ ˈhwopɪŋ etc
whore hɔ(r)
who're ˈhuə(r)
whoremonger ˈhɔmʌŋgə(r) $ ˈhɔr-
whorl wɔl $ hwɔl etc
who's huz weak-form: uz
whose huz weak-form: uz

whosoever ˈhusəʊˈevə(r)
why waɪ $ hwaɪ etc
whyever ˈwaɪˈevə(r) $ ˈhwaɪ- etc
Wichita ˈwɪtʃɪtɔ
wick wɪk
wicked bad ˈwɪkɪd
wicker ˈwɪkə(r)
wickerwork ˈwɪkəwɜk $ -kər-
wicket ˈwɪkɪt
wicket-keeper ˈwɪkɪt kipə(r)
Wicklow ˈwɪkləʊ
wide waɪd
wide-awake ˈwaɪd əˈweɪk £ ˈwaɪd əweɪk
widen ˈwaɪdn
wide-spread waɪd ˈspred
widow ˈwɪdəʊ $ ˈwɪdə
widower ˈwɪdəʊə(r)
width wɪtθ wɪdθ
wield wild
wife waɪf
wig wɪg
wiggle ˈwɪgl
wigwam ˈwɪgwæm $ ˈwɪgwam -wɔm
wild waɪld
Wilde waɪld
wildebeest ˈwɪldəbist -dɪ-
wilderness ˈwɪldənəs $ -dər-
wildfire ˈwaɪldfaɪə(r)
wildfowl ˈwaɪldfaʊl
wild-goose waɪld ˈgus
wild-goose chase waɪld ˈgus tʃeɪs
wile waɪl
Wilfred ˈwɪlfrɪd
wilful ˈwɪlfl -fʊl
will auxil v usu form: 1 strong-form: wɪl
    other weak-forms: wl wəl əl
will n, main v wɪl
William ˈwɪlɪəm
willing ˈwɪlɪŋ
will-o'-the-wisp ˈwɪl ə ðə ˈwɪsp
willow ˈwɪləʊ
willow-pattern ˈwɪləʊ pætn $ pætərn
willowy ˈwɪləʊɪ $ ˈwɪlə
wilt wɪlt
Wilton ˈwɪltən
Wiltshire ˈwɪlt-ʃə(r) $ -ʃɪər etc
wily ˈwaɪlɪ
wimple ˈwɪmpl
win wɪn
wince wɪns
wincey ˈwɪnsɪ
winch wɪntʃ
Winchester ˈwɪntʃɪstə(r) $ -tʃestər etc

wind wɪnd
windbag ˈwɪndbæg
windbreak ˈwɪndbreɪk
windcheater ˈwɪndtʃiːtə(r)
windfall ˈwɪndfɔl
wind-instrument ˈwɪnd ɪnstrʊmənt
wind-jammer ˈwɪnd dʒæmə(r)
windlass ˈwɪndləs
windmill ˈwɪndmɪl
window ˈwɪndəʊ $ ˈwɪndə
window-cleaner ˈwɪndəʊ kliːnə(r)
window-dressing ˈwɪndəʊ dresɪŋ
window-pane ˈwɪndəʊ peɪn
window-shopping ˈwɪndəʊ ʃopɪŋ
windpipe ˈwɪndpaɪp
windscreen ˈwɪndskriːn
windscreen wiper ˈwɪndskriːn waɪpə(r)
wind-shield ˈwɪnd ʃiːld
Windsor ˈwɪnzə(r)
wind-swept ˈwɪnd swept
windward ˈwɪndwəd £ -wʊd $ -wərd
wine waɪn
wineglass ˈwaɪnglɑːs $ -glæs
winepress ˈwaɪnpres
wing wɪŋ
wing-commander ˈwɪŋ kəˈmɑːndə(r) $ kəˈmændər
wing-span ˈwɪŋ spæn
wink wɪŋk
winkle ˈwɪŋkl
Winnie ˈwɪnɪ
winning-post ˈwɪnɪŋ pəʊst
Winnipeg ˈwɪnɪpeg
winnow ˈwɪnəʊ
winsome ˈwɪnsəm
Winston ˈwɪnstən
winter ˈwɪntə(r)
wintry ˈwɪntrɪ
wipe waɪp
wire ˈwaɪə(r)
wire-cutters ˈwaɪə kʌtəz $ ˈwaɪər kʌtərz
wire-haired ˈwaɪə heəd $ ˈwaɪər hərd
wireless ˈwaɪələs $ ˈwaɪərləs
wiring ˈwaɪərɪŋ
wiry ˈwaɪərɪ
Wisconsin wɪsˈkonsɪn $ -sn
wise waɪz
wisecrack ˈwaɪzkræk
wisdom ˈwɪzdəm
wisdom-tooth ˈwɪzdəm tuːθ
wish wɪʃ
wish(ing)-bone ˈwɪʃ(ɪŋ) bəʊn
wishy-washy ˈwɪʃɪ woʃɪ $ wɔʃɪ etc

wisp wɪsp
wistful ˈwɪstfl
wit wɪt
witch wɪtʃ
witchcraft ˈwɪtʃkrɑːft $ -kræft
witch-doctor ˈwɪtʃ doktə(r)
witch-hazel ˈwɪtʃ heɪzl
witch-hunt ˈwɪtʃ hʌnt
with wɪð $ wɪθ
withal wɪðˈɔl $ wɪθˈɔl
withdraw wɪðˈdrɔ $ wɪθˈdrɔ
withdrawal wɪðˈdrɔl $ wɪθ-
withdrawn wɪðˈdrɔn $ wɪθ-
withdrew wɪðˈdruː $ wɪθ-
wither ˈwɪðə(r)
withhold wɪðˈhəʊld $ wɪθ-
within wɪðˈɪn $ wɪθ-
without wɪðˈaʊt $ wɪθ-
withstand wɪðˈstænd $ wɪθ-
witness ˈwɪtnəs -nɪs
witticism ˈwɪtɪsɪzm
wittingly ˈwɪtɪŋlɪ
witty ˈwɪtɪ
wives waɪvz
wizard ˈwɪzəd $ ˈwɪzərd
wizened ˈwɪznd
wo! wəʊ
woad wəʊd
wobble ˈwobl
wobbly ˈwoblɪ
Wodehouse ˈwʊdhaʊs
woe wəʊ
woebegone ˈwəʊbɪgon $ -gɔn etc
woke wəʊk
woken ˈwəʊkən
wold wəʊld
wolf wʊlf
wolf-cub ˈwʊlf kʌb
wolf-hound ˈwʊlf haʊnd
woman ˈwʊmən
womankind ˈwʊmənˈkaɪnd ˈw- k-
womb wuːm
wombat ˈwombæt ˈwɔm-
women ˈwɪmɪn
womenfolk ˈwɪmɪnfəʊk
won wʌn
wonder ˈwʌndə(r)
wonderland ˈwʌndələænd $ -dər-
wondrous ˈwʌndrəs
wonky ˈwoŋkɪ
wont wəʊnt $ wɔnt etc
won't wəʊnt $ wʌnt
woo wuː

wood wʊd
woodbine ˈwʊdbaın
woodcock ˈwʊdkok
woodcut ˈwʊdkʌt
woodcutter ˈwʊdkʌtə(r)
wooden ˈwʊdn
woodland ˈwʊdlənd
woodman ˈwʊdmən
woodpecker ˈwʊdpekə(r)
woodpile ˈwʊdpaıl
woodpulp ˈwʊdpʌlp
woodshed ˈwʊdʃed
woodwind ˈwʊdwınd
woodwork ˈwʊdwɜk
woof of dog, hi-fi wʊf
woof of fabric wuf $ wʊf etc
wool wʊl
wool-gathering ˈwʊl gæðrıŋ
wool(l)en ˈwʊlən
woollies ˈwʊlız
woolly ˈwʊlı
Woolsack, the ˈwʊl-sæk
Woolwich ˈwʊlıdʒ
Woolworth ˈwʊlwɜθ £ -wəθ
word wɜd
word-perfect ˈwɜd ˈpɜfıkt
wore wɔ(r)
work wɜk
workaday ˈwɜkədeı
work-basket ˈwɜk baskıt $ bæs-
work-bench ˈwɜk bentʃ
workbook ˈwɜkbʊk
workhouse ˈwɜkhaʊs
working ˈwɜkıŋ
working party ˈwɜkıŋ patı $ partı
workman ˈwɜkmən
workmanship ˈwɜkmənʃıp
workout ˈwɜkaʊt
work-people ˈwɜk pipl
workroom ˈwɜkrʊm $ £ rum etc
workshop ˈwɜkʃop
work-shy ˈwɜk ʃaı
work-study ˈwɜk stʌdı
world wɜld
worldly ˈwɜldlı
world-wide ˈwɜld ˈwaıd
worm wɜm
worm-gear ˈwɜm gıə(r)
worm-hole ˈwɜm həʊl
wormwood ˈwɜmwʊd
worn wɔn $ wɔrn
worrisome ˈwʌrısəm $ ˈwɜısəm
worry ˈwʌrı $ ˈwɜı

worse wɜs
worship ˈwɜʃıp
worst wɜst
worsted n ˈwʊstıd $ ˈwɜstıd
worth wɜθ
-worth suffix wəθ $ £ wɜθ
worthiness ˈwɜðınəs
worthwhile wɜθˈwaıl $ wɜθˈhwaıl etc
worthy ˈwɜðı
would usual form after 'I, he, she,
  we, you, they': d strong-form: wʊd
  weak-form used elsewhere: əd
would-be ˈwʊd bi
wouldn't ˈwʊdnt
wouldst wʊdst
would've ˈwʊdəv
wound n, v wund
wound v past of 'wind' waʊnd
wove wəʊv
woven ˈwəʊvn
wrack ræk
wraith reıθ
wrangle ˈræŋgl
wrangler ˈræŋglə(r)
wrap ræp
wrapper ˈræpə(r)
wrath roθ $ ræθ
wreak rik
wreath riθ
wreathe rið
wreck rek
wreckage ˈrekıdʒ
wren ren
wrench rentʃ
wrest rest
wrestle ˈresl
wrestling-match ˈreslıŋ mætʃ
wretch retʃ
wretched ˈretʃıd
wrick rık
wriggle ˈrıgl
wright raıt
wring rıŋ
wrinkle ˈrıŋkl
wrist rıst
wristband ˈrıstbænd
wristlet ˈrıstlət
wrist-watch ˈrıst wotʃ $ wɔtʃ
writ rıt
write raıt
write-off ˈraıt of $ £ ɔf
write-up ˈraıt ʌp
writhe raıð

writing-desk ˈraɪtɪŋ desk
writing-ink ˈraɪtɪŋ ɪŋk
writing-paper ˈraɪtɪŋ peɪpə(r)
written ˈrɪtn
wrong rɒŋ $ rɔŋ *etc*
wrong-headed ˈrɒŋ ˈhedɪd $ ˈrɔŋ *etc*

wrote rəʊt
wrought rɔt
wrung rʌŋ
wry raɪ
wych-hazel ˈwɪtʃ heɪzl
Wyoming waɪˈəʊmɪŋ

X

X x eks
xenophobia ˈzenəˈfəʊbɪə
xerox ˈzɪəroks

Xmas ˈkrɪsməs
X-ray ˈeks-reɪ
xylophone ˈzaɪləfəʊn $ ˈzɪl-

Y

Y y waɪ
yacht jɒt
yacht-club ˈjɒt klʌb
yachting ˈjɒtɪŋ
yachtsman ˈjɒtsmən
yah jɑ
yahoo jɑˈhu
yak jæk
Yale jeɪl
yam jæm
yank jæŋk
Yankee ˈjæŋkɪ
yap jæp
yard jɑd $ jɑrd
yardstick ˈjɑdstɪk $ ˈjɑrd-
yarn jɑn $ jɑrn
yashmak ˈjæʃmæk
yaw jɔ
yawl jɔl
yawn jɔn
ye ji
yea jeɪ
year jɜ(r) $ £ jɪə(r)
yearbook ˈjɜbʊk $ ˈjɪər- £ ˈjɪə-
yearling ˈjɜlɪŋ $ ˈjɪər- £ ˈjɪə-
year-long ˈjɜ ˈlɒŋ $ ˈjɪər ˈlɔŋ £ ˈjɪə
yearn jɜn
yeast jist
yell jel
yellow ˈjeləʊ $ ˈjelə
Yemen ˈjemən
yen jen

yeoman ˈjəʊmən
yeomanry ˈjəʊmənrɪ
yes jes jeəs *informal:* je jeə
yesterday ˈjestədɪ -deɪ $ -stər-
yester-year ˈjestəjɜ(r) -jɪə(r) $ ˈjestərjɪər
yet jet
yew ju
Yiddish ˈjɪdɪʃ
yield jild
YMCA ˈwaɪ em si ˈeɪ
yodel ˈjəʊdl
yodelling ˈjəʊdlɪŋ
yoga ˈjəʊgə
yog(h)(o)urt ˈjogət ˈjəʊgət $ ˈjəʊgərt
yogi ˈjəʊgɪ
yoke jəʊk
yokel ˈjəʊkl
yolk jəʊk
yon jon $ jɒn
yonder ˈjondə(r) $ ˈjɒn-
yore jɔ(r)
York jɔk $ jɔrk
Yorkshire ˈjɔkʃə(r) $ ˈjɔrkʃɪər -ʃə(r)
you ju *familiar weak-form:* jə
you'd jud
you'll jul jɔl
young jʌŋ
youngster ˈjʌŋstə(r)
your jɔ(r) $ £ jʊə(r)
informal weak-form: jə(r)
you're jɔ(r) $ £ jʊə(r)
yours jɔz jʊəz $ jʊərz jɔrz

yourself jɔ'self jʊə'self jə'self
$ jʊər'self jɔr'self jər'self
yourselves jɔ'selvz jʊə'selvz jə'selvz
$ jʊər'selvz jɔr'selvz jər'selvz
youth juθ
youth-club 'juθ klʌb
youth-hostel 'juθ hostl
youths juðz $ juθs

you've juv *familiar weak-form:* jəv
Yukon 'jukon
Yugoslavia 'jugəʊ'slɑvɪə
yule jul
yule-log 'jul log $ lɔg *etc*
yum yum 'jʌm 'jʌm
Yvonne ɪ'von i'von
YWCA 'waɪ dʌbļju si 'eɪ

Z

Z z zed $ zi
Zagreb 'zɑgreb
Zaire zɑ'ɪə(r)
Zambezi zæm'bizɪ
Zambia 'zæmbɪə
zany 'zeɪnɪ
Zanzibar 'zænzɪbɑ(r)
zeal zil
zealot 'zelət
zealous 'zeləs
zebra 'zibrə £ 'zebrə
zenith 'zenɪθ $ 'zinɪθ
zephyr 'zefə(r)
zero 'zɪərəʊ $ 'zirəʊ
zero hour 'zɪərəʊ aʊə(r) $ 'zirəʊ
zest zest
zigzag 'zɪgzæg
zinc zɪŋk

Zion 'zaɪən
zip zɪp
zip-fastener 'zɪp 'fɑsnə(r) $ 'fæsnər
zipper 'zɪpə(r)
zither 'zɪθə(r) 'zɪðə(r)
Zoë 'zəʊɪ
zodiac 'zəʊdɪæk
zombie 'zombɪ
zone zəʊn
zoo zu
zoological 'zəʊə'lodʒɪkl zu'lodʒɪkl
zoologist zəʊ'olədʒɪst zu-
zoology zəʊ'olədʒɪ zu-
zoom zum
zoophyte 'zəʊəfaɪt
zounds 'zaʊndz
Zulu 'zulu
Zurich 'zjʊərɪk $ £ 'zʊərɪk

Key to symbols

Vowels and diphthongs

1	i	*as in*	see si	11	ɜ	*as in*	fur fɜ(r)	
2	ɪ	*as in*	sit sɪt	12	ə	*as in*	ago əˈgəʊ	
3	e	*as in*	ten ten	13	eɪ	*as in*	page peɪdʒ	
4	æ	*as in*	hat hæt	14	əʊ	*as in*	home həʊm	
5	ɑ	*as in*	arm ɑm $ ɑrm	15	aɪ	*as in*	five faɪv	
6	o	*as in*	got gɒt	16	aʊ	*as in*	now naʊ	
7	ɔ	*as in*	saw sɔ	17	ɔɪ	*as in*	join dʒɔɪn	
8	ʊ	*as in*	put pʊt	18	ɪə	*as in*	near nɪə(r)	
9	u	*as in*	too tu	19	eə	*as in*	hair heə(r)	
10	ʌ	*as in*	cup kʌp	20	ʊə	*as in*	pure pjʊə(r)	

In certain words taken from French several of the above vowels are given a nasal quality. For example, 3̃ *as in* restaurant ˈrestrɔ̃.

Consonants

1	p	*as in*	pen pen	17	h	*as in*	how haʊ
2	b	*as in*	bad bæd	18	m	*as in*	man mæn
3	t	*as in*	tea ti			*syllabic* m̩	*as in* government
4	d	*as in*	did dɪd				ˈgʌvm̩ənt
5	k	*as in*	cat kæt	19	n	*as in*	no nəʊ
6	g	*as in*	get get			*syllabic* n̩	*as in*
7	tʃ	*as in*	chin tʃɪn				happening ˈhæpn̩ɪŋ
8	dʒ	*as in*	June dʒun	20	ŋ	*as in*	sing sɪŋ
9	f	*as in*	fall fɔl	21	l	*as in*	leg leg
10	v	*as in*	voice vɔɪs			*syllabic* l̩	*as in*
11	θ	*as in*	thin θɪn				settling ˈsetl̩ɪŋ
12	ð	*as in*	then ðen	22	r	*as in*	red red
13	s	*as in*	so səʊ			*syllabic* r̩	*as in*
14	z	*as in*	zoo zu				measuring ˈmeʒr̩ɪŋ
15	ʃ	*as in*	she ʃi	23	j	*as in*	yes jes
16	ʒ	*as in*	vision ˈvɪʒn	24	w	*as in*	wet wet

/ˈ/ *represents* principal stress *as in* about əˈbaʊt.

/ˌ/ *represents* subordinate stress *as in* academic ˌækəˈdemɪk.

(r) An r shown in curved brackets is heard in British pronunciation when the next word begins with a vowel sound and follows without pause. Otherwise it is omitted. In American pronunciation no r of the phonetic spelling should be omitted.

$ Preferred recommendations appear in **bold** type, alternatives in medium weight type. If only one bold transcription is recorded, it is for both British and American English. Preferred recommendations for American English that differ from British English are preceded by a bold **$**.

$ Alternative American English forms which are not British alternatives are preceded by a medium weight $.

£ If an alternative form is for British English only it is preceded by £.

etc The use of *etc* is to indicate that the preferred form given for British English is also an alternative American form.

- Hyphens preceding and/or following parts of a repeated transcription indicate that only the repeated part changes.

See pages ix–xiii for a full explanation of the arrangement of the entries.